Petrosian Year by Year

Volume I (1942-1962)

Tibor Karolyi and Tigran Gyozalyan

Petrosian Year by Year: Volume I (1942-1962)

Authors: Tibor Karolyi and Tigran Gyozalyan

Typesetting by Andrei Elkov (www.elkov.ru)

Front cover: Tigran Petrosian plays against Konstantin Klaman in the Soviet Championship Semi-Final, Tbilisi (round 9), 1949. Photo from the private archive of David Gurgenidze

Follow us on Twitter: @ilan_ruby

www.elkandruby.com

ISBN 978-5-6041770-2-0

CONTENTS

4

Index of Games

Game	White	Black	Opening	Year
88	T. Petrosian	A. Lutikov	King's Indian Defence	1959
89	A. Matanovic	T. Petrosian	Caro-Kann Defence	1959
90	A. Kotov	I. Boleslavsky	Trompowsky Attack	1945
91	I. Boleslavsky	V. Smyslov	Queen's Gambit Accepted	1950
92	R. Fischer	T. Petrosian	Caro-Kann Defence	1959
93	P. Keres	T. Petrosian	Fragment	1959
94	T. Petrosian	E. Gufeld	King's Indian Defence	1960
95	T. Petrosian	N. Krogius	Fragment	1960
96	T. Petrosian	W. Unzicker	Queen's Gambit Declined	1960
97	S. Holm Pedersen	T. Petrosian	Fragment	1960
98	T. Petrosian	R. Wade	Fragment	1960
99	T. Petrosian	V. Korchnoi	Fragment	1961
100	T. Petrosian	V. Smyslov	Fragment	1961
101	S. Furman	T. Petrosian	Pirc Defence	1961
102	D. Ciric	T. Petrosian	Fragment	1961
103	M. Bertok	T. Petrosian	Fragment	1961
104	T. Petrosian	L. Pachman	Fragment	1961
105	T. Petrosian	M. Bertok	Fragment	1961
106	T. Petrosian	M. Bertok	Queen's Gambit Accepted	1962
107	T. Petrosian	S. Schweber	King's Indian Defence	1962
108	T. Petrosian	M. Tal	Reti Opening	1962
109	M. Filip	T. Petrosian	Pirc Defence	1962
110	T. Petrosian	S. Gligoric	Fragment	1962
111	A. Dueckstein	T. Petrosian	Caro-Kann Defence	1962
A1	G. Bakhtadze	T. Petrosian	Fragment (exchanges)	1944
A2	T. Petrosian	Zhuk-Tripolitov	Fragment (exchanges)	1945
A3	T. Petrosian	A. Buslaev	Fragment (exchanges)	1945
A4	T. Petrosian	N. Petrovsky	Fragment (exchanges)	1945
A5	T. Petrosian	S. Oganesian	Fragment (exchanges)	1948
A6	A. Kalantar	T. Petrosian	Fragment (exchanges)	1948
A7	T. Petrosian	K. Klaman	Fragment (exchanges)	1949
A8	I. Bondarevsky	T. Petrosian	Fragment (exchanges)	1951
A9	V. Simagin	T. Petrosian	Fragment (exchanges)	1951
A10	J. Lokvenc	T. Petrosian	Fragment (exchanges)	1953
A11	D. Bronstein	T. Petrosian	Fragment (exchanges)	1956
A12	T. Petrosian	F. Olafsson	Fragment (exchanges)	1959
B1	T. Petrosian	B. Kopelevich	Fragment (test)	1944
B2	T. Petrosian	A. Ebralidze	Fragment (test)	1945
B3	T. Petrosian	N. Grigoriev	Fragment (test)	1945
B4	T. Petrosian	G. Bakhtadze	Fragment (test)	1945
B5	T. Petrosian	Gongadze	Fragment (test)	1947
B6	V. Simagin	T. Petrosian	Fragment (test)	1950
B7	T. Petrosian	D. Bronstein	Fragment (test)	1951
B8	A. Kotov	T. Petrosian	Fragment (test)	1952
B9	V. Smyslov	T. Petrosian	Fragment (test)	1953

Game	White	Black	Opening	Year
B10	T. Petrosian	H. Corral	Fragment (test)	1954
B11	T. Petrosian	A. Bannik	Fragment (test)	1954
B12	A. Chistiakov	T. Petrosian	Fragment (test)	1956
B13	A. Tolush	T. Petrosian	Fragment (test)	1957
B14	A. Matanovic	T. Petrosian	Fragment (test)	1957
B15	T. Petrosian	A. Tolush	Fragment (test)	1958
B16	T. Petrosian	P. Benko	Fragment (test)	1959
B17	T. Petrosian	A. Suetin	Fragment (test)	1960
B18	D. Bronstein	T. Petrosian	Fragment (test)	1960
B19	T. Petrosian	E. Gufeld	Fragment (test)	1961
B20	A. Khasin	T. Petrosian	Fragment (test)	1961
B21	L. Polugaevsky	T. Petrosian	Fragment (test)	1961
B22	T. Petrosian	L. Schmid	Fragment (test)	1961
B23	M. Germek	T. Petrosian	Fragment (test)	1961
B24	T. Petrosian	A. Pomar	Fragment (test)	1962
B25	T. Petrosian	V. Korchnoi	Fragment (test)	1962

Foreword by Levon Aronian

As a chess player from a country where the name of Petrosian is held sacred, I am delighted at the opportunity to write about one of the most mystical chess players in the world.

When you think of post-war world champions and elements of nature, the following analogies come to mind: Botvinnik – Earth, Smyslov – Air, Tal – Fire, and Petrosian – Water.

Tigran Vartanovich's style was unhurried, even sometimes languid, with slow development in the opening. It was similar to a mountain brook, and often the pace of the game changed its course, just as the river and current accelerated. Most of his games follow this logic, which is elusive to nearly all other players.

Perhaps I began to study Petrosian's games too early. My relatives, like many chess lovers in Armenia, were proud and remembered the days when Tigran Vartanovich became the world champion, so it was natural that *Reliability Strategy* became one of my first books.

After the brilliant cavalry attacks by Alekhine in his *300 Games* I now had to figure out why I should exchange a good knight for a blunted bishop or give up space, and then try to build a blockade in positions with pawn chains. It was at the age of 13, when already playing at master level, that I read that book and began to understand my compatriot's wealth of ideas and depth of his plans. Now, many years later, having had the opportunity to study the games of players with a universal style, as well as the strongest computer programs, I am increasingly convinced that the chess style of the future will in many respects resemble Tigran Vartanovich's. You don't have to go far for examples: look at the games from the AlphaZero–Stockfish match or at openings that are coming into fashion: 1.e4 c6 2.♘f3 d5 3.d3 – elasticity, modest ambitions and a focus on manoeuvring; 1.e4 c5 2.♘f3 e6 3.g3 is another attempt to get away from the beaten track and focus on a slight advantage.

The names of the authors of this book – Tibor Karolyi and Tigran Gyozalyan – are well-known to serious chess players. Having raised many grandmasters, they continue to coach and at the same time write books on interesting subjects. I am sure that the rare games analysed in this book will help chess fans to discover the fascinating world of one of the least studied world champions.

Levon Aronian

Introduction by Tibor Karolyi

All world champions contributed greatly to the development of chess, and they all brought something new to chess culture. Their play has been illuminated by many authors. I was lucky enough to have the opportunity to write a three-volume treatise on Tal and three books on each of Kasparov and Karpov, as well as books on several other all-time greats. I managed to discover elements to their chess that I had never heard before, like how often Kasparov played on the a- and h-files, how many times Karpov checkmated his opponents in endgames or how well Tal played endgames. Also, I was able to spot for example that among the great players Portisch was a master of bishop pairs, and Beliavsky was incredibly strong at using his queen in the endgame and won so many games due to this, as well as how brilliantly he handled positions with unbalanced material. These giants of chess were not even aware of all the features of their own play and they were surprised. Regarding Petrosian, he was famous for his exchange sacrifices, but never read about how masterfully he often exchanged a bishop for a knight, or about another speciality he often surprised and beat opponents with: taking an a- or h-pawn with a b- or g-pawn.

I think Tigran Vartanovich is one of the least understood champions. Tal appeared on the world stage and, in games with huge stakes, he dared to play risky chess like no one else before him and, probably, after as well. Petrosian qualified for the world championship match with an extremely rational attitude. He recorded a very special accomplishment: he did not lose a single game in the interzonal or Candidates Tournament in that world championship cycle until the final.

The three Soviet and post-Soviet republics in the Caucasus have made an incredible contribution to chess. Kasparov, who many consider the greatest player of all time, was raised in Baku. Woman world champions Gaprindashvili and Chiburdanidze came from Georgia, European champion Azmaiparashvili as well. Aronian had a realistic chance of becoming world champion. Armenia won the Chess Olympiad 3 times. The Azeri team have achieved a lot as well. Vaganian, Mamedyarov and Radjabov are great players. On top of that, these nations have produced genius composers such as Henrik Kasparian and David Gurgenidze, and I could keep mentioning their achievements.

But Tigran Petrosian was the first great chess player from the region. I guess no one has contributed to the chess boom in that part of the world as much as he did. Only a very few chess players have made accomplishments like his. They named a street in Yerevan after him and his picture is on an Armenian banknote.

My junior trainer, International Master Peter Szilagyi, who later became my friend, was a great fan of the Armenian world champion. He talked about him so much that his tremendous respect for him definitely affected me. I visited Peter in hospital just a few days before he passed away and I was happy to tell him that I had the chance to write a treatise on Petrosian. He was weak and could hardly talk, but said what great news that was. He simultaneously smiled a bit, and that smile will remain in my mind for the rest of my life. It is such a pity that he will not read this book.

When I worked in Singapore, I was part of a team that included two fellow trainers who were Armenians in the Singapore Chess Academy. I took long walks and chats with my friends Tigran Gyozalyan and Ashot Nadanian. Tigran's devotion to the ninth world champion shined through when he talked about his fellow Armenian. He shared his personal memories on the occasions he was welcomed to Petrosian's home in Moscow with charming affection.

Ashot and Tigran influenced me and I started to investigate his play. I discovered a few things about it I had not read earlier. He was able to use his rooks and king originally. Tigran told me that Petrosian had once said that his strategy against weaker players was to hold and to spot holes in his opponent's calculations. I found quite a few marvellous examples of this. Portisch faced him many times; he spoke of him with special respect and liking. Ribli and Sherwin told stories as well.

Back in 2004 to 2005, Tigran and I were already thinking about writing a book on Petrosian. When I got an offer to write my books about Tal, there was also a discussion about writing on Petrosian as well. Looking back, I think it was lucky they stuck with Tal, as it was a magical experience writing about the great Misha. Ever since Singapore, I had a strong desire to write in detail about the ninth world champion. As a chess author, I did not and do not have the luxury to choose the subject I write on. But given the choice about whom I would write a book on, I would have selected Petrosian.

So I was excited when the chance came up and contacted Tigran. It was clear to me that his devotion to Petrosian would add a lot to my work. I can speak Russian and have access to some chess literature in Russian, but his Russian is close to native and his ability to reach out to many Armenian people and access more chess literature in Russian raised the level of this book. In addition, Tigran is an extremely well-educated chess player. I am looking forward very much to seeing our joint effort in print.

We hoped to find lesser known masterpieces of the maestro, and while we agree with the subtitle of Keene and Simpole's book on Petrosian "Master of Manoeuvre", we also wanted to discover less obvious features. We hoped to show all his masterpieces. I felt in my Tal book I was able to include all his good games. We hoped that feeling would come after the Petrosian book as well, and now after finishing the book we believe these hopes have been fulfilled. Most authors in the past were not able to investigate his games with a computer; yet scrutinising his games with modern tools would surely add a lot to his gems and uncover hidden beauty in them. The 9th world champion left so much to chess in his career that devoting a book to just part of it is another justified approach. There are examples of this: Yanvarjov covered only his play in the King's Indian, while Keene and Simpole wrote about his games versus the Elite.

Once on an airplane from Sydney to Singapore an Armenian lady was sitting next to me. We had a nice chat and when their world champion's name popped up she asked me if he was so successful because his opponents did not understand his thinking. And indeed, Botvinnik said to Spassky that he was unable to anticipate Petrosian's moves.

***

Vladimir Goldin, who was Armenian champion in 1952, told Tigran Gyozalyan that he had once held a conversation with Petrosian and told him "Tigran you must be a happy man, because your whole nation loved you!"

It is a bit unique in chess, but three nations can be proud of him. Regarding Armenians, the reasons are obvious as he was an Armenian, and their huge support contributed to his success. But he learned chess in Georgia, the country of his physical birth and his birth as a chess player, and he became great in Russia. The chess environments of these three countries were important elements of his accomplishments.

We cite Mikhail Tal: "Petrosian made an indelible impression on me because he always tried to play correct chess, he believed in the logic of the game. Amazingly, in any situation he believed in the formula: chess is a logical game. Petrosian is an absolutely phenomenal chess talent. Sometimes, he found ideas for rivals that they had never thought of. For me, he was perfect."

***

In this 2-volume treatise we cover his exceptionally successful career in chronological order. Actually, Petrosian planned to build his own book like that, but he passed away before he could write it and so the book *Reliability Strategy* was compiled posthumously under the editorship of the late Eduard Shekhtman for the Soviet state publishing house *Fizkultura i sport* in 1985. That book was updated in Russian by Russian Chess House in 2015, who renamed it *My Best Games*, edited by Oleg Stetsko, and it was then translated into English with some editorial and game selection differences and published by Quality Chess that same year with the title *Python Strategy*. However, the current treatise is very different. Very few games are covered in both works, and of those that are, we have considerably revised the analysis.

A careful reading of the sources suggests that Shekhtman originally cooperated with Petrosian on what was intended to be Petrosian's book.

In the 1985 book *Reliability Strategy*, Shekhtman wrote in his introduction "The world champion himself knew it was high time [to publish his games collection]. By that time *we* [my emphasis] had already managed to collect and systematise practically all the games that he had played." Interestingly, the 2015 Russian version completely dropped Shekhtman's introduction (one can speculate that it was for copyright reasons) while although his introduction was restored in *Python Strategy*, the latter reworded the introduction to "the Champion already understood perfectly well that the moment had come: he had already collected and classified practically all the games he had ever played," which removes the reference to Shekhtman's involvement. Whether this removal of the important fact of Shekhtman's collaboration with Petrosian was deliberate or accidental we don't know, but we prefer to think that Shekhtman did indeed initially collaborate with Petrosian. (His ongoing collaboration with Petrosian's widow Rona over two further works on Petrosian mentioned below suggests this, as one would not have expected her to collaborate with somebody who had misrepresented his relationship with her husband in the 1985 book.)

Pergamon Press also published a two-volume collection of Petrosian's games back in 1991 called *The Games of Tigran Petrosian*, also edited by Shekhtman, and it seems that this work was produced directly for Pergamon as there is no known Russian language equivalent. More recently, it has been republished by Ishi Press. However, that work is also very different, containing about 2,000 games, very few of which are annotated, but which are perhaps the origin of many Petrosian games found in today's database (in this book, by 'database' we refer to the ChessBase database). Pergamon's intention had been to include all the games of Petrosian which were known at the time. Those games were of course not subject to modern computer analysis, but this immense work was of great importance and serves as a point of reference for games and dates. References to "Shekhtman" in this book in terms of where and when games were played are generally taken from *The Games of Tigran Petrosian*.

In between those dates, in 1989, Shekhtman published another, much smaller set of works by Petrosian in Russian, also with *Fizkultura i sport*, called *Chess Lectures* (and published in English by Ishi Press in 2012 as *Petrosian's Legacy*). It contains a small amount of information that was of use in our treatise.

Finally, a much older and hence less important work of reference for historical facts about Petrosian's career was *Tigran Petrosian His Life and Games* written by Viktor Vasiliev and translated into English into 1974 by Batsford. It too has been reissued by Ishi Press. The original Russian version dates to 1969, authored by Vasiliev and Alexei Suetin. A different Russian version was published in 1973. Vasiliev's book makes pleasant reading and isn't only interesting for chess improvers. However, it is written in Soviet propaganda style and much of the infomation given is questionable.

***

Generally speaking, we deeply analyse 3-8 of his best games every year of his career. We do of course look at the most important games that he played, but we mainly search for his deepest and most interesting masterpieces. Our priority is quality of the games. In this first volume, we deliver 61 deeply analysed full games, fragments from 48 games, 12 positions in the Petrosian's Remarkable Exchanges chapter, 25 positions in the It's Your Move chapter, two studies, and 7 full games and 17 fragments in the commentaries. We introduce his trainers and seconds, who contributed a lot to his success. We do so through their games – we analyse a few of their greatest gems as well.

Petrosian's intention in his planned book was to show what went on in his and his opponents' minds, and he just wanted to keep the analysis that he made right after his games, adding little or nothing. We try to incorporate this element, but we are both trainers of juniors and want to help players learn from the maestro.

Interestingly, he very rarely placed a question-mark against his opponents' moves. It would be interesting to know whether he was being tactful towards them or actually did not want to help them. Timman once wrote that Karpov never showed the key highlights of his games in his analysis. Smyslov said something like "I want to make 40 good moves and if my opponent does the same we draw". Yet when I investigated Smyslov's play for my book *Kasparov: How His Predecessors Misled Him About Chess* I surprisingly noticed how much he risked and how much he played for a win. Portisch told me for my interview-based book with him that he had played so many games versus Karpov and never realised just how much he calculated. When he was Karpov's second he was shocked at how much he calculated in his games. Soviet sources often said about the twelfth world champion that he just feels where to put his pieces. I do not know whether Smyslov misjudged his own play or whether Karpov was aware of the above-mentioned feature of his own games, but I suspect that they both knew and just wanted to mislead their rivals. Professional players can't speak openly for as long as they have ambitions.

Petrosian very sadly never enjoyed being retired as he died so early, and amazingly he was ranked 19th in the world even when he passed away. Quite possibly, he was the strongest ever world champion when he breathed his last: Alekhine was still the champion, but his play had already deteriorated. So this is another reason why it is worth investigating Petrosian's play: as he was never retired he was unable to speak entirely sincerely.

Also, we think he did not care too much when selecting which of his early games to analyse. For example, he once analysed one of his games against Bondarevsky where virtually nothing happened, nobody even gave a check in the game, and in addition it was not played in a vital moment of his career.

Petrosian, T – Bondarevsky, I
Armenian Championship,
Yerevan, 1947

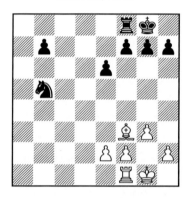

White to play and the game was drawn here. Instead of this, we show games from his career in where his genius shined. For instance, in the next masterpiece, he outplayed Bronstein with a stunning idea, though we have not come across any analysis of this game by Petrosian.

Petrosian, T – Bronstein, D
Soviet Club Championship
Moscow, 1974

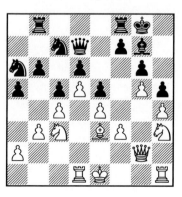

22.a4

A move which closes the queenside is not outwardly special, yet after this in just four remarkably purposeful moves he was winning.

22...♖be8 23.♘e2 ♘b8 24.♘g3 ♖e7 25.♘f2 ♖fe8

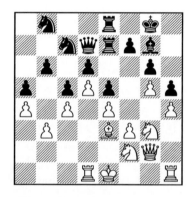

26.♖g1!

It is so hard to read Petrosian's thinking. He continued his stunning plan: 27.♘fh1!!, then 28.♘xh5!! and 29.♘g3, and he obtained a winning position by taking the h5-pawn. Petrosian closed the queenside four moves ago, and from then on he wasted no time and played this sacrifice in the most purposefulness way. Earlier, the great David could have tried Petrosian's speciality of evacuating his king, but would you believe he no longer could do anything about the winning knight sacrifice? Dear Reader, do you agreed that this idea is very much worth analysing? You will find it covered in detail in Volume II of this treatise.

We found improvements in several of his well-known games, for example, we think that Botvinnik could have saved a game in their match when commentators thought the game was already beyond salvation. We also found study-like ideas in famous endgame thrillers against Fischer and Geller.

Petrosian and Fischer produced one of the most exciting endgames in chess history, if not the most exciting. Fischer analysed it in his legendary book *My 60 Memorable Games* and Petrosian also analysed it in detail. We managed to find an idea that neither player considered.

Petrosian, T – Fischer, R
Portoroz Interzonal (13), 1958

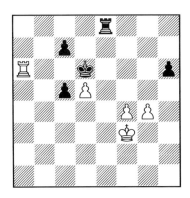

55...c6!! Black gives up the pawn, as without the second c-pawn the black rook can support the remaining c-pawn. With this stunning move Black can draw with far less effort than after the game continuation. This ending is analysed in detail in this first Volume, game 86.

Just like with Karpov, who in his youth was unable to play without inaccuracies, but who had already found some truly grand ideas, many of these Petrosian games were in the database but had never been analysed. We managed to shed light on quite a few deep concepts like the one against Bronstein.

There are two authors of this book. We selected the games together. I was responsible for the analysis, but we discussed the games and I made a lot of changes based on what Tigran suggested. We also finalised the book together.

Tigran Petrosian is one of the most mysterious chess champions, if not the most. Please join us in exploring his art!

We had so much pleasure writing this book together, and we believe that reading our work will bring you a lot of joy, too.

International Master
Tibor Karolyi

Introduction by Tigran Gyozalyan

My first encounter with Petrosian took place in Yerevan in 1972, when I played in the Higher League of the Armenian Championship. I had just turned 15 and, naturally, we did not engage in any conversation. Then I saw him at the Soviet championships and other competitions. But we personally got to know each other in 1978 outside Moscow at his dacha.

My friend International Master Igor Yanvarjov, who was already well acquainted with him, recommended me to call Tigran Vartanovich and kindly provided me with his telephone number. By the way, Tigran Vartanovich personally attended the viva of Yanvarjov's thesis at the University of Physical Education and Sports, where the latter wrote about the ninth world champion. I, like all Armenians, idolized Tigran Petrosian, and I had to pretty much overcome my excitement to call him, although Igor told me that I should not worry, because Petrosian was a very nice person in every way.

I asked Tigran Vartanovich for a meeting to look at my games and give me some advice. I was immensely happy when he agreed. I was struck by his kindness during our friendly conversation. I travelled by train to his place. I saw the face of the ninth world champion from the train window. I knew his face well, so it was easy to spot him at the station. I saw his familiar expressive head, and for a moment I was struck with nerves. My pulse was probably 120-150 beats per minute. But I was able to relax at the meeting, as the world champion treated me in our conversation as though we were old friends. He lived in Armenia for only three years, but remembered the chess players from my hometown Kirovakan (now Vanadzor): Artsrun and Lazar Sarkisian, the latter being my coach. I could feel his genuine interest in the state of chess in Armenia.

He introduced me to his wife Rona Yakovlevna and his sister. "Do you know what his name is !?" And he answered with a prompt: "Tigran!"

***

I have studied Petrosian's games a lot, and I used them so many times as a coach. Still, I did not even think of writing a book on my chess hero for many years. Then the idea came up during the time Tibor and I spent together in Singapore. The idea slept for long, and when in 2019 Tibor mentioned the idea again, I got very excited.

I thought I knew Petrosian's games well; still, I was surprised that he produced so many unknown masterpieces. On a good day he was a very deep young player as well. I was also surprised to spot so many new elements even in his most legendary games.

For me, Tigran Petrosian was not only a phenomenal champion. He is one of the best known Armenians of all time. I admire him not only for what he accomplished in chess, and I am grateful for his kindness to me.

It was a special joy working on Petrosian's career and fully worthwhile investigating it in such detail. I hope our work will bring pleasure to many players, and that juniors and improvers will significantly deepen their chess understanding from the games of the phenomenal player Tigran Petrosian.

FIDE Master
Tigran Gyozalyan

The authors together

A Brilliant Youngster

The ninth world champion was born on 17th June 1929 in Tbilisi, in the Georgian Republic of the Soviet Union. By nationality he was Armenian. There was nothing usual about that: according to the 1926 state census, 34% of the Georgian capital's population consisted of Armenians. His father, Vartan Petrosian, was a caretaker of an Officers House, while his mother was possibly a housewife. He had a brother Amaiak and a sister Vartush; Tigran was the youngest in the family. His parents named their boy after the Armenian king Tigranes the Great, who ruled from 95 to 55 B.C. Under him, the country became, for some time, the strongest state to Rome's east. We feel lucky to be able to show their picture in our photos section.

He learned checkers early on. When still very young he played board games like checkers and backgammon against older people in the Officers House. His remarkably good scores against them made his father happy.

Much of what we know about his early years comes from Vasiliev's book, but different sources state different ages when he learned to play chess. Perhaps Petrosian himself did not remember. Some say

8, some say 11, though the level he displayed when he beat the world class player Flohr in a simul in 1942 strongly suggests that it was closer to 8. Petrosian mentions in *Chess Lectures* that he first learned to play chess at a pioneers camp in 1940. He would have been 10 or 11, but of course one never knows with a boy with such exceptional abilities.

Moreover, Petrosian said in that book that when he saw the Ortueta-Sanz game at the age of 10, it thrilled him so much that it was a major factor in binding him to chess forever:

Ortueta, Martin - Sanz, Jose
Madrid, 1934

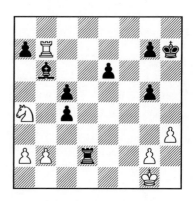

31...♖xb2!! 32.♘xb2 c3! 33.♖xb6 c4!! 34.♖b4 a5!! 35.♘xc4 c2 0–1

By the way if Black had no e6-pawn then he would have had a good fortress if the white knight took the a5-pawn in the final position.

One has to have a reasonable level of understanding to be able to enjoy this incredible game. This also suggests that Petrosian started chess closer to the age of 8.

One of his uncles was a chess lover, and maybe he influenced him in gaining a deeper interest in the game. Tigran enjoyed attending the 73rd Armenian School and he did very well there. He remembered some of his teachers very fondly. Petrosian must have increasingly focused on chess gradually. His father warned him to concentrate on his studies, as chess would not provide a living for him. His mother told her husband that Tigran was still doing excellently in his studies.

Coming from a nation with a difficult history, one which suffered genocide, helps to develop certain features: it creates will power, a feeling of solidarity for each other, and teaches the nation to survive. The ability to survive was to be an important feature of the world champion. Your Armenian author remembers that he spoke Armenian superbly; the family probably spoke it at home. They say he spoke Russian with an Armenian accent; also he used words suggesting he was an Armenian.

His nationality meant a lot to Petrosian, for example, when he first visited Yerevan, seeing that all the inscriptions were in Armenian made him cry.

After the 2018 Chess Olympiad in Batumi I (TK) returned home and on the tennis court I mentioned to my opponent, Ferenc Szakacs, that I had very much enjoyed my stay in Georgia. He told me that he had visited it during Soviet times, and he liked his visit as well. I said something like I can't tell exactly why it is so nice for me to be there, but it is. He answered instantly: because of their ancient culture. I realised immediately that he was right. Armenia became the very first Christian state in 301, while Georgia followed shortly after. Both nations have their own unique alphabets.

Becoming a great requires several elements to fall into place. One of them is to have a chess environment. Later, the chess environment in Georgia and the other two republics of the Caucasus would boom, but the roots must have been there in the forties. Let me remind you that Georgia would become the most successful country at women's chess, and they would have a male European champion. In addition, Georgia produced a lot of great chess composers, including two of the all-time greatest Henrik Kasparian (another Armenian by nationality) and David Gurgenidze. For that to happen, I believe that in the forties ordinary candidate masters and masters must have been at decent levels. But becoming a powerhouse started with Petrosian. He was the first world class player and the first male world champion of the region. His influence had a lot to do with the chess boom in the Caucasus and no great player contributed as much to chess development there as Petrosian.

Having a good, qualified trainer at a young age is perhaps not necessary, but very beneficial; Petrosian, like most great players, had one great mentor, his Nikitin, his Koblencs. However, he worked with Ebralidze for much less time than Kasparov and Tal worked with their mentors. According to Vasiliev, it was only for one and a half years. Still, a player's talent, dedication and ambition are the most important elements to becoming an all-time great at any sport. Petrosian was blessed in this respect.

The building on Rustaveli Avenue in Tbilisi, where the Petrosian family lived. Recent photo. Provided by Giorgi Khomeriki

1942

.

Chess books had a strong effect on Petrosian's progress and, probably, on his style as well. Archil Ebralidze, his first trainer, strengthened his love for chess books, and encouraged him to read them. He read Maizelis's textbook. But Nimzowitsch's books affected him the most. His father gave him money for breakfast, and he saved some of those roubles and bought chess books. Many people who knew him personally mentioned his excellent sense of humour. He was heard to joke: *today I breakfasted on Nimzowitsch.*

Portisch was also brought up on Nimzowitsch's *My System*, and there were strong similarities between their play. A reporter asked Petrosian before one of his world championship matches which book influenced him the most, and he answered Nimzowitsch's. What did Tigran like so much in the writings of the great Riga-born player? Nimzowitsch described a system, and its elements were logical. He read it so much, he ended up knowing that book by heart. Petrosian also read Spielmann's *The Art of Sacrifice in Chess* and liked it.

Capablanca's games also impressed him a lot. Petrosian called Nimzowitsch and Capablanca his "soul fathers in chess". He read the books from diagram to diagram. Tigran believed memorising positions to be very beneficial for him. He recommended playing blindfold and also played blindfold chess with another young boy, Vitya Bravinsky, who later according to Petrosian sadly dropped out of chess completely. Petrosian acquired the title of fourth category player at his very first event and, one year later, at his third event, gained the second category title.

The very first game in the database featuring Petrosian is against Flohr in a simul. Flohr was a great player who faced all the world champions from Lasker to Spassky, excluding Tal. It would be nice to know details about the conditions at the simul, such as how many opponents Flohr faced. Your Hungarian author once played against him in a simul in the seventies, and Flohr took the game seriously.

The simul giver usually plays White, so the following game is somewhat unusual. I wonder whether Flohr knew who were the strong players among his opponents in the simul. Had he known in advance the blooming ability of the young boy, perhaps he would have handled the opening more carefully. In a way, the fact that great players gave simuls during World War II shows the extent to which chess was important in the Soviet Union.

Game 1

Petrosian, Tigran – Flohr, Salo
Simultaneous, Tbilisi, June 1942
Budapest Gambit

1.d4

In his early years Petrosian played 1.e4 as well. By the way, Ebralidze was predominantly a 1.d4 player.

1...♘f6 2.c4 e5

Flohr had employed the Budapest Gambit only once before in a known game.

3.dxe5 ♘g4 4.e4

Tigran would face the Budapest Gambit only once more. He stuck to this line, which Alekhine liked as well.

4...h5 5.h3 ♘xe5

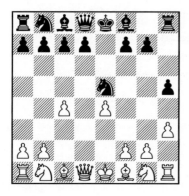

6.♗e3!

White prevents ♗c5. It would be nice to know whether he found it over the board.

6...♘bc6?!

Flohr unnecessarily allows the knight to develop on c3. 6...♗b4+! looks preferable. 7.♘c3 (7.♘d2 d6

8.a3 ♗c5 would be fine for Black) 7...♗xc3+ 8.bxc3 and Black would do better than in the game.

7.♘c3 ♗b4 8.♕d2

Petrosian avoids taking on doubled pawns.

8...d6 9.f4 ♘g6?

The knight is misplaced on g6, Flohr will want to solve its problem, but the tactics favour White. 9...♘d7 followed by ...♘c5 is stronger.

10.♘f3 ♕e7

The grandmaster attacks the centre. 10...♕f6 11.♖c1 ♘h4 was somewhat less problematic for Black.

11.♗d3 f5 12.exf5

Petrosian is not worried about a direct confrontation, and he opens up the position: his better development justifies it. 12.♘g5! would result in a large advantage.

12...♘xf4

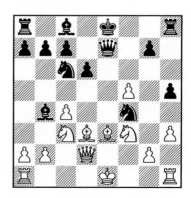

13.0-0-0

Such castling shows control over what White was doing and also indicates that White was no amateur. However, castling short would have been stronger, the reasons being that White's rook would defend the f5–pawn and, no less importantly, the White king would be less exposed to checks on the kingside. 13.0-0! ♝xc3 14.bxc3 ♞xd3 15.♛xd3 ♝xf5 (15...0-0 16.♞g5 or 16.g4 are strong. Please note the rook protects the f3–knight so Black can't play ♝e6!) 16.♛xf5 ♛xe3+ 17.♚h1! ♜f8 18.♛xh5+ ♚d7 19.♜ae1. Unlike after castling long here, the black queen has no check, therefore Black would be in trouble.

13...♝xc3   14.bxc3   ♞xd3+ 15.♛xd3 ♝d7?

This is a serious mistake. Black has two ways to stay in the game, none of which is easy to find, especially when one is playing a simul and on top of that finds himself in an opening he is not very familiar with. Black could obtain a playable game after 15...0-0 16.g4 ♝e6!! or 15...♝xf5! 16.♛xf5 ♛xe3+ 17.♚b2 ♜f8!, a subtle move. 18.♛xh5+ ♚d7 19.c5 and Black does alright after 19...♜ae8 or 19...♛f4.

16.♜he1

This move keeps some advantage, but it's not the best as it allows Black to castle. If 16.♝g5! ♛f7 17.♜he1+ ♚f8 18.♞h4 White wins as the h8 rook will be out of play.

16...0-0-0?

A losing mistake. The grandmaster panics and gives up the exchange to consolidate his position. After 16...0-0! 17.g4 ♛f7

18.♞g5 ♞e5 19.♛c2 Black would be living dangerously, but would be alive.

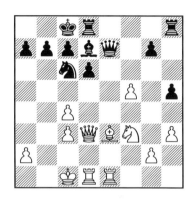

17.♝g5

The young talent wins the exchange. White's doubled pawns are not really vulnerable, therefore, White is clearly winning.

17...♛f7 18.♝xd8 ♜xd8 19.g4 ♞a5 20.♛d5!

Exchanging queens seals Black's fate. His liking for exchanging queens will remain with him all his career.

20...♛xd5 21.cxd5 ♜f8 22.♜e7 g6 23.fxg6 hxg4 24.g7 ♜g8 25.♜f7

The young Tigran allows his opponent to prolong resistance. Keeping the g7–pawn and playing 25.♞g5 would end the game quickly.

25...♝e8 26.♜f8 ♜xg7 27.♜xe8+ ♚d7 28.♜e3 gxf3 29.♜xf3

White is still winning easily, but it takes time to convert the advantage.

29...♞c4 30.♜df1 ♞e5 31.♜e3 ♜h7

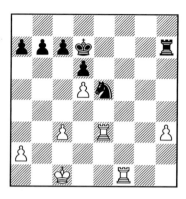

32.♖f4

White gets ready to advance the h-pawn. The edge pawn decides the outcome of the game. Petrosian plays the technical part perfectly.

32...c6   33.c4   ♔c7   34.♔b2 ♔b6 35.dxc6 bxc6 36.♔c3 ♔c5 37.h4

Black has no tools to handle the h-pawn.

37...♖b7 38.♖g3 a6

39.h5   ♖h7   40.♖g5   a5   41.♖f6 ♖b7

Black wants to make a few more moves.

42.h6 ♖b1 43.♖h5 ♖c1+ 44.♔d2 ♖a1 45.h7 1–0

Petrosian will meet Flohr over the board next time in the 1949 Soviet Championship Final. They will play 6 games in total together.

The young Petrosian was already able to get an advantage even though he did not control the tactics perfectly. After coming out on top from the opening he confidently converted the exchange advantage. This is good play from a 13-year-old boy. It is a pity there are no games from when Petrosian started chess, as by this time he was surely no amateur. When I wrote books on Karpov, I gained the impression that they intentionally published only his best early games. It would be interesting to know in Petrosian's case whether he had not kept the scoresheets or lost them during the war or when moving to other cities. Or whether, simply, the Soviet authorities did not want to publish them. In Tal's case, his blindfold match games and his Kasparov blitz match were published long after his death[1]. Hopefully, some unknown games will pop up in Petrosian's case as well.

Petrosian has no more games from 1942 and none from 1943 in the database. As the War progressed,

---

[1] The 14 blitz match games against Kasparov were published for the first time in *Coaching Kasparov, Year by Year and Move by Move, Volume I: The Whizz-Kid (1973-1981)* by Alexander Nikitin (Elk and Ruby, 2019)

there was probably less chess activity or perhaps no tournaments at all available to him. Maybe Petrosian lost his scoresheets. Also, the front drew increasingly closer and living standards kept falling. Hardships of the war affected everybody in the Soviet Union. Petrosian's family was hit harshly. His older brother Amaiak was conscripted to join the Red Army. After a while, letters stopped coming from him and his mother was informed, incorrectly as it turned out, that he had died.

His mother was so deeply saddened that she got ill and died in 1942, without discovering that Amaiak was still alive. His father Vartan was in his sixties by then. We asked Vartan, Petrosian's son, what disease had caused her death. He said that his father had not talked about it. Petrosian's aunt then took care of the family. Petrosian got a serious illness, though no source mentions what exactly happened to him, and for half a year he was unable to attend school. He also had little or no time for chess. Maybe he still thought a lot about chess and that was a nice way for him to escape reality.

Archil Ebralidze

Petrosian's junior trainer was born in the west Georgian town of Poti on the Black Sea coast in 1908. He participated in the 1937 Soviet Championship Final held in Tbilisi, the only time he featured in the final. We thought it would be interesting to know whether he qualified for the final of the championship or whether he was granted a wild card as a local player. On the chess.pro website Mikhail Vrona provided the answer. For various reasons, Botvinnik, Romanovsky, Ryumin and Bogatyrchuk declined to participate: Botvinnik was preparing for the viva of his dissertation, while Romanovsky and Ryumin informed the organisers they would not play due to illness. Bogatyrchuk just failed to show up without informing the organisers, and Ebralidze was admitted instead of him. He finished last at the very strong event, scoring 5 points from 19 games with no wins.

We checked Archil's games. In our opinion, he was one of the strongest players strategically at the event, or at least in the opening and early middlegame, but a lot of bad blunders crept in or he gradually got outplayed. He was also unable to convert clear advantages. In round 2, his opponent, Ragozin, left a rook en prise, yet Archil did not take it and lost. In round 4, he was a piece up against Bondarevsky and only drew, and maybe he was unable to recover after that. In general in his career, his winning rate was quite low, but he played modern openings and had a good feeling for how to build the position.

Actually, let me illustrate Georgia's chess level at the time: Goglidze finished well, sharing 6th-

8th place. The other Armenian from Georgia, Kasparian, scored two points more than Ebralidze.

They opened a chess club for young players in the Pioneers Palace of Tbilisi in 1941, and Ebralidze started to train the young Tigran there at the end of the year, bringing with him a huge chess book library according to *Chess Lectures*. He was only 33, and it would be interesting to know why he took up that job. The effect of World War II must have been felt strongly; maybe he was lucky not to be drafted to the Red Army. According to *Reliability Strategy*, there were group sessions with other talented boys such as Arumitian, and Ebralidze considered Alexander Buslaev the most capable. We do not know how much he worked with the 12-year old Tigran, but the level that Petrosian showed in his simul game against Flohr suggests that our hero spent a lot of time over the chessboard and possibly worked closely with Ebralidze.

Later, Petrosian's junior trainer apologised to his by then world class former pupil for not fully recognising his talent, as he had felt there were boys there with more shining talent. Ebralidze also died young, in 1960, from suicide due to psychological illness compounded by alcoholism, and was not fortunate enough to see his pupil become world champion. However, he did see him become one of the world's best players. We look at Ebralidze's chess a bit and in what ways he influenced Petrosian's play.

Game 2

Ebralidze, Archil – Lubienski, Tadeusz
Soviet Championship Semi-Final, Tbilisi (10), 1949
Dutch Defence

1.d4 d5 2.c4 e6 3.♘c3 c6 4.e3 ♘d7

Two rounds earlier, Archil had faced his former pupil, who played more conventionally: 4...♘f6 5.♘f3 ♘bd7 6.♕c2 dxc4 7.♗xc4 ♗d6 8.0-0 0-0 9.♘e4 ♘xe4 10.♕xe4 ♕e7 11.♕c2 e5 12.e4 ♔h8 13.♗g5 f6 14.♗e3 exd4 15.♘xd4 ♘e5 16.♗e2 ♘g4 17.♗xg4 ♗xg4 18.h3 ♗d7 19.♘f5 ♗xf5 20.exf5 a6 21.♖fe1 ♖fe8 1/2 Ebralidze, A – Petrosian, T, Tbilisi, 1949.

5.♘f3 f5 6.♕c2 ♘h6 7.♗d2 ♗d6 8.♖c1

As the game went, this move may seem superfluous, but if needed it may support an invasion on the c-file.

8...0-0 9.♗d3 ♔h8

10.♘e2!

Ebralidze starts a strategic plan.

10...♘f6 11.a3 ♘e4?!

Black should play 11...a5. Maybe the game would continue something like 12.0-0 ♘e4 (12...♘f7 13.♗c3) 13.♘e5 and White would have a small edge.

12.♗b4!

This is an excellent exchange, as it helps to gain control over the e5–square.

12...♘f7 13.♗xd6 ♕xd6

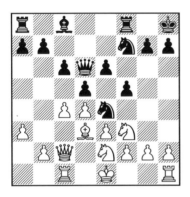

14.cxd5!

Ebralidze makes it harder to carry out c5. If 14.h4 ♗d7 15.♘f4 c5 Black would almost equalise.

14...exd5

Now one can see the point of placing the rook on the c-file, as Black would struggle after 14...cxd5?! 15.♕c7 ♗d7 16.♘e5.

15.h4!

This helps the knight to reach the e5–square, by stabilizing the f4–square for it. 15.♘f4?! would be hasty because of 15...g5!.

15...♗d7 16.♘f4 ♖ae8 17.♗e2!

An instructive square-clearing.

17...♗c8

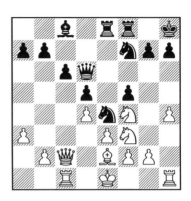

18.0-0!

The Georgian master continues to play in a subtle way. He is not worried by Black's attack and he is still trying to plant a knight on e5. Starting this by 18.♘d3 would be premature. 18...♕h6 19.g3 (19. ♘de5? ♘xe5 20.♘xe5 f4 and Black wins) 19...g5 20.♖h2 g4 21.♘fe5 ♘xe5 22.♘xe5 c5 and Black would obtain the upper hand.

18...♕e7

After 18...♘h6 19.b4 a6 20.♕b2 ♘g4 21.a4 White would be somewhat better.

19.g3!

White with this and the next brilliant move improves his defence on the kingside.

19...♖g8 20.♔g2! g5?

This mistake makes the worse position bad, as in the ensuing position White's play on the h-file is stronger than Black's on the g-file. Waiting passively with 20...a6 would lead to a typical minority attack squeeze after 21.b4 ♗d7 22.a4.

21.hxg5 ♘fxg5

If 21...♘exg5 then 22.♖h1.

22.♘e5

The plan to exchange the dark-squared bishop has borne fruit.

22...♘e6 23.♖h1 ♕c7?

23...♘xf4+ 24.exf4 would be better but still bad (we wonder whether the moves were recorded incorrectly and Black actually played 23...♘xf4+, with the alternative move order eventually aligning with the text).

24.♗h5

Ebralidze builds his attack, but taking the pawn with 24.♘xd5 would win in a simpler way.

24...♖e7 25.♖h3 ♘xf4+ 26.exf4 ♖eg7 27.♖ch1

White is winning.

27...♗e6 28.♕e2 ♕e7 29.♕d1

29.♗g6 would already win.

29...♕c7

30.b4

Ebralidze keeps playing strategically. This is instructive, as he is exerting pressure on the queenside as well, but he misses a direct win with 30.♗g6! It is not only beautiful, but lethally effective as well. 30...♖xg6 31.♕h5 ♖8g7 (31...♖6g7 32.♘g6+) 32.♘xg6+ ♖xg6 33.♕xg6 and White wins.

30...a6 31.♕c2 ♕e7 32.♕b2 ♗d7 33.♖e1

Was he short of time or did he not find a win and just wanted to tire his opponent? We may never know.

33...♗e8 34.♗e2 ♕d8 35.♗d3 ♕d6 36.♖eh1

Ebralidze gets back to the kingside.

36...♕d8

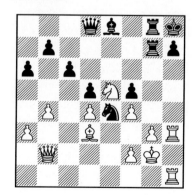

37.♕a1!

A fantastic idea! One may think that Ebralidze is just waiting, but this move and the next deep moves are part of a subtle plan.

37...♕b6?

It is dangerous to pull the queen away from defending the king.

38.♖1h2! ♖e7

Black expects ♕h1 and gets ready to play ♖g7 after the queen move, but the move has a tactical drawback.

39.♗xe4!

Going through Ebralidze's games one can see that he was frequently unable to convert his advantage, but this time he finishes the game.

39...fxe4 40.f5!

The f-pawn moves decisively, now White threatens f6 and f7.

40...♗d7

40...♖f8 41.♕h1! White deserved to be allowed to play this brilliant move. After 41...♕c7 42.♘g6+ ♔xg6 43.fxg6 Black would be desperately lost.

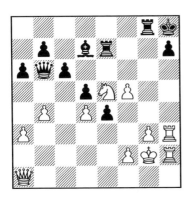

41.♖xh7+!

This neat rook sacrifice leads to checkmate.

41...♖xh7 42.♖xh7+ ♔xh7 43.♕h1+ ♔g7 44.f6+ ♔xf6 45.♘xd7+ 1−0

White wins the queen and it forces Black's resignation, however, a check with the queen would have led to checkmate. In this game, apart from one move, Ebralidze played both strategically and tactically as well as his great pupil did in his prime.

Game 3

Keres, Paul – Ebralidze, Archil
Georgian Open Championship,
Tbilisi (10), 1946
Spanish Opening

1.e4 e5 2.♘f3 ♘c6 3.♗b5 ♘f6 4.♕e2 ♗e7 5.0-0 d6 6.c3 0-0 7.d4 ♘d7 8.♘a3 ♗f6 9.♗e3 a6 10.♗xc6 bxc6 11.dxe5 ♘xe5 12.♘xe5 ♗xe5 13.♘c4 ♖e8 14.♖ad1

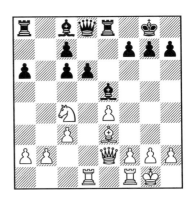

14...♕h4

Archil is not scared of his great opponent and plays actively.

15.♘xe5 ♖xe5 16.f3 c5 17.b4!

Keres weakens Ebralidze's queenside.

17...cxb4 18.cxb4

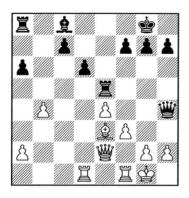

18...♖h5!

An imaginative move, and again a part of a plan. This rook manoeuvre allowed him to push his h-pawn 7 moves later!

19.g3 ♕e7 20.♕c4 ♗b7

A confident move. Black bases his play on his active piece, not worrying that the e4-pawn would choke the bishop. 20...♗e6 21.♕c6 ♖b8 22.a3 a5 would be equal.

21.♖c1 ♖c8 22.♖f2

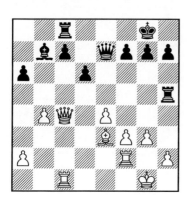

22...♖e5!

Again, this is neat planning. Archil doesn't just move the rook; he has an idea what to do with it.

23.♗d4 ♖e6 24.♗b2

Maybe Keres was worried about c5.

24...♖g6

It was such an original idea to transfer the rook from h5 to g6.

25.a4

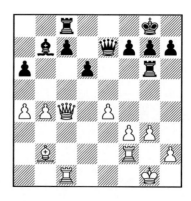

25...h5!

Ebralidze attacks.

26.♖fc2 h4 27.g4 h3

The pawn on h3 is unpleasant to live with. It seems Ebralidze was ahead of his time, as later Petrosian and Kasparov would employ his edge pawn like this.

28.♕f1?

This is an example of how difficult chess is to play. In our opinion, while great players like Korchnoi or Geller were extremely strong, only Rubinstein and Keres were on the level of the world champions in the 20th century. And even such a player can go wrong. White has no time to grab the pawn. It is always a risk to place the queen on the edge of the board. After 28.♕d4 the position would be equal.

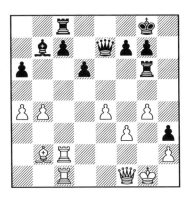

28...d5!

Black takes control. The fact that the b4–pawn is not protected makes this move strong.

29.exd5 ♗xd5 30.♖c5

Other moves were not any better.

30...♕e3+ 31.♔f2 ♕xf3 32.♕xf3 ♗xf3 33.g5 ♖d8 34.♔f2

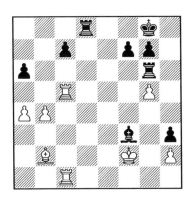

34...♖d2+

Black simplifies to a rook ending. Keeping the bishops with 34...♗d1

was promising as well. After 35.a5 ♖d2+ 36.♔g3 ♗b3 37.♗c3 ♖g2+ 38.♔xh3 ♖2xg5 White would be in big trouble.

35.♔xf3 ♖xb2 36.♔g3 ♖xb4 37.♔xh3 ♖xa4

The dust has settled, and Black should win easily with the extra pawns.

38.♔g3 ♖d6

39.♖1c4

Keres is worried about the safety of his king. After 39.♖1c3 ♖dd4 40.h3 ♖a1 Black is very likely to win.

39...♖d3+ 40.♔g4 ♖a2 41.♖c2 ♖d4+ 42.♔f3 ♖a3+ 43.♖2c3 ♖xc3+ 44.♖xc3

Black has two extra pawns, but has to overcome some difficulties. For example, 44...♖d8? 45.♖xc7 ♖a8 46.♖c4! a5 47.♖a4 ♔h7 48.♔g4 ♔g6 49.h4 f5+ 50.gxf6 ♔xf6 only draws.

44...♖d5!

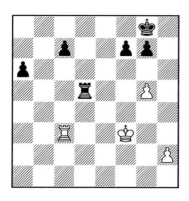

45.g6!

Keres had earlier made a clear mistake, but his resistance lives up to his reputation of a great player. If White manages to swap all kingside pawns, it will be a draw.

45...c5

45...fxg6 46.♖xc7 is not a clear win.

46.♔e4 ♖h5 47.gxf7+ ♔xf7 48.♖c2

White has to defend the h2–pawn.

48...♔e6 49.♔d3 ♔d5 50.♖g2

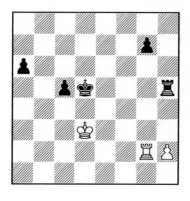

50...g5

Black definitely has to keep the g-pawn. And he can't afford to drop one of his queenside pawns either.

51.♔c3 a5 52.♔b3 ♔e4

The king can force a win on the kingside. Yet 52...♔c6 followed by pushing the queenside pawns should win easily. It would be practical, too, as the game was soon to be adjourned.

53.♔a4!

Taking the a-pawn first gives better chances than going after the c-pawn at once, as White's king will be closer to the kingside.

53...♔f3 54.♖g3+ ♔f4 55.♖g2 ♖h8 56.♔xa5 ♖c8

56...♖b8 57.♖c2 ♔g4 58.♖xc5 ♖b2 is very simple.

57.♖c2 c4 58.♔b4

58...♔g4

This unnecessarily allows the White king to block the pawn and later return to the centre. Pushing the c-pawn was simpler. 58...c3! 59.♔b3 ♔e3 60.♖g2 c2.

59.♖g2+ ♔h4 60.♔c3

Keres grabs his best chance.

60...g4 61.♔d4 c3 62.♖c2 ♔h3 63.♔e4

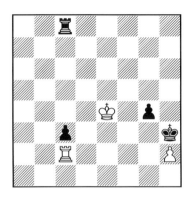

63...♖f8

Intending to place the rook on d2 with 63...♖d8 is the simplest way to win for a human. If 64.♔f5 ♖d5+ (64...♖d2?? 65.♖xc3+ ♔h4 66.♖c4 draws) 65.♔f4 ♖d2 66.♖xc3+ ♔h4 and Black wins.

64.♔e5 ♖f1 65.♔e4 ♖g1

Black goes for the kill. It would have been more practical to mark time until the game adjourned and work out the win at home.

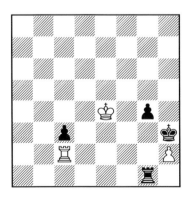

66.♔f5!!

A sign of genius. Keres sets a wicked trap. If the more natural 66.♔f4? then 66...♖g2 67.♖xc3+ ♔h4! would win.

66...♖g2??

After 66...♔h4! 67.♖xc3 ♖f1+ 68.♔e4 ♖f2 Black would still win. Black has another win as well: 66...♖f1+! 67.♔g5 ♖f3 68.♖e2 ♖d3 69.♖c2 ♖d5+ 70.♔f4. Now Black has several ways to win: 70...♖d2, 70...♖c5 or 70...♖d3.

67.♖xc3+ ♔h4

67...♔xh2 68.♔g5 g3 69.♔h4! and Black can't win.

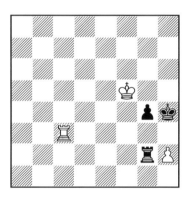

68.♖c4!

This pin saves the game.

68...♖f2+ 69.♖f4 1/2

Credit to Keres, but he was far beyond Ebralidze's level. It is unfortunate, but chess is a sport, and a fighting spirit and ability to concentrate for long is an important element of success.

Ebralidze had some great skills at chess: his planning was superb, and he was able to pass that on to his young pupil. Petrosian developed the ability to calculate superbly, and the combination of these elements made him such a great player.

This game affected the great Estonian, who in the same year composed the following study.

Game 4

Keres
1946

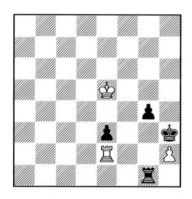

White to play and draw

1.♔f5! ♖f1+

1...♖g2 2.♖xe3+ ♔h4 (2...♔xh2 3.♔g5 g3 4.♔h4 ♖g1 5.♖a3=) 3.♖e4 ♖f2+ 4.♖f4!=

2.♔g5 ♖f3 3.♖e1! g3

3...♔g2 4.♔xg4 ♔f2 5.♖a1 e2 6.h4=

4.hxg3 ♔xg3 5.♖e2!!

Black is in zugzwang.

5...♔h3 6.♖a2!

White holds.

Ebralidze surely had a strong and positive impact on the future world champion as well.

***

Reliability Strategy contains the following incredible story: during a game at a Georgian championship qualifier in 1942 Tigran was told that his father, who had been seriously ill, had just passed away. According to the book, he failed to react to a check, picked up another piece and lost the game. Well, it is bad enough losing both parents at the age of 13 when the child inherits a fortune, but in Tigran's case it was even worse than that as he had already started to work to earn money. Tigran had been forced to undertake his father's job ever since the latter turned ill. He probably had to work for years, though maybe the end of the war eased the situation.

Many of the great chess champions were brought up with no father around, among others Fischer, Kasparov, Spassky, and Korchnoi. Losing both parents at such a young age and in such a short time is especially sad and unfortunate, but it makes the child strong as well.

1943

In January-February, Petrosian finished equal first with 11.5/15 in a second category Qualification Tournament in Tbilisi.

1944

This is the first year from which we have tournament games featuring Petrosian. There are 16 games available, which are enough to gain a realistic picture of his chess level.

First Category Tournament, Tbilisi

Although Petrosian was not yet a first category player, his level of play was well known and Alexander Blagidze, the head of the Pioneers Palace club, arranged for him to be allowed to play at the Georgian championship of first category players.

There are three games recorded for the event. We follow Shekhtman's order of the games throughout 1944 and 1945 and we believe it likely that he followed the order of the rounds. Petrosian was White in his game against Kopelovich. He played a main-line Chigorin Ruy Lopez properly, whereas his opponent made some mistakes. You can see how Tigran exploited them in the It's Your Move chapter.

We look at his game against Aghamalian (his name is without an 'h' in the database), who has only 6 games in the database, 5 against Petrosian and one against Keres. Out of these games, he beat Petrosian once and lost the rest, but the chemistry between him and the future world champion worked well and produced interesting games. It is not known what type of tournament that game was played in.

Game 5

**Aghamalian, Vartan –
Petrosian, Tigran**
First Category Event, Tbilisi, 1944
French Defence

1.e4 e6

Ebralidze liked Nimzowitsch's and Capablanca's styles and he passed his devotion on to his young pupil. Capablanca seldom employed the French and not really successfully, as he lost to Lasker and Alekhine with it. On the other hand, Nimzowitsch regularly played the French successfully. Petrosian employed the French a lot.

2.d4 d5 3.♘c3 ♗b4 4.a3

Smyslov would play this line a few times in his 1954 World Championship match against Botvinnik.

4...♗xc3+ 5.bxc3 dxe4 6.♕g4 ♘f6 7.♕xg7 ♖g8 8.♕h6 c5 9.dxc5

According to the database, this move was not played before and would never be repeated. Opening the position for the bishop pair is logical, but it creates isolated doubled pawns.

9...♘bd7 10.♗g5?

Trying to exert pressure on the kingside is over optimistic. White should keep the queenside together instead. After 10.♘e2 ♘xc5 11.♗e3 ♖g6 12.♕h4 ♕a5 13.♖d1 the position is roughly balanced.

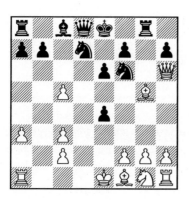

10...♖g6! 11.♗xf6

White gives up the bishop pair to return the queen to the centre. But it leaves his position underdeveloped. 11.♕h4?! ♕a5! 12.♘e2 b6 13.♗xf6 (13.♗d2 ♕xc5 is not much better) 13...♘xf6 14.cxb6 ♗a6 and White is in trouble.

11...♘xf6 12.♕e3 ♕a5 13.♕d4

It is not nice to move the queen when all the white pieces are still on their starting square.

13...♗d7 14.♕b4

After 14.♘e2 0-0-0 15.♕b4 ♕c7

16.♖d1 Black's advantage would be smaller than in the game.

14...♕c7 15.♖b1?

Aghamalian hopes to create problems for Black on the b-file, but they will be neutralised easily, so the rook should be placed on the d-file.

15...0-0-0 16.♘e2 e5 17.c4

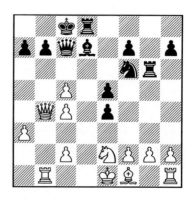

17...e3!

Black is far ahead in development, therefore, opening the position is justified.

18.f3

Taking the pawn with 18.fxe3 is no fun, but still resisted: 18...♘g4 19.♖b3 ♗c6 20.h3 (20.♘g3 ♕e7 21.♘f5 ♕f6 and Black wins) 20...♘h6 (20...♘f6 21.♖d3 is also better for Black) 21.♖g1 ♘f5 22.g3 and Black has an edge, but White would not be lost.

18...♗c6 19.♘c3

19.♕c3 White could take the annoying pawn, but that was slow: 19...e4 20.f4 ♕d7 would not help, and neither would 19.♖b3, for instance 19...e4 20.♖xe3 exf3

21.gxf3 ♔b8 and Black would win.

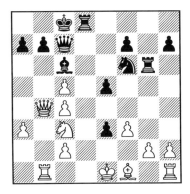

19...a6!

A Petrosian signature move; he could go after the opponent and obtain a winning position, but he prevents his opponent's play first. Attacking at once with 19...e4! was equally good, as after 20.♘b5 ♗xb5 21.♕xb5 exf3 22.gxf3 White's position is in ruins with 22...♘d7 or 22...♖g5.

20.♕b6

Aghamalian finds a move that gives him decent practical chances.

20...♕e7!!

Petrosian finds his way well in the complications.

a) 20...e4 21.♕xc7+ ♔xc7 22.f4 exchanging queens gives some advantage, but not that much.

b) 20...♕b8 intending e4. Then 21.g3! looks frightening for Black, but 21...♗xf3 (21...♘d7 22.♕a5 ♗xf3 23.♘d5 and White is no worse) 22.c6! (22.♗h3+ ♘d7 wins) 22...♗xh1

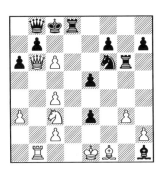

23.♘d5!!

b1) 23...♗xd5 24.cxd5 ♘xd5 25.♗h3+ ♖e6 26.cxb7+ ♔d7 27.♗xe6+ fxe6 28.♕xa6 and White has compensation for the piece.

b2) 23...♘xd5 24.♗h3+ ♖e6 25.cxb7+ ♔d7 26.cxd5 ♗xd5 27.c4!= White is a rook down, but he is no worse.

21.♕a7?

White goes down without a fight. 21.g3! bringing the bishop into play would have given Tigran chances to go wrong.

a) 21...♕e6! 22.♕a7 ♕f5 (if 22...e4?! 23.f4 still resists) 23.♖b6 ♖d2 and Black would keep some advantage.

b) 21...♗xf3 22.♕a7

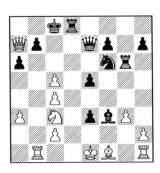

22...♔d7!! The later Petrosian would surely have seen this king walking away, and possibly the very young one also spotted it (22...♗xh1 23.♗h3+ ♘g4 24.♘d5 ♗xd5 25.cxd5 ♕c7 26.c6 ♕b8 27.♕xe3=) 23.♕xb7+ ♗xb7 24.♖xb7+ ♔e8 25.♖xe7+ ♔xe7 26.♗d3 ♖g4 and Black's advantage is considerable.

21...e4 22.f4

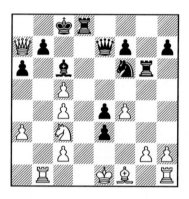

22...♘h5!?

Petrosian finds a good way to crack White's rather suspicious position, but his idea is still not the best. 22...e2! 23.♗xe2 ♖xg2 wins.

23.g3 ♘xf4! 24.♘a4??

Aghamalian wants to be active, but probably misses Black's lethal threat and goes down without putting up a fight. 24.♘d5! would not equalise, but would allow White to stay narrowly in the game. 24...♘xd5 25.cxd5 ♗xd5 (25...♖xd5?! 26.♗xa6!) 26.♗h3+ ♔c7 27.0-0 e2 (if 27...♖f6 28.♗g4 White avoids instantly losing and gets back in the game) 28.♖f2 ♗c6 29.♖xe2 ♖d5 30.c4 (30.♖f1? ♖f6!) 30...♕xc5+ 31.♕xc5 ♖xc5 32.♖f1 when White would be a pawn down, but it would require skill to convert the pawn advantage.

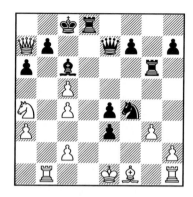

24...♕f6! 0–1 According to Shekhtman, White lost on time. The Black queen would invade decisively anyway.

Petrosian knew the spirit of the opening; he made a remarkable preventive move and maybe did not yet find his way as confidently as he would at his peak, but showed very good tactical vision which brought his opponent down. In the third available game, Petrosian was White against Lebedev in a Queen's Gambit Accepted. Petrosian sacrificed a pawn, he pressed for some time but Lebedev slowly took control. Eventually, they drew in a rook ending. The game lasted 40 moves.

From the known three games, Petrosian scored 2.5 points. He finished in second place, qualifying for the final of the national championship with 8.5/11 points.

Whoever gave him the advice to purchase *The Art of Sacrifice in Chess* by Rudolf Spielmann brought a lot of benefit to the young talent. Perhaps it was Ebralidze's recommendation, as he realised that Tigran's less developed calculating ability was stopping him from progressing even more.

Calculating superbly was one of the important elements of Tigran's chess throughout his career.

Championship of the Georgian Republic, Tbilisi

The event took started in November and ended in December. We will look at three of his games from this event, where he faced strong masters for the first time. He started the event as Black against Bakhtadze. It was a 1.c4 e5 English. Petrosian equalised and part of the middlegame can be seen in the chapter Petrosian's Remarkable Exchanges. Petrosian won the game nicely on move 27, catching White's king.

In round two, Petrosian faced a real test against Kasparian.

Game 6

**Petrosian, Tigran –
Kasparian, Henrik**
Championship of the Georgian
Republic, Tbilisi (2), 1944
King's Indian Defence

1.d4 ♘f6 2.c4 g6 3.♘c3 ♗g7 4.♘f3 0-0 5.g3 d6 6.♗g2 c6 7.0-0 ♘bd7 8.b3 ♖e8 9.♗b2 e5

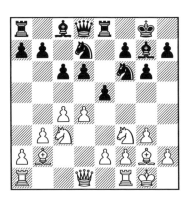

10.e3
To our surprise, this innocent looking move has been played more

than 60 times. Kasparian was 19 years older than Petrosian, so maybe the boy wanted to avoid a sharp variation.

10...♕c7 11.♕d2
On the other hand, there is no other game with this move in the database; players probably want to keep this square free for the knight.

11...h6 12.♖ac1 e4 13.♘e1 ♘f8 14.f3 exf3 15.♘xf3
The position is even.

15...♗g4 16.♘h4 ♕d7 17.e4 ♗h3
17...♘8h7 was reasonable as well.

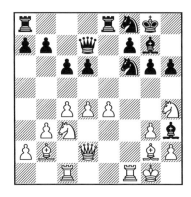

18.♘f5!?

An imaginative and somewhat confident move.

18...♘xe4

After 18...♗xg2 19.♘xg7 ♗xf1 20.♘xe8 ♖xe8 21.♖xf1 ♘xe4 22.♘xe4 ♖xe4 23.d5 White would have enough compensation for the pawn.

19.♘xh6+ ♗xh6 20.♕xh6 ♗xg2 21.♔xg2 ♘xc3

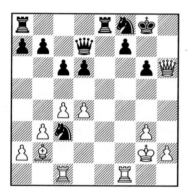

22.♗xc3

The dust has settled and the position is equal.

22...♖e2+ 23.♔g1?!

23.♖f2 is safer.

23...d5 24.♖f4 ♕e6 25.♗d2 ♖e8 26.♖h4 ♕f6 27.♖f1 ♕g7

28.♕xg7+

Both players are ready to settle for an endgame. Against such an outstanding endgame specialist this contains some risk.

28...♔xg7   29.♗h6+   ♔g8 30.♖hf4 f5 31.♗xf8

The four rook ending is still even.

31...♖xf8

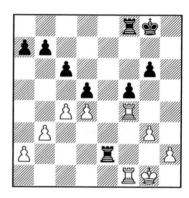

32.g4

Petrosian is not only looking for safety with 32.♖1f2, but is ready to enter a fight.

32...♖xa2 33.cxd5 cxd5 34.gxf5

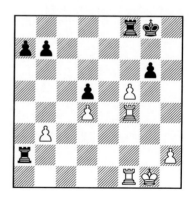

34...♖f6

Kasparian wants to battle the endgame out. After the more peaceful 34...♖xf5 35.♖xf5 gxf5 36.♖xf5 ♖b2 37.♖xd5 ♖xb3 the position would be equal.

35.fxg6 ♖xg6+ 36.♔h1 ♔h7 37.♖f7+ ♖g7 38.♖xg7+ ♔xg7 39.♖f5 ♖a5

Black avoids simplifying.

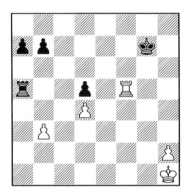

40.♔g1

After 40.h4 White could keep the b3–pawn. If 40...♖b5 41.♖f3 ♔g6 42.♔g2 ♖b4 43.♖d3 ♔f5 44.♔g3 ♔e4 45.♖f3 ♔xd4 46.h5 the endgame would be even.

40...♔g6 41.♖e5

Petrosian effectively agrees to swap the b3–pawn for the one on d5. This is somewhat risky, as Black will have connected passed pawns.

41...♖b5 42.♔f2

Playing passively is suspicious, for example: 42.♖e3 ♖b4 43.♖d3 ♔f5 44.♔f2 ♔e4 45.♔e2 ♖xd4 46.♖xd4+ ♔xd4 when Black would win the pawn ending.

42...a5 43.♔e2 ♖xb3 44.♖xd5 a4 45.♔d2

If it were Black to move, b6 or b5 would win, which shows that White has to be alert.

45...a3 46.♖a5 b5

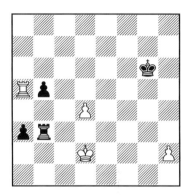

47.♔c2?!

This doesn't give away the draw, but it loses a tempo and makes it less effortless to obtain it. If 47.h4

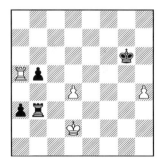

White can push the h-pawn first to send the black king away, which is simpler.

a) 47...b4 48.h5+ ♔h6 49.d5 ♖c3 50.d6 ♖c6 51.d7 ♖d6+ 52.♔c2 ♖xd7 53.♔b3 and White holds.

b) 47...♖b2+ 48.♔c1 (if 48.♔c3 b4+ 49.♔c4 White holds here as well) 48...b4 49.h5+ ♔h6 50.d5 ♖g2 51.♔b1 ♖d2 52.♖b5 and White is about to take the b-pawn, but 52.d6 ♖xd6 53.♖b5 also draws.

47...♖b2+ 48.♔c1

This is the only move here.

48...b4

49.h4

After 49.d5 ♖xh2 the only move to hold is 50.♔b1! The king move would stop a2.

49...♖h2 50.d5??

Petrosian probably just made this move without calculating at all. The punishment is rather heavy. 50.h5+ giving up the pawn is still fine. 50...♖xh5 51.d5 (51.♖a6+ and 51.♖a8 draw, but interestingly 51.♖a7?? would lose) 51...♖h2 52.♔b1 and White obtains the draw. White has another way to hold: 50.♔b1 ♖xh4 51.♖b5 ♖xd4 52.♔a2 when Black can't win according to Kasparian.

50...a2 0–1 Petrosian had to resign, as b2 will come with a huge check.

Losing the game must have been a bitter pill to swallow, but there were several positive sides. He played

freely and entered tactics, holding his own, even in the endgame against a magical endgame composer, until one blunder prevented him from obtaining the half point.

Let us show a fantastic study by the great Kasparian. We think that this Petrosian game generated the idea.

Game 7

Henrik Kasparian
Shakhmaty v SSSR, 1946

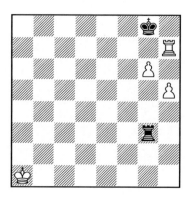

1.♔a2!!

The point of this fantastic move is to arrive at f2 on time and set up a zugzwang.

1.♔b1 ♖b3+=; 1.♔b2 ♖h3

a) 2.♔c1 ♖c3+! (2...♖g3? 3.♔c2+–; 2...♖h1+ 3.♔c2 ♖h3 4.♔d2+–) 3.♔d1 ♖d3+ 4.♔e1 ♖e3+ 5.♔f1 ♖f3+ 6.♔e2 (6.♔g2 ♖a3=) 6...♖g3=

b) 2.♔c2 ♖g3 3.♔d2 ♖h3 4.♔e2 ♖g3 5.♔f2 ♖h3. This is the key position of this brilliant study, as it is mutual zugzwang. 6.♔g1 (6.h6

♖h5=) 6...♖a3 7.♔g2 ♖b3 8.♔h2 ♖a3 9.♔g2 ♖b3 10.♔f1 ♖f3+! 11.♔e2 ♖g3=

1...♖d3

1...♖h3 2.♔b2 ♖g3 3.♔c2 ♖h3 4.♔d2 ♖g3 5.♔e2 ♖h3

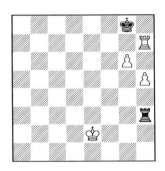

6.♔f2 and now Black is in zugzwang.

2.♖b7 ♖h3

2...♖g3 3.♔b2 ♖g5 4.♖h7 ♖g3 5.♔c2 ♖h3 6.♔d2 ♖g3 7.♔e2 ♖h3 8.♔f2 wins.

3.♖b5

Now the rook is not passive anymore, though it still takes time to win.

3...♔g7 4.♖g5! ♖h4

4...♖c3 5.h6++−

5.♔b3 ♖h1 6.♔c4 ♖c1+ 7.♔d5 ♖d1+ 8.♔e6 ♖e1+ 9.♔d6 ♖d1+ 10.♖d5 ♖a1 11.♔e7 ♖a6

11...♖e1+ 12.♔d8! ♔h6 13.♖d7! ♔xh5 14.g7 ♖g1 15.♔e8 ♔h6 16.♔f8+−

12.♖d7 ♖b6

12...♖a8 13.♔e6+

13.♔d8+ ♔g8 14.♖e7 ♔f8

14...♖a6 15.♔d7 ♖b6 16.♖e6 ♖b7+ 17.♔d6 ♖b6+ 18.♔e5 ♖b5+ 19.♔f6 and White wins.

15.♖f7+ ♔g8 16.♔e7 ♖a6 17.♖f6 ♖a7+ 18.♔e6 ♖a6+ 19.♔f5 ♖a5+ 20.♔g4 ♔g7 21.♖f7+ ♔g8 22.h6+−

In round 3, Petrosian faced Gamrekeil, another decent player who participated in the 1941 Georgian championship and in the 1955 one as well, among others. Playing during such a long period in the championship of a country with such a great chess tradition speaks for itself.

Game 8

Gamrekeil, Givi – Petrosian, Tigran
Championship of the Georgian
Republic, Tbilisi (3), 1944
Caro-Kann Defence

1.e4 c6

Petrosian replied 1...c5 the most frequently of all, but the Caro-Kann was the defence he employed the second most.

2.d4 d5 3.e5 ♗f5 4.♗d3 ♗xd3 5.♕xd3 e6 6.♘f3

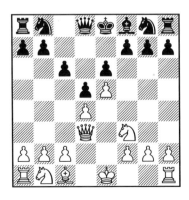

6...♕a5+!

This check and the next move demonstrate that Petrosian was already an educated player.

7.♗d2 ♕a6 8.♘c3

The knight doesn't stand well on c3, and if Black can exchange on d4, the e5-pawn may weaken.

8...♘e7 9.0-0 ♘f5 10.a3 h5 11.b4 ♕xd3 12.cxd3 ♗e7 13.♘a4

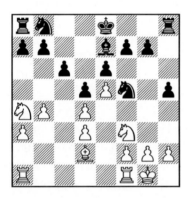

13...g5!

After developing calmly, Petrosian plays an imaginative space-gaining move.

14.♗xg5 ♗xg5 15.♘xg5 ♘xd4

Gaining a d-pawn for a g-one is usually beneficial.

16.♘c5?

White wants to play subtle chess, but it is not worth investing two tempi on provoking b6. The position would be even after 16.f4 and the game might continue 16... a5 (16...♘d7 17.♔f2) 17.♘b6 ♖a6 18.♘c8.

16...b6 17.♘a4

After 17.♘b7 ♔e7 the knight would not do enough on d6.

17...♘d7 18.f4 ♖g8

Black sends the knight back to improve his safety.

19.♘h3 ♔e7

Petrosian finds the best square for his king.

20.♖a2

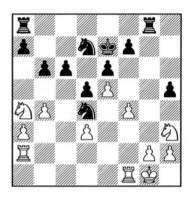

20...a5!

Switching to the queenside gives a large advantage.

21.♖fa1 ♖a6 22.♔f2 ♖ga8 23.♘g1 b5 24.♘c3

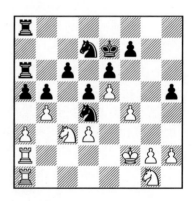

24...♘b3

After a few natural improving moves he wins a pawn with the help of small tactics.

25.♖b1 axb4 26.♘xb5 cxb5 27.♖xb3 ♖xa3 28.♖bxa3

28.♖ab2 ♘c5 loses on the spot.

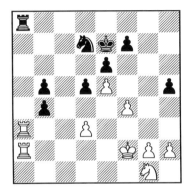

28...bxa3

The two connected passed pawns are decisive. The rest is elementary, and requires no comment.

29.♘e2 ♘c5 30.♘d4 ♘xd3+ 31.♔e3 ♘b4 32.♖a1 a2 33.♔d2 ♖c8 34.♘xb5 ♖c2+ 35.♔e3 ♖xg2 0–1

There was nothing especially remarkable about this game, but Petrosian played purposefully, and made no mistake at all.

In round 4, Petrosian was White against Nerzanov, who blundered badly and lost after White's 16th move. In round 5, Petrosian was Black against Malashia, and grabbed the b2-pawn with his queen. He was better when he blundered badly and resigned after Malashia's 19th move. In round six, Petrosian was White against Mikenas, who equalised in an Alekhine Defence. Mikenas won a pawn in the middlegame,

Petrosian had chances to hold with a fortress, but gave away a second pawn, perhaps in time trouble, and went on to lose. He lasted 41 moves against the legendary player. In round 7, Petrosian was White against Smorodsky. He gained an edge in a 1.c4 e5 English and pressed, but his opponent managed to hold. In round 8, Petrosian was White against Alexander Blagidze in a g3 King's Indian. Black equalised in the opening, got an edge in the middlegame and won the game on move 40. In round 9, Petrosian was Black against Sereda in a main-line Slav. The complex position was balanced for a long time. Petrosian gave up a pawn in an endgame, then he nicely spotted that he would draw a pawn down in a bishop ending. The game ended in a draw after Petrosian's 43rd move.

Game 9

Aghamalian, Vartan – Petrosian, Tigran
Championship of the Georgian Republic, Tbilisi (10), 1944
Grunfeld Defence

1.d4 ♘f6 2.e3

Of course, such a move doesn't hurt Black. Younger players tend to know openings, and it is likely that Aghamalian knew openings but just wanted to avoid a theoretical battle in this game.

2...g6 3.g3 ♗g7 4.♗g2 0-0 5.b3 d5 6.♘d2 c5 7.♘gf3 ♘c6 8.♗b2

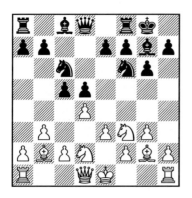

8...♗f5

All Petrosian's moves are healthy; he has found the best places for his minor pieces.

9.a3 ♘e4 10.0-0 ♖c8 11.♖c1 ♕a5 12.c3 ♖fd8 13.♘h4 ♘xd2

Petrosian doesn't want doubled pawns.

14.♕xd2

14.♘xf5? loses an exchange after 14...♘xf1 15.♘xg7 ♘xe3 16.fxe3 ♔xg7.

14...♗e6 15.♕d1

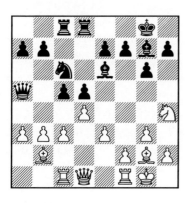

15...♕b6!

Nicely spotting that the b3–pawn is vulnerable.

16.♘f3 ♗g4

Petrosian stops the knight from defending the b3–pawn.

17.♗a1 ♘a5

17...e5 is also nice for Black.

18.♖b1 cxd4!

Opening the c-file is beneficial for Black as he may occupy it and invade on it.

19.cxd4

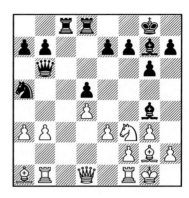

19...♗f5

Petrosian could just build the position with 19...♖c7 and enjoy a clear advantage, but he forces matters.

20.♖b2 ♕d6 21.♖a2 ♕c7 22.♘e1

22.b4 ♘c4 would consolidate, but it would be settling for long-term suffering. 22.♘d2 ♗c2 23.♕c1 ♗xb3 would lose a pawn.

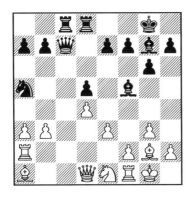

22...♛c1!

It is a good quality to know which piece to exchange.

23.♝f3 ♛xd1 24.♝xd1 ♜c1 25.♞f3 ♝g4!?

Petrosian wins a pawn, but misses an opportunity to finish the game faster. 25...♝b1! 26.♜b2 (26. ♜d2 ♝e4) 26...♜dc8 when White is paralysed.

26.♔g2 ♞xb3 27.♝b2

Or 27.♝xb3 ♝xf3+.

27...♜b1 28.♝xb3 ♝xf3+ 29.♔g1 ♜xf1+ 30.♔xf1

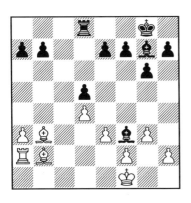

30...♜c8

Black is not only a pawn up, his pieces stand more actively. It is worth looking at how he converts his advantage.

31.♔e1 e6 32.♔d2 ♝f8 33.♝c3 f6

Petrosian prepares to gain space in the centre.

34.♝a4 ♔f7 35.♝b5 ♝d6 36.a4 e5 37.a5 ♝g4 38.♜b2 ♔e7 39.♝f1 ♜c7 40.♜b5

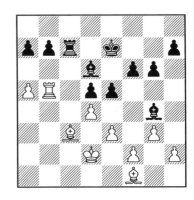

40...♝d7!

A clever way to send the rook away.

41.♜b1 e4 42.♝e2 ♝c6 43.g4 h6 44.h4 ♔e6 45.♜f1 b5

45...f5 46.gxf5+ gxf5 47.♜g1 ♔f6 48.♜g8 f4 was also promising.

46.a6?

This pawn is likely to fall thanks to this move. I suspect they had not adjourned on the 40th move, as Aghamalian would not have committed such a mistake after home analysis. 46.axb6! axb6 47.♜b1 and White would restrict Black somewhat. White's position would not fall apart on its own, and Black would have to work for the win.

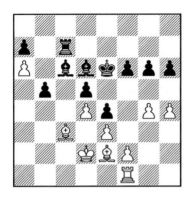

46...b4!

Petrosian uncovers a forced win.

47.♗b2 ♗a4 48.♗d1 ♗b5 49.♖g1 ♗xa6

The outcome of the game is decided by winning the second pawn.

50.f4 ♗b5 51.f5+ ♔f7 52.g5 fxg5 53.hxg5 h5 54.♖h1 ♖c8 55.fxg6+

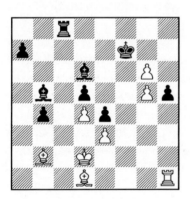

55...♔g7

A clever finish.

56.♗xh5 ♖h8 0–1

This was already a quality game by Petrosian.

The winter of 1944/1945 was cold and, unusually for Tbilisi, it snowed a lot. Petrosian had to set his alarm clock for 3 am in the morning to sweep the snow, after that he went to school, after that he continued with the championship, and the next day he also started at 3 am... The next game shows how tired he must have been.

Game 10

Petrosian, Tigran – Tsintsadze, Viacheslav

Championship of the Georgian Republic, Tbilisi (11), 1944

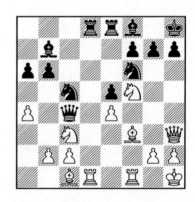

21.♖xd8?? ♖xd8? 22.♗g5?? ♕xf1# 0–1

After defaulting in the next two rounds, Petrosian rejoined the tournament and completed the event. In round 14, Petrosian was White against Sorokin, who played the Tarrasch Defence. Petrosian confidently sacrificed a pawn in an open position, and after some inaccuracies he brought down his opponent by catching his king in 23 moves. In round 15, Petrosian was Black against Mirzaev in a Sicilian side-line. Petrosian equalised, then his opponent gave away a pawn. Mirzaev fought hard, yet Petrosian's 61st move prompted Mirzaev's resignation. Tigran finished the event in 9th-11th place, scoring 7 points out of 15 games. He won an impressive 6 games, drew 2 and lost 5 over the board and two by forfeit.

It's best if we cite his lifelong friend, the chess player Tengiz Giorgadze, about these times[2]:

We were introduced in 1944 during the long snowy winter (in December). I saw him earlier at the Tbilisi Work Palace, where the 5th Georgian boys championship was held. We became friends from the start. At that time, the war was in progress. We lived in poverty, suffering from hunger. Tigran was wearing an extremely faded coat. I was wearing a body-warmer that I had been given at a factory in Zestaponi where I worked for 2 years, but we didn't worry so much about the hard times. We were young and we had chess.

We became friends mostly thanks to chess literature. I had lots of books and magazines. I had been collecting them even before the war, buying from second hand book shops with money saved from my meals. When Tigran saw my books... He would miss school. He would come in the morning and stay till the evening. He would read whilst I was at university (I was studying at the Tbilisi Railway Engineering Institute). When I returned home and whilst I cooked our modest dinner, he would tell me what he was reading about. At the same time, his eyes would shine so brightly that it was not difficult to guess his chess future.

Tigran also had good books in his possession. He knew nearly all of them by heart. Without mistakes, he could say what was written on which page. He could recite Aron Nimzowitsch's books My System *and* The Praxis of My System *like poems. He would tell me "these books' principles are in harmony with my soul." Tigran was already trying to play positional chess, in which his studies with Archil Ebralidze at the Pioneers Palace were of great assistance. The Georgian master was a big fan of the positional style.*

Friends called him Sanchik, but I called him Tigran. He was 4 years younger than me, but that did not affect our relationship. His mature attitude to chess earned him respect from us. Chess was his life's stimulus, his life's purpose.

When we became close friends, he told me his life story. In 1942, both his mother and father died. He was living with his aunt in a tiny apartment on Rustavely Prospect, next to the Officers House. He had a sister and brother but they were staying with other relatives. His elderly aunt was working as a cleaner

Interviews in Georgian magazine Lelo numbers 97 and 98, 1997

*in the Officers House. She would have to sweep the part of the street from the
Officers House to the Borjomi shop. Sometimes Tigran would help her. When he
became Georgian Champion in 1946* [Petrosian was Georgian Champion in
1945 but the championship ended in January 1946, and he was also Armenian
Champion in 1946] *and people could already recognise him, Tigran would wake
up at dawn to replace his aunt. He was embarrassed to bump into someone he
knew. He also told me that after he became an orphan, he would get up in the
middle of the winter night to secure his place in the queue for kerosene, which
he would then sell in order to bring home some money for bread. Sometimes, he
would work as a helper for the cinema mechanic at the Officers House.*

*In this hardship, Tigran matured quickly, becoming very single-minded. He
devoted all his time to chess. Thoughts about chess, being in the chess world,
participating in chess tournaments, reading chess books, all of that increased his
love for chess. Later, the World Champion Petrosian would write that reading
chess books without a chess set develops a player's technique, imagination and
thinking process. The teenager Tigran amazed me with composure, patience and
seriousness untypical of a young boy. I often heard him criticizing analysis by
the famous chess masters, such as Peter Romanovsky.*

In the database, there are 16 games from 1944. He scored 9.5 points out of
16: he won eight games, drew three and lost five.

It is a pity there are none of his games from when he was a beginner.
Analysing Karpov's, Fischer's, Carlsen's and Tal's games from their early
youth uncovers some features of the future great players. In Petrosian's case,
we sadly have to miss these games; perhaps some will pop up.

By this time, he was clearly no amateur, and he already had a repertoire.
A bit surprisingly, his wins mainly came via tactics. Of the five games he lost,
two were against superb players, Mikenas and Kasparian, who beat him in
long endgames. Moreover, their wins were in doubt right up until the very last
moment. He blundered twice, and he was outplayed strategically only once, by
Blagidze, which was impressive. That was a fantastic accomplishment at the
time, when it took youngsters longer to obtain a high level. The low number
of draws (only two) was somewhat surprising for a player who would later
become one of the most cautious players of all. His level in 1944 already shows
that he was likely to become a special player.

Petrosian's results in 1944

First Category Tournament, Tbilisi	8.5/11	
Georgian Championship	+ 6 = 2 – 7 (2 forfeits) 7/15	9th-11th place
Altogether	**15.5/26**	

Dear Reader, there may be a few small inaccuracies regarding the game data and the order of Petrosian's tournaments in this book. However, the sources we have rarely contradict each other, and when they do, we choose the information we think the most likely to be correct. We have made a big effort to trace and provide you with all the results.

1945

Junior event, Tbilisi

Petrosian won a junior event in Tbilisi, scoring 100 percent, we do not know in which month it was held or who else participated in the event.

Training games versus Grigoriev

Petrosian played some training games with Nikolai Grigoriev, and there are three games in the database. In the first game, Petrosian was Black and played 1...♘c6 versus 1.e4. There were quite a few mistakes in the game. Petrosian sacrificed a pawn then a piece and caught Grigoriev's king. In game 2, Petrosian was White. His opponent made an opening mistake in a main-line Sicilian, then Petrosian beautifully exploited it with a nice tactical idea, which can be seen in the It's Your Move chapter. Petrosian was Black in game 3, and after 1.d4 e6 2.c4 ♗b4+, they transposed into a Nimzo Indian. Grigoriev played poorly, and Petrosian nicely exploited his mistakes strategically and beat him convincingly. In these games he showed a kind of all roundness against a modest opponent.

Training Tournament, Tbilisi

A training tournament was held in Tbilisi in March and April.

In round 1, Petrosian was White against Kelendzheridze, who fell for a basic trap in the 3.♘c3 ♗b4 French Defence. Petrosian sacrificed an exchange (not a positional sacrifice) and his attack quickly forced his opponent to lay down arms, in 19 moves. Next, Petrosian was Black against Shtashvili; his opponent attacked in a ♗e2 Scheveningen with f4, g4, g5 and f5. Petrosian's king was caught early on and he resigned after White's 18th move. This game doesn't suggest that defending would come naturally to him. In game 3, Petrosian was White against Dzhaparidze in a King's Gambit He played the game fluently and won in 14 moves. Petrosian was Black against Buslaev next. He got a somewhat worse position in the g3 King's Indian but stirred up the position tactically. It was still bad for him, but the game then fluctuated and ended in a draw. In round 5, Petrosian was White against Chachua; he played the 1.d4 2.♘f3 with e3 and b3 setup. Tigran obtained a nice advantage in the opening, but it became smaller when he let his opponent exchange his strong bishop. In the end, he caught his opponent's king. He was White against Arnshtein next. He obtained a nice advantage in a Queen's Gambit Declined, but he let his advantage slip and the game ended in a draw.

In his first recorded or partly recorded event, he played much more as a tactician than as a strategist, while his endgame play was decent.

Tbilisi Championship

The championship of the Georgian capital was played in May and June.

Petrosian was White in round 1, and he faced Bakhtadze. It was a calm 1.c4 c5 opening and it looked like the game would end in a draw, but Black lost a pawn. Petrosian was winning easily, but after time control he made a bad mistake and the game ended in a draw after Black's 48th move. In round 2, Petrosian was Black against Malashia. The g3 King's Indian led to a complex middlegame. Petrosian outplayed and beat his opponent convincingly. In the next round, Petrosian was Black against Gershkovich in an Advance French. He took control at the end of the opening. Then the game started to fluctuate, from equal to advantage to Black. After time control, Petrosian was a pawn up and should have won, but the game ended in a draw. In round 4, Petrosian was White against Shishov. The Catalan resulted in a Stonewall position, and the fluctuating game ended in a repetition after Petrosian's 51st move. In game 5, he was Black against Giorgi Georgadse in an Old Benoni. He was lost for quite a few moves, but his opponent was eventually happy to simplify to a draw. In round 6, Petrosian faced Kasparian. Petrosian gave a check early on a4 in the Grunfeld, the great composer blundered in an equal position, and the rook ending was easily winning for Petrosian. In the next game, Petrosian was Black against Aghamalian. White exchanged queens in the Old Indian early on, then Petrosian nicely outclassed his opponent. The game lasted 34 moves. In round 8, Arutiunov played the 3...dxe4 French. The position was even for a long time, but Petrosian fell for a pin in the endgame and soon resigned. In round 9, Petrosian was Black against Nerzenov in an Exchange Slav. He got an edge, but it evaporated. Nerzenov hoped to win on the back rank, but blundered his rook and resigned. In round 10, Petrosian was White against Ebralidze in a 1.c4 e5 English. Tigran obtained a small edge and in a rook ending his trainer trapped his own rook. The way that Tigran exploited the trap can be seen in the It's Your Move chapter. Petrosian had a win against Blagidze next. He was probably Black, but we found no record of the game.

Kasparian won the championship with 8.5 points, but Petrosian was second with 8 points. He won 6 games, drew 4 and lost 1. Ebralidze was third with 7 points. Finishing just half a point below the established player Kasparian and beating him was a remarkable result for the young Tigran.

First Category Tournament, Tbilisi

A first category tourney was held in July and August. All we know about the event is that Petrosian had five recorded games.

Petrosian was White against Mirzaev and Buslaev, and he was too strong for his opponents. He was Black against Shishov, who played an early dxc5 in the Advance French. Petrosian was better, but played passively. Shishov took control and won the game with his 43rd move. Petrosian was White against Stintsadze. He gained an advantage in the g3 Grunfeld. His opponent equalised with a pretty move (Tigran may have missed it) and Petrosian lost a pawn soon after. Yet he struggled for a long time and managed to draw after his 74th move. Petrosian was Black against Blagidze, who gained a small edge in a main-line Nimzo Indian. Petrosian made an imaginative piece sacrifice to obtain a defended passed e-pawn. He soon equalised and the position was balanced for a long time. Petrosian's position became winning before time control, but the game ended in a draw after his 40th move. He was still winning, but maybe a draw was sufficient for him in the event or perhaps he did not realise that he had reached time control.

He won 2 games, drew 2 and lost 1 in this event.

Soviet Junior Championship, Leningrad

Petrosian travelled to the 1945 junior championship. He had a choice of playing the Soviet Championship Semi-Final or the junior championship; he opted for the second. It is somewhat amazing that less than two years after the devastating 872-day-long siege of Leningrad ended they held the USSR junior championship there. The city must have been in a much worse state than Tbilisi.

According to Vasiliev, somebody praised Reshko in a conversation before the event. Tigran played him as White in the first round, and he was worried when the game started. Petrosian gained a nice edge in a 3.♘d2 c5 Tarrasch French. Both young boys played very tensely, but once they reached an opposite-coloured bishops middlegame the Armenian talent occupied the driving seat. Petrosian checkmated Reshko on the 39th move. The final part of the game probably happened in time trouble. In round 2, Toradze went down quickly without putting up resistance. In the next game, Petrosian won with White against Petrovsky in a Closed Catalan, which can be seen in the chapter Petrosian's Remarkable Exchanges. In round 4, Petrosian was Black against Poliakov. The game ended in a repetition after Petrosian's 16th move. In round 5, Petrosian was White against Soboliev. He obtained some advantage, his opponent did not defend well, and Tigran won the one-sided game in 41 moves. In the next round, Petrosian was Black against Brazilsky. He equalised easily in a 3.♘c3 ♗b4 French, and there was not much excitement in the 28 move draw. In round 7, Petrosian beat an amateur, Korolkov, in 18 moves. In round 8, Soloviev as White turned the Spanish Opening into a dull draw. Petrosian played the g3 King's Indian as White against Glotov. In that game, he made a horrible strategic decision and was lucky to hold; probably, his opponent's time trouble saved him.

In round 10, Petrosian was Black against Vasilchuk. Tigran equalised in a main-line Caro Kann. The game sharpened up, first Petrosian was better, and the game fluctuated. They were probably in time trouble. Vasilchuk made a pretty 39th move forcing Petrosian's resignation, as he was powerless against White's unstoppable passed pawn.

We look at Petrosian's game from round 11.

Game 11

Petrosian, Tigran – Rudakov, Y
Soviet U20 Championship Final,
Leningrad (11), 1945
Slav Defence

1.d4 d5 2.c4 c6 3.cxd5 cxd5 4.♘c3 ♘f6 5.♘f3 ♘c6 6.♗f4 g6 7.e3 ♕a5

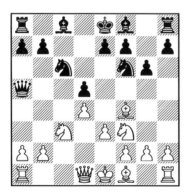

8.♕b3!
Petrosian prevents Black from pinning the c3–knight by ♘e4.

8...♗g7 9.♗e2 0-0 10.0-0
Perhaps starting Petrosian's idea with 10.h3!? was more precise, as it would save the f4–bishop.

10...♕b4
Exchanging queens doesn't solve Black's problems. Black should play 10...♘h5!? to exchange the f4–bishop. 11.♗g5 (11.♘xd5 ♗e6) 11...h6 12.♗h4 g5 13.♗g3 ♘xg3 14.hxg3 ♖d8.

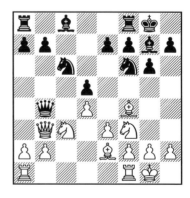

11.h3!
Petrosian finds a deep idea; he voluntarily accepts isolated doubled

pawns, which are rarely strong. After 11.♘e5 ♛xb3 12.axb3 ♖d8 13.♘xc6 bxc6 14.♖fc1 White would be somewhat better.

11...♛xb3

Black grabs the chance to create doubled pawns for White; not doing so would be unpleasant for Black, as after 11...♗e6 12.♘d2! ♖fc8 13.a3 he would face problems.

12.axb3 ♗f5 13.♖fc1 ♖ac8?!

An inaccurate move as the rook no longer defends the a-pawn. If 13...♖fc8 14.g4 ♗e6 White's position is promising after 15.♘e1!? or 15.♘e5.

14.g4

After 14.♘e5 a6 15.g4 ♗e6 16.♘d3 White's advantage is considerable, as 16...♘d7 17.♗f3 would be strong. Or if 14.b4 a6 15.b5 axb5 16.♗xb5 ♖fd8 17.♘a4 White has an edge.

14...♗e6

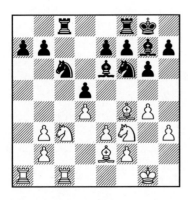

15.♘d2?

This knight move helps to consolidate the occupied space on the kingside and will work well in the game, but objectively it gives away

White's advantage. White could keep the advantage by exchanging one of the doubled pawns or improve the f3–knight with the move 15.b4! and if 15...a6 then 16.b5. White could also try 15.♘e5! ♘xe5 (15...a6 16.♘d3) 16.♗xe5 (16.dxe5 ♘e4 17.♖xa7 f6 18.exf6 ♗xf6 19.♖xb7: here Black is active, but has a two-pawn deficit) 16...a6 17.♗f3 when Black is passive.

15...h5 16.f3 hxg4 17.hxg4 ♘d7?

The strong 17...a6! would fully equalise, as it would take away the possibility of improving the d2–knight. After 18.♘a4 ♘d7 Black is doing alright.

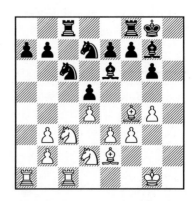

18.b4!

Accepting the doubled pawns pays off, as White can open the a-file and uses the b5 and b3–squares for his knights.

18...a6 19.b5

Petrosian's idea prevails. White gets rid of the doubled pawns and opens up the queenside a bit.

19...axb5 20.♘xb5 f6 21.♘b3

White improves the knight.

21...♗f7 22.♗g3 ♖fe8

22...e5?! 23.♘d6 would be unpleasant. After the stronger 22...♖a8!? 23.♔f2 e5 White's advantage would be smaller.

23.♔f2 ♗f8

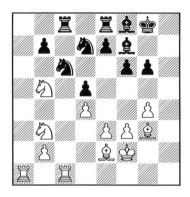

24.♘c7!

Petrosian's move is strong. There is another strong move: 24.♘a7! Exchanging the knight would help invade and win a pawn. 24...♖a8 (24...♘xa7 25.♖xa7) 25.♘xc6 bxc6 26.♖xa8 ♖xa8 27.♖xc6 and White's pawn advantage is enough to win.

24...♖ed8 25.♗b5?

Petrosian wants to remove the c6–knight, but he does it with the wrong piece. 25.♘a5! ♘xa5 26.♖xa5 e5 27.♖b5 and White wins.

25...e5 26.♗xc6 ♖xc7?

Black has to let one of his pawns go, but doesn't choose the best way of doing so. 26...bxc6! 27.♖xc6 ♖b8 28.♖c3 ♖b7 29.♘a6 and Black would not be worse, as White is tied up defending the b3–knight and can't do anything with his extra pawn.

27.♗xd7 ♖cxd7 28.dxe5 ♗g7 29.exf6 ♗xf6

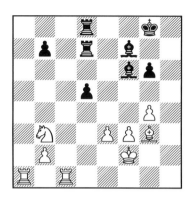

30.♘d4!

White threatens to win the b7–pawn with ♖c7, and this move decides the outcome of the game.

30...♗xd4

Simplifying to opposite-coloured bishops normally increases the chances of the weaker side, but this time it weakens the black king.

31.exd4 ♖e7

A blunder in an already hopeless position. After 31...♗e6 32.♗e5 Black's position would be beyond salvation because of the weak king.

32.♗h4 1–0

In this game, the young Petrosian shows special strategic vision, but some inaccuracies crept in. This neat game was an exception in this event, as in other ones he did not win in a strategic manner. In round 12, Petrosian was Black against Asaturian in a 4.♕c2 Nimzo-Indian. Petrosian was somewhat worse yet he rejected a repetition. He was still able to outplay his opponent, won a pawn, played well, and won the game. However, his opponent could have held with precise play. In game 13, Petrosian gained an advantage in a c4 c5 English against Zaneilli. Tigran outplayed him strategically and soon trapped his rook. In the 14th round, Petrosian was White against Lavrov. He played nicely and got a massive advantage in the Budapest Gambit. Lavrov did well to reach an ending the exchange down. The tablebase can prove that Tigran's position was winning, but he was unable to find a subtle plan. Had he won that game, he would probably not have had to share first place. According to the database, in the last round he played Zhurakov, but according to Shekhtman the game was against Yashin, yet they both show the same game. In a main-line ...♗f5 Caro-Kann, both players mainly looked for safety.

He finished 1st-3rd with Vasilchuk and Reshko; he lost to the first and beat the second. The players who shared first place with him became masters, but not great players. Petrosian scored 8 wins 6 draws and one loss (according to the database he won 9 with no losses, but the header of the Vasilchuk game in the database is incorrect).

Let's discuss how he won his games! Most of his victories came either by attack or outsmarting his opponents tactically. Interestingly, he played only two endings. He won 6 as White and drew two, which was great.

Apart from Petrosian, none of the players from the event would become well-known players. Perhaps it was too close to the war, and the two future giants of Leningrad, Korchnoi and Spassky, were too young. When he returned home he gained confidence and people in the local federation must surely have understood that they had a special talent on their hands.

Semi-Final of the Georgian Championship, Tbilisi

The event started in November and ended in December. After his performance at the Tbilisi championship, he surely must have been a favourite to qualify.

Petrosian's first game was against Sereda. He was White, but obtained no advantage in a Meran. In the middlegame, Petrosian gained a somewhat worse position with an isolated pawn, but he was able to hold. White against Bakhtadze in round 2, Petrosian obtained a big advantage in an unusual Sicilian. Bakhtadze escaped to a rook ending one pawn down, but Petrosian nicely converted his advantage. The end of the game can be seen in the It's Your Move chapter. Aghamalian gained an edge in a Reti in round 3. Petrosian lost a pawn in the middlegame and lost the game on move 41, when his king was caught. Petrosian was White next against Giorgi Georgadse. He obtained a small edge, but it disappeared in the middlegame. Black won a pawn through White's carelessness, yet lost the game soon after. Petrosian was Black in round 5 against Gabunia in a g3 Dragon. Petrosian made what was perhaps his first positional exchange sacrifice, and he won that game (it is shown in the notes to game 27). Tigran was White against Buslaev next in a main-line Queen's Indian. He gained a small edge and the game can be found in the chapter on Petrosian's Remarkable Exchanges. White wasted his advantage, but Buslaev made a big mistake, was punished for it and had to resign after Petrosian's 38th move. Lolua as White played the King's Gambit in round 7. Petrosian was better in the opening, but wasted his advantage. The see-saw game ended in a draw. If the game was recorded correctly, Petrosian was winning in the final position. Petrosian was White against Malashkhia in a Slav. Both sides made quite a few mistakes, and the game ended in a draw after the 34th move. Petrosian was too strong for Nerzanov in round 9. We look at his last game.

Game 12

Petrosian, Tigran –
Arutiunov, Albert
First Category Tournament,
Tbilisi (10), 1945
King's Indian Defence

1.d4 ♘f6 2.♘f3 d6 3.c4 g6 4.♘c3 ♗g7 5.g3 0-0 6.♗g2 ♘bd7 7.0-0 e5 8.e4 c6 9.h3 ♘h5

According to the database, Arutiunov plays a novelty. Later, Bronstein beat Botvinnik in their world championship match with this move. Bronstein spent a lot of time in Tbilisi during World War II, so maybe he got the idea from this game.

10.d5!?

Petrosian is ready to play a complex position. The variation pushing the pawn to d5 in another main line will be named after him.

10...c5

Closing the centre leads to a somewhat passive but solid position.

11.♘e1

White starts transferring the knight to d3.

11...♖e8?

The rook stands better on f8 then on e8.

12.♘d3 ♘b6 13.b3 f5 14.♖b1

I wonder whether he already foresaw the final destination of the rook.

14...♖f8

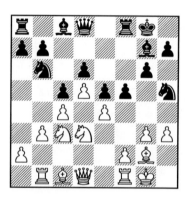

15.exf5!

Petrosian gains an outpost on e4.

15...♗xf5 16.♘e4 ♕d7 17.♔h2 ♘f6 18.f3 h6 19.♗e3 ♖f7

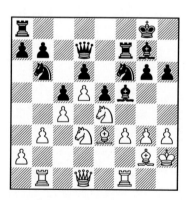

20.♖b2! g5 21.♖bf2!

Petrosian's rook manoeuvre was not great, yet it is remarkable. It is in the style of the future champion.

21...♗g6 22.♕d2 ♘xe4 23.fxe4 ♖xf2 24.♘xf2

Petrosian keeps the rook on the board. Having some space advantage it makes the defender's task harder.

24...♖f8 25.♕e2 ♘c8 26.♗f3 ♕e8

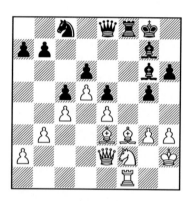

27.a3!

White starts gaining space. Playing on both sides increases White's pressure.

27...♘e7 28.b4 b6 29.♔g2 ♗f6 30.♕d2 ♕a4 31.♕c3 ♕e8

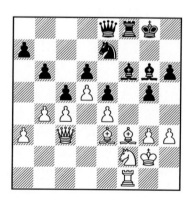

32.bxc5

This capture allows White to attack the a7–pawn, but it has a drawback as well, as it vacates the b6–square for the knight. 32.♗g4 would be stronger.

32...bxc5

If 32...dxc5 then 33.♖d1 would be careless because of the very clever 33...♘f5!, but 33.♕d3 keeps some advantage.

33.♕a5

33.♗g4 is also nice.

33...♕b8

After 33...♘c8 34.♗g4 ♘b6 35.♗e6+ ♔h8 (35...♗f7 36.♘g4) 36.♖c1 White is a bit better.

34.♕a6 ♘c8 35.♗g4 h5 36.♗d7

After 36.♗xc8 ♖xc8 37.♖b1 ♕xb1 38.♕xc8+ ♔h7 the position is equal.

36...♘e7?!

A pointless move. If 36...♕b3! Black could be active for the first time. 37.♗xc8 (after 37.♗xc5 dxc5 38.♗xc8 h4 White is not better) 37...♕xe3 and Black holds.

37.♕b5 ♕xb5

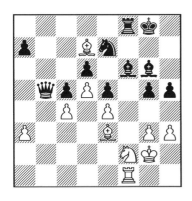

38.cxb5!

White creates chances to obtain a distant passed pawn.

38...♖b8 39.a4 ♔g7 40.♔f3

One may think that the king wants to ease the burden of the knight defending the e4–pawn.

40...♖b7 41.♗c6 ♖b8 42.♔e2!

Petrosian wants to improve the king.

42...♘c8 43.♔d3 ♗d8

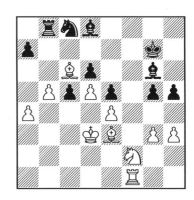

44.g4!?

Petrosian comes up with a surprising idea; he transfers the good-looking c6–bishop to f5.

44...h4 45.♖a1 ♔f6 46.♗d7

After 46.♘d1! ♘e7 47.♘b2 White's advantage would be large.

46...♗a5 47.♗f5 ♘e7

After 47...♘b6 48.♗d2 White would have an advantage.

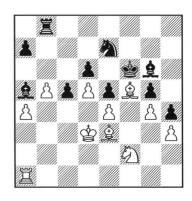

48.♔c4?!

This is an original idea, but not the best, as the knight would stand better on c4 than the king. 48.♘d1, 48.♖f1 ♗e8 49.♘d1 or 48.♗d2 are all very nice for White.

48...♗e8! 49.♖b1?!

A careless move allowing a pin. Nevertheless, the position remains equal after 49.♘d3 ♘xf5 50.exf5 (50.gxf5 ♗h5) 50...e4 51.♘f2 ♔e5 and Black is alive.

49...♘g6

With 49...a6! Black could take advantage of the fact that the rook is unprotected and create a target. 50.♘d3 (if 50.bxa6 the a-pawn is very strong, but Black's play is even stronger: 50...♖xb1 51.a7 ♗xa4 52.♔d3 ♖b2! 53.♗xc5 [53.a8=♕ ♗b5#] 53...♗b5+ 54.♔e3 ♗d2+ 55.♔f3 ♖a2–+) 50...axb5+ 51.axb5 ♗b4 and Black's problems would be behind him as the b5-pawn falls.

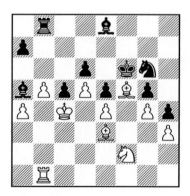

50.♗xg6!?

Giving up the strong bishop is a surprising decision.

50...♔xg6

After 50...♗xg6 51.♖f1 ♔g7 52.♔d3 (52.♗xg5 ♖f8) 52...♖f8 53.♔e2 ♔h6 Black is active enough.

51.♘d3

The knight had sat on the f2–square for the last 27 moves.

51...♖b7?

This move allows Petrosian to obtain an advantage. With 51...a6! Arutiunov has a chance to equalise fully. Let's see White's possibilities.

a) 52.♖b2. White has no time to move the rook to a defended square as after 52...axb5+ 53.axb5 ♗b4 the b5–pawn falls.

b) 52.♘xc5 dxc5 53.♗xc5 ♗d8 (53...axb5+ 54.axb5 ♗d8 55.b6 wins) 54.♖b3 axb5+ 55.axb5 ♖c8 56.♔b4 ♖b8 57.♔c4 and a repetition.

c) 52.bxa6 ♖xb1 53.♘xe5+ (53.a7 ♗xa4) 53...♔g7 54.a7 ♗xa4 55.♔d3 ♖b3+ (55...♗d1 56.a8=♕ ♖b3+ 57.♔c4 ♖b4+ 58.♔d3= and Black gives perpetual check) 56.♔e2 ♖b2+ 57.♔f1 ♗b5+ 58.♔g1 ♗d2 59.a8=♕ ♗xe3+ and White will give perpetual check.

d) 52.♗xc5 axb5+ (52...dxc5? 53.bxa6!! wins) 53.axb5 dxc5 54.♘xe5+ (54.♔xc5 ♔f6) 54...♔f6 55.♘c6 ♗xc6 and Black holds.

52.♖b2

After 52.♖f1 a6 53.bxa6 ♖a7 54.♖f8 White wins.

52...♖f7?

The rook had an important role to play, to hold the queenside pawns, and without it White will prevail easily. After the stronger 52...

♗d8 53.♗xc5 dxc5 54.♘xe5+ ♔f6
55.♘d3 White still had realistic
chances to win.

53.♖f2!

Exchanging the rooks paves the
way for White's queenside pawns.

53...♖xf2 54.♗xf2 ♔f6 55.♗e1

55.♘xc5 dxc5 56.♗xc5 ♗g6
57.♔d3 ♗c7 58.♗xa7 wins.

55...♗d8

56.♘b2!

The knight gets closer to its ideal
square.

56...♔e7

The king will not be able to
help.

57.♔d3 ♔d7 58.♘c4 ♗f6

If 58...♗f7 59.a5 ♗e8 60.a6 White
wins.

59.♗d2 ♗d8 60.a5 ♗e7

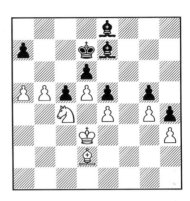

61.a6!

White's pawn gets too close to
promotion to enable Black to hold
the game.

61...♗c8 62.♗xg5!

White wins a pawn.

**62...♗f8 63.b6 ♔b8 64.♗xh4
axb6 65.♘xb6 ♔a7**

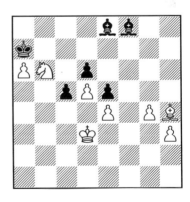

66.♗e7!

Both pretty and deadly effective.

**66...♗xe7 67.♘c8+ ♔xa6
68.♘xe7 ♔b5 69.♔c3 ♔b6 70.g5**

White is about to win a piece.

70...♚c7 71.g6 1–0

Arutiunov handled the opening passively, while Petrosian built his position nicely. Some moments he could have played more powerfully, but Petrosian brought his opponent down and he displayed some original moves. We know that from the 10 available games he scored 7.5 points, he won 6, drew 3 and lost 1 game. He qualified to the final, but it is not known whether he won the event.

Championship of the Georgian Republic, Tbilisi

The final of the 1945 Georgian championship started at the end of December 1945 and ended in January 1946.

Petrosian said that the 1945 Georgian championship was vital for his career. He became increasingly certain of his own abilities. This was probably when he decided to become a professional. Regarding the number of the rounds we can't be sure, as there are 14 games played by Petrosian of which 8 are White and only 6 are Black, so somebody must have withdrawn from the event. We were unable to find out in which round Petrosian rested.

Tigran started the event against Malashia in a side variation of the Slav. Petrosian nicely outplayed him and beat him in 40 moves.

Game 13

**Aghamalian, Vartan –
Petrosian, Tigran**
Championship of the Georgian
Republic, Tbilisi (2), 1945
Queen's Indian Defence

1.d4 ♞f6 2.♞f3 b6 3.g3 ♝b7 4.♝g2 e6 5.0-0 ♝e7 6.b3

This move obviously poses Black few problems.

6...0-0 7.♝b2 d6

Petrosian interestingly does not fight for the centre by pushing the c- or d-pawn two squares.

8.♞bd2 ♞bd7 9.c4 ♞e4

Petrosian fights for control of the e4-square. Undermining the centre with 9...c5!? was safer.

10.♞xe4?!

White plays too cautiously. There are two opportunities to create complications.

a) 10.d5 cutting off the bishop is strategically correct. Let's see how it works tactically! 10...exd5 (10...♞xd2 11.♕xd2±) 11.♞d4

a1) 11...♞ef6 12.♞f5 ♖b8 13.cxd5±

a2) 11...♞df6 12.cxd5 (if 12.♞f5 ♕d7 Black keeps the position together) 12...♝xd5 13.♞f5 ♕d7 14.g4 and White has nice compensation for the pawn.

a3) 11...c5 12.♘f5 ♗f6 13.cxd5 ♗xb2 14.♘xe4 ♗xa1 15.♕xa1 f6. The position is roughly balanced, and White has play for the exchange after 16.♘g5 or 16.♖d1.

b) 10.♘e5 and White could put his knight en prise. 10...f5 (if 10...♘df6 11.♘xe4 ♘xe4 12.♘d3 White has a small edge because of more space) 11.♘xe4 fxe4 12.♘xd7 ♕xd7 13.d5 (13.f3 d5) 13...exd5 14.cxd5 ♕f5 15.♖c1 ♗d8 (15...♖ac8 16.f3) 16.f3 ♕xd5 17.♕xd5+ ♗xd5 18.fxe4 ♖xf1+ 19.♔xf1. Here if 19...♗b7 then 20.e5 is slightly unpleasant, but after 19...♗e6 Black should hold.

10...♗xe4 11.♘d2

If White wants to occupy the centre with 11.♗h3 and ♘d2, Black would make his presence felt there with 11...c5.

11...♗xg2 12.♔xg2

12...f5

Tigran is looking for a fight and he is ready to take on a small disadvantage. 12...d5 or 12...c5 would both equalise.

13.f4

Aghamalian wants to carry out e4 under better conditions, but allows Black to prevent it. Instead, 13.e4! and White grabs the opportunity to play it straight away. 13...f4 (13...fxe4?! 14.♕g4) 14.♕g4 ♖f6 15.♘f3 ♕e8 and after 16.♖ad1 or 16.e5 White's better centre provides an edge.

13...d5!

Petrosian knows the limits to risk taking, and with this move he fights for the centre.

14.cxd5

After this capture, White will plant the knight on e5, but Petrosian correctly judges that the knight on e5 will not hurt him.

14...exd5 15.♕c2 ♗d6 16.♘f3

With 16.♕c6, Aghamalian could force an exchange of queens, but he wants to battle it out. After 16...♘f6 17.♘f3 ♕e8 Black should swap queens sooner or later. If 18.♕xe8 ♖fxe8 19.♘e5 a5 Black has a small initiative.

16...♕e8 17.♘e5 ♖c8 18.♖ac1 ♕e6 19.♕d3

19...♘xe5

Petrosian correctly judges that the protected passed pawn poses no problem for Black.

20.fxe5

After 20.dxe5 ♗e7 21.♖fd1 ♖fd8 22.♖d2 c5 the position would be even.

20...♗e7 21.♖f3?!

This is a step in the wrong direction. White gets nowhere by trying to exert pressure on the f-file. After 21.e3 c5 22.♕a6 c4 23.♖f2 it would be hard for Black to fight for an advantage. If 21.♖fd1 then 21...f4 could be played.

21...c5

Petrosian starts exerting pressure on the queenside.

22.♖cf1?!

White could just move the queen or exchange, and the position would be even after 22.♕d2 or 22.dxc5 bxc5 23.e3.

22...g6 23.e3?!

Perhaps moving back with 23.♖c1 was the simplest.

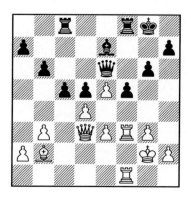

23...c4!
Black takes over on the c-file.

24.bxc4

If 24.♕d2 a5 25.♖c1 b5 26.bxc4 ♗b4 27.♕d1 bxc4 28.♖f2 White would be worse, but has reasonable chances to hold.

24...♖xc4 25.h4

Aghamalian takes a risk for activity, but after this move his king becomes slightly less secure.

If 25.♗a3 ♖fc8 26.♗xe7 ♕xe7 27.♖3f2 White should hold.

25...h5!

Petrosian seals his opponent's kingside.

26.♗a3 ♖fc8 27.♗xe7 ♕xe7 28.♖3f2 ♕e6!

Not a spectacular move, but a strong one. One function is clear: it helps Black to defend the d5 pawn, but has a hidden purpose as well.

29.♕b1

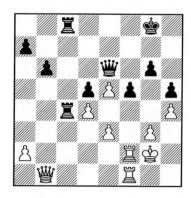

29...♔g7!!

It would be really nice to know why exactly he played this deep move. One possibility is that he knew that his opponent likes to go forward, and just waited. But there is a good chance he noticed something hidden. One may think it is a subtle prophylactic king move, but not quite! After 29...a6 30.g4 hxg4 31.h5 g3 32.♖b2 the players have equal chances, and after 32.♔xg3 ♕e7 33.♖g2 the position would also be equal.

30.♕b2

Aghamalian doesn't know what to do, so he decides to wait and see how Black will develop his play on the queenside. Not 30.g4?! hxg4 31.h5 g3! 32.♖d2 (32.♔xg3 ♕e7 loses)

32...♖h8! Here we finally see the point of Petrosian's idea: he vacated the 8th rank, enabling his rook to join the attack. After 33.♖h1 g5 White would face problems.

30...a6!

Petrosian plays on both flanks.

31.♖d2

31.♖e2 defending the e3-pawn was preferable. After 31...♖c3 Black could build play by ♖8c4 and b5.

31...♖c3 32.♔f3?

White carelessly protects the e3–pawn. After 32.♖e1 b5 Black would still be better.

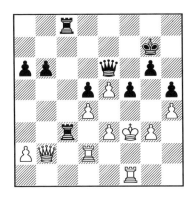

32...f4!!

This move is pretty and effective; Black could press positionally with 32...b5 as well.

33.gxf4?

This captures makes White's position fall apart. White should play 33.♔g2 and after 33...fxe3 34.♖e2 b5 35.♖f3 ♖8c4 36.♖fxe3 ♖xe3 37.♖xe3 ♕f5 White would still struggle on.

33...♕h3+

The invasion by the queen wins easily.

34.♔f2 ♕xe3+ 35.♔g2 ♕g3+

Petrosian win the practical way. The fancy 35...♖c2 36.♖xc2 ♕e4+ wins as well.

36.♔h1 ♕xh4+ 37.♖h2 ♖h3 38.♖xh3 ♕xh3+ 39.♔g1

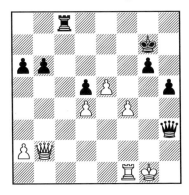

39...♖c3

The rook joins the attack, and it is decisive.

40.♖f2 ♖g3+ 41.♔g2 ♖xg2+

The simplification to a pawn ending wins effortlessly.

42.♕xg2 ♕xg2+ 43.♔xg2 b5 44.♔f3 b4 45.♔e3 a5 46.♔f3 a4 0–1

Petrosian played this game really well. He did not mind his opponent having a passed pawn. He nicely obtained pressure on the c-file. He found a subtle king move. When his opponent stepped into a tactical idea he beautifully exploited it and caught Aghamalian's king.

Petrosian's game against Sorokin is famous. Note the database says it was played in round 13, while Shekhtman places it third. We join the fluctuating game.

Game 14

Petrosian, Tigran – Sorokin, Nikolai
Championship of the Georgian Republic, Tbilisi (3), 1945

24...g6??

Sorokin wants to stop Petrosian's f-pawn from advancing. He had several reasonable defences; he could even play 24...♕xa3 with a balanced position, but chooses the most unfortunate one. According to Petrosian, 24...f5 would be more tenacious. The move he mentions is the most practical. 25.♘g5 ♖c2 (25...♖c6 would also be perfectly safe for Black) 26.♘xe6 ♖xe6 27.♖xe6+ ♔d7 28.♖e2 ♘c4 29.♘xc4 ♕xe2 and White would have to settle for a somewhat worse endgame: as White's extra pawn on the kingside poses no danger for Black it would be easier to play as Black even though Stockfish sees a dead draw here.

25.f5!!

White still plays it.

25...gxf5

26.♕xf5!!

A fabulous move; now Black's position falls apart as he loses the f7–pawn.

26...♕xd4+ 27.♔h1 ♗e7

27...♕g7 28.♕xd5 wins.

28.♕xf7+ ♔d7 29.♘f3 ♕h8 30.♗e5

Tal would win with 30.♘e5+ then 30...♔d8 31.♕f2 and continuing to attack the king. Tigran scores the point by simplifying to a piece ending.

30...♕h7 31.♕xh7 ♖xh7 32.♗xb2

Sorokin will play on for seven more moves.

32...♖c2 33.♗d4 ♗xa3 34.♘e5+ ♔d8 35.♘g5 ♖h5 36.♘xe6+ ♔e7 37.♘g6+ ♔d6 38.♘gf4 ♘xf4 39.♘xf4 1–0

In round 4, Petrosian was Black against Pkhakadze, and played the c6-d5 variation against the g3 Grunfeld. Petrosian unnecessarily sacrificed a pawn, yet he was able to hold with a remarkable fortress idea in a bishop endgame. It can be seen in the 1982 game against Browne in Volume II. In round 5, Petrosian was White against Nersenov. He gained a small edge in the Ruy Lopez. They reached an endgame, then White won a pawn and soon after the game. In round 6, Palavandishvili played a main-line against Tigran's Nimzo-Indian, but Petrosian gained a winning position early. He was winning for a long time, but made a big mistake in a rook ending. White found a very strong move and soon after, on move 41, the game ended in a draw. Petrosian was White next against Zhuk-Tripolitov, and he gained a

winning advantage in a main-line e3 Nimzo-Indian. A part of this game can be seen in the chapter Petrosian's Remarkable Exchanges. In round 8, Petrosian was Black against Kakabadze in an irregular 1.d4 opening. Petrosian's opponent made a very aggressive move, and Petrosian then missed a tactical shot. He lost a pawn and went on to lose in an opposite-coloured bishops endgame, resigning after White's 42nd move. In the next round, Petrosian was simply too strong for Tarsaidze.

Game 15

Sereda, Victor – Petrosian, Tigran
Championship of the Georgian Republic,
Tbilisi (10), 1945
King's Indian Defence

1.d4 ♘f6 2.♘f3 g6 3.g3 ♗g7 4.♗g2 0-0 5.0-0 d6 6.c4 ♘bd7 7.♕c2 e5 8.dxe5

This move, which has been played quite a few times, is somewhat tricky: Black can't be sure what is in White's mind, as it may be a sign of peaceful intentions, though White still can try to fight.

8...dxe5 9.♖d1 ♖e8

Petrosian deviates here from Goglidze-Flohr, Moscow, 1935. He may have known that game.

10.h3 c6 11.♗e3 ♕c7 12.♘c3 ♘b6

Black opens the diagonal for the bishop and attacks the c4–pawn.

13.♘d2 ♗e6 14.♘a4 ♘fd7 15.♘c5 ♘xc5 16.♗xc5 f5 17.♘f3

17...♖ad8

Black has completed his development; he has certainly equalised and obtained a pleasant game. 17...♗f6 would make ♗d6 harmless; it would take away the g5–square from the knight and prepare e4. 18.b3 (18.♗d6 ♕g7!) 18...e4∓.

18.b3 h6

If 18...e4! 19.♘d4 ♗f7 20.e3 ♘d7 21.♗a3 ♘e5 Black would be somewhat better.

19.g4?

This move doesn't stop Black's play in the centre and it weakens White's kingside. 19.e4 or starting by exchanging the rooks with 19.♖xd8 would keep the balance.

19...e4!

Black takes over in the centre.

20.♘d4 ♗c8

Petrosian could consider 20...♘d7!? at once as well.

21.e3

After 21.gxf5 gxf5 22.♖ac1 Black's advantage would be smaller.

21...♘d7!

Petrosian improves his knight. He plays a good move, but it is not the only effective one: 21...fxg4 22.♗xe4 ♕e5 23.♗xb6 axb6 24.♗xg6 gxh3 25.♘f5 ♗xf5 26.♗xf5 ♕e7! and White at least loses the exchange, meaning Black is close to winning.

22.♗b4 ♘e5 23.♗c3 ♘d3

Petrosian's move is strong. Black could win by 23...fxg4 24.♗xe4 gxh3 25.♗xg6 (25.♘f3 ♘xf3+ 26.♗xf3 ♗xc3 27.♕xc3 ♖f8) 25...♘g4 26.♘f3 ♘xe3.

24.gxf5 gxf5 25.♘e2 ♖d7

25...♔h7! was simpler, for example 26.♘g3 ♗xc3 27.♕xc3 ♖g8 28.♖d2 ♘xf2 wins.

26.♘g3 ♖f7?!

This allows White to exchange the d3–knight. 26...♖e6! builds the attack faster, then 27.♘h5 (27.♗xg7 ♖xg7) 27...♖g6. Here White has to give up the exchange to liquidate the d3–knight.

27.♘h5 ♗xc3 28.♕xc3 ♕e7 29.♘f4!

Sereda eases his position with this exchange.

29...♘xf4 30.exf4

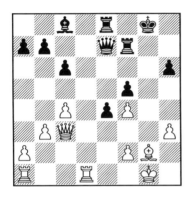

30...♖g7

It is natural to play on the g-file.

31.♕e3 ♔h7 32.♔h2 ♕h4 33.♖d2?

After 33.♖g1! ♖g4 (33...♖eg8 34.♖ad1) 34.♖ae1 ♖xf4 35.f3 White's chances to hold would be realistic.

33...♖eg8 34.♗h1

34.♖g1 ♖g4 would be nice for Black.

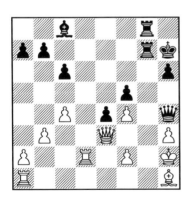

34...c5

Petrosian doesn't bother to win the pawn. If 34...♖g4 Black would checkmate after 35.♕xa7 ♖g3!.

35.♖ad1 b6

With 35...♖g6!! Black has a subtle way to go after White's king. He wants to transfer the queen to g7. 36.a4 (if 36.♖c1 then 36...♖g4, as if 36...♕f6 then 37.♕c3 resists) 36...♕f6 37.a5 ♕g7 and Black wins.

36.♖d6!

The rook stands on the sixth rank.

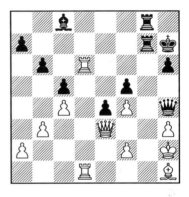

36...♖g4

This move pleases the eye and it frightens Sereda. It works well in the game, but White has an answer.

37.♖6d2?

37.♖c6!! They say it is easy to miss horizontal threats, and this brilliant move would create one. 37...♖4g7 (not 37...♖xf4? and the rook can't return after this capture: 38.♖d2 ♕g5 [38...♖fg4 39.♖dd6 wins] 39.♖c7+ ♖g7 40.♖xg7+ ♔xg7 41.♖d6 and White has the advantage regardless of his pawn deficit) 38.♖dd6 ♖d8=.

37...♖xf4

Black wins a pawn for nothing.

38.♖g1 ♖fg4 39.♖xg4 ♖xg4 40.♖d6

This no longer causes problems for Black.

40...♖g6! 41.♖xg6 ♔xg6 42.♗g2

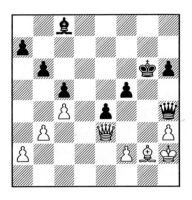

42...♔f6!!

Transferring the king to the centre is clever. It is a bit of a paradox, but the king has a better shelter in the centre and this takes away a lot of squares from the queen. Petrosian at his peak will make some sensational king moves. 42...♕g5 would be premature. 43.♕g3! ♗e6 (43... ♕xg3+ 44.♔xg3 ♔g5 45.h4+ ♔h5 46.♗f1 and Black can't win with the extra pawn as he can't penetrate the white camp) 44.♕d6 and White would be alive.

43.♕d2 ♔e7!

A nice square for the king.

44.♕e3

White can't open the position with 44.f3 as 44...f4 wins.

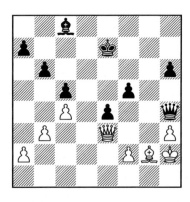

44...♕g5!

Now it is properly prepared, and therefore this wins.

45.♕g3 f4!

Petrosian simplifies to a winning bishop ending by giving the pawn back.

46.♕xg5+ hxg5 47.♗xe4 ♔d6 48.♔g2

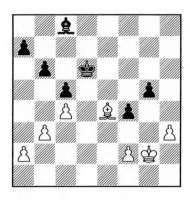

48...♔e5!

The dominant king decides the outcome of the game.

49.♗g6 ♔d4 50.♗h5 ♗f5

Having all the pawns on the colour of the opponent's bishop is usually a disadvantage, as they are vulnerable. White could resign here.

51.♗d1 a5 52.a4 ♗e4+ 53.♔h2 ♔d3 54.h4 gxh4 55.♔h3

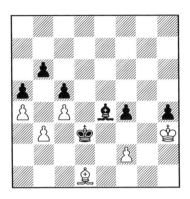

55...f3!

Black traps the bishop; of course Black had many ways to convert the advantage.

56.♔g4 h3 57.♔xh3 ♔d2 0–1

Petrosian made more inaccuracies than he would have liked, but made some original moves as well, and the contour of a genius can be seen. Two of the features of a world class player are evident: the original usage of his rook and his king.

In round 11, Petrosian was White against Tsintsadze. He obtained a clear advantage, but he was unable to win the promising position. They repeated moves in a knight versus bishop ending. Petrosian's opponent in round 12 was Tengiz Georgadze. In the game, Tengiz sacrificed the d4-pawn in the Caro-Kann, and soon after made a piece sacrifice for a pin and attack on the king: the sacrifice was a bluff. Petrosian was about to neutralise his friend's play, but instead of covering up his king he took a

pawn, after which his opponent rolled over him and checkmated him in a few moves. Petrosian is considered a great defender, and he unlike Korchnoi would take risky pawns only rarely. (Of course, an exception was in one of his most famous wins, against Kasparov at Tilburg in 1981.)

Tengiz wrote about this event. However, there are some inconsistencies compared with Shekhtman's information. Perhaps Tengiz remembered incorrectly and Petrosian was not due to play Sorokin in the next round. It is also possible that Shekhtman's order of games here was not correct. Perhaps Shekhtman mixed up the round 13 Kakiashvili game and the round 3 Sorokin game. In any event, we pass the word to Petrosian's childhood friend.

At the start of the competition, Tigran would plan out his performance. In order to secure the prize, how many games he would need to win, how many draws to make. At that time he needed a prize like air to breathe. He would achieve his aim, but in my opinion he was restricting his own creativity. The thing is, that often he would be satisfied with a draw only to make sure that he wasn't left without a prize. Later, this turned into a habit and sometimes a drawback when he was a grandmaster. Those draws also have another explanation. He would never betray chess logic. For him the opponent's personality didn't make a difference. He was doing what the position demanded. That's why he lost so few games. He was cautious and controlled his emotions. He always remembered what his target was.

Participants of the Georgian Championship in 1945 were told that the prize for the winner was going to be ... a coat. Tigran was close to his aim when we got to play each other. We had been preparing for the games together, but this time we decided that we would play the game seriously. So we played and I won. Tigran didn't manage to repel my attack in the Caro-Kann Defence. The next day he came to my house as usual.

"Auntie Nino, Tengiz made me lose a coat," he complained to my mother. Puzzled, my mother looked at me, as she didn't know that a coat was the first prize. She reassured him by saying that next time he would win, and that now he needed to fight till the end. He may yet win. We immediately set up the pieces and had a look at a few games of his next opponent, Nikolai Sorokin. We prepared an opening variation. Tigran won impressively and got his coat.

Next, Petrosian was White against Kakiashvili in round 13, which seems to have been his penultimate game in this 15-round tourney (see above for the explanation). He was too strong for his opponent. In Tigran's last game, he was White against Arutiunov. They played an Exchange Queen's Gambit. He castled long and quickly obtained a clear advantage. He won the game on move 41 by catching Black's king.

He won the national championship, scoring 10 wins, 3 draws and 2 losses according to *Reliability Strategy*. Malashia, Sorokin and Tsintadze finished joint-second with 10 points. As White, the young Tigran was incredible, he scored 7.5 points out of 8 games. In the database, he has 6 black games, scoring 2 wins, two draws and two losses. Interestingly, his losses came from blunders. His draws were somewhat awkward, as in two he was winning and made tactical mistakes, while he drew the other one from a pawn down. Most of his wins in the event came from attacking.

Petrosian's results in 1945

Junior event in Tbilisi	1st place
Training games vs. Grigoriev	+ 3 = 0 – 0 3:0
Training Tournament, Tbilisi	+ 3 = 2 – 1 4/6
Tbilisi Championship	+ 6 = 4 – 1 8/11 2nd place
First Category Tournament, Tbilisi	+ 2 = 2 – 1 3/5
Soviet Junior Ch., Leningrad	+ 8 = 6 – 1 11/15 1st-3rd place
Georgian Ch. Semi-Final, Tbilisi	+ 6 = 3 – 1 7.5/10 qualified
Georgian Championship, Tbilisi	+ 10 = 3 – 2 11.5/15 1st place
Altogether	**+38 = 20 – 7 48/65**

1946

We select a few more games from the first year after World War II than from most years. The reason is that apart from the most interesting games that year, he faced two great players for the first time. Against these giants, Keres and Korchnoi, he would play more than 100 games in total.

Georgian Open Championship, Tbilisi

The 1946 Georgian championship was held in March and April. There are 6 Petrosian games known from this event.

Tengiz Giorgadze recalls that he played Tigran, who was leading the event. Petrosian offered a draw, but Tengiz refused. Tengiz then managed to outplay him, and was winning in the adjournment. However, he made a wrong combination and Tigran won the game with accurate play. He was accused of throwing the game, but Tengiz denied it, both then and decades later in his interviews about his friend.

In these 6 games Petrosian played badly as Black and lost to Ebralidze. He made a few draws against lesser known players and beat Palavandishili. In round 15, Petrosian faced one of the strongest players of the time. In fact, after the war it was not clear whether Alekhine, Botvinnik or Keres was the best player in the world. Many talented players would have been happy to play safe and try to draw. Moreover, Keres crushed his opponents at the event, and the great Estonian had scored an incredible 13.5 points from the first 14 rounds.

Let's see whether the young Tigran would manage to withstand the intimidating threat of facing a mighty opponent in the 15th round.

Game 16

Petrosian, Tigran – Keres, Paul
Georgian Open Championship,
Tbilisi (15), 1946
Grunfeld Defence

1.d4 ♘f6 2.c4 g6 3.♘c3 d5

Although Keres scored very well with the Grunfeld, he employed it relatively rarely. He had probably already won the event by the time this game was played, so he could experiment with his opening selection.

4.g3

Combining ♘c3 with g3 is not considered dangerous; on the other hand, it gives Black relatively few options.

4...♗g7 5.♗g2 dxc4 6.♘f3 0-0 7.0-0

Petrosian plays with confidence: he is ready to sacrifice a pawn for no concrete compensation.

7...c6 8.♘e5 ♗e6 9.e4

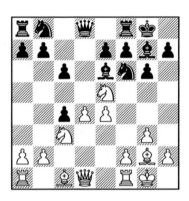

9...♘a6

The Estonian does not care to exchange the e5–knight. According to the database, this was a new idea.

10.♗e3 ♘e8 11.♕e2 ♘d6 12.♖ad1 ♕c8

12...♘b4 13.d5 would be unclear, or 13.a3 ♘d3.

13.a3 f6

Keres chases the well-placed knight away.

14.♘f3 ♘c7

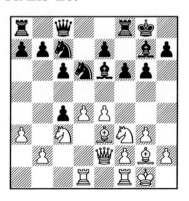

15.d5

Petrosian plays actively, though he could have built the position with 15.♗f4 or 15.♖fe1.

15...cxd5 16.exd5 ♗f5

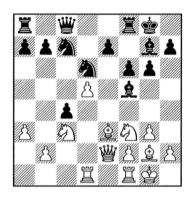

17.♗f4!?

Petrosian gives Keres a chance to win the exchange. White was not forced to do so, as after 17.♖fe1 ♗d3 18.♕d2 ♖d8 19.b3 the position would be balanced.

17...♗d3

Keres picks up the gauntlet. The position would be balanced after 17...♖e8 18.♖fe1 ♗d3 19.♕d2 as well. Vasiliev writes that Petrosian offered a draw in the game: perhaps this was the moment when the Estonian refused the offer.

18.♕xe7

Another confident move, as if he gave up the other rook for the bishop he would be more likely to gain a pawn on top of the compensation for the exchange. After 18.♖xd3 cxd3 19.♕xe7 ♖f7 20.♕e3 ♕d7 21.♕xd3 White would have good compensation.

18...♖f7 19.♕e3 ♗xf1 20.♔xf1 ♕d7?

Keres defends the knight, but this is a serious mistake as it allows White to push the passed d-pawn further. After 20...♘ce8! 21.h4 (21.♕e6 ♕d7) 21...♕d7 22.♘d4 the position would be balanced.

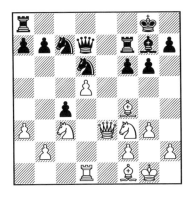

21.♗xd6!

He definitively clears the way for the d-pawn.

21...♕xd6 22.♘e4 ♕b6

If 22...♘xd5 23.♕d4 ♕c6 24.♕xd5 White's advantage is sufficient to win.

23.d6

23.♗xc4! would be more precise.

23...♖d7?

After 23...♕xe3! 24.fxe3 b5 White's advantage would be much smaller than in the game.

24.♗xc4+ ♔h8

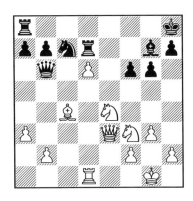

25.♕xb6?!

Petrosian simplifies to an endgame. His continuation gives him an edge, but he misses a clear win. Going after the king with 25.♕f4! would be decisive.

a) 25...♘e8 26.♘h4! Perhaps Tigran did not spot this winning move. 26...♕a5 (26...♗f8 27.♘xf6) 27.♗d5 ♗f8 and Black would be hopelessly lost after 28.♘xf6 or 28.♘g5.

b) 25...♕xb2 26.♘c5 ♖dd8 and White has a few winning moves, for example 27.♕e4 or 27.♘d4.

25...axb6 26.♖c1?!

Petrosian understandably wants to get out of the pin, but he should defend the rook rather than move it from the d-file. 26.♖d2! ♘a6 27.b4 and White would be much better. Or 26.♗b3! ♘a6 (26...♘e8 27.♗e6 ♖dd8 28.d7 ♘c7 29.♗a2 and Black would really struggle) 27.♗a4 ♖dd8 28.♘d4 f5 29.♘g5 ♘c5 30.♘de6 ♖db8 31.♗b5 and Black may not survive.

26...♘e8 27.♗b5 ♖xd6

Black liquidates the passed pawn to his relief. 27...♘xd6 28.♗xd7 ♘xe4 would be equal as well.

28.♘xd6

28.♗xe8? would be a mistake because of 28...♖e6.

28...♘xd6

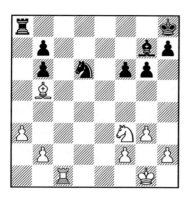

29.♗d3

The dust has settled. The endgame is even, despite the fact that Black has doubled pawns.

29...f5 30.♖c2 ♔g8 31.♔f1 ♗f6 32.♘d2 b5 33.♘b3 ♔f8 34.♘c5 ♔f7

This is a virtual draw offer.

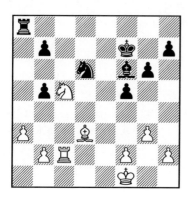

35.♘xb7

Petrosian accepts: he simplifies to a dead drawn endgame by swapping all the queenside pawns.

35...♘xb7 36.♖c7+ ♔g8 37.♖xb7 ♗xb2 38.♗xb5 ♗xa3 39.♗c4+ ♔h8 40.h3 ♗c5 41.♔g2 ♖c8 42.♗a6 1/2

Perhaps the game was adjourned here, but there was no point playing on. A very encouraging game for the young talent. Drawing in a fighting game against one of the very best players in the world was impressive. And he had moments when he could have won, while his superb opponent never did. This was indeed a confidence boosting game.

According to Vasiliev, Petrosian was so proud of this draw that he carried its scoresheet everywhere until he finally lost it. Keres kept all his scoresheets, though, and in 1964 he gifted our hero a copy of the scoresheet from their first encounter. When their first game later came up in their conversation they both laughed a bit.

Keres's personal score against Petrosian indicates just how great he was: they played 35 tournament games (they never played a match), and each player scored 3 wins while they drew 29 times.

In the 19-round championship, Petrosian finished in 5th place. He scored an impressive ten wins, drew five times and lost four games, which was probably a bit more than he might have expected. That said, he only lost to strong players: Mikenas, Zagoriansky, Ebralidze and Sorokin.

Petrosian was the titleholder and was unable to defend his title, but still this was not a bad performance, as the opposition was of a different calibre. Anyway, it is hard to form an opinion on Petrosian's play, as we know only 6 of his 19 games. Of these six games, none were against famous players. Tigran lost a poor game to Ebralidze, but it is always hard to play against one's own trainer.

Keres won the event, scoring an incredible 18 points out of 19. Mikenas 17.5, Zagoriansky 14 and Ebralidze 13 – these players finished ahead of Tigran. His junior trainer scored only half a point more than his former pupil.

Tengiz Giorgadze mentions something important from 1946.

From childhood, Tigran suffered from hearing problems in one ear. In 1946, at the request of the Georgian Ministry of Sport, the director of Tbilisi Chess Club, chess player and wonderful person Varvara Zargarian, travelled to Moscow with Tigran and took him to see ear, nose and throat specialists. Having checked Tigran, the doctors concluded that they couldn't offer any help. There was no cure for his condition.

Tigran calmly accepted it. He never complained about his partial deafness. During walks, he would try to turn his better ear to people with him. Once he said to me: "It isn't such a bad thing that I can't hear in one ear. At the big tournaments, when the audience is making a noise, I don't hear anything, while other players complain!" When his hearing got worse, he started using a hearing aid.

Armenian Championship, Yerevan

Petrosian made a very big decision: he moved to the Armenian capital, Yerevan. Kasparian possibly moved at the same time, as they both participated in the 1946 Georgian open championship and the 1946 Armenian one as well. There is no word why he chose to move. Maybe everything in Tbilisi reminded him of his parents; maybe the Armenian Chess Federation wanted to strengthen chess in the country and offered good conditions. We do not know whether other members of the family, his brother, sister and aunt joined him. Perhaps moving improved the wellbeing of the whole family. He does however state in *Chess Lectures* that he moved at the initiative of a senior chess official, Andranik Akopian.

The Armenian championship was held in June, and he started with 6 straight fairly easy wins. His opponents were not at his level and then, after two draws, he won one more. In round 10, he faced Kasparian. It is not known how Henrik stood in the tourney at the time, but knowing the level, he was probably not far behind. The older player failed to get any edge in the opening, then blundered a piece in the middlegame and went on to lose. According to *Reliability Strategy* Petrosian won the event outright, scoring 9 points out 10 games. Kasparian and Fridstein (who was invited from outside the republic to raise the level) scored 8 points. However, in the same year Tigran played a match against Kasparian and the header of the games says that it was a play-off, so perhaps the first two players were expected to play a match.

Soviet Under 18 Championship Final, Leningrad

His next tournament was a junior event in Leningrad. The header of the database calls it under 18, while Vasiliev calls it a Soviet junior tournament. Petrosian had a very inspired event, and we analyse 4 of his games from it. The headers of the games do not indicate the rounds, so we chose the order in the database. Unlike a year earlier, this time a lot of future strong players participated. Names like Korchnoi, Krogius, Nei, and Kotkov are familiar in chess circles even today.

Though Petrosian played the next game superbly it is not because of the quality that we look at it here: his opponent played poorly and put up little resistance. The reason the game made it to this book is different: it was Petrosian's first game against one of his fiercest, and perhaps absolutely fiercest rival, Victor Korchnoi. I guess neither of them foresaw the heated matches that they were to play against each other.

Game 17

Petrosian, Tigran – Korchnoi, Victor
Soviet Under 18 Championship Final,
Leningrad (6), 1946
Dutch Defence

1.d4 e6 2.♘f3 f5 3.g3 ♘f6 4.♗g2 d5 5.0-0 ♗d6 6.c4 c6 7.b3

This move demonstrates that Petrosian had followed the Soviet championships: Botvinnik used it against Ragozin at the 1939 final. One year earlier, Pirc introduced the move, and I wonder whether Botvinnik knew that game.

7...0-0?!

7...♕e7 grew into the main line; Ragozin first played that queen move in 1948.

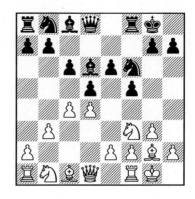

8.♗a3!

The idea is correct, as exchanging the dark-squared bishop favours White.

8...♗xa3 9.♘xa3 ♕e8 10.♘c2 ♕h5?!

Korchnoi ignores the development of his queenside. It will hard to choose which moves to attach a question-mark to; his whole play was bad.

11.♕c1

Petrosian stops g5 for a while.

11...♘e4

12.♘ce1!

White improves the knight, by getting to e5.

12...g5 13.♘d3 ♘d7 14.♘fe5!

Tigran gets ready to chase the e4–knight back.

14...♔h8?!

Korchnoi makes another optimistic move; he was probably looking for play on the g-file.

15.f3 ♘d6

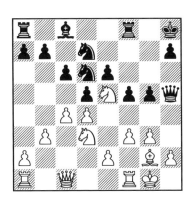

16.e4!

Black's king is so exposed that White can open the centre effectively.

16...♘f7

After 16...fxe4 17.fxe4 dxe4 18.♘xd7 ♗xd7 19.♘e5 White wins.

17.cxd5

Opening the position allows White to invade.

17...♘dxe5

Or 17...cxd5 18.♕c7 while 17...exd5 18.g4 is virtually winning.

18.dxe5 cxd5 19.exd5 exd5 20.f4

Petrosian's strong moves give Black no time to get organised.

20...♖d8

20...♗e6 21.♘c5 or 20...gxf4 21.♘xf4 ♕h6 22.♕b2 ♗e6 23.♗xd5 would win.

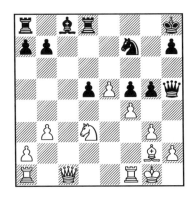

21.♕c7!

The queen is like a raging bull in a china shop, destroying everything.

21...b6

21...♗e6 22.♕e7 ♕g6 23.fxg5 or 21...g4 22.♖fd1 would both win.

22.fxg5 ♗a6

Black can do nothing against the loss of a piece.

23.♘f4 1–0

Petrosian played reasonably well; Korchnoi probably wanted to win very badly or they might have played a very early round and he underestimated his opponent, explaining why he chose such a risky opening.

Game 18

Dunaev, Vladimir – Petrosian, Tigran

Soviet Under 18 Championship Final, Leningrad (9), 1946
Sicilian Defence

1.e4 c5 2.♘f3 d6 3.d4 cxd4 4.♘xd4 ♘f6 5.♘c3 e6

Petrosian would later demonstrate remarkably original handling of a variation with a similar pawn structure. 5...a6 6.♗g5 ♘bd7 7.♕d2 e6 8.0-0-0 b5 9.♗d3 ♕b6 10.♗e3 ♘c5 11.f3 ♗e7 12.♔b1 b4 13.♘ce2 0-0 14.g4 ♘fd7 15.♘g3 a5 16.f4

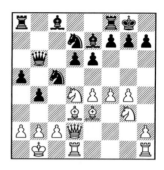

16...♗a6! Petrosian intentionally held the c8–bishop back and now develops it in a manner that is very unusual for a Scheveningen. White has been unable to create any attack on the kingside. Now, Petrosian starts his attack on the queenside by removing an important defending piece. 17.g5 b3! 18.axb3 ♗xd3 19.cxd3 ♖fb8 20.♘ge2 ♕a6 21.♕c3 ♖c8 22.♕c4 ♕b7 23.♖c1 ♖ab8 24.♖c2 ♕a8. Petrosian's original building of the attack yielded him a winning position and he went on to win soon after in Bondarevsky, I – Petrosian, T, Moscow, 1960.

6.♗e2 a6 7.a4

7.0-0 ♕c7 8.a4 ♘c6 9.♔h1 ♗e7 10.f4 0-0 11.♘b3 b6 12.♗f3 ♗b7 13.♕d2 ♖ab8 14.g4?

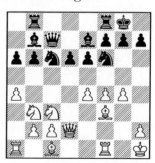

14...d5! 15.exd5 ♘b4 16.dxe6 ♗xf3+ 17.♖xf3 ♕b7 18.♔g2 ♘xg4 Bhend, E – Petrosian, T, Zurich, 1961.

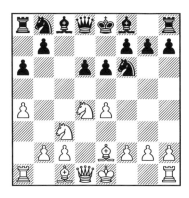

7...♗e7 8.♗e3?! ♕c7

Petrosian probably did not know the subtle nuances of the variation, yet he played it really well. It only became known decades later that White should play ♗e3 only after ♘c6.

9.♘b3 b6

The way Petrosian develops is the right one to expose the drawback of the early ♗e3; this move prevents White from gaining space by playing a5.

10.f4 ♗b7 11.♗f3

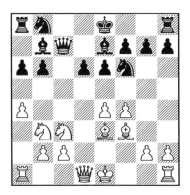

11...♘bd7!

The knight aims to put more pressure on e4 with ♘c5.

12.0-0 ♖c8 13.g4 ♘c5

Petrosian vacates the d7-square and improves the pawn structure.

14.♘xc5 bxc5 15.g5 ♘d7 16.a5?!

According to Petrosian, White had no idea how to attack. He suggests 16.f5 ♘e5 17.♗g4, but here Black could equalise with 17...exf5. Perhaps 17.fxe6 is stronger, as after 17...fxe6 18.♗h5+ g6 19.♗g4 White would be somewhat better.

16...♖b8!

Tigran wastes no time with castling, but starts his play on the queenside.

17.♕d2 ♗c6 18.♘a4?

Interestingly, Petrosian doesn't mention that this move is a mistake. White has no time for this. Instead, 18.b3 ♖b4 19.♕g2 c4 20.♘a2 would be equal.

18...♖b4!

This is strong, but Black would do well after 18...h6! as well. For instance, 19.g6 fxg6 20.♕g2 0-0 21.♕xg6 ♖f6 and Black would be much better. The winner writes that they both correctly thought that 18...♗xa4 19.♖xa4 ♖xb2 20.♕c3 was bad for Black.

19.b3

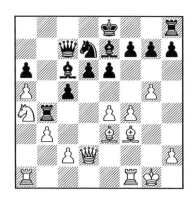

19...♖xe4!

This move is deep and surprising, but the simpler 19...♗xe4 worked well, too. If 20.♗xe4 (after 20.c3 ♗xf3 21.cxb4 ♗b7 22.bxc5 Petrosian preferred the game continuation compared with this position, but this would also be better for him after 22...♘xc5) 20...♖xe4 21.c4 h6! 22.♘c3 ♖xe3 23.♕xe3 hxg5 24.fxg5 d5! Black would be clearly better.

20.c4 h6 21.g6?

This pawn push helps Black to gain complete control over the e4–square. Let's see how White could defend.

a) 21.♘c3 ♖xe3 22.♕xe3 hxg5 23.fxg5 ♘e5 24.♗xc6+ ♕xc6. Petrosian calls this a hard to handle, complex position, but on the way Black had a win: 23...d5! 24.♕f2 ♘e5.

b) 21.♕g2! ♖xe3 (21...♕b7 22.♘c3 ♖xe3 23.♗xc6 ♕c7 24.♘a4 with mutual chances) 22.♗xc6 ♔f8 23.g6 ♗f6 with a slight edge for Black.

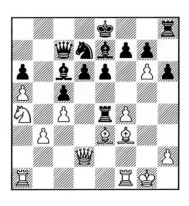

21...f5!

Black makes sure he controls the e4-square.

22.♘c3 ♘f6 23.♗xe4 fxe4

23...♘xe4 24.♘xe4 ♗xe4 25.b4 0-0 26.bxc5 ♖f6 wins as well.

24.♖ad1?

Dunaev doesn't know what to do. He could look for some counterplay: 24.b4 cxb4 25.♘e2 ♘g4 26.♘d4 ♗d7 or 24.♘e2 0-0 25.b4 ♘g4 26.bxc5 dxc5 27.♖a3 ♖f6, and in both cases Black should overcome some resistance.

24...d5 25.cxd5

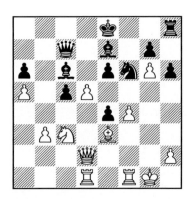

25...exd5

Black's pawns are rolling. White no longer has a chance to survive.

26.f5 d4 27.♗f4

White saves the piece, but loses two pawns. Black not only has a devastating attack, but he is ahead material-wise. The rest is simple.

27...♕c8 28.♘e2 ♕xf5 29.♗g3 ♕xg6 30.♘f4 ♕f7 31.♕c2 g5 32.♘e2 d3 0–1

That game became a classic; it was Petrosian's first. He will be famous for that exchange sacrifice.

Game 19

Petrosian, Tigran –
Khavsky, Sergey
Soviet Under 18 Championship Final, Leningrad (10), 1946

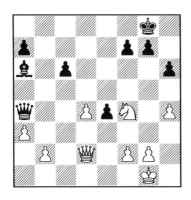

29.♔h2!!

This is a very deep move. It gives his opponent a chance to go wrong in a tactical way. Petrosian visualises the position 4 moves ahead.

29...♗d3?!

Khavsky sees his "tactical chances". 29...♕b5 or 29...♗c4 30.♕e3 then 30...♕c2 or 30...♗d5 would keep the position equal.

30.♘xd3

Petrosian goes along with Black's intention.

30...♕xd4   31.♕f4!   ♕xd3 32.♕b8+ ♔h7

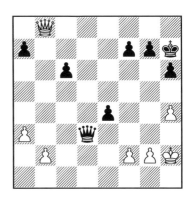

33.♕xa7

They have exchanged the d-pawn for the a-pawn, and now the distant a-pawn is stronger. Now one can see the idea behind Petrosian's king move: the black queen can't give a check on b1 and create its own passed pawn.

33...♕d6+?!

This move looks good, but things start getting unpleasant for Black. What should Black have done?

a) 33...♕b3. Attacking the b2–pawn like this is not a good idea, as White is somewhat better after 34.♕d4 ♕d3 (34...♕c2 35.b4) 35.♕c5.

b) 33...♕d5! Black tries to improve the queen with c5 and ♕d4.

b1) 34.♕c7 c5 35.a4 ♕d4 36.♕xf7 e3 37.fxe3 ♕xh4+ equalises.

b2) 34.♕e3 ♕e5+ (34...c5 35.a4) 35.g3 ♕xb2 36.♕xe4+ g6 and Black holds.

b3) 34.b4 ♕a2 35.♕e3 ♔g8. It is hard to progress with White.

b4) 34.g3 c5! 35.a4 e3 (35...♕f5 36.♔g1 e3 37.fxe3 ♕b1+=) 36.fxe3 ♕d2+ 37.♔h3 ♕d5 38.e4 ♕xe4=

c) 33...♕d2!? 34.♕xf7 (34.b4 ♕a2 35.♕e3 ♔g8 and White's edge is very small) 34...♕xb2 35.♕f5+ ♔h8 36.♕c8+ ♔h7 37.♕xc6 ♕xa3 38.♕xe4+ and White wins a pawn, but it is a theoretical draw.

34.g3 f5 35.♕e3

Petrosian stops any hope of exposing his king. His queenside pawns have more potential than one may think. In addition, it is not easy to do something useful with Black. Khavsky now brings out his king; objectively it doesn't lose, but it is safer to have a hidden king.

35...♔g6 36.b4 ♔f6 37.♕c3+

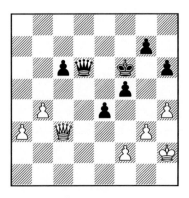

37...♔g6 38.h5+

A very clever move, but not the best. 38.a4!? f4 39.gxf4 would be stronger.

38...♔f7?

Khavsky is not worried at having his king somewhat exposed to checks. 38...♔xh5? is also bad because of 39.♕xg7. Black should play 38...♔h7!. In a queen ending the quality of the king's shelter is often a key element. Having the king covered,

Black would find it easier to play for f4 or attack the h5–pawn. 39.♕c5 (39.a4 f4 or 39.♕e3 ♕d1) 39...♕f6 (if 39...♕e6 Black plays to open the white king: 40.♕e3 [40.a4 f4] 40...♕d6 41.♕f4 ♕d5 42.a4 c5 and Black is no worse) 40.♔g2 (40.a4 f4) 40...♕e6 (40...f4?! 41.g4) 41.♔f1 ♕f7 and Black would not be worse.

39.a4!

White starts to deploy his ace, and he is ready to give up a pawn for it.

39...♕d5

39...♕d1 40.a5 or 39...♕e6 40.a5 f4 41.gxf4 ♕g4 42.♕c4+ and we can see the drawback of an unsheltered king: 42...♔f8 43.♕xe4 ♕xh5+ 44.♔g3 and White wins.

40.♕e3 ♕d1

Now the black queen will not track the a-pawn for a while.

41.a5 ♕xh5+ 42.♔g2 ♕d1

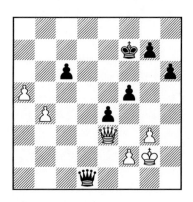

43.a6

The a-pawn has grown too strong.

43...♕a1 44.♕b6

44.a7 ♕a6 45.♕d4 would be faster.

44...♕c3

44...♕a3!? sets more problems

for White, though after 45.♔h2! (45.a7?? ♕f3+) 45...e3 (45...♕f3 46.♕e3) 46.♕b7+ ♔f6 47.♕xc6+ ♔g5 48.♕c7 White wins.

45.♔h2 f4

45...e3 46.♕xe3 or 45...♕f3 46.♕e3 would lose.

46.♕c7+   ♔g6   47.a7   ♕d4 48.♔g2 f3+ 49.♔h3 ♕d5

If 49...♕d1 50.♕xc6+ ♔h5 51.♕e8+ White forces checkmate.

50.♕f4

Attacking the e4 pawn is lethal.

50...♕d3

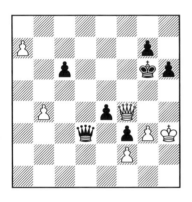

51.♔h2!

The king uses the h2-square for the second time. 51.♕g4+ ♔f6 52.♕h4+ ♔g6 53.a8=♕ would also win.

51...♕a3 52.♕xe4+

White either takes two pawns with check or exchanges queens.

52...♔g5 53.♕e3+ 1–0

Petrosian beautifully spotted that the a-pawn, though it was far from promotion, would have a chance to grow decisively strong. In the process, some small inaccuracies crept in, but

he still played really well and won the game. Again, not spectacular, but deep and strong play.

<hr/>

Game 20

Petrosian, Tigran – Petrovsky, Nikolai

Soviet Under 18 Championship Final, Leningrad (14), 1946

Bogo-Indian

1.d4 ♘f6 2.c4 e6 3.♘f3 ♗b4+ 4.♗d2 ♕e7 5.g3 ♘c6 6.♗g2

In those days this variation was just beginning, and 6.♘c3 has not been played yet.

6...♗xd2+ 7.♘bxd2 d5?!

Black nearly always plays 7...d6 here.

8.0-0 0-0 9.♖e1 ♖d8 10.e3 ♗d7

After 10...b6 11.a3 a5 12.♕a4 ♗b7 13.♖ac1 White is somewhat better.

11.♖c1 ♖ac8 12.a3 ♘a5 13.♘e5 c6?

A rather passive move. After 13...dxc4 14.♘dxc4 ♘xc4 15.♘xc4 b6 White's advantage is smaller than in the game.

14.c5

Petrosian gains space.

14...b5 15.f4 ♗e8 16.♕c2

16.b3!? would stop 16...♘c4.

16...♘d7!?

Exchanging a piece would ease Black's cramped position.

17.e4 f6

After 17...♘xe5 18.fxe5 ♘c4 19.♘b1 White's advantage is fairly big.

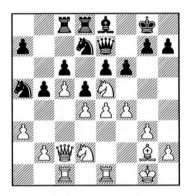

18.exd5!

An effective and somewhat surprising piece sacrifice.

18...fxe5

Perhaps not taking the piece with 18...cxd5 gives Black slightly better chances of survival. But after 19.♘d3 ♘c6 20.♕c3 Black would really struggle.

19.d6 ♕f8 20.dxe5

White has two pawns for the piece and the passed pawn is enormously powerful. 20.fxe5 would be winning as well.

20...g6

Another passive move, but it no longer matters as a more active one

would not change anything. 20...♗g6 21.♕c3 ♘b7 22.b4 ♘b8 23.♘f3 and White would sooner or later crack Black's very passive position.

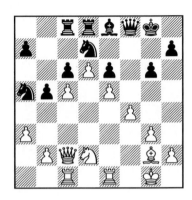

21.b4

Petrosian starts improving his position; Black has no counterplay, so White has oceans of time to do so.

21...♘b7 22.♘b3 ♕f7 23.♘d4 ♘f8

If 23...♘b8 24.a4 a6 25.axb5 axb5 26.♕b3 ♗d7 27.♖a1 White would be about to invade decisively.

24.a4 a6

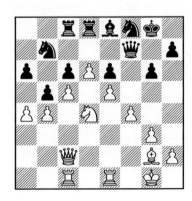

25.♖a1

White intends to invade on the a-file. Black is defenceless.

25...♕g7 26.♕e4 ♖a8 27.axb5 cxb5

After 27...axb5 White has many ways to win, one of which is 28.♘xc6.

28.♕xb7 1−0 White wins back the piece, so there is no point playing on.

Petrosian played this game imaginatively.

Petrosian's performance was phenomenal; he scored 14 points out of 15 games. Dropping only two draws requires not only being well above the level of the event, but special concentration to maintain the level of play.

His performance was noted by the best players of the Soviet Union. Duz-Khotimirsky wondered in an article how this little boy managed to go an entire tournament without losing a game. The great Levenfish described his play: he feels the positions well, he strategically outplayed his opponents and finished them off with a short tactical blow. He rarely makes a calculation error. He plays endgames well and defends difficult position stubbornly.

Let us add that one gets the impression from these games that all positions came naturally to him. He had only one lost position at the event, against Nei. The future Estonian champion went wrong tactically. Petrosian was fantastic: his talent shined through and it became clear to most people by then that he was destined to become an all-time great.

Petrosian – Kasparian Match, Yerevan

According to Vasiliev, the Armenian Chess Federation organised a match between the two best Armenian players, and the match was played in September and October. He mentions no play-off, whereas Shekhtman says the match was for the title of Armenian champion. He says the great composer never looked at him as a rival; rather, he regularly invited Tigran to his house and showed him his studies. They enjoyed friendly relations.

In game one of the match, Petrosian as White had some pressure, but missed a beautiful tactical shot and went on to lose. In the second game, Kasparian obtained a promising queenless position. Henrik let Tigran ease the pressure, and the long game ended in a draw. In game three, Petrosian obtained a clear edge in the opening, but let Kasparian back into the game. Close to time control, the older player chose not to avoid complications, but instead of an exchange sacrifice which would have led to a balanced position, he made a mistake which led to problems and soon after he made a losing mistake. By time control, he was a piece down. Kasparian put off resigning the game for as long as he could, but in vain. In game four, Petrosian as Black equalised in the opening, but had a bad day and after several unfortunate moves his king got caught. In game five, Petrosian as White got the upper hand, but let his advantage slip. Then, though, thanks to Kasparian's mistakes, he obtained an easily winning position. Petrosian allowed him to reach an endgame a pawn down, he still should have won, but after long suffering for Black the game ended in a draw. In game six, Petrosian as Black equalised. He sacrificed a pawn and the complications led to a position with 3 pawns for a piece, but Kasparian's king was somewhat exposed. Henrik created play against Tigran's king, and at the end of an exciting and somewhat seesaw game Petrosian got checkmated. Both players were probably in time trouble. In the seventh game, the last of the first half, Kasparian as Black played the opening far too riskily. He was lucky to stabilise his position, but he was always worse and resigned right after time control. Tigran was behind 3:4. In game eight, Kasparian risked the Alekhine, but Petrosian stepped aside from an opening discussion. Kasparian gained a small edge, the game simplified to an endgame, and peace broke out after time control. In game nine, Kasparian played the King's Indian. Petrosian gained an advantage early on and won a one-sided game convincingly. In game ten, Kasparian did not even play 2.d4 against the French. After the opening, he sacrificed a pawn for no reason, then another, and Petrosian forced his resignation on move 30. Kasparian had probably run out of both energy and patience. In game eleven, Petrosian mainly looked for safety, no player was able to create winning chances, and after time control they agreed to a draw in a rook ending. In game twelve, Kasparian started the game 1.f4 d5 2.♘f3 g6 3.e3. Petrosian kept playing healthy moves. Suddenly, Kasparian blundered and lost an exchange, but soon sacrificed a pawn to create a passed pawn. Petrosian somehow spoiled the win, maybe he was careless, maybe too tense, or maybe somebody was short of time. The game was drawn. In game thirteen, Petrosian handled the opening against the Pirc carefully. Kasparian won a pawn, but gained a passive position and the game ended in a draw. Maybe Tigran would have tried to win in a different situation.

We look at the last game. Petrosian needed a draw to win the match.

Game 21

**Kasparian, Henrik –
Petrosian, Tigran**
Match,
Yerevan (14), 1946
Caro-Kann Defence

1.e4 c6

Just like in the Armenian championship, Petrosian employs the Caro-Kann in this important game. So far in the match, against 1.e4 he had lost with both the Sicilian and 1...e5, drawn once each with the Caro-Kann and Alekhine, and won a French.

2.♘c3

Kasparian chose 2.d4 d5 3.exd5 cxd5 4.♗d3 in the second game of the match; he was able to press in most of that game.

2...d5 3.♘f3 ♗g4 4.h3

Kasparian deviates from their game of the Armenian championship. It continued 4.♗e2 e6 5.d4 ♘f6 6.e5 ♘fd7 7.0-0 ♗e7 8.♘e1 ♗xe2 9.♘xe2 c5 10.f4 g6 11.dxc5 ♘xc5 12.♗e3 ♘c6 13.♗xc5 ♗xc5+ 14.♔h1 ♕b6 15.♖f3 ♖d8 16.a3 0-0 17.♘d3 ♗e7 18.♕d2

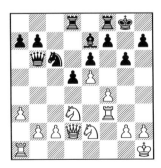

18...f5 and Petrosian obtained a pleasant position. Kasparian later made a big tactical mistake and lost. Kasparian, H – Petrosian, T, Armenian Championship, Yerevan (10), 1946.

4...♗xf3 5.♕xf3 e6 6.♗e2 ♘d7

Petrosian chooses to settle or concede the centre, as this knight move takes away the d7-square from his other knight. So after ...♘gf6, e5 would come with great force.

7.0-0 ♘gf6 8.d4

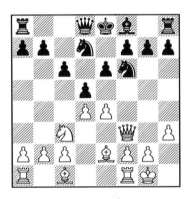

8...dxe4

Black will have a solid position with no weaknesses, but White has a little space advantage and the two bishops.

9.♘xe4 ♗e7 10.♗d3

10.c4!? probably gives better chances.

10...0-0 11.♘g3

The knight will do nothing on g3.

11...♖e8 12.c3

This is somewhat modest if one plays for a win.

12...♕c7 13.♖e1 ♖ad8 14.♗f4 ♗d6

Exchanging the bishops eases Black's position, as it provides more room for the remaining pieces.

15.♗xd6 ♛xd6 16.♖ad1 ♛c7 17.♘e4

This does not make the position worse, but with fewer pieces on the board it is harder for Black to go wrong.

17...♘xe4 18.♖xe4 ♘f6 19.♖h4

The rook looks dangerous, as it creates the threat of ♗xh7.

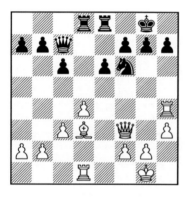

19...♛a5!

Petrosian meets the threat and starts improving his queen. If 19... h6? 20.♖xh6 wins; or if 19...♖d5 20.c4 ♖g5 and the position would be even.

20.♖e1

20.♖f4 ♖d5 21.c4 ♖d7 22.a3 ♛d8 and Black's position is safe.

20...♛d5!

Black's queen is standing well.

21.♛d1 g6

After this move, White has little chance of attacking successfully.

22.♖e5 ♛d6

22...♛xa2? runs into 23.♛f3 ♘d7 24.♖xh7.

23.♛d2 ♛f8

Maybe this is a bit too cautious.

24.g4?!

Kasparian still tries to play against the black king, but this weakens his own king.

24...♘d7 25.♖a5?

Kasparian probably hopes that placing the rook on the edge will be temporary, but the return will not happen. After 25.♖e1 c5 26.g5 ♘b6 Black's position would be only slightly better, but for the great endgame-composer drawing had no value in this game.

25...a6 26.f4?

This overly aggressive move crosses the red line, and after it White is lost.

26.g5! e5 27.♗f1 ♘c5 (Black could have an edge with the simpler 27...♛d6) 28.b4 b6 29.♖a3 ♘e6 30.♖xa6 ♛e7 would be interesting.

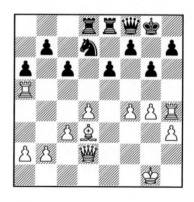

26...♛e7!

The queen sends the rook even further away.

27.♖h6

The rook stands pitifully on h6, but 27.g5 c5 would also be pretty bad.

27...c5!

Black has more force in the centre, so creating a fight is in Black's interest.

28.♗e4 ♘f6

After 28...cxd4 29.cxd4 ♘c5! 30.♗g2 b6 31.♖a3 ♕f6 Black would win, but 28...e5! would make White's position fall apart straight away.

29.♗f3 cxd4

29...e5 wins as well.

30.cxd4 ♕c7!

Petrosian finds a way to win; there are other ones as well.

31.♖e5

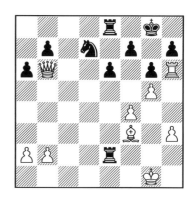

36...♘xb6

White is only one pawn down materially, but virtually a rook and a pawn down. Even an endgame magician like Kasparian can't produce a miracle here.

37.♗xe2 ♘a4 38.♗f3 b5 39.b3 ♘c3 40.a3 ♖d8 41.♔f2

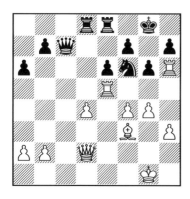

31...♕b6!

Now Black wins. Perhaps Kasparian played on as he was short of time, or because of the huge stakes on offer.

32.g5 ♖xd4 33.♕f2 ♘d7 34.♖e4 ♖d2 35.♖e2 ♖xe2 36.♕xb6

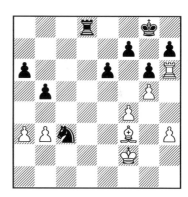

41...♘b1

Interestingly, Tigran allows the queenside pawns to disappear. He calculates well, but 41...♖d2+ 42.♔e3 ♖b2 would win with no calculation required.

42.a4 ♘d2

42...bxa4 43.bxa4 ♖d4 wins as well.

43.♗e2 ♘xb3 44.axb5 axb5 45.♗xb5 ♘d4 46.♗d3

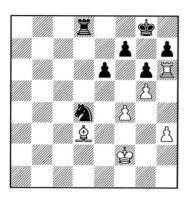

46...e5!

Black wins the second pawn and in addition the h6-rook is still absolutely out of play.

47.fxe5

Maybe 47.f5 gives more chances for Black to go wrong, but 47...gxf5 wins.

47...♘e6 48.♔e3 ♘xg5 49.♗e2

49.♖h4 ♖d5 50.♔f4 ♘e6+ loses.

49...♖d5 50.e6 ♖e5+ 51.♔f4 ♖xe2 52.♔xg5 ♖xe6 53.♖h4

53...f6+ 54.♔h6 ♖e5 0–1

A pretty zugzwang to checkmate on the next move, though its beauty probably gave Kasparian no pleasure. But Black was going to win anyway.

Winning the match was a big success. Something else, though, was probably more important. He may have noticed that his older opponent was getting tired towards the end of the event. Maybe Kasparian had also got tired at the end of the Armenian round robin championship. Here in the match, Kasparian obtained a two-point lead, and ended with a two-point deficit. I think this experience would help Tigran in choosing to fine-tune his tournament strategy in Curacao to qualify to challenge Botvinnik, and also when Botvinnik collapsed at the end of their match.

After the match, the Armenian Federation applied to the Soviet Federation to grant Petrosian the master's title. The request was denied. It would be interesting to know their reason.

So not long after his seventeenth birthday, he had already won the adult championships of both Georgia and Armenia, as well as the junior championship of the Soviet Union. Taken together, this was a stunning accomplishment. The Soviet Union had quite a few stars who had proved before the war that they were very strong, including Botvinnik, Keres, Lilienthal, Flohr and Mikenas, while Bronstein and Smyslov were also powerful players by then. But for the experts it must have been clear that one Armenian boy would soon join them.

Petrosian's results in 1946

Georgian Open Championship, Tbilisi	$+10 = 5 - 4$ 12.5/19 5th place
Armenian Championship, Yerevan	$+ 8 = 2 - 0$ 9/10 1st place
Soviet Under 18 Championship Final, Leningrad	$+ 13 = 2 - 0$ 14/15 1st place
Petrosian – Kasparian Match, Yerevan	$+ 5 = 6 - 3$ 8:6
Altogether	**$+36 = 15 - 7$ 43.5/58**

1947

Training match with Tengiz Giorgadze

Tengiz mentions that in 1947 he played a 4-game mini-match against Petrosian, which ended in a 2:2 draw. Sadly the games are not available, not even a summary. Tigran's friend mentions that he was never again able to catch his opponent's king, which suggests that he may have at least won a game.

Armenian Championship, Yerevan

The event took place in June. Only one of his games is in the database from the Armenian championship. They invited two strong players from outside Armenia, Bondarevsky and Duz-Khotimirsky, to raise the level of the event.

Reliability Strategy includes Tigran's analysis of his draw against Bondarevsky. It would be interesting to know why he analysed that game, in which virtually nothing happened, whereas we have never come across any analysis by him of his very exciting Keres game. Bondarevsky was a strong player who won the 1940 Soviet championship with Lilienthal ahead of Smyslov, Keres, Boleslavsky and Botvinnik, but he was still far from Keres's level. Petrosian shared 2nd-4th places with Duz-Khotimirsky and Kasparian. He scored seven wins, three draws and one loss. The *hors concours* Bondarevsky came first, meaning that Petrosian and Kasparian were champions.

Soviet Championship Quarter-Final, Tbilisi

In *Reliability Strategy*, this tournament is called the all-Soviet championship for candidate masters. The event was held in Tbilisi in July and August, and perhaps the warm memories of the city where he spent his childhood helped him in the event.

In round 1 as White, he convincingly beat Lipnitsky, and in the second round as Black he pressed Airapetov but drew.

His third game was confidence boosting, as he scored an impressive win over a reasonable player who was to beat Geller in 1949. We look at that game.

Game 22

**Petrosian, Tigran –
Pirtskhalava, Akaki**
Soviet Championship Quarter-Final,
Tbilisi (3), 1947
Dutch Defence

**1.d4 f5 2.c4 e6 3.g3 ♘f6 4.♗g2
d5 5.♘f3 ♗d6 6.0-0 c6 7.♘c3**

Petrosian deviates from his game against Korchnoi.

7...0-0 8.b3

According to the database, Petrosian plays a new move. Botvinnik played a game in 1940 against Ragozin when he took on d5 here and created an outpost on e5 for his knight.

8...♕e7

Vaiser would later play 8...b6!? against Hort and draw comfortably.

9.♗b2 ♘bd7 10.e3 ♘e4

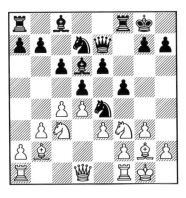

11.♘e2!

Just like in the Korchnoi game, Petrosian aims to occupy the e5–square with his knight, and he is ready to invest a few tempi to do so.

11...♕f6?

Black plays to attack the king, but he is too optimistic. He needed to play on the queenside: 11...a5 or 11...b5 are reasonable, but we would choose 11...b6 12.♘e5 ♗b7.

12.♘f4 ♕h6

Pirtskhalava continues to build his play against White's king.

13.♘d3 ♘df6?

Black is only playing on the kingside. In addition, he weakens his influence over the e5–square. After 13...b6! White's advantage is smaller than in the game.

14.♘fe5

He would later play a remarkable game after a similar knight move:

Petrosian, T – Bondarevsky, I
Soviet Championship,
Moscow (17), 1950

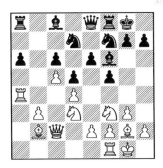

With 17.♘fe5 White paralyses Black in the centre. 17...♘fxe5 18.dxe5 ♗e7 19.f4 ♖b8 20.♖fa1 ♖b5 21.b4 h5 22.♗c3 h4 23.e3 ♘b8

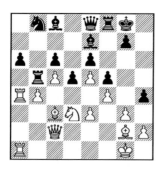

With 24.♘e1! Petrosian switches his attention to the kingside out of the blue. 24...♖b7 25.gxh4 is another small surprise. 25...♗xh4 26.♘f3 ♗d8 27.h4! and White puts his defensive line in front. 27...♕h5 28.♗e1 ♗d7 29.♕f2 ♔f7

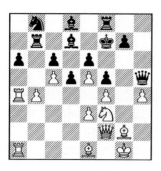

30.♗f1! After accomplishing his original aim of paralysing Black's play on the kingside, Petrosian changes side again. With his next move, Tigran took the a6–pawn with a winning position. Petrosian went on to win by keeping play on both sides of the board.

Let us show another subtle Petrosian game in a Stonewall position.

Petrosian, T – Savon, V
Moscow Spartakiad (2), 1972

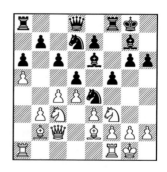

13.♗d3! ♗f7 14.♘e2! ♖c8 15.♖fd1 ♘g5 16.♘e5 ♘xe5 17.dxe5 ♕c7 18.f4 ♘e4 19.♗a3 ♖fd8

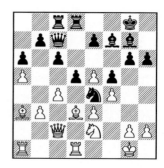

20.♗xe4! Petrosian displays one of his specialities, another great swap of a bishop for a knight. 20... dxe4 21.♗c5 ♖xd1+ 22.♕xd1 ♕d8 23.♘d4 ♔h7 24.♕e1 e6 25.♕b4 ♕d7 26.♖d1 ♖d8 27.♗b6 ♖g8 28.♕d6 ♕e8 29.♘c2 g5

30.♕d7 Petrosian obtained a winning position and went on to win.

Now back to our game:

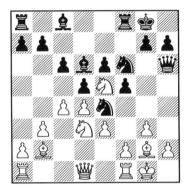

14...♘g5 15.f3

Black is getting pushed back.

15...♘f7 16.♕e2 g5?!

This move just weakens the black king without allowing Black any attacking chances against the white king.

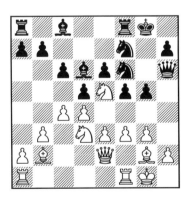

17.♖ae1

Tigran brings his last piece into play.

17...a5 18.e4!

White is better developed, so he is justified in opening up the centre. Black is already lost.

18...♗b4 19.♖d1 dxe4 20.fxe4 ♘xe5 21.dxe5 ♘xe4

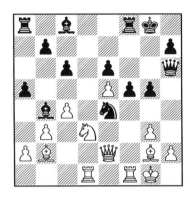

22.♗xe4

Black's pieces are so far away from White's king that there is no danger in giving up the g2–bishop.

22...fxe4 23.♘f2

23.♘xb4 axb4 24.♗d4 ♗d7 25.♗c5 would also win.

23...♗c5 24.♗d4!

Preserving the knight is the strongest move.

24...♗e7 25.♘xe4 ♗d7

Developing the bishop is too late.

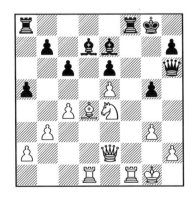

26.♗c5!

Exchanging the bishop provides an access route to invade.

26...♖xf1+ 27.♖xf1 ♗xc5+ 28.♘xc5 ♗e8 29.♖f6

Petrosian wins a pawn and Black's king remains weak, while the rook on a8 has still not made any move.

29...♗g6 30.♘xe6 g4 31.♘f4 ♛g5 32.♘xg6 hxg6

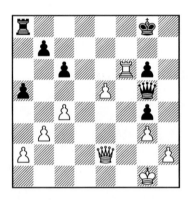

33.♖f4

Petrosian goes for winning a second pawn.

33...♔g7

33...♖e8 34.♖xg4 ♖xe5 35.♖xg5 ♖xe2 36.♖xg6+ ♔f7 37.♖h6 and White wins with a two-pawn advantage, although 34.e6 ♛e7 35.♖e4 would lead to a quicker win.

34.♛e3 ♛d8

Black is reluctant to move the a8–rook in this game.

35.e6 ♛e8 36.♖f7+ 1–0 Black resigned.

This was a very one-sided game, but Petrosian played it instructively. It shows his superior level compared

with most players in the quarter-final.

In round 4, he treated the opening aggressively against Tengiz Giorgadze. He gained an advantage and beat his friend convincingly. In round 5 as Black, he pressed against Shcherbakov, but the strong player was able to hold. In round 6, having the white pieces, he convincingly beat Gongadze, and the exciting part of that game can be found in the It's Your Move chapter. In round 7, he was Black against Solmanis, and a sharp game ended early in perpetual check. They might have agreed to a draw in advance, though, as Black missed a number of ways to win. In round 8, Petrosian was White against Alexandrov, and he opted for a very complex middlegame. Shortly before time control, Petrosian made a losing mistake, but by time control he had stabilised the position and had to work for another 10 moves to draw. In round 9, he was Black against Ter-Pogosov, and used the Armenian Variation of the French Defence. Ter-Pogosov pressed for long, but suddenly blundered a bishop and went on to lose. In round 10, Petrosian was White against Muchnik, who bravely sacrificed an exchange for some play. Tigran probably could have tried to win, but went for safety and simplified to a draw. In round 11, Blagidze handled the opening sharply, but Petrosian spotted a hole in his calculation and gained a clear advantage, winning the game convincingly. In round 12, Petrosian as White looked for sharp play by castling long against Buslaev. This game can be seen in the commentary to game 34 against Sidorov. Black did well to avoid getting checkmated, but was unable to create drawing chances and lost. In round 13, he probably played Levitas. The game is not in the database, but according to chess.pro Petrosian won that game.

In round 14, Petrosian as White pressed against Shishov. Black was close to losing, but held. One gets the impression that Petrosian did not seal the best move. In the last round, a quick draw against Alekseev perhaps assured him of first place. He won the quarter-final with 11.5 points out of 15, half a point ahead of Shishov. His 8 wins and 7 draws were impressive. And he of course qualified for the semi-final.

Individual championship for Spartak Players, Riga

Soviet master Mikhail Beilin said that he first met Petrosian in a tournament in Riga, but there are no Petrosian games from the tournament in the database and it is not mentioned in our main sources. Thanks to Mikhail Vrona for finding the cross-table of the event, which was held in the autumn of 1947. Petrosian scored 10.5 points out of 19; he won 6 games (5 of them were against the 5 bottom players), drew 9 and lost 4. He finished 10th, 4.5 points behind the winners Simagin and Furman, and 3.5 behind Saigin.

Soviet Championship Semi-Final, Moscow

Petrosian started the event as White against the strong Konstantinopolsky and played cautiously. However, he then blundered a pawn in an equal position. He cleverly created some difficulties for his opponent, who let his advantage slip, possibly in time trouble. Soon after time control, they agreed to a draw. In game two as Black, he drew against the theoretician Panov. The position simplified after the opening, and there was little to play for when the draw was agreed. In the third round, Petrosian as White gained a nice advantage against Kholmov, and then he obtained a winning position with a passed pawn. However, he then blundered his advantage away, and after another mistake Kholmov should have won a queen ending, but he allowed Petrosian back in. Petrosian pushed his passed pawn too early and lost it, and had he given some precise checks first he would not have lost this seesaw game. In round 4, Petrosian's original opening handling against Kan worked poorly.

Tigran ended up with a hopeless position in the opening and lost the game without a chance. The header of his Friedstein game doesn't indicate the round number, but only the fifth is missing. Petrosian was White. They reached a fighting position and Tigran won a pawn. In a complex position, Petrosian soon took control and won convincingly. In round 6, Podolny as White castled long, and according to Vasiliev Petrosian dared to walk with his king in the middlegame for the first time. Podolny obtained a somewhat better queenless middlegame, but Petrosian was able resist his opponent's bishop pair and obtained a draw. In round 7, Kamishov played the opening somewhat wildly. Petrosian missed a tactical win in one move, and soon after he was badly lost. However, his opponent gradually wasted his advantage, and after time control the position calmed down into what should have been a draw. Yet Kamishov rejected a repetition, soon after gave away a third pawn for the exchange, and lost. So Petrosian reached 50 percent. In round 8, Petrosian equalised in the opening as Black versus Zagoriansky. After the opening, they swapped queens and Petrosian obtained a slight edge, but Zagoriansky's good defence earned him a draw.

In round 9, the position was more or less equal during most of the game, and it is still balanced when we join it. In this fragment, Petrosian's genius shines through!

Game 23

Petrosian, Tigran –
Liublinsky, Victor
Soviet Championship Semi-Final,
Moscow (9), 1947

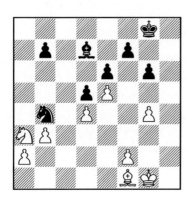

35.f4

Petrosian gains space and gets ready to centralise his king.

35...♘xa2 36.♔f2 ♘c1

With 36...♘b4 the position would be equal and the game would probably end peacefully. Liublinsky hopes to create chances.

37.b4 g5

Black wants to create complications. Jumping with the knight was interesting: 37...♘a2 38.b5 ♘c3 39.♗d3 ♘d1+ (39...♘a4=) 40.♔e2 ♘b2 41.♗c2 ♘c4 42.♘xc4 ♗xb5 43.♔d2 when Black wins a pawn, but it is a draw as Black has no means of penetration.

38.fxg5 ♔g7

After 38...♘a2 39.b5 ♔g7 Black

probably gets away with the pawn deficit.

39.♔e3

The king is doing more than just centralising.

39...♗a4?

Black hopes to rescue the knight.

a) 39...♔g6 40.♔d2 ♘a2

a1) 41.b5 ♔xg5 42.♔c2 (42. ♗d3!) 42...♔f4! 43.♔b2 ♔e3 44.♔xa2 ♔f2! 45.♗d3 ♔e3 46.♗c2 ♔xd4 and Black probably holds.

a2) 41.♗d3+! White should go after the knight with the bishop, not the king. 41...♔xg5 42.b5 f6 (42... ♔xg4 43.♗b1 or 42...♘b4 43.♗b1 wins) 43.♗b1 ♘b4 44.♔c3 and White may win.

b) 39...b5! Black could still hold by fixing the b4-pawn. 40.♘c2 (40.♔d2 ♘a2) 40...♘a2. The c2–knight defends b4 but unfortunately it blocks both the king and the bishop, preventing them from going after and winning the a2–knight.

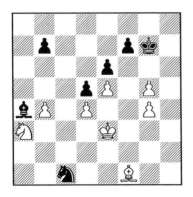

40.♔d2

Petrosian a bit surprisingly goes for trapping the knight.

40...♘a2 41.b5 ♘b4

41...♔g6 would lose as well. 42.♗d3+ ♔xg5 43.♗b1 ♗b3 44.b6! ♔xg4 (44...♘b4 45.♔c3 ♘c6 46.♔xb3 ♘xd4+ 47.♔b4 and the b6–knight decides the outcome) 45.♗xa2 ♗xa2 46.♘b5 ♔c4 47.♘d6 ♗a6 48.♘xf7 ♔f5 49.♘d8 and Black is in a lethal zugzwang.

42.♔c3!

If 42.♘b1 ♘c2 43.♔c3 b6 44.♗e2 ♘e3 Black would get away with it.

42...♘a2+

43.♔b2!

Petrosian subtly spots that the king stands better here than on d2.

43...♘b4 44.♘b1! ♔g6

a) If 44...♘c2 45.♘c3 and the king takes away the b3–square, which is why the king stands better here than on d2.

b) 44...♗c2 would force White to find a great idea: 45.♘c3 b6. It looks like this move sets up zugzwang for White, while other moves would lose instantly (if 45...♗d3 46.♔b3, 45...♔g6 46.♔a3 or 45...♗g6 46.♘a4 and White wins)

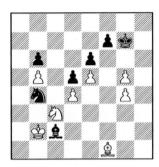

b1) 46.♘a2 ♗d3 47.♗xd3 ♘xd3+ 48.♔c2 ♘e1+ 49.♔d2 ♘f3+ 50.♔e3 ♘xg5 51.♘c3 ♔f8 52.♘a4 ♔e7 53.♘xb6 ♔d8 and Black may hold the position despite the pawn disadvantage.

b2) 46.g6!! A very deep idea; White closes the kingside to invade on the queenside, and it has a tactical justification (46.♔a3 ♘d3 47.♗xd3 ♗xd3 48.♔b4 ♗c2= as White can't invade. Or 46.♗e2 ♔g6 47.♔a3 ♘d3 48.♘a4 ♘f4!= and here one can see that the bishop stands much worse on e2 than on f1) 46...fxg6 (46...♔xg6 47.♔a3 ♘d3 48.♘a4 as Black can't take on a4 because the king unfortunately stands on g6) 47.g5! This prevents any counterplay on the kingside (if 47.♘e2 Black could play 47...♗d1 though White may win as well) 47...♔f7 (47...♗d3 48.♔b3) 48.♔a3 ♘d3 49.♗xd3 ♗xd3 50.♘a4! ♗xb5 51.♘xb6 and Black loses as the kingside is closed.

45.♘c3 ♗xb5

Giving up the bishop is a desperate attempt, but Black is lost anyway.

45...♗c2 46.♔a3 ♘d3 (46...♗d3 47.♔xb4 ♗xf1 48.b6 ♔xg5 49.♘a4 wins) 47.♗xd3+ ♗xd3 48.♔b4 ♔xg5 49.♘a4 and White soon wins the b7–pawn and the game.

46.♗xb5 ♔xg5 47.♔b3 ♘a6

48.♗xa6!

Luckily for White there are enough pawns on the board.

48...bxa6 49.♘a4 ♔xg4 50.♘c5 a5

After 50...♔g5 51.♘xa6 f6 52.exf6 ♔xf6 53.♘c5 the knight would arrive in time.

51.♘b7 ♔g5 52.♘xa5 f5 53.exf6 ♔xf6

54.♘c6

The knight saves the last pawn, so now it is an elementary win.

54...♔f5 55.♔b4 ♔e4 56.♔c5 ♔f5 57.♔d6 ♔f6 58.♘d8 1−0

The next game is perhaps more important for his career than one may think.

Game 24

Abramov, Lev − Petrosian, Tigran
Soviet Championship Semi-Final,
Moscow (10), 1947
French Defence

1.e4 e6 2.d4 d5 3.♘d2 ♘f6 4.e5 ♘fd7 5.♘gf3 c5 6.c3 ♘c6 7.♗d3 ♕b6

This move was played twice before this game.

8.0-0

According to the database, Abramov was the first to sacrifice this pawn. Later, Kasparov would play it as well.

8...cxd4 9.cxd4

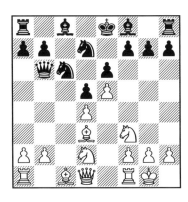

9...♘xd4

Petrosian later said that he likes to defend. This is the first game we noticed in which he intentionally defends. Earlier, he often played the opening cautiously, but rarely took risky pawns. Maybe this was indeed the first time he intentionally opted for defending.

10.♘xd4 ♕xd4 11.♘f3 ♕b6 12.♗e3

12.♕a4 and 12.♕c2 have become the main lines.

12...♕d8?!

This looks artificial. Maybe Petrosian wants to control the g5–square. 12...♕xb2 13.♖b1 ♕c3 looks playable, while 12...♗c5!? is the most natural move.

13.♕a4 ♗e7 14.♕g4! ♔f8

Petrosian gives up the right to castle. 14...g6 would weaken the black squares. Black could consider giving up the exchange with 14...0-0!? 15.♗h6 g6.

15.♖ac1

This paralyses Black a bit.

15...b6 16.b4!

While this restricts Black's pieces even more.

16...h5

16...a5 17.a3 maintains the grip.

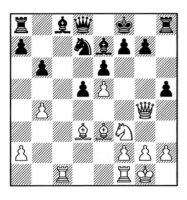

17.♕d4

17.♕f4! keeping the d4–square was very strong, and in addition it stops g6.

a) 17...a5 18.♘d4 ♔g8 19.♘c6 ♕e8 20.bxa5 ♗a6 (20...bxa5 21.♘xe7+ ♕xe7 22.♖c7 and White wins) 21.♗xa6 ♖xa6 22.♕a4 and Black would be in trouble.

b) 17...♔g8 18.♖c3 when White will dominate along the c-file, and the pawn is not enough for this. 18... a5 (18...♘f8 19.♖fc1) 19.bxa5 bxa5 (19...♖xa5 20.♘g5 ♗xg5 21.♕xg5 ♕f8 22.♖c7 and Black is struggling) 20.♖fc1 ♘f8 21.♖c7 ♗d7 22.♘d4 and Black can hardly move.

17...a5 18.bxa5?!

Opening on the queenside helps Black. It would be interesting to know how Petrosian would have tried to finish developing had he faced 18.a3. Perhaps he would have

chosen 18...axb4 19.axb4 ♗a6, as 18...g6 19.♖c2 or 19.♕b2 with ♘d4 were somewhat unpleasant.

18...♖xa5 19.♕f4 ♔g8?

This move works superbly in the game; however, it is a clear mistake. With 19...♘c5! the knight covers the c8–bishop. After 20.♗c2 ♗a6 (20... ♔g8) 21.♖fe1 ♗c4 Black would have preferable chances.

20.♘d4?

This not only lets the advantage go, but leads to a lost position. 20.♘g5! ♗xg5 21.♕xg5 ♕e8 (21... ♕xg5?? 22.♖xc8 and here one can see what was wrong with Petrosian's king move) 22.♖c7 and Black has serious problems.

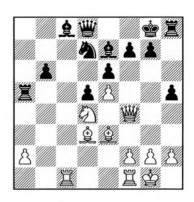

20...g5!

Tigran exploits Abramov's mistake and wins another pawn, and in addition he makes room for his king.

21.♕g3 h4 22.♕h3 ♘xe5

Now White is simply lost.

23.♗d2 ♖a3 24.♖c3 ♖xa2

24...♖xc3 25.♗xc3 ♗c5 would win as well.

**25.♕e3 ♗f6 26.♖fc1 ♗d7
27.♗e2 ♔g7 28.h3 b5**

28...♖a4 29.♔h1 ♘g6 30.♘c6 d4 wins faster.

29.♖c5

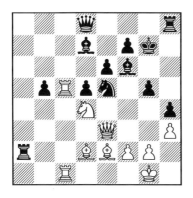

29...♘g6

Petrosian gives back the pawn a bit unnecessarily. Keeping the pawn with 29...♘c4 was decisive as well.

**30.♗xb5 ♗xb5 31.♖xb5 ♘f4
32.♗c3 ♕d7**

32...e5 33.♘f5+ ♔h7! (33...♔g6?! 34.♗xe5 ♘e2+?! [34...♖e2] 35.♔f1 ♘xc1 36.♗xf6 and White is no worse) 34.♗xe5 ♘e2+ and Black wins.

33.♖b2 ♖xb2 34.♗xb2

34...e5

Interestingly, Petrosian doesn't bother bringing the rook into play yet.

35.♘f3 d4 36.♕e4 ♕d5

A confident move, this gives back a pawn to swap queens.

**37.♕xd5 ♘xd5 38.♖e1 ♖b8
39.♗a3 d3**

The d-pawn is too strong.

40.♗d6 ♖d8 41.♗xe5

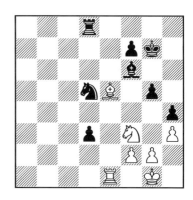

41...♘c3

This forces an exchange, while 41...♗xe5 42.♖xe5 f6 43.♖e1 ♘c3 wins as well.

42.♗xf6+

42.♗xc3 ♗xc3 43.♖d1 ♔g6

a) 44.♘e1 ♗xe1 45.♖xe1 ♔f5 (45...d2 46.♖d1) 46.♔f1 ♔d5 47.♖d1 (47.♔g1 d2) 47...♔e4 48.♔e1 ♔d4 and Black wins.

b) 44.♔f1 ♔f5 45.♖c1 d2 46.♖d1 ♔f4 47.♔e2 g4! A nice move. 48.hxg4 (48.♘xh4 ♖e8+ 49.♔d3 gxh3 50.gxh3 ♖e1 51.♔c2 ♗b4 and White is in zugzwang) 48...h3 49.gxh3 ♖e8+ 50.♔d3 ♖e1 and Black wins.

42...♔xf6 43.♘d2 ♔g6 44.g3

White has no useful move. 44.♔f1 ♖a8 45.♘f3 (45.♖e3 ♖a1+ 46.♖e1 ♖a2) 45...f6 46.♖c1 ♖a2 wins.

44...f5 45.♔g2 ♘e4 46.♖d1

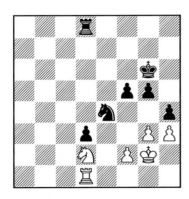

46...hxg3

After this exchange the invasion comes easily.

47.fxg3 ♔f6 48.♔f3

48.♘f3 d2 wins; 48.g4 ♘xd2 49.♖xd2 fxg4 50.hxg4 ♔e5 51.♔f3 ♔d4 is hopeless for White.

48...♔e5 49.♔e3 ♘xg3 50.♘f3+ ♔f6 51.♘d4

51.♖xd3 f4+ 52.♔d2 ♘e4+ 53.♔c2 ♖xd3 54.♔xd3 ♘f2+ 55.♔e2 ♘xh3 and Black wins.

51...d2 52.♘f3 ♘e4 53.♘d4 ♖h8 54.♖f1 ♖xh3+ 0–1

Petrosian won a pawn. He did not defend perfectly, but his play was good enough to win the game.

In the 11th round, Petrosian played the minority attack in the Ragozin as White against Veresov. His opponent allowed him to gain pressure. At one point, he missed a win, then Veresov made another

mistake and Petrosian exploited it. Finally, his opponent overstepped the time limit in a hopeless position. The 3-game winning streak came to an end in round 12 against Ravinsky. Petrosian equalised in a Ruy Lopez, and they manoeuvred for a long time. Just before time control, Petrosian gave away a pawn. His opponent converted his advantage in a knight ending. In the next round, it was another Ruy Lopez, but this time he was White. Averbakh's play grew too strong in the Marshall. Tigran held off the attack by giving up an exchange, but it was hopeless and Averbakh convincingly won the game. In the 14th round as Black, he sacrificed a pawn. Kasparian probably missed a move and lost the exchange. But his position did not collapse. Henrik lost on time when his position was not even worse. The header of the Simagin game in the database says that it was played in round 13, but according to Vasiliev the game was played in the last round and the stakes were very high. A draw meant the master's title and winning qualification to the Soviet final. Petrosian was White, he gained a small edge in the Ilyin-Zhenevsky Dutch, and he offered a draw. However, Simagin refused. Tigran's advantage grew and he again offered a draw, but his opponent still wanted to continue. Simagin in a worse position made a clearly losing move on move 24 and offered a draw. Petrosian accepted and he finished the strong event in fifth place. He won 6, drew 5 and lost 4.

He needed some rounds to get used to the level, but after that he played well. The event most likely contributed to his development. Petrosian was rewarded with the master's title together with two decent players, Kholmov and Vistaneckis.

Years later, Averbakh remembered him from this event: "His ease of play, quick thinking, and dispassionate judgment of positions attracted attention. One got the feeling that he was a chess player with exceptional talent and a bright future ahead."

Petrosian played for the Spartak club in Armenia. Kolobov, who was a trainer in the Spartak Moscow team, recalls the idea of Petrosian moving to Moscow. Petrosian was a great football and ice hockey fan, he would be glad at the free tickets to these sports events. Maybe that was an element, but the level of chess in Armenia was not sufficiently high for Petrosian even when he moved there in the first place, and he needed stronger opponents to fully improve. In the 1946 championship, he beat all Armenian players, apart from 2 draws. The next year, apart from Kasparian, only 8 other Armenian players managed a draw against him. In Moscow, there were many world class players, while the support of the Armenian people would be with him regardless of where he lived. It was clear that sooner or later he had to move to the Soviet capital to improve his chess.

Petrosian's results in 1947

Petrosian – Giorgadze training match	2:2
Armenian Championship, Yerevan	+7 = 3 – 1 8.5/11 2nd-4th place
Soviet Championship Quarter-Final, Tbilisi	+ 8 = 7 – 0 11.5/15 1st place
Championship of Spartak Clubs, Riga	+ 6 = 9 – 4 10.5/19 10th place
Soviet Championship Semi-Final, Moscow	+ 6 = 5 – 4 8.5/15 5th place
Altogether	**+ 27 = 24 – 9 41/64**

1948

According to the sources, Petrosian only played his first games that year in June. His first event was the Armenian championship. Round 1 was unusual in Petrosian's career, in that it was a wild game. We don't know whether in Yerevan he trained on his own or with a local player or anybody else.

Game 25

Petrosian, Tigran – Manoian, R
Armenian Championship, Yerevan (1),
1948
French Defence

1.e4 e6 2.d4 d5 3.♘c3 ♗b4 4.e5 c5 5.a3 cxd4?!

A pretty weak variation.

6.axb4 dxc3 7.♘f3

This is not one of the main lines, yet it gives White an edge.

7...♘e7 8.♗d3

If 8.bxc3 ♘g6 9.c4 White is somewhat better.

8...♘g6 9.0-0 ♘c6

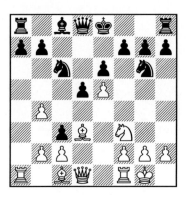

10.♗xg6

Petrosian gives up the bishop pair to get the pawn back.

10...hxg6 11.bxc3 ♕c7 12.♖e1 ♘e7 13.♕d3 ♗d7 14.♗g5 ♘f5

After 14...a6 Black can afford to leave his king in the centre.

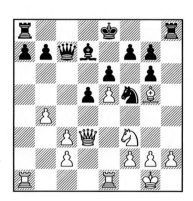

15.g4

Petrosian doesn't wait. He could have chosen a different move and pushed the pawn once Black castled, when the knight could only retreat to h6. 15.b5 and 15.♖eb1 were reasonable.

15...♘e7 16.♘d4 a6 17.♖e3

A nice multifunctional move; one

can miss the fact that the rook can get to h3.

17...♘g8

The position would still be easier to play with White after the more natural 17...♖c8!? 18.♖h3 ♖f8 19.♖e1.

18.f4

Building play with 18.♖ae1 is somewhat more natural, but that day Petrosian was in a pugnacious mood and he gets ready to sacrifice a piece.

18...♕c4 19.♕d2 f6

Black picks up the gauntlet; he goes for a tactical battle.

20.exf6 gxf6

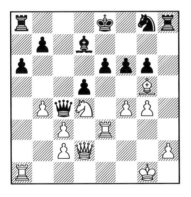

21.♘xe6

This is not the only way to sacrifice material. 21.♕e1 fxg5 22.♖xe6+ ♗xe6 23.♕xe6+ ♔f8 (23...♔d8 24.♕d6+) 24.♕d6+ (24.♕e5 ♖h7 25.♘e6+ ♔e8 26.♘c7+ ♔f8 and it looks like perpetual check) 24...♘e7 25.♕f6+ ♔g8 26.♕xe7 ♕xc3 and one side will give perpetual check.

21...♗xe6

21...fxg5 22.♘c7+ wins.

22.♖xe6+ ♔f7

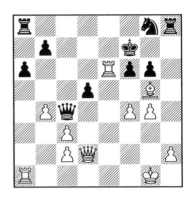

23.♖b6!

Using the rook horizontally is an imaginative way to attack. 23.♖ae1 fxg5 24.♖1e4 dxe4 (24...♕xe4 25.♖xe4 dxe4 26.♕d5+ ♔f8 and the position is balanced) 25.♕d7+ ♔f8 26.♕d6+ and White has to keep giving check.

23...fxg5 24.♖xb7+ ♔f8?

Black commits a mistake in defence. Here is the right continuation: 24...♘e7 25.♖e1 ♖ae8 (25...♖he8 26.♕e3 ♕e4 27.♕g3! gxf4 28.♕h4 and White wins) 26.♕f2 (26.♕e3 ♕e4 27.♕f2 [27.♕g3?? gxf4] 27...♕xf4 28.♕e2 ♔g8 and the position is even) 26...♖h7 27.fxg5+ ♔g8 and the position is balanced.

25.♖f1 ♔e8 26.♖e1+ ♔f8 27.♕e3?

Petrosian's concentration slips and he misses a win. If 27.♕f2! Black would lay down arms quickly, for example after 27...♘f6 28.♖e6 or after 27...gxf4 28.♕b6 White invades and wins.

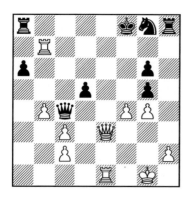

27...♕c8!

The queen attacks both the rook and the pawn.

28.fxg5??

It would be interesting to know why he played this blunder. After 28.♕b6! ♕xg4+ 29.♔h1 ♕f3+ 30.♔g1 Black must give perpetual check.

28...♕xb7 29.♖f1+ ♔g7

29...♕f7? 30.♖xf7+ ♔xf7 31.♕e5 wins.

30.♕e5+ ♔h7 31.♖f3

Petrosian plays in Tal's style.

31...♘h6

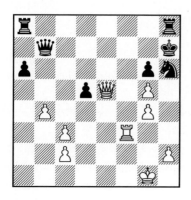

32.♖h3

White is a rook and a knight

down. His attack is very dangerous, but not irresistible.

32...♕g7??

Just like in many Tal games, the pressure takes its toll and the opponent plays a losing move. The cold-blooded king move 32...♔g8! would take the sting out of White's attack. After 33.gxh6 (if 33.♕d6 then 33...♖f8 or 33...♕f7 would win) 33...♖h7 34.♖f3 ♖f8 White runs out of play.

33.♖xh6+ ♔g8 34.♕e6+

This check wins easily, though 34.♕xd5+ would lead to checkmate.

34...♔f8 35.♖xg6 ♕e7

35...♕xg6 would not prolong the game for long.

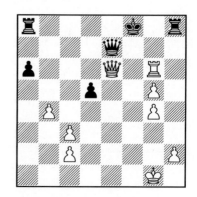

36.♖f6+

White wins everything.

36...♔e8   37.♕c6+   ♔d8
38.♕xa8+   ♔d7   39.♕c6+   ♔d8
40.♖d6+ 1–0

Tigran played this game in Tal's style. In my Tal books, I realised that the Magician from Riga programmed himself before the game. If he wanted, he was able to play disciplined, superb positional chess. Here we saw that Petrosian could play wild chess. Had he kept on playing like this, he would have got used to it and would have become extremely strong as well. It was not a great game, but we wanted to show you that he was able to play like this.

We look at the game from the next round as well. Quite possibly, the name of his opponent is not correctly given in the database. In the cross table of the event there is no player with such a name, and moreover, "Marine" is a female Armenian name. However, there are two other players with the same surname.

Game 26

Avetisian, Marine –
Petrosian, Tigran
Armenian Championship,
Yerevan (2), 1948

1.d4 ♞f6 2.c4 g6 3.♞c3 ♝g7 4.e4 0-0 5.♞ge2 d6 6.g3 e5

Kasparian played this move first; maybe Henrik suggested this move to his younger fellow Armenian.

7.♝g2 exd4 8.♞xd4 ♞c6 9.♞xc6

There was a Botvinnik-Yudovich game, Leningrad, 1939, with this opening, and the future World Champion played 9.♞c2 here.

9...bxc6 10.0-0 ♝e6 11.b3 ♞d7 12.♝b2

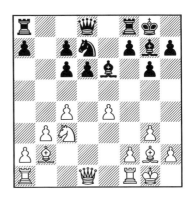

12...a5!
Petrosian wants to create a weakness on b3.

13.♞a4 ♝xb2 14.♞xb2 ♛f6 15.♛c2 ♞c5
Petrosian doesn't mind exchanging the knight.

16.♞d3 ♞xd3 17.♛xd3

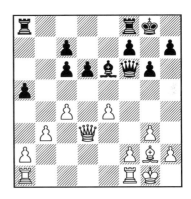

17...a4
Petrosian creates a target.

18.e5
Avetisian simplifies, but some tension remains.

18...dxe5 19.♝xc6 ♜ad8 20.♛f3
Exchanging the bishop with 20.♝d5! would be beneficial for White. 20...♝xd5 (20...c6 21.♛f3

saves the piece, or after 20...♗h3 21.♖fe1 ♖fe8 22.♕c3 c6 23.♗g2 White has nothing to worry about) 21.cxd5 c6 (21...♖d6 22.♕c4) 22.♕a6 axb3 23.♕xc6 and the queenside pawns disappear, therefore White holds.

20...♕xf3

Petrosian reduces material; this allows his opponent less time to prepare to meet his play.

21.♗xf3 axb3 22.axb3

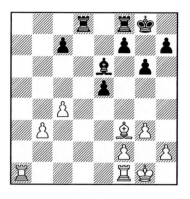

22...♖d3 23.♗d1?

The bishop will be passive here. Exchanging the bishop with 23.♗d5! would allow White to get rid of the queenside pawns and reach a 3 pawns versus 3 pawns drawn rook ending. 23...♗xd5 (23...♗h3 24.♖fe1 ♖e8 25.♖e3 and White is safe) 24.cxd5 ♖xb3 25.♖a7! This makes sure that the c7–pawn will be exchanged (25. ♖fc1 ♖b7 26.♖c6 ♖d8 27.♖ac1 ♖d7 would probably be enough to hold as well) 25...♖c3 26.♖b1 ♖d8 27.♖bb7 ♖d7 28.d6 It would be interesting to know whether 70 years ago they knew that this was a draw.

23...♖fd8 24.♔g2 f5!

This gains space and opens the way for the king. After 24...♖d2 25.♗f3 ♖8d3 26.♖a7 White would get away with it.

25.♖e1?!

A passive move, as it doesn't really attack the e5 target. With 25.♗c2! White could take advantage of the fact that the d8-rook is unprotected. Exchanging a pair of rooks (especially getting rid of the passive e1–rook) is beneficial for White. After 25...♖d2 26.♖fd1! ♖8d6 (26...♔f7 27.♔f1) 27.♖xd2 ♖xd2 28.♗d1 White may hold by transferring the king to e1.

25...♔f7 26.♖b1

The other rook becomes passive as well. 26.♔f1 was better, as it retains chances of attacking the c7–pawn.

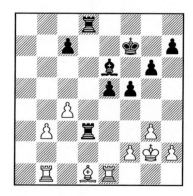

26...♖d2!

Petrosian seals the fate of the d1– bishop.

27.♗e2 ♖a2!

Petrosian not only gets ready to double rooks on the second rank, but takes the a-file away from White. The d-file is less useful for the white rook, as it can't attack anything on that file.

28.罝a1

Occupying the d-file does not help, as after 28.罝ed1 罝xd1 29.奧xd1 e4 30.曾f1 g5 White would be in trouble.

28...罝dd2 29.罝xa2 罝xa2 30.曾f3

30.h4 e4 is enough as well.

30...曾f6

Perhaps 30...g5!? was more precise.

31.曾e3

31.h4! would ease White's position a bit.

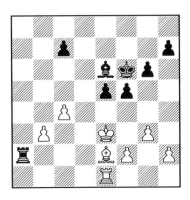

31...g5!

Petrosian pushes Avetisian back.

32.曾d3?

White is just marking time. He needed to stop the black pawns with 32.f4, even if that cost a pawn. It would would pose Petrosian a dilemma: to win a pawn or press further.

a) After 32...gxf4 33.gxf4 exf4+ 34.曾xf4 罝b2 35.奧d1 (35.奧f3 罝xb3 36.奧d5) 35...罝xh2 36.奧f3 it is hard to tell whether Black will win.

b) 32...罝b2 33.fxg5+ 曾xg5 34.h4+ 曾f6 35.奧d1 罝g2 36.曾f3 罝h2 and White struggles.

32...c5 33.曾e3 f4+

Black's advanced pawns secure a win.

34.gxf4 exf4+ 35.曾f3 h5 36.曾g2

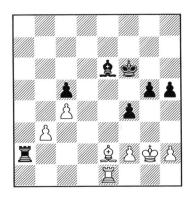

36...g4!

White gets completely pushed back.

37.奧d1 罝a1 38.曾f1 h4

Petrosian tightens the screws. White has no air to breathe.

39.奧c2

39.曾e2 奧f5 is also hopeless.

39...罝xe1+ 40.曾xe1 曾e5 41.曾e2 奧f5 42.奧d1

42...♔d4

Black's domination is complete.

43.♔d2 g3

Petrosian creates a winning passed pawn. After 43...f3 White would be in zugzwang.

44.fxg3 fxg3 45.hxg3 h3

Black's h-pawn will be a queen very soon.

46.♗f3 h2 0–1

In round 3, he got a small edge against Oganesian as White in the opening, but it slipped away. The position was equal for a long time, but in the endgame Petrosian subtly exchanged many pieces, and his win can be seen in the Petrosian's Remarkable Exchanges chapter. In round 4, Petrosian was Black against Kalantar, and his win can be seen in the Petrosian's Remarkable Exchanges chapter, too. The game turned into a bishop versus knight ending. Kalantar did not just wait with his king. Petrosian cleverly played to exchange his bishop for the knight. His opponent failed to smell a rat, and he lost the pawn ending. According to the database, Tigran lost as White in round 5 to Kalashian, but that is unlikely, as Petrosian probably won the game, in which case he would have been Black. But that would have meant three black games in a row, so maybe this game was not played in round 5. In any event, the game against Kalashian was balanced, but Black gained the upper hand in an ending after time control.

Sakuni – Petrosian, Tigran
Armenian Championship,
Yerevan (6), 1948
Sicilian Defence

1.e4 c5

Petrosian played the Sicilian relatively rarely in his early years, and he kept changing his lines in it. He and Kasparian both had 5 out of 5 at this point, so it was worth taking risks.

2.♘f3 ♘c6 3.d4 cxd4 4.♘xd4 ♘f6 5.♘c3 d6 6.♗b5

This is a relatively harmless move. Petrosian also played a remarkable game in another line in this variation.

6.g3 g6 7.♗g2 ♗d7 8.0-0 ♗g7 9.♘de2 0-0 10.a4 ♖c8 11.♗e3 ♘g4 12.♗f4 ♘b4 13.♖c1 a6 14.♕d2 ♕c7 15.h3 ♘e5 16.b3

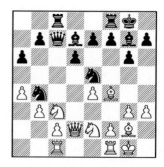

16...♗xh3! This exchange sacrifice is good but not spectacular, however, it is special, as it was probably Petrosian's first of many such sacrifices. Some of them will become eternal. **17.♗xe5 ♗xe5 18.♘d5**

♘xd5   19.♗xh3   ♘c3   20.♗xc8
♖xc8 21.♘xc3 ♗xc3 22.♕d3 ♗b2
23.♖cd1 ♕xc2, when Petrosian got a
slightly preferable position and went
on to win, Gabunia, T – Petrosian, T,
Tbilisi, 1945.

**6...♗d7   7.♗e3   g6   8.f3   ♗g7
9.♕d2**

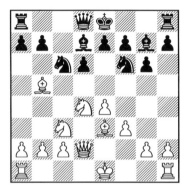

9...♘e5!

Exchanging bishops helps place
the knight on c4. He felt which
pieces to swap with finely tuned
senses.

10.♗xd7+ ♕xd7 11.♗h6 ♘c4

Petrosian looks to get rid of
White's dark-squared bishop; this
makes sure that White has no
attack.

**12.♕e2   ♗xh6   13.♕xc4   0-0
14.♖d1 a6 15.0-0 b5 16.♕d3 ♕b7
17.♘b3**

17.a3 and 17.♘de2 were more
resilient.

17...♖ac8

17...♖fc8 looks nice as well.

18.♔h1 ♗g7 19.♘e2

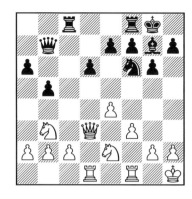

19...♘d7!

The knight aims to get to c4; the
move improves the bishop as well.

**20.c3 ♘e5 21.♕d5 ♕b6 22.♕d4
♕c7**

Petrosian keeps the queens on,
though he could have swapped them
as well, as 22...♕xd4 23.cxd4 ♘c4
24.♖b1 e5 25.♖fd1 ♖fd8 is also
promising for Black.

23.♕f2 ♘c4 24.♘f4

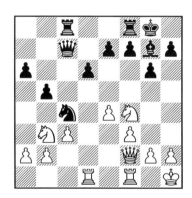

24...e6!

Petrosian has just placed his
knight on a great outpost, and now
he prevents his opponent from doing
the same.

25.♖fe1 ♖fd8 26.♘d3 a5

Tigran starts pushing back his opponent on the queenside.

27.♘d2 a4 28.a3

If 28.♘xc4 bxc4 29.♘b4 a3 30.♕d2 axb2 31.♕xb2 ♕c5 Black would be clearly better as well.

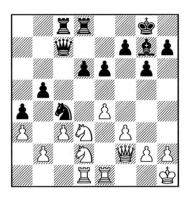

28...♘xb2!

A nice and somewhat surprising sacrifice: the two connected passed pawns backed by the bishop will win.

29.♘xb2 ♕xc3 30.♖b1 ♕xa3 31.♘f1 b4 32.♕e2

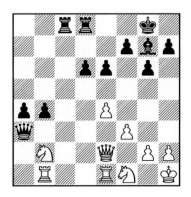

32...b3

The connected passed pawns are irresistible, and the rest is simple.

33.♘e3 ♕b4 34.♘d3 ♕b6 35.♕d1 ♖c3 36.♕e2 a3 37.♘d1 ♖c6 38.♘c1 b2 39.♘a2 ♕b3 40.♘dc3 ♗xc3 41.♘xc3 ♖xc3 0–1

In round 7, Petrosian was Black against Mokatsian. White played really cautiously, Tigran took a huge risk and was worse, but in a direct confrontation he outplayed his opponent. He won a pawn and converted it into a win. In round 8, he was Black against Allakhverdian. White played poorly, gradually reached a losing position by move 15, and lost without resistance. In round 9, he was White against Oltetsian, who also lost without resistance. According to the header in round 10, he was White again and his opponent was Agababean; the numbers of the rounds are probably mixed up. Petrosian gained a winning position in the opening, but let most of his advantage slip away. Around time control, he won a pawn and managed to win the game. Petrosian played the game of the event against Kasparian (there is no information showing in which round it was played). The middlegame with no queens was heading for a draw, but Petrosian then played some strange moves and gave up the only open file. Kasparian then unnecessarily exchanged off his strong bishop. Petrosian still had to work hard for the draw but obtained it. Petrosian beat two more players, but those games are not in the database.

Petrosian and Kasparian both scored an incredible 12.5 points out of 13. On the one hand, this shows that they were very good, but on the other it indicates that the young talent needed better opposition.

Championship of the Republics of the Caucasus, Tbilisi

The next tournament was played in Tbilisi: the championship of the republics of the Caucasus. Playing in the city he was raised in must have been nice. Perhaps he met old friends. But on the other hand, it might have been hard to keep concentrating on the event. We know seven of his thirteen games, but the headers do not say the numbers of rounds.

He was Black against Blagidze. The game was even all the way and they drew. He easily beat Amirkhanov as White. Petrosian was White against Ebralidze; it looks like Petrosian did not try particularly hard to beat his trainer. The way he treated the opening suited his former trainer. The position was balanced all the way, and they repeated moves in an equal ending. Pirtskhalava as White in an equal position carelessly exchanged a few pieces, which led to the loss of a pawn. Petrosian never let him back into the game. Petrosian was Black against Shakhtakhtinsky; they manoeuvred in a closed position for some time. The position simplified to a queen ending. Tigran was a pawn up, but his king had no good shelter. After time control, White made a blunder, allowing the exchange of queens, and he resigned. His opponent withdrew after this game, and has no other game in the cross-table of the event, so maybe they played it in round 1. Shishov as White treated the 3.e5 Caro-Kann wildly; he was clearly lost for a long time. However, Petrosian then made a careless move. Shishov found a nice pawn sacrifice and got away with a draw. Petrosian played the Orthodox Queen's Gambit as Black against Sorokin. He created complications riskily in a solid position, but the position remained balanced all the way. They had probably adjourned the game for the second time when they agreed to a draw. He played six more games, of which he won 4 more with two draws; sadly, the games are not in the database.

He finished the event with 7 wins, 6 draws and no loss. He scored 10 points out of 13, but the 9 points that counted for the event earned him second place. The winner was Makogonov with 10 points.

One may think that this event was a qualifier for the Soviet Championship, as in 1948 Tigran didn't participate in the quarter-final or semi-final. However, neither he nor Makogonov played in the Soviet final. By the way, Ebralidze finished third, scoring 8 points. Something important happened during this event, which is mentioned in *Reliability Strategy*. He went for a walk with

Makogonov, and Tigran told him that he was invited to move to Moscow and was not sure what to do. The strong player told him not to worry and move, as his development would profit a lot from it. It took some time until Petrosian finally made the very beneficial decision.

Sadly, in 1948 Petrosian played too few games against strong players. He lost no games at all, which also shows his level. Had the Soviet authorities managed him better and found proper tournaments for him, he quite possibly would have got to challenge Botvinnik earlier.

Petrosian's results in 1948

Armenian Championship, Yerevan	$+ 12 = 1 - 0$ 12.5/13 1st-2nd place
Championship of the Republics of the Caucasus	$+ 7 = 6 - 0$ 10/13 2nd place
Altogether	**$+ 19 = 7 - 0$ 22.5/26**

1949

Just like in the previous few years, Petrosian started the year at the championship of his republic.

We show the following game partly because it is the only available game from that championship, but also to demonstrate that most players of the event were far behind Petrosian. Mokatsian played this game poorly, but later he became a reasonable player.

Game 28

**Petrosian, Tigran –
Mokatsian, Akob**
Championship of the Armenian
Republic, Yerevan, 1949
King's Indian Defence

1.d4 ♘f6 2.♘f3 g6 3.c4 ♗g7 4.♘c3 d6

Petrosian, who had a nice sense of humour, once said that he was very grateful for the King's Indian Defence as it helped him feed his family for years. He also allegedly said that if he did not win against the King's Indian he was having a bad day. He scored well against it.

5.e4 0-0 6.g3 ♘c6

Provoking d5 is not worth two tempi.

7.d5 ♘b8 8.♗g2 ♘bd7 9.0-0 ♘g4 10.♕e2 ♘ge5

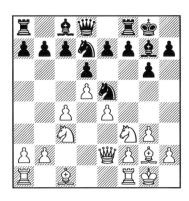

11.♘xe5!

Petrosian plays to bring his pieces out fluently, rather than trying to choke his opponent's pieces with 11.♘d2.

11...♘xe5 12.♗e3 b6

This is a bit pointless. Perhaps Mokatsian wants to stop c5. Black should try 12...c5!?, which results in a smaller disadvantage.

13.♖ac1 ♗d7 14.h3 ♗c8 15.f4

Petrosian gains space and pushes back his opponent's piece.

15...♘d7

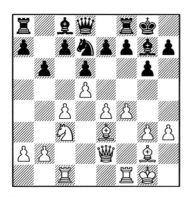

16.♘b5!

Tigran employs another main weapon in closed positions: he improves one of his pieces.

16...a5?

Black's position becomes even more static.

17.♗d4!

Petrosian aims to weaken Black's king by exchanging the g7–bishop.

17...♘c5

Black can't act in the centre, as after 17...e5 18.dxe6 fxe6 19.♗xg7 ♔xg7 20.e5 White wins.

18.♗xg7 ♔xg7

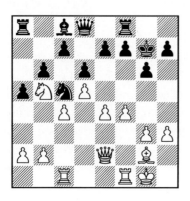

19.e5!

White's space advantage in the centre is huge. He is already winning.

19...♗d7 20.♘d4 f5

Black fights for space, but weakens the king.

21.♖c3 ♖b8 22.e6

This pawn is too powerful to live with.

22...♗e8 23.b3 ♖c8

24.g4!

Tigran starts opening up Black's king, and Black is powerless against it.

24...♖f6 25.♖g3 ♔h8 26.♕b2

White can win at will, for example 26.gxf5 gxf5 27.h4 a4 28.h5 a3 29.♖g5.

26...fxg4 27.hxg4 ♔g8 28.g5 ♖f5 29.♖h3

Petrosian doesn't even bother to take the exchange.

29...b5 30.♖ff3

This makes ♖xh7 a threat.

30...h5

31.♖xh5 1–0 It was pretty, but one-sided as well. Perhaps some of the remaining players at the event were unable to put up resistance.

Petrosian badly needed better opposition than in this game. He finished the event with 12 wins, 1 draw and 2 losses. It earned him the silver medal. We only know that Mokatsian played, but have no other names. The two losses and second place suggest that some strong players were invited from outside the republic.

Soviet Championship Semi-Final, Tbilisi

The Georgian capital occupies a special place not only in Petrosian's personal life, but in his chess career as well. He qualified for the Soviet final for the first time in his home town. He probably managed to channel the emotion of thinking of his family and meeting his trainer and childhood friends in the right direction: specifically, he met Tengiz at this tournament.

In the first round, Petrosian was Black against Salmonis. In the 3.exd5 cxd5 4.♗d3 Caro-Kann the position was always balanced and soon after time control they agreed to a draw. In the second round, he was Black against Vasiliev (though maybe the headers of the early Petrosian games in the database are not correct). Petrosian equalised in a g3 King's Indian, but he made a mistake by giving up his bishop for a knight. His position was close to lost, but he gradually decreased his disadvantage and by time control they agreed a draw in an equal position. In round 3, Petrosian was White against Novotelnov. He got a small edge and sacrificed a pawn. Then, his opponent blundered, and Tigran confidently converted his advantage. In the next round, Petrosian as Black against Lubienski accepted hanging pawns in a Nimzo-Indian. His opponent wanted to carry out a smart little combination, but it resulted in the blunder of a piecc. In thc fifth round, Petrosian as White in an English Opening played originally. His opponent, Aramanovich, was able to keep the position balanced for some time, then blundered a piece. Petrosian convincingly converted the advantage with the extra piece. In the sixth round he drew with Pirtskhalava, who withdrew, so that game did not count.

We look at his game from round 7.

Game 29

**Petrosian, Tigran –
Pogrebissky, Iosif**
Soviet Championship Semi-Final,
Tbilisi (7), 1949
Grunfeld Defence

**1.d4 ♘f6 2.c4 g6 3.♘f3 ♗g7
4.g3 0-0 5.♗g2 d5 6.cxd5 ♘xd5
7.0-0 c5**

According to the database,
Mikenas first played this move to
beat Alekhine. It was played a lot
in the 1948 Salsjobaden Interzonal.
Kotov, Boleslavsky and Szabo all
employed it.

8.e4

Petrosian plays an ambitious
move.

8...♘f6 9.e5 ♘fd7

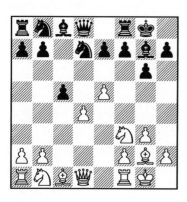

10.♘g5?!

This is a rare move; it is probably
not a dangerous one.

10...cxd4 11.f4

After 11.e6 ♘e5 Black would be
better.

11...♘c5?!

11...♘b6! is more difficult to
meet for White, as it would require
an effort to get rid of the d-pawn.

12.b4

Sending the knight back isolates
the d-pawn a bit.

12...f6

This leads to an exciting
middlegame. After 12...♘e6!?
13.♘xe6 ♗xe6 14.♗xb7 ♗d5
15.♗xa8 ♗xa8 Black has nice
compensation for the exchange.

13.exf6 exf6

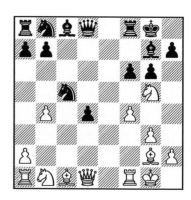

14.♘xh7!

White wins back the pawn.

14...♔xh7 15.bxc5 ♘c6?!

Pogrebissky should have tried to
get rid of the c-pawn. After 15...♘a6
16.♗a3 ♖e8 17.♘d2 d3 18.♖c1 the
position would be complex.

16.♗b2 ♕c7?

The queen will be surprisingly
out of play on c7. If 16...♗f5 17.♘d2
♖e8 18.♘c4 ♗f8 the position would
be balanced.

17.♘d2 ♗e6 18.♘e4 ♖ad8

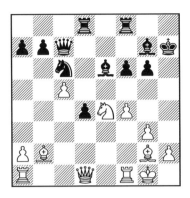

19.h4!?

Petrosian spots that Black's king is vulnerable. After 19.♘d6 f5 20.♕a4 ♖d7 21.♖fe1 White's position would be promising.

19...♕d7?!

Improving the queen is a bit late. Black should send the e4 knight away. 19...♗c4! 20.♖f2 f5 21.♘d6 (21.♘g5+ ♔h6) 21...♖xd6 22.cxd6 ♕xd6 23.♖c1 though Black would still be somewhat worse.

20.h5

Petrosian starts opening Black's king.

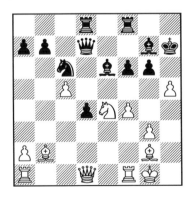

20...♗g4?

Pogrebissky doesn't sense the danger. After 20...f5 21.♘d6 b6

22.hxg6+ ♔xg6 23.g4 ♘e7 24.♗a3 White would have the upper hand in a complex position.

21.hxg6+ ♔xg6 22.f5+

This pretty move traps Black's king.

22...♗xf5

22...♕xf5 23.♕b1 wins as well.

23.♘d6 ♗g4

If 23...♗e6 24.♗e4+ f5 25.♕g4+ ♔h7 26.♘xf5 Black's king is still caught.

24.♗e4+ ♔h5

25.♖f4!

Petrosian leaves the queen en prise; it is a joy to play such a move.

25...f5 26.♖xg4

Another eye pleasing move.

26...fxg4 27.♕d2 ♖h8

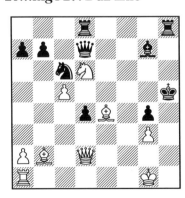

28.♔g2 1–0

And the final sweet move, with checkmate in 3. There was another way to checkmate, too: 28.♗c1 would finish the game in no time.

In round 8, Petrosian was Black against Ebralidze. The game was a peaceful matter, they exchange a lot and after the opening they agreed to a draw. It was the last meeting between the trainer and his pupil in a tournament game. In round 9, Petrosian was White against Klaman. In the King's Indian Black got no play on the kingside, while Petrosian took control on the queenside and won convincingly. This game features in the Petrosian's Remarkable Exchanges chapter and is the game from this book's cover. Against Ilivitsky, he as Black drew in an Orthodox Queen's Gambit; not much happened in the game. In round 11 versus Nezhmetdinov, Petrosian as White exchanged queens early and soon after created doubled pawns for his opponent. White won a pawn and after time control he won the game. In round 12 against Chistiakov, Petrosian as Black based his play on the activity of his pieces, accepting weaknesses in his pawn chain. However, he ran out of activity, lost a pawn and was unable to save the game. In the next round, Petrosian as White tried the closed Sicilian against Makogonov. They exchanged no pawns. A bit before time control, Black sacrificed two

pieces for a rook and pawn. Petrosian had chances, but he wanted to win with insufficient preparation, and the game ended in a draw. In game 14, he was Black versus Grechkin. In the 4...♗f5 Caro-Kann, White got the bishop pair and played on for a long time, but Petrosian held firmly. In round 15, Petrosian gained a small edge in a Tarrasch French against Kasparian. The game was equal for a long time, but Kasparian blundered and Petrosian quickly won the game. In the penultimate round, Petrosian was Black against a rival in the event, Kholmov. In the Caro-Kann, Tigran gave up the bishop pair and he had to work for a draw, but never looked troubled and drew. In the last round, he was White against Geller, and sharing the point meant qualification for the final for both. They pretended to play, exchanged all pieces and agreed to a draw. By the way, Petrosian and Geller would end up playing each other 43 times despite playing no match against each other. Qualifying for the final was a superb accomplishment. Geller won the event, scoring 11.5 points out of 16; Petrosian finished half a point behind. He won 7 games, drew 9 and lost one. It was a pity that Pirtskhalava withdrew from the event. In fact, this Georgian player beat Geller, but his games did not count for the event. Petrosian scored 6 wins and one draw against the bottom 7 players. Kholmov finished third with 10 points.

Soviet Championship Final, Moscow

Petrosian must have been looking forward to his first final. It was the ultimate challenge for a young player in his country to prove his talent. In those days, just to obtain the right to line up was a most impressive accomplishment in itself. Petrosian moved to Moscow in 1949 (some sources say it was 1950, though Petrosian states in *Chess Lectures* that it was 1949), most probably that winter. Going to live in the Soviet capital was beneficial for his chess. Petrosian later said the early fifties were the happiest years of his life.

The championship started in the second half of October, and maybe he already lived in the Soviet capital. Petrosian's play had been affected by something in his first ever semi-final game when he played way below his level. This then happened in his first game at the final of the championship as well. He blundered badly as Black against Kotov. First he gave away a pawn for free, and soon another one. He resigned on move 13. Playing the first game at such a prestigious event for the first time probably created too much tension for Petrosian. In the second round, he faced one of the very best players in the world, Smyslov. Petrosian chose an open Sicilian, the position was even in the Scheveningen, but he missed a pawn sacrifice. Tigran made another mistake and lost a pawn; he fought on, but with no chance. Soon after time control he resigned. Petrosian's tribulations did not end in round 3. Flohr smelled a rat and castled long against Petrosian's Old Indian. Black was almost lost soon after the opening. Petrosian worked his way back, but got carried away and made an aggressive, but bad move. Flohr had a chance to give forced checkmate. A careless check allowed Tigran to get back, but he made another mistake and soon had to resign. In the fourth round, Petrosian was White against Geller. He played the variation of the King's Indian that would be named after him, although it had been played by Flohr in 1948 and Lilienthal beat Geller with it in round 2 in this championship. Tigran unnecessarily gave up the bishop pair and made a losing move on move 16; he played on until move 27 with no hope. In round 5, he and Keres reached an unusual middlegame in another King's Indian. Petrosian's position was playable and a small tactical skirmish occurred, Tigran made a bad mistake and ended up with a hopeless position. He fought on, but in vain. Losing 5 in a row is tough, but life had earlier treated him tragically, which helped mould his iron personality.

Round 6 was a pivotal moment for Tigran, where we look at his first win against a world class opponent.

Game 30

Petrosian, Tigran – Lilienthal, Andor
Soviet Championship Final,
Moscow (6), 1949
Four Knights Game

1.e4 e5 2.♘f3 ♘c6 3.♘c3 ♘f6 4.♗b5

This is a clever choice when one is not doing well: it is hard for Black to play for a win. By the way, although he beat Geller, Lilienthal did not start the event well either and was on minus two before this game

4...♗b4 5.0-0 0-0 6.d3 ♗xc3 7.bxc3 d6 8.♗g5 ♕e7 9.♖e1

Petrosian deviates from Keres's play. That game went: 9.♗xc6 bxc6 10.c4 c5 11.♘d2 h6 12.♗xf6 ♕xf6 13.♖e1 ♖b8 14.♘f1 ♗e6 15.♖b1 ♖b6 Keres, P – Lilienthal, A, Leningrad, 1947, and it ended in a draw.

9...♘d8 10.d4 ♘e6 11.♗c1 c5

This is a common line, closing the centre, but it leaves Black's position static. 11...c6 and 11...♖d8 are played more often.

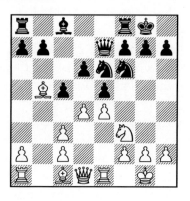

12.♗f1!

The bishop may move to g2.

12...♕c7?

Lilienthal deviates from his own winning game. He beat Bondarevsky with 12...♖d8. The game move is unfortunate, as the knight will stand worse on d8 than on f8 and the queen will be misplaced on c7.

13.d5 ♘d8

13...♘f4?! 14.♗xf4 exf4 15.♕d2 ♘h5 16.e5 and White would have a clear advantage.

14.♘h4!

White improves his knight and gets ready to gain space with f4.

14...♘e8

Placing all the pieces on the back rank can be played, as the position is quite closed, but it is still unattractive. 14...♕e7 and 14...♖b8 do not equalise either.

15.g3 ♕e7

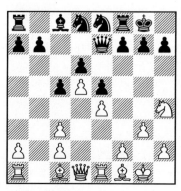

16.♘f5 ♗xf5

Or 16...♕f6 17.♕f3

17.exf5

A knight is often stronger than a bishop, but the bishop pair is usually stronger than the knight pair.

17...♕f6 18.♕g4 ♕e7

18...g6 19.♗g5! wins an exchange.
19.♗g5 ♕d7

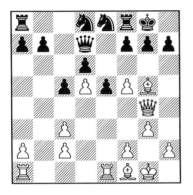

20.a4

Petrosian plays across the entire board.

20...f6 21.♗d2 g6

Lilienthal is in deep trouble. He wants to ease White's grip, but the position opens up for the two bishops.

22.♗h3 ♕xf5 23.♕xf5 gxf5 24.♗xf5 ♘g7 25.♗d3 f5

Black tries to be a bit active, but waiting was also joyless.

26.f4 e4 27.♗e2 ♖c8 28.c4 ♘e8

Perhaps 28...♖c7 is a bit better, and maybe 28...h5 is Black's best try, as it will probably lead to a fewer number of pawns.

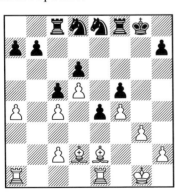

29.h3!

Petrosian's move is good, but 29.g4 could be played at once.

29...♘f6 30.g4 fxg4 31.hxg4 ♖c7 32.♔f2

After weakening the e4–pawn, he goes after the h7 one.

32...h6 33.♖h1 e3+

This is a desperate attempt to create complications.

34.♗xe3 ♘e4+ 35.♔g2 ♘f7 36.♗d3 ♖e7 37.♖ae1 ♖fe8 38.♗c1 ♘c3 39.♖xe7 ♖xe7

Black can do nothing with the e-file, and the c3–knight is far from its camp.

40.a5 b6?

40...♘a2 would lose, but at least saves the knight.

41.axb6 axb6 42.♗d2

Petrosian wins the knight.

42...♘e2?

42...♘a4 43.♖a1 wins.

43.c3 b5 44.♔f3 1–0

This was a one-sided game, but beating a world class player for the first time must have been very pleasing.

In round 7, Petrosian was Black against Aronin. They played the Two Knights line of the Caro-Kann Defence. Petrosian gave up the bishop pair and he equalised with purposeful play. The game ended in a draw after Black's 18th move. In the next game, Petrosian was Black against Kholmov. In a French Defence, Tigran unnecessarily gave up the bishop pair, but Kholmov failed to capitalise on it. Petrosian sacrificed a pawn, they castled on opposite sides, and then agreed to a draw in a wild position. Petrosian had 8 minutes for the next 25 moves until time control.

In round 9, Petrosian as White treated the Orthodox Queen's Gambit Exchange sharply, by castling long. Mikenas skilfully neutralised his play by exchanges. The position is equal when we join the game.

Game 31

Petrosian, Tigran – Mikenas, Vladas
Soviet Championship Final, Moscow
(9), 1949

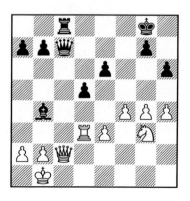

30.♕d1!?
Petrosian avoids exchanging queens; had he swapped the position would be equal. After this move, White has no advantage, but Black can go wrong more easily as his king is slightly less secure.

30...♕b6?!
The strong Lithuanian grandmaster makes a mistake. Black is too optimistic; he hopes to get some play against White's king, but moves his army far away from his own king.

a) Black could bring the queen close to his king with 30...♕f7. Then 31.g5 (31.a3 ♗e7 32.g5 hxg5 33.hxg5 b5 would be a balanced position) 31...hxg5 32.hxg5 ♕g6 and White has no attacking chances.

b) The surprising 30...♗e1 wins a pawn. After 31.♘e2 ♗xh4 32.♘d4 ♕d7 33.f5! the position would be even.

31.g5!
Petrosian takes his chance and starts playing against Black's deserted king.

31...hxg5 32.hxg5 g6?
Petrosian threatens g6. Now that threat is stopped, but this move is not the best. 32...♗c5? would not work, as White wins after 33.♖b3! (33.g6? ♗xe3) 33...♕d8 34.♕h5. But 32...♗e7! although not equalising keeps Black in the game. 33.♘e2! (now White can't attack the black king, as 33.g6 ♗f6 is strong, or if 33.♕h5?! then White has no time to attack on the h-file. 33...♕b4! 34.♖d1 ♕a4 and the position is equal) 33...♕a6

34.♘d4 (after 34.g6 the pawn would be unpleasantly close to the black king) 34...♖c7 35.♘f3 and White would be clearly better.

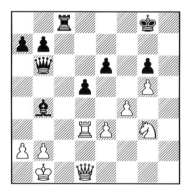

33.♖b3!

A brilliant move! Out of the blue, White has two threats.

33...♕a5 34.♕d3!

The rook vacated the d3–square for the queen.

34...♔f7 35.♘f1?

Petrosian probably wants to prepare a3 and put the knight on a defended square. It would be interesting to know how much time the players had here. Perhaps one or both were short of time. Maybe that generated this mistake; otherwise Petrosian would have found one of the ways to win. 35.f5! gxf5 36.♘xf5 ♕c7 37.a3 would win in no time. Or 35.a3 gets the point a bit more slowly after 35...♗e7 36.♖xb7 ♕e1+. Petrosian probably thought that this works by continuing 37.♔a2 ♕xg3 38.♕d4. In fact, White not only wins, but checkmates after 38...♔e8 39.♕g7 or 38...♖e8 39.♕f6+.

35...♗e7?

Mikenas feels that the bishop should return to the king, but chooses the wrong square. 35...b6! 36.a3 ♗f8. The bishop will go to g7 and solve Black's problems. Or 35...♕c7! 36.a3 ♗f8 and Black is safe here as well.

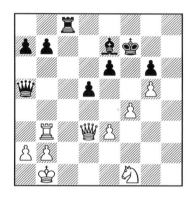

36.♘d2!

The knight aims to get to f3.

36...♕c7?

Mikenas fails to find the only resisting move and makes a losing one in a very difficult position: 36...♖h8!! is the only way to stop the knight. Still, after 37.♖xb7 ♖h1+ 38.♔c2 ♖h2 39.♕d4 ♔e8 40.a3 White is close to winning.

37.♖c3 ♕d7 38.♘f3

38.♘c4 is prettier.

38...♗d6 39.♕d4

This move wins, but allows Black to prolong the game. The more precise 39.♖xc8! wins almost instantly. 39...♕xc8 40.♕d4 ♕e8 41.♕f6+ ♔g8 42.♘d4.

39...♖xc3   40.♕f6+   ♔e8 41.♕xg6+

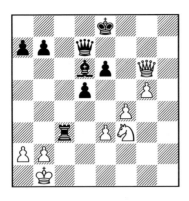

41...♕f7

Black escapes to an ending a pawn down.

42.♕xf7+ ♔xf7 43.bxc3 ♗c5 44.♘e5+ ♔g7 45.♘g4 b5

Mikenas reduces the number of pawns, whereas centralising the king would lead to a quicker loss: 45...♔g6 46.♔c2 ♔f5 47.♘e5 ♗d6 (47...♗xe3 48.g6 ♔f6 49.♘g4+ wins the bishop) 48.♘f3 ♔e4 49.g6 ♗f8 50.♘d4 and Black can't save the bishop.

46.♔c2 b4 47.cxb4 ♗xb4 48.♘e5 ♗d6 49.♘c6 ♔g6 50.♔d3 ♗c5 51.♘e5+ ♔f5

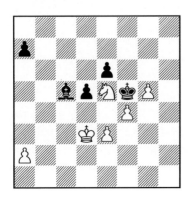

52.a4!

It is beneficial for White to push the pawn as close to promotion as possible, and this move also fixes the a7–pawn.

52...♗b6

52...a5 53.♘c6 ♗b6 54.♘e7+! and White promotes the g-pawn.

53.♘c6 ♔g6 54.a5 ♗c5 55.♘e5+ ♔g7

55...♔f5 56.g6 ♗f8 57.a6 and Black would be in a lethal zugzwang.

56.a6 ♗b6 57.♘d7

57.e4 wins as well.

57...♗a5 58.♘e5

Petrosian probably repeats the position to seal the move and adjourn the game.

58...♗b6 59.♘c6 ♔g6

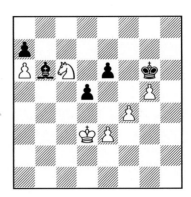

60.e4!

White opens the way for the king.

60...dxe4+

60...♗c5 61.♘d8 wins.

61.♔xe4 ♔f7 62.♘d4 ♔e7

If 62...♗c5 then 63.♔e5 would follow.

63.♘b5

Petrosian prepares the invasion with his king.

63...♗g1 64.♔e5 ♗b6 65.g6 ♗c5

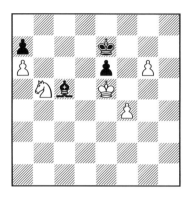

66.g7

Petrosian finds a forced win, though 66.f5 would win as well.

66...♔f7 67.♘c7

Petrosian wins a second pawn. 67.g8=♕+ ♔xg8 68.♔xe6 would win as well.

67...♗b6 68.♘xe6 ♔g8 69.♔f6 ♗e3 70.f5 1−0 Black resigns. This was not perfect play, but Petrosian looked for a fight, played imaginatively and was good enough to beat a very strong player.

Maybe scoring 3 points out of his last 4 games used up too much energy, and in round 10 he lost to Goldberg as Black. In a closed Sicilian, he obtained a pleasant position, but he then strangely gave up his g7-bishop. Then his opponent let him back into the game from a lost position. After that, Goldberg won two pawns and was winning, but made a losing blunder before time control. Petrosian failed to exploit this and went on to lose. In the next round, Petrosian was

White against Bronstein; he played too ambitiously by castling long in a ♕c2 Nimzo-Indian. He was worse, but managed the keep his position together and draw. In the twelfth round, Petrosian was Black against Levenfish; they manoeuvred in a g3 King's Indian Defence for a while. Petrosian opened the position with a pawn sacrifice. His opponent was somewhat better, but blundered an exchange and lost soon after. In round 13, he was White against Boleslavsky. Black did not play 5...♘xc3 in the Grunfeld after 5.e4, and instead played the dubious 5...♘b6. Petrosian was winning all the way. However, Boleslavsky was still stronger than him and survived. In round 14, Petrosian was Black against Furman. They played a King's Indian, but after the opening Tigran made an unfortunate move and got into big trouble. Karpov's future trainer allowed him back into the game, but a tactical mistake cost Petrosian the exchange and, later, the game. In round 15, Petrosian as White got an advantage in a 5...exf6 Caro-Kann against Sokolsky. He was close to winning, but let his opponent back in. Still, some small advantage remained. He squeezed for long, then won two pawns. Strangely, he gave back a pawn two moves after time control (perhaps he was not aware that time pressure was over) and the ensuing rook ending was a draw. In round 16, Kopylov as White tried the closed Sicilian. Petrosian first equalised, then gradually outplayed his opponent. He was close to a win, but Kopylov got away with a repetition after time control. Petrosian started the last three rounds as White against Taimanov in a main-line Queen's Indian. No player was able to create winning chances and the game ended in a draw after White's 32nd move. In the penultimate, 18th round, Ragozin took on d5 and played 4.♗d3 against the Caro-Kann. They exchanged queens and Petrosian gradually outplayed his opponent. In a rook ending, Petrosian's advantage grew to winning, but in a race to queen with rooks still on the board he went from winning to losing. In the last round, Petrosian was White against Liublinsky. After 1.d4 ♘f6 2.♘f3

e6 he played 3.♗g5. He started an attack, his opponent made a serious mistake, and Tigran's attack broke through fairly quickly.

Petrosian scored 7.5 points and finished 16th out of 20 players. He won 4, drew 7 and lost 8 games. It was a good school, and he surely learned a lot. Smyslov and Bronstein came first with 13 points, while Geller and Taimanov ended up with just half a point less than the champions. Geller lost in the last round to Kholmov.

Although Botvinnik did not play in the championship, it was an extremely strong event. Tigran started horribly, but once he settled down he did well. Altogether, it was not a bad result for a debutant in such an event.

Tashkent

At the end of the year, Petrosian played in the capital of Uzbekistan, Tashkent. No game is known from this event, and all we know is that he shared first and second place. He won 11 games, drew 3 and lost one. It must have been a good event for him.

Petrosian's results in 1949

Armenian Championship	+ 12 = 1 – 2	12.5/15 2nd place
Soviet Championship Semi-Final, Tbilisi	+ 7 = 8 – 1	11/16 2nd place
Soviet Championship Final, Moscow	+4 = 7 – 8	7.5/19 16th place
Tashkent	+ 11 = 3 – 1	12.5/15 1st-2nd place
Altogether	**+ 34 = 19 – 12**	**43.5/65**

Note: excluding his draw with Pirtskhalava

1950

Unknown Moscow event

Petrosian played a game against Simagin that year. It is not known exactly when it was played or what event it was. Simagin sacrificed a pawn in the Two Knights Variation of the Caro-Kann. Petrosian gave it back. It was an equal position when Simagin missed a tactical shot; it can be seen in the It's Your Move Chapter. Petrosian won a pawn and converted his advantage.

Spartak-Dynamo Team event

Petrosian joined the Spartak Moscow club. His team played a match against Dynamo in March and Petrosian was White against Baturinsky. They played a Saemisch Nimzo-Indian, and the middlegame was complex and balanced throughout. Black made a mistake and Petrosian caught his king in no time. His opponent lost on time.

Moscow Championship

Petrosian participated in the Moscow championship in August. There are 14 games in the database. One is missing, but can be found in the Internet, against Soloviev. As we know in which round only a few games were played, we first discuss the games where Petrosian was White.

Against Averbakh, he played cautiously, and the game ended in a draw after the opening. Averbakh mentions that their relations became closer after Tigran moved to Moscow. They often met at each other's homes and celebrated new year's eve together. "We got closer during this championship." They prepared together for the 1949, 1950 and 1951 championships and they analysed adjourned games together.

Against Chistiakov, he obtained a winning position in a g3 Benoni. The resilient master somehow survived in a long game which was probably adjourned. He obtained an edge against Golovko's King's Indian. Approaching time control, it grew into a winning edge. Black found a great trick. Petrosian carelessly took a pawn and his opponent got back into the game. Then Petrosian again reached a winning endgame, but he made a careless king move, this time should have taken a pawn, and credit to Golovko: he obtained a draw with very good play. Tigran obtained no advantage in the Saemisch Variation of the

Nimzo-Indian against Kan. Petrosian was alert and the game ended in a draw. Next up, Panov played the King's Indian. Petrosian got a winning position with neat play, but he missed a tactical shot and was lost. He made time control, but soon after got checkmated. Shcherbakov played the Queen's Indian Defence. He made a risky move against Petrosian's e3 variation. Shcherbakov, still in the opening, sacrificed a piece for two pawns, one of which was a well defended passer on c3. Petrosian patiently manoeuvred a lot and gradually won the game. Against Zagoriansky, he attacked in a Ruy Lopez. It looked like Petrosian had started to have problems, when Black simplified to a draw.

He played one more white game and we selected this one for analysis.

Game 32

Petrosian, Tigran – Beilin, Mikhail
Moscow Championship, 1950
Queen's Gambit Declined

1.d4 d5 2.c4 e6 3.♘c3 ♘f6 4.♗g5 ♗e7 5.e3 h6 6.♗h4 0-0 7.♖c1

Petrosian is looking to deviate from the main line. Euwe played a few games featuring this rook move. Later, Petrosian would also try ♘f3 and ♖c1 with no e3.

7...b6 8.cxd5

White is ready to exchange a few pieces to create a backward pawn on c7.

8...♘xd5 9.♘xd5 exd5 10.♗xe7 ♕xe7 11.♗e2

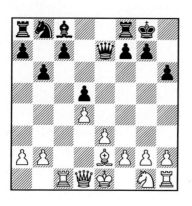

11...♕b4+

Exchanging queens results in a small but long lasting advantage for White. According to the database, this had not been tried before.

12.♕d2 ♕xd2+ 13.♔xd2 c6 14.♘f3 ♗g4

Beilin looks for more simplifications.

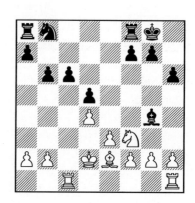

15.♘e5

Petrosian is ready to keep swapping, and he gets closer to Black's soft points.

15...♗xe2 16.♔xe2 ♖c8 17.♖c3 f6 18.♘d3 a5?!

Bringing the king over at once is preferable. White's advantage would

be a bit smaller after 18...♔f7!?
19.♘f4 ♘a6 20.♖hc1 ♘b4 21.♖b3
♘a6, when Black's position is more
solid than in the game.

**19.♖hc1   ♔f7   20.♘f4   ♖d8
21.♖b3 ♖a6**

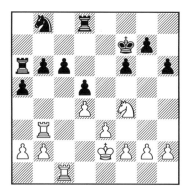

22.h4!

This poses a rather unpleasant
problem: Black either tolerates the
knight on a good square or gives
White a target to bite at.

22...♔e7

Black doesn't take action on
the kingside. Driving the knight
away probably led to a slightly less
one-sided game. 22...g5!? 23.♘d3
♔e6 24.g4 ♔d6 25.f4 ♘d7 26.hxg5
hxg5 27.fxg5 fxg5 28.♖bc3 c5
29.♖h1. Black's position would be
unpleasant, but perhaps preferable
to the game.

23.h5!

The pawn fixes Black's pawns
and creates an outpost on g6, and
not only there. It is not easy to read
Petrosian's idea.

**23...♔d6 24.♖bc3 ♖a7 25.♘g6
♖ad7**

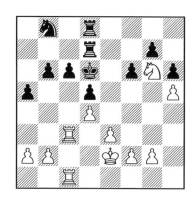

26.♘h4!

The knight is looking to put
pressure on g7. I wonder when
Petrosian visualised this idea. It was
hard for the opponent to anticipate
it in advance.

26...♔c7

If 26...♔e6 then 27.g4 would be
played.

27.♘f5 ♔b7 28.♔f3!

This is a subtle move. Petrosian is
not lazy, he makes the effort to find
the ideal square for his king as well.

28...♖e8!

This is a good move; it stops ♔f4
and the rook may head to e6 to free
the knight.

29.a3 b5?

This is a mistake; he wastes time
on bringing the knight into play and
in addition weakens the c5–square.
Black still has chances to hold.
With 29...♖e6 Black should defend
c6 at once and try to improve the
knight. Then 30.♔g3 (30.♔f4 ♘a6
31.f3 ♘c7 32.♖h1 ♘b5 and Black
neutralises the f5–knight with ♘d6)

a) 30...♖f7 and Black just waits.
31.e4 (31.f3) 31...♖d7 32.exd5 cxd5

(32...♖xd5 33.♔f4) 33.f3 and White could press for long.

b) 30...♘a6 31.f3 ♘c7 32.♔f4 ♘b5 33.♖3c2 where Black is passive, but it is not easy for White to progress. 33...a4 (33...♖c7 34.e4 ♖d7 35.exd5 ♖xd5 36.♘xg7 and White is better) 34.g4. It would be interesting to see how Petrosian would press here.

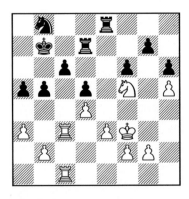

30.♔g3!
Petrosian gets ready for e4.
30...♖e6 31.f3 ♘a6 32.♔f4 ♘c7 33.e4
Petrosian gets closer to opening up the centre.
33...dxe4 34.fxe4 ♘e8

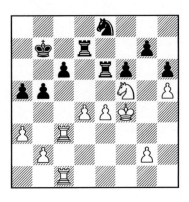

35.♖c5!
The rook is decisive on this square.
35...♘c7
35...a4 36.d5 wins.
36.a4 bxa4?
Beilin runs out of patience and allows White's invasion at once. If 36...♘a6 37.♖5c3 ♘c7 (37...bxa4 38.♖a3) 38.axb5 ♘xb5 39.♖b3 ♔a6 40.♖c4 Black's position is about to fall apart.
37.♖xa5 ♘b5?
He blunders the knight, but nothing would resist for long.
38.d5! 1–0
A beautifully constructed game.

Let's switch to Petrosian's black games! Let's start with the one against Soloviev. It was a Caro-Kann, Soloviev sacrificed a pawn, Petrosian took it, but soon gave it back to simplify. He outplayed his opponent from a harmless position and won a pawn with a small combination. Petrosian won the game with firm hands. Next, Petrosian was Black against Ravinsky. The position became rather sharp, but the tension disappeared and they agreed to a draw before time trouble. Bonch-Osmolovsky played 3.♗b5+ against the Sicilian. No player had a chance to create anything and they drew after 24 moves. Against Simagin, Petrosian introduced a novelty in the sharp Saemisch Variation of the Nimzo-Indian. His opponent reacted poorly and got a lost position in the opening. Simagin strangely kept on playing with no hope. Against Estrin,

Tigran won a pawn in a French Defence, but his position was a bit passive and they agreed to a draw in a balanced position. Against Fridstein, he played the King's Indian, then in the early middlegame all queenside pawns disappeared and he was justified in settling for a draw. Moiseev castled long against the Old Indian. Petrosian exchanged the dark-squared bishops and it was reasonable for Tigran to agree a draw.

Petrosian finished the event with 9 points out of 15; it earned him third place, behind Averbakh and Chistiakov, who both scored 11 points. He won 4 games, fewer than expected after the Soviet final, drew 10 and lost one. Third place is not bad for a player who was not in good form.

Soviet Championship Semi-Final, Gorky

There were 7 quarter- and 5 semi-final groups in the Soviet Championships. Tigran was only required to start in the semi-final. He participated in the one held in the city of Gorky (now Nizhny Novgorod, its historical name). The event took place in October and November. The rounds are not indicated in most of the headers of the seven known games. We start with one whose round is not known.

Game 33

Ratner, Boris – Petrosian, Tigran
Soviet Championship Semi-Final,
Gorky, 1950
King's Indian Defence

1.d4 ♘f6 2.c4 d6 3.♘c3 e5 4.♘f3 ♘bd7 5.g3 g6 6.♗g2 ♗g7 7.0-0 0-0 8.♕c2 ♖e8 9.b3 c6 10.e3 ♕a5

Bronstein had played this move earlier.

11.h3 ♘f8 12.dxe5

Often, taking on e5 in the King's Indian is a timid move at best; here it is reasonably strong, though, as Black wants to play e4. For example, after 12.♗b2 e4 13.♘d2 d5 Black has a pleasant position.

12...dxe5 13.♗b2

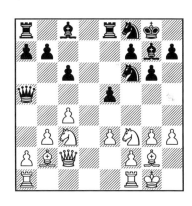

13...♗f5

Petrosian wants to provoke e4.

14.♕e2

If 14.e4 ♗c8 (14...♗e6 15.♘d1 ♘6d7) 15.♖fd1 ♘e6 the position would be a fighting one.

14...♘e4 15.♖ac1 ♘c5

15...♘xc3 16.♗xc3 ♕c7 would be fine as well.

16.e4 ♗d7 17.♕c2

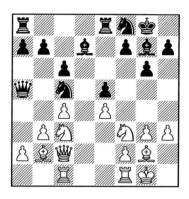

17...♕b6!?

Petrosian interestingly stops a3 and b4. After 17...♘ce6 18.♘e2 ♖ad8 19.a3 ♕c7 the position would be balanced.

18.♘e2 a5 19.♗c3

Maybe Ratner wants to play against the e5–pawn, or maybe wants to prepare b4. If 19.♖cd1 Black would play 19...f5.

19...f5

Petrosian plays actively.

20.♘d2 ♘fe6 21.♘f3 ♘f8

This is a remarkable way to repeat moves.

22.♘d2

22...fxe4

After testing Ratner, Petrosian tries to exert pressure differently. Black's play easily compensates for the isolated pawn. 22...♖ad8 looks nice as well.

23.♘xe4 ♗f5 24.g4 ♗xe4 25.♗xe4 ♘fe6 26.♖cd1 ♖ad8

26...♘xe4 27.♕xe4 a4 is also unpleasant for White.

27.♗g2?!

If 27.♖xd8 ♖xd8 28.♘g3 ♘d4 29.♕b1 White's disadvantage is smaller than in the game.

27...♘d4 28.♕b2

28...♖f8!

This is a fantastic practical idea; Petrosian tries to sell a dummy. He spots that White has no useful move and this sly move allows a good-looking combination. Many players would play 28...a4!?, which would keep an edge, but it is not wicked, unlike Petrosian's move.

a) 29.♘c1 axb3 (29...♘ce6 30.bxa4) 30.axb3 ♘ce6 31.♖fe1 and Black's advantage is small.

b) 29.♘g3 axb3 30.axb3 ♕xb3

(30...♘dxb3   31.♘e4)   31.♕xb3
♘dxb3 32.♘e4 and Black has a
small edge, but White's bishop pair
are not easy to counter.

29.♘xd4?

Ratner starts biting at the hook.
After 29.♘g3 ♘ce6 30.♘e4 ♘f4
Black would be somewhat better.

29...exd4 30.♖xd4??

Ratner falls for the clever
trap and executes a good-looking
combination. Instead of this capture,
30.♗xd4?? ♖xd4 31.♖xd4 ♘e6
would also lose. But with 30.♗d2!
he still resists, and after 30...♘a4
(30...♘e6 31.♕a3) 31.♗xa5 ♕xa5
32.bxa4 ♖f7 although Black would
dominate the dark squares with
decent winning chances, it would
not be over.

30...♘a4!!

This brilliant move wins on
the spot. Ratner hoped for 30...
♗xd4 31.♗xd4 and after that he
had play for the exchange. Once
Simagin asked Petrosian how he
almost always beat weaker players.
In the Soviet Union they often

mentioned that Chigorin had special
inspiration. Petrosian, who had an
excellent sense of humour, answered
something like I keep the position
and wait for my opponents to get
"Chigorin's inspiration" in order
to spot a hole in their combination.
Petrosian demonstrated many such
counter combinations and one could
write a long article on them.

31.bxa4 ♕xb2 32.♗xb2 ♗xd4

Ratner has no compensation at all
for the exchange, so he could resign
already.

33.♗a3 ♖f4 34.♗c1

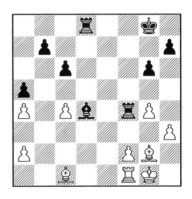

34...♖xf2

This was pretty, but easy to see.
The rest needs no comment.

35.♖xf2 ♖f8 36.♔h2 ♖xf2
37.♔g3 ♖xa2 38.♗g5 ♖a3+
39.♔h2 ♖xa4 40.♗f1 ♖a1 41.♗d3
a4 42.c5 a3 43.♗c4+ ♔g7 0–1

A game by a matured player with
excellent tactical vision.

We continue with Petrosian's
other black games. Against Byvshev,
the 6.d4 Ruy Lopez line led to a
balanced position. Petrosian cleverly

transferred his a8-rook via b8 and b6 to g6, then overdid his originality with ♖e8, and a mistake led to a bad position. Byvshev went for the kill the wrong way; Petrosian saved the game in a small direct confrontation. Against Dubinin, he played the French. In a complex middlegame Tigran took control quickly and won convincingly.

Let's switch to Petrosian's white games! The one we look at was contested close to the finish.

Game 34

Petrosian, Tigran – Sidorov, Anatoly
Soviet Championship Semi-Final,
Gorky (12), 1950
Queen's Gambit Exchange Variation

1.♘f3 ♘f6 2.d4 d5 3.c4 e6 4.♘c3 c6 5.cxd5 exd5 6.♕c2 ♗d6 7.♗g5 0-0 8.e3 ♘bd7 9.♗d3 ♕c7?!

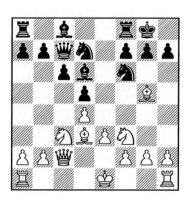

10.0-0-0!?
Petrosian faced a new move. He reacted aggressively, by castling long.

Let's see some other games in this variation when he castles long.

Petrosian, T – Buslaev, A
Tbilisi 1947

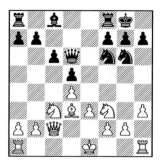

13.0-0-0 ♖e8 14.♔b1 b6 15.g4 ♕e7 16.♗xg6 hxg6 17.♘e5 c5 18.f3 ♗b7 19.h4 ♘d7 20.f4 f6 21.♘xg6 ♕xe3 22.♖d3. Petrosian obtained a winning advantage and went on to win.

Petrosian, T – Tolush, A
Soviet Championship,
Moscow (2), 1950

12.♗xf6 gxf6 13.g4! fxe5 14.fxe5 ♗e7 15.0-0-0! ♗g5 16.gxh5 ♔h8 17.♕f2 f5 18.h4 ♗e7 19.♕f4 1–0.

Petrosian, T – Vaitonis, P
Saltsjobaden/Stockholm (1), 1952

17.g4 ♖c8 18.♕h2! ♗e7 19.♔h1
fxg4 20.hxg4 ♘f7 21.♘xf7 ♗xf7
22.♗e5 ♗f6 23.f4 ♗xe5 24.dxe5
♕e7 25.♘e2 a6 26.♘d4 ♘e6

27.♘f5! gxf5 28.gxf5 ♘f8
29.♖g1+ ♔h8 30.♕h6 ♘g6 31.fxg6
♗xg6 32.♖xg6 1–0

Petrosian, T – Stoltz, G
Saltsjobaden/Stockholm (20), 1952

20.h4 and White is already
winning. 20...c5 21.dxc5 ♕c7
22.♘xe6 ♗xe6 23.h5 ♗f7 24.hxg6
♗xg6 25.♘d4 ♕e5 26.f4 ♕e7
27.♗xe4 ♕xe4 28.♕xe4 dxe4
29.♖c1 ♗e8 30.♖h6 ♗g6 31.c6 ♖ac8
32.♖h2 bxc6 33.♖xc6 ♖xc6 34.♘xc6
♖f7 35.♖d2 ♖c7 36.♖d6 1–0

Back to the game:
10...♖e8

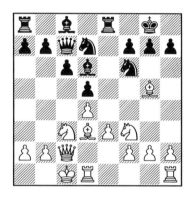

11.g4
Petrosian plays purposefully.
11...♔h8?!
This is a bit mysterious. Sidorov
possibly wants to threaten to capture
the g4–pawn. 11...h6 12.♗xf6 (if
12.♗h4 ♘xg4 White would have
compensation) 12...♘xf6 13.g5 hxg5
14.♘xg5 with a complex position.
12.♖dg1 b5 13.♗xf6
Giving up the bishop accelerates
White's play on the kingside. After
13.♗h4 b4 14.♘a4 ♘e4 the position
would be very complex with mutual
chances.
13...♘xf6 14.g5 ♘e4?!
Sidorov sacrifices a pawn,
leading to serious difficulties.

The best move is 14...♘h5 but then 15.♗xh7 g6 16.♗xg6 and this sacrifice provides White with a dangerous attack: 16...fxg6 17.♕xg6 ♘g7 18.♕h6+ ♚g8 19.g6 ♘f5 20.♕h5 ♕g7 21.♘g5.

15.♘xe4 dxe4 16.♗xe4 ♗e6

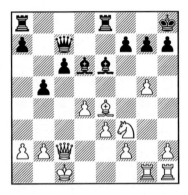

17.g6!!

Petrosian attacks not only with great imagination, but with a lot of power as well. 17.♚b1 defending the pawn first would be strong, too. 17...♖ac8 (17...♕e7 18.♘e5) 18.g6! (18.♖c1 ♕a5; 18.♗f5 ♕d7 19.♗xe6 ♕xe6 20.g6! – otherwise Black would stabilize and it would be hard for White to progress as his knight stands loose. 20...fxg6 21.♘g5 ♕f6 and White has an edge) 18...fxg6 19.♘g5 would work as well.

17...hxg6?

Sidorov chooses the worst recapture. 17...♗xa2 18.♘g5 would also be bad. But the other move was clearly preferable, though no fun either. 17...fxg6! 18.♘g5 ♗d5 (18...♗g8 19.♗xg6 hxg6 20.♕xg6 wins) 19.h4 ♖xe4! This exchange sacrifice

keeps Black in the game (19...♚g8 20.♗xg6 [20.♚b1 is also promising] 20...hxg6 21.♕xg6 ♚f8 22.h5 and Black is lost). Then 20.♘xe4 ♕e7 and White would be better, but still has to work hard to win.

18.♘g5

The main strength of this knight move is to destroy the e6–bishop.

18...f5

After 18...♚g8 19.♘xe6 (19.h4 ♗d5 20.♗xg6 is also very powerful) 19...♖xe6 20.h4 Black would be in trouble.

19.♘xe6 ♖xe6

20.♗f3

White has an irresistible attack, while Black has no attack. 20.♗xc6 ♖c8 21.d5 would win as well.

20...♖c8 21.h4

Opening the h-file is decisive.

21...c5 22.d5!

White naturally closes the centre.

22...♖f6 23.h5 g5

The pawn sacrifice does no more than prolong the end.

24.♖xg5 c4 25.♚b1 ♖cf8 26.♖hg1 ♖8f7 27.♖g6 ♗e5

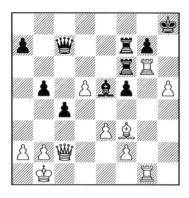

28.h6

This opens up the black king.

28...gxh6 29.♖g8+ ♔h7 30.♗h5

The bishop joins the attack.

30...♖f8 31.♖xf8 ♖xf8 32.f4 ♗g7 33.♗g6+ ♔h8 34.♗xf5 ♕c5

Maybe Black had no time to resign. The rest is simple.

35.♕g2 ♕e7 36.♕g6 ♖xf5 37.♕xf5 ♕xe3 38.♖d1 ♕f2 39.♕c2 ♕xf4 40.d6 ♕f8 41.d7 ♕d8 42.♕g6 1–0

This was a very nice attacking game. Today we know a lot of games in the English Attack of the Scheveningen and Najdorf variations of the Sicilian involving the sacrifice of the g-pawn in a similar way, but Petrosian had probably not seen such an idea earlier and found it over the board.

Let's discuss the rest of Petrosian's white games! Against Levenfish, Petrosian sacrificed a pawn in a main-line Slav for a strong bishop and nice files for his rooks. His 61 year-old legendary opponent gave the pawn back. Then Black made a big mistake, sacrificing a piece to create complications. Petrosian neutralised his play and won before time control. Against Furman, Petrosian gained an advantage in a complex four knights middlegame. He made a mistake and got into trouble. After time control, Furman sacrificed an exchange. Tigran was always on the defence and went on to lose. Petrosian chose the Saemisch against Makarov's King's Indian. Tigran castled long. Black wanted to create play on the queenside and he was successful in a way, but he created play for the young Armenian. Petrosian beat him nicely in a one-sided game. Petrosian won a lot of games, 8, drew only 4, and lost 3; he finished in second-third place with Liublinsky on 10 points. Aronin won the event with 10.5 and Furman was fourth with 9.5. Petrosian did well, as he again qualified for the Soviet Championship Final.

Soviet Championship Final, Moscow

Botvinnik and Bronstein were going to play the world championship final against each other the following year and so prepared for the match instead of lining up at the 1950 championship. Still, without them it was extremely strong. The event started in November and finished in December.

Petrosian started the event as Black against Suetin, in a 6.d4 Ruy Lopez instead of the 6.♖e1 main line. Petrosian began to have problems in the opening and lost a pawn for nothing. He fought for long, but had to admit defeat on move 60. In round 2, he was White against Tolush, who made a serious mistake in the Queen's Gambit Exchange Variation. Petrosian finished him off in a mere 19 moves. See the conclusion of the game in the comments to the 1950 Sidorov game. In round 3, he was Black against Mikenas. White always had more space, and got an almost winning position. To create complications, Petrosian sacrificed a piece, and with one bad move Mikenas allowed his young opponent back into the game. Not long before time control Petrosian made a big mistake, and resigned on move 41. In the fourth round, Borisenko sacrificed a pawn as Black in the Saemisch King's Indian. Tigran was able to reach an endgame, and he nicely converted his advantage into a win. After four decisive games, Petrosian as Black drew versus Sokolsky. A Classical Sicilian transposed into a harmless Dragon, and peace broke out in an even position after 19 moves. In round 6, he met Aronin as White, when the Queen's Gambit Exchange Variation simplified into an endgame. Aronin pressed imaginatively, but at one point he made a losing move. Petrosian missed the opportunity to set up a surprising zugzwang. Maybe he realised what he had missed, as Tigran fell apart and lost soon after. In round 7, Petrosian as Black played the French against Liublinsky. He instructively built his position, but it was still even when his opponent blundered a pawn. Petrosian gave him no chance and won the game on move 41. In the 8th round, Petrosian was White against one of the championship favourites, Boleslavsky. Black created doubled pawns on the c-file for his opponent in the Nimzo-Indian, they manoeuvred for some time, and then Petrosian was able to exchange his doubled pawns. He was better with the bishop pair, but surprisingly agreed to a draw when he could have played on. In round 9, Petrosian played the King's Indian as Black. Flohr handled the position carefully, and after some exchanges they agreed to a draw on the 22nd move. In the tenth round, Alatortsev was White. Petrosian played the Nimzo-Indian. They reached a hanging pawns middlegame, then launched a series of exchanges, and soon a dead drawn position occurred. In round 11, Petrosian as White faced the Slav Gambit, and Averbakh made a mistake in a complex position. Petrosian found a neat piece sacrifice. However, he unnecessarily closed the queenside and Averbakh took control. Petrosian resisted for long, but in vain. Up until then, he had always bounced back with a win in the next round after each loss, but not this time. Petrosian played the Bogo-Indian passively as Black against Lipnitsky, who after a long squeeze invaded with his king in a four-rook ending. He was winning, but a careless move gave Tigran the chance to save the game. He missed it and went on to lose quickly.

In round 13, he played an already established great player, who had finished 2nd in the 1948 World Championship and third in the 1950 Candidates Tournament, Vassily Smyslov. They produced an exciting game and we look at it in detail.

Game 35

**Petrosian, Tigran –
Smyslov, Vassily**
Soviet Championship Final, Moscow
(13), 1950
Queen's Gambit Accepted

1.d4 d5 2.♘f3

Smyslov was Black with 2.c4 dxc4 3.♘f3 a6 against Botvinnik in 1948, and, more importantly, against Tolush in round 5 of this championship, so Petrosian probably wanted to avoid it.

2...♘f6 3.c4 dxc4

Smyslov played only a few Queen's Gambit Accepted games, but some of them were in 1950.

4.e3 c5 5.♗xc4 e6 6.0-0 a6 7.♕e2 b5 8.♗b3 ♗b7 9.a4

This variation often leads to sharp tactical positions.

9...♘bd7 10.e4

Petrosian plays the move with which Kotov beat Flohr in the 1950 Candidates Tournament.

10...cxd4

Taking the pawn is risky: 10...♘xe4?!. 11.d5 exd5 12.♗xd5 ♗xd5 13.♘c3

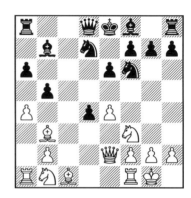

11.e5?

This is a bad novelty, but it is unpleasant to receive it unless the black player has analysed the sharp move in advance.

11...♘g4?!

Not a bad move, but clearly not the best. Perhaps Petrosian had missed the simple 11...♗xf3! during home analysis. After 12.gxf3 ♘c5 13.♗d1 d3 Black would be much better.

12.axb5 ♗c5

Smyslov makes a developing move, and it is reasonable. There are several other playable possibilities. For example, after 12...♘c5 13.♗c4 d3 14.♕d1 ♗xf3 15.♕xf3 ♘xe5 16.♕f4 f6 17.bxa6 Black is no worse in the complications. Or if 12...axb5 13.♖xa8 ♗xa8 14.♘xd4 ♘gxe5 15.♘xb5 ♗c5 Black would be safe.

13.bxa6 0-0

After 13...d3 14.♕xd3 ♘xf2 15.♖xf2 ♕b6 the position would be very complex, almost wild.

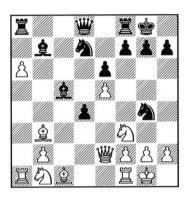

14.axb7

Petrosian sacrifices an exchange for a dangerous pawn on the seventh and some play against the g4–knight.

a) after 14.♗f4 ♗xf3 15.gxf3 d3 16.♕e1 ♕b8! Black equalises with this double attack.

b) 14.♘bd2!? means White no longer wants to take on doubled pawns. 14...♕c7 (14...d3 15.♕xd3 ♘xf2 16.♖xf2 ♕b6 and the position would be unclear) 15.♗c2 ♘gxe5 (15...♗d5 16.♘b3) 16.♘xe5 ♘xe5 17.♘b3 ♗d5 18.♘xc5 ♕xc5 and White is somewhat better.

14...♖xa1 15.♕e4

15.♗c2 ♕c7 (15...g6 16.h3) 16.♗f4 d3 17.♗xd3 ♘xf2 18.♖xf2 ♕b6 19.♗g3 ♕xb7 with a roughly balanced position.

15...♘xf2

a) 15...d3 16.♕xg4 (16.♕xd3? ♘xf2 17.♖xf2 ♖xb1 18.♕xb1 ♗xf2+ 19.♔xf2 ♕b6+) 16...♖xb1 17.♗h6 ♖xf1+ 18.♔xf1 g6 19.♗xf8

♘xf8 and the b7–pawn gives White an advantage.

b) 15...♕b6 16.♕xg4 (16.♗c2 f5; 16.♗c4 ♖xb1 17.♘g5 g6 18.♕xg4 ♘xe5 19.♕h4 h5 20.♘e4 and the position is unclear) 16...♖xb1 when the position is sharp. White has to play accurately to keep the balance. 17.♗c2 ♖xc1 18.♖xc1 ♕xb2 19.♗xh7+ ♔xh7 20.♘g5+ ♔g8 21.♖f1 ♗e7 22.♘xe6 fxe6 23.♕xe6+ ♖f7 24.♕xd7 ♗f8 25.b8=♕ ♕xb8 26.♕xd4 should end in a draw.

16.♔xf2 d3+?

The position is so complex that even great talents start making mistakes. After 16...♗a7 17.♗g5 ♕b6 18.♗c4 ♘c5 19.♕h4 ♕xb7 20.♘bd2 ♕xb2 the position is balanced.

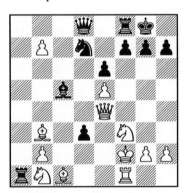

17.♔g3!

Petrosian finds a good square for his king. Suddenly, the black king is in danger.

17...♖xb1

17...♕b6 18.♘g5 g6 19.♖xf7 ♖xf7 20.♗xe6 wins, or 17...♗e7 18.♗e3 ♕c7 19.♖c1 ♘c5 20.♗xc5 ♗xc5 21.♗c4 wins.

18.♕xd3?!

Tigran doesn't find the best move. 18.♗g5! ♕b6 19.♖xb1 ♕xb3 (19...h6 20.♗d2) 20.♕c6 (maybe Petrosian missed this possibility to threaten the d7–knight) 20...f6 21.exf6 gxf6 22.♗d2 ♕d5 23.♕xd5 exd5 24.♗f4 and Black would be in serious trouble.

18...♖xc1!

This is the only move to stay in the game.

19.♖xc1 ♕c7 20.♕b5

20.♔h3 ♕xb7 21.♗a4 ♘b6 22.♖xc5 ♘xa4 23.♖b5 ♕a6 and Black gets away with it.

20...♗f2+?

20...♖b8! Black should take the pawn first. Then 21.♗a4 ♗f2+ 22.♔xf2 ♕xc1 23.♕xd7 ♕xb2+ 24.♔g3 ♕xb7. The position would be a dead draw, leaving the players nothing to play for.

21.♔xf2 ♕xc1 22.♕xd7 ♕xb2+

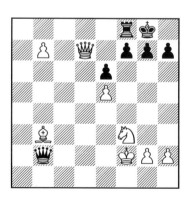

23.♘d2

The knight defends the bishop; it allows protection of the passed pawn. White is winning because of the b7-pawn, but he still has to navigate some difficulties.

23...♕xe5 24.♗d1?!

It is a bit careless to place the bishop on the same file as the knight. 24.g3 ♕b8 25.♕c6 ♕a7+ (25...♖d8 26.♘c4 wins, but this move will not work in the game as the bishop will stand on d1) 26.♔e2 h6. White easily wins with 27.♘e4 or 27.♗c2.

24...♕b8! 25.♕b5

Or 25.♕c6 ♖d8!.

25...♖d8 26.♔e1

The subtle 26.♕a5! indirectly defends the b7–pawn. 26...♕f4+ (26...♖d7 27.♗f3) 27.♔e1 ♖b8 28.♕c3 h5 29.♗xh5 wins.

26...♕d6

After 26...♕xh2 27.♗f3 ♕c7 28.♘c4 Black should lose.

27.♕b2?!

27.♕a5! defends the knight and attacks the rook, winning time to defend b7, and if 27...♖e8 then 28.♗f3 wins.

27...♕xh2

Smyslov bags a pawn, which is an accomplishment.

28.♗f3 h5

Or 28...♕c7 29.♕b4 ♖b8 30.♘c4 and White wins.

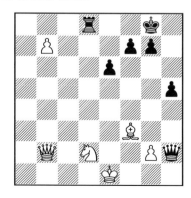

29.♘f1?

The knight drops out of play and can no longer help the b7–pawn. After this mistake, White can probably no longer win. Whereas after 29.♘e4! h4 (29...♕c7 30.♕c3) 30.♕b6 ♕b8 31.♔f1 White can soon play ♘c5 and win.

29...♕f4 30.♗xh5

Petrosian allows simplifications to a draw. Black is likely to hold after 30.♔f2 h4.

30...♕h4+ 31.g3 ♕xh5

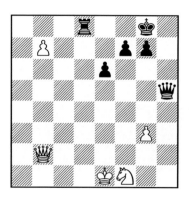

32.b8=♕ ♖xb8 33.♕xb8+

White has won an exchange, but has only one pawn left, therefore Black can hold. Note the position would be a draw without the queens on the board as well.

33...♔h7 34.♕f4 e5 35.♕e4+ g6 36.♘e3 ♕g5 37.♔f2 ♕f6+ 38.♔g2 ♕d6 39.♘d5

Quite possibly they were in time trouble; it was worth trying the move 39.♘c4. Though after 39...♕b4 (39... ♕d4? 40.♕xd4 exd4 41.♘e5 and White wins only with this move) 40.♕d5 f6 41.♘d6 (41.♕d7+ ♔g8)

41...♔h6 and Black gets away with it.

39...f5

40.♕c4 ♔g7 1/2

They agreed to a draw, as there was no point in adjourning.

In the next round, Petrosian was Black against Konstantinopolsky. He castled by hand in the Ruy Lopez. Tigran even made a careless move, but he was able to hold after struggling and they repeated moves before time trouble. Against Geller as White, Petrosian tried a reverse Pirc. He was slightly worse until he blundered a pawn and resigned 10 moves later. In the penultimate round, he was Black against Keres. In a French after 3.♘d2 ♘c6 4.c3 he risked 4...f5. After the opening, Petrosian was almost hopelessly lost. However, the great Estonian player either lost his sense of danger or missed something, and let Tigran back into the game. Then Paul sacrificed a piece, and Petrosian took it and took control, soon winning the game. In the last round, Petrosian was White against Bondarevsky. He outplayed and beat his opponent convincingly in the Dutch Stonewall. The key part of the game can be seen in the comments to game 22 of this book against Pirtskhalava.

He improved compared with a year before, scoring 8 points out of 17. He won 5, drew 6 and lost 6. He shared 12th-13rd place with Bondarevsky. Keres was able to recover and won the championship, scoring 11.5 points out of 17. Second-fourth places were shared between Lipnitsky, Tolush and Aronin. Stars like Smyslov, Boleslavsky, Geller and Flohr finished disappointingly.

Petrosian's results in 1950

Game vs. Simagin	1 : 0
Spartak – Dynamo (vs. Baturinsky)	1 : 0
Moscow Championship	+ 4 = 10 – 1 9/15 3rd place
Soviet Championship Semi-Final, Gorky	+ 8 = 4 – 3 10/15 2nd-3rd place
Soviet Championship Final, Moscow	+ 5 = 6 – 6 8/17 12th-13th place
Altogether	**+ 19 = 20 – 10 29/49**

1951

Lithuanian Championship

Petrosian started the year in Vilnius; it shows his strength that he was sent there to raise the level of chess in the Baltic republic. There are only two Petrosian games in the database from this tourney. We look at one of them in detail.

Game 36

Petrosian, Tigran – Chukaev, Egor
Lithuanian Championship, Vilnius,
1951
London System

1.d4 ♘f6 2.♘f3 e6 3.♗g5
Petrosian played this move quite a lot. He has 21 white games in the database, of which he won 12 and lost only one. Taimanov, Mecking and Unzicker were among his victims.
3...d5 4.e3 ♗e7 5.♘bd2

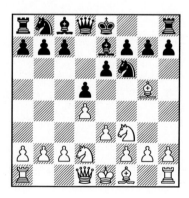

5...0-0
Castling early in 1.d4 openings when White plays no c4 exposes

Black to the danger of a kingside attack.
5...♘bd7 6.♗d3 c5 7.c3
a) 7...0-0 8.♘e5 ♘xe5 9.dxe5 ♘d7 10.♗f4 f5 11.h4 c4 12.♗c2 b5 13.♘f3 ♘c5 14.g4 b4 15.gxf5 exf5 16.♘g5 g6?

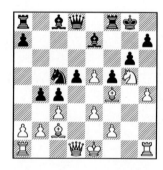

17.h5!. Black is in trouble after this strong attacking move. 17...♘d3+ 18.♗xd3 cxd3 19.hxg6 hxg6 20.♕xd3 bxc3 21.bxc3 ♗xg5 22.♗xg5 ♕a5 23.♗f6 ♖e8 24.♕d4 ♔f7 25.e6+ ♖xe6 26.♗d8 1–0 Petrosian, T – Liublinsky, V, Moscow, 1949.
b) 7...b6. This is what he played as Black when he beat Spassky during their 1966 world championship match.

6.♗d3 c5 7.c3 ♘c6

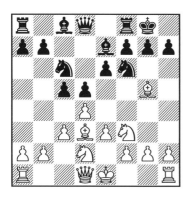

8.♘e5

White starts active play in the centre.

8...♘e8

Releasing the tension with 8...♘d7!? looks a bit better.

9.♗f4 ♗d7 10.h4

Petrosian bases his play on his kingside attack.

10...♖c8 11.♘df3 cxd4?!

This capture prevents Black from playing actively in the centre, as he will have to endure the strong knight on the e5 square. 11...f6 or 11...♘xe5 12.dxe5 (12.♘xe5 ♘d6) 12...f5 are reasonable for Black, as he would not have to put up with the e5–knight.

12.exd4 ♘f6

Black decides to live with the powerful e5-knight. After 12...f6 13.♘g5 f5 (13...g6 14.♘xd7 ♕xd7 15.♘xh7! ♖f7 16.♗xg6 and Black's king is in trouble) 14.♘xd7 ♕xd7 15.♕e2 White would enjoy long-lasting pressure.

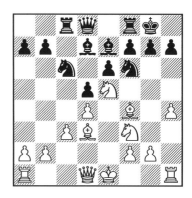

13.♘g5!

Petrosian brings another piece closer to Black's king.

13...♗e8

Attacking the knight with 13...h6 gives Whte the chance to bite at Black's pawn chain. 14.♕e2 (14.♘gf3 ♘e4) 14...♗e8 15.♘gf3 and White may attack with g4.

14.♖h3

Petrosian brings the rook into play very originally. 14.♘g4!? g6 15.h5 is perhaps even more promising.

14...♕a5?

Black's position is already tough, as he has only passive choices. But the queen should stay in the centre.

a) 14...♕b6 if Black wants to move the queen, as maybe this would give White more chances to go wrong. However, after 15.♕e2 (15.♘g4 ♘e4) 15...h6 (15...♘a5? 16.♖g3 and White breaks through after 16...h6 17.♘h7 or 16...g6 17.h5) 16.♔f1 ♘a5 (16...♖d8 17.♖e1) 17.♖e1 White's attack is very strong.

b) Black should play 14...♗d6! as this adds a piece to the defence.

15.♕e2 ♗c7 (15...♘e7) 16.♔f1 and now if 16...♘e7 17.♘g4 is unpleasant, but after 16...h6 Black's position will not fall apart on its own.

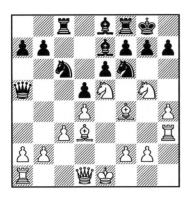

15.♔f1!

The king steps out of the pin, but he moves to a good square and vacates the e1 square for the rook.

15...b5 16.a3

16.♖g3 would already work well.

16...♕b6

Black can do nothing but wait. He cannot chase the knight away, for example after 16...h6 17.♖g3 ♔h8 (17...hxg5 18.hxg5 ♘e4 19.♗xe4 dxe4 20.♕h5 and White wins) 18.♘xc6 ♗xc6 19.♗e5 Black would be in big trouble.

17.♖g3

White overpowers Black's king with the rook. Now ♘xh7 is a devastating threat.

17...g6

If 17...h6 18.♘h7 wins.

18.h5 ♘d8

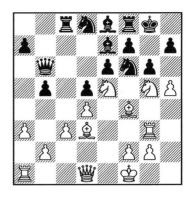

19.♘xh7!

This sacrifice has animal power, and it destroys Black's king. Black can't resist.

19...♘xh7   20.hxg6   fxg6 21.♘xg6

This is slaughter. Chukaev plays on just about until he gets checkmated.

21...♗xg6   22.♖xg6+   ♔h8 23.♖h6 ♖xf4 24.♖xh7+ ♔g8

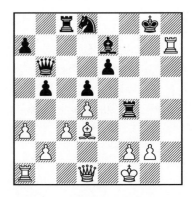

25.♕h5   ♘f7   26.♗g6   e5 27.♗xf7+ ♔f8 28.♖h8+ ♔g7 1–0

A nice attacking game.

In the other known game, he was White against Kholmov. Ratmir took control in the Slav at the end of the opening and won the game convincingly.

Kholmov won the event with 10.5 points. Petrosian finished joint-second with Lilienthal and Simagin.

He scored 9.5 points out of 14 games. He won 8, drew 3 and lost 3. He also lost to Mikenas and Ostrauskas. His 8 wins were impressive, the three losses a bit much, but the result was not bad at all.

Mukhutdinov – Petrosian Match, Tashkent

Petrosian was invited to the Uzbek capital Tashkent to play a match against the local master Mukhutdinov, who were he to win the match would have received the master's title. The match was held in April and May.

Petrosian started the match as Black. Petrosian won a pawn in the Saemisch Nimzo-Indian and he gradually converted his advantage. In the second round, they played an off-beat Queen's Gambit. Mukhutdinov played riskily, then Tigran offered a pawn in an equal position. Black took it and got problems. The local player resigned on move 40. In game 3, Mukhutdinov switched to 1.e4; Petrosian took on an isolated pawn against 3.♘d2 in the French. White gained an edge, but allowed a sacrifice which let Black equalise. In the ensuing rook ending, Petrosian seemed to have good chances, but the game ended in a draw. Maybe Petrosian did not want to humiliate his opponent. In the fourth game, they opted for a Catalan. Mukhutdinov as Black played way below par on the day, lost a pawn early and resigned after White's 23rd move. In game 5, Petrosian faced the 2.♘c3 + 3.♘f3 variation of the Caro-Kann. He equalised, they manoeuvred and after some simplifications they agreed to a draw on move 29. In round 6, Petrosian after 1.d4 f5 played 2.♘c3. They reached a complex middlegame, Mukhutdinov played well and held. After time control, the game ended in a draw. In the seventh game, the Uzbek player handled the opening poorly, and continued to have a bad day. He resigned before his 23rd move. In round 8, probably desperate to win a game, Mukhutdinov tried the Albin Counter Gambit. Petrosian played a side-line, and gave back the pawn. Surprisingly, Black did alright, then Petrosian attacked a pawn. Black defended it by setting a small trap. The trap saved the pawn, but lost a bishop, Mukhutdinov played on for a while, but of course lost. The next game, was a Sicilian Sozin. Mukhutdinov lost his composure, playing 9.♘de2 and on the next move moved it back to d4. Petrosian simplified, but blundered an exchange; his broken opponent missed it and the game soon simplified to a draw. In game 10, play was even more bizarre. Mukhutdinov played ...♘fd7 in a main-line King's Indian, then he retreated to f6 with the same knight, and that was not all, as in the next two moves he played ♔h8 and the f6 knight went to g8. It must have been hard for Tigran to remain serious, but he nicely increased his advantage with some knight manoeuvres (his were not only sensible, but strong). Black resigned after time control. In game 11, Petrosian tried a rather dubious line of the Accelerated Dragon and he was close to losing. However, he managed to survive the opening a pawn down. Mukhutdinov was unable to convert his advantage to a win. The twelfth game is not available, but it ended in a draw. In the penultimate game, Petrosian equalised with the 4...♘d7 Caro-Kann. Mukhutdinov started a rather risky attack. White's position was playable for some time. In the complications, White lost an exchange and resigned. In the last game, Petrosian faced the Ilyin-Zhenevsky line of the Dutch Defence, and he was better when they repeated moves. He won the match convincingly by 10.5:3.5. He had 7 wins and 7 draws. Once he had broken his opponent, he probably could have scored more points, but he was nice to his hosts.

Moscow Championship

Tigran participated in the Moscow championship in 1951 as well. We were not able to find out in which month this event took place. Logic suggests that it was held before the Soviet Championship Semi-Final. Actually, it might have been a qualification event for Moscow players to the semi-final. Only nine of the twelve games are in the database.

Unfortunately, there is no information as to in which round the games were played. We discuss Petrosian's white games first. Against Estrin, the future world chess correspondence champion, he obtained no advantage in a main-line Tarrasch Defence (Estrin was a good writer, by the way, and your Hungarian author read his books on the openings a lot as a junior player). Black had an isolated pawn, but unnecessarily accepted doubled pawns when they exchanged queens and the position became unpleasant for him. Petrosian was able to win a pawn, then a second one and soon after the game. Against Khachaturov, Petrosian was White in a reversed Closed Sicilian; the position was balanced for some time, and when it opened in the mid-twenties Petrosian quickly took control and checkmated his opponent before time control. Against Moiseev, he developed his bishop to g5 and his knight to d2 against the Orthodox Queen's Gambit. When the direct confrontation started his greater ability came into play and he was winning soon after the opening. Petrosian scored a win without allowing his opponent back into the game. Next, Zagorovsky, another future world chess correspondence champion, was unable to equalise in the g3 line of the King's Indian. After the opening, White won a pawn, then a second, and he was three pawns up in an opposite-coloured bishops ending. He won in 46 moves.

Let's switch to his black games! Against Chistiakov, his King's Indian resulted in a Benoni pawn structure middlegame. Petrosian's disadvantage was sometimes smaller, sometimes bigger. White did not even win an exchange when the opportunity arose, and it was so obvious that he must have rejected it on purpose, yet Petrosian's stubborn defence earned him a draw. Fridstein played the 3.♘d2 Tarrasch against the French. Petrosian obtained a clear edge, then his opponent blundered and the game lasted only 17 moves. Petrosian got a pleasant middlegame against Poliak in a Boleslavsky Sicilian. White carelessly exposed his king with a g4. Petrosian took control and beat him in no time. Tigran played the Orthodox Queen's Gambit against Simagin. He equalised, and soon after the opening offered a draw, to which Simagin agreed. Petrosian took more risk in the openings than usual. He won the event, scoring 9.5 points out of 12. He won 7 games and drew 5 with no losses. Zagorovsky finished second with 8.5 points. Simagin scored 8, and Averbakh and Moiseev 7 each. Scoring 2.5 points more than Averbakh with whom he drew was impressive indeed.

Game 37

**Petrosian, Tigran –
Koliakov, Alexander**
Moscow Championship, 1951

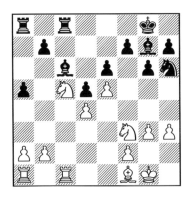

22.g4!
Petrosian takes away the f5–square from the black knight.
22...♗f8

It is natural to bring the bishop into play.
23.♖c3 b6?!
Black is probably too optimistic. He should just patiently wait and keep improving his pieces. 23...♔g7 24.♖ac1 ♗e7 (24...♘g8 25.♗b5 ♖a7 and Black may hold his position together) 25.♗b5 ♗xb5 26.♘xe6+ fxe6 27.♖xc8 ♖xc8 28.♖xc8 ♗c6 and Black is no worse.

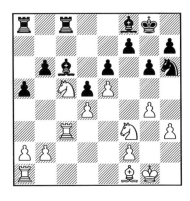

24.♘a6!

The knight moves far away from its camp, which always contains some risk. However, it achieves a surprisingly large amount on the edge of the board.

24...♗d7?!

After 24...♗b7?! 25.♘c7 ♖ab8 26.♖ac1 ♗e7 27.♗a6 White gains control over the c-file. Black's best try is 24...b5! and after 25.♘c5 ♗e8 26.♖ac1 ♖cb8 he is somewhat passive, but has good chances to hold.

25.♘c7!

Petrosian doesn't allow Black to swap a pair of rooks.

25...♖a7 26.♖ac1 ♗b4?

Keeping the rook on the c-file helps White. After 26...♖b8!? 27.♘b5 ♗xb5 28.♗xb5 ♔g7 Black's position would be passive, but it is hard to tell whether White's clear advantage is sufficient to win.

27.♖3c2 ♗a4

The bishop move attacks the rook, but doesn't avoid White's threat. 27...♖b8 28.♘b5 was still possible and still very hard to play.

28.b3 ♗e8

28...♗d7 29.♘xd5 exd5 (29...♖xc2 30.♘f6+) 30.♖xc8+ ♗xc8 31.♖xc8+ ♔g7 32.♖d8 and White gets the d-pawn with a decisive advantage.

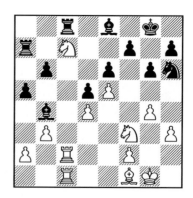

29.♘xd5!

Petrosian wins a pawn with this small combination. Black's position falls apart.

29...♖xc2 30.♘f6+

The knight doesn't only win a pawn, but finds a superb outpost.

30...♔f8 31.♖xc2 ♘g8

After 31...♖a8 32.♘g5 White would win another pawn.

32.♖c8!

The pin is lethal.

32...♖e7 33.♗b5 1–0 Black lost on time, though his position is hopeless as he loses a piece.

Soviet Championship Semi-Final, Sverdlovsk

The group Petrosian was in played in the Russian city of Sverdlovsk (now Yekaterinburg, its historical name) in May to June.

In round 1, Petrosian was Black against Dubinin. In a main line of the Ruy Lopez White did not prepare d4 with 8.h3 but pushed the d-pawn two squares straight away. Petrosian made one inaccurate and one bad move and found himself a pawn down in a pretty bad position. Dubinin was not purposeful, though. Petrosian nicely built an attack. He created realistic chances, but it probably took him too much time. He played inaccurately, Dubinin regained the advantage, and Petrosian blundered his queen and resigned a few moves before time control. The next game we found was in round 7. Konstantinov played the closed variation against Petrosian's Sicilian. The position was balanced for a long time, but then the Russian master gradually outplayed Tigran. Black was lost for quite some time. When White exchanged queens the situation became less problematic, and luckily for Tigran his opponent exchanged rooks as well, which meant he survived. It would be interesting to know whether Konstantinov was short of time or whether he respected Petrosian so much that he was always looking for a draw. In round 9, Petrosian played the King's Indian against Cherepkov. After the opening, he could have sacrificed a knight, but did not. In the middlegame, his play on the kingside looked slower than his opponent's on the other flank. But as the experienced Russian master did not play accurately Petrosian's play grew more active. His opponent was worse when, possibly in time trouble, Petrosian made a horrible mistake. His position fell apart in a mere 4 moves. In the tenth round, Petrosian was White against Ilivitsky. In a main-line Nimzo-Indian, Petrosian built an attack with an isolated pawn against Black's king. After a surprising exchange of a bishop for a knight, he sacrificed a piece, his initiative enabled him to break through, and he won the game. The last game we know is from round 16. Petrosian was Black against Veltmander, who did well overall as he finished the event joined 5th with two others. White obtained the two bishops in the 4.♕c2 Nimzo-Indian. Petrosian built his play against Black's king and gained space nicely. Veltmander defended somewhat passively. Petrosian switched his attention to the centre and the queenside; he established a super knight on d4. Not long before time control, Veltmander sacrificed two exchanges, but soon resigned. Saigin withdrew from the event without playing the last three games. The game against Petrosian was one of these three, so Petrosian won the point without playing. Petrosian won the event scoring 13.5 points out of 19. He won 9, drew 9 and lost only 1. Geller came second with 13 points, and two other strong players, Boleslavsky and Averbakh, were joint third. Naturally, with this major success he qualified for the final again.

Soviet Republics' Team Championship, Tbilisi

According to the database, the team championship of the Soviet Republics took place in September between the semi-final and the final of the Soviet championship. It must have been an emotional event, as it was held in Tbilisi. Tigran was selected for board 3 of the Moscow team. It would be interesting to know who played the higher boards ahead of him in his team. Only two of his games are known from the event. In one of them, he was Black against Bannik. In a main-line Nimzo-Indian, Petrosian sacrificed a pawn, the position was complex, and Tigran had two knights versus Bannik's bishop pair. One inaccurate move and the position turned bad suddenly. Bannik beat him convincingly. In his other known game he was White against Tolush. It was a Nimzo-Indian as well. Black equalised in an isolated pawn position. Black won a pawn, but White had the bishop pair. In an open position Petrosian made a mistake, and lost another pawn and the game. He also won two games, one against Amirkhanov of Azerbaijan and Abdullaev of Uzbekistan. He drew one against Novotelnov of the Russian Republic. Sadly, the moves of these three games are not known.

Masters Tournament, Tbilisi

According to *Reliability Strategy* Petrosian played a masters tournament in Tbilisi, though only his result is mentioned. However, thanks to the great endgame composer David Gurgenidze who provided us with Georgian archival information, readers can now learn more about this event, which started in the middle of September and ended in October. Suetin won the event, scoring 11.5 out of 15.

Petrosian and Bannik were joint 2nd with 9.5 points. Joint 4th-6th places were taken by Kasparian, Shishov and Aronin with 8.5. It is worth looking at some of the other names in the tournament: Furman, Karpov's future trainer, Bukhuti Gurgenidze and Firkhsvala gained 8 points. Karseladze, Nona Gaprindashvili's future trainer, finished the event with 4.5 points. Petrosian won 7 games overall, drew 5 and lost 3.

Andor (Andrei) Lilienthal

Petrosian got himself a trainer in 1951, the former world class player Andor Lilienthal (he went by the name of Andrei in the Soviet Union). It is not known how the working relation started, whether the federation appointed him, the Hungarian grandmaster offered his services, or Petrosian asked him. In any event, knowing the level that Tigran reached by the end of 1952, it was an extremely fruitful cooperation. Andor was born in Moscow in 1911, but raised in Budapest. He moved back to Moscow and got married there in 1935. Your Hungarian author met his then wife Zhenya in the seventies. She was in her fifties or sixties. A very decorative lady, it was clear that she was exceptionally beautiful when they married.

He played all the world champions from Lasker to Petrosian with the sole exception of Tal. He personally knew more champions as well. At his peaks in 1934 and 1942 he was certainly a top 10 player in the world, and at his very best maybe he was even in the top 5. His score against Lasker was 1 win, 2 draws with no loss, against Capablanca 1 win, 2 draws, 1 loss, against Alekhine 1 draw, 1 loss, against Euwe 1 win, 1 draw, no loss, and against Botvinnik he won 2, drew 5 and lost 5. He played the most games against Smyslov among the world champions: he won 4, drew 8 and lost 7. He played twice against Petrosian, but lost both games.

Let's see his most famous game!

Game 38

Lilienthal, Andor –
Capablanca, Jose Raul
Christmas Congress 1934/35 Hastings
Premier tournament (5), 1935
Nimzo-Indian Defence

1.d4 ♘f6 2.c4 e6 3.♘c3 ♗b4 4.a3 ♗xc3+ 5.bxc3 b6 6.f3 d5 7.♗g5 h6 8.♗h4 ♗a6 9.e4 ♗xc4 10.♗xc4 dxc4 11.♕a4+ ♕d7 12.♕xc4 ♕c6 13.♕d3 ♘bd7 14.♘e2 ♖d8 15.0-0 a5 16.♕c2 ♕c4 17.f4 ♖c8 18.f5 e5 19.dxe5 ♕xe4

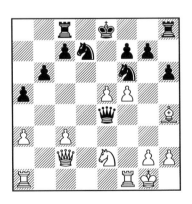

20.exf6‼ ♕xc2 21.fxg7 ♖g8 22.♘d4 ♕e4 23.♖ae1 ♘c5 24.♖xe4+ ♘xe4 25.♖e1 ♖xg7 26.♖xe4+ ♔d7 1-0

During the game, Capablanca told Euwe, "either I win or I get checkmated," and the great Cuban soon had to resign.

When Fischer lived in Budapest he spent quite a lot of time at the Lilienthals' home. The way Andor got acquainted with Fischer was remarkable. It started in 1992 when Lilienthal and his second wife Olga visited the Fischer-Spassky rematch in Yugoslavia. At a reception, Andor was standing with the help of his stick. Fischer went up to him and without introducing himself or any greetings came out with appreciation in his voice: "Pawn takes f6". He was referring to the famous Lilienthal-Capablanca game shown above.

By the time Petrosian started to play, Lilienthal was past his peak. Petrosian and Andor had something in common: they had both lived a very tough childhood. Andor's mother was an opera singer, but she lost her voice during World War I and was unable to continue performing. Further, his father left the family and his mother was left with three children. He states in his book *Chess Was My Life* that as a child during WWI he lived in poverty and experienced hunger, that later it was a struggle to make a living as a chess player, but his life was pleasant in the Soviet Union and due to that he was unable to keep fighting the same way. By the end of the forties he had also started to tire more quickly.

He also told your Hungarian author an interesting story, that when he was leading in the 1940 Soviet championship other players started to throw games to Bondarevsky, which was how they got to share first place. (I think the authorities ordered them, and that Bondarevsky had nothing to do with it.) Then he figured out that it was safer not to get any stronger. After the championship, he was sent to give simuls in the Central-Asian Soviet Republics. Then, in the middle of the tour, he was told to return immediately to Moscow and play in the 1941 USSR Absolute Championship, so he had just a few days to prepare, while for example Botvinnik knew about the event earlier and prepared properly. Originally, he should have played a match against Bondarevsky for the Soviet Champion's title. However, making him fight over 20 games against 5 players (Botvinnik, Smyslov, Keres and Boleslavsky were the others) made it far harder to become champion than beating one strong opponent.

In the seventies, he moved back to Hungary. I was fortunate to meet him there and analysed a few times with him. Uncle Andor as I called him was simply brilliant at it. He attacked so fluently, and good moves came so naturally to him. He was a good-hearted person. Fischer did not like either Soviet or Jewish people, yet he still spent a lot of time with the Lilienthals.

Older Hungarian players told me that when Andor lived in Hungary before the war he was a flamboyant young man, but that he changed in the Soviet Union. He witnessed the terror of Stalin in the thirties; he was always somewhat worried and cautious even when he visited Hungary. I only witnessed similar behaviour from certain Romanian players who lived in Ceausescu's time. Yet, he had no reason to be worried in Hungary in the late seventies; everybody liked and respected him greatly.

Interestingly, he spoke no language as a mother tongue, as he spoke both Hungarian and Russian with a foreign accent. While I can't say anything about his Russian, he spoke Hungarian with no linguistic mistakes. Andor also possessed a good sense of humour, which is useful when one has to endure long training sessions, and it helps during those many-hour long sessions.

Sadly, we do not know how he and Tigran worked together. They probably analysed a lot, and Andor was probably able to give a lot of advice about how to play against the top players because of his personal experience against them. I recall him talking about Botvinnik; of course, he had tremendous respect for the sixth world champion and generally liked him. He said that when Botvinnik played he would try to create tension and build a feeling of enmity towards his opponent. Once, the day before he was due to play Botvinnik, Andor encountered him in the streets of Moscow. Mikhail Moiseevich declined to greet him and instead crossed over to the other side of the road. He told this with a kind of laugh and found this behaviour a bit stupid. Such little things could help Tigran in knowing what to expect against other world-class players.

Of course, his psychological support could have helped. As far as I know, the Lilienthals had no children, and maybe Andor considered Tigran a bit like his child. Andor's leg was paralysed when he was young and he was unable to participate in several kinds of sport, though he liked swimming a lot. Perhaps he influenced Tigran to keep his body in good shape.

One thing is certain: their successful work in 1951 and 1952, as Tigran transformed from a strong player into not only a silver medallist at the Soviet championship, but a steady world-class player. Their work continued at least until 1960. He was not one of Tigran's official seconds at the world championship matches, but they most probably consulted. Actually, some sources say they kept working together until 1970.

Petrosian talked much more in his interviews about Ebralidze, which possibly contributed to the fact that people do not realise Lilienthal's impact on his career. Of course, Petrosian was Armenian, but maybe it was simply more pleasant for him to talk about Ebralidze, as that prompted him to recall Tbilisi and Georgia, to which he also felt emotionally attached. For whatever reason, he talked more about his junior trainer. Both of their roles were very important in his life and it is hard, perhaps impossible, to compare their effects: Ebralidze helped to make Tigran love chess and did a lot to build his foundation, while Lilienthal helped to raise the level of an already very strong young man to that of a world-class player in a short period of time.

Soviet Championship Final, Moscow

The Soviet championship, which was held in Petrosian's new home city, started in November.

Petrosian's first opponent was Kopylov. Tigran was White and they played the Nimzo-Indian. Black played the opening very aggressively and sacrificed an exchange. His attack was frightening, but objectively he was bluffing. Petrosian failed to find the win. In the middlegame, the position was more or less balanced. But on move 30 Petrosian, possibly with little time left, went wrong and lost quickly. In round 2, Petrosian was Black against Aronin. In a main-line Ruy Lopez White mistakenly gave away the b2-pawn. Petrosian then blundered a pawn and his advantage. In just a few moves Aronin outplayed Petrosian, who had to resign one move before time control. Once again, he had started an event nervously – but he was often able to bounce back. In round 3, Petrosian as White won a pawn against Geller in a King's Indian, and they soon repeated moves. In the final position, Geller had a nice advantage, but perhaps the draw was prearranged and the repetition was to avoid criticism. If the idea was to recover, then it worked, as Petrosian started a magical run which demonstrated that he had become a world-class player. In round 4, Petrosian as Black against Bondarevsky reached a Benoni position via a King's Indian, with White taking on d5 with the e-pawn. White was unable to exploit his small advantage. Petrosian equalised and with a subtle exchange took control. Soon after, Tigran won a pawn, though it took him a lot, almost 50 moves, to convert the advantage into a win. His win can be seen in the Petrosian's Remarkable Exchanges chapter. In round 5, Petrosian was unable to gain an advantage with the g3 line against the King's Indian. Kotov started to make a few poor moves, and Petrosian beautifully took control and won an exchange. Kotov fought on for a long time, but in vain. In round 6, Petrosian was Black against Averbakh; he gave up the two bishops in a Caro-Kann Two Knights Variation. The closed position remained balanced and the game ended in a repetition on move 29. In round 7, Petrosian was White against Moiseev; the pawn centre disappeared in a main-line Nimzo-Indian. Petrosian started tactical play and eventually gained compensation for a pawn. He pressed, but Moiseev held the draw. In round 8, Petrosian was Black against Flohr; he got a small disadvantage in a very closed position. Flohr played on for a long time, but had no real winning chances.

In round 9, Petrosian faced the greatest player of the previous generation, the reigning world champion Mikhail Botvinnik. This event was the latter's first individual event since he obtained the world title.

Game 39

Petrosian, Tigran –
Botvinnik, Mikhail
Soviet Championship Final, Moscow
(9), 1951
Queen's Pawn Game

**1.d4 ♘f6 2.♘f3 e6 3.♗g5 h6!
4.♗h4**

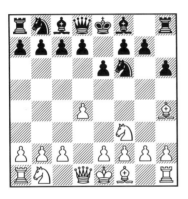

4...g5!?
According to the database,
Botvinnik introduces a novelty. He
was known for his very good opening
preparation and superb squeezing in
endings. In this game, Petrosian gets
a taste of it.
5.♗g3 ♘e4 6.♘bd2 ♘xg3
Exchanging the bishop results
in a complex fight. White gets play
on the h-file and some development
advantage.
7.hxg3 ♗g7 8.c3
It is reasonable to restrict the g7–
bishop.
8...d6 9.e3
White will score better with
9.e4.

**9...♘c6 10.♗d3 ♗d7 11.♕c2
♕e7**
Botvinnik cleverly hides where
he wants to castle.

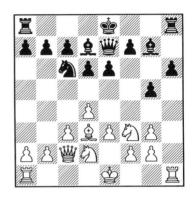

12.0-0-0
Petrosian could hold back his
castling by 12.b4!? or 12.g4.
12...a5?!
Mikhail Moiseevich optimistically
wants to exert pressure on White's
king. Acting in the centre looks
preferable: 12...f5 13.e4 (13.♔b1
0-0-0 and the position would be
complex and balanced) 13...♕f6
14.exf5 exf5 would be unclear.
13.e4
13.g4! was better, as White
should manoeuvre the knight to
h5. If 13...a4 (13...0-0-0 14.♘e4 or
14.♘f1) 14.♘e4 a3 15.b3 White
would transfer the knight to h5 and
would be somewhat better.
13...a4 14.a3
Stopping the a-pawn is a
practical decision, as the position
will be sharper without it.
However, Black equalises thanks
to the hole on b3. 14.♘f1 a3

could lead to extremely complex positions. It would be hard to handle the complications even for these great players. 15.b3 (15.b4 is unclear) 15...g4 (15...h5 16.♘e3 is unclear) 16.♘h4 b5 17.f4 (17. ♗xb5?? ♕g5+) 17...gxf3 (17... b4 18.d5) 18.gxf3 b4 19.d5 with a highly complicated game.

14...♘a5!

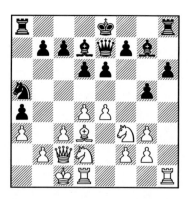

15.♖de1

Petrosian doesn't simply wait, but prepares e5; he is looking for a fight.

15...0-0-0 16.♔b1

16.e5 at once was reasonable as well.

16...♔b8 17.e5 d5

Botvinnik keeps the position closed. After 17...h5 18.exd6 cxd6 19.d5 the position would be unclear.

18.g4 ♖c8?!

Preparing c5 like this is an inaccuracy. Doing it with the b-pawn would be more precise. 18...♕e8 19.♕d1 b6 or 18...b6!? 19.♕d1 c5 20.dxc5 bxc5 would be equal.

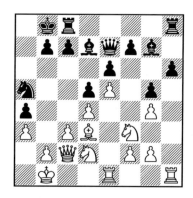

19.♕d1!!

This is a very subtle idea, he starts exerting pressure on the a4-pawn out of the blue.

19...c5 20.♗c2! ♕e8

If 20...b5 21.dxc5 ♖xc5 22.♖e3 White would have a small edge.

21.dxc5!

Petrosian vacates the d4-square for the knight.

21...♖xc5

If 21...♗f8 22.♘d4! (22.♘xg5?! ♗xc5 23.♘h3 ♖g8 and Black has compensation for the pawn) 22... ♗xc5 23.♘2f3 White's knights are strong.

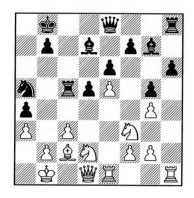

22.g3?!

This is a somewhat mysterious move, and maybe Petrosian wants to hide his intentions. After 22.♘d4! ♘c6 (22...♖f8 23.♖e3) 23.♘xc6+ ♗xc6 24.♘f3 White would be somewhat better planning ♘d4 and ♖e3 followed by g3 and f4.

22...♘c6!

This commits White's knight to defending the e5–pawn, so it can't occupy the d4–square.

23.♖e3

Or 23.♗xa4 ♘xe5 24.♗xd7 ♘xd7.

23...♖a5 24.♖he1 ♗f8?

Botvinnik commits a tactical error. Instead, the position would be equal after 24...♕d8 25.♗xa4 (25. ♔a1 ♕c7) 25...♘xe5 26.♘xe5 ♗xa4 27.♕e2.

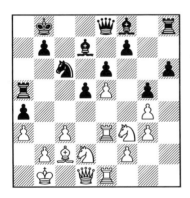

25.c4?

Petrosian misses a golden chance. Opening up the position helps Black's bishop. After 25.♖3e2 ♗c5 26.♖h1 the position would be even, but White has something even better: 25.♗xa4! Taking the pawn

would favour White. 25...♘xe5 (25...♗c5 26.♗xc6 bxc6 [26...♗xc6 27.♘d4] 27.♘b3 ♗xe3 28.♖xe3 and Black would struggle despite the extra exchange) 26.♗xd7 ♘xd7 27.♘b3! and White would win a pawn for nothing after 27...♖a6 (27... ♖b5 28.a4) 28.♕xd5.

25...♗c5 26.♖3e2 ♘e7 27.♔a1 ♕d8

27...♕c8!? would be more precise.

28.♖h1?!

Petrosian is not tuned in to deliver a punch. 28.cxd5! exd5 (28...♘xd5 29.♘e4) 29.e6! This sacrifices a pawn to change the structure. After 29...fxe6 (29... ♗xe6 30.♗xa4) 30.♘e5 ♗b5 31.♗d3 ♗e8 (31...♘c6 32.♘df3) 32.f4 White has compensation for the pawn.

28...♗a7!?

Botvinnik opens the rank for the rook. He has another promising continuation as well: 28...b5! 29.cxd5 (29.cxb5 ♗xb5) 29...exd5 30.e6 ♗xe6 31.♘e5 ♕c7 32.♘df3 f6 33.♘g6 ♗xg4 34.♘xh8 ♗xf3 35.♖xe7 ♗xe7 36.♕xf3 ♕xc2 37.♕xd5 and Black would be somewhat better.

29.♕b1?

Petrosian finds a worse square than d1 for the queen. 29.♖h2 or 29.♗d3 would not equalise, but would still not be as unfortunate as the game continuation.

29...♖c5 30.cxd5

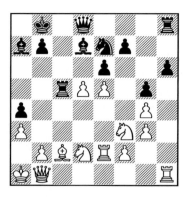

30...exd5!

Suddenly, Black's bishops are too strong.

31.♗f5?

Giving up the two bishops worsens the position. White should just give up a pawn and try to survive.

a) 31.e6 ♗xe6 32.♖he1 ♖c7 33.♘e5 White would be a pawn down, but Black still has to convert it, which would require good play.

b) 31.♘d4 ♗xg4 32.f3 ♗d7 33.e6 White gets rid of Black's bishop pair. 33...fxe6 34.♘xe6 ♗xe6 35.♖xe6 ♕c8! 36.♗f5 ♘xf5 37.♕xf5 and Black is a pawn up, yet it would not be over.

31...♘xf5 32.gxf5 ♗b5! 33.♖ee1 ♖c7

Suddenly, the bishop pair are working with immense power.

34.♖h2 g4 35.♘h4 ♕g5!

Botvinnik wins a pawn, though going after White's king with 35...♕c8! and getting the rook to c2 wins quickly. 36.f4 ♗d4 (36...♖c2 wins as well) 37.♘f1 ♖c3! would win beautifully.

36.f4 gxf3 37.♘hxf3 ♕xg3

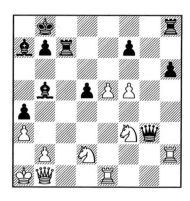

38.e6!?

Petrosian doesn't want to go down without a fight. He is lost; nevertheless, he creates some problems for Botvinnik. Reducing the number of pawns reduces the number of weaknesses.

38...fxe6?!

Perhaps Botvinnik was short of time and wanted to get closer to the 40th move, but this exchange increases White's chances of surviving. It vacates the f5–square for the white queen, and if she gets there, then White will gain some activity. 38...♗f2! 39.♖e5 (Black wins after 39.♖eh1 ♗e3) 39...♖hc8 40.♖h1 f6 (40...♕f4 wins as well.) 41.♖xd5 ♗c6 42.♖d3 ♕f4 and Black would win as White would be tied up.

39.fxe6 ♖hc8

39...♗f2 would not be as strong as it was one move earlier. 40.♖e5 (40. ♖eh1 ♗e3) 40...♖hc8 and now after 41.♖h1 or 41.♕f5 Black would be better, but both moves would give White chances to survive.

40.♖xh6!

Reducing the number of pawns increases White's drawing chances.

40...♗f2

After 40...♗e3 41.♖h5 ♗xd2 42.♘xd2 ♖c5 43.e7 White would have chances to survive.

41.♖eh1 ♕g4 42.♖g6 ♕f4 43.♖g5

Petrosian rightly wants to take the d5–pawn.

43...♕d6?

The queen defends the pawn, but this move gives away the win. It is possible they were in time trouble and when the reigning world champion made this move he was not aware of having reached time control. Hence, he defended the pawn in a hurry. Black would win after 43...♗e2! 44.♖f5 ♕d6 45.♖f6 ♖c3 or 45...♗e3.

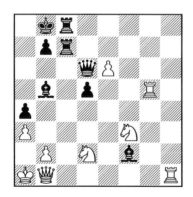

44.♕f5!

White gets back into the game.

44...♗e3

44...♗c6 45.♖d1.

45.♕xd5?!

Petrosian plays for a fortress idea and gets the draw, but the subtle 45.♕e5! would even stop any squeezing. 45...♕xe5 (45...♕c5 46.♖g7) 46.♖xe5 ♗xd2 (46...♗f4 47.♖f5) 47.♘xd2 ♖c1+ (47...♖c2 48.♘b1) 48.♖xc1 ♖xc1+ 49.♔a2 and White would be safe.

45...♕xd5 46.♖xd5 ♗c6

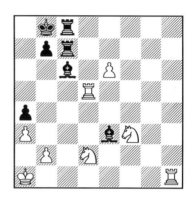

47.♖hh5

The only move to save the piece. White loses the exchange, but so few pawns remain on the board that he can hold.

47...♗xd5 48.♖xd5 ♖e7 49.♖e5!

The rook chases away the well placed bishop.

49...♗h6

Exchanging the bishop still gives Black slight hopes of winning. 49...♗xd2 50.♘xd2 ♖c6

a) 51.♖a5 ♖exe6 52.♖xa4 ♖e1+ 53.♔a2 ♖e2 54.♘b1 ♖b6 55.♖b4 ♖xb4 56.axb4 when the Lomonosov tablebase proves it is a draw.

b) 51.♖e4 ♖a6 52.♖b4 ♖exe6 53.♘e4 ♖e5 54.♘c3 ♖ea5 when Black is very much tied to defending his a-pawn, and I don't think he can win.

50.罝e4 罝c6

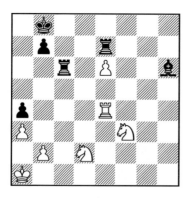

51.罝xa4

After this capture, Botvinnik squeezes for long, but Petrosian was always safe. Petrosian would probably hold by just doing nothing, though at one point he started to push his pawns. The game ended after an 11-hour fight.

51...罝exe6 52.罝e4 罝f6 53.含a2 含c7 54.罝e7+ 含c8 55.罝e2 罝c2 56.含b1 罝cc6 57.匊d4 罝cd6 58.匊2b3 盦g7 59.含a2 罝f1 60.匊c2 罝f5 61.罝g2 盦f6 62.匊b4 含d7 63.罝h2 含c7 64.匊c2 罝g5 65.匊d2 罝e6 66.匊b4 盦g7 67.含b3 罝e3+ 68.含a2 罝e6 69.含b3 罝e3+ 70.含a2 罝e8 71.含b3 含b8 72.匊b1 罝e3+ 73.匊c3 罝eg3 74.罝d2 罝g2 75.罝xg2 罝xg2 76.匊d3 罝h2 77.含c4 罝d2 78.a4 含a7 79.匊b5+ 含b6 80.b4 罝c2+ 81.含b3 罝g2 82.匊c3 罝g3 83.含c4 罝g4+ 84.含b3 罝g3 85.含c4 盦xc3 86.a5+ 含c7 87.含xc3 含c6 88.含c4 罝g4+ 89.含c3 含b5 90.匊c5 罝c4+ 91.含d3 罝xb4 92.匊xb7 含c6

93.a6 含d5 94.匊d8 罝d4+ 95.含e3 罝e4+ 96.含d3 罝f4 97.a7 罝a4 98.匊f7 罝xa7 99.匊g5 罝a3+ 100. 含e2 1/2

Holding one's own against the reigning world champion increases one's self confidence. Maybe after this game Petrosian thought that he would have the chance to obtain the chess crown. He finished the event amazingly.

In round 10, Petrosian was Black against Lipnitsky. He risked the Hungarian Defence in the Italian, and he still equalised. The position sharpened up in the middlegame. Petrosian managed to outplay Lipnitsky and won the game at time control. In round 11, he was White against Bronstein. The position was balanced for a long time, then Bronstein sacrificed two pawns close to time control. But he went too far, though Petrosian missed a few winning chances. Bronstein survived to time control when Petrosian found a brilliant move, which can be seen in the It's Your Move chapter. Tigran obtained some advantage; he pressed until move 59, but had to settle for a draw. In round 12, Petrosian was Black against Novotelnov. White played the 6.盦e2 line against the Najdorf but his setup was harmless. After the opening, Petrosian made a nice breakthrough and won the game convincingly.

Game 40

Petrosian, Tigran – Smyslov, Vassily
Soviet Championship Final, Moscow
(13), 1951
Slav Defence

**1.d4 d5 2.c4 dxc4 3.♘f3 ♘f6
4.♘c3**

Petrosian deviates from the opening of their previous game and chooses a sharper line.

4...c6 5.e4

Petrosian plays the Slav Gambit, a sign he was playing for a win. It was also a surprise, as he had not played this variation before. At this stage of the tourney, Smyslov had scored 7 wins and two losses. Botvinnik, Bronstein, Geller and Taimanov were among his victims.

5...b5 6.e5 ♘d5 7.a4 e6

Smyslov played an exciting game with the move 7...♗e6. Then 8.axb5 ♘xc3 9.bxc3 cxb5 10.♘g5 ♗d5 11.e6 fxe6 12.♕g4 h5 13.♕f4 ♕d6 14.♕f7+ ♔d7 15.♗a3 ♕c7 16.♗e2 ♘c6. This was followed by a blunder in a better position: 17.♗xh5??. After 17...♘e5!! Black was winning and went on to win in the game Tolush, A – Smyslov, V, Leningrad, 1947.

8.axb5

One year earlier, Geller got a promising position against Smyslov, yet Petrosian deviates from that game. 8.♗e2 ♗b7 9.♗g5 ♘xc3 10.bxc3 ♕c7 11.0-0 h6 12.♗h4 ♘d7 13.♘d2 ♘b6 14.♘e4 c5 15.♗f3 cxd4 (15...♘xa4!?) 16.♕xd4 ♗xe4

17.♕xe4 ♘d5 18.♕g4 h5 19.♕g5 and Black was in trouble in Geller, E – Smyslov, V, Moscow, 1950, which ended in a draw.

8...♘xc3 9.bxc3 cxb5 10.♘g5 ♗b7

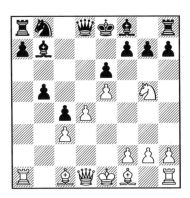

11.♕h5

Petrosian plays the novelty which Furman deployed against Lilienthal in the same year's semi-final.

11...g6!

Lilienthal answered 11...♕d7 and the game ended in a draw.

In 1952, the same players had this position, and Petrosian deviated here. 12.♕h3 ♗e7 13.♕h6 ♗f8 14.♕h3 ♘d7 and Smyslov rejects a repetition. Then 15.♗e2 ♗e7 16.♗f3 Petrosian, T – Smyslov, V, Gagra/ Voronovo, 1952. The game ended in a draw, though at certain moments Tigran was in trouble.

12.♕g4 ♗e7 13.♗e2

Seven years later, Petrosian continued differently. 13.h4 h6 (13...h5 is also possible) 14.♘e4 h5 (14...♕d5!? looks stronger) 15.♕f4 ♘d7 16.♗e2 ♘b6 17.♘d6+ ♗xd6

18.exd6 ♘d5 19.♕e5 ♕f6 20.♕g3
♕f5 21.0-0 0-0 22.♖a5 a6 23.♖e1
♔h7 24.♗f3 ♕d3 25.♖a3 ♖a7??

26.d7! ♘xc3 27.♕g5 ♗xf3
28.♕h6+ ♔g8 29.♕xf8+ ♔xf8
30.d8=♕+ ♔g7 31.♗h6+ ♔h7
32.♕f6 1–0 Petrosian, T – Ignatev,
F, Moscow, 1958.

13...♘d7 14.h4

14.♗f3 was to become more
common. Szabo later tried it against
Petrosian himself. 14...♕c8 15.♗a3?
(15.♘e4!?) 15...♗xf3 16.♘xf3 ♕a6
17.0-0 (if 17.♕e4 0-0 18.♗b2 ♕c8
19.♗c1 f5 Black wins) 17...♗xa3
18.♖a2 b4 (18...0-0 19.♖fa1 ♕b7
20.♖xa3 a5 21.♖xa5 ♖xa5 22.♖xa5
♖a8 is more decisive) 19.cxb4 c3
20.♕e4 ♖c8 21.♖fa1

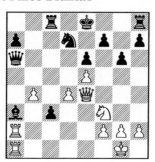

21...c2 22.♖xc2 0-0 23.♘e1 ♘b6
24.♖c5 ♖xc5 25.dxc5 ♕c4 26.♕b1

♗xb4 27.cxb6 a5 28.♕d1 ♕b5
29.♘f3 ♕xb6 and Black was winning
in Szabo, L – Petrosian, T, Budapest,
1955. Petrosian went on to win.

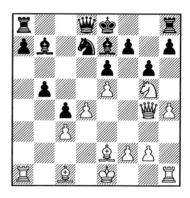

14...h5 15.♕g3 ♘b6

Black could consider 15...♗d5!?
as well.

16.0-0 a5!

This move stops ♗a3, and
given the chance Black may create
connected passed pawns by pushing
the b-pawn. Kasparov writes that
Smyslov felt comfortable about
the break, otherwise he would
have played 16...♗d5 17.♖b1 ♗c6
18.♗d1, which would have been
unclear. 16...♘d5 is also possible.

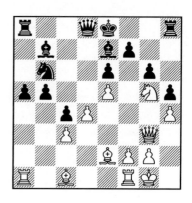

17.d5!!

Petrosian finds an imaginative idea to create play by opening the centre. Interestingly, Petrosian attaches a ?! mark to it, but his move is the one that gives the best practical chances. Incredibly, Geller had the same position in the same round versus Flohr. He continued 17.♖b1? and soon got into a lost position. 17... b4 18.f4 ♕d7 19.♗a1 b3. Geller was unable to create play and Black's passed pawns decided the outcome of the game. It would be interesting to know whether Petrosian or Geller made the move first in this position. One suspects that Geller was the one.

17...♘xd5

There is nothing wrong with this capture. According to Petrosian, Black should have taken with 17...♗xd5!? to prevent the knight from getting to e4. He actually played this capture to create a masterpiece 30 years after this game, covered in Volume II. After 18.♖d1 ♕c7 Gazarek played 19.♖d4 against Petrosian in 1981 at Oberwart and lost. Kasparov thinks that after 19.♗e3 White has strong pressure, but it looks like Black can castle long after a few careful moves. After 19...♕c6!? 20.♕f4 (20.♗d4 ♘a4) 20...♗xg5 21.♕xg5 ♘d7 Black may play b4, and perhaps his chances are somewhat better.

18.♖d1 ♕c7

Commentators do not mention the 18...♗xg5!? capture, though perhaps it is reasonable. Black may not need the dark-squared bishop if he pushes the a-pawn and will try to walk with his king to the queenside. After 19.♗xg5 ♕c7 Black should be better.

19.♘e4 0-0-0

According to Petrosian, although queenside castling entails considerable danger, it is already hard to suggest a fully satisfactory defence for Black. However, he is only partly right. Black has a safer place for the king. Let us add that long castling is also playable. What else can be tried? If 19...0-0?! then 20.♗xh5! is very strong. Suetin came up with walking to the kingside via 19...♔f8!?. Actually, he was sceptical about it, but it looks alright. For example, after 20.♘d6 ♗c6 Black seems to be doing well. His rook can move to d8 and he can play b4, when we do not see a way for White to keep some play. 19...♗c6 looks fine as well, and in fact after 20.♗g5 ♔f8 Black would stand better.

20.♗g5!

Petrosian exchanges an important defender.

20...♗xg5

After 20...a4 21.♗xe7 ♕xe7 22.♘d6+ ♖xd6 23.exd6 the position would be balanced.

21.♕xg5 a4

This move is somewhat passive, but it is still reasonable; it has the merit that the queen no longer has to defend the a-pawn.

a) 21...b4 22.cxb4 axb4 23.♘d6+ ♔b8. Crouch analyses this position and reaches the conclusion that the sharp position would be balanced.

b) 21...f6!? Kasparov says that this move, which takes away the d6 check from White, was discovered in the nineties. 22.exf6 ♘f4 23.♖xd8+ ♖xd8 24.♗f3 ♗d5 and Kasparov stops here, saying that Black would be better. However, White can still create play with the subtle 25.♔h1!, which prepares g3. (Stepping aside from the check with 25.♔f1 would work as well.) Then 25...b4 (25...a4 26.g3) 26.cxb4 axb4

27.♘c5!! This sacrifice aims to drag the queen into a pin. 27...♕xc5

28.♖a8+ ♔d7 29.♖xd8+ ♔xd8 30.f7+ ♔d7 31.♕h6 and the game will end in a draw.

22.♕g3 f5?

According to Kasparov, after this move Black has to sacrifice the exchange under less favourable circumstances. Perhaps Black can still hold, but it's unclear, and, if he can survive, then his path is very narrow. Interestingly, nobody mentioned 22...♗c6!? before. Black wants to place his king on a6 so the bishop defends the b5–pawn. 23.♘d6+ (23.♗f3 ♔b7 24.♘d6+ ♔a6 and Black is better) 23... ♖xd6 24.exd6 ♕d7 25.♗f3 ♖d8 26.♗xd5 exd5 27.♕f4 ♕e6 (27... ♔b7 28.♖db1 ♔a6 and Black would be better) 28.♖e1 ♕xd6 29.♕xf7 d4 and Black will have very dangerous passed pawns.

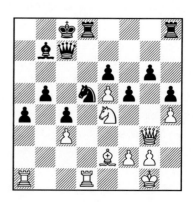

23.♘d6+ ♖xd6 24.exd6 f4?

Smyslov commits a losing mistake; this move loosens Black's pawn chain.

a) All commentators suggest 24...♕g7?? as a move which gives chances, but it is wrong as Black loses by force.

a1) If 25.♗f3 then 25...♘xc3?? would lose to 26.d7+!, but 25...♔d7 or 25...♕f6 26.♗xd5 exd5 would keep Black in the game.

a2) 25.♗xc4!! They missed this brilliant tactical shot. After 25...bxc4 26.♖xa4 ♔d7 27.♖xc4 White threatens ♖xd5 and ♖c7 with check. 27...♗c6 (27...♖c8 28.♖xc8 ♔xc8 29.♕d3 or 29.c4 would win) 28.♖xc6 ♔xc6 29.d7 wins.

b) 24...♕d7! This move has not been analysed before. 25.♗f3 (25. ♕xg6?? ♘f4; 25.♖ab1 ♔b8) 25...♖d8 26.♖ab1 (if 26.♕xg6 ♘xc3 or if 26.♖d2 ♕xd6 27.♕xg6 ♕e7 28.♖ad1 ♔c7 Black is in the game) 26...♕e8 (26...♗c6 27.♗xd5 exd5 28.♕xg6 ♕xd6 29.♕xf5+ and Black would be in trouble, as his pawns are immobile) 27.♖d2 (27.d7+ ♕xd7 28.♕xg6 ♗c6 and Black would be worse, but still alive) 27...f4 28.♕g5 ♖xd6 29.♕e5 ♖d8 30.♕d4 ♕c6 and Black has three pawns for the exchange, but White is much more active. Black would be clearly worse, but maybe not yet lost.

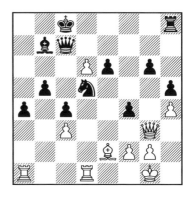

25.♕xg6
Now White's position is winning.
25...♖xd6 26.♗f3 ♗c6 27.♖e1 ♖e8

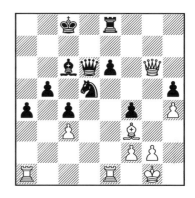

28.♗xd5!?
Petrosian simplifies to a winning endgame. After 28.♖ad1! ♔c7 29.♕xh5 White would win more quickly, as Black has virtually no move.
28...♕xd5 29.♖ad1! ♕f5
Black has no choice other than to play the endgame.
30.♕xf5 exf5 31.♖xe8+ ♗xe8

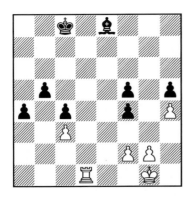

32.f3

Petrosian gets ready to centralise his king. The pawn on f3 restricts the bishop as well.

32...♔c7 33.♔f2 ♔b6 34.♔e2 ♔a5

Smyslov chooses to place his king on the edge. Heading towards the centre was not any better: 34...♔c5 35.♖b1 a3 36.♔d2 b4 37.cxb4+ ♔d4 38.♖a1 c3+ 39.♔c1 ♔e3 40.♖xa3 ♔f2 41.♖xc3 ♔xg2 42.♔d2 and White wins, as Crouch pointed out.

35.♖b1 a3

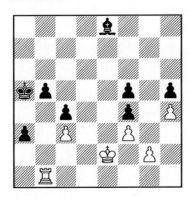

36.♔d2 b4

Otherwise, White would play ♔c2 and ♖b4, winning the key a3–

pawn. Or 36...♔a4 37.♖b4+ ♔a5 38.♔c2 would win.

37.cxb4+   ♔a4   38.♔c3   a2 39.♖a1 ♔a3

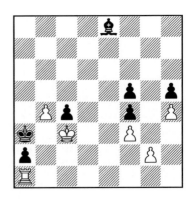

40.♔xc4!

White wins the promotion race. It would be nice to know how many moves in advance Petrosian had calculated this rook sacrifice as winning.

40...♔b2 41.♖e1

According to the database, Petrosian placed the rook on the d-file, but other sources say the e-file. Sacrificing the rook would win here as well. 41.♖xa2+ ♔xa2 42.b5 ♔b2 43.♔c5 ♗d7 44.b6 ♗c8 45.♔d6 ♔c3 46.♔e5 ♔d3 47.♔xf4 ♔e2 48.g4 (48.♔g5 ♔f2 49.♔xh5 ♔xg2 50.f4 wins) 48...fxg4 49.fxg4 hxg4 50.♔g3 would win.

41...a1=♕

Had the rook moved to the d-file, 41...♗a4! would save the game.

42.♖xa1   ♔xa1   43.b5   ♗d7 44.b6   ♗c8   45.♔d4   ♔b2   46.♔e5 ♔c3   47.♔xf4   ♔d4   48.♔g5   ♔e5 49.♔xh5 ♔f6

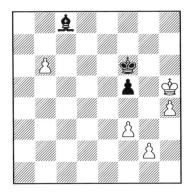

50.g4!

The only winning move. Black can't hold back three passed pawns. Perhaps Petrosian visualised this as early as move 28, so he may have seen it 22 moves in advance.

50...♗b7 51.♔h6 1–0

This was a vital win over one of the best players in the world.

In round 14, Petrosian as Black played the semi-Tarrasch against Simagin. The Russian player had an isolated queen's pawn and he was unable to do anything with his position. Petrosian beautifully exchanged White's strong b1-bishop, then Simagin pushed his g-pawn, Tigran brilliantly uncovered White's soft points by swapping more minor pieces. Petrosian won a pawn, then another, and he converted his advantage into a win. The game can be seen in the Petrosian's Remarkable Exchanges chapter.

Petrosian had 9 points when he met Taimanov, who trailed him by half a point. Petrosian obtained an edge in the opening, sometimes it

grew a bit, sometimes it decreased. We join the game at move 23.

Game 41

Petrosian, Tigran – Taimanov, Mark
Soviet Championship Final, Moscow (15), 1951

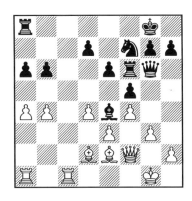

23.♗xa6!

White bags a pawn. But the game is far from over.

23...♖xa6   24.♖c8+   ♘d8 25.♖xd8+ ♖f8 26.♖xf8+ ♔xf8

White is a pawn up with potential to create a distant passed pawn, but Black has a stronger bishop and his king is safer.

27.♕e2 ♖a8

27...♖a7!? looks slightly better, to keep the rook closer to the a-pawn. 28.♔f2 (28.a5 h5 29.a6 ♕g4 is safe for Black) 28...h5 29.h4. It is hard to tell whether White can do anything with his extra pawn.

28.a5 bxa5 29.bxa5

The a-pawn is a strong card in White's hand.

29...♕e8

Taimanov wants to transfer the queen to the queenside.

29...h5!?: maybe Black should keep White busy on the kingside. 30.♔f1 (30.♔f2 h4 31.♖g1 hxg3+ 32.♖xg3 ♕h6 33.h3 ♖c8 and Black holds) 30...♕g4 (30...h4 31.gxh4 ♕h6 32.♗e1 and it is hard to tell whether White could win here) 31.♕xg4 hxg4 and Black probably holds as the pawn is only on the fifth rank.

30.a6 ♔g8?!

Taimanov is too cautious. 30...♕c8!? is probably more precise, as he would start building his play at once.

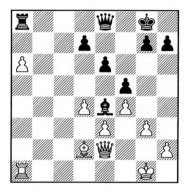

31.d5!

It is a good practical idea to open the diagonal for his bishop.

31...♗xd5 32.♗c3 ♕c8

Taimanov tries to be active with his queen on the queenside. 32...d6 looks good enough to hold, providing that Black can defend on the seventh rank. The pawn takes away two dark squares from the white bishop and

queen. 33.a7 (if 33.♕d2 ♕h5 the black queen poses serious danger to White on the kingside, and after 34.♕d4 ♕g4 35.a7 h5 36.♖b1 ♔h7 Black is not in danger of losing) 33...h6 34.♗d4 ♔h7 and Black has better chances to hold than White has to win.

33.♕d3 ♕c5

It would be interesting to know how much time the players had here. Did they have time to work out for whom swapping queens would be beneficial, or were they short of time and playing one move at a time? After 33...♕c7! 34.♕d4 d6 Black is likely to hold.

34.♖a5?!

After 34.♕d4!? ♕e7 White had good chances to win. White has another promising continuation as well: 34.♗d4!? ♕c8 (34...♕c6 35.a7 d6 [35...♗e4 36.♕b3] 36.♕c3 would be hard to defend with Black) 35.a7 h6 and Black would be alive, but with a hard life. 35...♗b7?! would be weaker because of the strong 36.♕b5!.

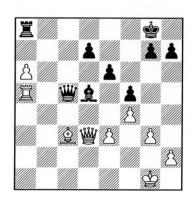

34...♕c4?

This is a pivotal moment. Exchanging queens most probably loses. If 34...♕c6? then 35.♕d4 would win. But Black has a good alternative: 34...♗c4! This subtle intermediate move allows Black to grab the a-pawn.

a) 35.♕d2

a1) 35...♗b5 36.a7 ♕c4 (36...♖xa7 37.♗d4) 37.h3 (37.♕e1 ♗c6) 37...♕f1+ 38.♔h2 ♗c6 and Black is safe.

a2) 35...♕b6 36.♗b2 (36.♔f2 d6) 36...♖xa6 37.♕c3 ♔f7 38.♕xg7+ ♔e8=

b) 35.♖xc5 ♗xd3 36.♖c7 ♗xa6 37.♖xd7. The rook does less damage on the seventh rank than usual:

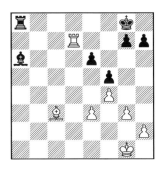

37...♖c8! The active rook keeps the balance (37...g6 38.♖g7+ ♔f8 39.♖xh7 and White is better) 38.♖xg7+ (38.♗xg7 ♖c1+ 39.♔f2 ♖c2+ and Black gets away with it) 38...♔f8 39.♗e5 ♖c1+ 40.♔g2 ♖c2+ 41.♔h3 ♗f1+ 42.♔h4 ♖xh2+ 43.♔g5 ♖h3 and Black holds.

35.♕xc4 ♗xc4 36.a7 d6?!

Giving up the pawn leads to a loss, but keeping it would mean more obstacles to overcome. Let's see what

happens if Black just tries to hold the position: 36...♗d5 37.♗e5!? The bishop aims to trap the rook. (37. ♗d4 ♖c8 38.♖b5 ♖a8 39.♖b8+ ♔f7 40.♔f2 ♔e7 and Black resists) 37...♖c8

a) 38.♔f2 ♔f7 39.♔e1 g6 (39...♔e7 40.♗xg7) 40.♔d2 ♗f3 (40...♔e7 41.♖xd5 wins) 41.♖a4 ♔e7 42.♖d4 (42.e4 ♗xe4 43.♖xe4? fxe4 44.♗b8 e3+!) 42...h6 43.♗d6+ and White wins.

b) 38.♗b8 ♗a8 39.♖a1 ♔f7 (39...♖c2 40.♖d1 and White wins) 40.♖d1! and White drags the king to the 8th rank. 40...♔e8 (40...♔e7 41.♗d6+ ♔e8 42.♖b1 wins) 41.♗e5 ♗f3 (41...♖c2 42.♖b1) 42.♖b1 ♗a8 (42...♖a8 43.♗b8) 43.♖b8 ♔d8 44.♗d6 and Black is paralysed.

37.♗b4 ♗d5 38.♗xd6 ♖c8

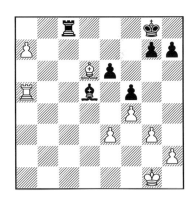

39.♗c5!

Petrosian restricts the rook's activity and gets ready to invade with his king.

39...♔f7 40.♔f2 ♔e8 41.♔e2 h6

Keeping the pawns on the kingside where they are would lose

as well. For example, White could open a path with h3 and g4.

42.♔d3 g5

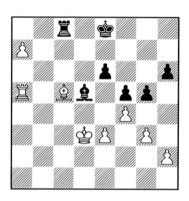

43.♖b5

The game must have been adjourned somewhere here. It is a bit of a surprise that Taimanov keeps on playing.

43...♔d7 44.♔d4 g4 45.♖b8 h5 46.♗b6 ♗f3 47.♔e5 ♗d5 48.♔f6 ♖e8

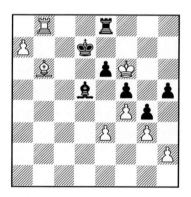

49.♔g5

The king collects the second pawn.

49...♖c8 50.♔xh5 ♗e4 51.♔g5 ♗d5 52.♔f6 ♖e8 53.♗d4

Transferring the bishop is strong.

53...♖c8

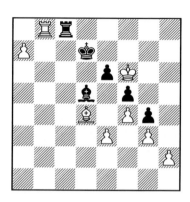

54.♗e5 ♖e8

If 54...♗e4 Petrosian probably would not go for exchanging rooks, as the opposite-coloured bishops ending might be a draw even with a 3-pawn advantage, given that it is questionable White can create another passed pawn. Instead, 55.♔f7 wins.

55.♔f7 ♖c8 56.♖b6

Activating the rook finishes the game in no time.

56...♗c6

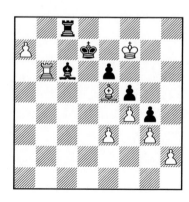

57.♗b8 1–0 Black is in complete zugzwang.

In the penultimate round, Petrosian was White against Keres, who was leading the event with Geller. Keres made a careless move in the opening and Petrosian won a pawn, but he allowed Keres to simplify to an ending with rook and 4 pawns vs. rook and 3 pawns on the kingside, a theoretical draw. Petrosian pressed for some time, but had no real chance to win. Before the last round, Keres had 11 points, while Petrosian, Smyslov and Geller had 10.5. Petrosian as Black faced Tergupov in the last round. Tigran played the opening unusually riskily. Tergupov built up a strong attack, but was unable to do anything with the position. Petrosian equalised fairly quickly and soon after took control. He scored a victory one move before time control. His 7 points out 8 games at the end of the event was a phenomenal run. His rivals Keres and Geller won as well, while Smyslov drew.

Keres won the championship with 12 points, while Petrosian and Geller finished joint-second with 11.5. Smyslov scored 11 points, while the reigning world champion Botvinnik finished fifth with 10 and his challenger Bronstein was joint 6th-8th with Averbakh and Taimanov.

Petrosian won 8 games, drew 7 and lost only 2. Only he and Keres were beaten twice, whereas all the other participants lost more games. Petrosian was awarded a prize for scoring the most points against grandmasters. His overall silver medal was a great success; it was certainly a performance of a world class player. He importantly qualified for the interzonal tournament of the world championship cycle.

Petrosian's results in 1951

Lithuanian Championship, Vilnius	+ 8 = 3 – 3 9.5/14 2nd-4th place
Petrosian – Mukhutdinov Match, Tashkent	+ 7 = 7 – 0 10.5:3.5 winner
Moscow Championship	+ 7 = 5 – 0 9.5 /12 1st place
Soviet Championship Semi-Final, Sverdlovsk	+ 9 = 9 – 1 13.5/19 1st place
Soviet Team Championship, Tbilisi, 3rd board	+ 2 = 1 – 2 2.5/5
Masters Tournament, Tbilisi	+ 7 = 5 – 3 9.5/15 2nd-3rd place
Soviet Championship Final, Moscow	+ 8 = 7 – 2 11.5/17 2nd-3rd place
Altogether	**+ 48 = 37 – 11 66.5/96**

1952

Maroczy Memorial, Budapest

Petrosian's results, especially joint-second place in the Soviet championship, earned him the opportunity to play in a foreign country. Petrosian's first event abroad took place in Budapest. Hungary's best player until then, Geza Maroczy, had died in 1951. The country and ruling Communist Party decided to organise a big event for their player, who had produced the best results in the world between 1905 and 1907. The line-up was fantastic, especially the Soviet players, including the world champion Botvinnik.

In round 1, Petrosian was White against Smyslov. Smyslov equalised in a 1.c4 e5 English Opening, they swapped queens, and Vassily offered a draw soon after. It was reasonable to take it, especially knowing how poorly Petrosian had started the other events that he had experienced for the first time.

In the second round, Petrosian faced another powerhouse, Keres, and we look at this game.

Game 42

Petrosian, Tigran – Keres, Paul
Maroczy Memorial,
Budapest (2), 1952
Nimzo-Indian Defence

1.d4 ♘f6 2.c4 e6 3.♘c3 ♗b4 4.e3 0-0 5.♘f3 d5 6.♗d3 c5 7.0-0 b6

Keres plays a rare variation. According to the database, it was first employed by Pirc in 1939. Novotelnov gave it a try against Bronstein in the 1951 Soviet champioship final. By the way, Keres would employ this variation a few more times, he would not lose with it anymore, and he beat Gligoric with it.

8.dxc5

This will remain a rare move.

8...bxc5

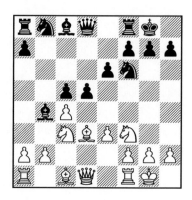

9.♘e2!?

This move will not even be repeated. The opening probably

surprised Petrosian, and all he wants is to find an idea which his opponent probably hadn't analysed in detail.

9...♘bd7! 10.b3 e5!

Keres handles the opening ambitiously.

11.♗b1?!

After the stronger 11.♗f5 or 11.a3 ♗a5 12.♘d2 the position would be equal.

11...e4

If 11...dxc4!? 12.bxc4 ♗b7 Black would have a small advantage.

12.♘d2 ♗a6

Keres plays another nice developing move.

13.♗b2 ♕a5?

Keres gets carried away and misses White's tactic.

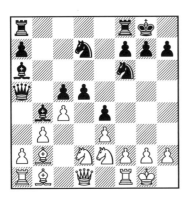

14.♘xe4!!

White obtains the two bishops with this subtle, small combination.

14...dxe4 15.a3

White traps the bishop.

15...♗d2 16.b4 cxb4

Black has no pleasant continuation, for example if 16...♕b6 17.♕xd2 ♗xc4 18.♖c1 ♗xe2

19.♕xe2 cxb4 20.axb4 he can't really take White's last queenside pawn. That is why White has a neat advantage thanks to his bishop pair.

17.♕xd2 ♗xc4 18.axb4 ♕g5?!

The queen doesn't stand well here, but it would not stand well on any available square. Had Keres kept the queen on the queenside the game would have possibly lasted longer, but he would probably still have lost. If 18...♕b6 then 19.♖c1 would be strong.

19.♖a5 ♕h4

20.h3!

Petrosian prevents an attack.

20...♖fb8

Black hopes to get rid of the b4–pawn, but has only very little chance of accomplishing that.

21.♘g3!

Keres wanted to attack on the kingside; surprisingly, Petrosian creates a big threat, and he spectacularly moves a pinned knight.

21...♖b5

21...♗xf1 22.♘f5 would trap the black queen.

22.♖xb5 ♗xb5 23.♖c1 ♗d3

Giving up the pawn doesn't stabilise the position, but loses by force.

24.♗xd3 exd3 25.♗d4 ♘e4

Bringing the queen back doesn't help. 25...♕g5 26.♕xd3 ♕d5 27.♘f5 and White wins.

26.♕xd3 ♘xg3 27.fxg3 ♕xg3

Other moves were hopeless as well: 27...♕e7 28.♖c7 or 27...♕d8 28.♕e4 would win.

28.♕e4!

The queen's power is decisive. Black's position falls apart.

28...♖d8

28...♖f8 29.♗xa7 or 28...♕b8 29.♕g4 would be decisive.

29.♕e7 ♕b8 30.♗xa7! ♕xa7

30...♖a8 31.♖c7 would win. Maybe Keres had no time to resign; he plays on with an exchange deficit.

31.♕xd8+ ♘f8 32.♕e8

This prevents any hope of giving perpetual check.

32...♕a3 33.♖c7 ♕b3 34.♕e7 ♕d5 35.♔h2 h6 36.♖c8 1–0

Beating the reigning Soviet champion was quite an accomplishment and surely meant a lot to him.

In the next round, Petrosian faced his first ever non-Soviet opponent, Pilnik from Argentina. The South American was White and he defended his e4-pawn with 5.d3 in the Ruy Lopez. Petrosian acted fairly aggressively and based his play on a kingside attack. However, his play there came to a standstill. Pilnik gained a clear advantage, but Petrosian was able to come back into the game. Yet a big mistake crept in, and although lost, Petrosian fought on, managing to adjourn the game, though he was unable to save it. We now know that Petrosian couldn't be broken, and indeed he bounced back against Sliwa. He was White against the Polish player. Black equalised in the e3 Nimzo-Indian. However, Petrosian started to outplay his opponent soon after the opening. Black lost a pawn and, when an exchange was going to drop, he resigned. In round 5, Petrosian was Black against Geller. In the Orthodox Queen's Gambit Declined no player had a chance to take control, and the game ended in a draw on move 23.

Game 43

Petrosian, Tigran – Golombek, Harry
Maroczy Memorial,
Budapest (6), 1952
Queen's Indian Defence

1.♘f3 ♘f6 2.c4 b6 3.d4 e6 4.e3

Petrosian would regularly employ this fighting variation, usually once or twice a year. He was not unscathed in it, but still achieved a solid plus score.

4...♗b7 5.♗d3 c5

Let's look at some of his other good wins with this variation. Interestingly, he would also outplay his opponents despite the opposite-coloured bishops after 5...♗b4+. See Petrosian, T – Fuller, M, Siegen, 1970.

5...d5 6.0-0 ♗d6 7.b3 0-0 8.♗b2 ♘bd7 9.♘c3 c5 10.cxd5 exd5 11.♖c1 ♕e7 12.♕e2 ♖ad8 13.♖fd1 ♘e4 14.♗a6 ♗a8 15.♗b5 ♘df6 16.♘e5 ♘xc3 17.♗xc3 ♘e4 18.♗b2 f6 19.♘d3 ♔h8 20.♘f4 ♕f7 21.♕g4 f5 22.♕e2 ♗b7 23.♗d3 ♘xf4? 24.exf4 ♖fe8 25.♕c2 ♖c8

26.dxc5! Tigran opens the long diagonal, and he will win the game thanks to it. 26...♖xc5 27.♕b1 ♖xc1 28.♕xc1 ♘c5 29.♗e5 ♖c8 30.♕b2 ♘xd3?! 31.♖xd3 ♖c6 32.h3 h6 33.♖e3 ♖g6 34.♗d4 ♔h7 35.♕c2 ♕d7 36.♔h2 ♗c8 37.♖c3 ♗a6 38.♖c7 ♕e6

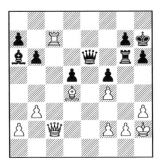

39.g4 ♗f1 40.♕xf5 ♕xf5 41.gxf5 ♖g2+ 42.♔h1 1–0 Petrosian, T – Polugaevsky, L, Soviet Championship Playoff, Moscow, 1970.

6.0-0 ♗e7 7.♘c3 d6?

7...cxd4 8.exd4 d5 9.b3 0-0 10.♗b2 ♘c6 11.♕e2 ♖e8 12.♖ad1 ♖c8 13.♖fe1 ♗f8 14.♗b1 g6 15.♘e5 ♗g7 16.h3 a6 17.cxd5 exd5 18.♕f3 b5 19.♘e2?

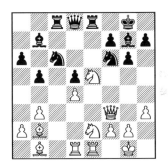

19...♘xe5! Black takes control. 20.dxe5 ♘d7 21.e6 ♖xe6 22.♗xg7 ♔xg7 23.♘d4 ♖xe1+ 24.♖xe1 ♕f6 25.♕g4 ♘e5 (25...♘c5!) 26.♘f5+ ♔h8 27.♕d4 ♖e8 28.♖e3? (White should defend the rook differently: 28.♔f1! gxf5 29.f4 would be equal) 28...gxf5 29.♕f4 d4 30.♖g3 d3 and Petrosian went on to win with the extra piece in Tal, M – Petrosian, T, Moscow, 1971 blitz game.

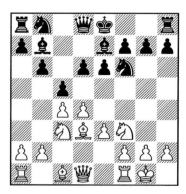

8.d5!

Petrosian exploits Golombek's serious inaccuracy and gains space in the centre while leaving the b7–bishop passive on the diagonal.

8...exd5 9.cxd5 0-0 10.e4 ♗a6 11.a4

The Benoni structure is risky for Black; here Black in addition has the passive bishop on e7. Unlike in most Benoni positions, Black has no active play.

11...♗xd3 12.♕xd3 ♘bd7

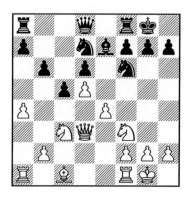

13.♘d2

Petrosian defends the e4–pawn in advance, while the knight may do well on the queenside.

13...♖e8 14.a5!

White bites at Black's pawn chain.

14...♗f8 15.f3 ♘e5 16.♕e2 bxa5

This helps White, but at least Black also gets hopes of active play. After 16...♖b8 17.axb6 axb6 18.♘b5 Black would be very passive.

17.♘b3 a4 18.♖xa4 ♖b8?

Black should play 18...a5! followed by ♕b6 or ♘ed7 and White's advantage would not be that big.

19.♘a5

The knight is very strong on a5.

19...♖b4 20.♖a2 ♕c7

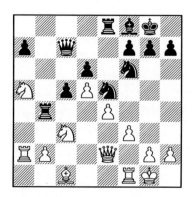

21.♗f4!

Petrosian wants to take the e5–knight to place his own knight on c6.

21...c4

Golombek prefers to die quickly and actively than live longer passively.

22.♗xe5!

This exchange makes sure the a5–knight reaches the c6–outpost.

22...dxe5 23.♔h1 ♘h5 24.g3!? ♕d7

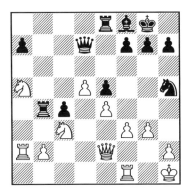

25.♔g2!?

Petrosian prevents any attack against his king.

25...♕d6

25...f5 26.♘c6 ♖b7 27.♕xc4 wins.

26.♘c6   ♕g6   27.♔h1   ♕h6 28.♖g1 ♗c5

Black is ready to swap off a few minor pieces. After 28...♖b7 29.♕xc4 Black would also lose.

29.♘xb4 ♗xg1 30.♔xg1 ♕b6+ 31.♔f1 ♕xb4

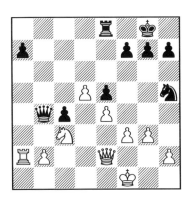

32.♖xa7

White wins a pawn for nothing; the outcome of the game is decided.

32...♖c8 33.f4!

Petrosian wins another pawn.

33...♕b8 34.♖e7 ♔f8 35.♖xe5 g6 36.♕d2 ♕d6 37.♘b5 ♕d7

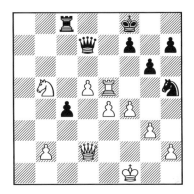

38.d6

The pawn is irresistible.

38...♖a8 39.♔g2 ♖a1 40.♘c3 ♖a6 41.♖d5 ♘f6 42.♕d4 1–0

In round 7, Tigran was Black against Stahlberg, and after 1.d4 ♘f6 2.♘f3 c5 3.d5 b5 Petrosian obtained the bishop pair, but he was behind in development. Soon, Petrosian started to have structural problems. In addition, his bishop pair got halved. Petrosian was already lost in the opening and was unable to last longer than 27 moves. In round 8, Petrosian was White against Szabo. In an e3 Queen's Indian, he exchanged a pair of pawns and knights. Black obtained the upper hand as early as the opening when Tigran blundered. The local grandmaster gave up two pieces for a rook, probably unnecessarily, which prolonged the game, but he gradually converted his advantage, and won against our hero on move 65. In round 9, Petrosian was Black against Gereben. Petrosian equalised in a g3 King's Indian. His attack started to grow after the opening. Petrosian had many chances to knock his opponent out, but failed to take them. Gereben managed to exchange queens and hold. In round 10, Petrosian faced Szily. In a Queen's Gambit, Petrosian obtained a tiny advantage, but his opponent defended accurately and held. In the next round, Tigran was Black against Benko. It was a g3 King's Indian with no c4. White had an isolated pawn in a complex middlegame. The Hungarian chess magazine Sakkelet writes that they got into time trouble. Benko took control and soon won a pawn and then the game on the 62nd move. Petrosian fell back to minus 1, but he had already demonstrated that he wanted to bounce back, and he had the ability and the determination to do that. In the 12th game, Petrosian was White against Kottnauer. He tried the King's Indian Attack, got no advantage, and the position fairly quickly simplified to a draw. In round 13, Petrosian was Black against O'Kelly. The Belgian grandmaster was unable to put Tigran under pressure in the g3 King's Indian. Rather, Petrosian started to create some play, but O'Kelly defended well and Petrosian's small edge evaporated. There was nothing left to play for by the time they agreed to a draw. In round 14, Petrosian as White employed the Saemisch Variation against Troianescu's Nimzo-Indian. The Romanian player sacrificed a pawn for very little. A bit strangely, Black sacrificed another pawn for virtually nothing. Petrosian exchanged queens and a pair of rooks, and Troianescu resigned a few moves later. In round 15, Botvinnik surprised him with 1.e4. Petrosian probably did not want a strategic battle and so opted for a Najdorf Sicilian. Botvinnik was unable to create any pressure. After the opening, on move 22, they agreed to a draw. In round 16, Petrosian was White against Barcza and he played the King's Indian Attack starting with 1.♘f3. He built his play on the kingside, and the Hungarian player did likewise on the other wing. The position was balanced. When Petrosian pushed his pawn to h5, Barcza panicked and gave away a pawn for nothing. Petrosian was soon winning, and the local player resigned shortly after time control. In the last round, Petrosian was Black against Platz, who only had 2 points. They reached a complex position in the King's Indian Saemisch, but while still in the opening Petrosian took control and won an exchange and soon after the game. He finished joint-seventh with Pilnik.

He scored 9.5 out of 17. His 6 wins were 2 fewer than at the Soviet championship, and the 4 losses were too many. He did well against the strong Soviets, but possibly misjudged the level of the better foreign players. Maybe he had played so much in 1951 that he did not have enough time to work on his openings. Keres won the very strong event with 12.5 points, while Geller finished second with 12 points, and Botvinnik, Stahlberg and Smyslov were joint-third with 11. Szabo came sixth with 10.5.

Training Team Event, Gagra/Voronovo

There are 7 games in the database from a team event which took place in May. The header of the games says Gagra/Voronovo. Perhaps the players played for these towns, but it was much more likely a double round event divided into two parts, with the first half held in Gagra. The town is in Abkhazia, which was a part of Georgia at the time (and still is in the opinion of most countries). It lies on the coast of the Black Sea, with a pleasant climate. Interestingly, our sources other than the database do not even mention this event.

The first Petrosian game of this event was against Botvinnik. It was probably played in Gagra. Playing in the republic he was born and raised in usually brought the best out of Petrosian.

Game 44

**Botvinnik, Mikhail –
Petrosian, Tigran**
Match/Training Team 1–Team 2,
Gagra/Voronovo, 1952
Sicilian Defence

1.e4 c5 2.f4

It would be interesting to know why Botvinnik chooses such a harmless line.

2...♘f6 3.d3 d5 4.e5 ♘g8

Petrosian wants to develop the bishop to f5 or g4.

5.♘f3 ♘c6 6.c3

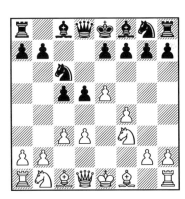

6...♗g4

Petrosian voluntarily gives up the bishop for the knight. He slightly preferred knights over bishops; here was an example of this.

7.h3 ♗xf3 8.♕xf3 e6 9.♕f2

This is somewhat awkward; White has all his pieces on their

starting square and makes another move with his only developed piece, the queen. However, the position is closed, therefore, development is less important than usual.

9...h5 10.♗e3 ♕b6

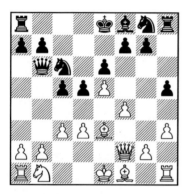

11.♕c2

The queen has to make another move in order to develop the knight to the d2-square. 11.b4? doesn't come into consideration as a possibility because 11...d4 almost wins.

11...h4!?

Petrosian keeps playing strategically. He fixes White's kingside.

12.♘d2   ♘h6   13.♗f2   ♘f5 14.♘f3 ♗e7 15.♗e2

If 15.b4, then again 15...d4 would be the answer.

15...♖g8!?

Petrosian plans to castle long. His move has deeper intentions than just postponing castling. If 15...f6 then 16.b4 could be played.

16.♕d2 0-0-0 17.0-0 d4!

Petrosian restricts the movement of the f2-bishop. This move gains space and separates the e5-pawn a bit.

18.♖fc1 ♔b8 19.♖ab1

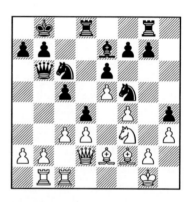

19...g5!

After placing the king on a safer square, Petrosian opens the g-file.

20.fxg5 ♕c7 21.♕f4 ♖d5 22.b4

Had White played a waiting move, Black could have played the slightly unpleasant 22...f6. If 22.c4 Black could sacrifice the exchange, but moving the rook back is also reasonable.

a) 22...♖xe5!? 23.♘xe5 ♕xe5 24.♕xe5+ ♘xe5 25.a3 ♗xg5 and Black has a pleasant game.

b) 22...♖dd8 23.a3 f6 24.♕e4 (after 24.gxf6 ♗xf6 25.b4 ♗g7 26.bxc5 ♗h6 Black would be somewhat better) 24...fxg5 25.b4 and the position would be unclear after

25...cxb4 26.axb4 ♘xb4 or after 25...♖df8.

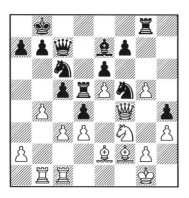

22...♘xe5

Taking on e5 is a small accomplishment. It opens up the position, and from now on inaccuracies must be treated as full mistakes and they may become expensive.

23.cxd4 ♘xf3+ 24.♕xf3 c4

After 24...♖xg5 25.bxc5 (25.dxc5 ♗f6) 25...♘xd4 26.♗xd4 ♖xd4 Black would be safe, and maybe even have a small edge.

25.dxc4 ♘xd4 26.♗xd4 ♖xd4 27.♕xf7

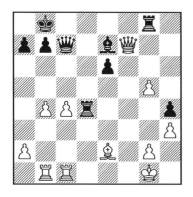

27...♖xg5

The dust has settled. The middlegame with opposite-coloured bishops will be complex, but more or less balanced. Botvinnik produced several masterpieces in such positions. Just some examples: he beat Kotov in 1939 in the last round of the Soviet championship to join his opponent in first place; his win against Gligoric in Palma de Mallorca in 1967; and his win against Matulovic at the 1970 Soviet Union-Rest of the World match in the Pirc Defence.

28.♕f2

Stepping on this diagonal contains risks. 28.♗g4 a5 would be equal. It would be interesting to know whether after 28.♔h1 the players would have settled for perpetual check or kept on fighting:

a) 28...♕g3 29.♗g4 ♗d6 30.♕e8+ ♔c7 31.♕f7+ and White keeps checking.

b) 28...♖xg2 29.♔xg2 ♕g3+ 30.♔h1 ♕xh3+ and here Black would give the checks.

c) 28...♖d2 29.♖d1 (29.♗f1 would result in a balanced position) 29...♖xe2 30.♕e8+ ♕c8 31.♕xe7 ♖gxg2 leads to another perpetual check.

28...♖d2 29.♖d1

29.♕e3 ♖xa2 30.♗g4 would keep the balance.

29...♖xa2

The rook wins a pawn and in addition it remains active.

30.♖a1?

Keeping the queen on the same diagonal as the king is dangerous. White's position would be perfectly playable after 30.♕f3! ♖f5 31.♕d3, after 30...♖g3 31.♕e4 and after 30...♖e5 31.♗f1.

30...♖xa1 31.♖xa1

31...a5!!

Petrosian wins a pawn and his bishop gets a few available squares. This probably came as a cold shower to Botvinnik, who was probably already short of time. It is always very dangerous if the opponent starts attacking in an opposite-coloured bishops middlegame.

32.♔h1

This is the only move.

32...♗xb4 33.♖d1??

Botvinnik wants to be active and doesn't find the second only move in a row: 33.♕xh4! The queen is more active on h4, and the rook doesn't lose sight of the a-pawn. 33...♕e5. The double attack is not lethal. 34.♖d1! (34.♖a2 ♗d6 wins) 34...♖xg2!?. This sacrifice gives Black excellent winning chances, but 34...♖g7 and 34...♔c7 would also give him a slight edge. 35.♕d8+ ♔a7 36.♔xg2 ♕xe2+ and White would struggle with his

exposed king, though it is hard to tell whether Black would win.

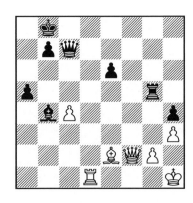

33...♕g3!

Exchanging queens now wins, as White, unlike if he had taken on h4, has no passed pawn.

34.♕xg3+ ♖xg3

34...hxg3 would win as well.

35.♗f3

After 35.♖a1 ♖e3 36.♗f3 ♗d6 37.♔g1 ♗g3 38.♔f1 a4 Black wins.

35...♔c7

35...a4 36.♖d7 ♖xf3 37.gxf3 a3 38.♖d1 ♗c3 would also win.

36.♔g1

After 36.♖a1 b6 37.♔g1 ♔d6 Black would win.

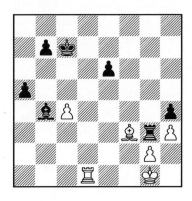

36...a4

The passed pawn is too strong for the world champion.

37.♖b1 ♗c5+ 38.♔f1 b6 39.♔e2 a3 40.♔d3 ♖g5 41.♖e1 ♔d6 42.♗e4

42...♖e5!

The rook pins the bishop. Black has two passed pawns, therefore, White can't exchange rooks.

43.♖e2 ♔e7!

Improving the king is decisive. It would be interesting to learn whether the players knew here that they had passed time control. It is also possible that they adjourned the game somewhere here.

44.♖a2 ♔f6 45.♖a1 ♔g5 46.♖f1 ♗d6 0–1 Botvinnik resigns, as the rook is about to move behind the pawn on a5 to push the pawn. With 47.♖f2 ♖a5 48.♖a2 ♗e5 Black would trap the rook on a2 with the bishop and win effortlessly.

This was his first win over the reigning world champion, Botvinnik. Doing it in a training game is a bit less sweet than at a normal event, but it still must have brought immense pleasure. Such a win delivers self-confidence and motivation to repeat the feat at an ordinary event.

In round two, he was Black against Kotov, in the London System versus g6 and ♗g7. Kotov made a careless move and Petrosian refuted it. Black obtained a passed pawn on b2 and a winning position. Kotov fought on, but he never had a chance of surviving. The game can be seen in the It's Your Move chapter. In his next game in the database he was White against Botvinnik. (Perhaps the second set of games against the same opponents was held in Voronovo, a town close to Moscow.) Petrosian played the Exchange Slav and he again gave up a bishop for a knight. Botvinnik was able to open up the position in his favour, then when he gave a check, Petrosian moved his king in the wrong direction and ended up with a lost position. Botvinnik never let him back into the game. In the fourth round, he was White against Keres (the only player whom he played only once at this event). Keres took on an isolated pawn in the Tarrasch Defence. The Estonian sacrificed a pawn to get rid of the isolani. Petrosian was close to winning with a distant passed pawn, maybe he was even winning, but Keres was able consolidate the position by swapping the passed pawn for an f-pawn and he held. In the Kotov return game,

Petrosian played 3.c3 4.♘f6 ♗d3 against the Sicilian. In a seemingly calm position Kotov made a very interesting piece sacrifice. Soon after, the Russian grandmaster made a subtle silent move that trapped Petrosian's queen. Had Tigran played well, he would have got quite a lot of material for the queen and would have stayed in the game, but he blundered and, as he got only two pieces for the queen, he had to resign at once. As White against Smyslov, he played the Exchange Slav. They repeated the opening of their game from the 1951 Soviet championship. Petrosian deviated and offered a move repetition, but Smyslov played on. At one point, Petrosian made a serious mistake, but Smyslov failed to find the refutation, and after that Petrosian was able to hold. In the rematch against Smyslov, Petrosian as Black played the King's Indian. He accepted a passive knight on a6 in return for exchanging the e2-bishop with his other knight. Smyslov obtained an edge on the queenside, while Petrosian's play on the other side remained modest. Petrosian got into serious trouble, but Smyslov let him back in. Instead of an almost equalising move, Petrosian made a pretty one, but that had a hole in it and Smyslov made a pretty move in return that was so strong it forced resignation.

Petrosian's 2 wins, 2 draws and 3 losses were a reasonable result against such strong opposition: Botvinnik, Keres and Smyslov were among the very best in the world at the time and Kotov was strong as well. Scoring two wins against these players showed his playing strength.

In 1952, the Soviet Union participated in the Chess Olympiad for the first time. Maybe Botvinnik's modest result at the Maroczy memorial and at the training event made the Soviet Federation come up with a surprising decision: they lined up without him. Their team was so strong that they didn't need Petrosian either. Perhaps Tigran was disappointed, but he surely knew that his time would come. Indeed, the Soviet team won the event with 21 points in the final; Argentina was second with 19.5 and Yugoslavia third with 19.

Marriage to Rona

In the early fifties, Petrosian once travelled on a train and met a young and charming lady called Rona Yakovlevna Avinezer. Afterwards, they started to date. Petrosian and Rona often went to chess events together. They say that Geller and Furman were not indifferent to her, either. Gossip was that she said she would see how Petrosian and Geller would perform at the interzonal... But she denied the story.

According to Averbakh, Rona liked both Tigran and Furman and asked a well-known player who was more talented at chess. Tigran was the answer. This helped her to make a decision and they got married in 1952. In fact, there are also other versions of this story.

Lilienthal and Averbakh were present at the wedding. According to Averbakh, they were a happy couple, never regretting marrying each other.

Some sources say that by the time of the upcoming interzonal tournament they were already officially a couple. She was an English teacher and interpreter. Rona was born in 1923 and had a son, Mikhail, from her first marriage. Rona's first son adopted the surname Petrosian.

Rona helped Tigran a lot, and virtually became his manager. Unlike Tal's first wife Sally Landau, who became her close friend, her husband's career was her priority.[1] Her contribution to Petrosian's performance was highly beneficial and the results speak for themselves. She passed away in 2005.

Interzonal Tournament, Saltsjobaden/Stockholm

The interzonal tournament was held in two places in Sweden. Of the 21 rounds, 14 were held in Saltsjobaden (18 kilometres from the Swedish capital) and 7 in Stockholm. According to Vasiliev, Petrosian was not thinking about winning the event or finishing second, he just wanted to qualify.

One gets the impression that Petrosian adopted this approach based on the earlier events of the year. He just wanted to play safe and achieve the goal with as few losses as possible.

In the Exchange Queen's Gambit in round 1 he beautifully outplayed Vaitonis strategically and finished the game with a neat piece sacrifice. (See the key moments in the notes to the 1950 Sidorov game.) By the way, Tigran's last win in a world championship cycle would come against Bouaziz 30 years later, in 1982. It was an exceptional accomplishment to keep up this level for so long. In round 2, Petrosian was Black against Gligoric, who lost to Stahlberg in round 1. They both played cautiously in the Tarrasch French and they agreed to a draw after Black's 14th move. In round 3, he was White against Prins, who cleverly chose the Semi-Tarrasch; they reached a Queen's Gambit type of middlegame. Petrosian tried to create some initiative, sacrificed a pawn, then his opponent gave the pawn back and got some advantage, so it

---

[3] Sally Landau's amazing biography, *Checkmate! The Love Story of Mikhail Tal and Sally Landau*, was published by Elk and Ruby in 2019. 5* recommendation from Matthew Sadler in New In Chess magazine and shortlisted for the 2019 English Chess Federation Book of the Year prize

would have been irrational to refuse the offer. In round 4, Petrosian was Black against Unzicker; he equalised with the Bogo-Indian and after White's 19th move they agreed to a draw. In round 5, Petrosian as White played 1.♘f3 ♘f6 2.d4 b6 3.♗g5 against Golombek. He got a tiny edge and kept on playing; in the ensuing knight ending the English player had to make important decisions before time control, but after Black's 40th move he already had to resign.

In round 6, Petrosian was Black against Pilnik. Tigran got a pleasant position with an Accelerated Dragon. After some small fluctuations, when Petrosian was already short of time, his Argentinian opponent started to play quickly to take advantage of his time trouble and he missed Petrosian's winning exchange sacrifice. We join the game when Petrosian has to make his 40th move.

Game 45

**Pilnik, Hermann –
Petrosian, Tigran**
Saltsjobaden/Stockholm
Interzonal (6), 1952

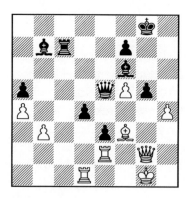

40...♗xf3!?

Petrosian was probably in time trouble, and that could be the reason for finding the second best move. After 40...d3! 41.♗xb7 dxe2 42.♕xe2 ♖xb7 White would be hopelessly lost, a piece down.

41.♕xf3 ♕f4?

Because of his lack of time, Petrosian had not recorded the

preceding 15 moves and was not certain that they had reached time control. So now he makes an additional move to be safe. However, he squanders the win for the last time in this game. Grabbing the pawn with 41...gxh4! would win, as Black simply would have too many pawns for the exchange. 42.♕a8+ ♔h7 43.♖g2 ♔h6 and White would be lost.

42.♕a8+!

Black has to play accurately. This was White's sealed move, and Petrosian in his room realised to his horror that what he thought to be the natural 42...♔g7? is very bad. 43.hxg5 ♕g4+ (43...♗xg5 44.♖f1 d3 45.♖xf4 dxe2 46.f6+! and White wins with this neat intermediate move) 44.♕g2 ♕xg5 (after 44...♕xg2+ 45.♔xg2 ♗e5 46.♔f3 White would win) 45.♕xg5+ ♗xg5 46.♖xd4 and White has excellent winning chances.

42...♔h7 43.hxg5

If 43.♖f1 d3 44.♖xf4 dxe2 45.♖f1

exf1=♕+ 46.♔xf1 the game would end in a draw.

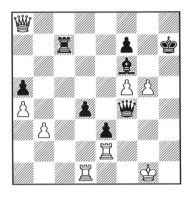

43...♖c2!!

A magical move. The rook is placed en prise, when the black bishop is also hanging. Black wants the e2-rook to move so he can win the d1-rook. Black has no other move, for example after 43...♗xg5? 44.♖f1 d3 45.♖h2+ ♕xh2+ 46.♔xh2 e2 (46...d2 47.f6) 47.♖h1 White would win. It is worth citing him from *Reliability Strategy* regarding this spectacular move. "Everybody who came to see me listened with a sceptical smile, as I complained about this disaster. No one wanted to believe that such a sharp change in the position – from clearly won to critical – could have occurred without blunders. Salo Flohr showed up. He lectured me just like everybody else, but when we got down to analysis, he too failed to find an adequate defence for Black. After complaining a little more, he was about to leave, making the remark as he did so that such a

position could not possibly be lost. Then he seemed to accidently move a piece. After the door closed behind Solomon Mikhailovich I noticed that my rook was now en prise, and – like a sudden revelation – we had found the draw! To this day I am still unsure whether Flohr realised how strong ...♖c7-c2 was or whether he moved the piece by accident."

44.♕h1+

Pilnik was surprised by Black's fantastic resource and he naturally settled for a draw.

44...♔g8 45.♕a8+ ♔h7 1/2 A sad draw from Petrosian's point of view.

In the next round as White, he agreed a quick draw with Averbakh, which they may have arranged in advance. In round 8, Petrosian was Black against Wade. White played awkwardly against the Najdorf by developing his bishops to g2 and b2. Petrosian took control, and they reached an endgame. Petrosian was a pawn up. A bit before time control Tigran made a careless move, and Wade should have played a move which possibly drew. Wade missed it and went on to lose. In round 9, Petrosian was White against Pachman, who played the Ragozin. Tigran played some innocent moves. Pachman had a bad day, failing to develop the b8-knight and a8-rook. Petrosian sacrificed a piece and won easily. In round 10, Petrosian was Black against Matulovic. The Yugoslav grandmaster gained no advantage in the two knights line against the Caro-Kann. After the opening, they swapped queens. Soon after, Petrosian obtained an edge, but Matulovic was able to withstand Tigran's pressure. The peace treaty was agreed on move 42. Petrosian had performed well in the first half. He was joint-second with Stahlberg with 7 points, trailing the inspired Kotov by 1.5 points. Geller and Taimanov had 6.5.

In the next round, Petrosian was White versus Sanchez. Tigran chose a side-line against the Semi-Tarrasch, but he was unable to exert any pressure, and Black offered a draw on move 23. Petrosian had no chance to win. His opponent did not understand Tigran, but after a little conferment the draw was sealed. This was a disappointing game for him. Once in a conversation, before the idea of a Petrosian book was a reality, I asked grandmaster Ribli about Petrosian. He said that he was a kind and well educated person, but had just one awkward thing about him – he did not speak any Western language. He had many interests, including music and football, but languages were not among them.

In the 12th round, Stahlberg played the opening with the intention to draw, and when on move 12 he offered to share the point, Petrosian accepted.

Petrosian's next opponent was Barcza. We look at that game.

Game 46

Petrosian, Tigran – Barcza, Gedeon
Saltsjobaden/Stockholm
Interzonal (13), 1952
King's Indian Attack

1.e4 c5 2.♘f3 ♘c6 3.d3
This move works well in this game, but a young player should play like this only rarely. Playing like this in the opening isn't the best way to improve.
3...e6 4.♘bd2 d5 5.g3 ♘f6 6.♗g2 ♗e7 7.0-0 0-0 8.♖e1 b6

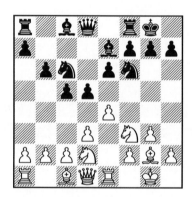

9.e5!
According to the database, this move was first played in a game between these players earlier that year. White will score well with this move introduced by Tigran.
9...♘e8?!
Barcza deviates from the previous game, but this move is not better.

A few months earlier in Budapest these players had reached the same position, via a different move order with 1.♘f3. Black continued 9...♘d7 and Petrosian suggests this move, but one should pay little attention to what an active professional says about an opening, as he doesn't want to help his rivals. 10.♘f1 ♗a6 11.h4 ♕e8 12.♗h3 ♗d8 13.♗f4 ♗c7 14.♘1h2 ♘d8?! 15.♕d2 d4 16.♗g2 ♗b7 17.♖e2 ♘c6 18.♖ae1 b5 19.c3 dxc3 20.bxc3 b4 21.cxb4 ♘xb4 22.♘g4 ♘d5 23.♗g5 ♔h8 24.♘fh2 ♖b8 25.h5 f6? 26.exf6 gxf6

27.♖xe6 winning.

10.♘f1 ♔h8?

This move is pointless, and it wastes time.

11.♗f4 f5

After 11...f6 12.♕d2 ♕d7 13.c3 fxe5 14.♘xe5 ♘xe5 15.♗xe5 ♘d6 White would be a little better.

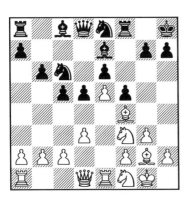

12.h4!

Petrosian stops g5 and secures the f4–outpost for himself.

12...♘c7 13.♘1d2 ♗b7

Petrosian mentions that after 13...d4? White could plant a knight on d6. He shows its tactical justification: 14.♘c4 ♘d5 15.♗g5 b5? 16.♘d6 ♘xe5? 17.♘xe5 ♕xd6 18.♗xd5 followed by 19.♗xe7 would win.

14.c3 b5?!

Barcza's idea weakens the c5 pawn a bit. Ragozin prefers 14...d4, but maybe Black should gain space with 14...a5!?.

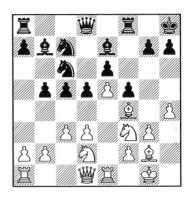

15.♘b3!

Petrosian plays very deeply; he spots that the c5 pawn is vulnerable.

15...a5 16.♗g5!

If 16.a4 Black would play 16...b4.

16...♘a6 17.d4! c4

Barcza keeps the position closed. Petrosian mentions 17...cxd4 18.cxd4 and he evaluates it as better for White. The b3-knight would be transferred to the f4 outpost. Ragozin suggests the weaker 17...

h6, but after 18.♗xe7 ♕xe7 19.h5 White's advantage would be fairly big.

18.♘c1 ♘c7

18...b4!? looks more resilient.

19.♘e2!

The knight is getting closer to its ideal square.

19...♔g8

Maybe 19...b4 20.♘f4 ♕e8 is slightly better than in the game.

20.♘f4 ♕e8

Maybe 20...b4 or 20...♖b8 are preferable.

21.♗xe7 ♕xe7 22.♘g5!

Petrosian gets closer to Black's camp; the position is very close, yet a bit surprisingly the move already creates a threat.

22...g6?

Barcza misses Petrosian's threat. However, his move would be bad even without it, as it gives White a chance to bite at Black's pawn chain on the kingside. 22...a4 would resist better.

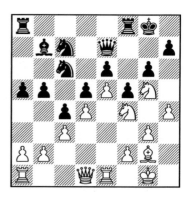

23.a4!!

After just moving his knight on the kingside he most imaginatively continues with a pawn move on the a-file. This breaks up Black's strong-looking pawn chain in the centre.

23...♗a6?

The Hungarian grandmaster eases Petrosian's task, but he is lost anyway.

a) 23...♘d8. Just holding the centre doesn't work. 24.axb5 ♘xb5 25.b3!? (after 25.♘gxe6! ♘xe6 26.♘xd5 ♕f7 27.♕a4 White would win) 25...♘xc3 26.♕c2 and Black's position falls apart.

b) 23...b4. This is relatively best, but not good enough.

b1) 24.♘fxe6 ♘xe6 25.♗xd5 ♘cd8 26.♗xc4 ♔g7 27.d5 (27. ♘xe6+? ♘xe6 28.d5 f4 is bad for White) 27...♘xg5 28.hxg5 ♕c5 29.b3 when the position would be unclear.

b2) 24.b3! White undermines Black's centre. If 24...bxc3 (after 24...cxb3 25.♕xb3 ♖ad8 26.♖ec1 Black is unlikely to keep the position together) 25.bxc4 dxc4 (after 25...

②b4 26.罝c1 c2 27.罝xc2 ②xc2 28.豐xc2 White would dominate regardless of the exchange deficit) 26.d5 (26.豐c1! wins in a simpler way as the queen can take on c3 on the next move) 26...c2 27.豐xc2 ②b4 28.d6 ②xc2 29.dxe7 罝fb8 30.皇xb7 罝xb7 31.罝ed1! wins.

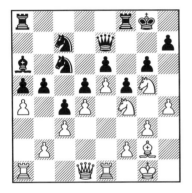

24.②fxe6!

This sacrifice, which was featured in Sakkelet, wins. Actually, White loses no material, as he wins it back quickly by force.

24...②xe6 25.皇xd5 罝ad8

25...②cd8 26.皇xa8 wins.

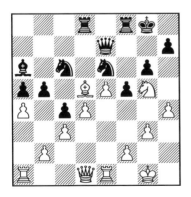

26.皇xe6+

Black has lost two pawns for nothing; in addition, the connected central passed pawns are irresistible. Black would risk nothing by resigning.

26...❀g7 27.axb5 皇xb5 28.d5 f4 29.豐g4 h6 30.②h3 1–0

This game illustrates Petrosian's playing level in 1952. He had already obtained tremendous strength, but did not yet have a world class white repertoire.

In round 14, Petrosian was White against Geller. They played the King's Indian, but neither played for a win and they drew after just 20 moves. In round 15, Petrosian had a big game against Szabo, the strong Hungarian grandmaster who stood on plus three. They both wanted to battle it out. Petrosian as Black chose the Najdorf. In a roughly even position, Szabo somewhat naively allowed an exchange sacrifice on c3. In the ensuing complex position they each made what were at the very least inaccuracies. Petrosian was worse most of the time. According to Sakkelet, Petrosian offered a draw with little time left on the clock, Petrosian doesn't mention it in his analysis, though, and the Hungarian number one player refused it. However, Szabo chose an unfortunate moment to simplify to an ending by exchanging queens. By time control, Black had too many pawns for the exchange. They probably adjourned the game, and Petrosian won on the 47th move. In the next three rounds, Petrosian made three quick draws against Kotov, Taimanov and Steiner. The first two were probably agreed in advance. The longest of these three games lasted 19 moves.

With three rounds to go, Kotov was leading on 14.5 points and had virtually won the event. Petrosian had 12, but only two games left to play (due to the system of byes). Taimanov and Geller had 11.5, Averbakh and Szabo 10.5, and Stahlberg 10.5 with only two games to play. Gligoric had 10 points.

Petrosian was Black against Eliskases in round 19. The King's Indian promised a fight, but the players treated the position cautiously and Petrosian offered a draw after his 24th move. With two rounds to go, things looked bright for him, as he was due to play against two players from the bottom. In the penultimate round, he was White against Stoltz, who scored almost no points against the top players, but scored well versus the bottom players. It was a Queen's Gambit Exchange, and Stoltz made a big strategic mistake in the opening by giving up the e5-square. He sacrificed a pawn in a lost position, but did not cause Petrosian any

problems. Our hero beat him neatly (see the key moments in the notes to the 1950 Sidorov game). In the last round, Tigran probably had a bye.

Petrosian finished joint-second with Taimanov, scoring 13.5 points out of 20 games. He won 7 and drew 13 with no defeat. Kotov won the event with an amazing 16.5 points, while Geller finished 4th with 13. Averbakh, Stahlberg, Szabo and Gligoric also qualified for the Candidates Tournament, scoring 12.5 points. At the closing ceremony, FIDE president Folke Rogard announced that with their results at the interzonal tournament, Petrosian, Taimanov and Averbakh had obtained the title of grandmaster.

The Soviet Chess Federation offered Petrosian the choice between participating in the Soviet championship or the following year's Bucharest tournament; he opted for the latter.

By the end of 1952, Petrosian with his silver medals at the Soviet championship and the interzonal, having beating almost all Soviet stars, including Botvinnik, Smyslov and Keres, was now a regular world class player.

Petrosian's results in 1952

Maroczy Memorial, Budapest	+ 6 = 7 − 4 9.5/17 7th-8th place
Training Team Event, Gagra/Voronovo	+ 2 = 2 − 3 3/7
Saltsjobaden/Stockholm Interzonal	+ 7 = 13 − 0 13.5/20 2nd-3rd place
Altogether	**+ 15 = 22 − 7 26/44**

1953

Bucharest

Petrosian had the chance to participate in a strong event in the Romanian capital in January and February. Lilienthal, his trainer, joined the delegation.

He started the event as Black against Barda. Tigran equalised in the King's Indian against the g3 line. One careless move would have allowed Barda to gain an edge with a nice pawn sacrifice. However, he missed it and soon after offered a draw. The position was even, but with Petrosian's strength he could have played on. In round 2, Petrosian after 1.d4 ♘f6 2.♘f3 b6 played 3.♘c3 against Golombek. They soon reached an awkward position where both sides had double e-pawns. Petrosian sacrificed his front e-pawn to create triple pawns in Black's camp. They played on, and Golombek's mistakes allowed Tigran to reach a winning endgame. It looked like Petrosian had given him some chances to escape, but he eventually won the game. In round 3, Szabo as White played the g3 line against the King's Indian. Tigran gave up the bishop pair for some pressure on the centre. He was slightly worse, but gradually equalised and they agreed to a draw after Black's 24th move. In round 4, Petrosian agreed a quick, probably prearranged draw against the young sensation Spassky. It would be interesting to know why, as he should have played for a win. In the next round, he was Black against Smyslov. They played a peaceful Queen's Gambit and agreed to a draw on move 20. In round 6, Petrosian as White employed the Saemisch Variation against the King's Indian. Petrosian's aggressive handling worked well and he had a clear edge. However, a careless move allowed Black to free his position and they sealed the draw after White's 32nd move. In the next round, Milev failed to develop his b1-knight in a Benoni and Petrosian quickly obtained an edge. He was already winning out of the opening and went on to take the full point. In round 8, Petrosian was Black against Tolush; it was an Accelerated Dragon, and not much happened in the 17-move draw. In the 9th round, he was White against Radulescu. He carried out his pet idea of castling long in the Queen's Gambit Exchange. Radulescu lost a pawn at the end of the opening. However, Petrosian unnecessarily sacrificed a pawn, and had Radulescu taken it White's advantage would have been only slight. According to the database, Petrosian gave away a pawn for nothing, but I suspect that somebody was short of time and they made mistakes when entering the game (Shekhtman shows the same move order). Petrosian won the game soon after time control.

In the 10th round, Petrosian gained a pleasant position against Troianescu's King's Indian Attack, then made a losing blunder, but it was not exploited. We join this famous game a little after the missed opportunity.

Game 47

Troianescu, Octavio – Petrosian, Tigran
Bucharest (10), 1953

25...♖xe4! 26.♗xe4 ♗xe4

Petrosian obtained a somewhat better position with this pretty exchange sacrifice and went on to win. However, this game is already well known and we prefer to analyse lesser known games in detail, such as the following from round 12.

In the 11th round, Petrosian tried the King's Indian attack against Sajtar's Sicilian, but he obtained no advantage. He sacrificed an exchange in the middlegame, and the game soon ended in perpetual check.

Game 48

Stoltz, Gosta – Petrosian, Tigran
Bucharest (12), 1953

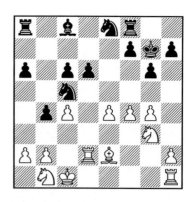

19...a5!?

An interesting idea. Black wants to push back his opponent on the queenside.

20.♗d1 ♖a7

Petrosian improves his rook in an imaginative manner. 20...♘f6 would lead to a reduced number of pawns. 21.♖xd6 ♘cxe4 22.♘xe4 ♘xe4 23.♖xc6 ♘f2 24.♖g1 ♘d3+ 25.♔c2 ♘xf4 26.♖d6 and Black would be somewhat better.

21.h3

21.f5 ♖e7 would give Black a slight advantage.

21...♖e7 22.♗c2 a4 23.b3

Stoltz stops the possibility of pushing him back further.

23...axb3 24.axb3

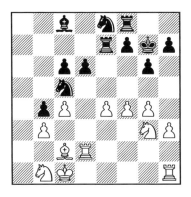

24...f5!

Petrosian finds a beautiful idea to soften White's pawn chain. White covers the f5 square four times, yet Petrosian still carries out the pawn push.

25.gxf5

After 25.exf5 ♖e3 26.♖g1 ♘xb3+ 27.♗xb3 ♖xb3 Black would be somewhat better.

25...gxf5 26.♖g2

After 26.exf5 ♖e3 27.♖g1 ♘xb3+ White is suffering.

26...fxe4   27.♘xe4+   ♔h8 28.♘xc5

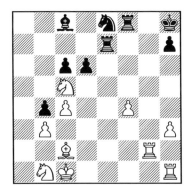

28...dxc5

Black has an interesting pawn chain on the queenside.

29.♖g5 ♖xf4 30.♖hg1?!

This move makes it harder to get at the c5–pawn. Further, as the game continues this move is a pawn sacrifice. White could weaken the choking pawn chain by 30.♖xc5, and 30...♖f2 should lead to a draw.

30...♖g7 31.♘d2 ♗xh3 32.♗xh7

Stoltz reduces the number of pawns. After 32.♘e4 ♗f5 33.♘xc5 ♗xc2 34.♔xc2 White would get away with the pawn deficit.

32...♖xg5   33.♖xg5   ♔xh7 34.♖h5+ ♔g6

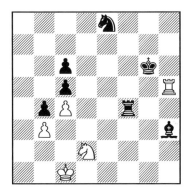

35.♖xh3

The dust has settled. Black is a pawn up and White has been pushed back, but Black has no passed pawn and it is hard to touch White's root pawn on b3.

35...♘d6 36.♖e3

White bases his defence on cutting off Black's king along the e-file. 36.♘f3!? transferring the knight to d3 to keep an eye on the c5–pawn was good enough to hold. 36...

♖e4 (36...♔f5 37.♘e1 ♘e4 38.♘d3 and White is safe) 37.♔d2 ♖e8 38.♘e1 ♘e4+ 39.♔e2 ♔f5 40.♖e3 ♔e5 (40...♖a8 41.♘d3) 41.♖f3 ♖a8 42.♔e3 and White probably holds.

36...♔f6 37.♖f3

If 37.♘f3? ♘f5 38.♖d3 ♘d4 Black wins. But 37.♖e2!?, continuing to cut the king off, looks simpler. 37...♖h4 38.♔c2 ♔f5 (38...♖h3 39.♘e4+ exchanging knights makes it easy for White to hold) 39.♘f3 ♖h3 (39...♖h8 40.♘e1) 40.♘e5 and White holds.

37...♔e5

37...♖xf3 38.♘xf3 ♘f5 39.♘e1 ♔e5 40.♘d3+ ♔d4 41.♔d2=

38.♖e3+

38.♖xf4 ♔xf4 wins, mainly because the white knight is passive. It is remarkable how exchanging rooks sometimes wins and sometimes doesn't.

38...♔f6

Petrosian retreats rather than sacrifice a pawn. 38...♔d4 would force White to defend precisely: 39.♖e6 ♘f5 40.♖xc6 ♖g4 41.♖f6!

♘e3 42.♘f3+ ♔c3 43.♖e6! ♘g2 44.♖e2 ♖g3 (44...♔xb3 45.♔b1 ♖g3 46.♘d2+=) 45.♘d2 ♔d3 46.♖e7 (if 46.♘f1? White loses after 46...♔xe2 47.♘xg3+ ♔d3) 46...♖e3 47.♖xe3+ ♔xe3 48.♔c2 ♘e1+ 49.♔d1 ♘f3 50.♘xf3 ♔xf3 51.♔d2 and White gets away with it.

39.♖f3 ♔f5

39...♖xf3 40.♘xf3 ♔f5 41.♔d2 ♔f4 42.♘e1 ♔e4 43.♘d3 ♔d4 44.♘f2 ♘f5 looks ugly, but it is a draw.

40.♖h3

Now White can't exchange. 40.♖xf4+? ♔xf4 41.♘f1 (41.♔c2 ♘f5 42.♔d3 ♘g3 43.♘b1 [or 43.♔c2] 43...♔f3 44.♘d2+ ♔f2 45.♘b1 ♔e1 46.♘d2 ♔d1 47.♘f3 ♘e2 48.♘e5 [48.♘d2 ♘c1+ 49.♔e3 ♔c2–+] 48...♘c1+ 49.♔e3 ♘xb3 50.♘xc6 ♘c1 wins) 41...♘f5 42.♘d2

42...♘g3! The key square for the knight. 43.♔d1 ♔e3 44.♘e1 ♔d4 45.♔d1 ♔d3 46.♘b1 ♘e4 47.♔c1 ♔e3 48.♔c2 ♔e2 49.♔b2 ♘d2. Black swaps the knight and wins.

40...♔e5 41.♔c2?

A mistake as it gives up control over the e-file.

a) 41.♘f3+! improving the knight is good enough to hold. 41...♔e4 (41...♔f5 42.♘e1 and White would be safe) 42.♘d2+ ♔d4 43.♘f3+ ♔d3 44.♘g5+ ♔e2 45.♖h2+=.

b) 41.♖e3+ Maybe he did not repeat the position, as he was worried about 41...♔d4, but we saw that the frightening move would not be enough.

41...♘f5! 42.♔d3?

The game was probably beyond salvation after this move. Instead:

a) 42.♖h5? ♔d4 43.♖h3 ♘e3+ (43...♖g4 44.♘f3+ ♔e4 45.♘d2+ ♔e5 46.♘f3+ ♔f4 47.♘d2 ♖g2–+) 44.♔c1 ♔d3 45.♘f3 ♖f5 and Black wins.

b) 42.♖h8!? White activates the rook. We do not see a forced win for Black. 42...♘d4+ 43.♔d3 ♖g4 44.♘e4 ♘xb3 45.♖h5+ ♔f4 46.♖h1! (46.♘xc5 ♖g3+ 47.♔c2 ♖g4 48.♖e5 ♖c3+ 49.♔b2 ♘d2 and Black wins) 46...♖g8 47.♖h4+! gives White drawing chances if the rooks get swapped despite the two-pawn deficit.

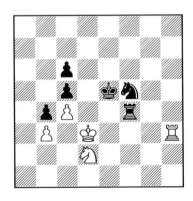

42...♖g4!!

The rook move sets up a zugzwang to place the black rook on the h-file.

43.♖f3 ♖d4+!

A subtle check; it forces White to choose a flank for the king.

a) 43...♖g3? 44.♖xg3 ♘xg3 45.♘f3+! White must free the knight. 45...♔f4 46.♘h4 and White holds, but not giving the check on the 45th move would be bad: 45.♔c2? loses, though it takes a lot of time and a lot of skill to win it with Black. Moves with an exclamation mark in the following line indicate they are the only moves to win, and this line includes the longest way for White to resist: 45...♘f5 46.♔d3 ♘d4 47.♔e3 ♔f5 48.♘e4! ♘xb3 49.♘d6+ ♔e5 50.♘f7+ ♔f6 51.♘d6 ♘a5 52.♘e4+ ♔e5 53.♘d2 ♔f5 54.♔e2 ♔f4 55.♔d3 ♘b7 56.♘e4 b3 57.♘c3 b2! 58.♔c2 ♔e3 59.♘d1+ ♔d4 60.♘xb2 ♘a5 61.♘d3

61...♘xc4! The two c-pawns provide a win only because White's pieces stand awkwardly (61...♔xc4? 62.♘e5+ ♔d5 63.♘d3=) 62.♘f4 ♘e3+ 63.♔d2 ♘d5 64.♘e6+ ♔c4 65.♔c1 ♘e7 66.♔c2 ♘g6 67.♔d1 ♘e5 68.♔c2 ♔b4 69.♘f4 c4 70.♘e2

♘f3!! (70...c5?=) 71.♘c3 ♘e1+
72.♔b2 ♘d3+ 73.♔c2 ♘f4 74.♘a2+
♔b5 75.♘c3+ ♔c5 76.♘e4+ ♔b4
77.♘c3 ♘d5 78.♘a2+ ♔a3 79.♘c1
c5 80.♘e2 ♔b4! 81.♘g3 ♘c3
82.♘f1 ♘b5 83.♘d2 ♘d4+ 84.♔d1
c3 85.♘e4 ♔c4 86.♔c1 ♘c6 87.♘g5
♘b4 88.♘e6 ♘d3+ 89.♔c2 ♘e1+
90.♔c1 ♔b4 91.♔b1 ♘d3 92.♔c2
♔c4 93.♔b1 ♔b3 94.♔a1 ♔c2–+

b) 43...♖g2 44.♖h3 ♖g7! Black
should still send his rook to the
d-file (44...♖g3+ 45.♖xg3 ♘xg3
46.♘f3+=) 45.♔c2 ♘d4+ 46.♔d3
♖d7 47.♔e3 ♘f5+ 48.♔e2 ♖d8
49.♘f3+ ♔f4 50.♘d2 ♘d4+ 51.♔f2
♖e8 and Black wins.

44.♔e2

With 44.♔c2 one can see why
setting up a zugzwang was important.
44...♖h4! 45.♖d3 (after 45.♔d3 ♖h2
46.♖f1 ♖h3+ White loses the rook)
45...♖h2 46.♔c1 (if 46.♖d8 ♘d4+
47.♔c1 ♖h3 48.♔b2 ♖d3 White
would be lost) 46...♖h1+ 47.♔b2
♘d4 48.♖e3+ ♔f5 49.♖e8 ♖h2
50.♔c1 ♖h3 and Black's position is
about to fall apart.

44...♖d8

45.♖h3

Maybe Stoltz should release the
cut-off of the king with 45.♖d3!?,
as the win for Black requires very
long and precise play. We illustrated
the win in the comment on move 43.
Here it would be 45...♖xd3 46.♔xd3
♘d4 47.♔e3 ♔f5 48.♘e4 ♘xb3–+

**45...♘d4+   46.♔e3   ♘f5+
47.♔e2 ♔f4**

The king steps aside to open the
file for the rook.

48.♖f3+ ♔g4

49.♖d3

Not ceding the f-file with 49.♖f2
would cause Black more difficulty.
49...♖e8+ 50.♔d1 ♘d4 51.♔c1
(51.♖f6 ♖e3 52.♖h6 [52.♖d6 ♖d3]
52...♔g5 53.♖d6 ♖d3 wins) 51...
♖e3 52.♔b2 ♖e5 53.♖f6 [53.♔a2
♔g3] 53...♖e2 54.♔c1 ♔g5 and
remarkably the black king will take
away some squares from the rook.
55.♖f8 ♔g6 56.♖f1 ♔g7 57.♖f4
♖g2 58.♖f1 ♖h2 and White is in
zugzwang; it is instructive how
the black pieces took away all the
squares from the rook on the f-file.

49...♘d4+

Exchanging the rook would throw the win away: 49...♖xd3? 50.♔xd3 ♘d4 (50...♔f4 51.♘e4=) 51.♔e4=.

50.♔f2 ♖f8+ 51.♔e1 ♖e8+ 52.♔f2

52...♔f4

The king move sets up a zugzwang.

53.♔f1

If 53.♘f3 ♖e2+ 54.♔f1, then 54... ♖e3 would win instantly.

53...♖e3

The exchange grants easy access to win the second pawn.

54.♖xe3 ♔xe3 55.♔e1 ♔d3 0–1

A very nice and effective squeeze.

In the 13th round, Petrosian was White against Stefan Szabo. He gained no advantage in the Exchange Slav, they exchanged a lot of pieces, and agreed to a draw on move 28. In the 14th round, Petrosian was Black against Barcza and they played out an 18-move draw. In round 15, Petrosian was White against the local player Reicher. Black equalised in a reverse main-line Sicilian. Play was equal

for a long time, but Black gradually fell apart from around move 30. By time control, Petrosian was two pawns up and went on to win. In round 16, Sliwa as White played the Saemisch against the King's Indian. They castled on opposite sides, and a sharp game was more or less balanced all the way. They agreed to a draw soon after time trouble.

Game 49

Petrosian, Tigran – Filip, Miroslav
Bucharest (17), 1953

23.♕xb6 ♕e4

Black is obviously worse, but has excellent chances to demolish the c4 pawn and obtain a theoretically drawn position. Going after c4 with the queen is not the most accurate move, as Black will have to defend the c5–pawn.

a) 23...♖fb8 24.♕c6 ♖c8 25.♕d5 ♕xd5 and Black may hold.

b) 23...♖a4! Going after the c4–pawn at once with the rook should be enough to hold. White has to play well to keep the c4–pawn. 24.♖c1 (24.♖d5 ♕c3 25.♖xc5 ♖xc4 and Black holds) 24...♖b4 25.♕a5 (25. ♕c6 ♖d8) 25...♖fb8 26.♖fd1 ♔g7 27.h3 ♖b2 and Black is easily active enough to hold.

24.♖c1

After 24.♕xc5 ♖ac8 25.♖d4 ♕xg2+ 26.♔xg2 ♖xc5 White would have chances.

24...♖fc8 25.♖fd1 ♖ab8

25...♖a4 can be tried here as well. 26.h3!? followed by ♕f6 is rather unpleasant for Black. If 26.♕f6 then 26...♖ca8 would be played. Pushing the pawn one square forces the rook to defend the c5–pawn for longer. Now the pawn is poisoned, as 26... ♖xc4?? 27.♕a6 wins a rook.

26.♕f6! ♖b4

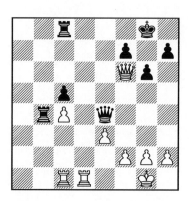

27.♕c3

Petrosian has stabilised the extra pawn advantage, but winning the game still requires a lot of work. 27.♖d7? would run into 27...♕xc4!.

27...♖cb8 28.h3 ♖b1

Black wants to stop the d1–rook from getting to the seventh rank.

After 28...♕e7 29.♖d5 or after 28... ♖b3 29.♕f6 ♖3b4 30.♖d7 Black would struggle.

29.♕f6 ♖xc1 30.♖xc1 ♖b1

Going for a queen ending is a reasonable decision, as 30...♖b4 31.♔h2 is no fun for Black either.

31.♖xb1 ♕xb1+ 32.♔h2 ♕e4 33.♕c3

After 33.♕f4 ♕xf4+ 34.exf4 f5 Black may get away with the pawn ending.

33...h5 34.f3 ♕e6

35.♕d3! ♔g7 36.f4!

Petrosian wants to bring the king closer to the centre. After 36.♔g3 ♕e5+ 37.f4 ♕a1 38.♔f3 ♕e1 Black would be safe.

36...f5

The Czech grandmaster plays actively and wants White to push his pawns.

a) 36...♔g8. Just waiting doesn't look sufficient. 37.♔g3 ♔g7 38.♔f3 ♔g8 39.♕d5 ♕e7 40.f5! ♔g7 41.e4 (41.fxg6 fxg6 42.♕e4 looks promising as well) 41...♕f6 (41... ♕c7 42.fxg6 fxg6 43.e5 and White would be about to win) 42.♕xc5 ♕c3+ 43.♔f4 ♕d2+ 44.♔e5 ♕xg2 45.f6+ (45.♔d6 ♕xe4! and Black holds) 45...♔g8 46.♕e7 and Black would not last for long.

b) 36...h4! and Black cages White's king. Continuing 37.♔g1 (37.e4 ♕f6 38.♔e3 ♔g8 and it looks hard to progress) 37...♕f6 it is rather hard to progress after 38.♕a3 ♕d6 or 38.♕d5 ♕c3.

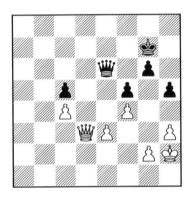

37.♔g3!

Petrosian tries to improve his king.

37...♔h7?

Filip wants his king to be less exposed to checks, but moving away from the centre prevents Black from exchanging queens.

a) 37...♔f7!? 38.♔f3 h4 39.e4 (39.♕d5?? would even lose after 39...♕xd5+ 40.cxd5 ♔e7) 39...fxe4+ 40.♕xe4 ♕f5 41.♔e3 ♔f6 and White probably has no forced win.

b) 37...♕e7! and Black can stop the king from invading on the kingside. 38.♔f3 h4 39.e4 (39.♕d5 ♕a7 40.♕d8 ♕b7+) 39...♕b7

40.♔e3 ♔h6 41.♕c2 fxe4 42.♕xe4 ♕b3+ 43.♕d3 ♕b2 and Black may hold.

38.♔f3 ♕b6?

Black wants to get closer to White's king, but his own king gets caught. This is a nice example of how dangerous it is to move the queen out of play. After 38...h4 39.e4 ♔g7 (39...♕c6? 40.♕d5!) 40.♕d5 fxe4+ 41.♕xe4 Black would struggle, but would not necessarily lose.

39.♕d7+ ♔g8 40.♕e8+ ♔g7 41.♕e7+

The queen is ideally placed on e7.

41...♔g8 42.♔g3!! 1–0

Petrosian brilliantly returns to g3 to invade with his king. Let's see why Black resigned!

a) 42...♕b4 43.♕e6+ (or 43.♔h4 ♕xc4 44.♔g5 ♕f7 45.♕xc5 and White wins.) 43...♔h7 44.♔h4 ♔h6 (44...♕e1+ 45.♔g5) 45.♕e5 ♔h7 46.♔g5 and Black's king would be caught.

b) 42...♕c6 43.e4 (or 43.♔h4 ♕xg2 44.♕xc5 and White wins as the c-pawn would be irresistible) 43...fxe4 44.♔h4 ♕c8 45.g4 and White wins.

In the last two rounds, he agreed quick draws against Boleslavsky and O'Kelly.

Petrosian finished the event second, scoring 13 points out of 19. He was undefeated, winning 7 games and drawing 13. Tolush won the event with 14 points. Among this strong field, Smyslov finished third with 12.5 points. Three players finished joint 4th-6th on 12 points: Boleslavsky, the very young Spassky and Laszlo Szabo. Petrosian lived up to the level of a world class player, and staying undefeated was an amazing achievement. However, there was one negative; he played arguably 6 draws with no real fight.

Perhaps he would not have scored more than 3 points out of those 6 games anyway, but playing them to the end could have accelerated his development, as he would have learned from them. Altogether, he performed well and showed his class.

Training Event, Gagra

In May 1953, Petrosian played in Gagra again. He started the event with special inspiration; we look at exciting fragments of the first two games.

Game 50

**Petrosian, Tigran –
Kotov, Alexander**
Training Team Tournament,
Gagra (1), 1953

31.♘xd7
An interesting exchange. The position is balanced.
31...♕xd7 32.♕c5 ♕d8
After 32...♘e4 or 32...♘c4 33.♗xc4 dxc4 34.♕xc4 ♕b7 35.♕e2 ♕e4 Black would be safe.
33.♔f1!?

Petrosian starts an original and remarkable idea. Black will still enjoy equality, however.
33...♔g7 34.♔e2 h5 35.♔d1 ♘e8
35...♘f5 is the simplest.
36.♔c2 ♘f6 37.♔b3 ♘g4
37...h4!? would be interesting.

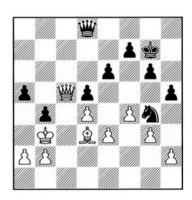

38.♔a4
The great six-move march has ended; White will soon take the a-pawn.
38...♘xh2?
After 38...♕a8 39.♕xa5 ♕c6+

40.♔b3 ♛c1 41.♕xb4 ♕xe3 42.♕c3 the position would be unclear.

39.♕xa5 ♕c8 40.♕c5 ♕a8+

After 40...♕d8 41.♕xb4 White's advantage would be smaller.

41.♔b3 ♘g4 42.♕xb4 ♕c8

If 42...♘xe3 then 43.a4 would be strong.

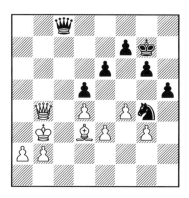

43.♕c5

Instead of going for repetition, 43.a4! or 43.♕e1! would give White a clear advantage.

43...♕b8+ 44.♕b5 ♕c7 45.♕c5 ♕b8+ 46.♕b4 ♕c7 47.♕d2?!

The position is the same as on move 43, and White could play 47.a4 or 47.Qe1 here as well

47...♕b8+ 48.♔c2

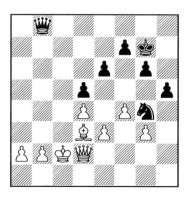

48...g5! 49.a4 h4!

Kotov obtained some counterplay and was able to hold.

Game 51

Taimanov, Mark – Petrosian, Tigran
Training Team Tournament, Gagra (2), 1953

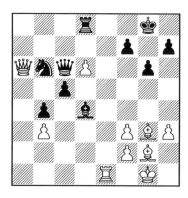

29...♖xd6

Petrosian sacrifices an exchange to get rid of the powerful passed pawn.

30.♗xd6 ♕xd6 31.♖e4??

A careless move. Taimanov doesn't realise the power of the b4–pawn. After 31.♖d1! ♔g7 Black would be slightly better.

31...♔g7?!

Petrosian misses a direct win: 31...c4! 32.bxc4 b3 33.♖e1 b2 34.♖b1 ♕f4.

32.f4?

Retreating the queen would take a great deal out of Black's coming break, but Black would still be better after 32.♕e2 ♘d5 or 32.♕a2 ♘d5.

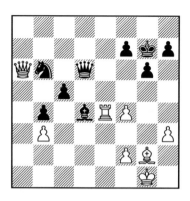

32...c4!

This break is decisive. Tigran did not spot it earlier, but doesn't miss it the second time.

33.♗f1

33.bxc4 b3 34.♖e1 ♕xf4 wins.

33...♕d5!!

This intermediate move is a killer. 33...c3? 34.♕d3 would equalise.

34.♖e5

34.♗g2 cxb3 wins.

34...♕f3! 35.♕a2 ♗xe5 36.fxe5

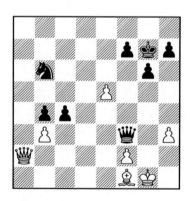

36...c3

The pawn wins the game.

37.♕a7 c2 38.♕c7 ♕c3 0–1

In round 3, Petrosian as White gained a decisive advantage against Tolush, who played the Benoni. Strangely, he missed many chances to win, and in the middlegame he unnecessarily allowed an exchange sacrifice. The position became unclear and the game ended in a draw soon after time control. In the next round, he had a bye, and then in round 5 Petrosian was White against Keres. In the reverse Schmidt Benoni, the position was more or less even. They played until the Estonian grandmaster had a wrong-coloured bishop and h-pawn ending, after which they agreed a draw. In round 6, Petrosian was Black against Geller, who played a side-line in the French. Petrosian gave up the two bishops for fluent development. Geller sacrificed a pawn. Tigran started to face difficulties after an inaccurate move, but soon after Efim Petrovich blundered and resigned on move 26. In round 7, Petrosian was White against Averbakh. He started a minority attack in a ♗g5 Grunfeld. They agreed to a draw after White's 23rd move, when there was little to play for. In the next game, Petrosian played the Sicilian with 2.♘f3 d6, and Boleslavsky tried 3.♗b5+. Petrosian sacrificed a pawn in the opening. In a queenless middlegame, he sacrificed another pawn to create tripled pawns in White's camp. His imaginative play looked like obtaining a draw, but some mistakes crept in probably with little time before time control, and Petrosian got caught in a checkmating web. In round 9, Smyslov as Black in the Grunfeld cxd5 and e4 line answered ...♘b6. Black followed up with ...a5 and ...a4, after which Petrosian quickly gained a winning advantage and did not let Vassily back into the game.

Game 52

Ragozin, Viacheslav – Petrosian, Tigran
Training Tournament,
Gagra (10), 1953

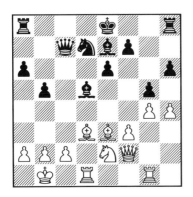

21...gxh4
Petrosian takes a pawn. Black has only one problem: his king isn't allowing his rooks to be connected. Castling would solve that, but neither side would be safe.

**22.♘c3   ♗b7   23.♗d4   ♖g8
24.♗h7**
Ragozin plays against the rook. Instead, 24.♕e2 ♕f4 would be unclear.

24...♖g5 25.f4

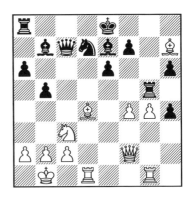

25...♖c5!?
Petrosian uses his rook imaginatively, offering to sacrifice an exchange.

26.♖ge1 ♖c4?!
After 26...b4! 27.♘e4 ♖d5 the position would be unclear.

27.♖xe6?
If 27.♗d3 ♖c6 28.f5 0-0-0 29.♘d5 White would be somewhat better.

27...fxe6 28.♗g6+

28...♔f8! Petrosian stood much better and went on to win.

Bondarevsky withdrew from the 11 player event after three games, granting two free days to his opponents after round 3; Petrosian finished with a bye in the last round. He won 4 games, drew four and lost one. Smyslov won the event with 6.5 out of 9, and in addition he beat Bondarevsky, whose games didn't count. Petrosian finished with 6 points.

Boleslavsky scored 5.5 out of 9 games, but in addition he also beat Bondarevsky. Averbakh, Kotov, Taimanov and Geller finished the event with 4.5 points out of 9 games. Keres missed the 50 percent mark by half a point, which shows the level of the event.

Neuhausen/Zurich Candidates Tournament

The tournament to determine who would challenge world champion Botvinnik, and which lasted nearly two months, started at the end of August.

Petrosian was the youngest of the 15 world class players at the event. 9 of them were from the Soviet Union: Reshevsky complained that there were too many. Petrosian was expected to fight for one of the higher places. The first 8 games were played in Neuhausen.

Petrosian started the event as White against Keres. Keres got a pleasant position in the English Opening. Petrosian stabilised his position with a pawn sacrifice, which created doubled pawns in Keres's camp, and he found a great square for his own knight. Petrosian firmly held the game and they agreed to a draw on move 41. According to Euwe in his book on the tournament, White's 41st move was the sealed one, while according to Najdorf in his book on the tournament Black sealed his 41st move. Bronstein says nothing about it in his book on the tournament.

In the second game, Petrosian produced one of his most famous games, the exchange sacrifice against Reshevsky. This game has been analysed in many publications already, so we just show a fragment. Reshevsky gained an advantage. He had several ways to increase the pressure and tried to push his central pawns. When we join the game, Tigran has to stop these pawns.

Game 53

**Reshevsky, Samuel –
Petrosian, Tigran**
Candidates Tournament,
Zurich (2), 1953

25...♖e6!!

This is Petrosian's most famous
strategic exchange sacrifice.

26.a4 ♞e7!

With two stunning moves,
Petrosian eliminates Reshevsky's
initiative in the centre.

27.♗xe6 fxe6

By rendering White's pawn chain
rigid in the centre and obtaining a
superb outpost for his knight, Tigran
equalised, and after time control
the game was adjourned. They
analysed at the hotel and agreed to a
draw.

In the third round, Petrosian
was White against Bronstein; it
was an open Catalan, and the game
ended in a repetition after 17 moves.
In round 4, Petrosian took a risk
with his opening selection. Gligoric
employed the g3 line against the
Benoni. Black equalised, and the
game remained balanced all the
way until the 41st move, when
they agreed to a draw. In round
5, Petrosian played the e3 line
against Taimanov's Queen's Indian.
Petrosian created complications
and got a rook and two pawns
for two minor pieces. Soon after,
Taimanov rejected repeating moves
and gradually took control, winning
the game after time trouble. In
round 6, Petrosian employed the
King's Indian against Najdorf, and
he gave up the two bishops in the
g3 line. Najdorf exchanged the g7-
bishop. Petrosian gained a passive
position; he sacrificed a pawn
for some tactical chances against
White's rook. Najdorf neutralised
his play and Petrosian's position fell
apart. After he lost another pawn,
Petrosian resigned. Petrosian drew
number four at the drawing of lots;
this resulted in a bye for round 7.
In round 8, he was White against
Averbakh; the 13-move draw was
probably prearranged. Having a
rest was a good idea, as he gained
energy and started to perform well.
Probably, he hoped that moving
from Neuhausen to Zurich would
change his luck, and it did indeed.
In round 9, he was Black against
Szabo. He employed the Orthodox
Queen's Gambit Declined. He
took on hanging pawns and at one
point declined to repeat moves. The
position transformed, with a black
passed pawn on c4. The Hungarian

grandmaster took a risk by capturing the c4-pawn. Petrosian pinned Szabo's knights. White objectively could have held the position, but made a mistake and ended up with a piece deficit. He played on for a short while and resigned.

In round 10, Petrosian was White against Euwe, who with plus 2 stood well in the event. Petrosian treated the Reti Opening harmlessly, but the ex-world champion got into difficulties when he awkwardly developed a knight on a6. Euwe was in serious trouble, but managed to reduce it. Then he suddenly gave up the bishop pair, which is where we join the game.

Game 54

Petrosian, Tigran – Euwe, Max
Candidates Tournament,
Zurich (10), 1953

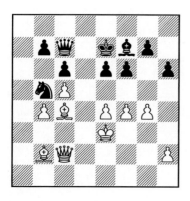

34.e5!
Petrosian correctly opens the position for his bishop pair.
34...♛d8

According to Stetsko, 34...♛d7 was more tenacious, as the queen would threaten to capture the g4-pawn.

35.exf6+   gxf6   36.h4   ♞c7 37.♛c3 ♞d5+

Petrosian writes that he earlier wanted to avoid opposite-coloured bishops, but now he needs to accept them. Black's move is, however, driven by desperation. The Dutchman probably hoped to give perpetual check.

38.♗xd5 ♛xd5

39.♛xf6+
Petrosian wins a pawn. Surprisingly, his own king is properly covered even though there is hardly any pawn around it.

39...♚e8 40.♛h8+ ♚d7 41.♛g7
This was the adjourned position. Home analysis convinced Petrosian that White was winning.

41...♚e8 42.♗f6 ♛b3+ 43.♗c3 ♛d1 44.♛h8+ ♚d7

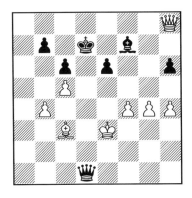

45.♕b8!

Surprisingly, White can afford to move the queen out of play to attack the b-pawn.

45...♕c1+

45...♕g1+   46.♔e4   ♕xg4
47.♕xb7+ ♔e8 48.♕xc6+ wins.

46.♗d2 ♕g1+ 47.♔d3 ♕f1+
48.♔c2 ♕a6

Black has to move his queen out of play, as 48...♗g6+? 49.f5 wins, or after 48...♕c4+ 49.♔b2 ♕d4+ 50.♗c3 ♕f2+ 51.♔a3 Black runs out of checks and loses.

49.h5!

Petrosian fixes the h6–pawn and stops the bishop.

49...♕a2+ 50.♔d3 ♕b1+ 51.♔e2

It is remarkable how White changes the flank where he places his king.

51...♕e4+   52.♔f2   ♕d4+
53.♗e3 ♕xb4

Taking the pawn changes nothing.

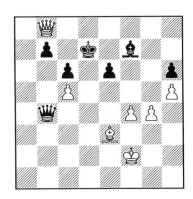

54.♕f8

Black can't stop the check on d6; the end is approaching.

54...♕b2+   55.♔g3   ♕f6
56.♕d6+ ♔c8 57.♗d4 ♕d8

Exchanging queens is the only way to prolong the game.

58.♕xd8+ ♔xd8

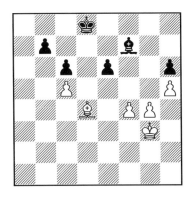

59.♗g7

Taking the h-pawn means game over for Black.

59...♔c7 60.♗xh6 b6 61.cxb6+ ♔xb6 62.♔h4 1–0 Euwe resigns.

In round 11, Petrosian was Black against Stahlberg. In a g3 King's Indian the Swedish grandmaster gave up the bishop pair, then made another inaccuracy allowing Black to fix the queenside, and in addition he blundered a pawn. The position was very closed, so Stahlberg was still able to make a lot of moves. He resigned on move 64. After 11 rounds, the standings among the leaders were Reshevsky 7.5 (11), Smyslov 7 (10), Najdorf 6 (10), Boleslavsky, Keres and Petrosian 5 (10), and Euwe and Bronstein 5 (11). In round 12, Petrosian was White against Boleslavsky in a reversed Closed Sicilian. Petrosian exerted pressure on the queenside, and Isaac on the other wing. Tigran offered a draw on move 21 when he was a bit better and Boleslavsky agreed to it. In round 13, Petrosian was Black against Kotov, and a great fight took place in the Old Indian. They played well in the complex position and agreed to a draw after Black's 32nd move. In round 14, Petrosian and Geller did not pretend to fight, but drew in a mere 14 moves. In the last game of the first half of the tournament, Petrosian as Black repeated against Smyslov the opening he had played against Reshevsky earlier, and he deviated on move 18. But his improvement was not good enough to equalise. After exchanging rooks, Petrosian was already lost. Smyslov missed a direct win by pushing his passed

pawn after some preparation. The Russian then gave a lot of checks to reach time control. Petrosian's sealed move was not the best. Interestingly, according to the computer, they made mistakes in a sharp position soon after the adjournment. On the 45th move, Petrosian found a great idea that was good enough to draw; a few months later, a Swedish amateur found a subtle move that would have given Smyslov a win. To make matters even more absurd, modern tools can find a better move, a piece sacrifice, instead of Petrosian's deep idea. It gives chances to hold and this game can be seen in the It's Your Move chapter.

The standings among the leaders after the first half of the event were: Smyslov 9.5, Bronstein and Reshevsky 8.5, Najdorf 8, and Boleslavsky, Euwe and Petrosian 7.5. As our hero was the youngest, he was likely to cope better in the 14 games of the second half of the event.

Petrosian started the second half, round 16, with an especially tough game: he was Black against Keres. The Estonian grandmaster chose a setup with c4, ♘f3, ♗f4 and e3 against the King's Indian. The opening went unpleasantly for Petrosian. He had a backward pawn, yet surprisingly he made a few exchanges. Keres built up play on the h-file nicely. The game worsened for Petrosian around time control. After Tigran took the c-pawn, his position fell apart quickly.

In the 17th game, Petrosian was White against Reshevsky in the

King's Indian. It was balanced for some time. Reshevsky declined to repeat moves. Then the American grandmaster played three suboptimal moves in a row. We join the game when it's Petrosian's turn to move.

Game 55

Petrosian, Tigran – Reshevsky, Samuel
Candidates Tournament,
Zurich (17), 1953

23.f5!?

White would be better after almost any move, for example 23.b3 or 23.♗e3 would provide a small advantage, as the black knights are on the edge of the board. Petrosian plays an imaginative and surprising move. Reshevsky is known for his time trouble, and Petrosian may have wanted to take advantage of it with this sacrifice.

23...♕d7?

23...gxf5!?. Black should take the pawn. It would be interesting to know what Petrosian planned against it.

a) 24.e6 fxe6 (24...♕c8 25.exf7+ ♖xf7 26.♗f4 is easier to play with White) 25.♕xe6+ (25.♗f4 ♕c6 and nobody has the upper hand) 25...♖f7 26.♗f4 ♕c6 and White has compensation for the pawn, but the position would be balanced. For instance, after 27.♕e2 e5 28.♗xe5 ♖e7 29.♕f1 the position would be equal.

b) 24.♘h3 ♗e4 25.♘f4 (25.♗f4 ♕c6 26.♖ad1 ♕g6 and Black would be in the game, 25.e6 fxe6? would be bad because of 26.♘fg5, but 25...♗d3 would be reasonable) 25...♗xe5 26.♘xe5 ♕xe5 27.♘xh5 and the position would be balanced.

24.e6

Another imaginative move, but White would be almost winning after 24.fxg6!? fxg6 25.♗f4. He may continue with b3 and Rad1.

24...♕d5

24...fxe6?? would lose to 25.fxg6.

25.exf7+ ♕xf7 26.fxg6 ♕xg6

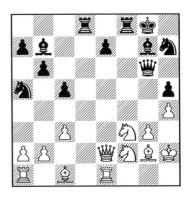

27.♘g5

Petrosian is looking for exchanges to get closer to Black's weak kingside.

White has another promising move as well. 27.♗f4 e5 (27...♘c6 28.♘e4 would be nice for White) 28.♘xe5 ♗xe5 29.♗xe5 ♗xg2 30.♔xg2 ♖de8 31.♕e4 is also much better for White.

27...♗xg2 28.♔xg2 e5?

Reshevsky misses a chance to ease his position. 28...♘xg5! 29.♗xg5 ♖d5! After this strong move, White's advantage is not very big, for example 30.♖ad1 ♖e5.

29.♕e4

Sax delivered a lecture on a tournament in Vrsac, when he praised Petrosian a lot. But he also made one remarkable point: if he decided to draw a game before it began, he would not change his plan regardless of how good a position he obtained. Tal also said that if Petrosian had decided to play for a draw, no force in the Universe could change his mind. After 29.♘xh7! ♔xh7 30.♘e4 or 29.♘ge4! ♘c6 30.♗g5 White would be close to winning.

29...♖f5

Maybe Reshevsky knew that with no queens on the board it would be harder to offer a draw.

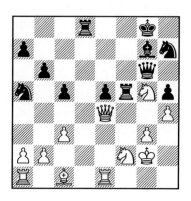

30.♘xh7 ♔xh7 1/2

According Bronstein, White is far better. If the queens are exchanged Black's pawns will become excellent targets, whereas if the queens remain on the board, his exposed king will be a continual problem for Black. Maybe he was told by the authorities to go for a draw to help Smyslov win the event, or maybe he wanted to avoid tension. Whatever the reason, had he played on he would have had decent chances to score a victory.

In the next game, he was Black against Bronstein. David played the unusual 4.♗g5 after 1.d4 ♘f6 2.c4 d6 3.♘c3 ♘bd7. Petrosian quickly exchanged the bishop. Both sides castled long. After the opening, Petrosian made some bad moves and got into a poor position. Bronstein made a serious mistake, which allowed Petrosian back into the game. Later, Tigran won a pawn, but the position was still unclear when Bronstein offered a draw and Petrosian took it. According to Bronstein, Petrosian had a good continuation available, but with little time on the clock he just did not see a follow up and hence agreed the draw. In fact, Bronstein was wrong; White had a move which would have forced Petrosian to play well to draw.

Game 56

Petrosian, Tigran – Gligoric, Svetozar
Candidates Tournament,
Zurich (19), 1953

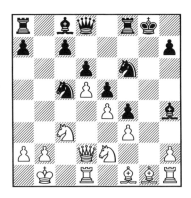

20.♗xc5!
This is a subtle exchange.
20...dxc5 21.♘c1 ♕e7 22.♘b3 ♗d7

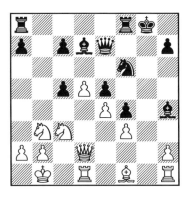

23.♕g2+!
Petrosian finds an original way to win the c5–pawn. 23.♘b5 and 23.♗b5 would also be strong.
23...♔h8 24.♕g1!
Petrosian will have a fantastic idea in a similar position.

Petrosian, T – Kluger, G
Hungary-Soviet Union,
Budapest (6), 1955

15.♔d2!
The start of a fascinating plan.
15...g5 16.h3 h5 17.♕g1!!
Petrosian brilliantly uses his queen.
17...a6 18.g4 fxg3 19.♕xg3?
Sadly, in Petrosian's most imaginative play a mistake creeps in. Here after 19.♘xg3! ♔h8 20.♗e3 White would be clearly better. In the next part of the game, Kluger will superbly outplay Tigran but close to time control (uncle Gyula was famous for his time trouble) Petrosian was able to get back into the game. Kluger was in time trouble from the 27th move.
19...♘h7 20.♗e3 h4 21.♕g2 ♔h8 22.♖hf1 ♗h6 23.c5 ♗d7 24.a4 ♘ef6 25.♘g1 ♘h5 26.♖fb1 ♘f4 27.♕h2 ♘f6 28.♗f1 ♘6h5 29.♘d1 ♕e8 30.a5 ♘g3 31.♘c3 ♕c8 32.♖c1 ♕e8 33.♗c4 ♗g7 34.♔c2 ♖f6 35.♔b3 ♗f8 36.♕c2 ♖g6

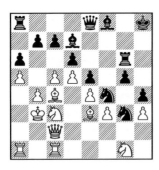

37.♗xf4!

A surprising decision, the point of it being to weaken Black's pressure on the d5–square.

37...gxf4

37...exf4 was stronger. After 38.c6 bxc6 39.dxc6 Bxc6 40.♘d5 White would have some compensation for the pawn.

38.c6!

This is a neat pawn sacrifice to get closer to Black's camp.

38...bxc6 39.dxc6 ♗xc6

40.♗d5!

Another very strong swap.

40...♖g7

After 40...♗xd5+ 41.♘xd5 c5 42.♕c4 the position would be complex.

41.♗xc6 ♕xc6 42.♘d5 ♕b7?!

This was the adjourned position. Here after 42...♕xc2+ 43.♖xc2

c5 Black should be careful on the queenside. Barcza mentions that the Hungarians made a mistake in their home analysis.

43.♕c6 ♕b8?

After the correct 43...♕a7! White's advantage would be smaller.

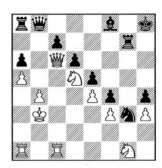

44.b5! axb5?! 45.♘xc7

Petrosian obtained a winning position and went on to win the game.

Back to the main game!

24...♘e8

24...♖fb8 25.♕xc5 is also rather bad for Black.

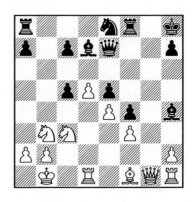

25.♕xc5

Petrosian has obtained a winning position. At one point in time trouble he allowed a nice rook sacrifice. Interestingly, both Petrosian and Bronstein missed a subtle string of White moves that could have driven away Black's bishop, which would have kept the advantage. Regardless of this stunning possibility, Petrosian deservedly beat the Yugoslav number one player. Gligoric resigned after time trouble.

In round 20, Taimanov had the white pieces. Petrosian repeated the Nimzo-Indian line which he had played against Reshevsky and Smyslov. Taimanov deviated on move 11. He also got a big advantage. Petrosian again tried an exchange sacrifice, but this time it did not work and he had to resign on move 40. After 20 rounds, Smyslov was leading with 12.5 (19), Reshevsky was second with 12 (19), Bronstein 11.5 (19), and other players had little chance of winning the event: Keres had 10.5 (19), Najdorf 10 (20), Boleslavsky 9.5, and Petrosian had 9 out of 19 games.

In round 21, Petrosian got no advantage with the e3 line against Najdorf's Queen's Indian. They agreed to a draw after Petrosian's 15th move. After a bye in the 22nd round he was Black against Averbakh. The quick draw may have been prearranged. In the 24th round, Petrosian was White against Szabo; the Hungarian grandmaster sacrificed a pawn in the English Opening. Petrosian quickly neutralised his play. Black sacrificed a knight and a rook to create complications. After the turmoil, Petrosian was a piece up, and Szabo resigned on move 41. In round 25, Petrosian as Black played the Old Indian versus Euwe. He gradually equalised, and the game ended peacefully after White's 23rd move. This was to be the last ever game between these two world champions. According to Kasparov in his *My Great Predecessors* (no source is given by Kasparov, though) Euwe once said of Petrosian: "If we look in chess history for a 'double' of Petrosian, we arrive at Capablanca. Petrosian is not a tiger that pounces on its prey, but rather a python that smothers its victim, or a crocodile waiting for hours for a convenient moment to land a decisive blow. Petrosian is an outstanding strategist. If he should begin to combine a little, he will be impossible to play against." In this round, Smyslov beat Reshevsky in perhaps the most critical game of the event. In the 26th round, Petrosian was White against Stahlberg. He looked for a prolonged fight with the King's Indian Attack. White gained a tiny advantage in the opening, and after some manoeuvring Petrosian found a breakthrough which was highly praised by Bronstein. Tigran won a pawn before time control. He firmly converted his advantage in the adjournment. We cite Bronstein: "This entire game is an excellent illustration of Petrosian's style: its highly individual positional pattern and its logical consistency combine to create a harmonious whole and an artistic achievement. Curiously, none of the annotators of this game, Stahlberg among them, could find a single sizeable error on Black's part! The contemporary game operates on such fine nuances that they prove difficult to isolate, even in analysis, to say nothing of over-the-board play." In the 27th round, he was Black against Boleslavsky. Isaac sacrificed a pawn in the Caro-Kann, and the game remained balanced all the way until move 24, when peace broke out. In the 28th round, Petrosian was White against Kotov, who had started poorly, but in round 21 beat the leader Smyslov and in the 23rd another possible winner, Reshevsky. Petrosian as White played the g3 line against the King's Indian, and nobody really wanted to win in a 19-move draw. In the penultimate round, Petrosian played the Nimzo-Indian as Black against Geller. Tigran obtained fluent play for the bishop pair. He outplayed his countryman; then he released the pressure a bit. Geller made a mistake on move 28, an almost losing move, and offered a draw. We know that when Petrosian decided he wanted a draw it was almost impossible to dissuade him from the idea, and he accepted Geller's offer. In the last round, Petrosian finished the event with a 13-move draw against the winner, Smyslov.

Petrosian ended with 6 wins, 18 draws and 4 losses. He scored 15 points out of 28 games; 3 points less than the winner Smyslov and 1 less than three other players, Bronstein, Keres and Reshevsky.

As Black, he scored 6.5 out of 14 games, won 2, drew 9 and lost three. In his three losses the openings did not work well and he was in trouble in three more black games. As White, he won 4 games, drew 9 and lost only 1. It was a good score. By the way, of his 9 draws, 6 ended before the 20th move and one on the 21st. So he really fought only in 7 white games. Had he tried in more white games, perhaps he would have scored a few more points.

He again demonstrated that he was an established world class player. He surely gained a lot of experience for the future, and he must have noticed how tiredness can affect one's result: Reshevsky's running out of fuel was an example of that.

Here is how Sakkelet described him: "at the beginning he was a bit hesitant, but then he improved forcefully. His success comes mainly from his realistic judgement of positions. He is one of the very few players to never over-press and can be content with a draw as well. In some of his games, such as his first game against Reshevsky, he showed resourcefulness and versatility." Finishing 5th at the age of 24, sort of making him 6th in the world after Botvinnik, meant that sooner or later he would raise his level to challenge the world champion.

Austria – Soviet Union Match, Vienna

Less than a week later, Petrosian was selected for the Soviet national team against Austria. In the first game, he was Black against Lokvenc, whom he played against with both colours. In a main-line King's Indian Petrosian gained a small edge with a nice exchange. The Austrian player gave away a free pawn and soon was completely losing. Uncharacteristically, Tigran spoiled the position, and the position was even when Lokvenc lost on time. The game can be seen in the Petrosian's Remarkable Exchanges chapter.

Game 57

Petrosian, Tigran – Lokvenc, Josef
Austria – Soviet Union Match, Vienna (2), 1953

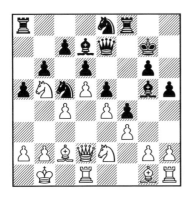

21.♗xc5!?

A bit surprisingly, White gives up the bishop pair. 21.♘ec3 with a3 and b4 would also give him an edge.

21...bxc5

21...dxc5 22.♘xc7 wins.

22.♗a4!

Petrosian is looking to exchange Black's light-squared bishop. By the way, in 1954 Petrosian produced a nice game against a

player who was prepared against this strategy. We take a brief look at that game:

Petrosian, T – Milic, B
Belgrade (8), 1954

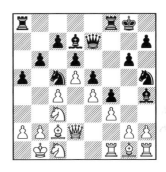

18.♗xc5!? bxc5 19.♗a4 ♗xa4 20.♘xa4 ♖fb8 21.a3 ♘f6 22.♘e2 ♘d7 23.♕c2 ♘b6 24.♘xb6 ♖xb6 25.♘c3 ♕d7 26.♘b5 a4

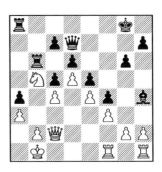

Milic probably knew the Lokvenc game and drew the conclusion to keep rooks on the board and organise Black's play on the queenside, avoiding doing anything on the kingside.

27.♔a2 ♖bb8 28.♖b1 ♖a6 29.♖hd1 ♖ba8 30.♖d3 ♔g7

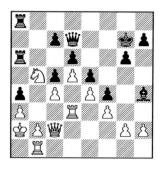

31.b4

After some nice preparation, Petrosian changes the structure.

31...axb3+ 32.♖dxb3 ♖a4 33.♕e2 h5 34.♘c3 ♖4a5

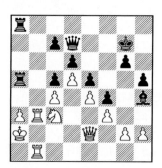

35.♔b2!

Petrosian with fantastic imagination sees a great square for his king in the centre.

35...♕c8 36.♖a1 ♕a6 37.♔c2 ♗d8 38.♔d3! ♕c8 39.♕b2 ♖5a6 40.♖b1 ♖b6 41.♖b5 ♕d7 42.a4 ♕e7?

After 42...♖aa6 43.♖a1 ♖a5 44.♖a2 White would be only somewhat better.

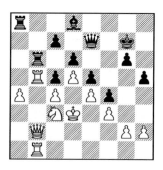

43.♖a1! ♖ab8? 44.a5! and the passed a-pawn soon decided the outcome of the game.

Back to the Lokvenc game.

22...♗h6 23.♘c1 ♕d8 24.♘c3 ♗xa4 25.♘xa4 ♘f6 26.♕c2 ♘d7 27.♘e2 ♗g5 28.♖d3 ♖b8 29.a3 ♘b6 30.♘xb6 ♖xb6

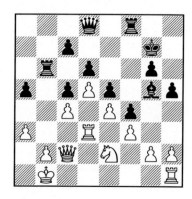

31.♖b3

Exchanging pieces brings an invasion closer.

31...♕d7 32.♘c3 ♗e7 33.♖xb6 cxb6 34.♕a4!

Tigran follows through his plan of exchanging.

34...♕xa4 35.♘xa4 ♖b8 36.♘c3
g5 37.h3 ♔f7 38.♔c2

Petrosian starts using his king.

38...♔e8 39.♔b3 ♔d7 40.♘a4
♖g8

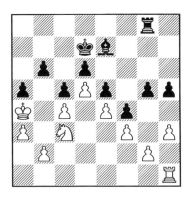

41.♔b5

The king march signifies danger
for Black. Petrosian as Black faced
a similar king against Lipnitsky at
the 1950 Soviet championship final.
He lost that game, but at one point
he could have saved it, so he was
probably aware that Black wasn't
necessarily losing.

**41...♔c7 42.♘a4 ♗f6 43.♖c1
♗e7**

43...g4? 44.hxg4 hxg4 45.♖h1
would win.

44.♖c3?!

The rook is misplaced on the
third rank.

44...♗f6?!

After 44...g4! 45.hxg4 hxg4
46.♖c1 ♖h8! Black would still be in
the game.

**45.♖b3 ♖b8 46.♖d3 ♗e7 47.b3
♖g8 48.♖d1 ♖a8**

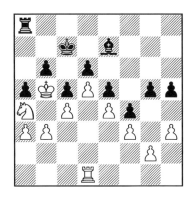

49.♖a1

It looks like he is just tiring out
his opponent, but this is part of a
plan.

**49...♗d8 50.♖a2! ♔b7 51.♘c3!
♗c7**

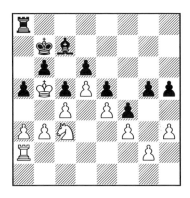

52.b4!

White progresses.

**52...axb4 53.axb4 ♖g8 54.♔a4
cxb4**

It is hard to form an opinion on
this move, which increases White's
options a bit. Instead, 54...g4!? looks
slightly preferable. After 55.hxg4
hxg4 56.♘b5 ♗b8 Black seems to
equalise by attacking the f3–pawn
with the rook.

55.♔xb4 ♖g7

55...g4!? Maybe the earlier he carries out this move the better.

56.♖a1 ♖g8 57.♔b5 ♖g7

Keeping the rook on the 8th rank would make White transfer his knight to b4 via a longer route.

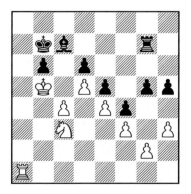

58.♘a2!

Petrosian improves his knight.

58...g4

Black has to act, as the knight would be too strong on c6.

59.hxg4 hxg4 60.♘c3 gxf3 61.gxf3 ♖g3 62.♖f1 ♖h3 63.♔b4

This leaves Lokvenc guessing.

63...♖g3 64.♘b5 ♗b8

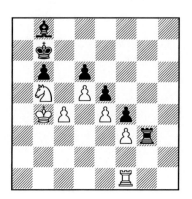

65.♔a4

The king vacates the b4–square. It is hard to read what Petrosian is trying to do.

65...♖h3 66.♘a3 ♗c7 67.♘c2 ♖g3 68.♘b4 ♖h3 69.♔b5 ♖h2

69...♖g3 70.♘c6 ♖h3 71.♖a1 ♖xf3 72.♖a7+ ♔c8 73.♘xe5 dxe5 74.♔c6 and White wins.

70.♖g1 ♖f2 71.♖g7 ♖b2

Lokvenc pins the knight. He could have taken the f3-pawn without punishment: 71...♖xf3

a) 72.♘a6 ♖b3+ 73.♔a4?? (73.♘b4=) 73...♖g3 and Black even wins.

b) 72.♘c6 ♖b3+ 73.♔a4 ♖b1 74.♘d8+ (74.♘xe5 dxe5 75.d6 ♔c6 is nice for Black) 74...♔c8 and Black would be safe.

72.♔a4 ♖b1

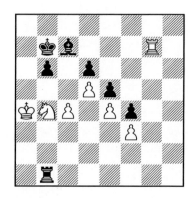

73.♘c6

The knight looks frightening on c6, but it is not decisive.

73...♖a1+

Black could take action or wait as well:

a) 73...b5+! Black could free his position in this way and he would be fine: 74.cxb5 (74.♔a3 bxc4 75.♘a5+ ♔c8 76.♘xc4 ♖f1 and Black would be safe) 74...♔b6.

b) 73...♖c1 74.♔b4 ♖b1+ 75.♔c3 ♖c1+ 76.♔b3 b5! 77.♔b2 ♖f1 78.c5 dxc5 79.♘xe5 ♔b6 80.♘d7+ ♔a5 81.e5 ♔b4 and Black is likely to hold.

74.♔b3 ♖f1?

The rook leaves the queenside, but after this mistake Black is sure to lose. What should Black do? 74...♔c8! 75.♔b4 ♖b1+ 76.♔a3 ♖a1+ 77.♔b2 ♖a4 probably holds. For example, 78.♔b3 ♖a1 79.♘e7+ ♔b8 80.♔b2 ♖a4. On the other hand, 80...♖f1? would not work, as 81.♘c6+ ♔b7 82.♘d8+ ♔c8 83.♘e6 wins.

75.♘d8+!

The knight sends the bishop away.

75...♔c8 76.♘e6 ♗b8 77.♔a4!

The king gets threatening.

77...♖b1

After 77...♖xf3? 78.♔b5 ♖c3 79.♖f7 ♖c1 80.c5 White wins.

78.♖g8+ ♔b7 79.♘d8+

The knight did its duty on e6.

79...♔a6

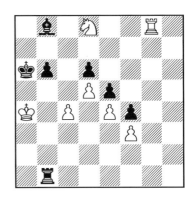

80.♖g7!

The rook traps the bishop.

80...b5+

This comes too late.

81.cxb5+ ♖xb5 82.♘c6 ♖b7

The game was adjudicated, and the verdict was 1–0. This was correct, as White is winning by force: 83.♖g8 ♗a7 (after 83...♗c7 84.♖a8+ ♔b6 85.♔b4 Black would be in complete zugzwang) 84.♖a8 and White will simplify to a winning pawn ending.

Beating Lokvenc 2:0 was a good performance.

Spartak Moscow – Iskra

According to the database, Petrosian played one game as White against Yudovich at a team event in Moscow. No other game from the event is known, so we do not know on which board they played. Tigran employed a King's Indian Attack to avoid a theoretical discussion. After the opening, Yudovich made a mistake, allowing Petrosian to obtain the bishop pair and creating doubled pawns in Black's camp. Petrosian paralysed him and beat him impressively.

Petrosian's results in 1953

Bucharest	+ 7 = 12 – 0 13/19 2nd place
Training Tournament, Gagra	+ 4 = 4 – 1 6/9 3rd place
Candidates Tournament, Neuhasen-Zurich	+ 6 = 18 – 4 15/28 5th place
Austria – Soviet Union match vs Lokvenc	+ 2 = 0 – 0 2:0
Spartak – Iskra Team Event vs. Yudovich	+ 1 = 0 – 0 1:0
Altogether	**+ 20 = 34 – 5 37/59**

Petrosian's family. Tigran is the baby in the hat. His parents died long before his chess successes. From David Gurgenidze's personal archive

Kasparian (left) against Ebralidze

Petrosian at the Soviet Junior championship in 1946. He dropped only two draws on the way to winning the event and beat Korchnoi

Petrosian with his friend and your Armenian author's coach Lazar Sarkisian, 1946. From the personal archive of Artur Sarkisian (Lazar's son). Lazar would sometimes call Petrosian 'Tiko' in conversations

Keres vs Palavandishvili, Georgian Championship, 1946 The picture illustrates the atmosphere under which Petrosian played his first game against Paul Keres

Armenian Championship 1946. Lazar Sarkisian is at the back left. Kasparian and Petrosian are sitting in the middle. From Artur Sarkisian's personal archive

Boleslavsky-Bondarevsky at a Soviet team event. According to the database, these two players met twice at Soviet team events, once in Leningrad in 1948 and once in Tbilisi in 1951

Participants of the 1948 Armenian Championship. Front row: Petrosian, Andranik Akopian, Henrik Kasparian, Akop Mokatsian. From Artur Sarkisian's personal archive

Against B. Gurgenidze

Probably from the fifties

Semi-Final of the Soviet Championship, Sverdlovsk, 1951

Peter Szilagyi with Andor Lilienthal. From the Szilagyi family archive

The players of the Amsterdam Candidates Tournament, 1956. Photographer Herbert Behrens, Anefo. Copyright holder Dutch National Archives

240

Petrosian with his son Vartan and wife Rona, 1957. Provided by Vartan Petrosian

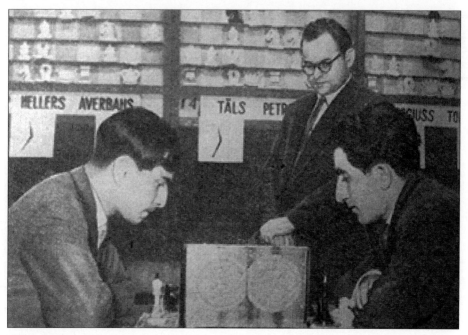

Tal and Petrosian are at the 1958 Soviet championship in Riga. Furman is standing

Petrosian with Tal and Spassky, probably at the 1958 Soviet championship in Riga

Petrosian-Fischer 1958, the first of the 27 games between them

242

Against Averbakh at the 1959 Soviet championship in Tbilisi

Zagreb 1959. Petrosian is the closest to the camera

With Nona Gaprindashvili in Tbilisi. From David Gurgenidze's personal archive

Against Geller

With Tal in Tbilisi, 1959. From David Gurgenidze's personal archive

In Tbilisi with Keres. From David Gurgenidze's personal archive

Petrosian-Larsen at the 1960 Nimzowitsch Memorial, Copenhagen. Petrosian had to win this game in the last round

Petrosian and Tal analyse Hort's game in Oberhausen, 1961. The position suggests it was against Keres

Stockholm 1962

248

In front: Keres, Geller, Tal, Petrosian, Korchnoi. At the back: Averbakh and Boleslavsky. At Amsterdam's Schiphol Airport on the way to the 1962 Candidates Tournament in Curacao. Copyright holder Dutch National Archives

Photographer: Harry Pot (Anefo)

1954

Soviet Championship Final, Kiev

This important event started in January. Kiev, the capital of Ukraine and the city in which Rona Yakovlevna had been born, hosted the event. Quite a few stars did not line up, including Botvinnik, Smyslov, Bronstein, Boleslavsky and Kotov, yet the championship was pretty strong, as Korchnoi, Averbakh, Geller, Taimanov, Furman and Lilienthal all participated.

Petrosian was White against Sokolsky in round 1. He played a King's Indian Attack against the Queen's Indian. The position was even for some time. Petrosian made a remarkable queen transfer to the queenside and started to play against the black king. Sokolsky allowed his king to be exposed. Petrosian's attack grew winning, but he exchanged queens. The ensuing ending was better for him; he managed to win on the queenside. In the second round, Livshin as White played 3.♗b5+ against the Sicilian. White played cautiously and the position simplified to a queen ending. Petrosian gained the upper hand, but Livshin was able to hold. In round 3 against Ilivitsky, he obtained a position as White which was not really better, but his enormous playing strength was likely to make itself felt. One serious mistake give the Armenian grandmaster a winning advantage, but instead of winning time with checks to reach time control he took a pawn, his king became exposed, and after reaching time control they agreed to a draw. In round 4, Tigran was Black against an opponent he had never faced before, Shamkovich. They exchanged pieces in the Bogo-Indian and agreed to a draw on the 24th move. In the next round, Petrosian was White against Bannik; he got an edge in a reverse Dragon, then the position simplified to a four-rook ending. It was still clearly better for Petrosian when they adjourned the game. The way he exerted pressure can be seen in the It's Your Move chapter. Possibly later, Black could have objectively held, but it was difficult in practice and Bannik failed to do so. In round 6 against Korchnoi, Petrosian equalised against the g3 King's Indian. All queenside pawns were swapped off. Maybe Petrosian was a bit too relaxed or was short of time. Korchnoi gained a winning advantage, but his moves suggest that he was in time trouble. Petrosian was able to hold with some fortune. In round 7, Petrosian was White against Flohr. After an opening when Flohr accepted doubled pawns, Tigran obtained a promising position. However, he was unable to crack Flohr's stubborn defence. In round

8, Petrosian was Black against Nezhmetdinov. In the 6.♗g5 ♘bd7 Najdorf the Tatar failed to play the opening well. At the end of the opening, Petrosian won a pawn and firmly converted the advantage. His analysis of this one-sided game is included in *Reliability Strategy*. In the next round, Petrosian after 1.d4 ♘f6 2.♘f3 e6 played 3.♗g5. Lisitsin neutralised Petrosian's play with exchanges, the game dried up and they agreed to a draw on move 23. In the 10th round, Petrosian played the Benoni against Kholmov. He was somewhat worse when he sacrificed a pawn. Kholmov took it. His play led to a balanced position, and they agreed to a draw after Petrosian's 27th move. In the 11th round, Averbakh, who went on to become the champion, played the Ragozin Variation of the Queen's Gambit. White's small initiative evaporated, and the draw took just 27 moves. Averbakh said in an interview for his 90th birthday that Rona, Tigran and he went to parties to visit her relatives several times during the tournament, but Rona noticed that Yuri won his next game after every visit, so these visits stopped. Yet according to Averbakh that was normal, as they were friends, but they both were fighting to win the championship.

In the 12th round, Petrosian accepted an isolated pawn in the French against Suetin. Neither player was able to gain an edge, the position simplified, and they agreed to a draw after Suetin's 28th move.

Game 58

Petrosian, Tigran – Geller, Efim
Soviet Championship Final, Kiev (13),
1954
Queen's Gambit Declined

1.d4 ♘f6 2.c4 e6 3.♘f3 d5 4.♗g5
Geller in the early part of his career rarely played any openings against 1.d4 other than the King's Indian. When he did, he usually opted for the Semi-Slav. If ...c6 Petrosian was possibly going to develop his knight on d2.

4...h6 5.♗xf6 ♕xf6 6.♘c3 c6 7.e3 ♘d7 8.♗d3 ♗b4 9.a3
According to the database this move was not played before this game.

9...♗a5 10.0-0 dxc4 11.♗xc4 0-0 12.♖c1 ♗c7

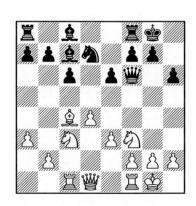

13.♗a2!
A clever move. White has more space and some development advantage, while Black has the bishop pair and no weakness. White

makes sure that Black will not win a tempo on the queenside by attacking the bishop, and also makes it harder for Black to carry out c5.

13...♖d8 14.♕c2 ♘f8?! 15.♘e4 ♕f5 16.♕b1 ♘d7

Jumping with the knight there and back reveals that Geller is not familiar with the position. Petrosian selected the opening well, as this position suits him better than Geller. Black could sacrifice a pawn to develop the queenside. 16...b6 17.♖xc6 ♗b7 18.♖xc7 ♗xe4 19.♕d1 ♖dc8 20.♖xc8 ♖xc8 and would have some, but not full compensation for it. Or Black could develop modestly with the solid but rather passive 16...♗d7 and ...♗e8.

17.♘fd2 e5

Geller runs out of patience and acts, but Petrosian is the better developed player.

18.d5! ♘b8

This redeveloping move is ugly, but other moves are not any better.

19.♖fd1 ♕g6

It would be interesting to know whether the grandmaster from Odessa was ready to live with a strong passed pawn, or whether he missed Petrosian's sweet idea. Black could also play differently: 19...cxd5 20.♖xc7 ♘a6 (20...dxe4?? 21.♖xf7) 21.♖c2 dxe4 22.♘xe4 ♗e6 23.♗xe6 ♕xe6 and White's advantage would be smaller than in the game.

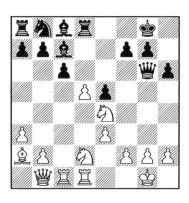

20.d6!

This is a brilliant idea. White has many more pieces in play, so it is no surprise that he has a tactical opportunity to improve his position.

20...♗b6

Not 20...♗xd6? as the pawn is poisoned. 21.♘xd6 ♕xd6 (21...♕xb1?? 22.♘xb1) 22.♘e4 (Ljublinski's 22.♘f3 ♕e7 23.♖xd8+ ♕xd8 24.♘xe5 is decisive as well) 22...♕e7 23.♖xd8+ ♕xd8 24.♖d1 ♕e7 25.♗xf7+ and White wins.

21.♘f3 ♘d7 22.♖c4!

The rook defends the knight to take over the queen's burden. But it may have another, hidden role.

22...♖e8 23.♕c1 ♗d8

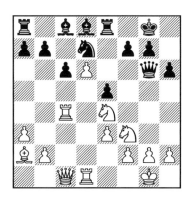

24.♘g3!

The knight opens the diagonal for the bishop and the rank for the rook.

24...e4

Geller finds a way to prolong the game. 24...♘f6 25.♕c3 e4 26.♘e5 ♕g5 and 27.♖c5 or 27.♘xf7 would win. Or 24...a6 25.♗b1 ♕f6 26.♖h4 would be the end.

25.♘d2 ♘f6 26.♘dxe4 ♘xe4 27.d7 ♗xd7 28.♖xd7 ♘d6 29.♖d4

Maybe 29.♖f4 ♖e7 (29...♗g5 30.♖g4) 30.♖xd6 ♕xd6 31.♘f5 would win more quickly.

29...♗e7 30.♖4xd6 ♗xd6 31.♗xf7+ ♕xf7 32.♖xf7 ♔xf7 33.♕c4+ ♔f8 34.♘e4

34.♘f5!? would win more material quickly.

34...♖ad8 35.g3 ♖e7

36.♔g2

Interestingly, Petrosian keeps the knight rather than win another pawn. After 36.♘xd6 ♖xd6 37.♕f4+ ♖f6 38.♕b8+ the a7 pawn would fall as well.

36...♗e5 37.b3 g6 38.h4 ♔g7

If 38...a6 39.♘c5 ♖d6 40.♕b4 and White wins.

39.♕c5

Petrosian wins the pawn.

39...♖dd7 40.♕xa7 ♗d4

Exchanging the bishop allows Black to prolong the game, but White is clearly winning.

41.♘c5 ♗xc5 42.♕xc5 ♖e6

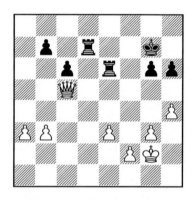

43.h5!

Opening up the black king makes it harder to defend it.

43...g5 44.♕c3+ ♔h7 45.♕c2+ ♔g7 46.♕f5 ♖de7

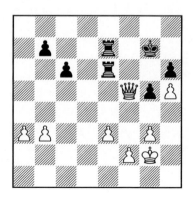

47.f4

White exposes Black's king further.

47...gxf4 48.exf4 ♖d6 49.♔f3 ♖e1 50.♕g4+ ♔f7 51.♕c8 ♖e7 52.♕f5+ ♔g7

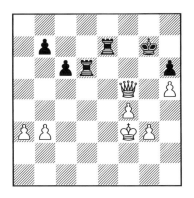

53.a4!

After checking Geller's alertness and tiring him, Petrosian progresses by pushing the queenside pawns. Maybe White would also win if he carried out g5 without acting on the queenside, but Petrosian's deep play vacates squares which only White will be able to use.

53...♖e1 54.♕g4+ ♔f7 55.♕c8 ♖e7 56.b4!

Petrosian gets on with his queenside play.

56...♖d3+ 57.♔g4 ♔g7 58.♕f5 ♖d6 59.♕c5 ♖dd7 60.♔h4 ♖e6 61.♕c3+ ♔h7 62.♕c2+ ♔g7 63.♕b2+ ♔h7 64.♕b1+ ♔g7 65.♕f5 ♖dd6 66.♔h3 ♖e7 67.♔g4 ♖ee6 68.♔f3 ♖e7 69.♕c2 ♖ee6 70.♕f5 ♖e8

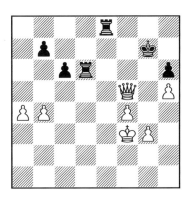

71.b5!

Petrosian had tired Geller for 15 moves, who had perhaps been trying to adjourn the game. Now Petrosian creates a weakness in Black's pawn chain. It is also possible he found it after adjournment analysis.

71...cxb5 72.♕xb5 ♖e7 73.g4!

The Armenian grandmaster plays across the whole board; he switches to the kingside to open up the black king more.

73...♖f6 74.a5 ♖fe6 75.♕b2+ ♔g8 76.♕b3

Without pushing the queenside pawns, White would not be able to use this square.

76...♔h7 77.♕d3+ ♔g8

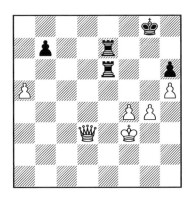

78.g5!

White wants to play g6, and he exchanges Black's last pawn on the kingside.

78...hxg5 79.fxg5

There are no more black pawns on the kingside so the black king is as exposed as it can be.

79...♖e5 80.♔f4 ♖5e6 81.g6

White is about to push the h-pawn as well; these pawns are devastating.

81...b6

Black has virtually no other moves, for example after 81...♔f8 82.h6 ♔e8 83.g7 ♔f7 84.♕d5 he could do nothing against ♔f5. Note that White can use the d5-square because Petrosian exchanged the c6-pawn.

82.a6 1–0

In the 14th round, Taimanov was White. He opened 1.c4, and against Tigran's King's Indian the Russian developed the bishop to g2 and pushed the d-pawn only one square. The position was always balanced, and they agreed to a draw after Petrosian's 30th move. In round 15, Petrosian was White against Bivshev. In the ♗f4 Grunfeld Black played c6. Petrosian surprisingly gave up the two bishops. White got an edge, but it evaporated. He again outplayed Bivshev, and sacrificed an exchange. Sadly, he then spoiled his position, possibly in time trouble, but was still able to hold. In the 16th round, Petrosian was Black against Lilienthal. In the Richter-

Rauzer Sicilian they reached a typical position with Black having doubled pawns on the f-file. White castled long and Black castled short. Lilienthal's play came to a halt on the kingside, while Petrosian won a pawn. The Hungarian reached a lost endgame the exchange down and resigned soon after time control. In the 17th round, Petrosian was White against Ragozin. They transposed into a main-line Nimzo-Indian. Black equalised, then Petrosian blundered in the middlegame, but Ragozin missed the right move, after which Petrosian held the game. In the penultimate round, Petrosian gave up the two bishops in a Queen's Gambit against Furman. It looked like they would soon draw, but Petrosian gave away a free pawn. Petrosian then had chances to hold. The game again deteriorated for him, but Furman missed a clear win and Petrosian held. In the last round, Petrosian was Black against Borisenko. In a main-line King's Indian Black played the rare 6...c5 7.d5 e5 setup. It looked like it would be a typical Petrosian masterpiece; I still wonder whether it pleased Tigran, though, as this time it was Borisenko who played beautiful strategic chess. However, approaching time control, when the direct confrontation started, inaccuracies started to creep into Borisenko's play. Perhaps he was in time trouble. He was still a bit better, but his 40th move was disastrous. Borisenko made 9 more moves, but without a chance. Petrosian finished the event joint fourth with Lisitsin. He remained undefeated, which was a serious accomplishment in the Soviet Championship Final, regardless of the fact that the champion Averbakh and the joint second-third placed Taimanov also achieved that. Petrosian won 6 games, while Averbakh and Korchnoi, also joint second-third, won 10 games each. Tigran won 3 games out of 9 as Black, which was good, but the 3 wins out of 10 games at White were not quite enough for a world class player. Such a result was not bad overall, however, Armenian fans would have hoped for more in a championship where a number of Soviet stars did not play.

Argentina – Soviet Union Match

In the spring of 1954, the Soviet national team went on a tour of South America. Perhaps it had a little to do with the political thaw in the Soviet Union after Stalin's death. They started out against Argentina, the team which had finished second at the 1952 Chess Olympiad. Petrosian played on the 8th, i.e. bottom board of the very strong Soviet team. He was to play 4 games against Pilnik. In the first game, Petrosian was Black, and he equalised in a 6.Be2 e5 Boleslavsky Sicilian. After the opening, Pilnik gained an edge. After his 24th move the Argentine player offered a draw, and it was reasonable to accept it. In the second game, Petrosian castled long in the Queen's Gambit Exchange, Pilnik equalised and they drew after move 23.

Game 59

Pilnik, Hermann – Petrosian, Tigran
Argentina – Soviet Union Match,
Buenos Aires (3), 1954
Sicilian Defence

1.e4 c5 2.♘f3 ♘c6 3.d4 cxd4 4.♘xd4 ♘f6 5.♘c3 d6 6.♗e2 e5 7.♘b3 ♗e7 8.0-0 0-0 9.♗e3 ♗e6 10.♗f3 a5

Petrosian plays actively on the queenside; he had no doubt prepared for this line, as Pilnik had played it a few times. In those days, the flow of information was much slower and smaller, but those Pilnik games were played at well-known events.

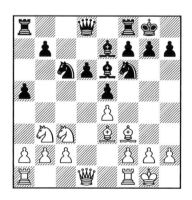

11.♘d5 ♗xd5 12.exd5 ♘b8

Petrosian deviates from the first game with a novelty. It had continued 12...♘b4 13.c3 ♘a6 14.a4 ♘d7 15.♗e2 ♘c7, when Petrosian deviated from the game Pilnik-Nedeljkovic 1952: 16.f4 exf4 17.♗xf4 ♘f6 (Black would equalise with 17...♖e8) 18.♗f3 ♖e8 19.♕d3 and White was somewhat better, Pilnik, H – Petrosian, T, Buenos Aires (1), 1954.

13.a4 ♘bd7 14.♗e2

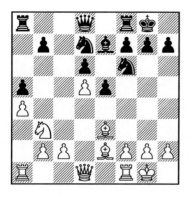

14...♘b6!?

An interesting idea. Petrosian invests two tempi to render White's queenside pawns less flexible.

15.c4 ♘bd7 16.♘d2 ♘e8

After stabilizing the queenside, Petrosian turns his attention to the kingside.

17.♔h1?!

White would do better if he kept the bishop pair. This move is pointless even if White doesn't mind swapping the bishop. After 17.g3!? ♗g5 18.f4 White's position would be better than in the game.

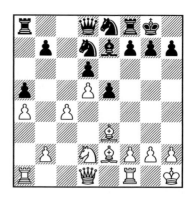

17...♗g5!

Exchanging the bishop is the right idea for Black, who obtains an initiative.

18.♗xg5 ♕xg5 19.♖a3 ♕e7 20.♖h3 ♘ef6 21.♗d3

The bishop is not really active on this diagonal, but no active role can be found for it.

21...g6

Black easily copes with White's attacking ideas, and this pawn move helps build Black's play.

22.♖e1 ♕d8 23.b3 ♔g7 24.♘f1

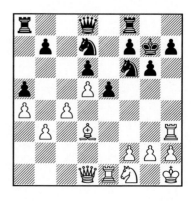

24...♘c5

The knight stands superbly on c5.

25.♗c2 ♘fd7 26.♕d2 ♖h8

Petrosian prepares to push the h-pawn; he may push two squares at once.

27.♘g3

The position would be even after 27.f4 h5 28.f5 ♘f6.

27...h5 28.♘e2 ♘f6 29.♘g1 ♖e8 30.♖he3 ♘g4 31.♖3e2

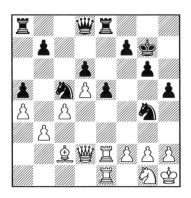

31...♕b6

Black's pieces stand a bit better, while White can do nothing but wait.

32.f3 ♘f6 33.♖e3

White can do nothing active.

33...♘cd7 34.♘e2 h4!

Black gains space.

35.♘g1 ♖h8 36.♘h3 ♖ae8 37.♕c3

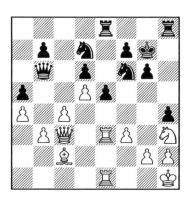

37...♕b4

Petrosian is happy as usual to exchange queens.

38.♕xb4 axb4 39.♘f2 ♘c5 40.♔g1

After 40.♘e4 ♘fxe4 41.fxe4 White would be passive, but had decent chances to hold.

40...♖eg8 41.g4?!

White has just moved his pieces for almost twenty moves without pushing a pawn. Now he decides to do so, but opening the h-file is beneficial for Black. 41.♘e4 would still be preferable.

41...hxg3 42.hxg3 ♘h5 43.♘h1

Pilnik plans to fight for the h-file. 43.♔g2 f5 44.♘h3 would be passive, but gives White some chances to hold.

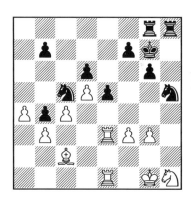

43...f5!

Petrosian gains space.

44.♖3e2 ♖h7 45.♖h2 ♖gh8 46.♖h3

46.♖ee2 would be more resilient. It would be interesting to know what way Petrosian was going to try to crack White's passive position.

46...♘f6 47.♖xh7+

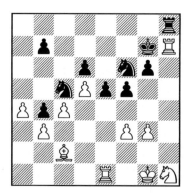

47...♞xh7!!

Closing the h-file which he wants to use is surprising. The course of the game suggests that Pilnik did not take this idea into consideration. It is especially remarkable as the game had probably already been adjourned, and if it was, then the whole Argentinian team may have analysed it.

48.♞f2

White has only ugly choices: 48.♜e2? ♞g5 49.♔g2 ♞xf3 wins, or 48.f4 exf4 (48...e4 is also strong) 49.gxf4 ♞f6 50.♞g3 ♜h4 51.♗xf5 ♞xb3 and White would struggle.

48...♞g5 49.♔g2?

The surprised Argentinian grandmaster makes an instantly losing blunder in a bad position. After 49.♗d1 ♔f6 50.♔g2 e4 Black would be much better.

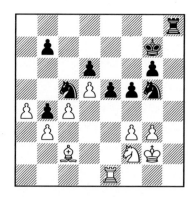

49...♜h2+! 0–1 This pretty move wins a pawn and the game.

In the last, fourth game, Petrosian played a hedgehog setup. After some slight fluctuations the game ended in a draw after time control. Petrosian won the mini-match 2.5:1.5. The Soviet Team won the event with the score of 20.5:11.5.

Uruguay – Soviet Union Match

The next stop on the tour was in Montevideo, the capital of Uruguay. Petrosian started the match against Corral. The Armenian grandmaster played his favourite Queen's Gambit Exchange. He won a very instructive game, but his opponent did not put up strong resistance. The end can be seen in the It's Your Move chapter. In the second game, Petrosian was Black against Olivera. White exchanged queens on d8 in the Saemisch King's Indian. Petrosian easily and instructively beat the probably amateur player. According to the database, the Soviet team won the match 19.5:0.5.

France – Soviet Union Match

In April, France hosted the Soviet team in Paris. Petrosian started as Black against Belkadi. He obtained an advantage against the King's Indian Attack and outclassed his opponent. Belkadi then played the King's Indian as Black, but he was unable to put up serious resistance. The Soviet team humiliated the French team as well, by the score 15:1.

USA – Soviet Union Match

It looks like the cold war had warm moments, too; one of them was that the US team hosted the Soviets in New York. The event took place in June and Petrosian was put on the seventh board. He started his mini match against Bisguier as White. In the King's Indian Attack he got a symbolic edge, they exchanged a lot and the game ended in a draw after Petrosian's 32nd move. In the second game, the American player attacked the King's Indian with the f4 line. In the middlegame, Petrosian allowed a tactical shot. He was worse, but created play with a pawn sacrifice. This game also ended after White's draw offer on the 32nd move. In the third game, they played a symmetrical 1.c4 c5 English. Bisguier handled the opening strangely, including playing ♔f8. He was somewhat worse when he made a serious mistake. Petrosian exploited it; a desperate piece sacrifice did not change the outcome. In the last game of the match, Bisguier as White decided to play sharply for a win. In a hedgehog type position he launched a pawn storm on the kingside. Petrosian was able to create counterplay on the a-file. He already enjoyed the luxury of choice to break with d5 or play e5, and then used his e5-pawn to establish a knight outpost on d4. Bisguier's attack came to a halt; Petrosian invaded on the queenside and won the game. Beating Bisguier 3:1 was a good performance. The Soviet team carried out a massacre with a 20:12 win over the home nation's team.

At the closing ceremony, *Chess Life* correspondent Eliot Hearst made observations of all the Soviet players, and here is what he said about Petrosian: "The baby of the Russian team, at 24, and who, though a native of Armenia, is described as Russia's Capablanca."

England – Soviet Union Match

In July, there was a match between England and the Soviet national team. Petrosian faced Milner Barry on seventh board. Petrosian got an edge in the main-line Nimzo-Indian. His opponent sacrificed a pawn, but was unable to create play and lost. The Soviet team won the first round with the stunning score of 10:0. In the second game, the Englishman played a harmless line against the Najdorf. Petrosian took control fairly quickly. He outclassed his opponent. 2:0 against England is always a good result. Russia amazingly beat England 18.5:1.5.

Sweden – Soviet Union Match

A few days after the match against England, the Soviet team played against Sweden in Stockholm. Tigran played a two game mini-match against Goode. In the first game, he got a neat position as White in the Saemisch Nimzo-Indian, but wasted his edge. In the endgame, Goode was up to the task and firmly held the draw. The second game was a g3 King's Indian. Goode made a big mistake at the end of the opening and Petrosian never let him back into the game. He won his mini-match 1.5:0.5, and his team defeated the Swedes 13:3.

Soviet Club Championship

Petrosian was not selected for the Soviet squad at the Amsterdam Olympiad. There were a lot of players on a similar high level, though it would be interesting to know how they selected the team. He was the youngest of the Soviet world class players At the same time, the Soviet team championship started. The event took place in the Latvian capital, Riga. Petrosian started the event as White against Suetin. It was a King's Indian and Petrosian played the 7.d5 variation that would be named after him. The move was first played in the game Grondman-Euwe 1923, and Flohr was the first world-class player to employ it, in 1948. But it is still rightly called the Petrosian Variation as he was so successful with it. He first employed it against Geller in 1949, and although he lost that game, it was his only loss out of 28 games: he won 16 games and drew 11 in his favourite line. A fine record! By the way, once he faced it as Black, against De Greiff, and drew. The Suetin win was his first win with the line. Suetin got very close to equalising, but he made some somewhat strange moves in the middlegame, including ♕f8-♕c8 and soon after ♕a6. Petrosian caught his king. Suetin had a bad day and resigned on move 40. In round 2, Petrosian was Black against Averbakh; it was a g3 King's Indian. The game was peaceful and Petrosian sacrificed a bishop to deliver perpetual check. In the third game, Petrosian as White gained a small edge against Chistiakov. Black got a bad pawn structure in the Ilyin-Zhenevsky Variation of the Dutch Defence with a horrible bishop against a knight with a great outpost. Chistiakov did really well to last as long as he did, but Petrosian forced resignation with his 65th move. In the fourth round, he was Black against a player who would stun the chess world like probably no other player ever did, the young Tal. Misha played 6.♗g5 against Petrosian's Najdorf. They repeated moves to draw in an equal position in the early middlegame. Petrosian next played in the 6th round, when he was White against Kan. They reached a highly complex position in a main-line Nimzo-Indian with e3-♘e2. Petrosian got a big advantage but missed a win. He was still somewhat better when, one move before time control, Kan made a bad mistake. He sacrificed an exchange, and Petrosian went on to win. Next, Petrosian was Black against Aronin in the Najdorf. The Russian player deviated from Tal's play at the same event. Petrosian handled the opening poorly but he escaped to an endgame the exchange down. Aronin had to play the endgame brilliantly to win.

In round 8, Petrosian was a bit better against Lisitsin. He is already better when we join the game.

Game 60

**Petrosian, Tigran –
Lisitsin, Georgy**
Soviet Club Championship Riga (8),
1954

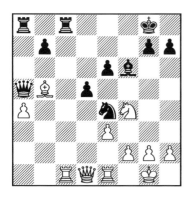

22...♘d6?
Lisitsin wrote some very good combination books, but maybe defending doesn't come to him naturally. After 22...♖xc1! 23.♕xc1

♕b6 or 23...♘c5 the position would be equal.
**23.♖xc8+ ♘xc8 24.♗d7 ♘b6
25.♗xe6+**
The bishop will be very strong when it comes to attack the king.
25...♔h8

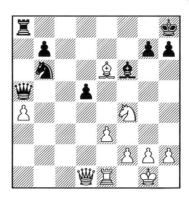

26.♖f1!
Petrosian places his rook on a defended square. Now the queen can go and attack the black king.

26...d4 27.♕f3 ♘xa4

If 27...dxe3 28.fxe3 ♘xa4 (after 28...♕xa4 29.♕h3 ♕e8 30.♗f5 White's attack breaks through) 29.♗d5 ♗g5 30.♘e6 ♗f6 31.♘g5 White wins.

28.♗d5!

Petrosian closes the fifth rank.

28...♕d8 29.♗xb7

White has time for this. Tal would probably want to mate his opponent directly by playing 29.♕h5. Taking the pawn shows Tigran's character: he makes sure to have the best conditions to continue if the attack fails to finish off his opponent.

29...♖b8 30.♗e4 ♘c3

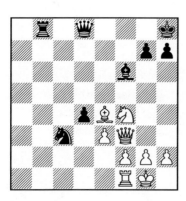

31.♕h3!

A nice attacking move.

31...h6

The bishop is poisoned: 31...♘xe4 32.♘g6+ ♔g8 33.♕e6 would be checkmate.

32.♗d3

One little move before the kill.

32...♕e8 33.♕f5 ♔g8 34.♗c4+ 1–0 Petrosian attacked very efficiently, and this game is a nice example.

In the 9th game, Petrosian was Black against Taimanov. It was a g3 King's Indian, and after a bit of turmoil they sealed a draw after Taimanov's 20th move. In the 10th round, Tigran was White against Korchnoi, in a 4.cxd5 5.e4 Grunfeld. The position simplified to a draw after the opening and they did not play on. In the last round, he was Black against Vasiukov[1]. White sacrificed a pawn for nothing in the Two Knights Variation of the Caro-Kann, and Petrosian ruthlessly punished him for his bad idea. Petrosian played well, he won 5 games and drew 4, but lost one as well. It was a good event for him.

Vartan Tigranovich Petrosian

After the Riga event, a special event happened in Petrosian's life on 18 September 1954: his son Vartan was born. We show in the photos section a picture of the Petrosian family from 1957. Vartan is 2 or 3 years old

---

For more on this fine attacking player who recently departed see *Evgeny Vasiukov, Chess Champion of Moscow* by Alexander Nikitin (Elk and Ruby, 2020)

in it. Petrosian had already adopted Rona's son Mikhail from her earlier marriage, but having his own issue must surely have brought him much joy.

It probably also changed the family's life. Maybe Rona had less energy to support her husband's career than in other years.

Actually, your Armenian author once saw a diagram with a combination played by Vartan in a Soviet chess magazine, but we were not able to trace it. Sometimes, Vartan would visit major chess events in Moscow. It is remarkable how much the adult Vartan resembles his father.

Your Armenian author spoke with Mikhail as well. He talked about his stepfather warmly and referred to him as his father.

Belgrade

Petrosian's last event of the year was in the Yugoslav capital, Belgrade. During Stalin's time there was big tension between the two communist countries. Now, though, Stalin was dead, and Petrosian and Bronstein became the first Soviet players to play in Yugoslavia. Petrosian started the event as White against Porreca. The Italian player risked the Albin Counter-Gambit, and Petrosian was not prepared for it. In the early part of the opening, Black enjoyed an advantage. Petrosian then solved his problems, took control and won the game. In the second round, Petrosian faced Rabar as Black. In a main-line Nimzo-Indian things looked alright for Petrosian, but he made a careless move and White got a clear advantage. Rabar was still much better when he offered a draw after his 22nd move. Petrosian understandably did not try his luck. In round 3, Petrosian after 1.d4 ♘f6 2.♘f3 b6 3.♗g5 ♗b7 played 4.♘c3 against Nievergelt. Black soon played g6. Petrosian attacked with h4 and got a big advantage; he refuted his opponent's desperate piece sacrifice and scored another victory. In round 4, Petrosian was White against Karaklajic. He handled the Meran originally by giving up castling with ♔f1. Petrosian was worse, but managed to equalise. He slowly took control. Karaklajic was able to simplify. Black was possibly able to hold, but Petrosian managed to squeeze the win.

In the next game, Petrosian was Black against Wade, and he equalised in the opening.

Game 61

Wade, Bob – Petrosian, Tigran
Belgrade (5), 1954

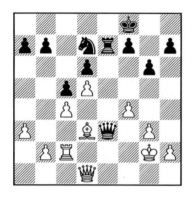

24.♖e2

Wade exchanges the rook; exchanging queens would be more practical. After 24.♕d2 ♕d4 25.♗e2 ♖e3 26.♔f1 White should hold.

24...♕d4 25.♕e1?

After 25.♖d2 ♘f6 26.♗f1 ♕e4+ 27.♕f3 White could keep his position together.

25...♖xe2+ 26.♕xe2 ♘b6!?

Petrosian wants to provoke a pawn move; he has a stronger way of acting on the queenside: 26...b5! 27.cxb5 (27.b3 bxc4 28.bxc4 ♕a1 wins) 27...♘b6 28.♕c2 ♘xd5 29.♔f3 ♘f6 and White's king would be dangerously open.

27.b3?!

This pawn move slightly weakens the queenside. It was probably better stopping ♘a4 with 27.♕c2 and planning to move ♗e2 and ♗d3.

27...♘d7 28.a4 ♘f6 29.♗c2 ♕c3

Petrosian's 26th move helped to provide the c3-square for the queen.

30.♗d1

Black will not swap queens; if 30.♕d3 then 30...♕e1.

30...h5 31.♕c2 ♕d4 32.♗f3 ♔e7 33.♕c1 ♔e8 34.♕c2 ♔d7

Black is probably just tiring his opponent.

35.♕c1

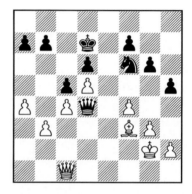

35...♘g8!?

A clever, practical idea. Black considers transferring the knight to f5, but also puts the ball in White's court and waits to see what he will do.

36.h3?!

After this move, if White's queen leaves c1 then Black could play the unpleasant h4. Instead, White could have created a weakness on the kingside with 36.f5, which would have kept the position balanced. 36...♘f6 (36...gxf5 37.♕g5) 37.fxg6 fxg6 38.♕g5 and White holds.

36...♘f6 37.g4

37.♕c2 h4 would be rather unpleasant.

37...hxg4

37...h4! would be strong as well.

38.hxg4 ♔d8 39.a5 ♘d7

Petrosian wants to improve his knight; he could play for zugzwang with 39...♔d7 40.g5 ♘e4 41.♗xe4 ♕xe4+ 42.♔f2 ♕d4+ 43.♔e2 ♔c7. Maybe White can survive, but the queen ending would be very difficult, as exchanging queens would be a win for Black.

40.♔g3

With 40.g5 White could make sure the knight remains cut off from the e5–square. However, 40... ♕d3 41.♕b2 ♕e3 42.♔g3 f6 (if 42...♕e1+ 43.♔h3 ♕xa5 44.♔g7 White is active enough) 43.gxf6 g5 44.fxg5 ♘e5 45.♕e2 ♕xg5+ 46.♗g4 ♕xf6 would be rather unpleasant for White to defend.

40...g5

The last move before time control is clever, but not the best. After 40... ♕d3! 41.♕d1 ♕c3 Black wins a pawn for nothing.

41.fxg5 ♔e7

After 41...♘e5 42.♕f4 ♕g1+

43.♔h3 ♕f1+ 44.♔g3 ♕e1+ 45.♔g2 ♕xa5 46.♕f6+ ♔d7 47.♕f5+ ♔e8 48.♕c8+ White may hold.

42.♗e2?

Wade is not sufficiently alert. After 42.♕f4 ♕g1+ 43.♔h3 ♘e5 44.♕f6+ ♔d7 45.g6 White would be alright. Or White would hold after 42.g6 fxg6 43.♕g5+ ♕f6 44.♕f4.

42...♘e5 43.g6

It is too late, as the knight can take the g-pawn.

43...♘xg6 44.g5

44.♔g2 ♔f6 would win.

44...♔f8

The king will not get checked, and moves closer to the g5–pawn.

45.♔g2 ♘h4+ 46.♔f1 ♔g7 47.♗d1

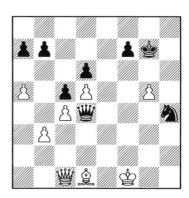

47...♘f5

The knight stands well; it covers its own king and attacks White's king. The queen and the knight will soon catch the white king.

48.♔e2 ♕g4+ 49.♔d3 ♕g1 50.♕b2+ ♔h7 51.♗h5 ♕g3+ 52.♔e4 ♘d4 53.♕d2 ♕h4+ 54.♕f4 ♕xh5 55.♕xd6 ♕f3+ 0–1

In the next round, Petrosian was White against Barcza. The Hungarian grandmaster played the Grunfeld and came out alright from the opening. They agreed to a draw after Black's 22nd move. In the seventh round, Tigran chose the Bogo-Indian against Nedeljkovic. No player was able to create chances in the 28-move draw. In round 8, Petrosian beat Milic in a nice game, and its highlights can be seen in the 1953 Lokvenc game. In the 9th round, Petrosian was Black against Ivkov. They played the Richter-Rauzer Sicilian, his position was alright, but he played too riskily and Ivkov managed to punish him. In the 10th round, Petrosian as White played the English Opening in too original a manner against Matanovic. The Yugoslav grandmaster acted powerfully and offered a draw after his 14th move. Petrosian agreed. In the 11th round, Petrosian was Black against Joppen. He equalised in a 3.♘c3 ♝b4 French. The German player made a mistake; Petrosian exploited it and won the game. In round 12, he made a quick draw with his fellow Soviet Bronstein. In the 13th round, Petrosian was Black against Janosevic. He handled the Caro-Kann Panov Variation too riskily. He was worse, but not lost, when he made a horrible move. He managed to prolong the game until resigning on move 74. In round 14, Petrosian was White against Pirc.

He got a small advantage in the g3 King's Indian, but his opponent was up to the task of holding. In the 15th round, Petrosian was Black against Pilnik. The Argentine player looked for safety in the 3.♘c3 French, and the draw was agreed after only 15 moves. In the 16th game, Djurasevic as Black equalised in the Exchange Queen's Gambit, his good play preventing Petrosian from applying any pressure. The game ended in a draw after Black's 40th move. In the 17th round, he was Black against Czerniak. He outplayed his Israeli opponent in a Sicilian sideline and won a complex game. In the penultimate round, he opened 1.e4 against Trifunovic. He got a nice advantage in the Scotch, yet after Black's twentieth move Petrosian strangely agreed to a draw in a better position. In the last round, Petrosian as Black tried the Old Indian against Gligoric, but the Yugoslav grandmaster outplayed him. Surprisingly, he wasted his advantage, but Petrosian blundered badly and got checkmated. Petrosian finished the event scoring 11.5 points out of 19. He won 7 games, drew 9 and lost 3. His joint 4th-5th place with Ivkov was disappointing. Bronstein won the event with 13.5 points. Tigran started well, but he was unrecognisable in the second half of the event. Perhaps he had some health issue, or something private happened to him.

Petrosian's results in 1954

Soviet Championship Final, Kiev	+ 6 = 13 – 0 12.5/19 4th-5th place
Argentina – USSR Match vs. Pilnik	+ 1 = 3 – 0 2.5:1.5
Uruguay – USSR Match	+ 2 = 0 – 0 2:0
France – USSR Match vs. Belkadi	+ 2 = 0 – 0 2:0
USA – USSR Match vs. Bisguier	+ 2 = 2 – 0 3:1
England – USSR Match vs. Milner Barry	+ 2 = 0 – 0 2:0
Sweden – USSR Match vs. Goode	+ 1 = 1 – 0 1.5:0.5
Soviet Club Championship, Riga	+ 5 = 4 – 1 7/10
Belgrade	+ 7 = 9 – 3 11.5/19 4th-5th place
Altogether	**+ 28 = 32 – 4 44/64**

1955

Soviet Championship Final, Moscow

This event was the qualification for the interzonal, so it mattered a lot for all the players. Petrosian had to finish in the top four to qualify, but if Botvinnik, Smyslov or Keres were ahead of him, they would not count, as the first was the world champion and the other two giants were seeded directly to the Gothenburg Candidates Tournament. The event was extremely strong, and only Bronstein who was sick did not participate from the stars.

Petrosian started the event as White against Kan. He could have gone for a sharp line with some advantage in the King's Indian Attack, but kept the position complex. Petrosian opened up Kan's king. Kan neutralised the attack by an exchange sacrifice, but this just prolonged the end a little. In the second game, Petrosian was White against Geller. He was unable to create chances in a 1.c4 c5 English Opening. They agreed to a draw after Geller's 26th move. In the third game, Petrosian as Black played the Old Indian against Kotov; they manoeuvred in a King's Indian type of position, and peace broke out after Kotov's 24th move. In the fourth round, he was White against Botvinnik. The world champion, who had started the event well with 2.5 out of 3 games, played the Slav Schlechter. Both players seemed content with a draw, which was agreed after the champion's 20th move. In the next game, Petrosian was Black against Spassky. They reached a complex position in the 6.♗g5 Najdorf. In the middlegame, Petrosian avoided a repetition, but did not play well. Not long before time control, Spassky sacrificed a piece. He was clearly winning, but his 40th move was a mistake. After Spassky's 42nd move, perhaps after analysing the position at home, they agreed to a draw, and Petrosian was fortunate in that game. In the 6th round, Petrosian was White against Averbakh, and the game ended in perpetual check in only 14 moves. They may have agreed to a draw in advance. In the seventh game, Petrosian was Black against Simagin. In the Richter-Rauzer Sicilian White created doubled pawns on f6 and took on c6 as well. In a complex position Simagin overrated his chances and sacrificed two pawns. He kept on playing when they swapped queens, but of course in vain. In the 8th round, Petrosian was White against Smyslov. It was another Schlechter Variation, and they drew in 16 moves. In the next round, Tigran was Black against Furman. Petrosian accepted an isolated pawn in the English Opening. He did not defend the pawn, but gave it away and changed White's pawn structure a bit. He instructively held the position. In the 10th round, Petrosian was White against Flohr in a reversed Benoni. Flohr's good play prevented White from creating chances to gain an edge. The game ended in a repetition after 27 moves. In the 11th round, Petrosian was Black against Ilivitsky. He gave up the two bishops for fluent play, took control and obtained a better endgame, but Ilivitsky's stubborn play earned him the draw. We now look at the masterpiece from round 12.

Game 62

**Petrosian, Tigran –
Taimanov, Mark**
Soviet Championship Final, Moscow
(12), 1955
Meran Semi-Slav

1.d4 ♘f6 2.c4 e6 3.♘f3 d5 4.♘c3 c6 5.e3 ♘bd7 6.♗d3 ♗b4!? 7.0-0 0-0 8.♕c2 ♗d6

This is somewhat illogical; it was hardly worth a tempo just to drag the queen to c2.

9.b3! dxc4 10.bxc4 e5 11.♗b2 ♖e8

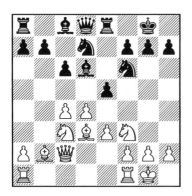

12.♘e4!

Petrosian exchanges to get closer to Taimanov's camp.

12...♘xe4 13.♗xe4 h6

After 13...g6 14.c5 ♗c7 White would have a few options, which gives a small edge. Perhaps 15.♖ad1 is the most promising.

14.♖ad1 exd4?!

This move makes the b2-bishop dangerously active. White is better developed, so opening the position should not favour Black. 14...♕e7 15.c5 ♗c7 16.♘xe5 ♘xe5 17.dxe5 ♗xe5 18.♗xe5 ♕xe5 19.♖d4 is not pleasant either but better.

15.♗h7+

Petrosian inserts a check. The commentators thought that 15.♖xd4 ♘f6 (15...♕e7! 16.♗h7+!) 16.c5 ♘xe4 17.cxd6 ♗f5 would be fine for Black, but they missed 18.d7! ♖e7 19.♘h4 ♗h7 20.♖fd1 and White would be much better.

15...♔h8 16.♖xd4!

Petrosian brings the rook into play. It is hard to anticipate what an amazing role this rook will have.

16...♗c5?

Taimanov plays optimistically; this move chases White's rook to a better square. Surprisingly, this mistake probably loses.

a) 16...♗f8 was recommended, but after 17.♖h4 f6 18.♗g6 it loses.

b) 16...♗c7 17.♗f5 c5 (if 17...♕e7 18.♖e4 ♕f8 19.♖h4 Black would be in trouble) 18.♖h4 ♘e5 19.♖h5 and Black is living dangerously.

c) 16...♕e7! would be the best defensive move. 17.♖fd1 (17.♖e4 ♕f8 18.♖d1 ♖xe4 19.♗xe4 ♘c5 is not worth much) 17...♗c7 18.♖e4 ♕f8 19.g3 and White would better, but clearly not winning.

17.♖f4! ♕e7

17...♖f8 18.♖d1! would be strong. After 17...f6 18.♖d1 ♖e6 (18...♕c7 19.♘h4 wins) 19.♗f5 ♖d6 20.♖xd6 ♗xd6 21.♖d4 Black would be in serious trouble.

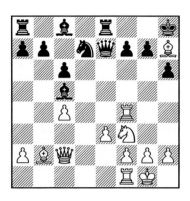

18.♖e4!

The rook chases the queen away, after which playing ♘f6 would result in doubled pawns in Black's camp. 18.♘h4 ♘f8 19.♗f5 is also very strong.

18...♕f8

After 18...♕d8 19.♗f5 Black would at the very least be in a very difficult position.

19.♖h4!

The rook moves again, and it forces a weakening of the g6–square.

19...f6

If 19...♘f6 the pretty 20.♖xh6! would win.

20.♗g6 ♖e7

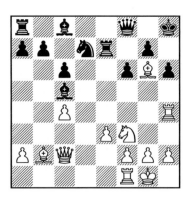

21.♖h5!

Petrosian employs his rook magically; he vacates the h4–square for the knight.

21...♗d6 22.♖d1 ♗e5 23.♗a3 c5

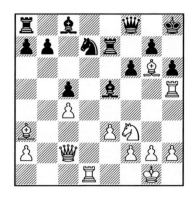

24.♘h4! 1–0 Taimanov resigns. Either the white knight reaches the g6-square or White's pieces invade decisively, for instance 24...♕d8 25.♗xc5 or 24...♖e6 25.♗f5 would win. 24...♕g8 would not be any better because of 25.♗e4 ♘f8 26.♖d8.

In round 13, Petrosian faced Borisenko as Black. He tried to create complications with the Dutch Defence. Borisenko played reasonably, and the game ended in a repetition after Petrosian's 27th move.

In the 14th round, Petrosian was White against Korchnoi. He played ♕c2 in the Meran and adventurously castled long. The game went wrong for him, though. He sacrificed an exchange to gain attacking chances, but by time control Petrosian was losing. When we join the game he is still losing.

Game 63

Petrosian, Tigran – Korchnoi, Victor
Soviet Championship Final, Moscow
(14), 1955

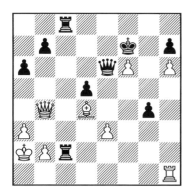

Black is an exchange up and has a dangerous passed pawn. White has a strong f6–pawn, and Black's king is not as safe as he would like it to be. Korchnoi now plays a reasonably good move but misses better ones, for example, 43...♖2c7! This move followed by ♖g8 is winning without

much difficulty. 44.♖h5 ♕c6! 45.♖g5 (after 45.b3 ♕c2+ 46.♔b2 ♕xb2+! Black would checkmate) 45...♖g8 and Black wins.

43...b5 44.♖h5!

This is a good move, which gives White practical chances to save the day.

44...♖8c4?

Leaving the 8th rank is a mistake. 44...♔g6! taking away the g5–square wins. 45.♖e5 ♕xf6 46.♖xd5 ♕e6 47.♕b3 ♖8c6 48.♗e5 ♔xh6 and White runs out of play and loses.

45.♕b3 ♕e4!

Korchnoi plays a fantastic idea; he threatens ♖c1 and cuts off the white queen from the g-pawn. But the idea has a hole in it. Attacking the king no longer works: 45...♔g6? 46.♖e5 ♕xf6 47.♕d3+ and White would win. After 45...♖f2 46.♖g5 ♖xd4 47.♖g7+ ♔xf6 48.♕c3 the position would be equal.

46.♖e5 g3

Black can't turn back along the way; he has to sacrifice the queen. 46...♕g6? 47.♖e7+ ♔f8

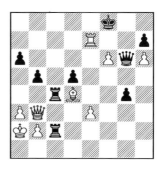

48.e4!! the pawn move vacates the third rank, enabling the queen to move to g3. 48...g3 (48...♖xd4 49.♕xc2) 49.♖g7 ♕xe4 50.♕xg3 checkmates.

47.♖xe4 dxe4

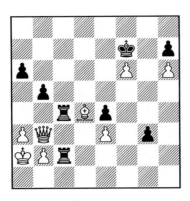

48.♗c3!!

Victor possibly calculated 48.♗e5? g2 49.♗h2 and he noticed that the fantastic 49...♖d2!! threatens to trap the white queen, and then after 50.♔b1 ♖d3 51.♕a2 Black would checkmate with ♖d1. Whereas 49...♖c1? may look like winning, but 50.a4! would save White. Petrosian's superb bishop move wins the c2-rook.

48...g2

48...♖f2?? 49.♕d1 would win. Black has no time to save the c2-rook: 48...♖c1 49.a4!! g2 50.axb5 axb5 51.♕xb5 ♖4xc3 52.♕d7+ ♔xf6 53.♕d6+ ♔f5 54.♕f4+ and White would definitely not lose.

49.♕xc2 g1=♕ 50.♕d2!

Petrosian improves the queen; he is safe, as the black king has no shelter.

50...♕g4 51.♔a1

After 51.♕d5+ ♕e6 52.♕h5+

♔f8 53.♔a1 White would be safe in the ensuing queen ending.

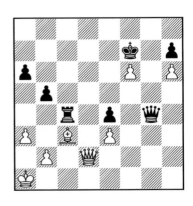

51...♕g1+

Korchnoi settles for repetition. He could still try and gain more with 51...♖c5 52.♕d6 ♖f5 53.♕xa6. White would be a fraction worse, but should hold.

52.♔a2 ♕g4 53.♔a1 ♕g1+ 54.♔a2 1/2

In the next round, Petrosian was Black against Lisitsin. He tried the King's Indian Defence. Not much happened in the 21-move draw. In the 16th round, Tigran was White against Keres. Petrosian accepted an isolated pawn position in the e3 Queen's Indian. The pawn structure changed, and Keres slowly took control. Petrosian managed to fight back, but mistakenly simplified to an ending with 1 rook each and opposite-coloured bishops before time control. After that he soon lost a pawn. After suffering for a long time, Petrosian managed to hold. In the 17th round, Petrosian was Black against Mikenas. They reached an exciting position in the Queen's Gambit Declined, and after the experienced grandmaster's 22nd move they agreed to a draw. In the penultimate round, Petrosian was White against Antoshin. The players manoeuvred in the Ragozin Variation of the Queen's Gambit, and when the direct fight started pieces disappeared quickly. After the 30th move there was nothing left to play for.

Here are the standings at the top before the last round: Geller 12, Botvinnik and Smyslov 11.5, Spassky 11, and Ilivitsky and Petrosian 10.5. In the last round, Petrosian was Black against Shcherbakov. The Russian master chose a side-line in the French. He somewhat mysteriously sacrificed a pawn early on, and he got no play for it. Petrosian created doubled pawns in White's camp, and had a superior knight to a bishop. Naturally, Petrosian won the game. Geller lost to Antoshin, Smyslov drew with Taimanov, Ilivitsky beat Furman, and Lisitsin was close to beating Spassky, but they drew.

Smyslov and Geller were joint winners. Petrosian finished joint-third with Ilivitsky, Spassky and Botvinnik; they all scored 11.5 points out of 19. Note that Botvinnik, who had been so successful at the Soviet championships, played his very last Soviet championship that year. Petrosian won 4 games and drew 15, remaining undefeated. He was criticized for playing passively, yet he risked losing against Spassky and Korchnoi, and struggled against Keres. He did not hold back in those games.

He recorded six draws which lasted no more than 22 moves, but they were mainly against top players like Botvinnik and Smyslov. Winning only 2 out of 10 white games was not satisfying. But sharing third place in the super strong Soviet final was a success. In particular, it provided him with a place in the upcoming interzonal in the world championship cycle.

Hungary – Soviet Union Match

In early May, the Soviet team won the World Students Team Championship, though strangely Petrosian, who at this point of his career was clearly stronger than Taimanov and Spassky, was not selected for the team. Perhaps this boosted his motivation to do well in his next event.

At the end of May, the Soviet team travelled to Budapest. Earlier, they had played independent countries; Hungary, though, was part of the Eastern bloc, which the Soviets controlled. In the fifties, Hungarian chess was not as strong as it would be in the late sixties and seventies, but it was far from weak.

In the first game, Petrosian was White against Bilek. They reached an isolated pawn position, the Hungarian neutralised Tigran's play, then when they simplified Petrosian made an inaccuracy. However, Bilek failed to exploit it, so Petrosian was able to avoid long suffering to obtain the draw with a pawn deficit. In the next game, he was Black against Szabo. The Hungarian number one played the Slav Gambit, and Petrosian's 14th move was a novelty. Soon after, Szabo sacrificed a piece, but it was a mistake, and Tigran exploited it. According to Barcza, Petrosian returned the piece in an exemplary way and won the game. The key highlight can be seen in the commentary of the 40th game of this book, in the 1951 Smyslov Soviet Championship game. In the third game, he was Black against Benko. It was a 13-move draw. In the fourth game, Barcza as Black chose a variation of the Exchange Queen's Gambit. Petrosian played a novelty on the seventh move, which became the main line. He saddled Black with doubled isolated pawns on the f-file. They reached a good knight versus bad bishop position. Petrosian scored another victory on the 60th move. In Petrosian's second game against Bilek, he played the 4...♘d7 Caro-Kann. They castled on opposite sides, the exciting fight was balanced, and a few moves before time control the battle ended in a repetition. In round 6, Petrosian and Kluger produced a fantastic game, which can be seen in the commentary to Petrosian's Gligoric Zurich 1953 game (game 56). Tigran won. In the last, 7th game, Petrosian as White played the Saemisch Variation against Benko. The Hungarian youngster made a bad mistake in the opening. He lasted until the 27th move.

Petrosian was rested in the last round. His 5.5 points out of 7 games comprised a world class performance. The experienced master Asztalos was so impressed after the event that he predicted that Petrosian would be Botvinnik's next challenger. We cite grandmaster Barcza: "The best personal performance was grandmaster Petrosian's. His technical skills are perfect; and they are combined with a very clever tactical arsenal."

The Soviet team beat the Hungarians 20:12, the same score they posted against the USA a year before.

Soviet Union – United States Match

In June, the Soviet team hosted the Americans in Moscow. Petrosian was selected on board 6 out of 8, behind Botvinnik, Smyslov, Bronstein, Geller and Keres. According to *Sports Illustrated* of 4 July 1955 "Russia's chess masters are mature men, well-groomed, dignified, their appearance suggesting a group of prominent professors. In comparison, the Americans suggest a group of revolutionaries—wild, unpredictable and unyielding in their resistance to Soviet chess authority."

In the first game, he was White against Horowitz. He got an edge in the 1.c4 c5 English and outclassed his opponent. In the second round, Petrosian played the Old Benoni with g6 as Black against Horowitz. He obtained a pleasant position in the opening. His opponent optimistically manoeuvred his queen to the edge of the board to hunt down a pawn. However, Petrosian exploited this journey and checkmated his opponent fairly quickly.

We look at his third game, where he played really well.

Game 64

Petrosian, Tigran – Pavey, Max
USSR – USA Match, Moscow (3),
1955
King's Indian Attack

1.e4 c5 2.♘f3 d6 3.d3 ♘c6 4.♘bd2 ♘f6 5.g3 e6 6.♗g2 ♗e7 7.0-0 0-0 8.c3 d5 9.♖e1 ♕c7 10.♘f1 ♗d7

Developing the bishop to d7 was only ever played in this game. It blocks the knight's path to its usual place, but still there is nothing terribly wrong with it.

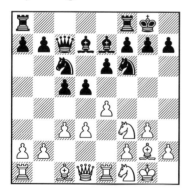

11.e5
Petrosian goes for closing the centre and soon starts an attack on the kingside.

11...♘e8 12.♗f4 ♕b6 13.♕e2 ♗d8?

Pavey launches an awkward idea. After 13...f5 14.exf6 ♘xf6 15.♘e5 White would have a small edge.

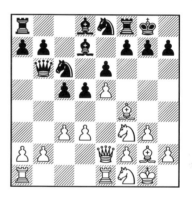

14.h4!
Petrosian launches an attack.
14...♕a6 15.h5 ♘e7?

The knight aims to help the king, but it fails to do so. Black should ease White's domination on the kingside and accept a backward pawn on the e-file. 15...h6 16.♕d2 f6 (16...b5 17.♗xh6 gxh6 18.♕xh6 ♕c8 19.♘e3 ♘g7 20.♗h3 followed by ♘g4 is clearly better for White, and if 20...f5 then 21.♘g2 would be strong) 17.♘e3 ♖c8 (17...♗e7 18.♗h3±)

18.d4 cxd4 19.♘xd5! when Black would be somewhat worse.

16.h6!

A pawn so close to the king is very annoying for Black.

16...g6

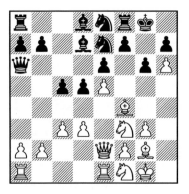

17.♗g5!

Petrosian is looking to exchange the dark-squared bishops.

17...♖c8 18.♘1h2

The knight joins the attack. It is hard for Black to do something beneficial.

18...♗b5 19.♗f1 ♘f5 20.♘g4 ♕b6 21.♕d2 ♗c6

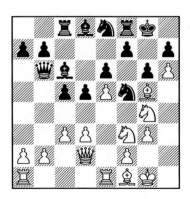

22.♗xd8!

Petrosian's strategy prevails, and the bishops get swapped.

22...♕xd8 23.d4

Petrosian makes room for his bishop.

23...♕e7

23...c4 24.♗e2 b5 25.♗d1 is also very difficult for Black.

24.♗d3 ♔h8 25.♔g2! ♖c7 26.b4!

Petrosian is patient; with his recent moves he has first improved those pieces which he can.

26...c4 27.♗c2 ♕d8

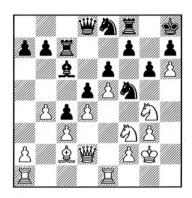

28.♕g5!

Petrosian wants to exchange in order to invade.

28...♕xg5

Black no longer has a good choice. For example, after 28...♖c8 29.a4 ♖b8 30.♘f6 Black's position is so passive that it would be beyond salvation.

29.♘xg5 ♘e7 30.♖e3!

Petrosian improves the rook; he most probably already anticipates the great ensuing tactical idea.

30...♘g8 31.♖f3 ♖e7

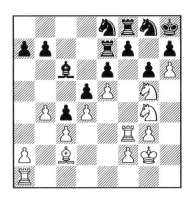

32.♗xg6!!

A highly unusual tactical shot, which opens up Black's position.

32...hxg6 33.h7 f5

Black could not just wait. If 33...b6 34.hxg8=♕+ ♔xg8 35.♖h1 a6 36.♖h7 White checkmates.

34.♖h1 ♘gf6

If 34...b6 35.hxg8=♕+ ♔xg8 36.♘e3 ♗d7 37.♖f4 White wins.

35.♘xf6 ♘xf6 36.exf6 ♖xf6 37.♖e3

White's knight is far superior to the bishop.

37...♖e8

After 37...f4 38.gxf4 ♖xf4 39.♖h6 White would win.

38.♖h4 ♗d7

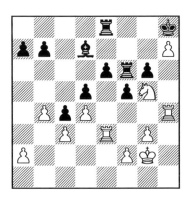

39.♔f3!

Petrosian finds a neat way to deliver the knockout punch.

39...♔g7 40.♔f4! ♗c8 41.♖e1 ♖ff8

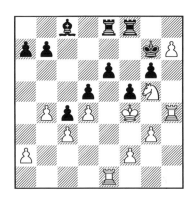

42.♔e5!

Petrosian uses his king elegantly.

42...♖h8 43.♖eh1 ♖e7 44.a4 ♖ee8 45.a5 ♖d8 46.♖h6 ♖de8

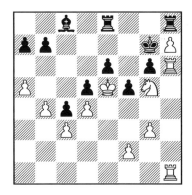

47.♘f3

Petrosian starts improving his knight. This will be his final improvement.

47...♖e7

This is an unfortunate square for the rook, but Petrosian's idea is

irresistible anyway. For instance, if
47...♗d7 48.♘h4 ♔xh6 49.♘xf5+
♔g5   50.♘e3   White   would
checkmate.

48.♘h4 1–0

In the fourth game, Petrosian
was Black again against Pavey.
They reached a main-line Ruy
Lopez Chigorin position. Pavey
acted aggressively, and Petrosian
reacted with a pawn sacrifice. Then,
the American sacrificed a pawn for
virtually nothing, and soon after a
rook. Petrosian took everything and

won the game. He scored 4 out 4 in
the event. He played against players
far below his level, yet he was very
impressive. The Soviets crushed the
Americans with a devastating score of
25:7, and three Soviet players scored
100 percent, Smyslov, Petrosian
and Kotov. The Americans had a
little bit of consolation: Reshevsky
beat the world champion Botvinnik
2.5:1.5. Maybe the one-sidedness of
the match contributed to the fact
that this was the last Soviet match
against the USA.

Interzonal Tournament, Gothenburg

The qualification competition for the next year's Candidates Tournament
was held in Gothenburg, Sweden. It started in the middle of August and the
players fought for 9 places. The Soviet players got certain numbers at the
draw that made certain they would face each other in the early part of the
event. The Argentine players were treated the same way.

Petrosian had a bye in the first round. In the second round, he was
White against Keres. In a main-line Nimzo-Indian Petrosian accepted
hanging pawns. He soon sacrificed a pawn, then got short of time early on.
He missed a win, and then forced a repetition. In the third round, Spassky
as White played the Two Knights Variation against the Caro-Kann. Boris's
handling was harmless; a draw was sealed after White's 24th move. In round
4, he drew with Geller in 14 moves. He and Ilivitsky also made just 14
moves. His draw against Bronstein lasted a bit longer, 19 moves. Pachman
in round 7 was his first foreign opponent. The Czech grandmaster employed
the g3 line against the King's Indian. After the opening, White started a
tactical confrontation, but the position simplified a lot, and Pachman did
not try to win with his symbolic advantage. In the 8th round, Petrosian
played the Mikenas-Carls Variation of the English Opening against Rabar.
He got a position in which it was hard to play for a win. The disappointing
draw ended after the 20th move of the Yugoslav player. His string of 7
draws came to an end in the 9th round. He was Black against Medina; the
Spaniard played the 6.f4 line against Petrosian's Najdorf. The position was
balanced for long, but on move 41 Medina sacrificed an exchange, and ten

moves later he resigned. In the tenth round, Petrosian was White against Bisguier. The Tarrasch transposed into a Queen's Gambit Accepted, Black's precise opening play neutralising White's attempts to win. The draw arrived after 20 moves. In the 11th round, Petrosian was Black against Panno. They reached an isolated pawn variation in a main-line Nimzo-Indian. They exchanged a lot of pieces, and the 4-rooks ending was always going to be a draw.

Petrosian's second half of the event started against Pilnik.

Game 65

Petrosian, Tigran –
Pilnik, Hermann
Gothenburg Interzonal (12), 1955
Sicilian Defence

1.c4 ♘f6 2.♘c3 g6 3.e4 d6 4.d4 ♗g7 5.♗e2 0-0 6.♘f3 c5 7.0-0

Petrosian will always play this move.

7...cxd4

Pilnik transposes to the Maroczy Bind. Tigran will play a game when his opponent avoids it: 7...♗g4 8.d5 ♘fd7 9.♗g5 ♘a6 10.♘d2 ♗xe2 11.♕xe2 ♘c7 12.f4 ♕e8 13.♖ae1 a6 14.♕d3 b5 15.b3 e5 16.f5 f6 17.♗e3 g5 18.cxb5 axb5 19.♘xb5 ♘xb5 20.♕xb5 ♖xa2 21.♖a1. White got an advantage and went on to win, Petrosian, T – Taimanov, M, Leningrad 1959.

8.♘xd4 ♘c6 9.♗e3 a6

Pilnik plays a rare move, Black has little chance to carry out b5. Ever since, Black players have tried to ease the position by exchanging pieces. 9...♗d7 10.♘c2 a6 11.f3 ♘e5 12.b3 ♖c8 13.a4 a5 14.♕e1 ♗c6 15.♖d1 ♘ed7 16.♔h1 ♕c7

17.♘d4 b6 18.♗d3 ♘c5 19.♗c2 ♗b7 20.♕h4 ♖fe8 21.♗g5 ♕b8 22.♖fe1 ♘e6 23.♘xe6 fxe6 24.♕h3 e5 25.♘d5 when Black was already in trouble and unable to hold in Petrosian, T – Rytov, B, Tallinn, 1979.

10.♕d2 ♗d7

This was a new move. Black's waiting stance is not good.

11.f3 ♖c8 12.♖fd1 ♖e8

13.♘xc6!

Petrosian follows a strong strategy. He exchanges a piece to gain space on the queenside and push Black back.

13...♗xc6

13...bxc6? would be clearly bad because of 14.c5!, but taking with the rook would lead to a somewhat better position than in the game. After 13...♖xc6 14.b4 or 14.c5 ♗e6 15.b4 White would have some advantage.

14.b4!

Petrosian gains space on the queenside. Black's position is solid with no weakness, but he has no active plan.

14...♘d7 15.a4! b6

15...♘f8 16.a5 would be more than unpleasant for Black.

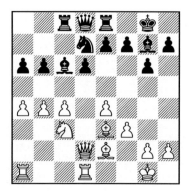

16.a5!

Petrosian creates a weakness in Black's camp.

16...b5?

After this mistake White will have a very strong pawn on a5, a potential passed pawn. 16...♗b7! 17.axb6 (or after 17.♗d4 bxa5 18.♗xg7 ♔xg7 19.♕d4+ f6 20.♖xa5 White would be better) 17...♘xb6 18.c5 dxc5 19.♕e1 ♗d4 20.♗xa6 ♕c7 21.♗xb7 ♕xb7 22.♗xd4 cxd4 23.♖xd4 and White would have an extra pawn but it would require some work and skill to win the game.

17.♖ac1 bxc4 18.♗xc4 ♗xc3

Pilnik has no good choice. Petrosian's subtle play made the bishop on g7 ineffective in this position. His move eases Black's problems on the queenside a bit, but weakens the king.

19.♖xc3 ♗b7

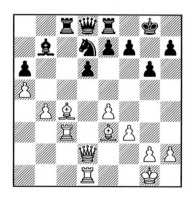

20.♗d4

Petrosian's move is strong, but 20.♗h6 or 20.♕d4 were equally powerful and somewhat more practical, as either would have prevented Pilnik from creating counterplay. Petrosian will have problems with his clock; it would be interesting to know whether time trouble was in the air already.

20...e6!

Pilnik's move leads to a lost position, yet it is a good one as in a hopeless position it creates play and problems for his opponent to solve. 20...♘e5? does not work because White would win after 21.♗xe5 dxe5 22.♕c1!.

21.♗e2 ♕e7 22.b5

White has many good options,

for instance 22.♖xc8 ♖xc8 23.♗b2 d5 24.exd5 exd5 25.♕d4 wins as well.

22...axb5 23.♗xb5 d5

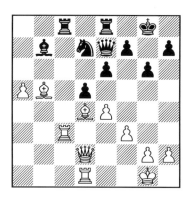

24.a6

The pawn is powerful, but that is not Black's biggest problem.

24...♗a8 25.♖xc8

White has many ways to win and this is one of them. 25.e5 or 25.exd5 ♗xd5 26.♕e3 would do as well.

25...♖xc8   26.♗xd7   ♕xd7 27.♕f4

There are simpler solutions: 27.♗f6 ♕d6 28.e5 ♕f8 29.♖c1 and Black would be absolutely lost, or 27.♕h6 f6 28.♗xf6 ♕f7 29.♗b2 dxe4 30.♕g5 and White wins.

27...♕a4!

Pilnik keeps Petrosian busy.

28.♖d2

28.♖d3 ♕xa6 29.♕f6 ♔f8 30.♖a3! ♕xa3 31.♕h8+ ♔e7 32.♕xc8 and Black would be caught.

28...♕xa6

Taking the passed pawn is an accomplishment; it gives him a bit of hope of surviving.

29.♕f6 ♔f8

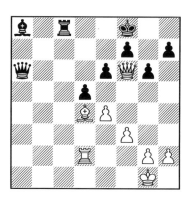

30.h3!?

With little time on the clock, Petrosian makes a practical decision, making room for his king. However, 30.♖c2! threatening mate in one if Black takes his rook would be decisive.

a) 30...h5 31.♖c7

b) 30...♔e8 31.♗c5 ♖xc5 32.♖xc5 dxe4 33.♕d4 exf3 (33...♕b7 34.♕d6+−) 34.♖c7 and White checkmates.

c) 30...♗c6 31.exd5 exd5 (31...♗xd5 32.♖c7) 32.♕d6+ ♔g8 33.♕e5 ♔f8 34.♗e3 ♔g8 35.♗h6 ♕a7+ 36.♔h1 f6 37.♕e6+ and it would be all over.

30...♔e8   31.♕h8+   ♔d7 32.♕xh7

Petrosian wins back the pawn; more importantly, he attacks the f7–pawn.

32...♖c1+ 33.♔h2

33.♔f2 ♖f1+ 34.♔g3 ♕d6+ 35.e5 ♕f8 36.♖c2 also wins.

33...♕d6+ 34.e5 ♕f8 35.♖a2 ♗b7

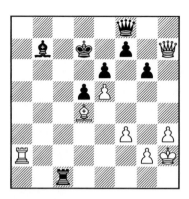

36.♖b2!?

After 36.♗b2! ♖c6 37.♗a3 the bishop stands well on a3 and, unlike in the game, it keeps the 4th rank open. In addition, it pushes the black queen to a poor square. After 37...♕e8 38.♖b2 ♗a6 39.♕h4 White would win by transferring his queen to the a-file.

36...♔c8 37.♕h4 ♖c4 38.♕f2 ♕h6 39.f4 ♕f8

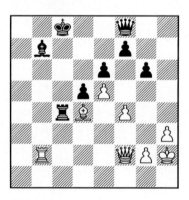

40.♕d2?

Petrosian's last move before time control is at the very least not the best, as he allows Black to activate his queen. After 40.♕e3! or 40.♖b3! Black would have to remain passive, while White could build play on the

queenside and sooner or later invade decisively.

40...♕a3!

The queen takes away a lot of squares from White. Pilnik saved several difficult positions in this event, and we can see why.

41.♖a2?

Perhaps Petrosian was not aware that he had completed his 40 moves and replied quickly, again making a mistake. After 41.♕f2 Black should still careful.

41...♕b4!   42.♕xb4   1/2

Swapping queens guarantees the draw.

Petrosian played very well, but he should not have left himself with so little time. Credit to Pilnik, who resisted well. It is a pity that such a masterpiece was spoiled.

In the 13th game, Petrosian was Black against Najdorf. He equalised in a main-line Queen's Gambit Declined. They played on, Petrosian started to press, and outplayed Najdorf, but his 40th move allowed his opponent to draw instantly. We look at his 14th game, where he played really well.

Game 66

Petrosian, Tigran – Guimard, Carlos
Gothenburg Interzonal (14), 1955
Queen's Gambit

1.c4 ♘f6 2.♘c3 e6 3.d4 d5 4.♘f3 ♗e7 5.e3

Petrosian wants a prolonged fight.

5...0-0 6.♗d3 dxc4 7.♗xc4 c5 8.0-0 a6 9.a4 ♘c6

Black has an extra tempo compared with a Queen's Gambit Accepted.

10.b3 cxd4 11.exd4 ♘b4 12.♘e5 ♗d7

Keeping the bishop pair with 12...b6 13.♕f3 ♖b8 is easier for Black than the game continuation.

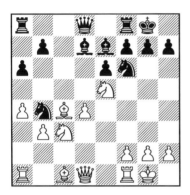

13.♗b2

The bishop is not exposed to any exchange here. It will not move again in this game, yet incredibly it will have a decisive effect.

13...♗c6 14.♕d2 ♘bd5

Playing 14...♖c8 and recapturing on c6 with the rook would result in a less complex position.

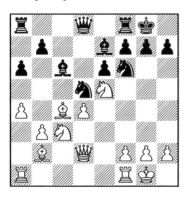

15.♘xc6

Petrosian changes the structure; objectively, this is not any better for White, but it is a more fighting continuation.

15...bxc6 16.♘a2!?

Petrosian start manoeuvring the knight, which embarks on a great journey. Black will enjoy a reasonable position with many good possibilities for a long time.

16...♕b8 17.♘c1 ♗b4 18.♕c2 ♗d6 19.g3 ♖d8

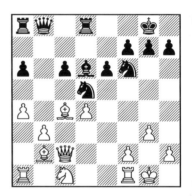

20.♕e2

Petrosian wants keep the knight, but 20.♘d3 ♘b4 would exchange it.

20...♘b4 21.♖d1 ♘fd5 22.♕e4

This frees up the e2–square.

22...♗e7 23.♘e2

The knight continues on its journey.

23...♗f6 24.♔g2

Petrosian treats the position originally, and he vacates another square.

24...a5

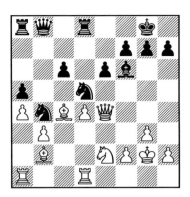

25.♘g1!

It is hard to read Petrosian's thinking.

25...♕b7 26.♘f3

The knight finds a new square.

26...♖ab8 27.♖ac1 h6 28.♔g1

Perhaps just throwing the ball into Guimard's court. The queen on b7 was unlikely to affect the king on g2.

28...♘b6 29.♗e2

Tigran preserves the bishop.

29...♘6d5

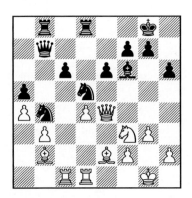

30.♘d2!?

The knight makes its seventh move; one may anticipate that it is heading for c4.

30...♗g5 31.♖c5 ♗e7

After 31...♕a7 32.♘c4 or 31...♗xd2 32.♖xd2 ♕b6 the position would be even.

32.♖xa5!

Petrosian dares to take a pawn, which requires precise calculation.

32...♘a2

Black is still doing alright, for example after 32...♕c7 33.♘c4 ♘a2 34.♕f3 ♘ac3 35.♗xc3 ♘xc3 36.♕xc3 ♗b4 37.♕e3 ♗xa5 38.♗f3 the position would be balanced.

33.♗d3 g6 34.♕f3 ♕c7?!

Guimard starts a decline. He has better continuations, for instance: 34...♗b4 35.♖a6 ♗c3 36.♗xc3 ♘dxc3 37.♖e1 ♘b4 38.♖a5 with mutual chances.

35.♖c5!

Petrosian finds a clever exchange sacrifice.

35...♗xc5 36.dxc5

The long-term passive b2–bishop becomes very active in no time.

36...♘ab4?!

The Argentinian plays a somewhat automatic move. Forcing matters was preferable.

a) 36...♞dc3 37.♖a1! (37.♖e1
♛d7) 37...♛e7 (37...♛d7? 38.♖xa2!
♞xa2 39.♛f6 would win) 38.a5 and
White's chances are better.

b) 36...♛a5 37.♗d4 ♞ac3 38.♖a1

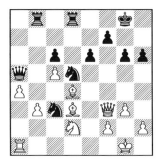

38...♞b1! An incredible move! (38...
f5 39.h4!). After 39.♞c4 (39.♞xb1 e5
40.♗b2 ♖xb3 41.♛e2 and White's
chances would be a little better) 39...
♞d2 (39...♛e1+ 40.♔g2 ♖xb3 41.♞e5
and Black's king is not fully safe)
40.♛g4 White is somewhat better.

37.♗c4 f5?!

Black takes away the e4–square,
but weakens his king. After 37...
♖e8 38.♞e4 f5 39.♞d6 ♖e7 Black's
problems are maybe smaller than in
the game.

38.♖e1 ♛e7 39.♛e2 ♖e8

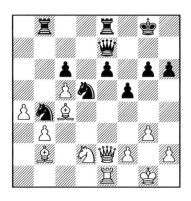

40.♞f3

The knight after a rest makes
another move; it makes sure Black
will not play e5.

40...♔h7

They reached time control. White
is winning, however, Black's position
will not fall apart on its own.

41.♛e5 ♛c7 42.♛e2 ♛e7 43.h4

This move was probably the
result of home analysis.

43...♞f6

43...♛xc5 44.h5 g5 45.♞d4
would win.

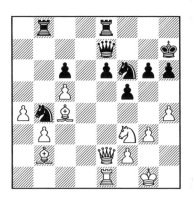

44.♗xe6!

Petrosian takes another pawn.
The position becomes rather tactical.
Petrosian will keep everything under
control

44...♞e4 45.♞d4 ♖bd8

45...♛f6 46.♗c4 ♞c3 47.♛d2
♖xe1+ 48.♛xe1 ♛xd4 49.♗xc3
♛xc5 50.♛e6 and White is about to
checkmate.

46.h5!

White blows open Black's king.

46...♖xd4 47.hxg6+! ♔xg6

48.♗xf5+!!

A beautiful bishop sacrifice drives the king out in the open. On the other hand, it was not difficult to calculate all the way to the end at home.

48...♚xf5 49.♕h5+

The check is devastating. White is a rook and a piece down, but his fluent attack leads to a win.

49...♚e6 50.♕g4+

50.♗xd4 would also win.

50...♚d5   51.♕f5+   ♕e5 52.♕d7+ ♚xc5 53.♖c1+ ♞c3

This prolongs the agony a bit.

54.♖xc3+ ♚b6

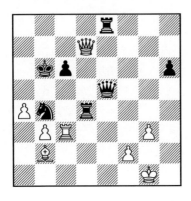

55.a5+!!

This neat little check exposes the black king. It is the only winning move and Petrosian had to see it many moves in advance.

55...♚xa5

Taking with the queen is no better, as after 55...♕xa5 56.♕xd4+ c5 57.♕d6+ ♞c6 58.♖c1 White would win.

56.♕a7+ ♚b5 57.♕b7+ ♚a5 58.♖c1 ♖d1+ 59.♖xd1 ♕xb2 60.♕a7+ ♞a6

After 60...♚b5 61.♕a4+ ♚b6 62.♕xb4+ ♚a6 63.♕c5 White is about to checkmate.

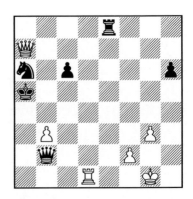

61.b4+!!

Another sweet little pawn move.

61...♚xb4

61...♚b5 62.♕b7+ would win instantly.

62.♕b6+ 1–0 Black had such a huge material advantage and yet is about to lose everything. A fantastic game! The opening was harmless for Black, but Petrosian kept the position alive by manoeuvring imaginatively, and when the position sharpened up he finished the game by sacrifices – great attacking play.

This win meant plus two, and it almost certainly guaranteed a qualification spot. In round 15, Petrosian was Black against Fuderer. He played the 3...c5 line against the Tarrasch French. Tigran accepted an isolated pawn and got a pleasant position. Fuderer offered a draw after his 27th move; Petrosian could have played on, but agreed to it. In the next round, Petrosian was White against Filip. He got no advantage in a main-line Nimzo-Indian, and peace broke out after his 19th move. In the 17th round, he played the Old Indian with g6 against Stahlberg. He equalised in the opening. The Swedish grandmaster sacrificed a piece for two pawns and the very closed position was more or less balanced. Approaching time control, Stahlberg had little time, so Petrosian created complications. This worked well, as Stahlberg soon made a big mistake, and he had to resign on move 41. In the 18th round, Tigran made a quick draw as White against Unzicker. Maybe it was not planned, and he simply got no advantage in a main-line Nimzo-Indian. In the 19th game, he was Black against Sliwa. He selected the Benoni and outplayed his opponent with ease, winning a pawn for nothing in the early middlegame. The Polish player, who finished the event last, resigned on move 36. In the penultimate round, Petrosian was White against Szabo. The Hungarian grandmaster equalised in the Grunfeld with ease, and the game ended after Tigran's 16th move. In the last round, Petrosian played the Modern Benoni as Black against Donner. He equalised, the game was balanced, and Tigran rejected a repetition in the middlegame. Donner made a big mistake a few moves before time control, and resigned on move 41.

Petrosian finished 4th, scoring 12.5 points out of 20. He won 5 (4 of them with Black and only 1 as White!) and drew all the other 15 games. He once again proved his special defensive ability, remaining undefeated. Bronstein won the event with 15 points; Keres scored 13.5 and Panno came third with 13.

By 1955 he had probably grown into the most difficult player in the world to beat. He easily qualified for the Candidates event; moreover, he could have scored more points. We cite grandmaster Barcza in Sakkelet: "Petrosian deployed his successful approach this time as well. Against less defensively strong players, he won five games and drew the rest. With this system, a good place in the event is almost always guaranteed, if it is combined with his own defensive strength. The drawback of it is that he cannot achieve an exceptional result."

Moscow Team Championship

The database suggests that Petrosian started the year at the Moscow team championship, but it was held in September. He must have rushed there after Gothenburg, and he probably joined the event after its start, which is why there are 4 draws from this event in the database – and one more game, a loss, can be found online. It would be interesting to know whether he was forced to play or his strong emotions for Spartak prompted him to help his team.

His first game was Black against Naranovich. His opponent handled the Queen's Gambit cautiously, and Tigran played on until move 40, but his opponent made no mistake and drew. In the second game, Petrosian as White tried the London System against Bronstein's Dutch Defence. David sacrificed a pawn, but Petrosian did not want to take risks and the game ended in a repetition on move 32. In the third game, he was White against Moiseev. The Russian player was able to withstand the pressure in the King's Indian Attack and the game ended in a draw after Petrosian's 41st move. In the fourth game, he was Black against Sudoplatov in the King's Indian Attack. White's careful play earned him the desired draw after time control. His black game against Vasiukov is not in the database but is available online. Vasiukov played the Advance Variation against the French. Petrosian chose a bad line; he made his way back into the game, but got a bad position with a few questionable moves. After time control, probably after adjourning the game, Petrosian resigned.

Amazingly, that was Petrosian's only loss in 1955. The fact that this included playing strong events such as the Soviet championship, world championship qualification, and matches against world class teams, makes this achievement even more special.

The four draws and one loss were a poor result, but his opponents played well, and the average Soviet players' level was impressive. That said, the probably tired Petrosian did not have enough determination in these last games. This year was the starting point for the world championship cycle, and he concentrated on events that mattered for that, consciously or unconsciously.

Petrosian's results in 1955

Soviet Championship Final, Moscow	+ 4 = 15 – 0 11.5/19 3rd-6th place
Hungary – USSR Match	+ 4 = 3 – 0 5.5/7
USSR – USA Match	+ 4 = 0 – 0 4/4
Gothenburg Interzonal	+ 5 = 15 – 0 12.5/20 4th place
Moscow Team Championship	+ 0 = 4 – 1 2/5
Altogether	**+ 17 = 37 – 1 35.5/55**

1956

Spartak – Torpedo Match

According to Shekhtman, Petrosian played in a team event in Moscow, while according to the database the game was played at the Moscow championship. Estrin as Black played the Ragozin Variation of the Queen's Gambit. Petrosian obtained the bishop pair early with an advantage. The game sharpened up and it was a fluctuating affair. Petrosian won in 31 moves.

Amsterdam/Leeuwarden Candidates Tournament

Petrosian's first tournament of the year was his most important event since 1953. The 10-player double round robin tourney was held in the Dutch capital and in Leeuwarden. He was determined and ready to fight in all of his games, and his attitude was a surprise. In order to prepare, he missed the final of the Soviet championship at the start of the year. The Soviet players started against each other.

Tigran's first opponent was Geller. Efim chose a main line against the Nimzo-Indian and Petrosian played the opening ambitiously. Geller gradually took control, then Petrosian sacrificed a piece for some pawns, but he did not get enough play and resigned after Geller's 46th move. In the second round, Petrosian was White against Bronstein. Perhaps David felt that this cycle was his last chance to challenge Botvinnik again. And maybe that generated the idea of playing for a win even with the black pieces and choosing a dubious line in the 1.c4 c5 English. Petrosian held a clear advantage throughout the game and by the time of Bronstein's 35th move his advantage had grown to almost winning. Yet David had less than a minute left when he attacked Petrosian's queen on his 35th move. Petrosian, who had 5 minutes left, did not realise that his queen was hanging. He made a move with his knight, and Bronstein took the queen for free. Tigran had to resign.

Bronstein: "I will never forget the look of horror with which Petrosian greeted the departure of his queen from the board. Then he silently stopped the clocks with an expression of hopeless resignation..." Vasiliev writes that at a dinner held in honour of the players by the people of Leeuwarden, the cooks prepared ice-cream in the shape of chess pieces. Bronstein took the queen and offered it to Petrosian: "Now we're quits!...Tigran smiled silently."

In the third round, Smyslov played the g3 line against Petrosian's King's Indian. On the 16th move, in a balanced position, he uncharacteristically made a bad mistake. Petrosian was clearly winning for a long time after that, but was unable to find the knockout punch. Smyslov escaped to an exchange down endgame and was able to hold. In the next round, Petrosian was White against Spassky. Boris made some inaccuracies in a slow opening, and when we join the game Tigran had already obtained an edge. Let's see what Tigran does with his advantage.

Game 67

Petrosian, Tigran – Spassky, Boris
Amsterdam/Leeuwarden
Candidates Tournament (4), 1956

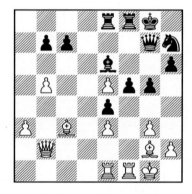

27.g4!
Petrosian breaks up Black's pawn chain with an original move. Now he will have a big advantage for many moves. We show this part with little commentary.

27...♕g6
After 27...fxg4 28.♗xe4 b6 29.♗b4 White's advantage would also be big.

28.♕b1 ♗d5 29.gxf5 ♖xf5 30.♖xf5 ♕xf5 31.♕d1 ♕e6 32.♕h5 ♖e7 33.♗h3 g4 34.♗xg4 ♖g7 35.h3 ♕e7

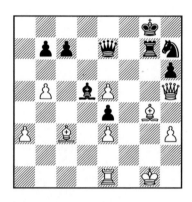

36.♗b4
36.e6! is the most convincing way to win here.

36...♕d7 37.♔h1
After 37.♖d1! it would be over for Spassky at once.

37...♗e6 38.♖d1 ♗xg4

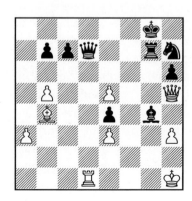

39.♕xg4

A highly unusual position.
39...♕xg4 40.hxg4 ♘g5

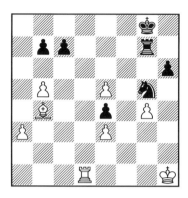

41.♔g2?

White would still win after 41.b6 cxb6 42.♔g2 or 41.♖d8+ ♔h7 42.♔g2 ♘e6 43.♖e8.

41...♘e6

Petrosian continued to press for another 30 moves, but Spassky was able to hold.

Instead of having 3 points out of 3 against Bronstein, Smyslov and Spassky that he could have achieved, only 1 point against them was written on the cross-table. In the next game, Petrosian got no advantage as White against Panno's Schlechter Defence. He made another one-move blunder, but the Argentine player missed the winning combination. The queenless position remained balanced. Petrosian survived time trouble and the game ended in a repetition. In round 6, Petrosian was White against Pilnik. Tigran faced his own opening, as the Argentine grandmaster played the Old Benoni with g6. Black made a big positional error by giving up the

key light-squared bishop. Petrosian won the one-sided game after his 50th move. In the 7th round, Filip played the King's Indian Attack as White. The Czech grandmaster allowed Petrosian to push him back. Filip resigned a bit before time control. So Petrosian had now worked his way back to 50 percent. He joked that he could have made 7 quick draws instead... In round 8, Petrosian was White against Szabo. He tried the e3+♘ge2 setup against the Nimzo-Indian. Black equalised and offered a draw after his 20th move, which Tigran accepted. In round 9, Petrosian was Black against Keres. Surprisingly, the Estonian grandmaster allowed an exchange of queens in a Sicilian Richter-Rauzer with the ...gxf6 pawn formation. Petrosian sacrificed a pawn and he always had enough play for it. The draw was sealed after time control.

In round 10, Petrosian started the second half of the tournament against Geller.

Game 68

Petrosian, Tigran – Geller, Efim
Amsterdam/Leeuwarden
Candidates Tournament (10), 1956
Queen's Gambit Tarrasch Defence

1.c4 c5 2.g3 ♘c6 3.♗g2 ♘f6 4.♘f3 e6 5.0-0 d5

Trying to surprise with the Tarrasch, an opening he rarely used.

6.cxd5 exd5 7.d4 ♗e7 8.♘c3 0-0

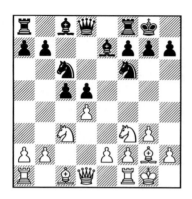

9.♗f4

This was a rare move then, and there were just 4 games with it in 1954 and 1955 by good players. White won all those four games.

9...cxd4

Geller plays a new move. 9...♗e6 and 9...♗g4 were the moves that would grow into the most common lines. Aronin would then play 9... c4 against Petrosian at the 1959 Spartakiad (team championship), and Petrosian would have to work hard for the draw in that game.

10.♘xd4 ♕b6 11.♘xc6

After this capture, the position is equal. White could try 11.♗e3!? ♕xb2 12.♘xd5 ♘xd5 13.♗xd5 and he would be somewhat better.

11...bxc6 12.♕c2 ♗e6 13.♗e3 ♕a5

13...c5 is also fine for Black. Petrosian mentions that White can't win the c5-pawn.

14.♕a4

Exchanging queens favours no side, and the position remains even.

14...♕xa4 15.♘xa4 ♘d7 16.♖fd1 ♖fc8 17.b3

If 17.♖ac1 then 17...♗f5 can be played.

17...♗a3 18.♗d4 ♗g4

Geller could just wait, but he keeps Petrosian busy.

19.♖d2 ♖e8 20.e3 ♗f5 21.♗b2 ♗xb2?!

Black would do better with the bishops on the board in particular, and with more pieces on the board in general. White's task is to bring the rooks to put pressure on Black's central pawns.

22.♖xb2 ♘b6?!

Geller wants to be active. Waiting with 22...♔f8 or 22...♖ec8 looks preferable.

23.♘c5

Petrosian naturally doesn't help Geller to reduce his number of pawn islands.

23...a5

After 23...♘d7 24.♖c1 ♘xc5 25.♖xc5 ♗d7 Black may hold by bringing the king to the centre.

24.♖c1

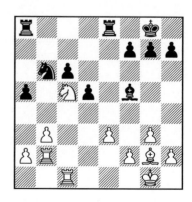

24...♖ec8?

Geller wants to avoid suffering for the draw.

a) 24...♔f8 25.♖d2 ♖a7 26.♖d4 and Black's disadvantage would be smaller than in the game.

b) 24...a4!? Giving up a pawn to exchange all queenside pawns should lead to a draw, but after some pain. 25.♘xa4 ♘xa4 26.bxa4 ♖ec8 27.♖b6 (27.♖b4 ♔f8) 27...♖xa4 28.♖bxc6 ♖xc6 29.♖xc6 ♖xa2 30.♗xd5 and Black should be able to hold, though White could play on forever.

25.e4!

Petrosian wants to get closer to the c6–pawn.

25...♗g6 26.f4!

Petrosian is looking to create a passed pawn.

26...f6 27.♗h3 ♖cb8

The move 27...♖e8 would not stop White from creating a passed pawn either. Then 28.♗e6+ ♔f8 and White would be somewhat better after 29.e5 or 29.exd5 cxd5 30.f5. White's advantage is clear after 28...♗f7 29.♗xf7+ ♔xf7 30.♘b7 as well.

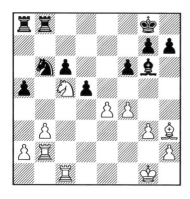

28.e5!

The passed pawn will be really strong.

28...fxe5 29.fxe5 a4

Geller, true to his nature, plays actively. It costs him a pawn, and although the extra pawn is a doubled pawn, the a2–pawn will really matter. 29...♖e8 30.♘e6 is also tough for Black.

30.bxa4 ♘c4 31.♖xb8+ ♖xb8 32.e6

White has two passed pawns, and they are much stronger than Black's c- and d-pawns.

32...♖b1

Exchanging rooks is bad, but everything else is bad, too.

a) 32...♖b2? 33.e7! ♔f7 34.♖e1 ♘d6 35.♗d7 wins.

b) 32...♖e8 33.♖f1 h5 34.♖f4 ♗b1 (34...♔h7 35.♗f1) 35.♖f7 ♗xa2 36.a5! ♘xa5 37.♖a7 ♘b3 38.♘b7 ♖e7 39.♖a8+ ♔h7 40.♘d8 and White wins.

33.♖xb1 ♗xb1

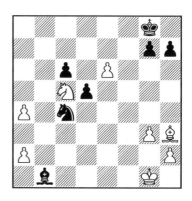

34.♗f1!

Petrosian clears the way for the pawn to draw closer to promotion.

34...♘d6

After 34...♘a5 35.♘b3 White would win.

35.a3 ♚f8 36.a5! ♘c8 37.♚f2

The king arrives in time to defend the c5–pawn.

37...♚e7 38.♚e3 ♚d6 39.♚d4 ♗f5 40.♗e2 ♘a7

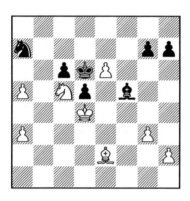

41.a6

Petrosian sealed this move. The pawn is really dangerous. Alternatively, inserting the move 41.g4 would make winning the ensuing promotion race easier, though White would have to overcome the fortress idea 41...♗xe6.

a) 41...♗g6 42.h4 h6 43.h5 ♗h7 (43...♗b1 44.a6) 44.♗d3 or 44.a6 and White would win effortlessly.

b) 41...♗xe6 42.♘xe6 c5+ (42...♚xe6 43.♚c5 wins) 43.♘xc5 ♘c6+ 44.♚e3 ♚xc5 45.a6 and White probably wins. Black would continue 45...g5

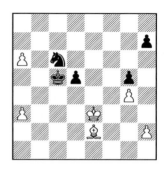

and then:

b1) 46.♗d3 h6 47.a4? According to Bondarevsky and Euwe this with ♗b5 wins, but we do not see how to penetrate with the king, as after 47...♘a7 Black has ♘c6 or ♘c8, and if White gets his bishop to d7 then Black replies ...♚d6.

b2) 46.♗d1! White keeps the a4–square vacant for his king. 46...h6 (46...♚b5 47.a7 ♘xa7 48.♚d4 ♚c6 49.♚e5 and White wins) 47.♗a4 ♘a7 48.♚d3 ♘c8 49.♗d7 ♘a7 50.♚c3 ♚d6 51.♗e8 ♚c5 52.♚b3 ♘c8 (52...♚b6 53.♚b4) 53.♗d7 ♘a7 54.♚a4! Here is the point of not pushing the a-pawn. 54...♚d6 55.♗e8 ♚c5 56.♚a5 and Black is in zugzwang.

b2.1) 56...♘c8 57.♗f7 d4 (57...♘a7 58.♗xd5 wins) 58.♚a4 d3 (58...♚b6 59.♚b4) 59.♚b3 ♚d4 60.♚b4 and White's king invades)

b2.2) 56...d4 57.♚a4 ♚c4 58.♗g6 d3 59.♗xd3+ ♚xd3 60.♚a5 ♘c8 61.♚b5 and White wins.

41...h3

After 41...♗xe6 42.♘xe6 ♚xe6 43.♚c5 ♚d7 44.♚b6 White wins the knight.

42.a4

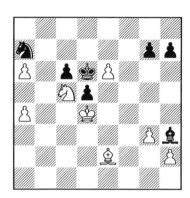

42...♞c8

42...g6 43.g4 (43.♞b7+ ♚xe6 44.♚c5 also wins)

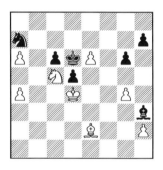

a) 43...h6 44.♚e3 (44.♞d3 ♝g2) 44...h5 45.♚f4

b) 43...♞c8 44.♞b7+ ♚xe6 45.♚c5 ♚d7 46.♞d6 ♞a7 47.♞f7 wins.

c) 43...♝g2 44.♚e3! White goes for trapping the bishop. Euwe's idea is not the only way to win, but it is stylish. 44...♞c8 (44...♚xc5? 45.e7) 45.♚f2 ♝h1 46.♚g1 ♝e4 47.♞xe4+ dxe4 48.♝c4 and White wins easily.

43.♞b7+

This enables the white king to penetrate.

43...♚xe6 44.♚c5 ♚d7

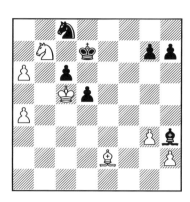

45.♞a5

The former world champion suggested 45.♞d6!, which looks faster as White also wins after 45...♞a7 46.♞b5 cxb5 47.axb5.

45...♚c7 46.♞xc6 ♞b6 47.♝b5 ♞d7+

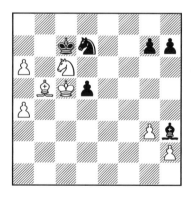

48.♚xd5?

Petrosian unnecessarily sacrifices a piece. Commentators thought that it actually squanders the win, and theoretically it does, but Black has to play more precisely than they thought, and actually requires a study-like solution. It would be

interesting to know what actually
happened, whether Petrosian missed
something in his analysis or did not
get as far as this position at home.
Instead, 48.♔d4! followed by taking
the d5–pawn with the knight was
not only far more practical, but
winning effortlessly.

**48...♗g2+   49.♔e6   ♗xc6
50.♗xc6 ♔xc6 51.a7**

51...♘b6?

Not long before the resumption
of this game, Geller lost an
adjourned game in which he played
a few moves impatiently. Maybe
that game affected his morale and
now caused his losing mistake. The
draw was tremendously difficult
to find: 51...♘c5+! would not only
force Petrosian to play with great
precision, but with the help of
incredible study-like motifs would
save the game. 52.♔f7 ♔b7 53.♔xg7
♘e4! A knight in endgames is a very
tricky piece.

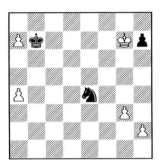

a) If the natural 54.♔xh7 then
Euwe pointed out that the fantastic
54...♘d2! draws, as White would
drop one of his kingside pawns after
55.g4 ♘f3 or 55.h3 ♘e4.

b) After 54.g4! ♘f2! (54...♔xa7
55.h4! ♔a6 56.g5 wins) 55.g5 ♘h3
56.♔f6 the white king plans to chase
away the knight: 56...♔xa7 57.♔f5

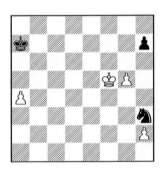

b1)   57...♔b6   58.♔g4   ♘f2+
59.♔g3 ♘e4+ 60.♔f4 ♘c5 61.h4
(61.a5+ ♔xa5!) 61...♔c6 – see 57...
♔b7 below.

b2) 57...♔a6? 58.♔g4 ♘f2+
59.♔g3 ♘d3 (59...♘e4+ 60.♔f4
♘c3 61.h4 wins) 60.h4 ♔a5
61.♔g4 ♔xa4 62.h5 and White
would win.

b3) 57...♔b7!! Black has an
amazing idea to save the game. The
king may move to the kingside from

this square and arrive in time and in that case can also hold back the a-pawn.

b3.1) 58.a5 ♔a6! The only move. 59.♔g4 ♘f2+ 60.♔g3 ♘d3 61.h4 ♔xa5 62.h5 ♔b5 and the black king arrives in time.

b3.2) 58.♔g4 ♘f2+ 59.♔g3 ♘e4+ 60.♔f4 ♘c5 61.h4. It looks like White wins, but... 61...♘c7! 62.h5 ♔d7 63.h6. It still looks winning for White, but... 63...♘e6+ 64.♔g4 ♔e7 (64...♘f8?? 65.a5 wins) 65.g6

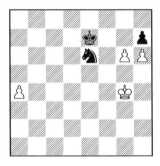

65...♘f8!! 66.g7 ♘d7! 67.♔f5 (67.g8=♘+ ♔f8 and Black holds) 67...♔f7 and White can't win.

52.a5 ♘a8 53.♔f7!

Chessbase attaches a question-mark to this good move and suggests the wrong 53.h4??.

a) 53...♔b7 54.♔f7 g5 55.h5 would indeed win.

b) But Black has a great idea: 53...g5!! 54.hxg5 (54.h5 h6! 55.♔f5 ♔d5!! and as the knight can always move, taking the h-pawn is not winning) 54...♔b7 55.♔f7 ♘c7 56.♔g7 ♘e6+ and Black holds.

53...g5 54.♔f6 g4

If 54...h6 55.♔g6 ♔b7 56.♔xh6 g4 57.♔g5 ♔xa7 58.♔xg4 White wins.

55.♔g5 ♔b7 56.♔xg4

Petrosian is winning: the Finalgen program proves it.

56...♘c7 57.♔g5 ♘d5

58.h3!

Petrosian gets ready to go after the h7–pawn. 58.♔h6? would be too hasty, as ♘e3! would hold. White has another way to win, too, which actually won a bit faster: 58.g4 ♔xa7 (58...♘e3 59.h3 ♘d1 60.h4 ♘e3 61.♔f4 would win) 59.♔h6 ♘f6 60.h3.

58...♘c3

Taking the pawn would not help. 58...♔xa7 59.♔h6 (59.g4? ♔a6

60.♔h6 ♔xa5 61.♔xh7 ♔b5 and
Black holds) 59...♔a6 (59...♘f6
60.g4) 60.♔xh7 ♔xa5 61.h4! and
pushing the g-pawn would spoil the
win, but pushing the more distant
h-pawn would win.

59.g4 ♘e4+ 60.♔f5

60.♔f4 ♘f6 61.♔f5 would be
faster.

**60...♘g3+ 61.♔f4 ♘e2+ 62.♔e3
♘c3 63.g5 ♘d5+ 64.♔e4 ♘e7**

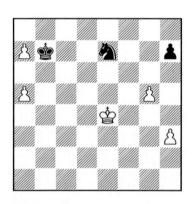

65.♔f4!!

Petrosian walks across a
minefield with enviable caution; his
move is the only winning one. After
65.♔e5? ♘g6+ 66.♔f6 ♘h4! Black
holds.

65...♘d5+ 66.♔f3

Petrosian has more than one way
to win. 66.♔e5 ♘e7 67.♔f6 ♘d5+
(67...♘g6 68.♔g7) 68.♔g7 ♘f4
69.♔xh7 ♘xh3 70.g6 ♘g5+ 71.♔g7
♘e6+ (71...♘e4 72.♔f8) 72.♔f7
♘d8+ 73.♔f6 wins.

66...♘e7 67.h4 ♔xa7

Taking the pawn doesn't help.

**68.♔f4 ♘g6+ 69.♔g4 ♘e7
70.h5 ♔a6**

71.♔f4! ♔xa5

71...♘d5+ 72.♔e5 ♘e3 73.h6
wins.

72.♔e5 ♔b6 73.♔e6 1–0

Geller resigned here, as after 73...
♘c6 74.♔f6 ♘d4 75.g6 hxg6 76.h6
White would promote to a new
queen. However, Petrosian's move
is not the only one. 73.♔f6 ♘d5+
74.♔f7! ♘f4 75.h6 also wins, but not
74.♔g7?? ♘f4 75.h6 (75.g6 ♘xg6!)
75...♘e6+ 76.♔f6 ♘xg5! and Black
holds.

In the 11th round, Petrosian as
Black played the King's Indian
against Bronstein; they reached a
closed position. Petrosian made a
surprising exchange, which can be
seen in the Petrosian's Remarkable
Exchanges chapter. They agreed to
a draw in an equal position after
Tigran's 29th move. In the next
round, Petrosian and Smyslov
agreed a 10-move draw. In the 13th
round, Spassky as White played
the e3+♘ge2 Nimzo-Indian; the
young grandmaster from Leningrad
played aggressively, but Petrosian
held back the attack. They reached

an equal rook ending and agreed to a draw after Spassky's 33rd move. In the 14th round, Petrosian opened 1.e4 against Panno. They exchanged queens in a sharp Dragon and a draw was concluded after 20 moves. In the 15th round, Petrosian as Black played the 4...♘d7 Caro-Kann against Pilnik; he equalised and seemed to take control on the kingside, but the Argentinian player defended well. At one point Pilnik could have caused problems, but the way he played led to a draw. In the 16th round, Petrosian was White against Filip. He played the opening disappointingly and offered a draw with his 22nd move. In the 17th round, Petrosian was Black against Szabo. The Hungarian number one played the Saemisch against the King's Indian. Petrosian obtained a small advantage, but White managed to equalise and they agreed to a draw after Petrosian's 31st move. In the last, 18th round, Keres as Black tried the Tarrasch. However, the Estonian lost the isolated pawn soon after the opening and offered a draw. Petrosian refused, but uncharacteristically was unable to progress with the extra pawn. After Petrosian's 23rd move Paul offered another draw; Petrosian was short of time and this time he accepted the offer.

He had thus ended the event with a string of 8 draws. In the first half of the tournament he played very ambitiously and had bad luck. He possibly paid for not being used to playing so many extremely tense games in a row. He slowed down for the second half. Petrosian scored 9.5 points out of 18 games; he finished joint-third with Szabo, Spassky, Bronstein and Geller. He failed to convert 4 winning games, only scoring 1 point from them. He and his fans surely hoped for more.

Euwe wrote: *Petrosian's play made a very favourable impression on the spectators, and on me personally. Thanks to his positional understanding he can exploit the tiniest positional advantage...* According to Vasiliev, not even the words of the ex-world champion could console him. Some people thought he should just improve his tactics, others, though, believed that he would never overcome his limitations to make a real bid for the world championship.

Yugoslavia – Soviet Union Match

Belgrade hosted the Yugoslavia – Soviet Union match in June.

Petrosian started the event with two fairly quick draws, against Milic and Matanovic. In the third, Petrosian was Black against Pirc; he got a pleasant position in the 1.c4 c5 English. In the middlegame, he gained a winning advantage with a tactical exchange sacrifice. He missed several ways to win, the players probably got into time trouble, and at one point Tigran made a losing blunder but Pirc failed to exploit it. After time control, there was nothing left to play for and they agreed to a draw. In the 4th game, he got no advantage in a main-line Nimzo-Indian against Djurasevic. They agreed to a draw after Black's 21st move.

He won a pawn in the fifth game, and we look at how he tries to convert his advantage.

Game 69

**Trifunovic, Petar –
Petrosian, Tigran**
Yugoslavia – Soviet Union Match,
Belgrade (5), 1956

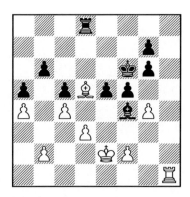

50...e4!
Petrosian changes the structure; he accepts tripled pawns, which is highly unusual, especially when one is playing for a win. An important element here is that Black's bishop will be stronger than White's.

51.dxe4
After 51.gxf5 exd3+ 52.♔xd3 gxf5 Black would have excellent winning chances, as Black has a potential passed pawn.

51...fxg4 52.♖g1 ♔g5 53.b3
Attacking the g4-pawn would be likely to lose as well. 53.♗e6 ♖d2+ 54.♔e1 ♖xb2 55.♖xg4+ ♔f6 56.♖xf4+ ♔xe6 and Black probably wins.

53...♖h8 54.♗c6 ♖h4 55.♗d7 ♗e5 56.♗c8 ♗d4
Petrosian tires his opponent a bit.

57.♖g2   ♔f4   58.♗d7   ♗e5 59.♖g1 ♔g5 60.♖g2

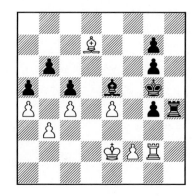

60...g3!
Black launches his play.
61.fxg3 ♖h1 62.♖f2 ♗xg3
Black   restores   the   pawn advantage.
63.♖f1   ♖h2+   64.♔f3   ♗e5

**65.♖f2   ♜h4   66.♖g2+   ♚f6
67.♗g4**

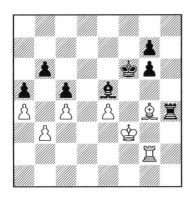

67...♜h1

Now White can't stop the h1–
rook from getting to the queenside.

68.♖d2 ♜b1 69.♖d3 ♜b2!

The rook ties up two of White's
three pieces.

70.♗c8

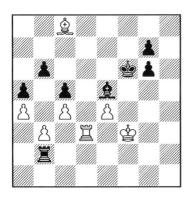

70...♚g5!

Petrosian starts improving his
king and, incredibly, sewing a mating
net.

71.♗d7 ♚h4 72.♗e6 g5 73.♗d7

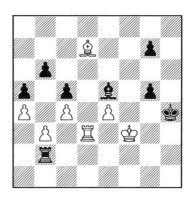

73...♗d4

Black threatens checkmate in
one.

74.e5 g4+ 75.♚e4 ♜e2+ 76.♚d5

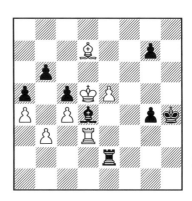

76...♗xe5

Black is completely winning.

77.♗xg4

This desperate piece sacrifice
postpones the end, but only by a
bit, as the second (previously, third)
g-pawn decides the outcome of the
game.

**77...♚xg4 78.♚c6 g5 79.♚xb6
♚f5   80.♚xa5 g4   81.♚b5 g3
82.♚xc5 g2 83.♖d1 ♗g3 0–1**

In the 6th game, he was White
against Gligoric. The g3 King's

Indian resulted in a Benoni type of position; he beautifully sacrificed a pawn for control over the light squares and outplayed the number one Yugoslav. Gligoric did not resign and, incredibly, Petrosian failed to make a capture, blundered his queen and resigned. He finished the event with two draws under 20 moves, one against Karaklajic and another against Ivkov. Petrosian's 4 out of 8 (1 win, 6 draws and 1 loss) was hardly satisfactory, and this below par performance probably contributed to his not being selected for the Soviet team for the Moscow Chess Olympiad. All the Soviets selected, Botvinnik, Smyslov, Keres, Bronstein, Taimanov and Geller, were superb players, yet Petrosian, who was younger than all of them, could have been among them. He probably would have played on board one in any other national team in the world.

Moscow Championship

Petrosian participated in the Moscow championship, which probably started in October. In order to qualify for the world championship cycle he had to qualify from the 1957 Soviet championship final, but as he missed the 1956 final, he had to participate at the semi-final stage. At his previous Soviet event he had performed poorly, so he decided to get used to Soviet events again by lining up at the Moscow championship.

According to the database, 18 players participated, though *Reliability Strategy* mentions 16. There are 8 Petrosian games from the event in the database. The order of his games is not known. Let's start with Petrosian's white games!

He played a symmetrical English against Gusev. Tigran obtained some advantage, but it evaporated and the game ended in a draw after White's 31st move. Then he was White against Osnos in a Boleslavsky Sicilian. Black equalised and offered a draw after his 28th move. It was reasonable to accept it. He faced another Ragozin against Uusi. The Estonian player handled the position well and Petrosian never had a chance to take control. They played on until time control and agreed to a draw in a pawn ending. Against Vasiukov's Leningrad Dutch, Petrosian developed the f1-bishop to g2 and did not play d4. Vasiukov built up an attack on the kingside. Petrosian did not live up to his reputation and did not defend his king well. He resigned after move 37, when facing checkmate (this game is analysed in full in Alexander Nikitin's book on Vasiukov mentioned earlier). In the games we know, Petrosian did much better as Black. He equalised against Chistiakov in a complex 3.♘c3 ♗b4 French, and when his opponent played poorly, he took control with an exchange sacrifice. Petrosian trapped the Russian player's king and won the game on move 29. This game can be seen in the It's Your Move chapter. He was then Black against Neishtadt in a Sicilian Richter-Rauzer. They reached a middlegame with a typical pawn structure with doubled pawns on the f-file. The position was complex for a long time. Tigran outplayed his opponent around time control and won after his 44th move. Simagin played 3.♗b5+ against the Sicilian. White created a Maroczy Bind type of pawn structure. Petrosian played actively. Simagin made a bad mistake, and he resigned 7 moves later after Petrosian's 25th move. Petrosian finished joint-first with Simagin. They scored 10 points. Antoshin was third with 9.5, while Bronstein surprisingly scored only 7 points. Petrosian won 6 games, drew 8 and lost one.

Petrosian-Simagin Playoff

Petrosian started the playoff match for the title of Moscow champion as White, later that same October in a best of six contest. He got nothing against the 3.♘c3 dxe4 4.♘xe4 ♘f6 5.♘xf6 exf6 variation of the Caro-Kann (with a slightly different move order) in the first round. They drew after 21 moves.

The next game was rather memorable for me, your Hungarian author, as it was the final example in an article on Petrosian. Simagin once asked him how come that you, Tigran, can beat patzers with such ease? To understand Petrosian's wittiness, one should know that in the Soviet Union they exaggerated how inspirationally Chigorin was able to play. Petrosian answered that he held the position and waited for the moment his opponent got "Chigorin's inspiration", after which Tigran would exploit the mistake. And he indeed produced many beautiful examples where he spotted a tactical hole in the play of his opponents. The very last example in the article was one where he outwitted Simagin himself. We join the moment when Simagin finds an "imaginative" idea, which turns out to be senseless.

Game 70

**Simagin, Vladimir –
Petrosian, Tigran**
Moscow Championship playoff (2),
1956

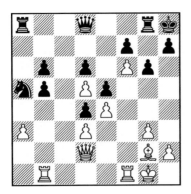

26.♗h3?
Simagin finds an "imaginative"
idea. The position would be equal
after 26.♖xb5 ♞b7 27.♕b4 ♞c5
28.♖xb6.
26...♞b7 27.♗e6
A beautiful-looking move, yet it
is absolutely harmless. White could
no longer play simple chess, as after
27.♖xb5 ♞c5 28.♖fb1 ♖xa3 Black
would win.

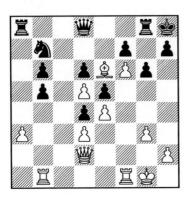

27...♕e8!
Petrosian doesn't take the piece,
but defends two pawns with one
move. What was Simagin hoping
for? After 27...fxe6? 28.dxe6 ♞c5
29.e7 ♕d7 30.f7 White would win
an exchange.
**28.♕h6 ♞c5 29.♖f3 ♕f8 30.♕h3
♖xa3 31.♗d7**
31.♖xb5 ♞xe4 and 31.♗g4 ♖xd3
win for Black.

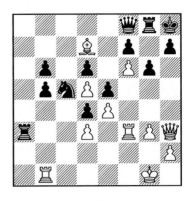

31...♞xe4
Petrosian starts harvesting.
32.♖ff1 ♖xd3 33.♖a1 h5

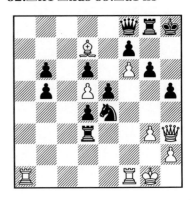

34.♗f5
It is again pretty, but again
ineffective.

34...♘g5 35.♕g2 gxf5

Petrosian finally takes the bishop. It is all over for the Russian player; Simagin makes a few more moves by inertia.

36.♕e2 ♘f3+ 37.♖xf3 ♖xf3 38.♕xf3 ♕h6 39.♖a7 ♕xf6 40.♕xh5+ ♔g7 0–1

In the third game of the event, Petrosian as White played 1.c4 followed by g3, ♗g2, ♘f3 and d3 against the King's Indian. Simagin again attacked too aggressively. He sacrificed a pawn, but Petrosian neutralised his play and beat him. In the fourth game, Petrosian played the Caro-Kann. They castled on opposite sides. Simagin obtained the two bishops and a small edge. In the middlegame, Petrosian won a pawn. Simagin's attack grew increasingly dangerous in a double-edged position. Before time control, he was already winning. He sent Petrosian's king to the centre and caught it, and Tigran resigned after Simagin's 52nd move. We look at their next, final game.

Game 71

Petrosian, Tigran – Simagin, Vladimir
Moscow Championship playoff (5), 1956
King's Indian Defence

1.♘f3 ♘f6 2.c4 c6 3.♘c3 d6 4.d4 g6 5.e4 ♗g7 6.♗e2 0-0 7.0-0 ♗g4 8.♗e3 ♘bd7

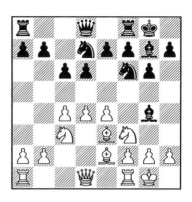

9.♘d2!

Maybe Petrosian needed 2 draws, but as he beat Simagin at the main event his Berger-Sonneborg score meant that 3 points were probably enough for the title. So he goes for safety, and anyway it is safer to head for positions with fewer pieces against such a dangerous tactician.

9...♗xe2 10.♕xe2 e5

If 10...e6 Petrosian planned to play 11.f4 d5 12.e5.

11.d5 c5 12.♖ab1

Petrosian naturally starts playing on the queenside. In his analysis, he prefers 12.a3.

12...♘e8 13.f3 f5 14.b4 cxb4

If Black plays 14...f4, the typical King's Indian type of attack has far less power without Black's light-squared bishop involved, mainly as Black can't sacrifice it on h3.

15.♖xb4 b6 16.a4 ♗f6

Exchanging the bishop is a standard plan in such positions.

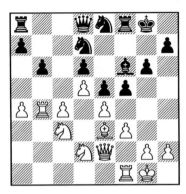

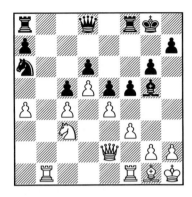

17.♔h1!?

Petrosian makes no comments on this move in the analysis included in *Reliability Strategy*, though it is an interesting idea to vacate the g1–square for the bishop. He does though mention that keeping the bishop is necessary to avoid ceding complete control of the c5–square to Black. 17.exf5 gxf5 18.a5 bxa5 19.♖a4 would also be somewhat better for White.

17...♗g5 18.♗g1! ♘c7 19.♖bb1 ♘a6 20.♘b3 ♘dc5?

Petrosian says no word about this move, though allowing the b-file to open clearly helps White. 20...f4 or 20...♔h8 were better.

21.♘xc5 bxc5

He attaches a question-mark to this capture and says nothing, but taking with the knight gave White more or less the same size of advantage. 21...♘xc5 22.exf5 gxf5 23.♗xc5 (23.a5!? would also be strong) 23...bxc5 24.♖b7 and Black's position would be loose, while he also has to tolerate the rook on b7. 24.g4 is also better for White.

22.exf5! gxf5 23.g4!

Petrosian plays like in the text books. It is a joy to see how he obtains control over the e4–square.

23...fxg4 24.♘e4 ♗f4

After 24...gxf3 25.♖xf3 ♗f4 26.♗e3 Black would be in big trouble as well.

25.♖b7 ♘c7 26.fxg4

White has obtained a strategically winning position.

26...♘e8

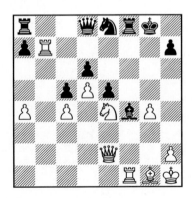

27.g5

Petrosian is looking to bring his queen into the attack via h5. Getting rid of Black's only active piece with 27.♗e3!? was winning as well.

27...♕c8 28.♖e7 ♕h3

28...♕d8 29.♖e6! would win.

29.♖f3

Petrosian is looking to win the game.

29...♕g4 30.♕d3?

Petrosian says nothing about this move or about the conditions it was played under. It would be interesting to know how much time both players had here, and also how far in advance he calculated. There are objectively better moves here; actually, White could win at once: 30.♘f6+! would force Black to lay down his arms. 30...♘xf6 (30...♖xf6 31.gxf6 ♘xf6 32.♕g2 would win) 31.gxf6 ♔h8 (31...♗g5 32.♕d3) 32.♕d3 ♕g8 33.♖g7 and it would be all over for Black. By the way, 30.h3 ♕h5 31.♕g2 ♔h8 32.♖e6 also wins.

30...♗xh2!

This is the only move; it is pretty and keeps Black in the game. If 30...♕h5 then 31.♖h3 ♕g6 32.♖exh7 would be decisive.

31.♖xf8+ ♔xf8

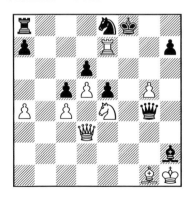

32.♖xe8+!

This is cute.

32...♖xe8 33.♗xh2 ♖e7?

Simagin lets his position fall apart by giving away the d6–pawn. 33...♖d8? would lose instantly because of 34.♕f1+, but 33...♕f5!, pinning the knight, would keep the position playable. After 34.♘xc5 it would be interesting to see whether Petrosian, who likes exchanging queens, would simplify here (34.♔g2 or 34.♕e2 would lead to equality) 34...♕xd3 35.♘xd3 and 35...♖c8 36.c5 would be unpleasant, but 35...♖b8 would lead to a balanced position.

34.♘xd6

After the departure of the d-pawn Black's chances disappear as well.

34...♕xg5 35.♕f1+ ♔g8

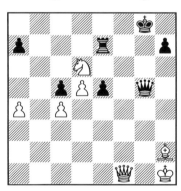

36.♘e4

Petrosian smells blood; Black's king is indeed weak. White could win by 36.♕g2 as well.

36...♕h4 37.♕e2 ♖g7 38.d6

38.♘xc5 ♕g5 39.♘d3 would win convincingly.

38...♕h6

After 38...h6 39.♕e3 ♔h8 40.a5 Black would lose.

39.♕d1?

39.♕f1 would win.

39...♕h4?

39...♕h3! Possibly Simagin was in time trouble, which would explain why he did not find this move that saved the game. 40.♕d5+ (40.♕e2 ♖g6 stopping the f6–check keeps Black in the game) 40...♔f8 41.♘d2 (41.♕a8+ ♔f7) 41...♕g4 42.♕f3+ ♔e8 and the position would be equal.

40.♕e2

40.♕d5+ and 40.♘g3 would also win.

40...♕h6

40...♕h3? 41.♘f6+ would win.

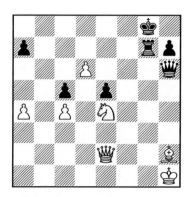

41.♕f1!

Petrosian sealed this winning continuation.

41...♖f7

Petrosian mentions how 41...♕e3 would lose. 42.♘f6+ ♔h8 43.d7 ♕d4 (let us add that 43...♖xd7 44.♘xd7 ♕e4+ 45.♔g1 ♕g4+ 46.♔f2 would avoid perpetual check) 44.♗xe5 ♕h4+ 45.♗h2 ♕d4 46.♕e1 and Black gets checkmated.

42.♕g2+ ♔f8 43.♘g5 ♕xd6

Petrosian wrote that this allowed an amusing finale. Simagin possibly showed his liking for Petrosian as he allowed him to finish the game brilliantly. He surely knew that Tigran had found the win in his home analysis. 43...♖d7 44.♕f3+ ♔g7 45.♘e4 would be hopeless as well.

44.♕a8+! ♔g7

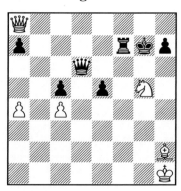

45.♗xe5+! ♕xe5 46.♕h8+!! ♔xh8 47.♘xf7+ 1–0

At the end of the magic White ends up with an extra piece.

This masterpiece was not without mistakes. Yet, Petrosian played deeply and the finishing combination was beautiful.

Petrosian won the playoff match 3.5:1.5.

Soviet Championship Semi-Final, Tbilisi

Petrosian was somewhat lucky to play his semi-final on home soil in Tbilisi. In the first round, he was Black against Antoshin, who played the Averbakh system against the King's Indian. The draw took 17 moves. In the second, he was White against Korchnoi in a 1.c4 c5 English. They swapped queens early on, and agreed to a draw after Korchnoi's 16th move. In the third round, Yukhtman played 3.♗b5+ against the Sicilian. Petrosian tried to create some play, but that led to a small disadvantage, and peace broke out after his 19th move. In round 4, he was White against Gurgenidze. He got the two bishops in a g3 King's Indian. Tigran gradually improved his position, and won in an endgame a bit before time control. In the fifth round, he met his friend from the Pioneers Palace Tengiz Giorgadze as Black. The Georgian played harmlessly against the Najdorf. Petrosian took control after the opening and he won the game soon after time control. In the 6th round, Petrosian as White faced Khalilbeili. After 1.d4 ♘f6 2.♘f3 e6 3.♗g5 Black quickly simplified with ♗e7 and ♘e4. Petrosian got nothing in the opening. He then tried to squeeze something, but was unable to as Black played well. In the seventh round, Petrosian played the French against Tal. It looked like White had an edge in the Advance Variation, but Petrosian held firmly and the game ended in a repetition in 26 moves. In round 8, he was White against Krogius. They reached a closed position in a King's Indian and it was equal for a good while. The pawn structure changed to an unusual one, after which he soon outplayed his opponent and Krogius resigned after time control. In the next game, he equalised against Chukaev. Let's see how he outplayed his opponent!

Game 72

Chukaev, Egor – Petrosian, Tigran
Soviet Championship Semi-Final
Tbilisi (9), 1956

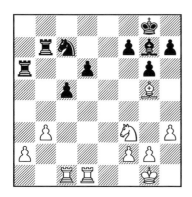

23...h6!

Petrosian opens the back rank and forces White to decide where to place the bishop.
24.♗f4
Chukaev hopes to put pressure on d6, but the bishop becomes a target. If 24.♗e3!? ♘b5 25.♖d2 ♘c3 26.♖cc2 ♖b5 27.♗f4 d5 28.♗e5 d4 29.♗xg7 ♔xg7 30.♘e5 Black would have a slight edge.
24...♘b5 25.♖c2 g5!
The pawn move forces White to decide whether to maintain watch over the d6 pawn.
26.♗e3?
The e3–square looks like a safe base for the bishop, but not against Tigran! 26.♗h2 f5 27.g4 (if 27.♖d5

f4 28.♖d3 ♘a3 29.♖c1 White still
has to work to be completely safe)
27...f4 28.h4 ♘d4 29.♘xd4 ♗xd4
30.♔g2 and Black is somewhat
better, though White may have time
to free the bishop.

26...♘c3 27.♖dd2

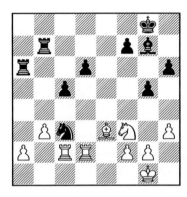

27...f5!
This pawn causes more problems
than one may think.

28.g3 ♖f7!
It is surprising that the well-
placed rook shifts to the other wing;
it forces White to give up a pawn.

29.♖d3 ♘xa2 30.♗d2 ♖b7
The main function of this move is
a bit hidden. Petrosian gets ready to
improve his king.

31.♖c4 ♔f7! 32.h4 g4 33.♘e1

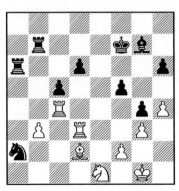

33...♘b4
Petrosian starts reducing
material.

**34.♗xb4 ♖xb4 35.♖xb4 cxb4
36.♘c2 ♗c3 37.♘e3**
37.♘d4 ♖a5 38.♘e2 ♗e5 39.f4
gxf3 40.♖xf3 ♔e6 41.♘f4+ ♔d7
and Black would soon surround the
b3–pawn.

37...♔e6 38.♖d5?
White gives up the b3–pawn.
38.♘d5 would resist better: 38...
♖a1+ 39.♔g2 ♖c1 40.♘c7+ ♔d7
41.♘d5 ♖b1 and Black has excellent
winning chances.

38...♖a3 39.♖xf5

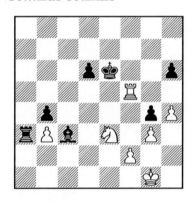

39...♖xb3
The b-pawn falls, and the distant
passer quickly decides the outcome
of the game.

**40.♖h5   ♖b1+   41.♔g2   b3
42.♖xh6+   ♔d7   43.♘c4   ♖d1
44.♖g6 ♖d4**
Black defends the g-pawn,
eliminating any drawing chances.

45.♘a3 ♖a4 46.♘b1 ♗e5 0–1
In the tenth game, he was White
against Kotkov. He was unable to
cause problems in a symmetrical

English and they agreed to a draw after Black's 21st move. In the 11th game, Tigran was Black against the newcomer Polugaevsky. He equalised in the g3 King's Indian. Polugaevsky made a careless move, and a tactical confrontation started which favoured Petrosian. Polugaevsky was never let back into the game. In the 12th round, Petrosian was White against Koblencs. He played the King's Indian Attack, Tal's trainer equalised, Petrosian manoeuvred, but Koblencs was able to neutralise his play and they settled for a draw after time control. In the 13th round, Gufeld as White chose the Exchange Slav. It looked like the game was heading for a draw quickly. In the middlegame, Gufeld offered some exchanges. However, during simplifications Petrosian gained a somewhat better position and Gufeld wrongly exchanged queens. Petrosian invaded the second rank with his rook and beat the Georgian master, who was unable to reach time control. In the 14th round, Zhurakov played the Queen's Gambit Ragozin passively, and Petrosian beat him easily in a one-sided game. In the 15th, he agreed a quick draw as Black versus Furman. In round 16, Petrosian was Black against Sakharov in a 3.♘c3 ♗b4 French. Petrosian equalised, but made an inaccurate move. White nicely took control and won an exchange. However, he allowed Tigran to equalise, and after blundering a pawn Sakharov got a lost position and resigned after time control. In the next two rounds, Tigran won two games by forfeit, the first against Voronkov and the second against Kasparian. This would have been their last ever game. In the final round, Petrosian as White did not really try to beat Buslaev, and drew in 22 moves.

Petrosian won the event with 14.5 out of 19. He won 10 games (including two forfeits), drew 9 and remained undefeated. He scored two points more than Furman, 2.5 more than Antoshin and Korchnoi, and 3 more than Tal and Gurgenidze. It was a superb result, proving that he was in a different class from other Soviet players except the very best grandmasters.

Petrosian's results in 1956

Spartak – Torpedo Team Event vs. Estrin	+ 1 = 0 – 0 1:0
Candidates Tournament, Amsterdam	+ 3 = 13 – 2 9.5/18 3rd-7th place
Yugoslavia – Soviet Union Match, Belgrade	+ 1 = 6 – 1 4/8
Moscow Championship	+ 6 = 8 – 1 10/15 1st-2nd place
Moscow Championship playoff vs. Simagin	+ 3 = 1 – 1 3.5:1.5 Winner
Soviet Championship Semi-Final, Tbilisi	+10 = 9 – 0 14.5/19 1st place
Altogether	**+ 24 = 37 – 5 42.5/66**

Note: including two wins by default in Tbilisi

1957

Soviet Championship, Moscow

The event started on the 21st January. Petrosian began as White against Furman, but he handled the opening awkwardly. After 1.d4 ♘f6 2.♘f3 e6 3.e3 he never managed to play c4. He fairly quickly found himself in a worse position, and in the middlegame he was quite lost. However, he made his way back, only to get lost again. After more seesawing he lost after time control. In the second round, he was Black against Boleslavsky. They played a main-line Nimzo-Indian, the sharp position simplified to an equal position, and they agreed to a draw after Isaac's 20th move. In round 3, Petrosian played the Saemisch too aggressively against Taimanov, and later he was clearly lost. Then, Taimanov, possibly in time trouble, wasted his advantage. We join the game at a point when the grandmaster from Leningrad was probably not aware that they had passed time control.

Game 73

Petrosian, Tigran – Taimanov, Mark
Soviet Championship Final,
Moscow (3), 1957

41...♕xe6??
Simplifying to a rook ending with an extra pawn looks like a chance to press. After 41...fxe6 42.♕e7 or 41...

♕f2+ 42.♖d2 ♕f5+ the game would end in a draw.
42.♕xe6 1–0 Taimanov resigns as after 42...fxe6 White would reply 43.♖d1! and in the ensuing pawn ending Petrosian will promote a queen, but not Taimanov.

In the fourth round, Petrosian was White against Stoliar. Black equalised in the e3 Queen's Indian, but in the middlegame made a poor move. Petrosian soon won a pawn and converted his advantage. In the fifth round, Petrosian was Black against Klaman. They reached an open position when Petrosian was able to grab a pawn; he went on to win the game in 27 moves. In round 6, Keres as Black played 1...e5 against 1.c4. The players risked nothing in the 20-move draw. In the next round, Petrosian was Black against Aronin in a French 3...♘f6 Tarrasch. Petrosian was somewhat worse, but equalised around time control and they settled for a draw. In the 8th round, Petrosian got a promising position as White in the King's Indian, but Gurgenidze defended well and they repeated moves not long before time control.

Game 74

**Tarasov, Vitaly –
Petrosian, Tigran**
Soviet Championship Final,
Moscow (9), 1957
Benoni

1.d4 ♘f6 2.c4 c5 3.e3 g6 4.♘f3 ♗g7 5.♘c3 0-0 6.♗e2 cxd4 7.♘xd4 ♘c6 8.0-0 ♘xd4 9.exd4 d5 10.c5 ♗e6 11.♗f3 ♕d7 12.♗f4 ♖fd8 13.♗e5

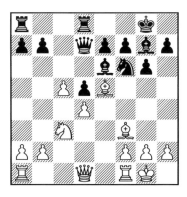

13...♘e4!?

Petrosian starts to breathe life into the position. In this championship he clearly made a

greater effort to win games than in earlier ones. The pawn sacrifice gives him practical chances.

14.♘xe4

Tarasov can't resist taking the pawn; yet it is safer not to take it. 14.♗xg7! ♘xc3 (14...♔xg7 15.♕c2) 15.♕b3 ♔xg7 16.♕xc3 and White would be a fraction better.

14...dxe4 15.♗xe4 ♗xe5 16.dxe5 ♕b5 17.♕c2

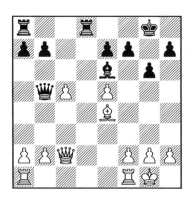

17...♖ac8

Black is ahead in development and White's pawns are somewhat loose, but White should be able to hold.

18.♖fc1

After 18.♖ac1 ♗xa2 19.b4 ♕xb4 20.♗xb7 White gets away with it.

18...♖d4!

Petrosian nicely spots that he can cause problems on the d-file.

19.b3 ♖cd8 20.h3

20.♖d1? ♕xc5 would exploit the unopened back rank.

20...♖d2!

Petrosian finds another area where he can harass his opponent and keep the game going.

21.♕c3

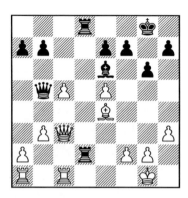

21...♕e2!

This is remarkable; he is a pawn down and yet plays for a win by exchanging queens.

22.♕f3 ♗d5! 23.♕xe2 ♖xe2

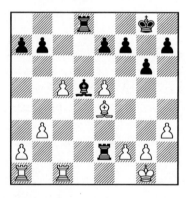

24.♗d3?!

If 24.♗xd5 ♖xd5 25.b4 ♖dd2 26.♖f1 White could hold this somewhat worse endgame.

24...♖xe5

Petrosian restores the material balance.

25.♖c3

25.♗f1 looks somewhat better.

25...♗c6 26.b4 a6 27.♖ac1?

This is a passive and pointless move, whereas after 27.a4! ♖ed5 28.♖aa3 White would hold.

27...♖ed5 28.♗c4 ♖d4 29.a3

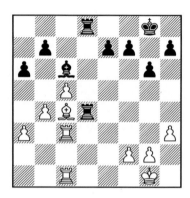

29...e6

Tigran builds the position; he has time, as White can do nothing but wait.

30.♖3c2 h5! 31.♖b2 ♖d2!

This exchange gets him closer to White's pawns.

32.♖xd2 ♖xd2 33.♖e1 ♖c2

Petrosian keeps his opponent busy with the next moves, by attacking targets.

34.♗b3　♖c3　35.♖e3　♖c1+ 36.♔h2

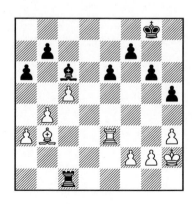

36...h4!

The white king is caged.

37.♖d3 ♖f1 38.♖d2 ♖a1!

After improving his position, Petrosian rightly aims for a bishop ending.

39.♖a2 ♖xa2! 40.♗xa2 ♔g7 41.f4 ♔f6

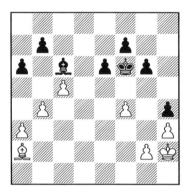

42.g3

It is not known when the game was adjourned, perhaps after this move. Here, Petrosian surprisingly missed a win by creating two connected passed pawns quickly: 42...♗d5! 43.♗b1 g5 44.fxg5+ ♔xg5 45.♗d3 f5 46.a4 hxg3+ 47.♔xg3 f4+ 48.♔f2 e5 49.b5 axb5 50.axb5 e4 51.♗e2 f3 and the pawns would decide the outcome. Later, he was winning too, but allowed his opponent to equalise. In the end, Tarasov made a big mistake and lost. It is a pity that the seesawing happened, all the more so after the Geller Candidates game. It is another example that his adjournment analysis was not without flaws.

A cold shower was waiting for him in the next round. He was White against Kholmov and they reached a Benoni type position. He was probably winning, or at least very close to it. He sacrificed a pawn, but was unable to deliver a knockout punch. His advantage evaporated, then close to time control he made a serious mistake and on the next move missed his opponent's checkmate in one. In round 11, Petrosian as Black played 1.e4 e5 2.♘f3 ♘c6 3.c3 d6 against Tolush's Ponziani Opening. They reached a King's Indian type of position. Still in the opening the Russian grandmaster carelessly castled long, missing a strong sacrifice. Petrosian didn't exploit it at once, but on the next move he employed a temporary knight sacrifice to take control and the rest was a slaughter. The key move can be seen in the It's Your Move chapter. In round 12, Petrosian used the variation named after him against Aronson's King's Indian. He gained the upper hand at the end of the opening. Aronson only resigned after Petrosian's 68th move, still, Tigran won the game comfortably. In round 13, Petrosian was Black against the sensation of the championship and the biggest star of the next 4 years, Mikhail Tal. In the 3.♘c3 ♗b4 French they reached a middlegame typical of the Poisoned Pawn Variation. Tigran was alright. He went for exchanging queens, but maybe did so a bit early. In the queenless middlegame, Tigran made a serious positional mistake;

he was treated to a dose of his own medicine, and the Latvian strongly converted his positional advantage. The next game was a quick draw as White against Bronstein. In the following round, Petrosian as Black played the Najdorf against Bannik. His position looked fine in the 6.♗g5 variation. It turned wild, then Tigran made a losing mistake; he was cruelly punished for it. In round 16, he did not try as White as he agreed an 18-move draw with Korchnoi. In round 17, Petrosian was Black against Nezhmetdinov. The Tatar played a side-line in the Spanish. They swapped queens, then Rashid sacrificed two pawns. Petrosian gave them back and the position simplified to a draw. In the 18th round, Petrosian played the Nimzo-Indian aggressively against Antoshin, but all he got was an unpleasant position. Black unnecessarily sacrificed a pawn, and after some precise defensive moves Tigran turned the tide around and started to attack. He won the game. In the 19th round, he was Black against Mikenas. He equalised in the Sicilian Richter-Rauzer. They swapped queens and the peaceful game ended in a draw after Vladas's 33rd move. In the penultimate, 20th round, he was White against Spassky in a reverse Saemisch King's Indian. Black castled long. Boris sacrificed a piece for two pawns in the middlegame. Petrosian gave back an exchange, and the position looked dangerous for the Armenian, but by time control he equalised and they agreed to a draw after Spassky's 42nd move. In the last round, Petrosian was Black against Khasin. They swapped queens in the King's Indian and Khasin did not try to press with his small edge.

Petrosian finished joint-seventh with Korchnoi, scoring 12 points. He won 7 games, drew 10 and lost 4. Tal, who had scarcely qualified from the previous year's semi-final, won the event with 14 points, while Keres and Bronstein scored 13.5. Petrosian, who had qualified from the semi-final by a clear margin, was surely hoping for more.

Soviet Union – Yugoslavia Match

The Soviet Union hosted the Yugoslav national team in Leningrad in July.

Petrosian started as White against Trifunovic. They played the Chigorin variation of the Ruy Lopez. The position opened up, then the Yugoslav player made a big mistake early in the middlegame. He was lost fairly soon after, and Petrosian won the game on the 48th move. Although he probably could have won the game faster, he never let his opponent back into it. In the second game, Petrosian deployed the Caro-Kann to meet Gligoric's 1.e4. He surprised his opponent with the 4...♘d7 line. Although Petrosian made a serious mistake in the opening, he managed to fight back and equalise. Gligoric made a losing move 30, but Petrosian's reply was also losing. In time trouble, he was a piece down and probably had no time to resign. Petrosian eventually managed to escape to a rook endgame where White had an h-pawn against Black's zero pawns. White had to play well to win, but Gligoric was up to the task. In the third game, Petrosian was White against Nedeljkovic. He avoided a theoretical opening with 1.d4 2.♘f3 and e3. The position opened up at the end of the opening. No player was able to take control and the draw arrived after 25 moves. In the next game, Petrosian was Black against Matanovic in the Ruy Lopez. Tigran made a spectacular move and the position simplified, ending in a draw after Matanovic's 18th move. The game can be seen in the It's Your Move chapter. Against Milic, Petrosian played the Najdorf, but after 6.♗c4 he transposed into an awkward Dragon with ♘bd7 and g6. The Yugoslav player got a nice advantage, but was ready to repeat moves. In the sixth round, Karaklajic tried the Ragozin as Black in a Queen's Gambit. Petrosian sacrificed a pawn, and although Black's position was playable, he made a serious mistake. Petrosian never let him back into the game and Nikola lost on time.

In the penultimate, 7th round, Petrosian was Black against Pirc.

Game 75

Pirc, Vasja – Petrosian, Tigran
Soviet Union – Yugoslavia
Leningrad (7), 1957

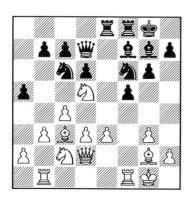

19...♘xd5
Petrosian changes the pawn structure, and in doing so he has to sacrifice a pawn. Later, White will have problems hanging on to it.

20.cxd5 ♘e5 21.♘d4
21.♗xa5 ♖a8 22.♘d4 (22. a4 ♘xd3) 22...♗h6 23.♗c3 ♖fe8 24.♖be1 c6 25.dxc6 bxc6 and Black has some compensation for the pawn.

21...♘g4 22.♖be1
Petrosian in his commentary prefers defending the pawn with the other rook and attaches a question-mark against this move, but it is neither weaker nor stronger than using the other rook. After 22.♖fe1 ♗h6 23.♘c2 ♕b5 24.a4 the position would be balanced.

22...♗h6 23.♘c2 ♕b5 24.h3 ♘e5 25.d4?

Giving up the e4–square is a mistake. After 25.♖d1 the position would be equal.

25...♘d7 26.♕e2 ♕xe2 27.♖xe2 ♘f6

27...b6 28.g4 ♘f6 29.gxf5 ♘e4 would be tough for White.

28.♗xa5 b6

28...♖e7 would be strong as well.

29.♗d2

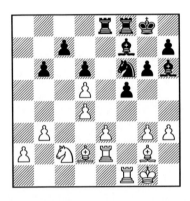

29...♗xd5

Ten moves after taking on d5, the pawn falls.

30.♗xd5+ ♘xd5 31.a4 ♖e4 32.♖ee1

If 32.♖fe1 c5 33.dxc5 bxc5 34.♘a3 ♔f7 White's position would be worse.

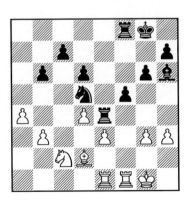

32...c5!

Exchanging the d4–pawn draws Black closer to White's queenside.

33.dxc5 dxc5 34.♔f2 c4

Petrosian wins a pawn.

35.♖b1 cxb3 36.♖xb3

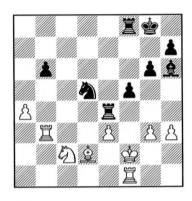

36...♖xa4

Black has won a pawn; in addition, his pieces stand better than White's. They soon adjourned the game, and Petrosian won comfortably.

37.♖fb1 ♖c8 38.♘e1 ♗g7 39.♔g1 ♖c5 40.♘f3 ♗f6 41.♖b5 ♗e7 42.♖5b3 ♔f7 43.♗e1 ♗f6 44.♔f1 g5 45.♗d2 ♔g6 46.♖d3 g4 47.hxg4 fxg4 48.♘d4 ♗xd4 49.exd4 ♖c7 50.♖e1 ♖f7+ 51.♔g2 ♖a2 52.♖e6+ ♖f6 53.♖e5 ♘b4 0–1

In the last game, Petrosian was White against Ivkov. He avoided a theoretical discussion and the game ended in a draw. Petrosian scored 5 points out of 8. He won 3, drew 4 and lost 1. The plus two result was not bad compared with the other Soviet players, though some players did better than that.

European Team Championship, Vienna/Baden

Finally, Petrosian was selected for the Soviet national team at an official event. The very first European team championship was held in the Austrian capital Vienna and Baden, in August. The matches were contested on ten boards, so it would have been very hard not to select him for the team. Petrosian was placed on board 6 in the mighty Soviet team.

They first had to eliminate Poland to qualify for the double round robin final, and Tigran was not put into the team for the two games against the Poles. Knowing how he typically started new events this made sense.

In the final, Petrosian started as Black against Czechoslovakia. His opponent, Sefc, opted for the 4.♛xd4 Sicilian. They reached a Maroczy Bind position where Petrosian gained a small advantage. This advantage grew bigger around time control, and Sefc resigned after move 59. In round 2, Petrosian was White against Heinecke in another Maroczy Bind. Petrosian got nothing from the opening, but the West German player made a horrible move and lost a piece, the game lasting just 23 moves. In the final round of the first half, Petrosian was White against Fuderer of Yugoslavia. They reached a Slav Exchange type of pawn structure, where Petrosian got a small edge. The Yugoslav player was able to withstand the pressure, and they drew soon after time control.

In the first game of the second round, Petrosian interestingly was Black against Sefc again. They played on a different board and we look at that game.

Game 76

Sefc, Jan – Petrosian, Tigran
European Team Championship Final
Vienna/Baden (4), 1957

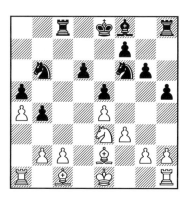

21.c4?

After this move, White's pawn structure becomes very rigid, and the light-squared bishop will be very passive. On the other hand, White's position is solid.

21...♗h6 22.b3 ♘fd7 23.♔f2 ♘c5

This is a nice outpost for a knight.

24.♖b1 h4 25.♖d1 ♖c6 26.♗d3 ♗f4 27.h3

27...♘bd7

The other knight is looking for an outpost as well.

28.♗c2 ♘f8 29.♗b2 ♘fe6 30.♘d5 ♗g5 31.♔f1 ♖f8

This move makes White address the threat of f5.

32.♖e1 ♔d7 33.♖bd1 ♔c8 34.♔f2 ♔b7 35.♘e3 ♘f4 36.♘d5 ♘h5 37.♘e3 ♗d8 38.♘d5

38...♘e6!

Petrosian is looking to exchange a pair of knights. After every exchange the c2–bishop becomes a bigger burden.

39.♔g1 ♘ef4 40.♗c1

40.♘e3 ♗b6 would be unpleasant.

40...♘xd5 41.♖xd5 ♗b6+ 42.♔h2 f6

Somewhere here they possibly adjourned the game.

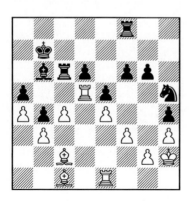

43.♗e3?

Keeping the bishop would limit the knight's movement. Petrosian rarely attaches a question-mark to his opponents' move, but this time he does, and says it increases Black's chances of winning. He suggests that White could still have held the position.

43...♗xe3 44.♖xe3 ♖a8

Maybe this was just to confuse his opponent, though it seems like Petrosian has not worked out a clear winning plan.

45.♔g1 ♘f4 46.♖d2 ♘e6 47.♖ed3

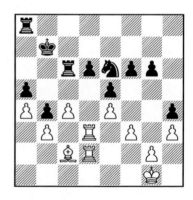

47...♘d4

He mentions he considered the exchange sacrifice in reply, but was not worried by it.

48.♔f1

White could think of giving up the exchange with 48.♖xd4 exd4 49.♖xd4.

48...♖f8

Petrosian wears out his opponent.

49.♔f2 ♔c7 50.♔f1 ♔d7 51.♔f2 ♔e7 52.♔f1 ♖a6 53.♔f2

♘e6 54.♖e3 ♘c5 55.♖d5 ♖aa8
56.♔f1 ♘e6 57.♖d2 ♘f4 58.♖e1
♖a7 59.♖ed1 ♖d7 60.♖e1

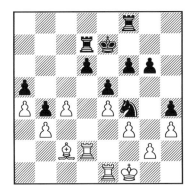

60...♖h8!

He probably already had the ensuing rook manoeuvre in mind.

    61.♖ed1 ♘e6 62.♖e1 ♘d4 63.♖ed1

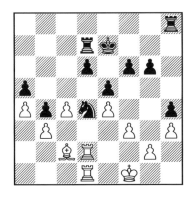

63...♔d8!

Petrosian looks for a better square for the king.

    64.♖e1 ♔c7 65.♖ed1 ♔c6 66.♖e1 ♔c5 67.♖e3 f5

Black makes his first pawn move in a long time.

    68.♔f2

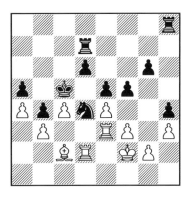

68...♖h5!

Petrosian here mentions his plan of doubling rooks on the g-file and placing the knight on f4, but White has a lot of resources to defend g2.

    69.♔f1 ♖g5 70.♔f2 ♖g3

This is an unusual square for a rook.

    71.♔f1 ♖f7 72.♔f2 ♖f8 73.♔f1 ♖h8 74.♔f2

74...♖h5!

Petrosian finds a great role for the second rook; it will be strong enough to bring the opponent down.

    75.♔f1?

According to Petrosian, this is the decisive mistake. Maybe White is not lost though.

After 75.♔g1 Black needs to find a way to increase the pressure. 75...♖hg5 76.♔h2 ♔c6 77.♖f2 ♔d7 (77...♘e6 78.♖ee2 ♘f4 79.♖d2 ♔c5 80.♔h1 and White keeps things together. Or 77...♔c7 78.♖d2 ♘e6 79.♖ee2 ♘f4 80.♖f2 ♔c6 81.♔h1 and White seems to hold) 78.♖d2

a) 78...♘e6 79.♖ee2 (after 79.♖ed3? ♔c7 80.♖e3 ♘f4 81.♖ee2 ♘xe2 82.♖xe2 Black probably wins by defending the d6 pawn with a rook and walking to f4 with the king) 79...♘d4 80.♖f2 (if 80.♖e3! ♖h5 see 78...♖h5 below) 80...♘xc2 81.♖xc2 fxe4 82.fxe4 ♖xb3 and Black wins.

b) 78...♖h5 79.♔g1 ♔c6 80.♗b1 ♖h7 81.♗c2 ♖g7

b1) 82.♗b1? f4 83.♖ed3 g5 84.♔h2 g4 85.fxg4 (85.hxg4 h3) 85... f3 and Black wins as 86.♖f2 ♖f7 or 86.♖b2 ♖f7 are decisive.

b2) after 82.♗d1! White has to change the diagonal of the bishop. 82...f4 (82...♘e6 83.♗c2) 83.♖ed3

b2.1) 83...♔c5 84.♔f2 g5 and one can't see how Black breaks through after 85.♗e2 or 85.♔f1.

b2.2) 83...g5 84.♗e2?

84...g4!! Black breaks through beautifully. 85.hxg4 h3 86.♗f1 ♔c5 87.♖d1 (87.♔h1 ♖h7 88.♔g1 ♖h6 wins) 87...♖g6 88.♖1d2 ♖h6 89.♗f2 (89.♖d1 ♘c2)

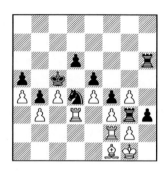

89...d5!! What a way to open up the position. 90.cxd5 (90.exd5 hxg2 91.♖xg2 [91.♗xg2 e4−+] 91... ♘xf3+ 92.♔f2 e4! wins) 90...♔d6!! and Black has time to clear the c-file for the rook. After 91.♖fd2 (91.♖d1 ♘xb3) 91...♖h7 the Black rook is about to invade decisively. This is all very nice, but on the way White can defend better and he may survive after 84.♔f2 or 84.♖xd4 exd4 85.♖xd4 ♖e7.

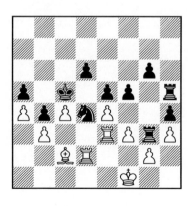

75...♖hg5 76.♖f2 ♔c6

Petrosian mentions that 76...♘e6 would be possible.

77.♖d2   ♔c7   78.♖f2   ♘e6 79.♖ee2 ♘f4 80.♖d2

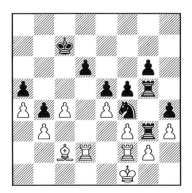

80...♔c6!

White is in zugzwang.

81.exf5

This is bad, but 81.♗b1 ♘xh3, 81.♗d3 ♘xd3 or 81.♗d1 fxe4 82.fxe4 ♖c3 would win for Black.

81...gxf5 82.♗d1 ♖g7 83.♗c2 ♖3g5 84.♗d3

White is again in zugzwang, and 84.♗b1 ♘xh3 would win.

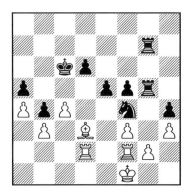

84...♔d7!

Petrosian improves his king.

85.♗c2   ♔e6   86.♗d3   ♖g3 87.♗c2 ♖g8

This sets up another zugzwang.

88.♗d3

88.♗d1 d5 89.cxd5+ ♘xd5 would win for Black, for example 90.♗c2 ♘e3+ or 90.♖fe2 f4.

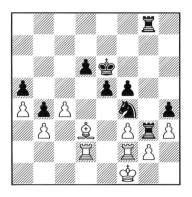

88...e4! 89.fxe4 ♘xd3

Petrosian wins a piece, it is all over.

90.♖xf5   ♘c5   91.♖fd5   ♖xb3 92.♖xd6+   ♔e7   93.♖6d4   ♖c3 94.e5 b3 95.♖xh4 ♖c1+ 96.♔f2 b2 0–1

Petrosian did not play against Germany, and in the last round he was Black again. Perhaps the captain noticed that his openings were stronger as Black. However, that was not the case against Yugoslavia, as he got into deep trouble in the 3.♘c3 ♗b4 4.e5 b6 French against the well prepared Nedeljkovic. Petrosian was probably lost when the Yugoslav player offered a draw. 4 points out of 5 games was a good result, but not exceptional for a player of his class.

Zenit – Spartak Moscow Match

Petrosian had failed to equalise against Terpugov at the point when we join the game.

Game 77

**Terpugov, Evgeny –
Petrosian, Tigran**

Zenit – Spartak Moscow, 1957

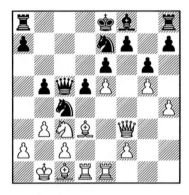

18...♗g7?!

Petrosian sacrifices a piece for the b-file. Objectively it is not the best idea, but it is rather imaginative. After the more conventional 18...♖b8 19.h5 a6 White would be somewhat better.

19.bxc4?!

White's accepting the knight sac is at least pleasant for Black. White could have obtained an edge with the help of a finesse.

a) 19.h5 ♘xe5 20.♗xb5+ ♔f8 21.♕e2 gxh5 and White would be somewhat better.

b) 19.♘xb5!

b1) 19...0-0 20.♗xc4 (after 20.a4 ♘xe5 [20...a6 21.♗xc4] 21.♖xe5 ♗xe5 22.♗a3 White would be

clearly better) 20...dxc4 21.♘d6 and Black would not have sufficient compensation for the pawn.

b2) 19...a6 20.♗xc4 axb5 21.♕e3!! Quite possibly, Petrosian missed this beautiful move, which prevents the black queen from reaching the a-file quickly (21.♗d3 b4) as if 21...♕c6 22.♗d3 b4 Black would not do well after 23.h5 or 23.f4.

19...bxc4 20.♗f1 0-0!

Black has time to build his play on the b-file. It is typical Petrosian, and it is hard to read his play. Starting with 20...♖b8+ at once would allow an interesting sacrifice. 21.♔a1 ♘c6 22.♘xd5!? exd5 23.♗a3 ♕a5 24.♖e2 (24.h5?? ♘d4) 24...♖b5 and the position would be balanced.

21.♔a1 ♖fb8 22.♘b1

White has no clear way to neutralise Black's play.

a) 22.h5 ♘f5 23.hxg6 hxg6 when Black would play ♕b4 and enjoy nice prospects.

b) 22.♕e3 ♕b4 23.a3 ♕a5

b1) 24.♘a2 ♘c6 25.♕c3 (after 25.f4? d4 26.♕e4 ♕b5 Black's attack breaks through) 25...♕b5 26.♗f4 ♗f8 and White's position is rather unpleasant.

b2) 24.♕d2 ♕a6 (24...♘f5 25.♘xd5; 24...♕b6 25.♕e3) 25.♘a2 ♘c6 26.♕c3 ♖b5 and Black's play on the b-file is nasty.

22...♘c6 23.♕g3?

Terpugov wants to hang on to all of his pawns; he can't afford to place his queen far away from his king. 23.♕c3 ♕xf2 (after 23...♗f8 24.♗a3 ♖xb1+ 25.♖xb1 ♕xa3 26.♕xa3 ♗xa3 27.c3 the position would be even) 24.h5 gxh5 25.♖e2 ♕f5 and White would struggle.

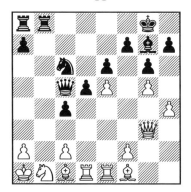

23...♖xb1+!

The sacrifice causes a decisive invasion.

24.♔xb1 ♖b8+ 25.♔a1 c3!

Black has time to cut off the white queen.

26.♗d2

This loses, but there is no defence. For example, if 26.♕f4 Black would also win with 26...♘b4 27.♖e2 ♕b5.

26...♘b4 27.♗d3

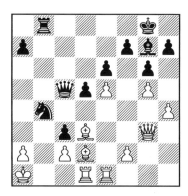

27...♕c4! 0–1 What a beauty. White can't avoid getting checkmated. A brilliant attacking game.

Petrosian played an exhibition game against Lilienthal during the Botvinnik-Smyslov match in March. Petrosian opened 1.e4 and he sacrificed a pawn. Lilienthal had to give up his queen, though he resisted until a bit after time control.

Match between
Metal Producers Cooperative Union and Moscow State University

Petrosian was White against Prokhorovich in a Slav Defence. Tigran accepted an isolated pawn and his opponent surprisingly castled long. In the middlegame, Petrosian was too strong for his opponent. It is not clear for which team Petrosian played.

Soviet Championship Semi-Final, Kiev

Petrosian's previous championship result was not good enough to give him an automatic place in the final, therefore, he had to line up in the semi-final in Kiev to qualify. The event started in November and finished in December. His first game was very promising indeed.

Petrosian, Tigran – Mikenas, Vladas
Soviet Championship Semi-Final,
Kiev (1), 1957
English Opening

1.c4 e5 2.♘c3 ♘f6 3.♘f3 ♘c6 4.d3 d5 5.cxd5 ♘xd5 6.g3 ♘de7 7.♗g2 ♘f5 8.0-0 ♗e7 9.a3 0-0 10.b4 ♗e6 11.♗b2 f6

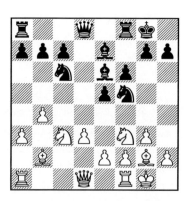

12.♘d2!?

Petrosian plays an original move. From now on Black has to consider White doubling the pawns on c6 and the knight getting closer to the c5–square.

12...♖b8 13.♕a4

This is another original way of putting pressure on Black's queenside.

13...a6 14.♖ac1

14.♗xc6 bxc6 15.♘ce4 (15.♕xc6 ♘d4) 15...a5 would be fine for Black.

14...♘fd4?

Mikenas plays for a combination. Instead, 14...♕d7 15.♖fd1 b5 16.♕c2 a5 17.♘xb5 ♘xb4 would be balanced.

15.e3! ♘b3?

A clever move, but a bad one. Objectively, it was better to admit his mistake and move the knight back. After 15...♘f5 16.♕c2 ♕e8 17.♘a4 White would clearly be better.

16.♘xb3 b5 17.♕xa6

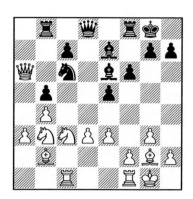

17...♖b6

Black traps the queen, but White gets too much material for it.

18.♕xb6 cxb6 19.♗xc6 ♗xb3

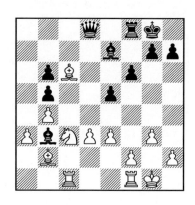

20.♗xb5!

There is nothing special about this capture, but what is remarkable is that Petrosian judged this position much better than his experienced grandmaster opponent.

20...♕a8?

Mikenas wants to bring the rook into play. After 20...f5! 21.♗c4+ (21.e4 ♗g5) 21...♗xc4 22.dxc4 f4 23.♘d5 White's advantage would be smaller than in the game.

21.e4! ♖d8 22.♘d5

Petrosian obtains the two bishops and a passed pawn.

22...♗xd5 23.exd5 ♔f8 24.♗c6 ♕c8

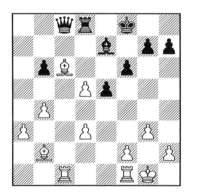

25.♖c4! ♕f5 26.♖e4 ♗d6 27.♖fe1 ♔g8

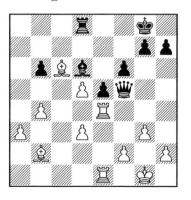

28.d4!

Getting rid of the doubled pawns leads to an easily winning position. Petrosian confidently converted his advantage.

28...♖f8 29.♖1e2 ♖f7 30.♔g2 h5 31.h3 g5 32.♗e8 ♖h7 33.dxe5 fxe5 34.♗xh5 ♖xh5 35.g4 ♕f7 36.gxh5 ♕xh5 37.♔h2 ♕f7 38.♗xe5 ♗xe5+ 39.♖xe5 ♕f4+ 40.♔g2 ♕h4 41.♖2e4 ♕h5 1–0

In the second round, Petrosian was Black against Sakharov in a 3.♘c3 ♗b4 French. White made a mistake early on; soon after, Petrosian took control, won a pawn, and won the game without any problem. He did not slow down in the third round. He was White against Khasin. His opponent won a risky pawn in a closed Catalan and his advantage quickly grew into a winning one. The game lasted 33 moves. In the fourth round, he agreed a short draw as Black against Kotov. This was followed by another short draw, this time as White against Furman. In round 6, he was Black against Sokolsky, and his position looked unpleasant in the King's Indian Saemisch. However, his opponent let his advantage evaporate and the game ended in a repetition after Sokolsky's 27th move. In the seventh round, Nikolaevsky tried the Old Indian developing the bishop to g7. Petrosian was able to create an exemplary knight on e4. They swapped queens; Tigran slowly but surely increased his advantage and won the one-sided game after his 60th move. In round 8, Petrosian as Black got a Maroczy Bind against Reshko. His opponent was glad to hold the balance, but a bit before time control Tigran made a serious mistake. He fought hard, but was unable to save the game. In the next round, he was White against Chistiakov. As usual, he castled long in the Queen's Gambit Exchange, but his opponent was well prepared. However, after an inaccurate exchange Petrosian gained an edge, but Black was able to hold the position. In the next round, he was Black against Vasiukov. The Russian player offered a draw in a theoretical position of the main-line Caro-Kann.

In the 11th round, he played the early middlegame cautiously and allowed quite a few exchanges against Goldberg. Then he gained a small edge, which he was able to extend. We join the game at this point.

Game 79

Petrosian, Tigran –
Goldberg, Grigory

Soviet Championship Semi-Final,
Kiev (11), 1957

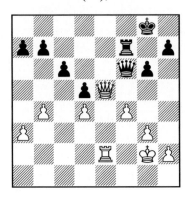

37.♔f3!

An imaginative way to prepare gaining space.

37...♔g7

White would have excellent winning chances after 37...♕d8 38.h4 or 37...♕xe5 38.♖xe5 ♖d7 39.g4.

**38.g4   ♔g8   39.♕e8+   ♔g7
40.♕e5 ♔f8**

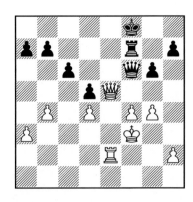

41.♕xf6!

Perhaps Tigran waited to exchange queens until the game was adjourned. White has very good winning chances in the rook ending.

41...♖xf6 42.g5 ♖f7 43.h4 ♔g7

After 43...♖e7 44.♖xe7 ♔xe7 45.f5 gxf5 46.♔f4 ♔e6 47.h5 the pawn ending would be winning. Maybe reducing the number of pawns with 43...h6 gives the best practical chances to save the day. 44.♖e6 (after 44.gxh6 ♖h7 45.♔g4 ♖xh6 Black might survive) 44...hxg5 45.hxg5 ♔g7 46.a4 a6 47.♔g4 ♔h7 48.a5 and White wins with f5.

44.♖e6 ♖c7

White would win after 44...h6 45.h5! or 44...♔f8 45.♔g4 ♔g7 46.♖e5.

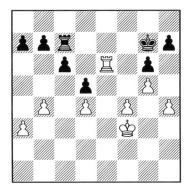

45.f5!

Petrosian creates a passed pawn. For a player well acquainted with Capablanca's games it is easy to find.

45...gxf5 46.♔f4 b6

Waiting passively would be hopeless, as White would take the f5–pawn and walk with the king to d6.

47.♔xf5   c5   48.bxc5   bxc5 49.dxc5 ♖xc5 50.♖e7+ ♔g8

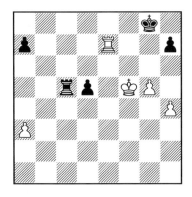

51.♖xa7

White wins a pawn. The position is winning easily because his king and rook are well placed and the a-pawn is very dangerous.

51...♖c4

51...d4+ 52.♔e4 ♖c1 53.a4 ♖h1 54.a5 ♖xh4+ 55.♔d3 h6 56.a6 ♖h3+ 57.♔xd4 ♖a3 58.gxh6 and White wins.

52.h5 ♖c1 53.♖d7 ♖f1+

53...♖a1 54.h6 (54.♖xd5? ♖xa3) 54...♖xa3 55.♖d8+ ♔f7 56.♖h8 and White's connected passed pawns win the game.

54.♔e6 ♖e1+ 55.♔xd5 ♖g1 56.♔c6 ♖xg5 57.♖d5 ♖g3 58.a4 ♖a3 59.a5 ♔f7 60.♖b5 1–0

Goldberg, who was tennis champion of Moscow, resigns.

In the 12th round, Petrosian was Black against Blagidze. It was a King's Indian Saemisch, but neither player was able to create winning chances and the game ended in a repetition after Tigran's 38th move. In the next game, Petrosian drew as White in 18 moves with Boleslavsky. In the 14th round, Petrosian was White against Shianovsky. He got a nice advantage in the g3 King's Indian. He surprisingly played on the kingside, instead of the standard queenside play. His advantage vanished, however. Then he sacrificed an exchange, and Shianovsky made a huge mistake and lost instantly in a direct confrontation. In the 15th round, he drew against Geller in 11 moves, which was reasonable as it was useful for qualification. In the next round, he was White against Bannik. He obtained a pleasant advantage in the g3 King's Indian, but nevertheless he agreed to a draw after Bannik's 22nd move. In the 17th round, he was Black against Bastrikov. His opponent handled the 3.♘c3 ♝b4 French poorly. Petrosian gained an advantage early on, won a pawn and scored a victory. In the last two rounds, he drew quickly against Nezhmetdinov and Bonch-Osmolovsky. Petrosian showed his class by winning the event, scoring 12.5 points out of 19. He scored 7 wins, 11 draws and one loss. Geller was second with 12 points.

Petrosian's results in 1957

Soviet Championship Final, Moscow	+ 7 = 10 – 4 12/21 7th-8th place
Soviet Union – Yugoslavia Match, Leningrad	+ 3 = 4 – 1 5/8
European Team Championship, Vienna/Baden b. 6	+ 3 = 2 – 0 4/5
Zenit – Spartak Moscow vs. Tergupov	+ 1 = 0 – 0 1:0
Team event vs. Prokhorovich	+ 1 = 0 – 0 1:0
Soviet Championship Semi-Final, Kiev	+ 7 = 11 – 1 12.5/19 1st place
Altogether	**+ 22 = 27 – 6 35/55**

1958

Petrosian's first tournament of the year was the Soviet Championship Final in Riga. The event was also the Soviet qualifier for the next world championship cycle. It was very strong, as of the stars only Botvinnik, Smyslov and Keres did not participate.

Petrosian started the event against Suetin; they played a King's Indian. Suetin carried out a somewhat flashy combination, which resulted in a passive position and Petrosian's advantage grew. By time control he was two pawns up, and Suetin resigned after Petrosian's 61st move. In the second game, Gurgenidze as White played 3.♗b5+ against the Sicilian. Petrosian gave up the bishop pair for healthy piece development. The game ended in a repetition on move 30. In the third round, he had a bye.

In the fourth round, he was White against Bannik, and we join the game when Petrosian had already obtained a huge advantage; this was one of Petrosian's most instructive games.

Game 80

**Petrosian, Tigran –
Bannik, Anatoly**
Soviet Championship Final,
Riga (4), 1958

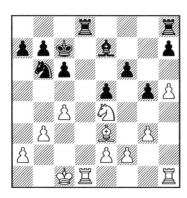

18.♗c5!

Petrosian exchanges Black's "bad" bishop. He explains that had he taken the knight, Black would have swapped rooks on the d-file and transferred the King to e6, building an uncrackable fortress. There is a short video of his lecture to juniors where he asked the pupils to analyse this position.

18...♖xd1+?!

When one has a serious problem, one should not exchange. Here, Black's best bet is to keep as many pieces on the board as possible with 18...♗xc5 19.♘xc5 ♖de8 20.f3.

19.♖xd1 ♗xc5 20.♘xc5 ♖e8 21.♘e4 ♖e6

21...♖f8 22.g4 ♘d7 23.f3 would also be bad.

22.g4 a5 23.♖d3 ♘d7 24.♔c2! b6

25.♖f3!

After improving his king, Petrosian ties Black's pieces to defending the pawn.

25...♔d8 26.a3 c5

Black stops b4 and c5, but it costs control over d5.

27.♔c3 ♔e7 28.♖d3 ♖c6 29.♖d5 ♘f8 30.♘g3 ♘e6 31.♘f5+ ♔e8 32.e3 ♘c7

Petrosian prefers transferring the knight to f7, but that would not change the outcome of the game.

33.♖d1 ♘e6

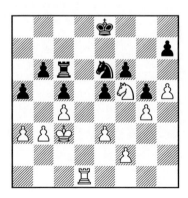

34.♔d3!

The king will play a strong role on e4.

34...♖c7 35.♔e4 ♖c6 36.♘d6+ ♔e7 37.♘f5+ ♔e8 38.♘d6+ ♔e7 39.♘f5+ ♔e8

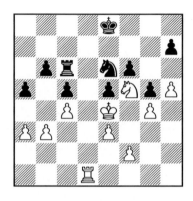

40.a4!?

Petrosian is focused on the practical and he waits to exchange rooks until the game is adjourned. 40.♖d6! would already win.

40...♘d8 41.♘h6

Petrosian sealed this move, which stops ♘f7. Bannik plays on in a hopeless position.

41...♘e6 42.♘g8 ♘f8

If 42...♔f7 the pretty 43.♖d7+! ♔xg8 44.♔d5 wins.

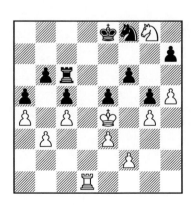

43.♖d2!

Petrosian explains he was playing for zugzwang. It was still possible to ruin the position: 43.♔f5? ♔f7 44.♘h6+ ♔g7 45.♖d8 ♘e6 and Black would escape.

43...♔f7

According to the maestro, 43... ♘d7 44.♔f5 ♔d8 45.e4 ♔e8 46.f3 ♔d8 47.♖xd7+! ♔xd7 48.♘xf6+ wins for White.

44.♘h6+ ♔e8 45.♘f5 ♘e6

After 45...♘d7 Petrosian shows a nice line: 46.♔d5 ♘b8 47.♘h6 ♔f8 (47...♔e7 48.♘g8+ ♔f7 49.♔e4!) 48.♔e4! ♔e8 49.♔f5 ♘d7 50.♘g8 and White wins.

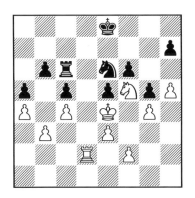

46.♖d6!

Exchanging the rook simply wins.

46...♖xd6   47.♘xd6+   ♔d7 48.♘b5 ♘g7

48...♘f8 49.♔f5 ♔e7 50.♘c3 ♘d7 51.♘d5+ ♔f7 52.e4 h6 53.f3! and Black would be in complete zugzwang.

49.h6 ♘e8

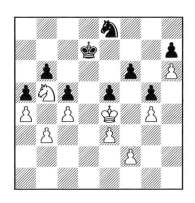

50.♔d5

The zugzwang forces Black to give up material in desperation. Strangely, Bannik plays on...

50...f5 51.♔xe5 fxg4 52.♘c3 ♔e7 53.♘e4 ♔f7 54.♔f5 g3 55.fxg3 g4 56.♘g5+ ♔g8 57.♔e6 ♘c7+ 58.♔d7 ♘a6 59.e4 ♘b4 60.e5 ♘d3 61.e6 1–0

In the next round, Petrosian as Black equalised in the Orthodox Queen's Gambit against Korchnoi, when he accepted an isolated pawn. He made some inaccurate moves and got into big trouble. Korchnoi was winning when, probably in time trouble, he made a tactical mistake. Tigran was able to escape with perpetual check. So he had again got into a lost position against Victor and survived. In the sixth round, Petrosian as White played a main line against Kotov's Nimzo-Indian. He was unable to create play and not much happened in the 26-move draw.

In the seventh game Petrosian was Black against the local hero, Tal, who also was on plus two. Mikhail obtained an edge in the opening. When we join the game, White still has the edge.

Game 81

Tal, Mikhail – Petrosian, Tigran
Soviet Championship Final,
Riga (7), 1958

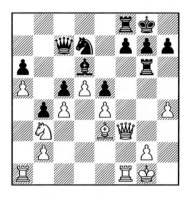

29...♛d8?!

Petrosian finds an imaginative idea, but this is not the best move, as after 29...♞f6 30.h5 ♜g4 31.♞d2 White's advantage would be small.

30.h5 ♜f6 31.♕g4

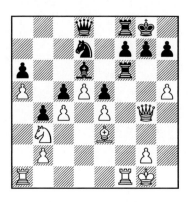

31...♜f4!?

Petrosian again sacrifices an exchange positionally. This time, the imaginative idea doesn't equalise.

32.♗xf4

Tal gets careless. Instead, 32.♜xf4 exf4 33.♗xf4 would have given him quite a nice advantage.

32...exf4 33.♞d2

After 33.♜xf4! ♞e5 34.♕h4 ♗e7 35.♕f2 White would be better.

33...♞e5 34.♕xf4?

34.♕h3 should be played.

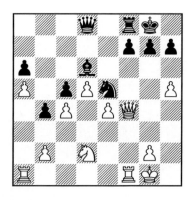

34...♞xc4

Petrosian has equalised, and later he took control. However, Tal's stubborn play yielded a draw.

In the eighth round, Petrosian was White against Taimanov. They reached a 1.c5 e5 type of position; Petrosian got play on the queenside, and Taimanov on the kingside. The game ended in a draw after Taimanov's 26th move, although Petrosian probably should have played on. In round 9, Petrosian was Black against Polugaevsky.

He equalised in the 4.f3 Nimzo-Indian. Polugaevsky played well and was able to keep the balance; they reached an endgame, and a bit before time control the game ended in a repetition. In the 10th round, Petrosian as White agreed a 19-move draw with Geller. In the 11th round, he won without play against the ill Borisenko. In the 12th round, Petrosian was White against Furman. The opening began 1.d4 ♘f6 2.♘f3 g6 3.♗g5, and Petrosian saddled his opponent with doubled pawns. In the early middlegame he brilliantly obtained an advantage, but allowed his opponent to equalise. Not long before time control, Semion unnecessarily went for a rook ending, then on move 40 he made a big mistake in a somewhat worse position. He lost the game after Petrosian's 45th move. In the 13th round, Krogius as White played the Keres Variation against the Scheveningen Sicilian. Black's position looked very dangerous, but he stabilised it. In the middlegame, in an equal position, Tigran made a big mistake, but Krogius failed to exploit it and offered a draw on the next move, which Tigran agreed to.

Game 82

Petrosian, Tigran – Gipslis, Aivars
Soviet Championship Final,
Riga (14), 1958

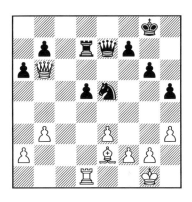

29.b4!?

Petrosian creates play in an unusual way; he doesn't try to play against the isolated pawn.

29...♘c6

After 29...♛d6 30.♛xd6 (30.♛a7 b5) 30...♖xd6 White's advantage would be small. Black should also hold after 29...♘c4 30.♛c5 ♛xc5 31.bxc5 ♘b2 or 31...♘e5.

30.♗xa6 ♘xb4

After 30...♛xb4 31.♛xb4 ♘xb4 32.♗c4 Black would be about to lose a pawn.

31.♗b5 ♖c7

After 31...♛d6 32.♛d4 ♘c6 Black should be able to live with White's small edge.

32.a3 ♘c2?

It is always dangerous when a knight moves far away from its camp. This time, it is a losing mistake, and Petrosian will exploit it with clinical precision. Black should have played 32...♕c5! 33.♕f6 and after 33...♘c6 Petrosian would probably press with 34.a4, as winning the pawn would lead to a theoretical draw given that Black could exchange the queenside pawns: 34.♗xc6 ♖xc6 35.♕d8+ ♔g7 36.♕xd5 (36.♖xd5 ♕xa3) 36...♕xd5 37.♖xd5 ♖c3 38.♖a5 b5 39.g3 ♖b3 40.h4 b4.

33.♖xd5 ♘xa3

If 33...♔g7 then 34.a4 could be played.

34.♕d4! ♖c8 35.♗d3! b5

After 35...♖e8 White has several ways to win, and here are two entertaining ones: 36.♗xg6 (36.♖d7 ♕e5 37.♕xe5 ♖xe5 38.♖xb7 ♖a5 39.♖b4 and White is about to trap the knight) 36...fxg6 37.♖d7 ♕e5 38.♕b6 ♕e6 39.♖d6.

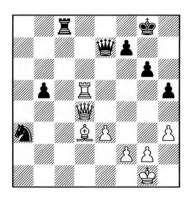

36.♗xg6!

This sacrifice decisively opens up black's king.

36...fxg6 37.♖d7 ♕f8 38.♕d5+ ♔h8 39.♕e5+ ♔g8 40.♕e6+ ♔h8 1–0

Gipslis resigned without waiting for Petrosian to play.

In the 15th round, Petrosian was Black against Spassky, who played the Giuoco Piano. Tigran handled the opening forcefully and the game ended in a draw after White's 20th move. In the 16th round, Tolush played the Stonewall Dutch as Black. They reached a complex and balanced middlegame. Tolush made a mistake and his position was about to fall apart when Tigran returned the favour. However, Tolush made another blunder and went on to lose. Its exploitation can be seen in the It's Your Move chapter. In the 17th round, Petrosian played the Accelerated Dragon against Bronstein. David did not choose a testing line. Still, he was able to get a small edge, but then surprisingly offered a draw. Petrosian was probably happy to accept. In round 18, Petrosian was White against Boleslavsky. They fianchettoed all 4 bishops in the English. In the middlegame, Petrosian started to gain a slight edge, but the game ended in a repetition after 25 moves.

Before the last round, Tal and Petrosian had 11.5 points each, with Bronstein on 11, and Spassky and Averbakh 10.5. The final pairings included Spassky-Tal, Averbakh-Petrosian and Bronstein-Korchnoi.

Petrosian played the Najdorf, and Averbakh chose the 6.♗e2

line, handling the 6...e5 variation positionally. Petrosian was able to set his position free. The centre disappeared and Yuri offered a draw. Maybe Tigran should have played on, as in the opposite-coloured bishops middlegame a mistake could have been fatal for White. Bronstein drew fairly quickly. Maybe his decision was influenced by the fact that he saw Tal struggling in his famous game again Spassky. That dramatic game was adjourned, and according to Vasiliev, Spassky met Petrosian before the resumption and told him that he would become Soviet champion that day. During the resumption, Tal managed to equalise and Spassky offered a draw. The brave Misha refused, despite its meaning qualification for the world championship cycle. Tal didn't want to risk losing his title which he had won in 1957 and beat the demoralised Boris. The Latvian, who scored 8 points out of the last 9 games, hence won the championship again, scoring 12.5 points.

Next were Petrosian with 12 and Bronstein on 11.5. Averbakh, who scored 11 points, also qualified, whereas Spassky's loss in the last round meant elimination. Petrosian beat the bottom 6 players (against Borisenko it was a default) and drew against the top 12. He was the only player who remained undefeated. This was a big success for him.

According to Averbakh, Petrosian was not really ambitious, and he was often pleased with second or third places, though he could have fought for first. At the end of the fifties, he finally set the target to fight for the world champion's title. This had much to do with the influence of Rona and Armenian fans. She was a highly ambitious person and did much to support her husband becoming world champion. Armenians in both Armenia, Moscow and other cities in the country dreamed that their hero would become the strongest player on the planet. They often wrote to him, even with questions such as *Dear Tigran, when will you finally become word champion? We are tired of waiting, please hurry up!*

Moscow Team Championship

Petrosian played a team event in March. He played the Slav Gambit as White against Ignatev. The game was balanced for a long time, but after Ignatev made a mistake Petrosian finished the game quickly.

Torpedo – Spartak Moscow Match

Shekhtman places this match after the Ignatev game with no month shown.

Lebedev played the Advance French as White. Tigran castled long, and his opponent sacrificed a pawn. The position was balanced, but in the early middlegame White made a serious mistake, Petrosian capitalised on it and never let him back into the game.

Gagra

According to Shekhtman, Petrosian played a training game against Bukhuti Gurgenidze in Gagra. Only one game is known from the event, but it is unlikely that Petrosian would have flown to the Black Sea to play only one game. Perhaps they were going to play a match and for some reason it was stopped.

Petrosian was Black and the Alekhine Defence transposed into an Alapin Sicilian. Petrosian obtained an easily winning position right in the opening, but he got careless and wasted his advantage. In the endgame, he committed a careless error and Gurgenidze beautifully took control. Maybe Tigran could have still held, but another mistake sealed his fate.

Team Event, Vilnius

In July, Petrosian played for the Moscow team in Vilnius. He was selected for board two behind Bronstein. We know all his opponents and results, but we have the moves of only three games.

In his first game, he was Black against Taimanov. Tigran was unable to equalise in a King's Indian, in fact he rarely had such a bad opening, even with Black. By move 20 he was already lost and had to resign eight moves later.

It is not known in which round his Uusi game was played. The Estonian would become a 6 times champion of the Baltic republic; he obtained his first title in that same 1958.

Game 83

Petrosian, Tigran – Uusi, Gunnar
USSR Team Championship,
Vilnius, 1958

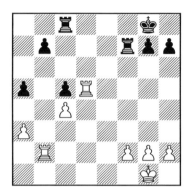

30...♖f4?

Black has no pleasant choice, but giving up a pawn would probably save the game: 30...♖cc7 31.♖d8+ (31.♖b5 ♖f4) 31...♖f8 32.♖xf8+ ♔xf8 33.♖b5 ♔e7 and Black's active king keeps the position balanced.

31.♖xb7 ♖xc4 32.g3 ♔h8?!

32...♖g4 33.♖dd7 is rather unpleasant for Black.

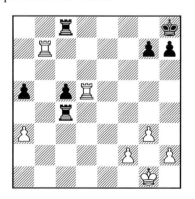

33.♖c7!

A neat way to divert the c8–rook.

33...♖a8 34.♖g5! g6?

Opening the seventh rank is a mistake. 34...♖g8 35.♖cxc5 would probably still win for White.

35.♖e5!

Petrosian's powerful play enables him to invade the seventh rank. This is much stronger than taking the pawn.

35...♖c3

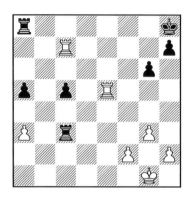

36.♖ee7!

The rest is simple.

36...♖xa3 37.♖xh7+ ♔g8
38.♖cg7+ ♔f8 39.♖xg6 ♖e8
40.♖c6 ♔g8 41.♖hc7 1–0

In the third game, Petrosian as Black played a main-line Spanish against Suetin. The game lasted 23 moves. All we know about his next game is that he beat Klavins, and then followed with two more wins against Mikenas and Bannik. He did not play against Georgia. Perhaps he did not want to play against the republic in which he was born and raised. In the last round, he drew with Polugaevsky. He scored 4 wins, 2 draws and 1 loss, meaning 5 points out of seven. Only Polugaevsky did better than him. The Moscow team won the event with 52.5 points.

Fischer visited Moscow in the summer of 1958, and he played blitz against Petrosian. Tigran reportedly won the first two games, and in the end he retained a plus two result.

Interzonal Tournament, Portoroz

The interzonal was held in August on the Slovenian coast in Portoroz. Petrosian was one of the favourites to qualify for the Candidates Tournament.

He started as White against Sherwin. The American chose the Queen's Gambit Accepted and Black got a small edge out of the opening. However, Sherwin made an unfortunate queen manoeuvre. Moreover, Sherwin was a player known to suffer from heavy time trouble, and the moves suggest that he was short of time here, too. Before time control, Petrosian won two pawns and was already winning. Sherwin did well to put off resignation until Petrosian's 58th move.

Once your Hungarian author was Sherwin's second, and he talked about Petrosian fondly. It was especially funny how he ordered food giving the sound of a chicken or acting like a crab.

In the second round, Petrosian was Black against De Greiff, and the Colombian played the Petrosian Variation against Petrosian in the King's Indian. It was a win-win situation for Tigran: either follow his variation, or an opening where he is very strong. The position was balanced for a long time and the game ended in a draw. The third round became part of chess history: Petrosian was White against Szabo, who played the Queen's Indian Defence, and Tigran played the variation which later would be named after him with a3. Szabo reacted well to the surprise and equalised, offering a draw after his 21st move, which Petrosian accepted.

Game 84

Pachman, Ludek – Petrosian, Tigran
Portoroz Interzonal (4), 1958
Old Indian Defence

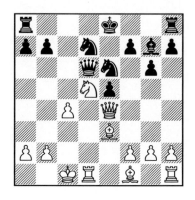

1.c4 ♘f6 2.♘f3 d6 3.d4 ♗g4
4.♘c3 g6 5.e4 ♗xf3 6.♕xf3 ♘fd7
7.e5 ♘c6 8.exd6 ♘xd4 9.♕e4 e5
10.dxc7 ♕xc7 11.♘d5 ♕d6 12.♗f4
♘e6 13.♗e3 ♗g7 14.0-0-0

14...0-0

Petrosian sacrifices his queen for material and activity.

15.♘b6 ♕xd1+ 16.♔xd1 axb6

The rook and knight are not full compensation for the queen, but Black is better developed.

17.a3?

The Czechoslovakian grandmaster gives away a tempo for free. After 17.♕b1 e4 18.h4 ♘dc5 19.h5 ♘a4 White's material advantage is enough to keep the balance.

17...♘dc5 18.♕c2 e4 19.f3?

Pachman weakens his position. Instead, Black's advantage would be small after 19.♔e1 ♘a4 20.♗e2 ♘xb2.

19...♖ad8+ 20.♔e1 ♘d4?!

Petrosian's move is good enough to keep a clear advantage, but there are other moves that would finish off Pachman faster. For example, Black would win quickly after 20...♗d4 21.♗xd4 ♘xd4 or 20...♖fe8 21.fxe4 ♘d4.

21.♗xd4 ♗xd4 22.fxe4

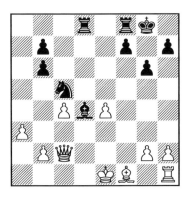

22...♘xe4

Black's development advantage is huge.

23.♗e2

White could prolong the game with 23.♕xe4 ♖fe8 24.♕xe8+ ♖xe8+ 25.♔d2 ♗xb2 26.a4 ♗e5 but Black has enough to win.

23...♖fe8 24.♖f1 ♖e7 25.♖f3 ♖de8 26.♖d3

After 26.♔f1 ♘g5 27.♖d3 ♖xe2 28.♕xe2 ♖xe2 29.♔xe2 ♘e6 White would have only a tiny chance to hold.

26...♗g1!

Black has to hurry to win; this nice move is played just in time.

27.h3 ♗h2 28.♗f3 ♗g3+

White's king is caught, and the rest is simple.

29.♔d1 ♘f2+ 30.♔d2 ♗f4+ 31.♔c3 ♘xd3 32.♔xd3 ♖e3+ 33.♔d4 ♗h6 34.c5 b5 35.♗xb7 ♗g7+ 36.♔d5 ♖8e6 0–1 Pachman lost on time before losing his queen.

Matanovic played the Ragozin Variation of the Queen's Gambit in the fifth game. Petrosian obtained a small edge. Then, the Yugoslav player made a careless move, and Petrosian beautifully increased his advantage. The reward for his powerful moves was a victory after his 23rd move. In the sixth round, he agreed a 13-move draw as Black against Filip. In round 7, he was White against Cardoso; Petrosian played the Saemisch Variation against the Filipino's Nimzo-Indian. He quickly got a clear edge, and then a winning advantage. Cardoso lasted until time control. In the 8th round, he played the Nimzo-Indian against Gligoric. The position was even for a long time; then approaching move 30 Petrosian's position became slightly preferable. They were probably in time trouble when they agreed to a draw after Svetozar's 34th move. If Tigran had had time he could have played on. In the 9th round, Petrosian was White against Neikirkh, and the two Soviet players agreed to a draw after Tigran's 16th move. Maybe it was prearranged. In the 10th round, he was Black against Fuster in a g3 King's Indian. He equalised and obtained a better position towards time control. By time control he was winning and Fuster resigned after Tigran's 51st move.

Game 85

Petrosian, Tigran – Rossetto, Hector
Portoroz Interzonal (11), 1958

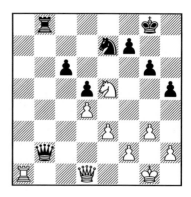

28.♖c1!
Petrosian attacks the backward pawn. It is very hard to anticipate what he will do.
28...♖b6
28...♕b7 29.♕f3 wins a pawn.
29.h3!!
He starts an unusual plan.
29...♔g7

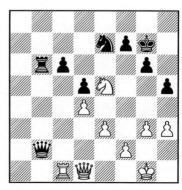

30.♔g2!
Petrosian probably planned ♕f3 and didn't want the rook to be hanging with a check.

30...♕a3?

30...♘f5! 31.♖c2

a) Darga suggests 31...♕b3, but after 32.♕c1! ♕b5 33.♘xc6 ♕d3 34.♘e5 ♕e4+ 35.♔h2 White would be a pawn up. White has other strong moves on the way, too: 33.♖a2! or 33.g4!.

b) 31...♕a3

b1) 32.g4 hxg4 33.hxg4 ♘h4+ 34.♔g3 g5 35.♕c1 ♕a7 36.♘xc6 ♕b7 37.♘e5 ♖b1 38.♖c7 and Black holds.

b2) 32.♕d2 ♕e7 33.♕c1 f6 34.♖xc6 ♖b7 35.♘f3 ♕e4 36.♕c2 ♔f7 37.♖c3! The rook defends the e3-pawn and White has a safe extra pawn.

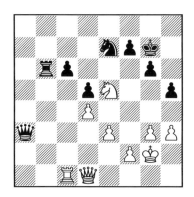

31.♖a1!

A brilliant idea. Petrosian takes his eye off the backward pawn, but he forces the queen to choose a diagonal and he attacks accordingly.

31...♕b2

If 31...♕d6 32.♖a7! ♕e6 33.♕a4 White will be almost winning with ♕a3 next move.

32.g4!

A highly unusual idea. White catches the black king, not from the usual 8th or 7th rank, but from the kingside. The pawn move takes away the f5 square from the knight. This is better than 32.♖a7?! ♖b7 or 32.♕f3 ♘f5.

32...hxg4 33.hxg4 ♖b7

If 33...♖b8 then 34.♕f3 invades decisively.

34.♖c1

Petrosian visualised the queen invasion but now misses a direct win. If 34.♕f3? ♕xa1 35.♕xf7+ ♔h8 White would have no more than perpetual check. However, after 34.♖a8! ♕b4 35.♕f3 or 35.g5 ♘f5 36.♕h1 he would win. How unusual to attack the king like this!

34...♕b5?

Gligoric and Matanovic suggest 34...f6? and they say that White can't take the pawn, because if 35.♘xc6 then 35...♖c7 would win. However, they are wrong, as 36.♖b1 would win. Black should play 34...g5! 35.♘xc6 ♘g6 36.♕c2 and White would be a pawn up for nothing, though White still has to win the game.

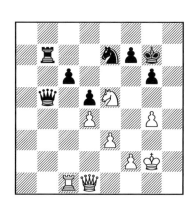

35.♕f3!

The queen decides the outcome of the game instantly.

35...f6

35...♘g8 36.♖h1 or 36.♖xc6 would win very quickly.

36.g5!

White hunts down Black's king.

36...♘f5

36...f5 37.♕h3 or 36...fxe5 37.♕f6+ ♔g8 38.♖h1 and White would also win.

37.gxf6+ ♔xf6 38.♖xc6+ ♔e7 39.♕f4 1–0 Another very original game!

After 11 rounds, Petrosian was leading with a superb 8.5 points.

In the next game, he was Black against Benko in an English. White built his position with ♘f3, c4, b3, ♗b2 and e3. Petrosian equalised, then he wanted to attack and made a somewhat risky move. Benko, with a small edge, offered a draw after his 21st move. Tigran did not take the risk of continuing.

Game 86

**Petrosian, Tigran –
Fischer, Bobby**
Portoroz Interzonal (13), 1958
English Opening

1.c4 ♘f6 2.♘c3 g6 3.g3 ♗g7 4.♗g2 0-0 5.♘f3 d6 6.0-0 ♘c6 7.d3 ♘h5 8.d4 e5 9.d5 ♘e7 10.e4 f5

Fischer prepared this unfortunate move. The game he wanted to improve on probably had a better move: 10...c5!? 11.♘e1 ♔h8 12.♘d3 f5 13.♖b1 ♘f6= Petrosian, T – Boleslavsky, I, Soviet Championship, 1957.

11.exf5 gxf5

Black has no pleasant way to recapture: 11...♗xf5 12.♘g5 is unpleasant, or if 11...♘xf5? 12.g4 ♘d4 13.gxh5 ♗g4 14.♘xd4 White would win.

12.♘xe5! ♘xg3

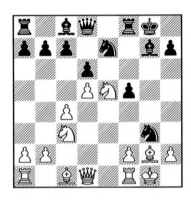

13.hxg3!

Fischer did not expect this capture, but he admitted Petrosian was right.

13...♗xe5

Fischer preferred 13...dxe5 keeping a fluid pawn centre; he was worried about 14.c5, although 14.♗g5 also looks strong.

14.f4!

White attacks the bishop and takes away the e5-square.

14...♗g7 15.♗e3 ♗d7 16.♗d4

Petrosian neutralises the g7-bishop. 16.♗f3 ♘g6 17.♕d3 or 16.c5 would also give him an edge.

16...♘g6 17.♖e1?

The American calls this move careless. Petrosian allows Fischer to get rid of his structural weakness. 17.♗f3!? or 17.c5!? dxc5 18.♗xc5 ♖e8 19.♕b3 and White's advantage would be bigger than in the game.

17...♖f7?

Fischer misses the chance to get rid of the isolated h-pawn. 17...♗xd4+ 18.♕xd4 h5! 19.c5 (19.♗f3 h4 20.♗h5 ♕f6 and the position is equal) 19...dxc5 (19...h4 20.c6) 20.♕xc5 h4 21.♖ad1 (21.d6 c6) 21...hxg3 22.♖d3 ♕h4 and Black would not be worse.

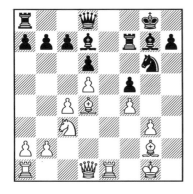

18.♗f3!

Petrosian stops the h-pawn. 18.c5 would be strong, too.

18...♕f8 19.♔f2!

A typical Petrosian move. He opens the route to the h-file and brings his king closer to the centre.

19...♖e8   20.♖xe8   ♕xe8 21.♗xg7 ♖xg7

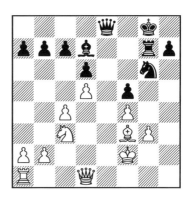

22.♕d4!

This is a sweet square for the queen.

22...b6 23.♖h1

23.b4! with c5 would be testing here as well, but Petrosian probably decided to keep the position closed. Fischer also prefers this idea.

23...a5

Fischer: *my first breath.*

24.♘d1 ♕f8 25.♘e3

Fischer: *Petrosian keeps building without getting sidetracked – even by good moves.* Fischer was more worried about the move 25.♗h5!, which he said would tie him up completely. The bishop would be ready to take the knight if needed. It stops 25...♖e7?? and Fischer mentions why it doesn't work: 26.♗xg6 hxg6 27.♖h8+. After 25...♘e7 26.♘e3 ♔h8 27.♗d1 (27.b3 ♘g8!) 27...♘g8 28.♗c2 White would be better.

25...♖f7 26.b3

No commentator mentions 26.a3!. Normally, the move 26...a4 would be a strong reply, but here White may aim to place his knight on b5.

The game could continue 27.♘c2 ♕g7 28.♕xg7+ ♔xg7 29.♘d4 ♔g8 30.♗d1 ♖f8 31.♖e1 and 31...♔f7 32.♘e6 or 31...♖f6 32.♘b5! would give White an edge.

26...♕g7

It is understandable that Fischer doesn't want to tolerate the strong queen forever.

27.♕xg7+ ♔xg7 28.a3

After 28.♗h5 ♖f6 29.♖e1 White could press.

28...♖f8

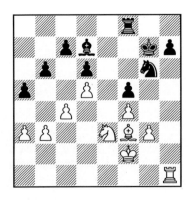

29.♗e2!

According to Fischer, Petrosian constantly finds ways to improve his position. 29.b4? would waste White's advantage because of 29...axb4 30.axb4 ♖a8.

29...♘e7 30.♗d3 h6 31.♖h5 ♗e8!

Fischer finds a clever idea to ease the pressure on f5.

32.♖h2

32.♖xf5 ♖h8! would win, as the rook on f5 would be trapped. Or 32.♘xf5+ ♘xf5 33.♖xf5 ♖h8! and White loses an exchange.

32...♗d7 33.♖h1

Petrosian wanted Black to move here.

33...♖h8

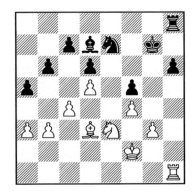

34.♘c2!

Fischer: *Headed for an even stronger post on d4. I was amazed during the game. Each time Petrosian reached a good position he managed to manoeuvre into a better one.*

34...♔f6 35.♘d4 ♔g7 36.♗e2 ♘g8

Fischer calls it panicking and attaches a question-mark to this move, but it doesn't make Black's defence more difficult. It is very much worth citing Bobby: *Petrosian likes to play cat-and-mouse hoping that his opponents will go wrong in the absence of a direct threat. The amazing thing is – that they usually do! Witness a case in point. I should have ignored the "threat" and played say 36...♖a8. If 37.♗h5 ♖c8 38.♖e1 ♔f6 now 39.♘e6 c6! would equalise, or after 39.♖e3 ♖b8 White is no doubt better, but we see no clear way how to crack Black's fortress-like position.*

37.b4! ♘f6 38.♗d3!

38.bxa5 ♘e4+ 39.♔e3 ♖a8 would give some counterplay.

38...axb4

If 38...♘e4+? 39.♗xe4 fxe4 40.bxa5 (40.♔e3 is also very nice for White) 40...♖a8 (40...bxa5 41.♔e3) 41.axb6 cxb6 42.♖b1 White would win, but Black could play 38...♔g6!? 39.bxa5 bxa5 40.♖b1 ♖e8 41.♖b7 ♘g4+ with counterplay.

39.axb4 ♔g6

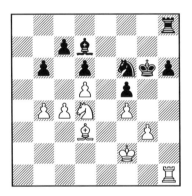

40.♖a1!

According to Fischer, White finally achieves his ideal setup, but Black's game is still tenable.

40...♘g4+ 41.♔e2 ♖e8+

I was wondering very much where the game was adjourned, and you will see the reason in the comments after White's 45th move. I was unable to find out who sealed the move and when. However, I asked members of a chess forum on Facebook. Nobody was able to answer for some time, but just when I had given up hoping Ton Bodaan messaged me that the game was adjourned here. Later he also sent

me some fantastic analysis by several commentators I was not aware of. I had to change an evaluation of a line of a key variation and Charles Sullivan's idea increased the already large size of the analysis. But these lines are amazing, as you will see.

42.♔d2 ♘f6 43.♖a6 ♖b8 44.♖a7 ♖c8

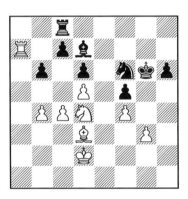

45.c5

Fischer says this pawn sacrifice caught him by surprise. Objectively, it gives away the advantage. Missing it might suggest that so far nobody sealed the move, but we know that this is not the case. It is a pity that Fischer doesn't mention what he was going to do against the move 45.♘f3!?, and if 45...♔h5 then 46.♔e3 could be played. Nobody mentions 45.♔c3!. Petrosian could have just waited and postponed the sacrifice, as Black is almost in zugzwang. 45...♘h5 (45...h5 46.♘f3) 46.c5 bxc5 47.bxc5 dxc5 48.♘f3 and White would be clearly better.

The next moves are virtually forced.

45...bxc5 46.bxc5 dxc5 47.♘f3 ♚f7 48.♘e5+ ♚e7 49.♘xd7 ♘xd7 50.♗xf5 ♖f8! 51.g4

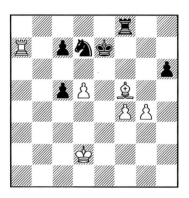

51...♚d6?!

Fischer says that this was the losing move, but analysis with the latest tools contradicts his view. Fischer does make his job extremely difficult, though, as after 51...♘f6! Black would hold fairly easily. 52.♗e6 ♘xd5! 53.♗xd5 ♖d8 and Black draws effortlessly. After 53... ♖xf4 Black would suffer in the rook and bishop versus rook ending.

52.♗xd7! ♚xd7 53.♚e3

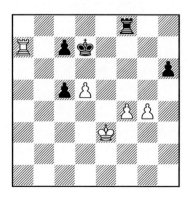

53...♖e8+!

The rook ending is about to became a promotion race, and it will be a thriller. Fischer gives a subtle check to chase the king away from the c-pawns. Some will find the next pages boring, but readers who love difficult and sophisticated endgames will find special joy.

A

53...♖g8 We decided to check whether Black can enter the promotion race with the rook on g8. 54.♚f3

a) 54...♚d6. This is not so relevant to the game, but the lines are beautiful so we show some of them.

55.♖a6+

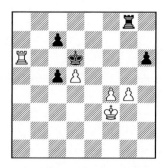

a1) 55...♚xd5 It looks like Black can draw with subtle play. 56.♖xh6 c4

a1.1) 57.f5 c3 58.♖h1 c5 (58...♚e5? 59.♖c1 c5 60.♖xc3 ♖c8 61.♖e3+ wins) 59.♚f4 ♖b8 60.♖c1 (60.♖d1+ ♚c4 61.f6 c2 62.♖c1 ♚d3 63.g5 ♚d2 64.♖xc2+ ♚xc2=) 60...♖b4+ 61.♚g3 (61.♚g5 ♖c4 62.♖c2 ♚e5 63.f6 ♚e6=) 61...♖b3 62.♚h4 ♚e5 63.♚g5 ♖b8 64.♖xc3 ♖g8+! 65.♚h5 ♚f6=

a1.2) 57.g5! c3 58.♖h1 ♖g6 59.♖d1+!! (59.♚g4 ♖c6 60.♚f5 c2

61.♖c1 ♔d6 62.♔f6 ♖d7+ 63.♔f7
♖c5 64.g6 ♖f5+ 65.♔g7 ♖xf4
66.♖xc2=) 59...♔c4 60.♔g4

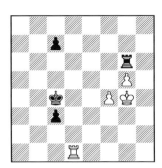

a1.2.1) 60...c2? 61.♖c1 ♔b3 62.f5+−
a1.2.2) 60...♖d6? 61.♖xd6! cxd6
62.g6 c2 63.g7 c1=♕ 64.g8=♕+
♔d4 65.♕g7+ ♔d3 66.♕g6+ ♔e3
67.♕e6+ ♔f2 68.f5!+− (68.♕xd6
♕g1+ 69.♔f5 ♕g3=)
a1.2.3) 60...c5!! 61.f5

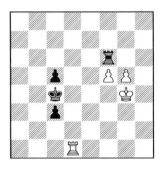

61...♖d6!! This is a brilliant move.
If White plays cleverly, Black must
find study-like ideas such as this one
to save the game.
a1.2.3.a) 62.♖xd6 c2=
a1.2.3.b) 62.♖c1 ♖d4+ 63.♔h5
(or 63.♔f3 ♖d3+ 64.♔e4 ♖d4+
65.♔e5 ♖g4=) 63...♖f4 64.♔g6
♔b3 65.f6 ♔b2 66.♖g1 c2 67.f7
c1=♕ 68.♖xc1 ♔xc1=

a1.2.3.c) 62.♖h1!

62...♖d4+!! (62...c2? 63.♖c1+−)
a1.2.3.c.1) 63.♔h5 ♖f4 64.f6 c2
65.♔g6 (65.g6 ♖f5+=) 65...♔b3
66.f7 (66.♔f7 ♔b2 67.g6 c1=♕
68.♖xc1 ♔xc1=) 66...♔b2 67.g7
c1=♕ 68.♖xc1 ♔xc1=
a1.2.3.c.2) 63.♔f3!!
a1.2.3.c.2.1) 63...♔d5? 64.g6 ♔e5
65.g7 ♖d8 66.♖h8 c2 67.♖xd8 c1=♕
68.g8=♕+−
a1.2.3.c.2.2) 63...c2? 64.♖c1
♖d3+ (64...♔c3 65.g6+−) 65.♔e4
♖d4+ 66.♔e5 ♔c3 67.f6+−
a1.2.3.c.2.3) 63...♖d3+!! This
is another subtle check. 64.♔e4!
♖d4+! (64...c2 65.♖c1+−)

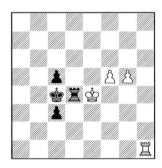

65.♔e5 ♖g4! and Black can start
pushing the c-pawn in time.

a2) 55...c6!! Black gives up the pawn, as without the second c-pawn the black rook can support the remaining c-pawn. 56.dxc6 (56.♖xc6+ ♔xd5 57.♖xh6 c4=) 56...♖c8 57.c7+ (57.f5 ♖xc6=; 57.♔e4 ♖e8+ 58.♔f5 ♖f8+=; 57.g5 hxg5 58.fxg5 c4=)

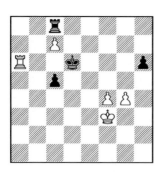

a2.1) 57...♔d5?? 58.♖xh6 ♖xc7 59.♖h5+!! This check makes Black either give way for the white king or move his own king far away from the white pawns. 59...♔d4 (59...♔e6 60.♔e4+− or 59...♔d6 60.♔e4 ♖e7+ 61.♖e5+−) 60.g5 c4 61.g6 c3 62.♖h7! ♖c8 63.♖d7+ ♔c4 64.g7 (64.♔e2+−) 64...c2 65.♖c7+ ♖xc7 66.g8=♕+ and White wins.

a2.2) 57...♔xc7! 58.♖xh6 c4 59.♔e2 (59.♖h5 ♔d7) 59...c3 60.♔d1 ♖g8 (60...♔d7=) 61.g5 ♖f8 62.♖h4 ♔d6 63.♔c2 ♔e6 64.♔xc3 ♔f5=.

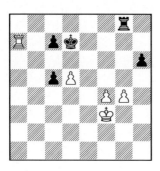

b) At the end of the analysis, we spotted that 54...♖c8!! in the above position draws fairly easily. 55.♖a1 (after 55.f5 ♔d6, 55.♖a6 c6 or 55.♔e4 ♖e8+ Black holds) 55...c6 56.d6 ♖f8 or 56...c4 easily draw.

B

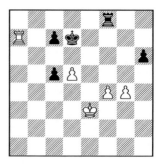

53...♔d6. Later, we realised that Black could play this at once. 54.♖a6+

a) 54...c6? 55.dxc6 (55.♖xc6+ ♔xd5 56.♖xh6 ♖e8+= is the simplest for Black here) 55...♖g8

(55...♖c8 56.c7+ ♔xc7

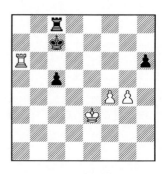

57.♖xh6+−. Interestingly, if the white king is on f3 it is a draw, but in this position White wins)

56.f5 c4 (56...♖xg4 57.f6 ♖g8 58.♔e4+−) 57.f6 c3 58.♔d3 ♔c7

59.f7 ♖f8 60.♔xc3 ♔b8 61.c7+
♔xc7 62.♔d4+−

b) 54...♔xd5! It is remarkable
that now the king move is the correct
one. 55.♖xh6 c4 (55...♖e8+!?)

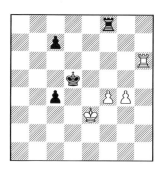

b1) 56.♖h1 c3 57.f5 ♔e5 58.♖c1
♖h8 (58...c5 59.♖xc3 ♖c8=) 59.♖xc3
♖h3+ 60.♔d2 ♖h2+ 61.♔d3 c5
62.♖xc5+ ♔f4=

b2) 56.♖h5+ ♔d6 57.♔e4
♖e8+! 58.♔d4 ♖f8 59.♖h6+ ♔d7
60.♔e5 ♖e8+ 61.♔d5 c3 (61...
c6+? 62.♖xc6!+−) 62.♖c6 (62.♖h3
c2 63.♖c3 ♖e2=) 62...♖e3 63.♖c4
♖d3+ 64.♔e4 ♖g3 65.g5 ♔d6
66.♔f5 c5 67.g6 ♔d5 68.♖e4 c2=
and the race would be even.

54.♔f3
54.♔d3 ♖g8=
54...♔d6 55.♖a6+

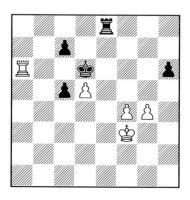

55...♔xd5

55...c6!! Neither of the giants
noticed that this move would
draw. 56.dxc6 (56.♖xc6+ ♔xd5
57.♖xh6 c4=) 56...♖c8 – see 53...
♖g8.
56.♖xh6 c4

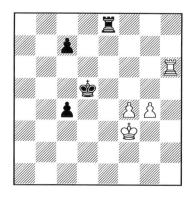

57.♖h1?!

Petrosian doesn't miss a win as he
thought, but doesn't find the most
testing continuation. From now on,
they both play very well.

57.♖h7!! Fischer mentions that
according to Petrosian this move
would win. Petrosian's analysis
was fantastic, yet not flawless.
Fischer used it in his fundamental
contribution to chess culture, *My 60
Memorable Games*.

A

57...c6. This is Petrosian's main
move, and his evaluation doesn't
look correct, though the position
is so complex that one cannot be
100% certain even with the most
modern tools. Some great ideas
were discovered by Charles Sullivan
in 2007 and he published them in

Karsten Muller's Endgame Corner.
58.♖d7+ ♔c5 (58...♔e6 59.♖d4
♖c8 60.♖xc4 c5 61.f5+ [61.♔e4
would win more slowly] 61...♔e5
[61...♔d5 62.♖c2+−] 62.♖e4+ ♔f6
63.♖e6++−) 59.♖d1 c3

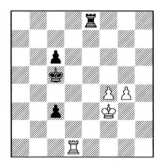

a) 60.f5 Maybe this gives Black
fewer options, but it is likely
to transpose to 60.g5. 60...♖d8
61.♖c1

a1) 61...♔d4? (for 61...♔b4!!
see 60.g5.) 62.♔f4 ♔d3 63.f6 ♔d2
64.♖a1 c2 65.g5 ♖a8 66.♖g1 (66.
♖xa8 c1=♕=) 66...♖e8 67.f7 ♖e1
68.♖g2+ (68.♖xe1 ♔xe1=) 68...
♖e2

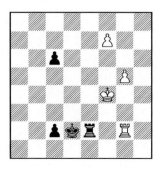

69.♔f3! ♖xg2 (69...c1=♕
70.♖xe2++−) 70.♔xg2 c1=♕
71.f8=♕+− wins as Sullivan pointed
out.

a2) 61...♔c4? 62.g5 ♔d3 63.f6
♖f8 (63...♔d2 64.♖g1 c2 65.f7 c1=♕
66.♖xc1 ♔xc1 67.g6+−) 64.♔f4

a2.1) 64...♔d2 65.♖g1 c2
66.♔f5 − when the black king
is on the d-file the white king
stands better on f5 (66.♔e5 ♖e8+
67.♔f5 ♖e1=) 66...♖e8 (66...c1=♕
67.♖xc1 ♔xc1 68.g6+−) 67.f7 ♖e1
(67...♖e3 68.g6) 68.♖xe1 ♔xe1
69.f8=♕ c1=♕ 70.♕b4+ ♔e2
71.♕e4+ and White wins easily by
swapping queens.

a2.2) 64...c5! Interestingly,
pushing this pawn gives better
practical chances.

a2.2.1) 65.♔e5 ♔d2 66.♖a1! −
with the king on d2 this is the right
side for the rook (66.♖g1 ♖e8+
67.♔d6 ♖e1 68.f7 [68.♖xe1 ♔xe1=]
68...♖xg1 69.f8=♕ ♖xg5=) 66...c4
(66...♖e8+ 67.♔d5 ♖d8+ 68.♔xc5
and White wins in 98(!) moves, or
if 68...♖g8 then 69.♖g1 wins) 67.g6
♖e8+ 68.♔f5 ♖e1 69.♖a2+ and
White wins the race to queen.

a2.2.2) 65.♔f5 ♔d2 66.♖g1 c2
67.g6 c4 68.g7 ♖g8

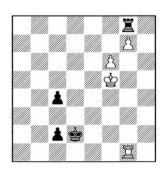

69.♔e4!! This is White's simplest
way to win. 69.♔e6? would be bad,

while 69.♔e5 would require more precision. 69...c3 70.f7 c1=♕ 71.♖xc1 (71.♖g2+ ♔d1 72.fxg8=♕+−) 71...♖xg7 72.f8=♕+−.

b) 60.g5 This is the way Petrosian starts the race in his analysis.

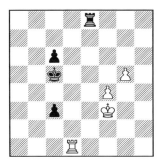

b1) 60...♖d8 Let me show you Huebner's analysis. 61.♖c1 (61.♖g1? ♔d4 62.g6 c2 63.♖c1 ♖d6 64.f5 ♔e5 65.♔g4 ♖d1 66.♖xc2 ♖g1+ 67.♔h5 ♔xf5=) 61...♔d4 62.♔g4 ♔d3 63.g6 ♔d2 64.♖h1 ♖e8 65.f5 ♖e1 66.♖xe1 ♔xe1 67.g7 c2 68.g8=♕ c1=♕ 69.♕b3+−

b2) 60...♔c4 61.g6 c2 62.♖c1 ♔c3 63.f5 ♖g8 64.♔f4 ♔d2 65.♖xc2+ ♔xc2 66.♔g5 c5 67.f6 c4 68.f7 ♖f8 69.g7 ♖xf7 70.g8=♕. The former no. 1 German grandmaster shows the instructive win 70...♖c7 71.♔f4 c3 72.♕a2+ ♔d3 (72...♔c1 73.♔e3 ♖h7 74.♕a3+ ♔c2 75.♕a4+ ♔c1 76.♕f4 ♖h3+ 77.♔e2+ ♔b2 78.♕b4+ ♔c2 79.♕e4+ ♔b2 80.♔d1 and White wins) 73.♕d5+ ♔c2 74.♔e3 ♖a7 75.♕d3+ ♔b2 76.♕b5+ ♔c2 77.♔d4 ♖c7 78.♕a5 and the rest is simple.

b3) 60...♔b4!! Sullivan found this fantastic idea, the point in many cases

being that Black amazingly does far better pushing the back pawn. He thought that the move draws, but it seems he missed a finesse. 61.f5 c5! Keeping the c4-square vacated for the pawn is the point of Sullivan's brilliant idea.

b3.1) 62.g6? It is remarkable that this push wastes the win. 62...♖g8 63.♔f4

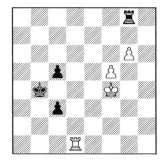

63...c4!! (63...c2 64.♖c1 ♔b3 65.♔g5 ♔b2 66.♖xc2+ ♔xc2 67.f6+−) 64.♔g5 (64.♔e5 c2 65.♖c1 ♔b3 66.f6 ♖xg6 67.f7 ♔b2 and the rook and c3-pawn will ensure a draw against the queen)

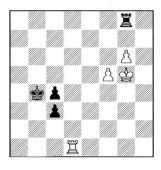

64...♖d8!! 65.♖c1 ♔b3 66.f6 ♔b2 (not 66...c2? 67.f7 and White has a winning position) 67.♖h1 c2

68.f7 c1=♕+= and White draws as Sullivan pointed out.

b3.2) 62.f6! This is the more testing way to advance the pawns. 62...♖f8

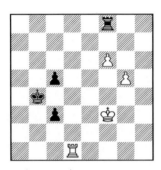

b3.2.1) 63.♖f1 and Sullivan analyses two moves here. 63...c2 (63...c4 is too slow now: 64.♔f4 ♔b3 65.♔e5 ♔b2 66.g6 c2 67.g7+−) 64.♔e4 ♔c3

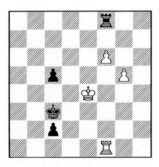

b3.2.1.1) 65.♔f5? c4! 66.g6 (66. ♔e6 ♔d2 67.♔e7 ♖a8 68.g6 c1=♕ 69.♖xc1 ♔xc1=) 66...♖d8! 67.f7 (67.g7 ♖d1) 67...♖d1 68.♖f3+ ♖d3= Sullivan

b3.2.1.2) 65.♔e5! Sullivan does not consider this move; it is very dangerous, but not winning. 65...♖e8+ (65...c4? 66.g6 ♖d8 67.f7 ♖d1 68.f8=♕ c1=♕ 69.♕f3++−) 66.♔f5

c4 (66...♖d8 67.f7 ♖d1 68.♖f3+ ♔c4 69.♖f4+ ♔b5 70.f8=♕ c1=♕±) 67.f7

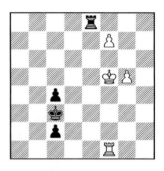

b3.2.1.2.1) 67...♖d8? 68.♔e5 ♔b2 (68...♖d1 69.f8=♕+−) 69.g6 ♖f8 (69...♖d1 70.f8=♕ c1=♕ 71.♕b4++−) 70.g7! (70.♖g1 c3! [70...c1=♕ 71.♖xc1 ♔xc1 72.♔d4!+−] 71.g7 ♖xf7 72.g8=♕ c1=♕=) 70...♖xf7 71.♖xf7 c1=♕ 72.g8=♕+−

b3.2.1.2.2) 67...♖f8! 68.g6 ♔b2 69.♔e4 (69.♔f6 c1=♕ 70.♖xc1 ♔xc1=)

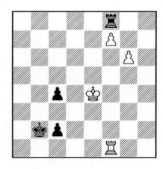

69...c3!! 70.g7 (70.♔d4 ♖d8+ 71.♔c4 ♖c8+ 72.♔d5 c1=♕=) 70... c1=♕ 71.♖xc1 (71.gxf8=♕ ♕xf1; 71.♖f2+ c2 72.gxf8=♕=) 71... ♖xf7=

b3.2.2) 63.♔f4 Helping the pawns with the king is more natural.

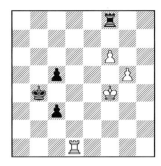

63...c4! Here again, Sullivan's great idea is the best (63...c2 64.♖c1 ♔b3 65.♔e5+−)

b3.2.2.1) 64.♔f5?! Sullivan only looks at this move. 64...c2 (64...♖d8 65.♖xd8+−) 65.♖c1 (65.♖g1 ♔b3 66.g6 ♔b2 67.g7 ♖g8 68.f7 ♖xg7=) 65...♔c3 66.g6 ♔d2 67.g7 (67.♖xc2+ ♔xc2=) 67...♖xf6+ 68.♔xf6 ♔xc1=

b3.2.2.2) 64.♔e5! This is what Sullivan does not consider in the analysis. At first I thought it would win, but it does not. The king stands well on e5 but it can be chased away. 64...♖e8+!

(64...c2 65.♖c1 ♔c3 66.g6 ♔d2 [66...♖e8+? 67.♔d6 ♔d2 68.♖xc2+ ♔xc2 69.f7+−]

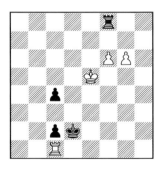

67.♖xc2+ If the white king were on f5 this position would be a draw

as the rook and the pawn could hold, but here it is a win. 67...♔xc2 68.g7 ♖e8+ 69.♔d4 c3 70.f7 ♖d8+ 71.♔e3+−)

65.♔f5 c2

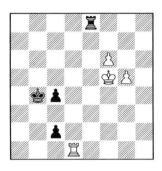

b3.2.2.2.1) After 66.♖c1 Black would not lose the race. 66...♔b3 67.f7 ♖f8!

(67...♖e2? 68.g6 ♔b2 69.♖xc2+ ♖xc2 [69...♔xc2 70.g7+−]

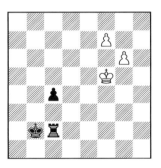

70.♔e4!!+−)

68.g6 ♔b2 69.♖xc2+ ♔xc2 70.♔e4 c3 and the rook and pawn hold against the queen.

b3.2.2.2.2) 66.♖f1 ♖d8 67.f7 ♔b3 68.g6 ♖d1 69.♖f3+ The rook on the f-file makes this check sensible, but not winning. 69...♖d3 70.♖xd3+ cxd3= (note if your computer states that White is winning then you need to use tablebases to see that it's a draw – in several cases in this game and of course elsewhere there will be contrasting endgame evaluations where the tablebases should be trusted).

b3.2.2.2.3) 66.♖g1 ♖d8 67.f7 (67.♖c1 ♔b3) 67...♔b3 (67...♖d1 68.f8=♕++−) 68.g6 ♖d1 69.f8=♕ c1=♕ 70.♕b8+ (70.♖xd1 ♕xd1=) 70...♔c2 71.♖g2+ (71.♕h2+ ♔b1 is a draw) 71...♖d2 72.♖xd2+ ♕xd2=

b3.2.2.2.4) 66.♖h1!? Moving to each file is different; the advantage of the h-file is that in a certain position the queen from b8 can defend the h2–rook. 66...♖d8 67.f7 ♔b3 68.g6 ♖d1 69.f8=♕ c1=♕ 70.♕b8+ ♔c2 71.♖h2+ ♖d2 (71... ♔c3?? 72.♕g3+ wins for White) 72.g7 ♕f1+ and wherever White exchanges queens the rook and pawn obtain the draw.

B

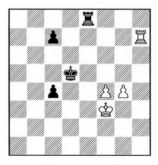

57...c5! This move also requires exceptional skill to hold. 58.♖d7+ ♔e6 59.♖d1 ♖b8! The latter is a difficult move to find, and is needed

in case the rook has to defend the front c-pawn from the side. 59... ♖a8! would possibly be good as well.

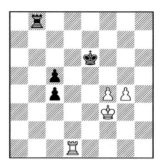

a) 60.g5? (60.♖e1+ ♔d5) 60...c3
a1) 61.♖c1 ♔f5 62.♖xc3 c4!=
a2) 61.♖e1+ ♔f7 62.♖c1 c4 63.f5 (63.♔e4 ♔g6 64.♖xc3 ♖c8=) 63... ♖b3 64.♔f4 c2 65.♖xc2 c3=
a3) 61.♔g4 ♖b4 (61...c2 62.♖c1 ♖b2=) 62.♖e1+ ♔f7 63.♔f5 c2 64.♖c1 ♖c4=

b) 60.f5+! A key position. Black has only one move, and it is very hard to find.

b1) 60...♔e7? 61.g5! (61.♖e1+ ♔f7 62.g5 c3 63.♖c1 c4 64.♔e4 ♖b3=) 61...c3 62.♔g4! c2 63.♖c1 ♖b2 64.f6+ ♔f7 65.♔f5 ♖b1 66.g6+

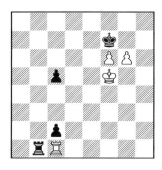

b1.1) 66...♔g8 67.♖xc2 ♖f1+ 68.♔e5 ♖e1+ 69.♔d5 ♖d1+ 70.♔xc5 ♖f1 71.f7+ ♔g7 72.♖g2 and White wins with ♔e5 and ♖g4.

b1.2) 66...♔f8 67.g7+! (67.♖xc2? ♖f1+) 67...♔f7 68.♖xc2 ♖f1+ 69.♔e5 ♖e1+ 70.♔d5 ♖e8 71.♖g2 ♖g8 72.♖f2 ♖c8 73.♖h2 and White wins.

b2) 60...♔f7? This was not analysed before. White has to play very accurately to win, but can. 61.♖d7+ (61.g5 c3) 61...♔g8

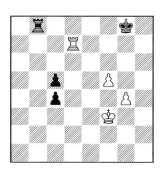

b2.1) 62.g5? c3 63.♖c7 ♖b5 64.♖c8+ (64.♔e3 c2 65.♔d2 c4=; 64.f6 c2 65.g6 ♖b8 66.♖xc5 ♖f8=) 64...♔f7 65.g6+ ♔f6 66.♖f8+ ♔g7 67.♖f7+ ♔g8=.

b2.2) 62.♖d5 ♖b5 (62...♖c8 63.♔e4 ♖e8+ 64.♔f4 ♖c8

65.♖d2 c3 66.♖c2 c4 67.♖xc3+−) 63.g5

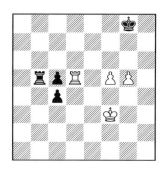

b2.2.1) 63...♔f7 64.g6+ ♔f6 65.♔e4 c3 (65...♖a5 66.♖d6+ ♔e7 67.♔e5+−) 66.♖d6+ ♔e7 67.♖e6++−.

b2.2.2) 63...c3 64.♔e3 c2 65.♔d2 ♖b3 66.♔xc2 c4 67.♖c5 ♖f3

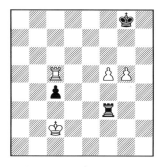

68.♔d2+−. Tablebases prove that White can win. 68...♔g7 69.♔e2 ♖g3 70.♖c7+ ♔g8 71.g6 c3 72.♖c5 ♔g7 73.♔f2 ♖d3 74.♖c7+ ♔f6 75.♖f7+ ♔e5 76.g7 ♖d2+ 77.♔f3 ♖d3+ 78.♔g4 ♖d1 79.♖e7+ ♔d6 80.♖e6+ ♔d7 81.♖g6 ♖g1+ 82.♔h4 ♖h1+ 83.♔g5 c2 84.g8=♕ c1=♕+ 85.♔f6 ♕c3+ 86.♔f7 ♕c4+ 87.♖e6 ♕d5 88.♕e8+ ♔c7 89.f6 ♕h5+ 90.♔f8 ♕h6+ 91.♔e7 ♕h7+ 92.♕f7+−

b3) 60...♔e5? 61.♖e1+! ♔d4 (61...
♔f6 62.♔f4 c3 63.g5+ ♔g7 64.g6
c2 65.♔g5 ♖b1 66.f6++−) 62.g5 c3
63.f6! c2 64.♖c1! (64.f7? ♖b1!=) 64...
♔e5 65.♖xc2 (65.♔g4+−) 65...♔f5
66.♖xc5+ ♔g6 67.♖e5+−

b4) 60...♔f6!! This superb move
in an almost study-like fashion holds
the game.

b4.1) 61.♖d6+

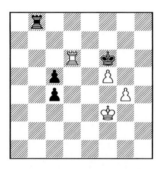

b4.1.1) 61...♔e7? 62.♖e6+ ♔f7
(62...♔d7 63.♖e5 [63.♖e2 c3] 63...
♔d6 64.♖e1+−) 63.♖c6 c3 64.g5
(64.♖xc5 ♔f6=) 64...♖b5 65.g6+
♔g7 66.♖c7+ ♔f6 67.♖f7+ ♔e5
68.g7 ♖b8 69.♖f8 c2 70.♖xb8 c1=♕
71.g8=♕+−

b4.1.2) 61...♔e5 62.♖e6+

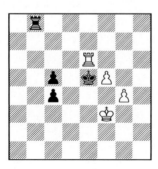

62...♔d4! Black hurries in the
race. (Even the slower 62...♔d5

draws, in the end a rook and the
c2-pawn hold against the queen.)
63.♖e2 c3 64.f6 ♖f8 65.g5 ♔d3
66.♖e5 ♔d4 67.♔f4 c2 68.♖e1 ♔d3
69.♔f5 ♔d2 70.♖f1 c1=♕ 71.♖xc1
♔xc1 72.g6 c4 73.g7 ♖xf6+ 74.♔xf6
c3 75.g8=♕ c2=

b4.2) 61.♔f4 c3 62.g5+ ♔g7!
(62...♔f7? 63.g6+ ♔f6 64.♖d6+ ♔e7
65.♖c6+−) 63.♖d7+! (International
Master Lawrence Day analyses only
63.♖c1, when Black can make a
much smaller effort against it than
against this strong check. Here is his
line: 63...♖b3 64.♔e5 ♔f7 65.♔d5
♖b2 [Day doesn't mention it, but
waiting on the third rank would
work as well.] 66.♖xc3 ♖g2 67.g6+
♔f6 68.♔e4 c4 69.♖xc4 ♖g4+!
70.♔d5 ♖g5! 71.♖f4 ♖g2 and Black
holds.)

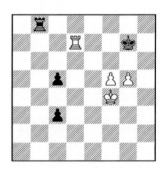

Just like on the previous move,
the black king has an only move.

b4.2.1)   63...♔g8?   64.♖d3
♖b4+ (64...♖b3 65.♖d8+! ♔f7
66.g6+! ♔e7 67.♖d5! ♖b5
68.♔e5+−) 65.♔e5 c2 66.♖c3
♖b2 67.f6! ♔f7 68.♔f5 c1=♕
(68...c4 69.g6++−) 69.♖xc1 (69.
g6+ probably wins as well) 69...

♖f2+ 70.♔e4 ♔g6 71.♖xc5 ♖e2+ 72.♔d4 ♖d2+ 73.♔c4 ♖e2 74.♔b5+−.

b4.2.2) 63...♔f8!

b4.2.2.1) 64.♖d3 ♖b3 (or 64...♖b4+ 65.♔e5 ♖b3 66.♖d1 c2=) 65.♖d8+ ♔e7 66.♖c8 ♔d6 67.♔e3 c2+ 68.♔d2 ♖g3 69.g6 ♖g2+ 70.♔c1 ♔e5 71.♖f8 c4 72.♔b2 (72.♖f7 ♔d4 73.♔b2 c1=♕+ 74.♔xc1 c3=) 72...c1=♕+ 73.♔xc1 c3 74.♖f7 ♔d4 75.g7 ♖g1+ 76.♔c2 ♖g2+ 77.♔b3 ♖b2+ 78.♔a3 ♖b8= (not then 79.♖f8? c2−+)

b4.2.2.2) 64.♖c7 ♖b5

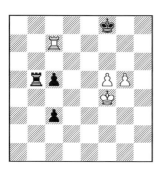

65.♖c8+ This check is very hard to meet, and Black has only one good square.

b4.2.2.2.1) 65...♔f7? 66.g6+ ♔e7 67.♔e3! (67.g7 c2) 67...c2 68.♔d2 ♖b1 69.♔xc2+−.

b4.2.2.2.2) 65...♔e7? 66.♔e3 c2 (66...c4 67.f6+ ♔e6 68.♖e8+ ♔f7 69.♖e7+ ♔g6 70.♖g7+ ♔h5 71.f7 ♖f5 72.♔e2 ♖f1 73.♔xf1 c2 74.f8=♕+−) 67.♔d2 (67.f6+ probably wins as well) 67...c4 68.f6+ ♔f7 (68...♔e6 69.♖e8+ ♔f7 70.♖e7+ ♔g6 71.♖g7+ ♔h5 72.f7+−) 69.♖c7+ ♔e6 70.♖e7+

♔d6 71.g6 ♖f5 72.g7 ♖xf6 73.♖e8+−

b4.2.2.2.3) 65...♔g7! The right square for the king. 66.f6+ (66.♔e3 c2 [66...c4 probably draws as well] 67.♔d2 c4=) 66...♔g6 67.♔e3 (67.♖g8+ ♔f7 68.♖g7+ ♔f8 69.g6 c2 70.♖f7+ ♔g8=) 67...c4 (67...c2? 68.♔d2 ♔xg5 69.f7+−) 68.♖g8+ ♔f7! 69.♖g7+ ♔f8 70.g6 ♖b6 71.♖f7+ ♔g8 72.♔e2 ♖d6=.

So Petrosian's 57.♖h7 was an amazing idea, but it looks like Black can hold with magical defences in several lines after both 57...c6 and 57...c5. Modern tools can contribute a lot to gaining amazing depth in such positions that are rich in ideas. However, they can't yet dissect them completely, so there is a little chance (we would estimate it as below 5 percent) that more advanced tablebases of the future will find a winning line for White.

Back to the game:

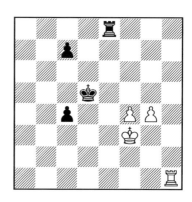

57...c3 58.g5 c5

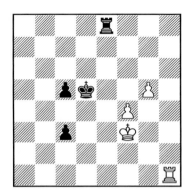

59.♖d1+

Alternatives:

a) 59.♔g4 ♖e2! (59...c2) 60.g6 ♔e6=

b) 59.g6 ♖g8 60.f5 ♔e5 61.♔g4 ♔f6 62.♖c1 ♖d8 (62...c4 63.♖xc3 ♖c8!=) 63.♖xc3 ♖d4+ 64.♔h5 c4 (64...♔xf5 65.g7+−) 65.♖g3 ♖d3=.

c) 59.f5 c2 60.♖c1 ♖e5 61.♔g4 ♖e2 62.♔h5 ♔e4 63.♔g6 ♔d3 64.f6 ♔d2 65.f7 ♖f2 66.♖h1 c1=♕=.

59...♔c4 60.g6 c2 61.♖c1

Or 61.♖g1 ♖d8 (61...♔d3 62.f5 ♖g8 63.♔f4 ♔d2 64.♔g5 c1=♕ 65.♖xc1 ♔xc1=) 62.♖c1 (62. g7? ♖g8!−+) 62...♔d3 63.f5 ♔d2 64.♖xc2+ ♔xc2=.

61...♔d3 62.f5

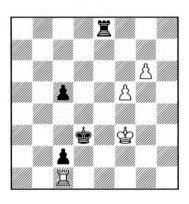

62...♖g8!

Stopping the pawn temporarily. This wins a tempo, and this time the tempo means survival. 62...♔d2? 63.♖xc2+ ♔xc2 64.g7 c4 65.f6 ♖g8 (65...c3 66.f7) 66.f7 ♖xg7 67.f8=♕+−

63.♔f4 ♔d2 64.♖xc2+ ♔xc2 65.♔g5 c4 66.f6 c3

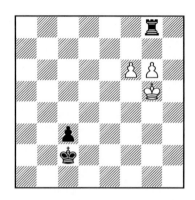

67.f7 1/2 The thriller ends.

Fischer writes: *I offered a draw, not realising it was bad etiquette. It was Petrosian's place to extend the offer.* Petrosian accepted it, as 67...♖xg6+ (or 67...♖c8 68.g7 ♔b1) 68.♔xg6 ♔b1 69.f8=♕ c2 would lead to a draw.

A fantastic game, one to rival the Ortueta-Sanz game that we mention at the beginning of this book. Petrosian would be the player to play the highest number of regular games against Fischer under the Soviet flag, 27 in total from 1958 to 1971. Spassky played more, but by the time of their second match in 1992 he was no longer a Soviet.

In the 14th round, Petrosian was Black against Bronstein. He chose the 4...♗a6 line against the Queen's Indian. He made some slightly awkward looking moves and at the end of the opening was in serious trouble. Approaching time control, Tigran considerably decreased his disadvantage, but on move 38 made a losing move. Yet Bronstein, probably with little time left, failed to spot the win. Petrosian was lucky to escape with a draw. In the 15th round, Petrosian was White against Averbakh in a main-line Nimzo-Indian. Neither player had a chance to gain the upper hand in a 22-move draw. Round 16 against Larsen was a reverse Dutch Stonewall, and Petrosian as Black got a slight advantage. Maybe he underestimated his opponent a bit and just waited too much for a mistake. The mistake actually came, but Petrosian committed it. Larsen forcefully took control, then a few moves before time control things turned really bad for the Armenian as Larsen doubled his rooks on the open seventh rank. Petrosian had to resign on move 41. This was a heavy blow to his chances of winning the event, but it didn't threaten his qualification. In the next round, Petrosian was White against Sanquinetti, and he got a neat advantage in the King's Indian. However, the Argentinian was able to hold the closed position as Petrosian was unable to crack his fortress. In the 18th round, Petrosian probably wanted to try to beat Panno as Black, but his King's Indian resulted in a worse position this time. They agreed to a draw after Tigran's 16th move. In the 19th round, Petrosian was White against Olafsson. He gained a clear edge in the King's Indian, and later was two pawns up, but he was unable to convert his advantage. After time control, Black had reasonable drawing chances, though Tigran kept trying until move 77. In the penultimate round, he was Black against Tal, who played an f4 King's Indian. After 22 moves they reached a dead draw, though it is hard to tell whether it was prearranged. Perhaps they wanted to make sure a Soviet player would win the event, and Gligoric was only half a point behind Tal with two games to go while Benko also had a theoretical chance of winning the event. Petrosian had a bye in the last round.

He had proved his extremely high level; this time he really tried to win the event and had chances to do so, but was unable to grab them. Tal won the tournament, scoring 13.5 points from 20 games. Gligoric scored 13 and Petrosian and Benko finished joint-third with 12.5 points. He won 6 games, drew 13 and lost one. Olafsson and Fischer also qualified with 12, but Bronstein, who was undefeated all the way but lost in the last round against a player from the bottom, Cardoso, missed qualifying by half a point.

Chess Olympiad, Munich

Finally, Petrosian was selected for the Soviet team for the Olympiad, which was to take place in Munich. The team was incredibly strong, so bringing Petrosian as the last, second reserve was understandable. The event started at the end of September and finished on 23rd October.

It was clever not putting him in the team in the first round. His disappointing starts at new events had happened much earlier, but they were always a risk. One of Tigran's best performances at the Olympiad started here, against Austria, in the preliminary group. Petrosian was White against Lokvenc. Tigran was in a different class, and Lokvenc lost on time in a hopeless position without even completing his 29th move. In his second game, he was Black against Padevsky in the 3.♘c3 ♗b4 4.♗d3 French. The Bulgarian player looked for safety and Petrosian was unable to create enough play. The game ended in a draw after Padevsky's 33rd move. In the next game, he was White against Contendini of Italy. Black played the Benoni poorly and lost a one-sided game. Against France, he was Black against Catozzi. The Frenchman avoided an opening discussion and two moves after the opening was completed Petrosian gained a clear edge. Catozzi managed to postpone resignation till time control with a hopeless exchange sacrifice. After sitting out against Ireland, Tigran was Black against Ravn of Denmark. The Dane handled the King's Indian aggressively and obtained a clear edge. They played on, and the game ended in a draw after Ravn's 32nd move, though Petrosian was still worse. In the last round of the preliminary group, Tigran was White against Llavandero of Puerto Rico. Petrosian won a pawn early, but played so cautiously that he only won after his 50th move.

In the first round of the final, he was rested against the USA. In the second round, he was Black against Lehmann of West Germany. Petrosian gained an edge in a Sozin Sicilian. After exchanging queens, Petrosian pressed for a long time, but Lehman was up to the task and held. After another rest against Bulgaria, he was Black against Fuderer. The Yugoslav player chose the main line of the Caro-Kann. The cautious play of both opponents resulted in a dead position, and they agreed to a draw after Petrosian's 17th move. In the next round, he was White against Kozma of Czechoslovakia, who made a serious mistake in the opening. We join this game.

Game 87

Petrosian, Tigran – Kozma, Julius
Chess Olympiad, Munich (5), 1958

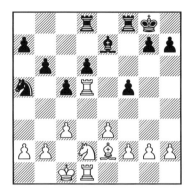

18.f4!

White gains space and stops Black from active play on the kingside.

18...g6 19.g3! ♖f6 20.e4

White gets closer to d6.

20...fxe4 21.♘xe4 ♖e6 22.♗f3 ♔g7 23.b3 ♘c6 24.♖5d3

With this and the next move, Petrosian nicely improves his bishop.

24...♘b8 25.♘f2 h5

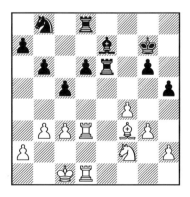

26.♔d2!

Petrosian makes an interesting decision, as there are too many pieces on the board to centralise his king. It is hard to read his idea.

26...♗f8 27.♗d5 ♖e7 28.♘e4

One may think that Petrosian wants to play against the d-pawn, but not only that.

28...♘a6

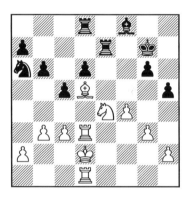

29.♔e3! ♘c7 30.♔f3!

The king has found a superb square. Now, White can play against the d6 pawn and think of pushing on the kingside. Petrosian won the game convincingly.

In the next game, he was Black against Llado of Spain. White played cautiously in the 3.♗b5+ Sicilian. Petrosian tried hard, but he was unable to cause the Spaniard any harm. There was nothing left to play for after Petrosian's 59th move. After a rest against Argentina, he was Black against Clarke of England. Petrosian took control in the Advance French fairly early. On move 30 he made a winning exchange sacrifice, and it can be seen in the analysis of the 1969 Zaitsev game in Volume II. The game lasted 41 moves. In the 9th round of the final he was White against East Germany. Pietzsch got saddled with a small disadvantage in a main-line Nimzo-Indian and he lost a pawn, but it was hard for Petrosian to do anything with his extra pawn. After time control, the East German did not simplify well. Petrosian's advantage quickly grew and he won the game. In the penultimate round, he sat out against Austria. In the last round, he was White against Nievergelt of Holland. Petrosian had a promising position in the Benoni, but after a direct confrontation his advantage evaporated. But then, the Dutchman made a very bad move, soon lost an exchange, and resigned.

The Soviet team naturally won the gold medal. Tigran scored 10.5 points out of 13 games; he won 8 and drew 5. It is hard to judge his play overall: he won several games effortlessly as he was far stronger than his opponents, but in others he was unable to create enough play to bring down his opponent. He scored the most points in the final among second reserves.

Petrosian's results in 1958

Soviet Championship Final, Moscow	+ 6 = 12 − 0 12/18 2nd place
Moscow Team events	+ 2 = 0 − 0 2/2
Gagra Training	+ 0 = 0 − 1
Soviet Republics' Team Event, Vilnius	+ 4 = 2 − 1 5/7
Portoroz Interzonal	+ 6 = 13 − 1 12.5/20 3rd-4th place
Chess Olympiad, Munich, 6th board	+ 8 = 5 − 0
Altogether	**+ 26 = 32 − 3 42/61**

1959

Soviet Championship, Tbilisi

Petrosian was probably very happy when he got the news that the Soviet championship would be held in Tbilisi, where he was raised. Quite possibly, he saw the chance to win. Tal had won the previous championship in his home town only half a point ahead of him. The event started in the middle of January and ended in February.

Botvinnik, Smyslov and Boleslavsky did not play, but all the other great players lined up. Petrosian started the event as White against Kholmov. The strong Russian master played the Bogo-Indian. Petrosian gained a small edge, he pressed for a long time, but never got close scoring a victory. In the second round, he played the Slav against Taimanov. Mark got a small edge, but a bit surprisingly he agreed to a repetition. In round 3, Tigran was White against Yukhtman. They played the King's Indian variation named after Petrosian. Black equalised, but he made a big mistake in the early middlegame, and got a lost position. After Petrosian's 31st move Yukhtman overstepped the time limit. In the fourth round, Petrosian was Black against Polugaevsky. He equalised in the Saemisch King's Indian, and they castled on opposite sides. Petrosian allowed the closing of the kingside. Polugaevsky beautifully took control on the queenside and won a pawn before time control. Tigran dug in very hard and survived the 76-move game. In the 5th round, he played as White an unexciting 20-move draw with Geller. In the 6th round, his draw came even more quickly, against Keres. The game lasted just 16 moves.

Game 88

Petrosian, Tigran – Lutikov, Anatoly
Soviet Championship, Tbilisi (7), 1959
King's Indian Defence

1.♘f3 ♘f6 2.c4 g6 3.♘c3 ♗g7 4.e4 0-0 5.d4 d6 6.♗e2 e5 7.d5 ♘a6 8.♗g5 h6 9.♗h4 c5

Lutikov plays a novelty. Petrosian played many games with this pawn structure as Black. Maybe it was not a sensible choice against him.

10.♘d2 ♗d7?!

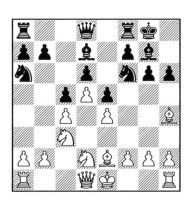

11.♘b5!

Petrosian thinks that Black's last move was inaccurate; he forces Black to defend the d6–pawn.

11...♗e8

Taking on b5 would be a big positional mistake, while 11...♕e7 would be roughly equivalent to the game continuation.

12.a3 ♕d7

If 12...♘c7 White would keep the knight with 13.♘c3! and play for b4.

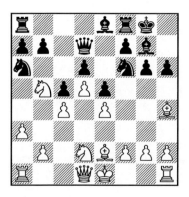

13.g4!?

Petrosian gains space and makes Black aware that carrying out f5 may cost the e4–square.

13...♘c7

If 13...♘h7 Petrosian planned 14.♗g3 and, possibly, after 14...♗f6 he would restrict the bishop with 15.h4.

14.♘c3!

With a space advantage you are not supposed to exchange pieces, as you want to keep the opponent's position cramped.

14...a6 15.a4

15.b4!? looks nice.

15...♕c8?!

King's Indian players do not like to play passively, but maybe here it was best to seal the queenside with 15...a5 and hope to hold on the other wing.

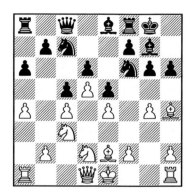

16.h3!

Tigran defends the g4-pawn and prepares ♕c2 and ♘d1–e3. Petrosian's suggestion was 16.g5!? to open the kingside a bit.

16...♖b8 17.♕c2 ♗d7

17...b5 18.axb5 (18.a5 ♗d7 is fine for Black) 18...axb5 19.♘xb5 ♘xb5 20.cxb5 ♗xb5 21.♗xb5 ♖xb5 22.♘c4 and White would be somewhat better.

18.b3 b6 19.♘d1

Tigran starts transferring the knight.

19...b5!

Lutikov responds correctly.

20.a5 ♔h8

If 20...bxc4 he planned 21.bxc4 and manoeuvring the knight to d3. Black's position would be passive, yet solid.

21.♗g3 ♘g8

If 21...g5? Petrosian suggests 22.♘e3 with ♘f5; White could also play the strong 22.h4.

22.♘e3 ♘e7

a) 22...bxc4?! 23.bxc4 ♖b4 24.0-0! (Petrosian suggests 24.♕c3 intending ♘c2, but that allows Black to free his position with 24...f5) 24...♘e7 25.♖fb1 and White's advantage is considerable.

b) 22...♘e8! Black should move this knight first, as it would take the sting out of White's play on the queenside. If 23.0-0 (23.b4 f5) Black can play 23...♘e7 or 23...f5, and although White would be better, the advantage would be small.

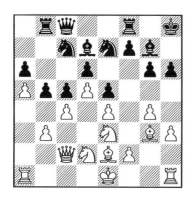

23.♗h4!

Petrosian makes a strong move; interestingly, he says nothing about it. According to Petrosian, 23.b4 at once is tempting, but not so good. He is right, but not in the way he thinks.

a) 23...f5? Tigran attaches an exclamation mark to this move. 24.bxc5 f4! 25.cxd6 fxe3 26.dxe7 (26. fxe3 ♘cxd5 is unclear) 26...exd2+ 27.♕xd2 ♖f7 Petrosian stops here

in his analysis, saying that "White's once formidable position is not as good as all that," but he probably just wrote what he was thinking during the game without checking, as here after 28.♖c1! or 28.c5! Black's position would be pretty bad: the passed pawns are stronger than Black's extra piece.

b) Black has a reasonable continuation: 23...cxb4! 24.c5 dxc5 25.♕xc5 (25.d6 c4) 25...♘exd5! It is a nice double piece sacrifice. 26.exd5 ♘xd5 27.♕xc8 ♖bxc8! 28.♘xd5 ♗c6 and Black's position would be playable.

23...♕e8?

23...♘g8

a) 24.b4 ♘e8 25.0-0 (25.♖c1!?) 25...cxb4 26.cxb5 would be somewhat better for White.

b) 24.0-0 f5? would be premature and would give up the e4–square. If 24...♗f6?! Petrosian planned 25.♗xf6+ ♘xf6 26.f4! with a nice advantage. Black should play 24...b4!, which would resist.

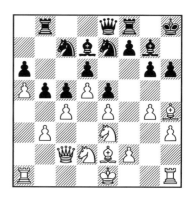

24.b4!

A beautiful breakthrough. Petrosian was to play another b4:

Petrosian, T – Hort, V
Hoogovens Wijk aan Zee (8), 1971

21.b4! What is special about it? The ease and the speed with which Petrosian obtained a winning position against a world class player.

24...♘c8?

Lutikov probably hoped to place his knight on d6, but it is destined to stay on c8 for the rest of the game and will not do much. Black should have taken the pawn. 24...cxb4 25.c5! ♖c8

a) 26.c6 ♘xc6 27.dxc6 ♗xc6 28.♕b3 According to Petrosian, Black doesn't have enough for the piece, but after 28...♕d7 29.0-0 d5 the position would be so complex it would not be easy to play either side.

b) 26.♗xe7 ♕xe7 27.c6 – here Petrosian mentions that 27...♗e8 is bad for Black, but after the strong 27...♘e6! the most White can hope for is a small advantage with 28.♕b1 or 28.♕b2.

25.bxc5?!

Tigran is keen to create a weakness in Black's camp, not noticing that after 25.♖c1! Black would have no useful move.

25...dxc5 26.cxb5 ♘xb5

Black has lost a pawn and stands poorly, but at least some of his pieces are at work.

27.♗xb5

According to Petrosian, 27.♕xc5? ♘d4 would give counterplay.

27...♖xb5

According to Petrosian, 27...♗xb5 gives better practical chances. After 28.♕xc5 ♕d7 29.♘ec4 White would be a pawn up.

28.0-0 f5

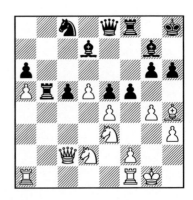

29.f3

Petrosian stops Black's play.

29...♖f7

a) According to Petrosian, it was essential to play 29...h5. However, taking on g4 would open up the position for White, and 30.♘dc4 or 30.♘ec4 could be played. So pushing the h-pawn would not solve Black's problems.

b) Improving the knight with 29...

♘d6! looks best, and after 30.♘dc4 ♘xc4 31.♘xc4 ♖b4 White's advantage would be small.

30.♘dc4 ♖b4

According to Petrosian, Black is already lost after this move.

31.♗e1! ♖b7 32.♗c3?!

Maybe Petrosian was playing against Lutikov's plan, but instead 32.gxf5 gxf5 33.♔h2 or 32.exf5 gxf5 33.♗c3 would give him a bigger advantage.

32...h5?

A horrible move. Black gives away a pawn for nothing at all. After 32...fxe4 33.fxe4 ♗b5 White's advantage would be small, and he would have to win the game all over again.

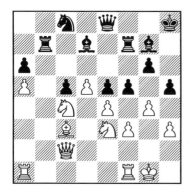

33.gxf5!

Petrosian takes the pawn, and his position becomes winning instantly

33...gxf5 34.exf5 e4

A desperate try; it is probably driven by the clock as well. 34...♕e7 35.♖ae1 would also be hopeless.

35.♔h2

The pawn could be taken as well. The rest is a slaughter.

35...exf3 36.♖xf3 ♗d4 37.♕d3 ♗f6 38.♖g1 ♔h7 39.♗xf6 ♖xf6 40.♕c3 ♕f8 41.♖g6 ♖f7 42.♖g5 1-0

The game was adjourned here, and Lutikov resigned without resuming.

In the 8th round, Petrosian was Black against Tal. It was a Chigorin main-line Ruy Lopez. He equalised fairly easily, the position was even and the game ended in a draw after Tal's 34th move. In the 9th round, Petrosian intentionally played as White a relatively unknown line to avoid Krogius's excellent theoretical knowledge. The Grunfeld led to a minority attack pawn structure and Petrosian beat him effortlessly. In round 10, he was White against Nezhmetdinov. He got into an unpleasant position in the Meran Semi-Slav, and it turned even worse, but Petrosian was able to equalise from this bad position. Tigran was already winning before time control and he soon wrapped up the win. In the 11th game, Petrosian was Black against Averbakh in a ♗e2 Najdorf Sicilian. Petrosian equalised and Averbakh failed to get a feel for the position. Yuri played ♘d5 followed by ♘e3, then his other knight retreated from b3 back to f1. He played ♕d3 then ♕e2 and, after ♖ad1, returned the rook to a1. Such off-day play got what it deserved. In the 12th round, Petrosian was White against Gufeld. The young Georgian wanted to repeat the Meran which had caused trouble for Tigran against Nezhmetdinov. Petrosian took on d5 and, after cxd5, Black did not fully equalise. Petrosian was a little better when Gufeld blundered horribly. 4 wins in a row was great form. In round 13, he was Black against Bronstein. In the Caro-Kann after 3.e5 ♗f5 David played 4.g4. It was a wild game. Petrosian sacrificed an exchange, but the position remained balanced and the game ended in perpetual check. In the 14th round, Petrosian was White against Vasiukov in a Dutch Defence. They reached a pawn structure similar to a Stonewall. Petrosian's play on the queenside grew increasingly stronger and he won the game convincingly. Petrosian was Black against Gurgenidze in round 15 and he took control in the Leningrad Variation of the Nimzo-Indian. It was a close matter; the Georgian player was able to hold. In round 16, Petrosian was White against Furman. He played the Exchange Variation in the Queen's Gambit and won with a minority attack with surprising ease. In the next game, he was Black against Spassky; it was also an Exchange Queen's Gambit. Petrosian held firmly, and peace broke out after his 25th move when they were already in a queen ending. In the 18th round, Petrosian was White against Kasparov's future coach Alexander Nikitin. It was a Grunfeld with ♘f3 and ♗g5. The position was more or less balanced all the way to the 50th move. In this round, Korchnoi and Tal adjourned their game, and,

according to Cafferty and Taimanov, Petrosian helped Victor to analyse the adjourned position. Tal lost the game, which meant that Petrosian was a point ahead of Tal and Spassky before the last round. In the last round, Petrosian was Black against Korchnoi. It was an Orthodox Queen's Gambit. He equalised and, after Korchnoi's 20th move, they agreed to a draw.

Tal and Spassky drew, so Tigran won the championship with a one point advantage. The support of the local Armenian community and of many Georgian people was no doubt beneficial for him. His final score was 13.5 points out of 19 games, while Tal and Spassky each scored 12.5.

Petrosian, the new champion, won 8 games, drew 11 and remained undefeated. Although he chose more fighting lines as Black, he was not lost in any games, and just had one truly worse position, against Nezhmetdinov.

What was different from the earlier times was that he scored 8.5 points as White out of 10 games. At one point, he won 6 white games in a row. This was a great achievement, during which he exploited the mistakes of his opponents. However, he produced fewer games with artistic value than usual. It seemed that he would commit fewer mistakes against stronger players at the Candidates events, but he needed to do more to qualify to challenge Botvinnik.

According to Vasiliev, winning the championship convinced Rona and Tigran that he had a good chance of becoming Botvinnik's challenger. Rona relieved him of everyday cares of the family and brought strict order to the household. Petrosian still made time to watch sport – ice hockey and, especially, his favourite soccer.

Leningrad – Moscow Team Match

Petrosian played two games against Taimanov in the Leningrad-Moscow match, which was held in the second most populated Soviet city. In the first game, Petrosian as White got a nice edge in a King's Indian. The opening part can be seen in the comments to the Pilnik game from 1955. He confidently converted his advantage. In the second game, Petrosian played the Orthodox Queen's Gambit. Taimanov treated the opening aggressively. Tigran made some inaccuracies and Taimanov got good attacking chances. Petrosian resigned just a few moves before Taimanov checkmated him.

Moscow – Belorussia Match

The Moscow team hosted Belorussia and Petrosian played two games against Suetin. The first game featured a Saemisch King's Indian, but neither player was able to take control, and they agreed to a draw in a dead endgame. In the second game, Petrosian played the 4...♘d7 Caro-Kann. He neutralised White's play and they agreed to a draw after his 27th move.

Petrosian probably celebrated his 30th birthday between this match and the next event. He could be proud of what he had achieved, but was probably hungry for more.

Soviet Union – Yugoslavia Match

In July 1959, the Soviet Union hosted the Yugoslav team in Kiev. Petrosian essentially played a four game mini-match against Matanovic. In the first game, Petrosian was White. Matanovic made an unusual move in the Nimzo-Indian. Tigran exploited it, gained an edge, and soon tricked him tactically. Matanovic resigned after White's 30th move. In the second game, Petrosian as Black conceded the bishop pair in the Caro-Kann Two Knights Variation. He got a small disadvantage, but was able to live with it.

The draw was agreed after 29 moves. The third game was a 1.c4 c5 English. Matanovic equalised as Black and it looked like the game would end quickly in a draw. The Yugoslav player simplified to a drawish rook ending a pawn down. Petrosian squeezed for long, but his opponent was able to find a rook and pawn versus queen fortress and the game ended in a draw after 81 moves.

Game 89

Matanovic, Aleksandar – Petrosian, Tigran

Soviet Union – Yugoslavia Match,
Kiev (4), 1959
Caro-Kann Defence

1.e4 c6 2.♘c3 d5 3.d4 dxe4 4.♘xe4 ♘d7

Interestingly, Petrosian played this line 20 times; he won 5 games and lost 4. All 4 who beat him were superb players: Fischer, Karpov, Gligoric and Romanishin. In none of these games did Petrosian get any problems in the early part of the opening, though against Gligoric he did make a bad move and was in trouble later in the opening.

Later that year, he would handle nicely this other line against Gligoric: 4...♗f5 5.♘g3 ♗g6 6.h4 h6 7.♘f3 ♘d7 8.h5 ♗h7 9.♗d3 ♗xd3 10.♕xd3 ♕c7 11.♖h4 e6 12.♗f4 ♗d6 13.♗xd6 ♕xd6 14.♘e4 ♕e7 15.0-0-0 ♘gf6 16.♘xf6+ gxf6 17.♕d2 ♘b6 18.♕a5 ♕d6 19.♖d3 ♕d5 20.♕a3 ♘c4 21.♕b4 ♘d6 22.b3 a5! Petrosian starts playing beautifully on the queenside. 23.♕d2 a4 24.c4

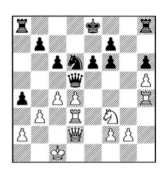

24...axb3! 25.axb3 ♕a5 26.♕xa5 ♖xa5 27.♘d2 ♔e7 28.♘b1 ♖g8 29.g3 f5 30.♘c3 ♖a1+ 31.♔d2 ♖g4 (31...b5!?) 32.♖xg4 fxg4 33.♔e3 b5 34.cxb5 cxb5 35.♔f4 ♖f1 36.♘d1? f5

37.d5 Gligoric, S – Petrosian, T, Bled/Zagreb/Belgrade 1959. Here he could have harvested the fruit of his brilliant play and won with the strong move 37...♘e4. Perhaps he was short of time.

5.♘f3 ♘gf6 6.♘xf6+ ♘xf6 7.♗c4 ♗f5 8.♕e2 e6 9.♗g5 ♗e7 10.0-0-0

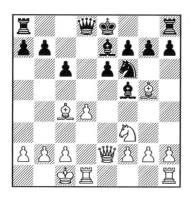

10...&g4!

There were only a few games with this position at the time, but his move, a novelty at the top level, would grow into the main line. Petrosian liked giving up a bishop for a knight ever since childhood. Here the point of the move was to reduce the number of pieces, which eases the problem of the small disadvantage.

11.h3 &xf3 12.#xf3 @d5 13.&xe7

After 13.&d2 b5 14.&b3 a5 Black would be active.

13...#xe7 14.&he1

Fischer in his game against Petrosian in Bled, 1961, will deviate with 14.&b1. Then 14...&d8 15.#e4 b5! 16.&d3 a5 17.c3 #d6 18.g3 b4! 19.c4 @f6 20.#e5

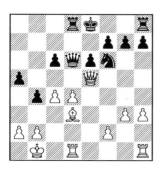

20...c5!? Petrosian plays for a win. (20...#xe5 21.dxe5 @d7 would lead to a draw) 21.#g5 – Fischer wants to battle it out as well. 21...h6!

a) If 22.#xg7? then Petrosian prepared the nice idea 22...&e7! 23.dxc5

a1) 23...#xc5 24.&he1 #g5 (24...&dg8?? 25.&xe6+!) 25.#xg5 hxg5. White interestingly can't hang on to the pawn due to 26.&f1 (26.&h1 @g4) 26...&xd1+ 27.&xd1 @e4

a2) 23...#c6 24.&g6 &df8 25.&he1 (25.&xf7?? #e4+! 26.&a1 &h7) 25...&hg8 26.&d6 &xg7 27.&xc6 &xg6 28.&c7+ and the position would be balanced as the black queenside pawns are weak.

b) Fischer actually played 22.#xc5 #xc5 23.dxc5 &e7 (after 23...&c8 White is the one who has less room to go wrong) 24.c6! &d6 25.&he1! &xc6 26.&e5 &a8 27.&e4. Here Petrosian should just have taken the bishop and settled for sharing the point, but he trailed the American in the penultimate round and therefore tried to win but went on to lose.

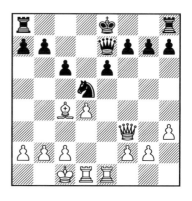

14...0-0 15.♔b1

White can't win a pawn, as 15.♗xd5 ♕g5+ would be inserted.

15...♖ad8 16.♗b3 ♕f6 17.♕e2

Matanovic probably just doesn't want to play an ending against Tigran.

17...♖d7 18.c3 b5 19.g3 ♖fd8 20.f4

The Yugoslav grandmaster plays actively, and doesn't just seek a draw.

20...b4!

Petrosian tries to open the b-file.

21.♕f3?

21.cxb4 ♘xb4 22.a3. It would be simpler to reduce material and not to open the b-file with 21.♗xd5!. After 21...♖xd5 22.cxb4 ♖xd4 (White could hold against other moves as well: 22...♕f5+ 23.♕e4 ♕xh3 24.♖d3 or 22...♕g6+ 23.♕d3 ♖xd4 24.♕xg6) 23.♖xd4 ♕xd4 24.f5 (24.a3) 24...♖d6 25.fxe6 ♖xe6 26.♖d1 the ending is even.

21...bxc3 22.bxc3 c5! 23.♖e5?

This move leads to difficulties. White should play 23.c4! ♘b4! 24.a3

♘a6 25.d5 and Black's advantage would be very small.

23...cxd4   24.♗xd5   ♖xd5 25.♖xd5

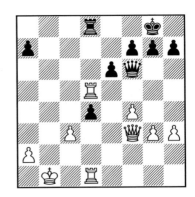

25...exd5!?

Petrosian keeps the position quite complex. 25...♖xd5 simplifying to a queen ending gives him fewer practical chances. Still, after 26.♖xd4 ♖xd4 27.cxd4 ♕f5+ 28.♔b2 g6 the endgame would be easier to play as Black, as the black king's shelter is much more reliable.

26.♖xd4 h6 27.g4?

Matanovic underestimates Black's play. 27.♕d3 centralising the queen would not equalise, but would be enough to hold, for instance if 27...♕e6 then 28.h4 can be played.

27.♖xd5 taking the pawn was not losing, but would lead to positions with difficulties.

a) 27...♕g6+ 28.♔c1 ♖xd5 29.♕xd5 ♕xg3 30.c4 White should be able to hold as the c-pawn would be strong enough.

b) Petrosian probably would choose 27...♖b8+ 28.♔c2 ♕b6. Here after 29.♕d3 a computer would hold, but for a human it would be hard to defend, especially approaching time control.

27...♕e7!

The queen gets active. Now White's king is under pressure.

28.♕f2

If 28.♕d1 ♕e3 White would be in big trouble.

28...♖b8+ 29.♔a1 ♕a3 30.♕c2 ♖e8 31.♖b4?

White has more stubborn defences. After 31.♖d1 ♖e3 32.c4 ♖c3 33.♕b2 dxc4 34.h4 it would be hard to tell whether Black's advantage is enough to win. Or after 31.♕d2 ♖e2 32.♖a4 ♕xa4 33.♕xe2 d4 Black will win a pawn, but White, unlike in the game, would not be clearly lost.

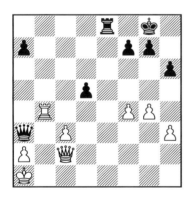

31...d4!!

This eye-pleasing pawn sacrifice leads to a queen ending a pawn up.

32.♖xd4 ♖e1+ 33.♖d1 ♖xd1+ 34.♕xd1 ♕xc3+ 35.♔b1 ♕xh3

Black is a pawn up, and in addition White's king is more exposed.

36.a4

Pushing the pawn is reasonable. White hopes he might be able to take the a7–pawn and create a passed pawn. After 36.♕e2 ♕h1+ 37.♔c2 ♕c6+ Black would win.

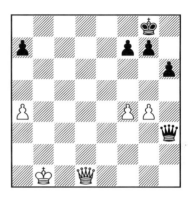

36...h5!

Petrosian weakens White's pawn chain on the kingside.

37.gxh5 ♕f5+ 38.♔b2 ♕xf4 39.♔b3 ♕f5!

Petrosian ties the white queen to defending the h5–pawn and closes the diagonal for possible future checks. Now his king aims to get to h6 and the h5–pawn will fall.

40.♔c4 ♔h7 41.♕d2 0–1 The position was probably adjourned here, and Matanovic resigned as he would lose the second pawn.

The Soviet team won the event 24.5:15.5. Beating Matanovic 3:1 was an impressive result and the quality of his play was really good.

Spartakiad, Moscow

An Olympiad was organised in Moscow for teams representing the 15 Soviet republics, Moscow and Leningrad. It was a big event with many sports, including chess. The database wrongly contains information that Tigran played for Armenia, but in reality he was the third board player of the Moscow team, behind Botvinnik and Smyslov.

In the first game of the group part of the event, he probably beat Seoev of Turkmenistan, although the game is not available. In the second game, Petrosian was Black against Gufeld, who played for Ukraine. White gained a small edge in the 6.♗g5 Najdorf. Petrosian managed to equalise, and the endgame ended in a draw. In the third round, he was White against Krutikhin. The player from Kirgizia played the Fajarowicz Variation of the Budapest Gambit, 3...♘e4. Petrosian reacted insipidly and they drew after 22 moves. In the fourth round, Mikenas was White against him. The Lithuanian grandmaster played the 1.c4 c5 English peacefully. After a careless pawn move, Petrosian nicely took control and won the game after his 40th move. In the last game of the preliminary section, he was rested against Uzbekistan. In the first round of the final, Petrosian was Black against Klavins in a Two Knights Caro-Kann. Petrosian equalised, then in the middlegame the Latvian player blundered his queen in one move. After that, he was rested against Georgia; he probably asked not to play against the republic where he was raised. In the third round of the final, he was Black against Korchnoi, who represented Leningrad. In an Exchange Queen Gambit, Petrosian soon accepted doubled isolated pawns on the f-file. The position was complex all the way. They drew on move 57, probably after they adjourned. In the last round, Petrosian was White against Aronin. The player representing the Russian Soviet Republic played the Tarrasch Defence; he improved on Petrosian's win over Geller from 1956. Petrosian found himself in a worse position and he had to play well to hold the draw.

Overall, he scored 5 points out of 7 games. He won 3 and drew 4 with no loss. The Moscow team won the event.

Isaac Boleslavsky

Boleslavsky played on the top board of the Belorussian team in the Spartakiad. Perhaps it was during this event that Petrosian approached Boleslavsky to become his trainer. Petrosian writes he was surprised that Isaac agreed. It was an extremely useful "move", one of the best in his life.

Isaac, a world class grandmaster, was born in 1919, so he was 10 years older than Petrosian. Now, at the age of 40, he had probably lost a great deal of his ambition. When I (your Hungarian author) interviewed Lilienthal, I knew that he had played many world champions, in fact all of them from Lasker to Petrosian. I asked him who was his most unpleasant ever opponent. I expected uncle Andor to say Botvinnik, Capablanca or Alekhine, but he instantly said Boleslavsky, adding that he was a highly subtle player.

Grandmaster Benko was present during that interview and stated that Boleslavsky had been an extremely good player, but suddenly put on a lot of weight in a short period of time and afterwards was unable to maintain his level.

What did he achieve? He won the Ukrainian championship at the age of 19 and defended his title in the next two years. He qualified for the 1940 Soviet championship and gained the master's title. He finished his first Soviet championship final 5th-6th. In the 1941 Absolute Championship he finished 4th. In the 1944 Soviet championship he took the bronze medal behind Botvinnik and Smyslov. In the 1945 championship he finished second behind Botvinnik. Two years later, he was second behind Keres. In the strong Chigorin memorial, he was joint-third together with Smyslov behind Botvinnik and Ragozin.

In 1948 in Saltsjobaden, he finished third and qualified for the Candidates Tournament. Bronstein won in Saltsjobaden and Szabo was second. In the 1950 Budapest Candidates Tournament he was joint-first with Bronstein. He and David played a play-off to challenge Botvinnik for the championship. The match stood 6.5:6.5, but he lost the last game under questionable circumstances. (See *The Rise and Fall of David Bronstein* by Genna Sosonko, Elk and Ruby, 2017, for a detailed discussion of this incident.) At the Helsinki Olympiad, he contributed 7 points from 8 games to the Soviet gold. However, by 1953 he had lost some of his powers and he was far from qualifying from the interzonal. After that, he no longer participated in the world championship cycle. His last Soviet championship was the 1961 final.

He was a player who felt dynamism in chess superbly. He was an expert in the King's Indian and a variation is named after him in the Sicilian.

So how was he helpful for Petrosian? He definitely had some opening ideas. The support of a great player and trust in Petrosian's talent must have meant a lot. But perhaps the best help was connected with the fact that in the sixties Petrosian's biggest rivals, Tal, Geller, and Spassky, were very dynamic players. Analysing a lot with Isaac did not turn him into a ferocious attacker, but probably taught him to face this style very well.

It would be interesting to know who paid Boleslavsky, the state or Spartak, Tigran's club. Tigran must have been living comfortably, but he probably was unable to afford him from his own money. He was the last world champion not to become a millionaire. Petrosian doesn't write how often or how long they trained. They probably did not reach the level of professionalism with which Karpov managed to build his own camp. However, the results that Petrosian accomplished prove that Isaac was very beneficial for him. Let's pay homage to Boleslavsky with two of his masterpieces. These games exemplify Isaac's style.

Game 90

Kotov, Alexander –
Boleslavsky, Isaac
Soviet Championship, Moscow, 1945
Trompowsky Attack

1.d4 ♘f6 2.♗g5 ♘e4 3.♗f4

According to the database, this move was a novelty then. Boleslavsky also played in an interesting game against Bondarevsky, who chose 3.♗h4.

3...d6

Isaac looks for dynamic play.

4.f3 ♘f6 5.e4 g6 6.♕d2 ♘bd7

Black wants to win a big tempo early on.

7.♗h6? ♗xh6 8.♕xh6

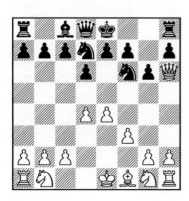

8...c5!

Black is better developed and this move is justified to open the position.

9.c3 ♕b6 10.♕d2 cxd4 11.cxd4 e5!

The young master triggers a direct confrontation.

12.♘a3?!

Kotov looks for original play; conventional moves would lead to equality.

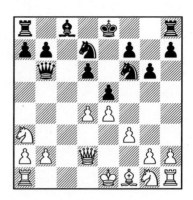

12...d5!

Boleslavsky opens the position powerfully.

13.dxe5?!

This move helps Black's development. After 13.exd5 ♘xd5 14.♘c4 (14.dxe5 ♘e3) 14...♕xd4 15.♕xd4 exd4 16.♘e2 White would equalise.

13...♘xe5 14.♗b5+ ♔f8!

After 14...♗d7!? 15.♗xd7+ ♘fxd7 Black would be better as well. If 16.exd5 (16.♕xd5? ♕xb2) 16...♖c8! Black obtains an edge by preventing long castling.

15.exd5 ♔g7 16.♘e2

If 16.0-0-0? then 16...♗f5.

16...a6 17.♗c4 ♖e8

17...♗h3 18.♘c3 ♖ac8 19.♗b3 ♗f5 20.0-0-0 ♘d3+ 21.♔b1 ♘f2+ 22.♔a1 ♘xh1 23.♖xh1 h5 24.h3 and White only has a bit of play for the exchange.

18.♖d1?

Kotov makes a losing mistake. 18.♔f1 is dubious, for instance the simple 18...♗d7 would be strong. However, White had a playable roller-coaster continuation: 18.0-0-0! ♗f5 19.♘g3 ♖ac8 20.♘xf5+ gxf5 21.d6 and White survives, as 21... ♕d8 22.d7! can be played.

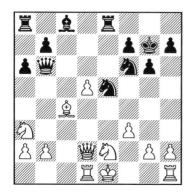

18...♗h3!

A brilliant move. Black develops quickly.

19.♔f1

White has no defence. If 19.f4 ♗xg2 20.fxe5 ♖xe5 21.♖f1 ♗xf1 22.♔xf1 ♖f5+ Black breaks through.

19...♘xf3 20.♕f4

20.♕c3 ♖e3 21.♗d3 (21.♖d3 ♗xg2+ 22.♔xg2 ♖xe2+ and Black checkmates in 3) 21...♖c8 22.♘c4 ♖xc4!. This is not only good looking, but highly effective as well. 23.♕xc4 ♘g4! 24.♘d4 (or 24.gxh3 ♖xe2 checkmates) 24...♖e1+ 25.♖xe1 ♘d2+ and Black wins the queen.

20...♘g4 21.♕xf3 ♘e3+ 22.♔e1 ♗xg2 23.♕f2

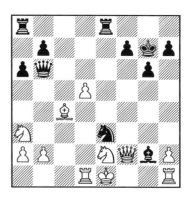

23...♗xh1

Black has ended up an exchange and a pawn up, as well as continuing to attack. White can resign here.

24.♖d3 ♕b4+ 25.♖d2 ♖ac8 26.♗b3 ♗xd5 27.♗xd5 ♘xd5 28.♕d4+ ♕xd4 29.♖xd4 ♘f6 0–1

Game 91

Boleslavsky, Isaac – Smyslov, Vassily
Candidates Tournament,
Budapest (6), 1950
Queen's Gambit Accepted

1.d4 d5 2.c4 c6 3.♘c3 ♘f6 4.♘f3 dxc4 5.a4 c5 6.e4 cxd4 7.♕xd4!

This is the right recapture.

7...♕xd4 8.♘xd4 e6

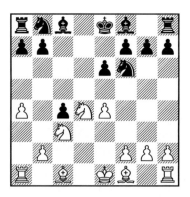

9.♘db5!

This is another strong move; it forces Black to place his knight on a6.

9...♘a6 10.♗xc4 ♗c5 11.♗f4!

Smyslov wants to keep the two bishops. He is optimistic and keeps the king in the centre.

11...♔e7

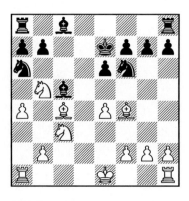

12.0-0!!

This is a subtle idea. Most players would keep the king in the centre with no queens on the board. White's advantage

would be small after 12.♔e2 ♘b4 13.♖hd1 a6.

12...♗d7?

Smyslov doesn't smell Isaac's idea. After 12...♖d8 13.e5 ♘d5 White would have an edge after any capture on d5.

13.e5 ♘h5

13...♘e8 would be less of a problem, though after 14.♘e4 ♗b4 15.♖fd1 White's advantage is still big.

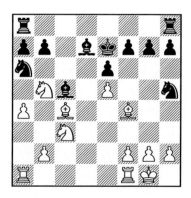

14.♗e3!

Here we can see the point of Boleslavsky's idea; he castled in order to place the rook on the f-file. He noticed the huge power of the rook on the f-file before the fxe3 capture took place and the f-pawn was still on its starting square, blocking the f-file. Great visualising and imagination.

14...♖hc8 15.♗e2 g6 16.♘e4 ♗xe3

After 16...♗b4 17.g4 ♘g7 18.♗g5+ ♔f8 19.♘f6 White wins.

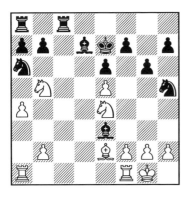

17.fxe3

Isaac's strategy prevails: his rook is mighty on the f-file.

17...罩c2 18.公bd6 罩f8

Black has no defence. 18... 罩xe2 19.罩xf7+ 含d8 20.公xb7+ 含c7 21.罩c1+ 含xb7 (21...含b6 22.a5+ 含b5 23.公c3+ would be over) 22.罩xd7+ 含b6 (22...公c7 23.罩cxc7+ 含a6 24.b4 and White is about to checkmate) 23.a5+! 含xa5

24.罩b7 and White checkmates.

19.兵xa6 bxa6 20.g4 公g7

20...f5 21.gxh5 fxe4 22.罩xf8 含xf8 23.罩f1+ 含g8 24.h6 兵xa4 25.罩f7 and White wins.

21.公f6 兵c6

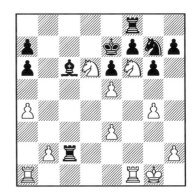

22.罩fc1 1–0 The rook did enough on the f-file. Smyslov, who was close to his prime, resigns. He was beaten like this very rarely.

Candidates Tournament, Bled/Zagreb/Belgrade

The Candidates Tournament was held in three cities in Yugoslavia, in Bled (Slovenia), Zagreb (Croatia) and Belgrade (Serbia). Petrosian, as the newly-baked Soviet champion, was one of the favourites. Tal, Smyslov and Keres also had decent chances to win the 8-player quadruple round robin event. Boleslavsky was Petrosian's second. Interestingly, FIDE and the organisers did not force the Soviet players to start against each other. The first 14 rounds were played in Bled.

Petrosian started against Olafsson. The Icelandic player improved on the Nimzo-Indian which Petrosian had played a few months earlier against Matanovic. He got a playable, balanced position. Petrosian, with subtle sense, swapped off the dark-squared bishop. This can be seen in the chapter Petrosian's Remarkable Exchanges. Then, Olafsson lost his way and did not know what to do. Fridrik got into time trouble, Petrosian took control, and the Icelandic player left a rook en prise before time control.

In the second round, Petrosian faced Fischer, and we now look at this superb game.

Game 92

Fischer, Bobby –
Petrosian, Tigran
Candidates Tournament,
Bled/Zagreb/Belgrade (2), 1959
Caro-Kann Defence

1.e4

Fischer opened with his king's pawn every time he had White against Petrosian.

1...c6 2.♘c3 d5 3.♘f3 ♗g4 4.h3 ♗xf3 5.♕xf3 ♘f6

Petrosian played 14 games in this position. 8 times he chose this knight move, while 6 times he pushed the e-pawn one square. He won 6 games, drew 7 and lost 1.

6.d3 e6 7.g3 ♗b4

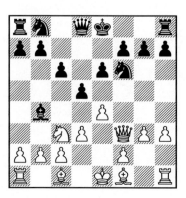

Petrosian plays this move for the first time. He had three games in this position after White's seventh

move, the previous time being in 1951.

8.♗d2 d4 9.♘b1 ♗xd2+

Keres and Benko would later play 9...♕b6 against Fischer at this event. Fischer says the queen would be misplaced on b6. The American writes in his book *Tal accused me of "bad judgement"* for preferring White here.

10.♘xd2 e5 11.♗g2 c5 12.0-0 ♘c6 13.♕e2

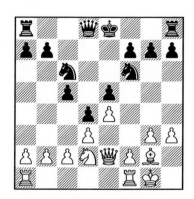

13...g5!?

Petrosian plays ambitiously; he aims to stop White on the kingside. The move will work really well in this game. In their next game with the same colours, Petrosian was worried about Bobby's preparation and instead played 13...♕e7, which plans long castling. 14.f4 0-0-0 15.a3 ♘e8 (according to Fischer 15...♘d7 is also playable) 16.b4 cxb4 (Fischer calls

16...f6 safer and he judges the position as equal) 17.♘c4 (the American grandmaster prefers 17.fxe5 and he thinks White would have an advantage) 17...f6! This strong move was a surprise for White (he expected 17...bxa3) 18.fxe5 fxe5 19.axb4 ♘c7 20.♘a5

20...♘b5! Fischer: *I already knew I got outplayed.* 21.♘xc6 bxc6 22.♖f2 g6 23.h4 ♔b7 (Fischer suggests 23...♖hf8! *exchanging and exchanging to reach a winning ending*) 24.h5 ♕xb4? (24...♖hf8 was still very good) 25.♖f7+ ♔b6 26.♕f2 a5 27.c4 ♘c3 (Fischer calls 27...♘d6 safer) 28.♖f1? (Fischer mentions that 28.♕f6! was the right move. Then 28...♖df8 29.♕xe5 ♖xf7 30.♕xh8 and he adds that Black's position would be risky after 30...♕d6 or 30...a4, although we see no win for White) 28...a4 29.♕f6 ♕c5 (29...♕d6!? 30.♕g7 ♖dg8 31.♖b7+ ♔c5 32.♕h6 ♖a8 33.♗h3 [33.♕g7 a3] 33...♖hd8 34.♕g7 a3 and Black would probably win)

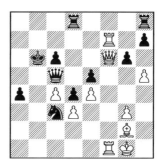

30.♖xh7 – Fischer here decided to play for a win. This move is not special, but to notice what he notices highlights his exceptional talent. 30...♖df8 31.♕xg6 ♖xf1+ 32.♗xf1 ♖xh7 33.♕xh7

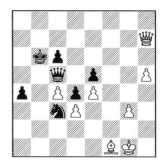

33...a3 It looks like Black clearly wins the race to queen, but Fischer realised in advance that although White promotes later, Black cannot do any damage with the two queens, and instead has to watch the h-pawn march and actually it will be White who can start attacking. 34.h6 a2 35.♕g8 a1=♕ 36.h7 ♕d6. Petrosian was in time trouble (if 36...♘e2+ Black could force a draw. 37.♔g2 ♘xg3 38.♕b8+ [38.♔xg3 ♕xf1] 38...♘a6 39.♕a8+ ♕a7 40.♕xc6+ ♕b6 41.♕a8+ ♕a7 42.h8=♕ ♕xf1+ 43.♔xg3 and Black would give perpetual check).

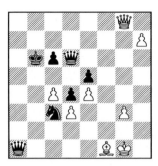

37.h8=♕ What a position! How rarely we play with 4 queens on the board. 37...♕a7? (37...♕e1=) 38.g4

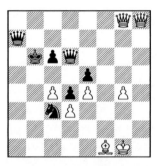

38...♔c5!! A great idea, as the king will be safer behind White's pawns. However, after the king move Black is still lost. 39.♕f8 (Fischer's suggestion 39.♕h2 is not convincing because of 39...♕a1! which Bobby doesn't mention and given the opportunity Black could then play ...♘d1. But 39.g5 should win: after 39...♔b4 40.♕h2 Black would lose as if 40...♔b3 then 41.c5+ wins) 39...♕ae7 40.♕a8? Fischer thought he would win (40.♕f5! ♔b4 41.g5 would be really strong. 41...♘d1 42.♕ff6 ♕de6 43.♗e2 and Black would struggle) 40...♔b4!! Petrosian finds a shelter for the king, and it is the only move. 41.♕h2

41...♔b3! After this move Bobby had to seal his move.

a) 42.c5!? (which was not played). Fischer: *After the game a kibitzer asked Petrosian if he thought this would have won for White. Petrosian, who must have analysed it for many hours (not knowing of course what my sealed move was) simply answered "I do not know."*

a1) 42...♕xc5. The bulletin mentions this move and gives the following line, but objectively it probably would not have saved the game. 43.♕g8+ ♔a3 44.♕c2 ♕b4 45.♕c1+ (45.♕a8+ ♕a4 46.♕c1+ (the bulletin misses this strong check) 46...♔b3 47.♕b8+ ♕ab4 48.♕g8+ ♔a4 49.g5 and White wins) 45...♔a4 46.g5 ♕f8 47.♕e6 and White probably wins.

a2) 42...♕de6 43.♕b8+ ♘b5 44.♗e2 ♔c2 (44...♔a3 45.♕b6 ♕b3 46.♕xc6 ♕b1+ 47.♗f1 ♕g5 and Black's position is no fun, but he is still alive) 45.♕a8 ♔b1 46.♔g2 ♕xc5 47.♕g1+ ♔c1 48.♕a1+ ♔xa1 49.♕xc1+ ♔a2, where Black is living very dangerously, but would have chances to survive.

b) 42.♕a1?! was Fischer's sealed move. 42...♕a3 43.♕xa3+ ♔xa3

44.♕h6 ♕f7 45.♔g2 ♔b3 46.♕d2
♕h7 Then an oversight 47.♔g3? but
Fischer had already lost his edge.

47...♕xe4 48.♕f2 ♕h1 Fischer:
*I offered a draw, afraid that he
wouldn't accept. Black certainly has
the edge now. After having fought for
a draw so long, however, Petrosian
was obviously unprepared to readjust
his frame and start playing for a
win.* Fischer, B – Petrosian, T,
Bled/Zagreb/Belgrade (16), 1959.
Another fantastic thriller!

Back to the game:

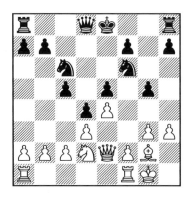

14.♘f3?!
Fischer plays against the g5–
pawn. Simagin suggests 14.f4 as

being better for White, but that is
not true. 14...gxf4 15.gxf4 ♕e7 (15...
♘d7 16.♕h5 ♕f6 17.♘c4 ♕g6
18.♕f5 ♔e7 and Black's position
would be fine with Rag8 to come:
19.fxe5 [19.♖f2] 19...♖ag8) 16.♘c4
0-0 (16...♘d7 17.♕h5) 17.♘xe5
♘xe5 18.fxe5 ♘d7 and Black would
be alright. Fischer stated that he had
intended to play 14.c3. Black could
play 14...♕e7, 14...♖g8 or 14...h6, as
all look playable.

14...h6 15.h4! ♖g8
15...g4? is bad, as after 16.♘h2
White would open the f-file with
17.f3. However, sacrificing the g-pawn
with 15...♕e7!? is at the very least
interesting. 16.hxg5 hxg5 17.♘xg5
0-0-0 18.♘f3 ♖dg8, and Black's
compensation is real, for instance
19.a3 (19.♘h4? ♖xh4 20.gxh4 ♘d8
and Black would take control) 19...
♘h5 20.♖fb1 ♘f4 21.gxf4 exf4
22.♔f1 ♕e6 and Black has nice play.
**16.a3 ♕e7 17.hxg5 hxg5 18.♕d2
♘d7**
Perhaps Tal would have sacrificed
the g5–pawn with 18...0-0-0.
19.c3 0-0-0 20.cxd4

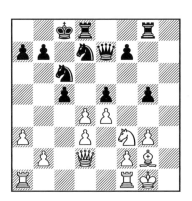

20...exd4!

Tigran hopes to take advantage of the e5–square. After 20...cxd4 21.b4 ♕f6 22.♖fc1 ♔b8 the position would be even.

21.b4 ♔b8 22.♖fc1

If 22.e5 g4 23.♘h4 ♘cxe5 24.♖fc1 ♕f6 25.bxc5 ♘f3+ White would be in trouble.

22...♘ce5

The position would be even after several other moves as well. 22...cxb4 23.axb4 ♘de5 (23...♕xb4? 24.♕a2 and White is better) 24.b5 ♘xf3+ 25.♗xf3 ♘e5 and the position would be balanced, or if 22...♖c8 23.♖ab1 g4 (23...♘ce5=) 24.♘h4 ♘ce5 the position would be more or less balanced.

23.♘xe5 ♕xe5 24.♖c4 ♖c8 25.♖ac1

If 25.♖b1 then 25...♖c7! 26.♕b2 ♖d8 would keep Black in good shape.

25...g4 26.♕b2 ♖gd8 27.a4

27.♗f1? ♕g7 28.♗e2? (28. ♖xc5 ♘xc5 29.♖xc5 ♖xc5 30.bxc5 ♖c8 and Black would have decent winning chances) 28...♕h6 29.♗xg4 ♘e5 30.♗xc8 ♖h8 and Black is about to checkmate White.

27...♕e7

28.♖b1?

A pivotal moment, and after Fischer's mistake his position becomes lost. 28.♖d1? would not be good either, as after 28...♘e5 29.♖xc5 ♖xc5 30.bxc5 ♕xc5 the knight would give Black an edge. White could keep the position even with 28.bxc5! giving up an exchange: 28...♘e5! 29.♖xd4 ♘xd3 30.♖xd3 ♖xd3 31.♗f1 (31.c6 is also good enough) 31...♖dd8 32.c6 The position would be balanced as the black king would not be safe enough.

28...♘e5   29.♖xc5   ♖xc5 30.bxc5

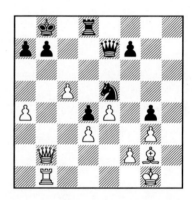

30...♘xd3

Petrosian chops White's key pawn, and now Black is winning thanks to the strong d-pawn.

31.♕d2 ♘xc5 32.♕f4+ ♕c7 33.♕xg4 ♘xa4

Petrosian plays cautiously. Perhaps the move 33...d3!? would bring the end faster than the game continuation. 34.♗f3 (34.e5 ♕xe5) 34...d2 (34...♘xa4 35.e5 ♘c5 wins easily) 35.♗d1 ♕e5 and White would be in trouble.

34.e5 ♘c5 35.♕f3

35...d3!

The passed pawn will have a paralysing effect.

36.♕e3 d2 37.♗f3 ♘a4

Petrosian probably just wants to reach time control. 37...♖d3 would finish the game quickly. 38.♕e2 ♕d7 39.e6 (39.♖d1 ♘a4–+) 39...fxe6 40.♕e5+ ♕c7

38.♕e4 ♘c5 39.♕e2

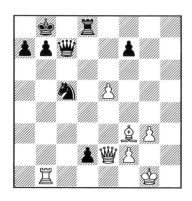

39...a6

Petrosian starts a glorious push of his queenside pawns.

40.♔g2 ♔a7

It is relaxing to get to time control.

41.♕e3

According to Simagin, the game was adjourned in this position. That probably meant that Petrosian sealed the move. Petrosian and Boleslavsky had time to work out the winning plan. It must have been hard for Fischer, realising that all he could do was to watch Petrosian make progress.

41...♖d3 42.♕f4 ♕d7 43.♕c4

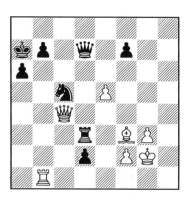

43...b6!

Black defends the knight, but this is another small pawn push.

44.♖d1 a5 45.♕f4 ♖d4 46.♕h6 b5!

The pawns draw closer to promotion.

47.♕e3

47.♕f8 ♕c7 (47...♘e6 48.♕a8+ ♔b6 49.♕b8+ ♔c5 is more flashy) 48.♕a8+ ♔b6 is the simplest way to win.

47...♚b6

The king moves forward as well; it is well protected. Petrosian's plan is not conventional; it takes time but is lethal.

48.♕h6+ ♘e6 49.♕e3 ♚a6 50.♗e2 a4!

The pawn gets closer to the first rank.

51.♕c3 ♚b6 52.♕e3 ♘c5 53.♗f3

Fischer can do nothing but wait.

53...b4!

The pawn marches on.

54.♕h6+ ♘e6 55.♕h8 ♕d8 56.♕h7 ♕d7

Petrosian gains time.

57.♕h8

57...b3!

The pawn move also provides a way for the king to get to a3.

58.♕b8+ ♚a5 59.♕a8+ ♚b5

59...♚b4. Even this "blunder" would win. 60.♗c6 ♕e7 61.♕xa4+ ♚c3 62.♕a6 ♕b4.

60.♕b8+ ♚c4! 61.♕g8 ♚c3

The king reaches an even safer area.

62.♗h5 ♘d8

62...a3 63.♗xf7 ♕d5+ 64.♚g1 ♕f3 or 62...b2 63.♗xf7 ♕b7+ 64.♚h2 b1=♕ would also win.

63.♗f3 a3

Black's pawns are devastating.

64.♕f8 ♚b2!

The king marches on.

65.♕h8 ♘e6 66.♕a8

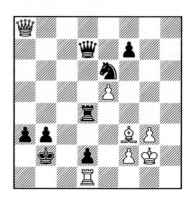

66...a2!

Now the pawn is just one move away from promotion.

67.♕a5 ♕a4 68.♖xd2+ ♔a3 0–1

Fischer resigns. A fascinating fight!

In the third round, Petrosian was White against Smyslov. It was a 1.c4 e5 English and the former world champion equalised easily. After exchanges, they reached a four-knights endgame. They played on for long, and the game ended in a repetition after 60 moves.

Game 93

Keres, Paul – Petrosian, Tigran
Candidates Tournament,
Bled/Zagreb/Belgrade (4), 1959

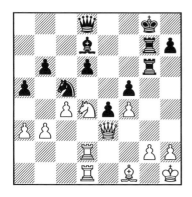

42...♕a8!?

Petrosian's position is very difficult. He gets ready for Keres to push the b-pawn. Keres had sealed his 41st move, and maybe Petrosian chose this move as the Estonian grandmaster might not have analysed it. It is almost impossible to imagine what this queen will do

to White's king just 10 moves later.

43.♔g1?!

Keres gets ready to meet ...♘d3. What else should White do? After 43.b4 axb4 44.axb4 ♘d3 White would be only somewhat better. White's best approach is to improve his knight with 43.♘b5! ♘d3 (if 43...♕f8 44.♘xd6 and White is winning) 44.♘c3! The knight wants to close the long diagonal. If 44...♗c6 45.♗xd3 exd3 46.♘d5 Black would be lost.

43...h5!

Petrosian starts building an attack on the kingside. If 43...♘d3? 44.♗xd3 exd3 45.g3 White would win.

44.♖b1

After 44.b4 axb4 45.axb4 ♘d3 46.b5 h4 47.♗xd3 exd3 48.♘f3 ♕e4 49.♕xd3 ♕xd3 50.♖xd3 ♖xg2+ 51.♔f1 ♗e6 White would be a bit better.

44...h4 45.♖bb2

Keres plays cautiously.

45...♖g4 46.♖f2

If 46.b4 ♘d3 47.♗xd3 exd3 48.bxa5 bxa5 49.♕xd3 ♖xf4 Black is just a bit worse.

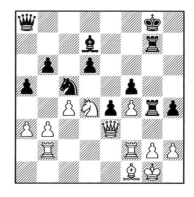

46...♕d8!!

Petrosian changes his target. He no longer focuses on the g2–pawn, but has spotted a fantastic tactical idea.

47.b4?

Keres misses Petrosian's idea; he chooses the wrong moment to send the knight away. After 47.♖fd2 ♕f6 48.b4 axb4 49.axb4 ♘d3 50.♗xd3 exd3 51.b5 White would have a small edge. White could instead have cleared a way for his king.

47...♖g3!!

Most of us can only dream about making such a fabulous move.

48.hxg3?!

This capture is not losing, but it is dangerous. 48.♕c1 ♘d3 would equalise.

48...hxg3 49.♖fd2 ♕h4 50.♗e2

Maybe Keres missed Petrosian's play in his adjournment analysis, and his annoyance now influences his concentration. He has a practical continuation: 50.♘f3! exf3 51.gxf3 ♖e7 52.♕d4 ♗c6.

50...♖h7 51.♔f1??

White could still avoid defeat before this move, but Keres probably did not see what was coming. After 51.♗h5! ♖xh5 52.♔f1 ♘d3 53.♘e2 ♘xb2 54.♖xb2 ♕f6 55.♘xg3 White has good chances to hold.

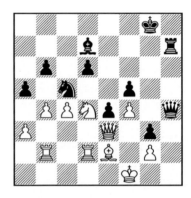

51...♕xf4+!! 0–1 This magical queen sacrifice leads to checkmate.

After his flying start with 3.5 out of 4, he agreed a quick draw with Tal. The fact that they produced four quick draws at this event suggests that they had agreed them beforehand. This slightly controversial act saved energy for both of them. It was within the rules, and at such an event one must follow the tactics one thinks the most beneficial. In round 6, he was White against Benko. He obtained a slight edge in the King's Indian. It looked like Benko would escape, but Petrosian sacrificed a pawn and soon won an exchange. He had chances to win, but inaccurate play allowed Benko to save the game. In the last game of the first cycle, Petrosian was Black against Gligoric. He beautifully outplayed the local hero, but blew up a winning position. The exciting part of the game can be seen in the comments to Petrosian's Matanovic 1959 game. In the 8th round, Petrosian was Black against Olafsson, when he chose the Ragozin Variation of the Queen's Gambit. He had a pleasant game, but one strange rook move was followed by a bad knight move. The Icelandic grandmaster exploited it, obtained a clear edge and soon after was already winning. However, he allowed Petrosian to reach a holdable ending a pawn down. It looked like he would draw, but Tigran surprisingly exchanged queens into a slightly worse rook ending, still a pawn down. Yet by time control the game turned worse for him and he was unable to hold the adjourned position. In the 9th round, Petrosian was White against Fischer. Their Nimzo-Indian interestingly led to a Stonewall pawn structure. Petrosian won the game almost effortlessly. Fischer resigned after Tigran's 31st move. In the tenth round, Petrosian was Black against Smyslov. Vassily avoided main lines in the King's Indian, holding back e4 but playing ♘f3 and ♗g5. Petrosian exchanged the bishop. They swapped queens. Petrosian had to play precisely to avoid a disaster. Sadly for his supporters, he was unable to change his mind and start playing for a win, though he would have been justified to play on. In round 11, Keres was Black against him. It was a 1.c4 e5 English, and

not much happened in the 25-move draw. Round 12 was another draw with Tal. In the penultimate round of the second cycle, Petrosian was Black against Benko. Pal sacrificed a pawn in the Reti for reasonable play, but an inaccurate move allowed Black to reach an ending a pawn up. Benko started to run out of time. He could have equalised, but went wrong and lost on time after Petrosian's 34th move, by which time his position was absolutely hopeless. In the 14th round, he was White against Gligoric. In a 1.c4 c5 English, Svetozar accepted an isolated pawn for active piece play. The 18-move game ended in a repetition.

Here were the standings of the leaders at half way, when the event moved to Zagreb: Keres 10, Tal 9.5, Petrosian 8.5 and Gligoric 8. The rest of the field virtually had no chance of winning the event. In his third game against Olafsson, he was White; Tigran got no advantage in a main-line Nimzo-Indian and started to struggle in the middlegame. He reached time control with a pawn deficit, but with reasonable chances of drawing. When they simplified to a rook ending it looked like it would be an easy draw. He reached a theoretical draw still a pawn down, but Tigran wanted to obtain the draw somewhat impatiently, fell for a brilliant trick and lost. Losing against the bottom player must have been a shock. In the 16th game, he played a thriller against

Fischer, which can be seen in the comments to the game from the second round above. In round 17, Tigran was White against Smyslov, who chose the Queen's Gambit Accepted. Petrosian made an inaccuracy and lost a pawn for nothing. He tried to attack, but was unable to create real chances and lost. This loss made certain that he would not win. In round 18, Keres played the Panov variation against the Caro-Kann. Petrosian equalised and the game ended in a draw after his 18th move. The next draw came against Tal. In round 20, Petrosian played the Leningrad Variation against Benko's Nimzo-Indian. In a complex middlegame, Benko missed a nice trick. Petrosian won a pawn, and he was winning by time control. There was no adjournment. The key part can be seen in the It's Your Move chapter. In the last round of the third cycle, Petrosian was Black against Gligoric. Petrosian was worse most of the game in the Poisoned Pawn Variation of the French Defence, but he was able to hold.

The standing after the third cycle was: Tal 15.5, Keres 14, and Petrosian and Smyslov 11.5. In the 22nd round, Petrosian was Black against Olafsson, and he kept the Orthodox Queen's Gambit complex. The Icelandic grandmaster started to attack. At one point, the Armenian missed a chance to get an edge in a complicated position

and then found himself clearly lost. Quite possibly there was time trouble, which he survived, and the game ended in a draw. In the 23rd round, Fischer played the Orthodox Queen's Gambit as Black. Petrosian had a small edge, but Fischer was able to hold. In the 24th game, Smyslov as White played a side-line in a 1.c4 c5 English. Not much happened in the 24-move draw. Then, he drew quickly against Keres as White, and then with Tal. This time they made more moves for the gallery. In the 27th round, Petrosian was Black against Benko. It was a Queen's Gambit Accepted. The position was balanced for a long time, then Petrosian lost a pawn. By time control, Benko had allowed him to simplify to a draw. In the last round, he played as White against Gligoric in the King's Indian variation named after him. White got a pretty big advantage. He won a pawn, but in time trouble made a somewhat impractical decision by exchanging queens. After exchanging knights as well, he missed a well-hidden win. By time control, he was two pawns up but Black's doubled rooks on the second rank were strong. Petrosian claimed that he made a move quickly to trigger a quick response. It worked, as Gligoric missed the drawing move. Gligoric thought over his sealed move for 40 minutes, but it was too late. Petrosian was probably happy to reach the end of a long tournament.

Tal won the event with 20 points, and Keres was second with 18.5. Petrosian's 15.5 points were a decent result, but the gap between him on the one hand and Tal and Keres on the other was bigger than he would have wished for. Smyslov finished 4th with 15 points, and the next players were Gligoric and Fischer way behind with 12.5. Tigran won 7 games, drew 17 and lost 4.

The results of his 4-game mini-matches were as follows: Tal 2:2, Keres 2.5:1.5 (Tigran was the only player with a plus score against him), Smyslov 2.5:1.5, Gligoric 2:2, Fischer 3:1, Olafsson 1.5:2.5, and Benko 3:1. The event was beneficial for his future. He and Boleslavsky saw what to improve and they also realised that their cooperation was working well.

Petrosian's results in 1959

Soviet Championship Final, Tbilisi	+ 8 = 11 – 0 13.5/19 1st place
Leningrad –Moscow Match vs. Taimanov	+ 1 = 0 – 1 1:1
Moscow – Belorussia Match vs. Suetin	+ 0 = 2 – 0 1:1
USSR – Yugoslavia Match,	
Kiev vs. Matanovic	+ 2 = 2 – 0 3:1
Spartakiad, Moscow	+ 3 = 4 – 0 5/7
Candidates Tournament,	
Bled/Zagreb/Belgrade	+ 7 = 17 – 4 15.5/28 3rd place
Altogether	**+ 21 = 36 – 5 39/62**

1960

Bewerwijk

Petrosian started the sixties and the year in Holland at the traditional Hoogovens tournament on the sea. In the first round, he was White against Van Scheltinga. He got no advantage in the Queen's Gambit Accepted and the game ended in a draw after Black's 14th move. In his first Black game, he was unable to create play against Toran in the 1.c5 e5 English, and the game ended in a repetition after the 19th move. This game can be seen in the commentary to game 7 from the Petrosian-Botvinnik 1963 world championship match in Volume II. In the third round, he won as White a one-sided game against Barendregt. In the fourth round, Petrosian was Black against Donner. He equalised, but played a bit impatiently and Donner took control. However, the Dutch grandmaster soon gave away his edge, the position sharpened up, and Dutch fans may have started to worry, but Donner held for a draw after the 42nd move. In round 5, Petrosian got a small edge as White against Matanovic in an Old Indian. He pressed with an exchange sacrifice. The Yugoslav player reached a drawish rook ending a pawn down. Tigran pressed for 40 moves, but in vain. In round 6, he was Black against Tan. His opponent got a clear edge in the 6.♗g5 Najdorf, but Tigran fairly quickly outplayed and beat him. In round 7, he was White against Bouwmeester in a 1.d4 ♘f6 2.♘f3 e6 3.♗g5 opening. The Dutch player equalised, but Petrosian took control in the middlegame, and won an exchange and the game. In the penultimate round, he drew against Flohr in 16 moves. Before the last round, he trailed Larsen by a full point. They were now going to play each other in the last round. Luckily for Tigran, he had the white pieces. He got a slight edge in an Old Indian. Larsen caused himself problems with three weak moves in a row. The Dane tried to create chances with an exchange sacrifice, but Petrosian never gave him any chance to hold. Petrosian and Larsen won the event, scoring 6.5 points out of 9 games. He won 4 games and drew 5.

Soviet Championship, Leningrad

The championship, which started at the end of January, was very strong, even though Tal and Botvinnik did not take part because of their match for the crown, and Keres was absent, too, visiting Cuba with an Estonian cultural delegation. Holding the tournament in Leningrad was a small advantage for the two local stars, Spassky and Korchnoi.

Petrosian started the event as Black against Geller. It was a 3.exd5 cxd5 4.&d3 Caro-Kann. The position was balanced and they drew after 25 moves. In the second round, Petrosian was White against Suetin. It was an e3 Tarrasch, and Alexei made far too many moves with his pawns. Petrosian sacrificed a pawn. Suetin then lost a rook, and when he resigned after Petrosian's 24th move his rook still stood on h8 and his bishop still on f8. The strong grandmaster lost this game like an amateur. A part of it can be seen in the It's Your Move chapter. In round 3, Tigran was Black against Lutikov. Both players were content with a quick draw. In the fourth round, he was White against Taimanov, but he got no edge in a 1.d4 &f6 2.&f3 e6 3.&g5 opening. In the middlegame, Mark missed a pin and lost a pawn, then blundered another pawn and then another. Taimanov played on for some time before losing in 44 moves. In round 5, Petrosian played the Hungarian Defence against Sakharov. They swapped queens. Tigran struggled for long, but he equalised closer to time control, and after his 39th move his opponent, a bit worse on the board, lost on time. In round 6, he was White against Nei. The Estonian defended the Exchange Queen's Gambit really well and managed to withstand Tigran's exceptional squeezing. In the seventh round, Petrosian was Black against Smyslov in a 6.&e2 e5 Najdorf. After the opening, Petrosian gained a solid, but somewhat passive position. Petrosian withstood the long pressure and the game ended in a repetition after 105 moves. In the 8th round, Petrosian as White played his favourite 1.d4 &f6 2.&f3 3.&g5 setup. Simagin replied with b6 and g6. Petrosian saddled his opponent with doubled pawns on the f-file. The Russian player offered a draw at the end of the opening, and Petrosian took it. In round 9, Petrosian played Black against Shamkovich. They swapped queens early on in the 3.&c3 &b4 French. It was even for quite some time. They reached a rook ending before time control. Soon after, Shamkovich made a mistake, which Petrosian exploited and he won the game.

We now look at the 10th game. In preparing this book, your Hungarian author asked Henrik Carlsen if he would be so kind as to ask Magnus what his favourite Petrosian game was. I was very much wondering what the answer would be. Well, the answer was Petrosian's next game. So this game is special not only because of Petrosian's remarkable moves.

Game 94

Petrosian, Tigran – Gufeld, Eduard
Soviet Championship Final, Leningrad
(10), 1960
King's Indian Defence

1.d4 ♘f6 2.c4 g6 3.♘c3 ♗g7
4.e4 0-0 5.♘f3 d6 6.♗e2 e5 7.d5
♘h5 8.g3 ♘a6 9.♘d2 ♘f6 10.h4 c6
11.♘b3 ♘c7 12.♗g5 cxd5 13.cxd5
h6 14.♗xf6 ♕xf6

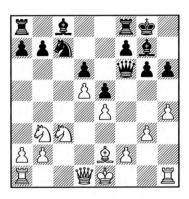

15.♗g4

Petrosian exchanges the dangerous c8–bishop. Gulko likes the idea, whereas Gufeld attaches a ?! mark to the move, preferring to push the h-pawn. If 15.h5 then 15...♕g5 or 15...♗d7 16.♗g4 ♗e8.

15...h5 16.♗xc8 ♖axc8 17.♕e2 ♗h6

Gufeld takes away the c1–square from the white rooks. Its effect can be countered.

18.♘a5

The knight ties the rook to defending the b7–pawn. Gufeld's analysis of this game mainly concentrates on Black's side, but White's play is much more original.

18...♖b8 19.0-0 ♖fc8

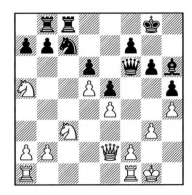

20.a4!

Tigran starts playing to place a rook on the c-file. To see the plan requires special vision.

20...♕d8

In this game, Black could have tried many plans, but we concentrate on Petrosian's play.

21.♘c4 ♘e8 22.♖a2!

Petrosian now makes another original move; it looks like the rook has nowhere to go to from a2.

Petrosian wrote in *Chess Lectures*: "There are many items in the treasury of chess lore which have impressed and are still impressive for me. Among them I can mention the game Lilienthal-Botvinnik from the 12th Soviet Championship, especially the move 14.♕d2...". So let us digress a little and see what move and game he was referring to:

Lilienthal, Andor – Botvinnik, Mikhail
Soviet Championship,
Moscow (17), 1940

14.♕d2! Interestingly, in Lilienthal's own commentary on this game in his autobiography he gives himself no exclamation mark. In our opinion, he was worried that Botvinnik would have got upset.

14...a5 15.a3 ♘a6 16.b4

Lilienthal paralyses the a6 knight.

16...♗f6 17.♗b2 ♕d7?

After 17...♗xb2 18.♕xb2 ♕f6 White's advantage would be much smaller than in the game.

18.♗xf6 ♖xf6 19.♘d3

It is natural to get closer to the e6–outpost.

19...a4!?

19...♕b5 was a better move than what the future world champion played.

20.♖ac1!

The beginning of a great role for the rook.

20...♕f7 21.♘f4 ♗c8 22.♖c3!

This is strong, but not extraordinary.

22...♗d7 23.♖fc1

This is strong and natural.

23...h6 24.h4!

Lilienthal makes sure the knight will not be sent away from f4.

24...♖a7 25.h5!

Lilienthal creates another outpost.

25...♖a8

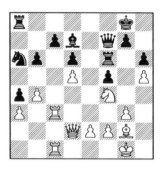

26.♖e3!!

This is not only strong, but brilliant.

26...♔h7 27.♖cc3!

Andor is ready to improve everything he can before he acts.

27...♖b8 28.♕d3!

Andor pins a black piece defending the a6–knight and the queen has an effect on the f5-pawn.

28...♖a8 29.♘g6!

Botvinnik rarely got destroyed strategically like this in his career.

29...♖xg6

This sacrifice is driven by desperation. After 29...♕g8 30.♗h3 ♕d8 31.♖f3 White would win.

30.hxg6+ ♔xg6

31.♖e6+!!

The rook has followed a glorious path: c1-c3-e3-e6+.

31...♔h7 32.g4!

Lilienthal goes after Botvinnik's king.

32...c5 33.b5 ♘c7 34.gxf5 ♘xb5 35.f6+ ♔g8

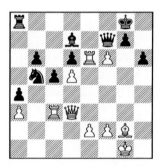

36.♖c4!

Another strong rook move.

36...♖e8 37.♖g4!

The rook forces a big weakening around the black king.

37...g5 38.♖xe8+ ♗xe8 39.♖e4

The stylish employment of the rooks seems never to end.

39...♔f8 40.♖e7!

Here, the rook is like a bull in a china shop, it destroys everything.

40...♕g6

40...♕xf6 41.♖xe8+ results in an extra piece for White.

41.♗e4 ♕h5 42.♗f3 ♕g6

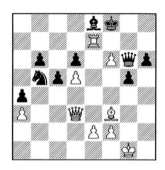

43.♖xe8+   1–0   Lilienthal deservedly forces the resignation of his great opponent with another sweet rook move. If 43...♕xe8 then 44.♕h7 would win instantly. Botvinnik, who at this point was probably the best player in the world, played poorly for his level, but Lilienthal was in his element. His play possibly influenced Petrosian's way of employing his rook in this Gufeld game.

Back to the game!

22...♕c7 23.b3

White has to defend the knight, and the pawn move suits his plan.

23...♕d7 24.♔g2 ♖c5

25.♖b1!

Another somewhat mysterious and original move.

25...♖cc8 26.♖c2

Petrosian finally places a rook on the c-file; he cleverly avoided the h6–bishop.

26...♘c7 27.♖bb2!

A small improvement is also an improvement.

27...♖f8 28.b4

It is such a joy to watch how Petrosian keeps building his play on the queenside.

28...♘e8 29.a5 ♘g7

29...a6? 30.b5 would win. After 29...♘c7 30.b5 ♘e8 31.a6 b6 32.♘a2 White's advantage would not be very big.

30.a6!

Petrosian progresses: he opens up the queenside.

30...bxa6

30...b6 31.♘a3 f5 (31...♖bc8 32.♘cb5 – now it can be seen why placing the rook on b2 was beneficial) 32.♘cb5 f4. Gufeld in his commentary misses 33.♖c7, the

winning move. Black could try 30...f5!? 31.axb7 f4 32.♕f3 and White's advantage would be small.

31.♘a5

White's advantage would be pretty clear after 31.♖a2 ♖xb4 32.♖xa6 ♘e8 33.♖ca2.

31...f5 32.♘c6 ♖be8?

The rook does nothing here; Gufeld should have kept it on the queenside. 32...♖b6 33.♖b3! A wonderful prophylactic move that defends the third rank. 33...f4 34.♘d1! a5 35.♖a2 and White would have a small edge.

33.♘b1?!

So far, it has been vintage Petrosian, but here an inaccuracy creeps in. Tigran overdoes things, playing one more original move than he should. The rook defends the third rank. Of course here, the players may have had little time. White should play 33.♕xa6!, as Black can't really avoid exchanging queens. 33...♖f7 34.♖a2 f4 35.♕d3 ♕g4 36.♕f3 and Black would struggle.

33...♔h7?!

After 33...♖f7 34.♖a2 ♖ef8 35.♖xa6 f4 36.f3 fxg3 37.♖xa7 ♕e8 the position would be unclear.

34.♖b3! fxe4?!

Black should still double rooks on the f-file with 34...♖f7.

35.♕xe4 ♖f5?

Black has insufficient play on the f-file. After 35...♘f5 36.♖a3 ♘d4 37.♖ca2 ♗g7 38.♘d2!? (38.♖xa6 ♖f4! would allow Black fully back into the game) 38...♘b5 White would have a small edge.

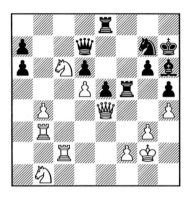

36.♖a3!

Another strong rook move.

36...♕b7?

Without the queen, Black hasn't enough fuel for his attack. Black could have obtained better practical chances with 36...♖ef8. However, White should still bring down his opponent: 37.♘c3! ♕f7 38.♘d1 g5 (38...♘e8 39.♘d8 and Black would be in trouble) 39.hxg5 ♕g6 40.♘c3 ♗xg5 41.♖xa6 and White wins.

37.♘c3!

Another patient move. Petrosian postpones harvesting, as after the careless 37.♕c4?! the reply 37...e4! would stir up complications.

37...♖ef8 38.♕c4!

Petrosian gets ready to harvest Black's queenside.

38...♖f3 39.♖xa6 ♗e3

This is a last desperate try to create chances in time trouble. It can be ignored.

40.♘e4 ♗h6

40...♗b6 41.♘g5+ would force the laying down of arms.

41.♖xa7 1–0 Gufeld resigns. Boleslavsky mentions that if 41...♕b6 then 42.♕a6 would exchange queens and win. How many knight moves did Petrosian make? Eight, and the last one prompted Gufeld's resignation.

In the 11th round, Petrosian as Black played the Slav against Liberzon. He equalised, and after his opponent played carelessly, he weakened his king. Uncharacteristically for Tigran, he missed a direct win, but he still won a pawn and gradually converted his advantage. In round 12, he agreed a 12-move draw versus Korchnoi as White. In round 13, Bronstein after 1.e4 c6 2.♘e2 d5 played 3.e5. The position became somewhat unusual. In the early middlegame, David naively grabbed an exchange and his position soon collapsed. The end can be seen in the It's Your Move chapter. He had to resign as early as move 23. In round 14, Petrosian was Black against Polugaevsky. In a main-line Nimzo-Indian, it looked like he had fallen for home analysis. He started to struggle early and resigned after Lev's 24th move. In the 15th round, he was White against Gurgenidze. The Georgian played the Grunfeld poorly, was a pawn down by the 10th move, and resigned on move 25.

After 15 rounds, Korchnoi and Petrosian were leading with 11 points. In round 16, he did not feel well and asked to play his game in his hotel room. He was Black against Averbakh. It is a bit awkward playing the King's Indian when one feels poorly. He was unable to equalise in the g3 line. Then, in the middlegame, he made two unfortunate moves and got into big trouble. He made it to move 40, but could not avoid getting checkmated. In the next round, he was White against Spassky. He played the Petrosian Variation against Boris's King's Indian. Spassky handled the opening dynamically, but he overdid it and got into a tough position. Petrosian never let him back into the game.

The standings among the leaders before the last two rounds were Geller 12.5 points, Petrosian and Korchnoi 12, and Bagirov 10.5. Petrosian was Black against Bagirov in the penultimate round, while Geller was White against Korchnoi. Tigran played a Scheveningen, the position simplified, and they agreed to a draw after Bagirov's 19th move. Korchnoi declined to repeat moves in an equal position, then Geller soon made a bad mistake and lost.

Before the last round, Korchnoi led by half a point ahead of Petrosian and Geller. In the last round, Korchnoi was White against Suetin, while Geller was Black against Bronstein. Petrosian was White against Krogius, and we look at that game.

Game 95

Petrosian, Tigran – Krogius, Nikolai
Soviet Championship Final,
Leningrad (19), 1960

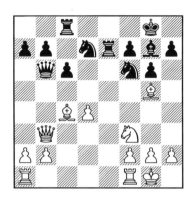

18.♕a3!?

Petrosian plays a slightly surprising move.

18...♖ee8 19.♗d2!?

Another move that was not easy to anticipate. White wants to play ♗a5.

19...♗f8

After 19...♕c7 20.♖ac1 (20.♖fe1 ♘b6) 20...♘b6 21.♗d3 ♘fd5 the position would be equal.

20.♕a4 ♕c7 21.♕b3 ♘b6

22.♗a5!

This pin is a bit annoying.

22...♘e4

After 22...♘fd5 23.♗xd5 cxd5 24.♗xb6 ♕xb6 25.♕xd5 ♗g7 Black is active enough to maintain the balance.

23.♖ac1 ♘d6

If 23...♕f4 24.♗xb6 axb6 25.♕xb6 ♗d6 Black would have sufficient compensation for the pawn. 26.♖fd1 ♘g5 27.♘e5 ♖e7=. Or 23...♗g7 24.♖fe1 ♘d6 25.♗d3 ♖xe1+ 26.♖xe1 ♖e8 and the position would be equal.

24.♗d3 ♗g7

25.h4!

Petrosian switches to the kingside out of the blue. His last move on that part of the board was 9.♗g5.

25...♖cd8?!

It is easy to underestimate the power of Petrosian's play. Black should continue 25...♘e4! 26.h5 ♕f4! when he intends to play ♘g5 to swap the f3-knight. 27.♗xb6 axb6 28.♗xe4 ♖xe4 29.♕xb6 and although White is a

pawn ahead, his advantage would be small.

26.h5!

This move leaves the g6–pawn hanging.

26...gxh5?

Krogius panics. Black has no pleasant choice, the least joyless being 26...♘f5!? 27.♗xf5 gxf5 28.d5 (or 28.♖c5 would also be reasonable).

27.♖c5!

The rook will be very powerful on the kingside.

27...♘e4 28.♖xh5 ♗xd4?

Krogius probably plays the rest with little time on the clock. He weakens the king considerably: 28...♘f6! 29.♖h4 ♖d5 would not lose quickly.

29.♖h4 ♘c5 30.♗xh7+ ♔g7 31.♕b4 ♗f6 32.♕g4+

Maybe 32.♖g4+ is a simpler win, though after 32...♔xh7 33.♕xc5 ♖d5 34.♕c2+ ♔h8 White still has to find 35.♗c3! and Black's defence would be demolished.

32...♔f8 33.♗b4 ♖d5

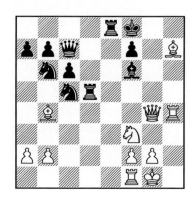

34.♖h5

After 34.♕g8+! White would win straight away: 34...♔e7 35.♖e1+ ♖e5 36.♘xe5 ♖xg8 37.♘g4+.

34...♘bd7 35.♕g8+?!

Petrosian was quite possibly short of time as well. In the next moves he gives away a part of his advantage. 35.♖xd5! cxd5 36.♘d4! would be decisive.

35...♔e7 36.♖e1+ ♘e5 37.♕g3?!

37.♕g4! would be stronger.

37...♔d8 38.♘xe5 ♖dxe5??

Krogius blunders the knight. After 38...♗xe5! 39.♕g4 Black would be only slightly worse.

39.♖hxe5 ♗xe5 40.♕h4+ ♔c8 41.♗f5+ ♔b8 42.♗xc5 1–0

Korchnoi was in trouble against Suetin in the last round, but by time control he was much better and won. The Bronstein-Geller game looked like it was heading for a draw, but David sacrificed a piece and lost. Korchnoi won the championship with 14 points out of 19 games, Petrosian and Geller finished joint-second with 13.5. Petrosian won 10 games, which was a great accomplishment; he drew 7 and lost 2.

A Childhood Friend Remembers

At the Soviet championship, his old friend Tengiz Giorgadze was Gurgenidze's second, and on his way home he visited Tigran at his Moscow residence. It is interesting to read what he shares about his visit in the articles mentioned earlier.

Whenever I was in Moscow, we would see each other. It continued like that until his death on 13th August 1984. In 1960, I was returning from Leningrad where I was Bukhuti Gurgenidze's second at the 27th Soviet Championship. On my way, I visited Tigran in Moscow. I spent the whole evening with him, we talked a lot. Tigran was always learning something new, even when he was already a strong and famous grandmaster. I always knew that I would learn a lot from him. He showed me some of his new books.

"Recently, I have been looking out for collections of Akiba Rubinstein's games. In our country, I can't find anything like that. I have to look abroad in second-hand book stores," Tigran said to me.

"But why would such an established player like yourself need to study those games? Surely you are not playing worse than Rubinstein!"

"In my opinion, there is no chess player with such a deep positional style as Rubinstein. I am trying to understand his secret," replied Tigran, and picked a book from the shelf that he found in Sweden containing a collection of Rubinstein's games. "Have a look at how he played," and he chooses a page with the game Rotlewi – Rubinstein. "You like games like that."

Rotlewi, G – Rubinstein, A
Lodz 1907

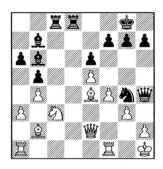

22...♖xc3!!   23.gxh4   ♖d2!!
24.♕xd2 ♗xe4+ 25.♕g2 ♖h3! 0–1

When he finished demonstrating the game, I asked if Capablanca's games were any worse.

"His games are different. Rubinstein's have more depth."

"Have you thought what Lasker's games are like?"

"Of course I have. Lasker is more difficult to understand. He is multi-faceted. I have not studied him yet. But I need to."

In those days, Tigran was working a lot on the classical legacy. He was concerned that not many collections of classical games were getting published: "One needs to study them in order to become a grandmaster." Akiba Rubinstein's biography would be published in our country a few years later, but there is still no collection of his games.

Once we started talking about wealth. Tigran didn't live poorly.

He had a lovely, big flat in the centre of Moscow and a grand cottage on the outskirts, in the village of Razdory.

"There are rumours that I am rich. I could have been if only I were smarter. I was brought up in poverty, wishing for a piece of bread, and now I am satisfied with little," Tigran said, and continued, "Here is one example of how I lost wealth. In 1954, I was in South America as a part of the Soviet team, participating in a friendly match. In Montevideo after the first match, we were invited to the city hall. At the end of the evening I was approached by a gentleman with a beautiful little box in his hand. He asked me to accept this small gift from the Armenian diaspora as a sign of gratitude. When I had a look inside the box, I was blinded by the golden jewels, worth tens of thousands of dollars. This priceless gesture frightened me. I was not used to it. In our delegation there was also a man from the KGB. He gave me a look and I had to make an excuse as to why I could not except such a gift. But the Armenian did not give up. The next day, at a similar reception, each member of the delegation received a gift. The gentleman who passed me the colourful box said to me in Armenian: 'Your jewels were divided amongst the 15 members!' What can I say?"

Petrosian's Position in the Chess World

The Botvinnik-Tal match was due to start in a few weeks. Petrosian probably wanted Tal to win, as it was probably going to mean one fewer rival at the Candidates events. It would be interesting to know what he expected from that match. Tal won convincingly, and Petrosian probably expected him to defend his title and Botvinnik not to participate in the Candidates. At times, Keres, Smyslov, Korchnoi and Geller were able to play slightly better than him, but he was likely to be on average the strongest player in the next Candidates Tournament. Noticing the chance probably made him and Boleslavsky work harder. By the way, Vasiliev writes that he asked Petrosian once it was clear that Tal would become the champion whether he thought that the rules needed some revision as a result? Tigran answered "No. Because sooner or later a chess player like Capablanca will become World Champion, who will bring order to chess."

Team Event in Tunisia

He won 2:0 against Tunisia and beat his Italian opponent in one game there. Petrosian was Black against Kaja in his first game against Tunisia. The amateur player quickly lost two pawns, but managed to postpone resignation until after Petrosian's 54th move. In game 2, Petrosian was White against Moosen. He was pleased with a small edge in the Queen's Gambit Exchange and chose to win the game slowly. Black resigned on move 48 when he had no sensible moves left. Finally, Petrosian was Black against Siveri. The Italian played the Sozin Variation against the Najdorf. Petrosian took control early and won the game with his 32nd move.

West Germany – Soviet Union Match

Hamburg hosted a friendly match at the end of June between West Germany and the Soviet Union. Petrosian started the event as White against Teschner. It was a closed Catalan and Tigran was too strong for his opponent. In round 2, Petrosian was Black against Troeger, who played the London System. Petrosian beautifully manoeuvred his knights and gained space. After a bit of pressure, he convincingly won the game in 42 moves. Petrosian's great opening play can be seen in the commentary to the 7th game of the 1966 World Championship Final match against Spassky in Volume II of this work. In the third game, Petrosian was Black against Lehmann; the English Opening transposed into the Grunfeld. Petrosian outplayed and beat his opponent with ease. In round 4, he was Black against Bialas. The German played the 3.♕xd4 Sicilian, and Petrosian's playing strength was too much for his opponent. In the fifth round, Petrosian was White against Pfeiffer in a main-line Slav. The German master was in the game for a long time, but it got difficult for him just before time control. Petrosian needed 65 moves to break Pfeiffer's resistance. In round 6, Petrosian drew quickly against Lothar Schmid. He could have played on. Perhaps his opponent, who was a millionaire, sponsored the event. In the last round, he faced Unzicker.

Game 96

Petrosian, Tigran – Unzicker, Wolfgang

West Germany – Soviet Union Match, Hamburg (7), 1960

Queen's Gambit Declined

1.d4 ♘f6 2.♘f3 e6 3.♗g5 d5 4.c4 c6 5.♕c2 ♗e7 6.e3 0-0 7.♘c3 h6 8.♗f4 ♘bd7 9.cxd5 cxd5 10.♗d3 a6 11.0-0 b5

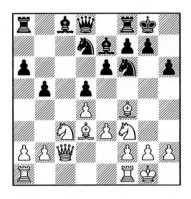

12.a4!

Petrosian bites at Black's pawn chain. If Black takes on a4, the a6–pawn will be vulnerable, whereas if he pushes past, the b3–square will become a great post for a white knight. It is also important that White is likely to gain control over the only open file.

12...b4 13.♘a2 ♘e8 14.♘c1 a5 15.♘b3 ♗a6

Black faces a dilemma: exchanging pieces makes it easier for White to invade, but keeping the bishop would mean one more passive piece.

16.♗xa6 ♖xa6 17.♕d3 ♖a7 18.♖fc1 ♘d6

If 18...♗d6 then 19.♘e5 would be strong.

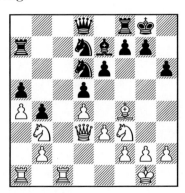

19.♗xd6!

Petrosian likes knights, and reducing the number of pieces helps to invade. 19.♖c2 would be strong as well.

19...♗xd6 20.♖c6 ♘b8

After 20...♘b6 21.♕b5 ♘c4 22.♘fd2 ♘xb2 23.♖b1 ♘c4 24.♘xc4 dxc4 25.♕xc4 Black would be very passive.

21.♖c2 ♘d7 22.♖ac1 ♘b6

Unzicker prefers to keep the queens on the board. Whatever he chooses, Black is going to suffer.

For example: 22...♕b8 23.♖c6 ♘b6 (after 23...♖d8 Black would struggle) 24.♕b5 ♘c4 25.♕xb8 ♗xb8 26.♖c2 ♗d6 27.♘fd2 and White would press.

23.♕b5 ♘c4

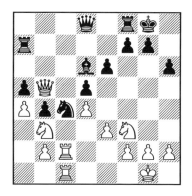

24.♘fd2

With fewer pieces on the board, White has more chances of invading.

24...♘xd2 25.♖xd2 ♕a8

The German player wants to keep the queens, as without them Black's position would be very passive. After 25...♕b8 26.♕xb8 ♖xb8 27.♖c6 ♗e7 White can try to invade with the rooks via 28.♖dc2 or play 28.f3 and when the opportunity arises exert pressure with e4.

26.♖dc2 ♖d8 27.♖c6 g6 28.g3 ♔g7

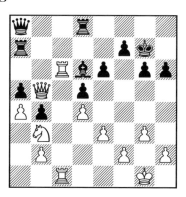

29.♔f1!

Petrosian starts a fantastic idea, which will prevail.

29...♔g8

If 29...♖b8 it looks better to keep the rook, at least for a while, so 30.♕d3.

30.h4

Tigran plays across the whole board, and he now threatens to push the h-pawn even further.

30...h5 31.♖1c2 ♔h7 32.♔e1 ♔g8 33.♔d1 ♔h7 34.♔c1 ♔g8 35.♔b1

The king has made it to the queenside.

35...♔h7

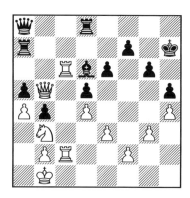

36.♕e2!

White threatens to open the kingside out of the blue.

36...♕b7?

Black should defend against g4 with 36...♔g7!.

a) 37.g4?! hxg4 38.♕xg4 ♖a6! and Black keeps the position together. 39.♖xa6 ♕xa6 40.h5 ♕d3 and Black is doing alright.

b) If Black would just wait, maybe Petrosian would try to exchange queens. 37.♖c1 ♗e7 38.♕c2 (38.f3 ♕b8) 38...♖b8. Here, White could try pressing with 39.♖c8 or 39.f3 ♖a6 40.♖c7.

37.♖c1

Petrosian vacates the c2–square for the c6–rook; now pushing the g-pawn can be more threatening. It is a pity that Petrosian doesn't finish the game quickly. After 37.g4! hxg4 38.♕xg4 ♕e7 39.f4 ♕f6 40.h5 White would be winning.

37...♔g7

After 37...♕a8? 38.g4 hxg4 39.♕xg4 ♖a6 40.♖6c2 White's kingside attack is huge. Black should play 37...♕e7!?, as the queen here stops the advance of the g-pawn. 38.♖a6 (38.♕b5 would also be unpleasant) 38...♖da8 39.♖xa7 ♖xa7 40.♕b5 and Black's position would be passive, though it might be possible for White to find a forced win.

38.♕b5 ♕a8

Exchanging queens loses by force: 38...♕xb5? 39.axb5 a4 40.b6 ♖ad7 (40...♖aa8 41.b7 ♖ab8 42.♘a5+−) 41.♘a5 ♖a8 42.♖xd6! ♖xd6 43.b7 ♖b8 44.♖c8+− and White will be a piece up. Black could however try 38...♕d7.

39.f4

Petrosian puts the ball in Unzicker's court. The German player is almost in zugzwang. White could gain more space with 39.e4 ♗e7 40.e5.

39...♔h7

After 39...♖b8 40.♖b6 (40.♕e2 ♗e7) 40...♖xb6 41.♕xb6 ♗e7?

42.♖c8! ♕xc8 43.♕xa7 White is probably winning, but after 41...♕b8 Black, although very passive, could maybe survive.

40.♕e2 ♕b7?

The last move before time control is a losing one. After 40...♔g7! White should keep pressing, as a direct kingside attack can be met. 41.g4?! hxg4 42.♕xg4 ♖a6 43.♖xa6 (43.♖6c2 ♖h8 44.♔g2 ♔f8 and Black is alive) 43...♕xa6 44.h5 ♕d3+ 45.♔a2 ♕xe3 and Black is in the game. Black should be alert to counter virtually any move in this line, as White could press on the queenside and if Black were to concentrate too much on the queenside a g4 could easily hurt. So even a waiting move like 41.♔a2 would pose problems. In addition, White could cause problems by transferring the knight to the kingside.

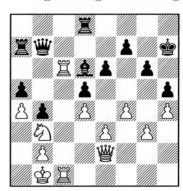

41.g4!

Now, White's attack brings down Black. Here we can see that transferring the king to the queenside was useful, as it makes the attack easier to carry out.

41...hxg4 42.♕xg4 ♕e7 43.h5!

Black has no defence on the kingside.

43...♕f6 44.♔a2 ♔g7 45.hxg6

45.♖g1 also wins.

45...♔xg6 46.♕h4 ♗e7

Or 46...♖h8 47.♕f2 wins.

47.♕f2 ♔f8 48.♘d2 ♖b7 49.♘b3 ♖a7

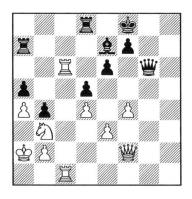

50.♕h2!

Black's days are numbered.

50...♗f6

After 50...♗d6 51.♖xd6! ♖xd6 52.f5 exf5 53.♖c8+ ♔e7 54.♕h8 White would catch Black's king.

51.♖c8! ♖ad7

51...♖xc8 52.♖xc8+ ♔e7 53.f5 ♕xf5 54.♕b8 finishes the game.

52.♘c5

The knight joins the attack, it is all over.

52...b3+

If 52...♖xc8 53.♘xd7+ ♔e7 54.♖xc8 or if 52...♖d6 53.f5 ♕xf5 54.♕xd6+ wins.

53.♔xb3 ♖d6 54.f5! ♖b6+ 55.♔a2 1–0

A great strategic game even by Petrosian's standards.

Petrosian's 6.5 out of 7 games was naturally a great result. Surprisingly, quite a few German national players were unable to resist. The Soviet team won the event 51:13, an amazing result.

Nimzowitsch Memorial, Copenhagen

Copenhagen organised a grandmaster tournament for the 25th anniversary of Nimzowitsch's death. The event started in early August. Petrosian was happy to pay homage to the great player and author he had learned a lot from.

He started the event against his likely main rival in the tournament, Geller. It was a quick, perhaps prearranged draw. In the second round, he was Black against Pietzsch. The East German as White played a side-line against the Benoni. Petrosian equalised. At the end of the opening, White had to sacrifice a pawn, but strangely Pietzsch gave up an exchange instead. Petrosian made a mistake and allowed his opponent some compensation, but White gave away his key pawn and lost quickly. In round 3, Petrosian as White chose the 3.♘f3 ♘f6 4.♕a4+ variation of the Queen's Gambit Accepted against Golz. In the ensuing position, White was saddled with doubled f-pawns but gained the two bishops. Petrosian gradually outplayed his opponent and beat him convincingly. In the fourth round, Petrosian was Black against Holm in a 4.g3 ♗a6 Queen's Indian. Petrosian made a big mistake in the opening; his opponent could have obtained a winning position by a piece sacrifice. Then his advantage declined. When we join the game, Petrosian is trying to stir up the position to create chances for his opponent to go wrong.

Game 97

Holm Pedersen, Sejer – Petrosian, Tigran
Nimzowitsch Memorial, Copenhagen (4), 1960

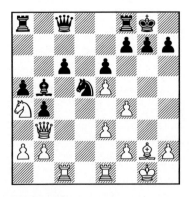

19...♕d8!?

One may think that Petrosian is just avoiding losing an exchange with ♗xd5 and ♘b6.

20.♕d1

After 20.♕c2!? ♕e7 White would have a small edge, but not 20...g5? because of the strong 21.f5!.

20...g5!?

Another original idea. Black aims at softening White's pawn chain. Petrosian avoids drawing simplifications with 20...♘xf4 21.exf4 ♕xd1 22.♖exd1 ♗xa4.

21.♘c5 gxf4 22.♕h5

The queen poses no danger for Black. After 22.exf4 ♘xf4 23.♕g4+ ♘g6 the position would be balanced.

Or if 22.e4, then after 22...♘e7 23.♘d7 ♘g6 the position would be complex.

22...fxe3 23.fxe3

After 23.♗xd5!? cxd5 24.♖xe3 ♔h8 25.♖h3 ♖g8+ 26.♔h1 ♖g7 27.♖g1 ♖xg1+ 28.♔xg1 ♕g8+ 29.♖g3 ♕f8 30.♘b7 f5 31.♘d6 ♗e8 the position would be balanced, though perhaps it would be easier to play it as White.

23...♕e7

The only move, but good enough.

24.♗xd5?

After 24.♔h1 ♔h8 the position would be equal. But Holm gets "Chigorin's inspiration" and sees a combination which he thinks forces a draw. Well, life is full of surprises...

24...cxd5

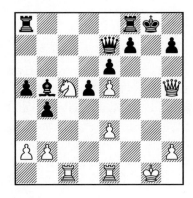

25.♘e4

This is a beauty, but in a lost position.

25...dxe4 26.♖c7!

White finds another brilliant move, but in a wrong concept.

26...♕d8!

After 26...♕xc7 White would give perpetual check with 27.♕g5+.

27.♖d1

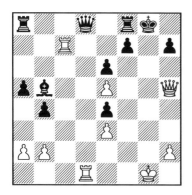

27...♗e2!!

A magical counterpunch, which spoils White's combination. I wonder what Holm's reaction was when he saw this stunning move. If 27...♗d3 White would do alright after 28.♕h6 or 28.♖d7.

28.♖xd8

If 28.♕xe2 ♕xc7 wins.

28...♗xh5 0–1 This great swindle resulted in Black being a piece up.

In the fifth round, Petrosian as White got an edge in the Old Indian against Larsen. The Dane made a big mistake at the end of the opening. Petrosian beat him with a crushing attack, but his task was quite easy, especially for a world-class player. In the sixth round, he was Black against Borge Andersen. He risked a dubious line in the King's Indian Saemisch,

managed to equalise, and when his opponent blundered, he exploited it with a pretty knight sacrifice. He had a simple way to win, but found a highly complicated one instead. In round 7, Hamann played a King's Indian with ♗g4 against the main line. Black sacrificed a pawn. They reached an interesting endgame where Petrosian had the bishop pair and 4 pawns on one side, while his opponent had a bishop, knight and three pawns on the same side. Tigran managed to win it. In the 8th round, he was Black against Kolvig. Petrosian equalised against a reverse Dutch and gradually outplayed his opponent, beating him. In the ninth round, Petrosian was White against Nielsen. Tigran after 1.d4 f5 played 2.♗g5. He quickly obtained an advantage and beat his opponent convincingly. In the 10th round, he played the Sicilian against Enevoldsen. His opponent played 3.♗b5+. Petrosian equalised, they swapped queens, Petrosian tried to outplay his opponent, but the game ended in a draw. In the 11th round, Petrosian played the Geller System against the Pirc versus Barendregt. He got a small edge, increased it and scored another victory. Petrosian played 1.d4 d5 2.♘f3 ♘f6 3.♗g5 as White against Stahlberg next, who performed well in the tournament. They reached an unusual position and it was balanced for a long time. Tigran managed to outplay the Swedish grandmaster before time control and beat him. In the last round, he was

Black against Orbaan. They concluded a 13-move draw in the 4...♘d7 Caro-Kann.

Petrosian scored 10 wins and 3 draws out of 13. 11.5 points out of 13 was a formidable result, and he scored 1 point more than the second-placed Geller.

Spartakiad, Moscow

That year, the team championship was held in the Soviet capital. Petrosian played on the second board of the Moscow team, behind Smyslov.

In the first round, he was Black against Tarasov of the Russian Republic. Tarasov played the Keres Variation against the Scheveningen. Petrosian equalised, and later he won a pawn, but White got a lost position only when he failed to grab a tactical chance to hold. Tarasov resigned after Tigran's 28th move. In the second game, Petrosian as White got an advantage against Petersons of Latvia. It was another 1.d4 ♘f6 2.♘f3 e6 3.♗g5. In the middlegame, Petrosian allowed Petersons to equalise. Black unnecessarily gave away the exchange and went on to lose. In the third round, Petrosian as Black risked the Old Benoni by developing the f8-bishop to g6 against Nei. The excellent Estonian player beat him convincingly. This time, he did not rest against Georgia. Buslaev as Black was his opponent. Tigran played an aggressive line against the Queen's Gambit Accepted. He positionally outplayed his opponent nicely in a queenless middlegame and scored a victory. After that, he took a rest against Azerbaijan. In the next round, he faced Taimanov as White. He employed 1.d4 ♘f6 2.♘f3 e6 3.♗g5 again. Mark got the two bishops, but made a large number of queen moves. Petrosian soon obtained a strong passed pawn on d6. In the middlegame, Taimanov mistakenly allowed Petrosian to establish a strong knight in the centre. From then on, it was a one way track. Taimanov made time control but then resigned. In the last two rounds, Tigran and Smyslov did not play. According to *Reliability Strategy* they had to go to the Olympiad, but there is a question-mark against that explanation, as the Leipzig Olympiad started 11 days after the end of the Soviet Team Championship. Korchnoi, who was also going to Leipzig, only missed the last round. Tigran's 4 wins and 1 loss comprised another good result.

Chess Olympiad, Leipzig

The Olympiad was held in the East German city of Leipzig. The event started at the end of October and finished in November. Petrosian was only the second reserve player and did not play the first game of the preliminary group, against Monaco.

In the second round, he won effortlessly against Seth of India. In his second game, he was Black against Kramer of Holland. He quickly got the two bishops in a side-line of a King's Indian, gained an edge and won the game nicely. In the next game, he won easily against Reyes of the Philippines. The same happened in his game against the Austrian Janetschek. Mercuri was his opponent against Italy, and it was also a one-sided game. Tigran was rested in the next two games, against Argentina and Poland. In the last round of the preliminary group, he obtained a small edge against Cardoso of Portugal. Petrosian won a pawn and the game.

He was rested in the first round of the final against Bulgaria. In the second game, he beat Vukcevic of Yugoslavia with surprising ease. He won a pawn, and possibly in his opponent's time trouble he trapped Black's rook. In the next round, he dropped his first half point. Prins of Holland played the Veresov as White. Petrosian made a careless move and from then on his position was unpleasant. According to both the database and Shekhtman, the game ended in a draw after Petrosian's 17th move. Maybe his last move was not correctly recorded. In the fourth round of the final, he was Black against Kluger and he risked a dubious Old Indian line. Tigran knew that his opponent regularly found himself in time trouble and played accordingly. However, he got into a lost position. Nevertheless, the strong Hungarian IM ruined his position and lost. Petrosian did not impress the selector of the Soviet team, as he was not put in the next two rounds, versus the United States and Argentina. His next game was against Pfeiffer of West Germany. Petrosian as White did not get any advantage in a Meran, but his opponent then made a careless move which allowed Petrosian to sacrifice a knight. Pfeiffer should not have taken the piece, but did and lost with little resistance. In the 8th round, he was Black against Ujtelky of Czechoslovakia. Petrosian equalised in an English Opening. He created complications, but his opponent was good enough to keep the balance. The game ended in a draw after Ujtelky's 31st move. In the next game, Petrosian was White against Pietzsch. The East German player got a reasonable position in the Old Indian, but allowed Tigran to build a nice outpost on d5. Petrosian's advantage grew bigger, but he allowed his opponent to reach a worse endgame. His advantage again grew big and he won the game. In the penultimate round, he had a rest against Romania. We join his last game against Wade of England.

Game 98

Petrosian, Tigran – Wade, Bob
Olympiad Final, Leipzig (11), 1960

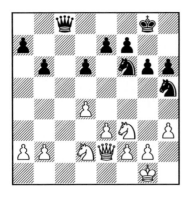

23.♕c4

Petrosian has gained no advantage at all so far, and now offers to exchange queens. Keeping queens on or exchanging them changes nothing in the evaluation of the position.

23...♕xc4 24.♘xc4 ♘d5

After 24...d5?! 25.♘ce5 ♔f8 26.♘c6 White would be somewhat better. But after 24...♘e8 25.♔f1 (25.e4 ♘hf6) 25...f5 26.♔e2 ♘hf6 Black's position would be easy to hold, as he could bring the king to the centre.

25.♔f1 ♘hf6 26.♔e2 ♔f8

After 26...♘e4 27.♘fd2 ♘xd2 28.♔xd2 f5 29.f3 ♔f7 Black would be absolutely safe.

27.♘e1

After centralising his king, Petrosian improves one of his knights.

27...♔e8 28.♘d3 ♔d7 29.f3

The Armenian starts gaining space.

29...♘c7

After 29...e6 30.e4 b5 Black would have nothing to worry about.

30.e4 ♘fe8

The point of retreating with the knight is to prepare a pawn push. If 30...e6?! then 31.e5 could come. However, Black has a few reasonable alternatives: 30...b5 31.♘a5 ♘a6 or 30...♘g8 31.d5 (31.♔e3 e6) 31...g5 32.♘b4 e6 and all of these should be good enough to hold.

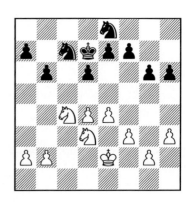

31.h4!?

Petrosian expands his space.

31...f6

If 31...e6 32.g4 f6 White's space gives him a small edge. Maybe Black should try 31...g5.

32.d5

White keeps pushing back the Englishman bit by bit. Now Black has only somewhat unpleasant choices.

32...e6 33.dxe6+ ♘xe6 34.♘e3 g5

34...♘d4+ 35.♔f2 and if 35...♘c6 36.♘f4 or if 35...♔e7 36.♘f4 and Black would struggle.

35.♘f5

35.h5 would also be strong.

35...h5 36.♔e3 ♘8g7

If 36...a5 then 37.a3 would be played.

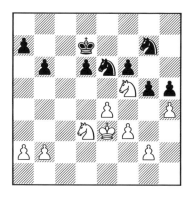

37.♘xg7!

Petrosian starts exchanging to open up the position in order to create chances to invade.

37...♘xg7 38.hxg5! fxg5 39.f4! gxf4+

39...♘e6 40.fxg5 ♘xg5 41.♔f4 ♘e6+ 42.♔f5 ♘d4+ 43.♔g5 ♘e2 44.e5 dxe5 45.♘xe5+ ♔e6 46.♘d3 and White probably wins.

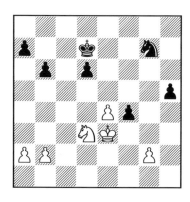

40.♘xf4 ♔e7

Black has to choose which side to move to. Wade chooses the kingside.

a) Staying in the centre with 40...a5 would lead to zugzwang. 41.♔d4 b5 42.♔d5 ♔c7 43.e5 (43.♘e6+? ♘xe6 44.♔xe6 ♔c6 and Black would get away with it) 43...dxe5 44.♔xe5 ♔c6 45.♔f6 and White wins.

b) Maybe heading to the queenside was Black's best chance. 40...♔c6 41.♔d4 a6 42.b4 a5 43.♔c4 b5+ 44.♔c3 and White probably wins.

41.♔d4 ♔f6

After 41...♘e6+ 42.♘xe6 ♔xe6 43.g3 White wins easily. If 41...♔d8 42.♔d5 ♔d7 43.g3 Black is in a lethal zugzwang: 43...b5 (43...♔c7 44.♘e6+ wins, or 43...a5 44.e5 dxe5 45.♔xe5 ♔e7 46.♘d5+ wins) 44.b4 a6 45.a3 ♔e7 46.♔c6 and White's king invades.

42.♔d5 ♔g5 43.♘e2 ♘e8

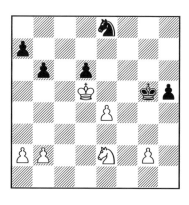

44.♔c6

White goes to collect the a-pawn.

44...♘f6 45.♔b7 ♘xe4

45...d5 46.exd5 ♘xd5 47.♔xa7
b5 48.♔a6 b4 49.♔b5 h4 50.♔c4
(50.a4? bxa3 51.bxa3 ♘c7+=) 50...
♘e3+ 51.♔xb4 ♘xg2 52.a4 ♔g4
(52...h3 53.♘g1) 53.♘g1 and the
queenside pawns win the game.

**46.♔xa7 ♔f5 47.♔xb6 ♔e5
48.a4!**

Edge pawns are enemies of a
knight, as the horse has fewer squares
around such a pawn.

48...d5 49.a5 d4 50.♘xd4

Petrosian plays to the gallery.
50.♘c1 ♔d5 51.a6 ♘d6 52.a7 ♘c8+
53.♔b7 ♘xa7 54.♔xa7 ♔c4 55.b3+
♔c3 56.♘e2+ ♔xb3 57.♘xd4+
♔c4 58.♘e2 would win here as well.

50...♔xd4

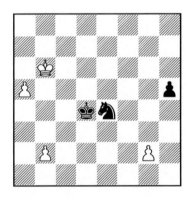

51.♔c6!
This is the only winning move.
51...♘c5 52.b4!

White has no other way to win.

52...♘d3 53.♔b5!

Yet another only move. White's
triangulation usually makes the
opponent move, but this time it is
taming the knight.

53...♔e5

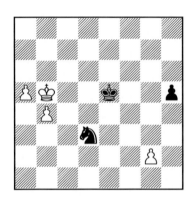

54.a6!
The pawn is not to be stopped.
Petrosian plays this one superbly,
just like in the Geller game.

54...♘xb4 55.♔xb4 1–0

Yes, Wade made some mistakes,
but Petrosian's highly instructive
play also contributed to bringing
down the New Zealand-born
Englishman.

Petrosian just dropped two
draws; he scored 12 points out of 13
games, the highest percentage of the
gold-winning Soviet team.

Moscow – Leningrad Match

Petrosian finished the year at the annual match between the teams of
the two most populated Russian cities. In 1960, Moscow was the host. He
played a mini-match against Bondarevsky. The first game was a Spanish

and Petrosian got no advantage as White. However, he started to gain an advantage before time control. He was probably even winning, but allowed his opponent to escape to a rook ending. It was going to be a draw for a long time, then he missed a win on his 64th move, and 3 moves later they agreed to a draw. In the second game, Petrosian handled the Sicilian in an original way, and he nicely outplayed and beat his opponent. The interesting part of the game can be seen in the comments to the Dunaev 1946 game. He thus beat Bondarevsky 1.5:0.5.

By the end of 1960, Petrosian had grown into the second best player in the world. Only Tal, the reigning world champion, had posted better results than him.

Petrosian's results in 1960

Bewerwijk (Wijk aan Zee)	+ 4 = 5 – 0 6.5/9 1st-2nd place
Soviet Championship Final, Leningrad	+10 = 7 – 2 13.5/19 2nd-3rd place
Tunisia – Soviet Union Match	+ 2 = 0 – 0 2:0
Soviet Union – Italy Match	+ 1 = 0 – 0 1:0
West Germany – Soviet Union Match	+ 6 = 1 – 0 6.5/7
Nimzowitsch Memorial, Copenhagen	+ 10 = 3 – 0 11.5/13
Soviet Team Championship, Moscow	+ 4 = 0 – 1 4/5
Chess Olympiad, Leipzig, board 6	+ 11 = 2 – 0 12/13
Moscow – Leningrad Match vs. Bondarevsky	+ 1 = 1 – 0 1.5:0.5
Altogether	**+ 49 = 19 – 3 58.5/71**

1961

Soviet Championship and Zonal Tournament, Moscow

Petrosian obtained everything in this cycle of the world championship. He would become the Soviet champion, Olympic champion and Soviet team champion. All that was left was to win the Candidates event. So he managed to focus intently on the world championship.

The Soviet championship was held in his home city, and the results of the previous three championships strongly suggested that to play in one's home base was an advantage. Tal and Botvinnik were to play their rematch, and FIDE had seeded Keres to the interzonal, so these players did not participate. The first four were to qualify for the next world championship stage.

Petrosian started the event as Black against Simagin. He managed to gain a small edge in a Nimzo-Indian. Then, he increased his advantage and won a pawn, but Simagin reached a tricky same-coloured bishops ending. White built a fortress, and surprisingly it did not crack. Then, Petrosian agreed a quick draw with Boleslavsky, who played his farewell championship. In round 3, he was White against Lutikov in a King's Indian (Petrosian Variation). Petrosian quickly took control and won the game convincingly. In round 4, Petrosian was Black against Bannik. The game ended in a repetition after 11 moves.

Game 99

Petrosian, Tigran – Korchnoi, Victor
Soviet Championship Final & Zonal,
Moscow (5), 1961

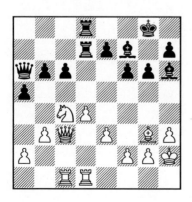

27.♖c2!

A very smart move. Petrosian allows Korchnoi to take a risk.

27...e5?

Victor bites on the hook. With the queen out of play, it is wrong to go for direct confrontation

28.♖cd2 e4

Black has only bad choices. 28...exd4 29.♖xd4 ♖xd4 30.♖xd4 ♖xd4 31.♕xd4 ♗xc4 32.♕d8+ ♔f7 33.♕d7+ ♔g8 34.♕e8+ ♔g7 35.♗d6 ♗g8 36.♗f8+ ♔h8 37.♗xh6 and he would be lost.

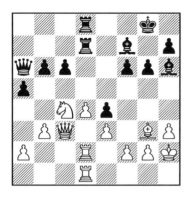

29.d5!

Tigran hurries to open the centre; he has an extra queen in the vicinity.

29...♗xd5

Perhaps with little time on the clock, Korchnoi failed to realise that this bishop on d5 can be demolished. But not 29...♖xd5? 30.♕xf6 ♖xd2 (30...♗g7 31.♕xd8+) 31.♖xd2 ♖xd2 32.♘xd2 and Black could resign after 32...♕c8 33.♗e5 or 32...♗g7 33.♕d8+.

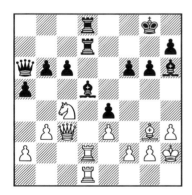

30.♕xf6?!

White's advantage will still be big, but he misses a clear win at once with 30.♖xd5! removing another defender. 30...♖xd5 (30...

cxd5 31.♕xf6 ♗g7 32.♕e6+ ♔h8 33.♘d6 wins as well) 31.♕xf6 and Black's defence cannot resist. 31...♖xd1 (other moves are also bad: 31...♗g7 32.♕e6+ ♔h8 33.♘d6 or 31...♖f8 32.♕e6+ ♔h8 33.♘d6) 32.♗e5 ♖1d7 33.♕h8+ ♔f7 34.♕xh7+ and White rolls over Black.

30...♗g7 31.♕g5 ♖f8!

White threatens both ♘e5 and f3. Korchnoi defends against both with one move. If 31...♕a7 then there follows a surprise with 32.f3! (32.♘e5 would be strong as well) 32...♖e8 33.fxe4 ♖xe4 34.♘d6 ♖e6 35.e4 and White wins. Maybe Black's best chance is 31...♗c3 32.♘e5 ♗xe5 33.♗xe5 ♖f8 34.♗b2 and his position would be extremely difficult to defend, but perhaps not lost.

32.♕g4 ♖df7

There is no time to bring the queen back, as 32...♕a7? 33.♘xb6 wins.

33.♘d6 ♖e7

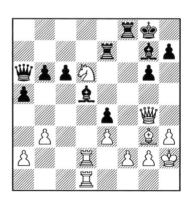

34.♖xd5! cxd5 35.♕g5 ♗f6?!

Bringing back the queen with 35...♕a7 would avoid a collapse. 36.♕xd5+ ♔h8 and White would be much better after 37.a4 or 37.♖c1. On the other hand, 37.♘xe4 is not convincing as Black could swap queens with 37...♕a8.

36.♕xd5+ ♔h8 37.♘xe4 ♗g7

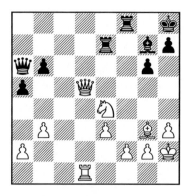

38.♘d6!?

Petrosian doesn't create a direct threat, but this move is unpleasant for a player with seconds on the clock. 38.♗d6 would win, but it would give Victor obvious moves. 38...♖d8 (38...♖d7 39.♕e6 ♖fd8 40.♗e5) 39.♗xe7 ♖xd5 40.♖xd5 h6 41.♘f6 and White would win, but slowly.

38...♕a8 39.♕b5

Tigran aims to take more pawns.

39...♕a7 40.♘c4 1−0 Korchnoi overstepped the time limit in a hopeless position. This win would be extremely important for the final result of the championship.

In round 6, he was Black against debutant Stein. It was a 3.♘c3 ♗b4 French, with White's position

preferable from early on. Petrosian allowed the opening of the f-file, and from then on things looked gloomy for Tigran. A blunder sealed his fate, and from this game on Stein started to fly.

Petrosian, Tigran – Smyslov, Vassily
Soviet Championship Final & Zonal, Moscow (7), 1961

18.♕a4!

Petrosian starts transferring his queen to the kingside. The idea contains more power than one may think.

18...♖fd8 19.♕e4!

Maybe the former world champion missed this subtle move, which creates a target in Black's pawn chain. 19.♕g4 would give away White's advantage because of 19...♗f8. In this game, Petrosian treats his queen in a similar way to how he used his rook against Taimanov in their 1955 game.

19...g6 20.♕g4! h5

Euwe shows a pretty sacrifice with 20...♔h7 21.♗xg6+ fxg6 22.♕xe6 ♖f8 23.♖d7 ♖ce8 24.♘g5+! hxg5 25.♕h3+ ♔g8 26.♕h8+ ♔f7 27.♕f6+ ♔g8 28.♕g7#

21.♕h3 f5

Perhaps this was Smyslov's ugliest move in his whole career. But other moves were bad as well.

a) 21...♖d6 22.g4! (Petrosian)

a1) 22...♖d5 23.♗xg6 fxg6 24.gxh5 ♖xh5 25.♕xe6+ ♔f8 26.♕xg6 ♘e5 27.♗xe5 ♖xe5 28.♖xc8+ ♗xc8 29.♕h6+ ♔g8 30.♕f4+−

a2) 22...♖cd8 23.gxh5 ♖xd3 24.♖xd3 ♖xd3 25.hxg6 fxg6 26.♕h8+ ♔f7 27.♘e5+ and White wins, as Petrosian pointed out.

b) 21...e5 22.g4 ♔g7 would at least force White to find a neat sacrifice. 23.gxh5 ♖h8 24.♗xg6!! fxg6 25.♕e6 ♖xh5 26.♖d7 and White would win as well.

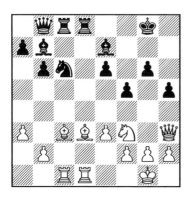

22.♗c4

Thanks to White's subtle queen moves he is completely winning;

the rest would be simple even for a decent amateur.

22...♖xd1+ 23.♖xd1 ♔f7 24.e4!

This pawn move softens up the king decisively.

24...♕f4 25.♖e1 ♕g4 26.exf5! ♕xc4 27.fxg6+ ♔e8

27...♔xg6 28.♖xe6+ ♔f7 29.♖xc6 would win.

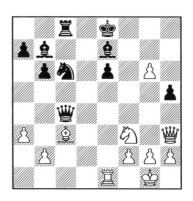

28.g7

The pawn is too strong for Vassily.

28...e5

28...♔d7 would be hopeless as well. 29.♖d1+ ♗d6 (29...♔c7 30.♕g3+) 30.♕g3 ♘d4 31.♘e5+.

29.♕xh5+ ♔d7 30.♖d1+ ♗d6 31.♗xe5 ♘d4 32.♘xd4 1−0

Smyslov had had enough of this game.

In the 8th round, Petrosian was Black against Cherepkov. Black equalised in the 4...Nd7 Caro-Kann. Cherepkov sacrificed a pawn, then another, soon after an exchange, Petrosian took everything and won the game. In round 9, he drew quickly with Geller.

Game 101

Furman, Semion – Petrosian, Tigran
Soviet Championship Final & Zonal,
Moscow (10), 1961
Pirc Defence

1.d4 g6 2.e4 ♗g7

Petrosian plays the Pirc for the very first time. He will play it with d6 20 times and will remain undefeated. He won 5 of those games. Surprising opponents with new openings was not part of Tigran's arsenal, and using such a weapon probably came from Isaac.

3.♘f3 d6 4.♘c3 ♘f6 5.h3 0-0 6.♗e3 c6 7.♗d3 ♕c7 8.0-0 e5 9.♖e1 ♘bd7 10.a4 ♖e8 11.♕d2 b6 12.♖ad1

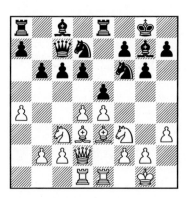

12...a6

Petrosian plays standard small space gaining moves.

13.♖a1?

This is strange from a strong grandmaster; he loses two tempi for nothing.

13...♗b7 14.dxe5

Petrosian cleverly selected the opening; Furman doesn't feel the position and doesn't know what to do with it.

14...dxe5

Petrosian takes like this because he wants to battle it out.

15.♗h6

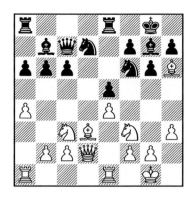

15...♕d6!

A confident and original move.

16.♗xg7 ♔xg7 17.♕e3 b5

Tigran naturally gains space.

18.♗f1

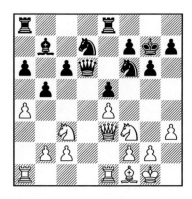

18...♕b4!

The queen harasses the b2–pawn. This was the reason for Tigran's subtle 15th move.

19.♘d1 ♕e7 20.♘d2

If 20.♘c3 Petrosian probably would have answered 20...♖ad8.

20...♘c5 21.♘c3

After 21.b3 ♖ad8 22.♘b2 the position would be equal.

21...♖ad8

Petrosian develops his last piece. He already has a small advantage. None of his moves were spectacular, yet his play was strong.

22.b4

If 22.♖ad1 both 22...♘e6 and 22...♖d4 would be strong.

22...♘e6 23.♘a2 ♘d4 24.♕c3

If 24.♖ec1 then 24...bxa4 (or Petrosian would perhaps try exerting pressure with 24...♕d6!?) 25.♘c3 ♕xb4 26.♖xa4 and White should be able to get away with it.

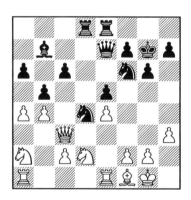

24...bxa4!!

A superb move, though it is easy to miss its point.

25.♗d3

Black's idea was to carry out c5 and play against the c2–pawn. Furman defends the c2–pawn in advance. If 25.♘c1 ♘b5 26.♕e3

♕xb4 Black will be at least a pawn up, still, White should try this rather than the game continuation.

25...♘h5!

Petrosian almost always keeps in mind that the chessboard has two flanks. He has just placed a pawn on the edge, and right after he places a knight on the other edge. And these moves are so strong! Note, though, that 25...c5! 26.bxc5 ♘d7 would also be very strong, and Black would be close to winning. Still, Petrosian likes to surprise his opponents.

26.♘c4

After 26.♗f1 ♘f4 27.♘f3 ♘xf3+ 28.♕xf3 ♖d2 White would struggle.

26...♘f4 27.♗f1

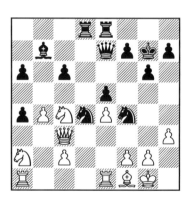

27...c5!

Black improves two pieces with one move, the bishop and the queen.

28.bxc5 ♕xc5 29.♘c1 ♗c6

Petrosian tries to hang on to the pawn. He is winning.

30.♕a3 ♕xa3 31.♘xa3

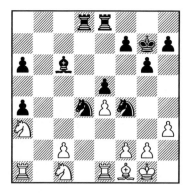

31...♘xh3+!

This sweet move wins two pawns.

32.♔h2 ♘xf2 33.♗d3 ♘b3!

Tigran naturally exchanges, as he has a three-pawn advantage. Furman could resign here. Maybe he was short of time. As he was a strong player perhaps it was hard to take that he was beaten in a teacher-pupil like game.

34.♖b1 ♘c5 35.♖b6 ♘cxd3

Petrosian no longer wants to win more pawns; he ruthlessly swaps off all the minor pieces.

36.cxd3 ♘xd3 37.♘xd3 ♖xd3 38.♖xc6 ♖xa3 39.♖c7 ♖e6 40.♖a7 ♖a2 41.♖e3 ♖f6 0–1

In the 11th round, Petrosian was White against Gufeld. The Georgian played an Old Benoni position with g6, but Petrosian got a clear edge. Gufeld did not want to suffer, but his active play worsened his position. Tigran made some original rook moves and got a winning advantage. His opponent then made a kamikaze attack in time trouble, but Petrosian gave him no chance. A part of it can be seen in the It's Your Move chapter.

After 11 rounds, Petrosian and Geller shared the lead with 8 points, while Spassky had 7. In round 12, Petrosian was Black against Averbakh in a Saemisch King's Indian. Petrosian neutralised Averbakh's play on the kingside, and the game ended in a draw after White's 20th move. In the next game, Petrosian as White agreed another 20-move draw, with neither he nor Bronstein really wanting to fight. In the 14th round, Petrosian was Black against Khasin, who played the Hungarian Defence too cautiously. Petrosian took control by obtaining the two bishops and won the game (it can be seen in the It's Your Move chapter). In the next game, Petrosian agreed a quick draw with Spassky, which they might have arranged beforehand. In the 16th round, Petrosian was Black against Polugaevsky. It was a main-line Nimzo-Indian, and this time Tigran equalised. In the middlegame, Lev made a careless move. Petrosian found a nice tactical idea and won the game convincingly. Its exploitation can be seen in the It's Your Move chapter. And he did not step on the brake, but beat Taimanov next. Petrosian played the Saemisch Variation against the King's Indian. He handled the opening cautiously, but while Taimanov tried to create play, he sooner created weaknesses in his own camp. Mark sacrificed a pawn, but was unable to cause problems and lost. In the penultimate round, he was Black against Borisenko. The Old Indian changed into an Old Benoni structure.

In the opening, Borisenko had an edge, but Petrosian took control. The game fluctuated, it was adjourned, Petrosian was a bit better, but the draw after the adjournment and another draw in the last round against Tarasov meant gold for the second time.

He finished with 13.5 points from 19 games. He won 9 games, drew 9 and lost one. Korchnoi, who beat Spassky in the penultimate round and Polugaevsky in the last, was second with 13 points. Geller safely qualified with 12 points. Stein played a dramatic last round game against Spassky, and he beat Boris and finished the event with the same number of point as Efim. Petrosian, Korchnoi, Geller and Stein qualified for the interzonal.

Winning the championship was a huge success for Petrosian. Korchnoi: "Before the tournament began, I considered the only 'certain' candidate for a place in the interzonal to be Petrosian. Now I am satisfied that I was not mistaken." His friend Geller: "Petrosian's first place was fully deserved, and in my opinion, he is now one of the strongest players in the world."

Moscow Team Championship

Shakhmatnaya Moskva No 8-9-1961, which was published at the end of April, reported on the event, so it probably took place earlier the same month. Petrosian as White played the reversed King's Indian against Aronin in the first round. He got a small edge, and close to time control Aronin made a serious mistake and got checkmated. Next up, Averbakh as White played the Saemisch variation against Petrosian's King's Indian. They castled on opposite sides, and it turned into a wild game. Averbakh came out on top and won in 28 moves. After that, Petrosian as White played an innocent line of the 1.c4 c5 English against Lublinsky. The game turned complex, but after time control there was nothing left to play for. Against Bonch-Osmolovsky, he was Black in a 6.g3 Najdorf. Petrosian got a nice position; he outplayed and beat his opponent. In total, he scored 2.5 points out of 4 games.

Yugoslavia – Soviet Union Match

In May, the annual Yugoslavia – Soviet Union match took place in Belgrade. Tigran started the event with a good game. He was White against Trifunovic in a King's Indian Attack. His opponent allowed him to build a huge centre. At the end, Tigran's central pawns choked his opponent. In the second round, he was Black against Matanovic. The Caro-Kann Panov resulted in White accepting an isolated pawn. Petrosian pressed beautifully, but the Yugoslav played well and he was able to hold. The day before Petrosian's third round, there was important news from Russia: Botvinnik had won his rematch against Tal. This was a bit of luck for Tigran, as a healthy and well prepared Tal would have been a more difficult opponent than the great but aging Botvinnik.

Game 102

Petrosian, Tigran – Ciric, Dragoljub
Yugoslavia – Soviet Union Match,
Belgrade (3), 1961

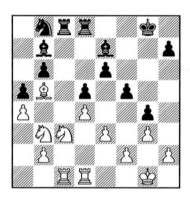

34.♔g2!!

The position is equal, but the way Petrosian poses his opponent problems is remarkable.

34...♔f7?!

34...♘d7! 35.h3 ♘f6 was stronger.

35.h3 h5 36.♖h1 ♖h8

36...♗f6 would be simpler.

37.♘e2! ♖xc1?

This exchange helps the knight come into play. After 37...♗d6 or 37...♗c6 38.♗xc6 ♘xc6 39.hxg4 fxg4 40.♘f4 h4 Black should be able to live with his small disadvantage.

38.♘bxc1 ♗f6

After 38...gxh3+ 39.♖xh3 ♗d6 (39...♘a6 40.♘f4) 40.♘d3 ♘a6 41.♘df4 ♘c7 42.♗d3 ♗c6 Black would lose a pawn but it would not

be over, as Black has chances to swap pawns on the queenside.

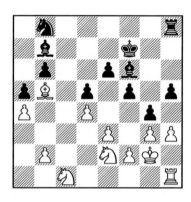

39.♘d3

The knights are threatening. Petrosian's knights often dominated his opponents' bishops.

39...gxh3+?

A careless capture. Now Black's position falls apart. After 39...♔e7! 40.♘ef4 ♔d6 Black would have chances to hold.

40.♖xh3 h4 41.gxh4 ♖xh4 42.♘e5+ ♔g8

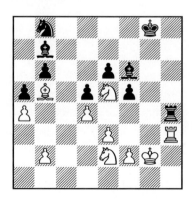

43.♖g3+!

This check is a killer and Ciric loses material.

43...♗g7 44.♘f4 ♖h6 45.♘d7 ♘c6 46.♘h5 ♖xh5 47.♘f6+ ♔f7 48.♘xh5 ♗h6 49.♖h3 ♔g6 50.♔g3 1–0

In the fourth round, Petrosian was Black against Matulovic. He handled the Caro-Kann Panov in a risky way. The Yugoslav was a fine positional player. Tigran himself would probably have enjoyed making White's moves, but instead he was constantly on the receiving end. After a while, Matulovic allowed Petrosian to improve his knight. The Armenian managed to equalise and they agreed to a draw after time control.

Game 103

Bertok, Mario – Petrosian, Tigran
Yugoslavia – Soviet Union Match,
Belgrade (5), 1961

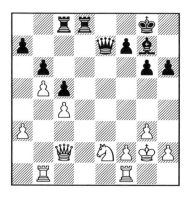

22...g5!?

Petrosian prevents the knight from reaching the d5 outpost. He

probably planned this move five moves earlier.

23.♖bd1

Had Bertok known the future, maybe he would have settled for a slightly worse endgame. 23.♘c3 ♗xc3 24.♕xc3 ♕e4+ (24...♖d4 25.♖fe1) 25.♔g1 ♕d3 26.♕f6 ♖d6 27.♕e7 and White should get away with it.

23...♕e6 24.h3 h5!?

Petrosian plays a move where it is very hard to read what he is doing. After 24...♖e8 25.♖d2 ♕e4+ 26.♕xe4 ♖xe4 27.♖c1 White survives.

25.♖fe1 ♖xd1 26.♖xd1 ♖e8 27.♖d2

After 27.♘g1 ♕e4+ 28.♕xe4 ♖xe4 29.♖d7 White is probably not worse.

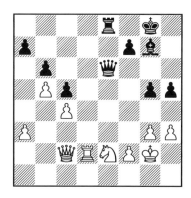

27...♗h6!

What a surprise: the bishop moves to the edge, to a blocked diagonal.

28.♘g1

White has a surprising pawn sacrifice available: 28.g4!? hxg4 (28...h4? 29.♘g1) 29.hxg4 ♕xg4+

30.♘g3 ♗g7 31.♖d5, when he has enough compensation for the pawn and the position would be balanced.

28...♕e4+

Petrosian likes exchanging queens, and here it gives him practical chances.

29.♕xe4 ♖xe4 30.♖c2?

Bertok plays passively. If 30.♖d7 ♖xc4 31.♖xa7 g4 32.hxg4 hxg4 33.♖a6 White is probably not worse.

30...g4 31.hxg4 hxg4 32.♘e2?!

After 32.f3! gxf3+ 33.♘xf3 White would have better chances to hold than Black to win.

32...♔g7 33.a4 ♔g6 34.♔f1 ♗g5 35.♔g2?

White decides to wait, but this stance will lead to disaster.

Good or bad, White should play 35.a5!. After 35...bxa5 36.♖a2 ♗d8 37.♖a4 ♔f5 (37...♗c7?! 38.♘c1) 38.♘c3 ♖d4 39.♔e2 White's fortress may hold.

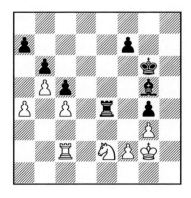

35...♔f5!

The king gets closer to the centre with this somewhat sly move.

36.♔f1 ♖e6!

The rook move allows an invasion by the king. The rook not just vacates the e4-square, but intentionally chooses the 6th rank and not another one.

37.♖a2 ♔e4!

Now the king turns into a monster.

38.♖a3 ♗d2 39.♔g2 ♖f6!

Maybe Bertok missed this neat move, which ruins White's fortress hopes.

40.a5

40.♔f1 ♖f3 wins.

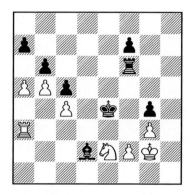

40...bxa5!

Petrosian, just like against Furman, likes doubled edge pawns. By the way, he also had them when he beat Taimanov a few months earlier in the Soviet championship. Later, Karpov would demonstrate similar captures, the game against Wahls in 1992 being a nice example.

41.♘f4 ♗b4 42.♖d3 ♖xf4 43.♖e3+ ♔d4 44.gxf4 ♔xc4 45.♖e7 f6 46.♖xa7 ♔xb5 47.f3 g3

0–1 White resigned as he could do nothing but watch the a-pawn walk all the way to a1.

Petrosian's 4 points out of 5 games was a formidable result, and his play was impressive as well. Interestingly, the match was surprisingly close, with the Yugoslavs losing only to 28.5-31.5, so Petrosian's contribution made the difference.

Zurich

At the end of May, Petrosian participated in a tournament in Zurich. He started as Black against Gligoric and equalised in the Orthodox Queen's Gambit. In the early middlegame, Svetozar had a small initiative, but it then swung to Tigran. Gligoric simplified to a rook vs. rook and bishop ending with no pawns. Petrosian tried to win for almost 40 moves, but Gligoric held. In the second round, Petrosian played the variation named after him in the Queen's Indian. Keres surprisingly played a bad line and Petrosian had a clear advantage, but he allowed too much counterplay. The great Estonian won an exchange. Paul needed another 25 moves to convert his advantage. In the third round, Petrosian as Black played the Scheveningen versus Bhend. In the ♗e2 line, the Swiss player chose an unfortunate moment to start an attack with g4. Petrosian took control with a nice d5 break in the centre; you can see it in the analysis of the 1946 Dunaev game. Bhend resigned after Petrosian's 28th move. In the fourth round, Petrosian was White against Matulovic. He got no advantage in a Benko Gambit type of opening. The position remained equal, and they agreed to a draw after Black's 32nd move. In the fifth round, Christoffel as White sacrificed an exchange at the end of the opening. Petrosian neutralised his play and he needed 58 moves to win the game. Petrosian's next opponent was Lombardy. The young American chose as Black the Queen's Gambit Accepted. Black got a solid, but passive position. Lombardy sacrificed a pawn. Petrosian won the game flawlessly. In the seventh round, Petrosian was Black against Keller. He equalised with a King's Indian, and the position was balanced for a long time. The Swiss player allowed Tigran the bishop pair. Petrosian took control before time control, and Keller resigned after playing his 59th move. In round 8, Petrosian was White against Lothar Schmid, who played the Modern Benoni. Tigran gained an advantage in the opening, and won the game instructively. The final part of the game can be seen in the It's Your Move chapter. In the ninth round, Petrosian was Black against Walther; he played the g6 line in the Caro-Kann Panov. They reached a queenless middlegame with the Swiss player accepting an isolated d4-pawn. Tigran won the game in a neat fashion. In the penultimate round, Tigran was White against Kupper, and his Swiss opponent played the Nimzo-Indian. It looked like the spectators would witness another Petrosian positional masterpiece, but strangely he gave away a pawn for nothing. Interestingly, this time his opponent had doubled edge pawns. Petrosian still tried to win, and perhaps at some point he could have played better, but Kupper's stubborn play earned him a draw. In the last round, Petrosian as Black played the King's Indian against Larsen. Black had a pleasant game, although Larsen's position was alright for a long time. Then, around the 30th move, the game turned increasingly difficult for him. By time control, Petrosian was winning and the Dane resigned after Tigran's 44th move. Meanwhile, Keres agreed a quick draw as White against Walther to secure first place.

Petrosian finished the event with 8.5 points out of 11, half a point behind Keres and 1.5 points more than the third-placed Gligoric.

European Team Championship, Oberhausen

The European Championship was held in Oberhausen in West Germany at the end of June. Petrosian was on board four, behind Botvinnik, Tal and Keres. The Soviet and Yugoslav teams were seeded to the final, which was a double round robin event.

Petrosian did not play in the first round against Spain. In the second round, he was Black against Bertok of Yugoslavia. He showed a positive and new aspect to his game, introducing a new idea in the Modern Benoni by developing his knight to e7. He got an edge in the opening and soon after time control won the game comfortably. In the third round, he was White against Jansa of Czechoslovakia. He played the Rossolimo Sicilian and got no advantage, but the young Czech made an ambitious move that weakened his king. Jansa resigned after Tigran's 29th move. In his third game, he was Black against Bilek. The Hungarian played the Sozin Variation against the Classical Sicilian. Bilek made two weak moves in the sharp opening and resigned after Petrosian's 19th move. In the fifth round, Petrosian chose a side-line in the Spanish Open as White against Teschner of West Germany. His harmless line brought him no advantage. Later, he was able to cause some problems, but Teschner found a remarkable fortress and drew. In the next game, he was White against Spain's Albareda. He got a nice advantage in the Benoni, but attacked a bit too early. They swapped queens, and though Tigran pressed for a long time, he had to settle for a draw. He seemed to have underestimated his opponent, something he rarely did. In round 7, the team played against Yugoslavia for the second time. Petrosian was Black against Matanovic. They played a Caro-Kann Panov, but not much happened in the 22-move draw. In the 8th round, Petrosian was White against Hort in a 1.c4 e5 English Opening. The position was balanced, but at the end of the opening Hort made a very poor move. Petrosian exploited it and won the game convincingly. Hort's resignation came after Tigran's 55th move. In the penultimate round, Petrosian was Black against Barcza of Hungary. He played the King's Indian setup against the English Opening. The Hungarian got a small edge, but Petrosian drew with ease. Petrosian did not play in the last round against Germany.

The Soviet team won the event easily. Petrosian was undefeated, and his 6 points from 8 games was a good result.

Bled

Bled organised a tournament to mark the 30th anniversary of the world class tournament held by the beautiful Slovenian lake. The event started in early September. The line-up was fantastic in 1961 as well.

In the first round, Petrosian was Black against Donner. The Dutchman played the Austrian Variation against his Pirc. Petrosian equalised, they swapped queens and agreed to a draw after Donner's 22nd move. In the second round, Petrosian was White against Parma. Their main-line Nimzo-Indian resulted in a symmetrical pawn structure. Tigran made a careless move. Parma got good attacking chances, but instead of settling for a somewhat better endgame he attacked with an exchange sacrifice. The young Yugoslav exchanged queens at the wrong moment, and another mistake sealed his fate. In the next round, Petrosian was Black against Darga. White played the ♗e2 line against the Scheveningen. Petrosian carried out the traditional ♘d7-f8-g6 manoeuvre. Then he played e5, they exchanged a lot, and in the endgame White was somewhat better when they agreed to a draw after White's 23rd move. Petrosian was White against Bisguier in round 4. The American played the Semi-Tarrasch. Tigran's opening was disappointing and he was unable to exert pressure. Black was slightly better when peace broke out after Black's 20th move. In round 5, Petrosian was Black against Germek. White looked for a draw by exchanging queens early in the Old Indian. Germek's plan did not work well, however, as Petrosian's superior playing strength brought him down. The end of the game can be seen in the It's Your Move chapter.

Game 104

**Petrosian, Tigran –
Pachman, Ludek**
30th Anniversary Tournament,
Bled (6), 1961

18.♖e4 ♖d8 19.♕xf6+!!

A fabulous sacrifice, which leads to checkmate. It is a bit of a pity that this sacrifice could have been played one move earlier as well. Petrosian's 18th move was still winning, though.

**19...♔xf6   20.♗e5+   ♔g5
21.♗g7!! 1–0** Pachman resigned without waiting for checkmate.

In round 7, Petrosian was Black against Portisch. The Hungarian grandmaster handled Petrosian's Old Benoni with g6 very well. However, later in the middlegame he allowed Tigran to equalise. Close to time control and probably in time trouble, Tigran blundered a piece and resigned. In the 8th round, Petrosian was White against Najdorf. They played a Saemisch King's Indian where Petrosian obtained a pleasant position. In the middlegame, the position reached a balance, but as they approached time control Najdorf chose a slow plan. Tigran decisively invaded on the queenside and Najdorf lost on time in a hopeless position. In the 9th round, Petrosian was Black against Ivkov. They played a ♗g5 Najdorf with ♗c4. The Yugoslav player got really aggressive, sacrificing a piece. Petrosian offered a draw after his 15th move. The position was wild, and objectively White was better, but Ivkov accepted the draw offer. Petrosian's next opponent was Tal. Tigran changed his white line against the King's Indian and opened the centre. Tal offered a draw after his 17th move, which Tigran accepted, and the position was indeed even. In the 11th round, Petrosian played the French. Olafsson got a small advantage in the 3.♘c3 ♗b4 line. Tigran managed to equalise, and soon after Olafsson lost a pawn. The Icelandic grandmaster launched an attack, but lost the game after Black's 32nd move. In the next game, Petrosian was White against Geller. Tigran deviated from his Tal game, and they agreed to a draw after Efim's 16th move. In the 13th round, Tigran was Black against Matanovic. It was a Tarrasch French with 5...♕xd5. They exchanged queens early and played in an equal position, but neither player was able to create winning chances.

Game 105

Petrosian, Tigran – Bertok, Mario
30th Anniversary Tournament,
Bled (14), 1961

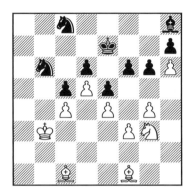

43.♗h3

Perhaps this was Petrosian's sealed move. Black is very passive, his h8 bishop can't move, and the b6 knight has to cover the a4–square. But it is not easy to penetrate Black's position.

43...♔d7

Closing the kingside with 43...g5? is not worth it because White gets the f5 outpost. 44.♗d2 ♔d7 (44...♔f7 45.♘f5 ♔f8 46.♗a5 and White wins) 45.♗a5 ♔c7 46.♘f5 ♔b7 47.♗xb6 ♔xb6 and White wins by transferring the bishop to a4 and invading on e8. 48.♔a4 ♔a6 49.♗f1 ♔b6 50.♗d3 ♔a6 51.♗c2 ♔b6 52.♔a3 ♔c7 53.♗a4 and White invades and wins.

44.♗d2 ♘e7 45.g5+

Petrosian opens up the kingside. As the bishop can always move to e6, the black king can't defend the queenside.

45...♔e8 46.♗a5! ♘ec8

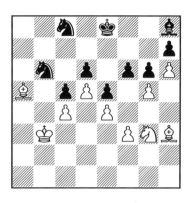

47.♘h1!

After tying up Black's knight, Petrosian finds a somewhat surprising move for his knight.

47...fxg5 48.♘f2 ♗f6 49.♗g4!

One may think that Bertok just moved with no aim, but Petrosian figures out his idea and prevents the freeing of the f6–bishop with the g4 pawn sac.

49...♗d8 50.♘h3 ♗f6 51.♗d2

So the knight went to the corner to recapture the g5–pawn.

51...♘e7

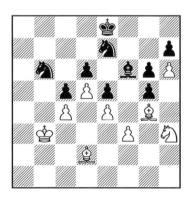

52.♘xg5

Petrosian feels so well when to choose bishops and when to choose knights. White still has to invade.

52...♗xg5 53.♗xg5 ♔f7 54.♗d2

Petrosian changes his focus. He now wants to throw the b6–knight off balance.

54...♘ec8

Bertok steps into losing simplifications. If Black just waited with 54...♔e8 then White possibly has several ways to win. Here is one: 55.♗e6! and both of Black's knights are paralysed.

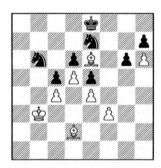

a) 55...♔d8 56.♗a5 ♔c7 57.♗f7 ♔b7 58.♗d2 ♔c7 59.♗g5 ♔d7 60.♗f6 (60.♗xe7?? ♔xe7 61.♗xg6 ♔f6 and Black would survive with a fortress) 60...♘bc8 (60...♔d8 61.♗xg6) 61.♔a4 and the white king invades on the queenside. In addition, White could add more power by playing f4 as well.

b) 55...♔f8 56.♗a5 (56.f4 wins as well: 56...exf4 57.♗xf4 ♘ec8 58.♗xc8 ♘xc8 59.♔a4 ♔e7 60.♔b5 ♔d7 61.e5 and White wins the c-pawn soon) 56...♘ec8 57.♗xc8 ♘xc8 58.♔a4 ♔e7 59.♔b5 ♔d7 60.♗d2 ♘e7 61.♗g5 and the bishop paralyses the knight.

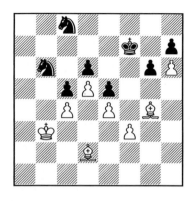

55.♗xc8!

Exchanging the knight wins, as the white king invades decisively.

55...♘xc8 56.♗g5!

Placing the bishop on this diagonal makes sure the knight will not win the h6–pawn.

56...♘b6 57.♗d8 ♘c8 58.♔a4 ♔e8 59.♗g5 ♔d7 60.♔b5 ♔c7

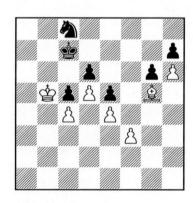

61.♔a6

Black is in zugzwang.

61...♘b6

Moving to the corner loses quickly as well. 61...♔b8 62.♗d8 ♘a7 (62...♔a8 63.♗c7) 63.♗c7+ and the pawn ending is easily won.

62.♗d8+ 1–0

In the 15th round, Petrosian was Black against Trifunovic. The Yugoslav player sought a draw, and Petrosian didn't mind. They played just 19 moves in the Queen's Gambit Accepted. In the 16th round, Petrosian was White against Udovcic. He got a clear edge in a Benoni, then Udovcic sacrificed a pawn for virtually nothing. The Yugoslav player did well to get to a 4-rooks ending and he lasted till Tigran's 71st move. In the 17th round, Tigran was Black against Keres, who trailed him by half a point. They played a main-line Caro-Kann and White's initiative was neutralised by exchanging queens. They agreed a draw after Tigran's 17th move.

Here are the leaders' standings before the 18th round: Tal 13.5 points, Fischer and Gligoric 12, Petrosian 11.5, and Keres 11. In the 18th round, he was Black against Fischer, while

Gligoric was White against Keres. Petrosian played the 4...♘d7 Caro-Kann. He played originally, risked and lost, and a good part of the game can be seen in the commentary to the Matanovic-Petrosian 1959 game. In the last round, he was White against Gligoric. He had to beat him to catch his opponent in the cross-table. Tigran went for a slow 1.c4 c5 English, developing with g3, ♗g2, ♘ge2, and b3. Gligoric started to experience problems when he unnecessarily gave up the two bishops. Black sacrificed one pawn and then another, but was unable to create play and resigned after Petrosian's 32nd move.

Petrosian finished the event with 12.5 points. He won 8 games, drew 9 and lost two. He was joint-third with Keres and Gligoric; they scored two points fewer than the winner Tal and one fewer than Fischer.

Soviet Team Cup, Tashkent

In early October, Petrosian participated in the Soviet Team Cup in Tashkent. In the preliminary group he played three games, though the order of these is not certain.

He was White against Cherepkov. His opponent was well prepared against his 1.d4 ♘f6 2.♘f3 e6 3.♗g5 opening and Black got a slight space advantage. The position simplified to a slightly worse 4-rooks ending. Tigran fell asleep and surprisingly lost. He got a taste of his own medicine, with his opponent playing in a way that he himself usually played to win games. In another round, Spartak played against the Armenian team. Mnatsakanian played the 3.e5 Caro-Kann very aggressively. Petrosian's counterpunch was strong and his 24th move triggered his opponent's resignation. Petrosian was also White against Suetin. Black gave up the two bishops voluntarily. Suetin was mistakenly ready to exchange all major pieces. However, Petrosian's advantage continued to grow, and in the end he simplified into an easily winning same-coloured bishops ending.

In the first round of the final, he was White against Geller. He played 5.♗e2 0-0 6.d5 against the King's Indian. Geller continued with normal moves, but Petrosian played a horrible h4 in the opening and from then on he struggled badly. He resigned after Geller's 50th move. In his next game, Petrosian was Black against Tal. The great Misha played a main-line Caro-Kann a bit awkwardly. Petrosian could safely castle short, but risked castling long, on the opposite side. That gave Tal a clear edge, but Tal went wrong and Petrosian took control. Still, his advantage in the endgame was not enough to win. In the third game, he was White against Smyslov. Petrosian after 1.c4 ♘f6 2.♘f3 b6 played 3.d3, and Smyslov of course equalised. They reached a hanging pawns position, where Petrosian made a very optimistic attacking move that allowed a combination. He soon made another mistake and was lost. Interestingly, Smyslov opted for a rook ending one pawn up instead of a queen endgame with a two-pawn advantage. Tigran resigned after time control. In the fifth game, he returned to his normal style, and he was White against Stein in a King's Indian. Stein buried his bishop on a8 for an attack, and Petrosian punished him for taking too much risk. In the last game, Petrosian was Black against Korchnoi. It was a 3.♘c3 ♘f6 4.♗g5 dxe4 5.♘xe4 ♗e7 6.♗xf6 gxf6 French, where they both castled long. Petrosian played b5, but he was soon struggling on the queenside. Tigran's resilience was enough to avoid resignation until the 68th move.

Petrosian was impatient in this team event; he scored 3 wins, 1 draw and 4 losses. It was a long time since he had finished an event with a minus score. This was disappointing even if one takes into consideration that the players who beat him were mainly world class opponents. Maybe it was a good lesson; he was able to find out how far he could go with risking to win.

Petrosian's results in 1961

Soviet Championship Final, Moscow	+9 = 9 – 1	13.5/19 1st place
Moscow Team Championship	+2 = 1 – 1	2.5/4
Yugoslavia – Soviet Union Match, Belgrade	+3 = 2 – 0	4/5
Zurich	+7 = 3 – 1	8.5/11 2nd place
European Team Championship, Oberhausen	+4 = 4 – 0	6/8
Bled	+8 = 9 – 2	12.5/19 3rd-5th place
Soviet Team Championship, Moscow	+3 = 1 – 4	3.5/8
Altogether	**+ 36 = 29 – 9**	**50.5/74**

Note that Shekhtman gives a different order of events, but we employ the order given in the database.

1962

Interzonal Tournament, Stockholm

Petrosian was about to face the toughest year of his career. Had one asked what would have been the more difficult task, to win through the Candidates events or beat the 51-year-old semi-retired champion in a long match, probably it was the former. The interzonal started in the Swedish capital at the end of January.

Petrosian started as White against Olafsson. He did not produce any surprise, but played 1.d4 ♘f6 2.♘f3 e6 3.♗g5. The Icelandic grandmaster was so well prepared, however, that Tigran was unable to equalise. By move 20 Olafsson was almost winning. Then Petrosian decided to try and win a pawn, and his position was clearly lost. However, a miracle happened. For several moves, virtually any move would have been winning for Olafsson, but maybe he was already short of time. Petrosian equalized and in the end Fridrik blundered a back rank checkmate. Yes, Petrosian was very lucky, but his formidable results in recent years probably weighed on Olafsson's mind and thereby contributed to his time trouble. In the second round, Stein as White aggressively played a main-line against the Caro-Kann, and after Petrosian's 18th move they drew the game. Tigran had a bye in round 3. In the fourth round, Petrosian was White against Geller, and they played the Petrosian Variation of the King's Indian. White obtained a clear advantage, but after Efim's 22nd move they agreed to a draw. Maybe Petrosian was too nervous, or maybe they had agreed the draw in advance. Perhaps, too, Geller wanted to mislead future opponents, or simply played carelessly. In round 5, Korchnoi opened with 1.e4, and in the main-line Caro-Kann exchanged Tigran's g6 bishop with ♘e2 and ♘f4. Petrosian strangely took a huge risk by castling long. One gets the impression that the tension was too much for him. However, Korchnoi went wrong and the game ended in a draw. In the sixth round, he was White against Filip. He obtained a small edge but went for a sharp confrontation; he created an isolated pawn in the Czechoslovakian player's camp, but at the cost of a misplaced knight on h3. They agreed to a draw after Filip's 21st move. In round 7, Petrosian was Black against Bolbochan. The Argentinian player opened the centre in a 1.c4 c5 English Opening, and the position simplified into a clear draw. Until this point, Petrosian was hardly recognisable. Partially perhaps because he was a favourite, and perhaps also because Petrosian knew that he would not have that many chances to become the challenger. In the 8th round, he was White against Bertok.

Game 106

Petrosian, Tigran – Bertok, Mario
Stockholm Interzonal (8), 1962
Queen's Gambit Accepted

1.d4 d5 2.c4 dxc4 3.♘f3 ♘f6 4.♘c3 a6 5.e3

Petrosian doesn't want to play a sacrificial line.

5...e6 6.♗xc4 c5 7.0-0 b5 8.♗b3 ♗b7 9.♕e2 ♘bd7 10.♖d1 ♗d6 11.e4 cxd4 12.♖xd4 ♗c5 13.♖d3

Other games reached this position in 1961, but Veresov was the first to play this move.

13...♘g4 14.♗g5 ♕b6

15.♘d5

Petrosian follows theory.

15...♕a5?

It would be interesting to know whether Bertok had analysed this at home, or improvised with this new move.

a) 15...exd5. Taking the piece is possible. 16.exd5+ ♔f8 17.d6 ♔g8 18.♗xf7+ (18.♕e7 ♖f8 19.♕xd7 ♘xf2 20.♗xf7+ would lead to a

repetition) 18...♔xf7 19.♕e7+ ♔g6 20.♕xd7 ♗xf2+ 21.♔h1 ♗c8 22.♕e7 ♗f5 and the position would be unclear.

b) 15...♗xd5 16.exd5 e5 (16...♘xf2 17.dxe6 ♘xd3+ 18.♔f1 fxe6 19.♕xd3 ♗e7 Koblencs, A – Klovans, J, Riga, 1962, 20.♗xe7 ♔xe7 21.♖e1 and White would be somewhat better) 17.♗h4 0-0 18.♘g5 ♘gf6 19.♘e6 fxe6 20.dxe6 ♔h8 21.exd7 and White was a bit better, Veresov, G – Suetin, A, Novgorod, 1961.

16.♖f1

16.♗h4! This bishop move would be stronger. After 16...b4 (16...♘ge5 17.♘xe5 ♘xe5 18.♖c3 ♖c8 19.♘f6+ and Black would be in trouble) 17.♗a4 ♕xa4 18.♘c7+ ♔f8 19.♘xa8 ♗xa8 20.♖c1 White would win.

16...♖c8 17.♘f4 ♘ge5

17...♗xf2+ 18.♖xf2 ♘xf2 19.♕xf2 (19.♖d6 ♘c5 brings huge complications) 19...♖c1+ 20.♖d1 and the position would be balanced.

18.♘xe5!

18.♘h5! would also be strong, as if 18...0-0 then 19.♘xe5 ♘xe5 20.♖g3 would win.

18...♘xe5 19.♖h3

After 19.♘h5! ♘xd3 20.♘xg7+ ♔d7 21.♕xd3+ ♔c7 22.♗xe6 fxe6 23.♗f4+ ♔b6 24.♘xe6 White's attack would be huge.

19...♘c4?

White is winning after this mistake, as Black will no longer have a piece on the kingside. 19...♕b4 20.♘h5 (or 20.♘xe6 fxe6 21.♗xe6 ♗d4 22.♖d1 and Black would be living dangerously) 20...♖g8 21.♖c3 and White would have a promising position as Black could no longer castle. Or 19...h6 20.♕h5 g6 21.♕e2 ♗e7 22.♗xh6 and Black stabilises his position, but it costs a pawn.

20.♖d1 ♕b6

20...0-0 21.♗f6 would be decisive.

21.♘h5!

Petrosian takes the castling option away from Black.

21...♖g8 22.♖hd3

22.♗xc4 bxc4 23.♗f6 would win as well.

22...♘d6 23.e5 ♘e4

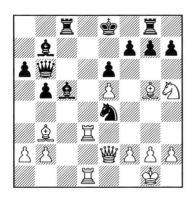

24.♗e3!

Now Black's position falls apart

faster than if White had won the queen with 24.♖d8+. White has one more rook in play.

24...♗xe3 25.♖xe3 ♕c6 26.♕g4 ♕e7 27.♖de1 f5

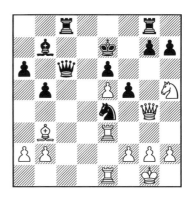

28.exf6+

Black defended the knight, but his king remains wide open.

28...gxf6 29.♕h3 f5

Or 29...♘g5 30.♖xe6+ ♔f8 31.♖xf6+ ♕xf6

32.♕xc8+! ♗xc8 33.♖e8+!! would win, whereas after 33.♘xf6 ♘f3+ Black would still resist.

30.f3 ♘g5 31.♕xf5 ♖cf8 32.♖xe6+ ♘xe6 33.♖xe6+ ♔d8 34.♕d3+ 1–0 Bertok has had enough and resigns.

The win had a calming effect on Tigran. In the ninth round, Petrosian was Black against Uhlmann, and they were content with a 17-move draw. In the 10th round, Petrosian was White against Teschner. He played a reversed King's Indian. The position was equal for a long time, but Tigran gained a small edge after the German player swapped queens. Closer to time control, Teschner missed Petrosian's threat and lost a pawn. He resigned after time control when he was going to lose another one. In the 11th round, Petrosian was Black against Benko in a Bogo-Indian. Tigran carelessly exchanged a pawn on d4. From then on, Benko's position was pleasant. The game then turned worse for Tigran, but he offered a draw after his 25th move and he was probably relieved when the American ex-Hungarian accepted it. In the 12th round, he was White against Aaron. He got a nice advantage in the 1.c4 e5 English. The Indian player gave away a pawn, and resigned on move 49. In the 13th round, Petrosian was Black against Portisch. The Hungarian grandmaster played a pawn sacrificing line against the Queen's Gambit Accepted. Tigran did not take it and equalised. They agreed to a draw after Lajos's 21st move in an equal position, when Tigran could have maybe played on. In round 14 against Bilek, Petrosian as White withdrew his knight to c2 in the Maroczy Bind. He looked for a prolonged fight by keeping pieces on the board. His plan worked and the Hungarian made a poor active move; from then on, Petrosian's structure was better. After Bilek unnecessarily exchanged queens, his position started to fall apart; the Hungarian played on for some time, but had to resign after Petrosian's 50th move. In the next round, he was Black against Barcza, and was happy to draw after the Hungarian's 13th move. In the 16th round, Petrosian had the white pieces against Bisguier. He gained an edge in the Orthodox Queen's Gambit after he carried out a combination resulting in his having a queen and two pawns versus three minor pieces. Soon after, in an unclear position, the American offered a draw, and Petrosian accepted it. It was smart to offer a draw against such a strong player when there was more chance than normal that Petrosian would agree to it. A draw offer has many elements, and Bisguier cleverly tested Petrosian's judgment. In the 17th round, Petrosian was Black against Fischer; he played a safe line of the 3.♘c3 French and easily held a slightly worse position. They agreed to a draw after Tigran's 40th move. In the 18th round, Petrosian was White against Pomar. The Spaniard strangely castled long in a typical Exchange Queen's Gambit. Petrosian won a pawn with a surprising queen move, which can be seen in the It's Your Move chapter. The one-sided game ended soon after time control. In the 19th round, Petrosian was Black against Gligoric. He settled for a slight disadvantage in the Caro-

Kann. Gligoric did not really try to hurt him, then Petrosian equalised by exchanging queens and the game ended in a draw after Gligoric's 30th move.

Game 107

Petrosian, Tigran – Schweber, Samuel
Stockholm Interzonal (20), 1962
King's Indian Defence

1.d4 ♘f6 2.c4 g6 3.♘c3 ♗g7 4.e4 d6 5.♗e2 0-0 6.♗g5
Petrosian rarely played the Averbakh Variation.
6...h6 7.♗e3 e5 8.d5 c6

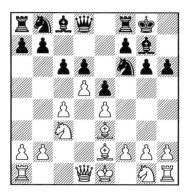

9.h4!
Petrosian plays a new move in a rare line.
9...cxd5
If 9...h5 White would probably place his knight on g5.
10.cxd5 ♘bd7 11.h5 g5
After 11...♘c5 12.♗xc5 dxc5 13.hxg6 fxg6 14.♕b3 White's advantage would be small.

12.f3
Petrosian gets ready to close the kingside.
12...a6 13.g4 b5

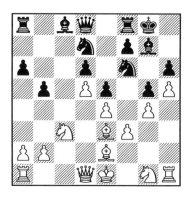

14.a4!
White weakens Black's queenside.
14...b4 15.♘b1 a5?
Black should try 15...♘b6!? with the idea of sacrificing on d5. After 16.♘h3 (if 16.a5 ♘bxd5 17.exd5 e4 Black would be fine) 16...♖e8!? the position would be playable for Black, but if 16...♗b7 then 17.♘d2 would still be unpleasant.
16.♘d2 ♘c5

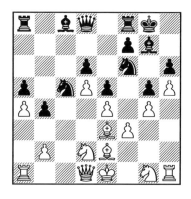

17.♗xc5!

Petrosian often gives up a bishop for a knight. Here, the c4–square comes with it.

17...dxc5 18.♗b5!

The bishop saves his knights.

18...♗b7 19.♘e2 ♘e8

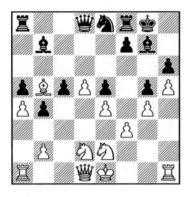

20.♗xe8!

Now he even gives up his second bishop. This eliminates Black's only piece which has a chance of obtaining some activity. White's advantage is winning.

20...♖xe8 21.♘c4 ♗a6 22.♕b3 ♕f6 23.♖c1 ♗f8 24.♘g3

Petrosian drags the b7–bishop to defending the f5–square.

24...♗c8 25.0-0 ♖d8 26.♔g2 ♖a7

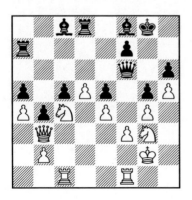

27.♖f2

Tigran gets ready to attack the c5–pawn.

27...♔h7 28.♖fc2 ♕a6?

Giving up the e5–pawn for free worsens Black's position. If 28...♗d7 perhaps Petrosian would play 29.♘h1 to transfer his knight to d3.

29.♘xe5! ♖c7 30.♘c4 ♗g7 31.♕d3 ♔g8 32.♖d2

32.e5 ♗e6 33.d6 would win as well.

32...♖e7

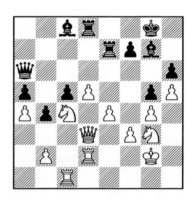

33.e5!

After this move, Black either gets choked by White's central pawns or reaches a hopeless ending.

33...♗xe5 34.♘xe5 ♖xe5 35.♕xa6 ♗xa6 36.♖xc5 ♗c8 37.♖xa5

White wins the second pawn; it is all over for Black.

37...f5 38.gxf5 ♗xf5 39.♘xf5 ♖xf5 40.♖b5 ♖df8 41.d6 ♖xb5 42.axb5 ♔f7 43.d7 1–0

In round 21, Petrosian as Black drew with Yanofsky in 10 moves. In the 22ⁿᵈ round, Petrosian was White against German. He got no advantage out of the opening in a 1.c4 c5 English but he gained a small edge when they swapped queens. He soon won a pawn and went on to convert his advantage in 65 moves. In the last round, he agreed a quick draw against Cuellar.

Petrosian ended the event with 15 points out of 22 games. He finished joint-second with Geller. Petrosian won 8 and drew 14 games, remaining undefeated. Fischer won the event, scoring 17.5 points, 2.5 more than the Soviet stars. Kotov was another player who once dominated the interzonal but did not then do well at the Candidates event. Actually, at the soccer world cup it is not usually beneficial to play well at the early stages either.

Despite his high level of creative play, this was a modest result for our hero. Nevertheless, he qualified, and at world championships only that matters.

Candidates Tournament, Curacao

The Candidates Tournament was held in Curacao. Playing the most important event in a place with a tropical climate was new for all participants. The competition, which lasted for almost two months, started in early May. Five of the eight players were from the Soviet Union, which was obviously too many. Tal and Fischer were the main pre-tournament favourites; the former had been the world champion a year earlier and had won the Bled tournament, while Fischer had won the interzonal by a big margin. Euwe, though, predicted a win for Petrosian. The fact that he had comfortably qualified despite playing at way below his best level gave Armenian fans reason to hope. Geller and Korchnoi were really strong, too, and were they to be in good form they had a chance.

Keres at the age of 46 was unlikely to last the pace in such a long event. Benko and Filip did not really have a chance of winning, but of course they were good enough to beat anybody. It would be interesting to know just how aware the Soviet players were of the seriousness of Tal's illness. In the first round, Petrosian faced Tal, one of the few players whom Tigran had not yet beaten. We look at that game.

Game 108

Petrosian, Tigran – Tal, Mikhail
Candidates Tournament,
Curacao (1), 1962
Reti Opening

1.c4 ♘f6 2.g3 c6 3.♘f3 d5 4.b3 ♗f5 5.♗a3

According to the database, Petrosian plays a novelty. It allows Black to develop in many different ways.

5...g6 6.d3 ♗g7 7.♘bd2 ♕b6?!

Later Tal usually just castled here, but this time he looks for action at once. 7...a5 or 7...0-0 both look preferable compared with the game move.

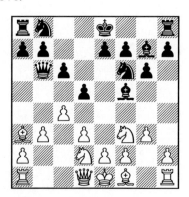

8.♗g2!

Tigran is not scared; he is ready to enter sharp positions.

8...♘g4?! 9.d4! ♘a6

Taking the pawn is bad: 9...♗xd4 10.♘xd4 ♕xd4 11.0-0 and then e.g. 11...dxc4 (11...♘f6 12.cxd5 cxd5 13.♘e4; 11...♘d7 12.cxd5 cxd5 13.e4) 12.♕c1 c3 13.♘f3 ♕g7 14.h3. White would be better in all variations.

10.0-0 ♘b4?!

This will help White to gain space on the queenside. 10...♘f6!? would put the ball back in White's court.

11.♗b2 0-0

11...♘c2? 12.♖c1 ♘xd4? 13.c5 would win a piece, but after 11...a5 12.a3 ♘a6 White's best continuation according to Timman is 13.♗c3 0-0 14.e3 with a solid advantage (*Curacao 1962: The Battle of Minds that Shook the Chess World*, New In Chess, 2005). After 13.♖c1 White would have a small edge.

12.a3 ♘a6 13.♖c1 ♖ad8 14.b4 ♘b8?!

After 14...♘f6 15.♕b3 ♘e4 White's advantage would be rather small.

15.♕b3 ♘f6

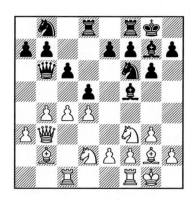

16.a4!

Gaining space on the queenside is strong.

16...♘e4 17.♖fd1 ♘d7 18.cxd5

Playing 18.a5! at once would reduce Black's possibilities. 18...♕a6 (18...dxc4 19.♘xc4) 19.cxd5 cxd5 with a small edge.

18...cxd5 19.a5 ♕d6?

The queen is exposed to a bishop attack here. The black queen has better squares: after 19...♕a6 20.♗f1 ♘df6 21.♘xe4 (21.e3 ♕e6) 21...dxe4 22.d5 White's edge would be small. Or 19...♕b5 20.♗f1 ♘df6 and Black should be able to live with his position.

20.b5 ♘xd2 21.♖xd2 ♖c8 22.♘h4

After 22.♖dd1! ♗h6 23.♗a3 ♕e6 24.e3 White's advantage is decent.

22...♖xc1+

Black would do alright after 22...♗e4 23.f3 ♗h6. Timman mentions 22...♗e6 23.♖xc8 ♖xc8 24.♗a3 ♕c7 25.♗xd5 ♗xd5 26.♕xd5 e6 27.♕d6, but Black is alright thanks to the tactical 27...♕xa5 28.♕xd7 ♖d8.

23.♗xc1

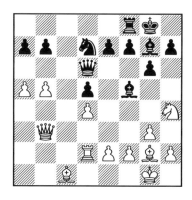

23...♕c7?

This is a big mistake, as Black should keep the bishop.

24.♘xf5 gxf5

Not 24...♕xc1+? as 25.♖d1 would win.

25.♗a3

Timman mentions that after 25.♖c2!? ♕xa5 26.♕xd5 he feels Petrosian was not certain about 26...♕a4. However, White could win by 27.♖c7 or 27.♕xf5.

25...♕xa5

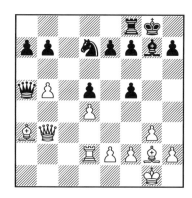

26.♕b4!?

A strong and especially unpleasant move for a player looking for complications. After 26.♖d1 ♘b6 27.♗xe7 ♖e8 28.♗c5 Black's position would be pretty bad as well.

26...♕b6

After 26...♕xb4 27.♗xb4 ♖c8 28.♗xe7 ♖c1+ 29.♗f1 ♗f6 White would be much better, but maybe not winning.

27.♗xd5

If 27.♕xe7 ♘f6 (27...♗xd4 28.♕g5+) 28.♕c5 ♖d8 White's advantage is close to winning.

27...e6 28.♗f3 ♖c8

Or 28...♖d8. The idea of this rook move is to take the sting out of the queen invasion. However, after 29.d5! (after 29.♕a4 ♗f8 30.e3 a6 White's advantage would be similar to the game) 29...♗f8 30.d6 ♘e5 31.♗h5 Black would be in trouble.

29.♕a4!?

Maybe 29.♕e7! is even stronger than Petrosian's continuation: 29...♘f6 30.♕xb7 ♕xb7 31.♗xb7 ♖c7 32.♗c6 a6

a) 33.d5 exd5 (after 33...axb5 34.dxe6 fxe6 35.♗xb5 White has decent winning chances) 34.♗d6 ♖c8 35.♗e5 axb5 36.♗xb5 and White would have excellent winning chances.

b) 33.♗d6! ♖c8 34.bxa6 ♖xc6 35.a7 ♖a6 36.♖c2 ♖xa7 37.♖c8+ ♗f8 38.♗xf8 ♖a1+ 39.♔g2 and it's bad luck for Black. Here, unlike in the game, Black has to push the h-pawn two squares. After 39...h5 40.♗e7+ White simplifies to a winning endgame.

29...♖c7

After 29...♗f8!?, had Petrosian played the same move that he played in the game, it would have given Black good drawing chances. But after 30.d5! (30.♗xf8 ♔xf8 31.♖a2 ♘f6 32.♕xa7 ♕xb5 33.♕xb7 ♕xb7 34.♗xb7 ♖c7 – probably having the knight and bishop on the board would increase Black's chances to hold, though Timman thinks this position would still offer White good winning chances) 30...♘e5 31.dxe6 fxe6 32.♗xf8 ♖xf8 Black's position would be rather unpleasant.

30.♔g2

After 30.d5! ♗f8 31.d6 ♖c8 32.e3 Black would be lost. Let's

cite Averbakh (Quality Chess's translation): "These last few moves are characteristic of Petrosian. He conducts the fight in a manner that guarantees him total safety, even though playing for complications might have been the quickest way to the goal." Very few people knew Tigran as well as Yuri.

30...a6

30...♗f8!?.

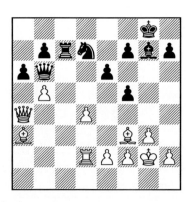

31.bxa6

After 31.d5 ♕xb5 32.♕h4 ♖c8 33.dxe6 fxe6 34.♕e7 Black should lose.

31...♕xa6

31...bxa6?? 32.♖b2 ♕xd4? would lose quickly to 33.♖b8+ ♘f8 34.♖xf8+.

32.♕xa6 bxa6 33.e3 a5 34.♖a2 ♖a7

After 34...♗f8 35.♗xf8 ♔xf8 36.♖xa5 ♘f6 perhaps it was preferable to keep the knight.

35.♗b4 a4 36.♗c6 ♗f8 37.♗xf8 ♔xf8

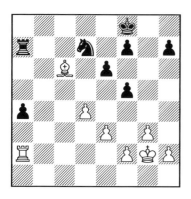

38.℞xa4

White wins a pawn, but the game is far from over.

38...℞c7

38...℞xa4 39.♗xa4 ♘f6 40.♔f3. Today's commentators can envy people of the future when programs will be able to dissect a position and tell for sure whether White wins or not. I discussed this position with the 8-times Hungarian champion Ferenc Berkes. It caught his imagination and he decided to take a deeper look at the position. I made a summary of his detailed analysis. He is not sure whether White could win, but thinks there is more chance of it being a win than a draw.

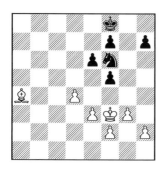

40...♘e4!

The knight aims to get to c3, where it will be surprisingly active. Waiting passively looks almost hopeless, as White carries out g4 and after fxg4 hxg4 White will place the bishop on b3, push the e-pawn to e5 and follow up with pushing the f-pawn to the fifth rank. 41.♗c2 ♘c3 42.♔f4 ♘e2+ 43.♔g5 ♔g7 44.h3

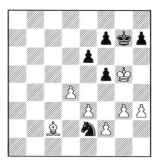

a) 44...♘g1 45.♔h4 ♘f3+ 46.♔h5 ♘g1. This looks sufficient to draw, but White has a remarkable plan. 47.g4!! ♘xh3 48.f4 ♔f6 49.gxf5 exf5 50.♔h4 ♘f2 51.♔g3 ♘g4

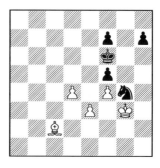

52.e4! h6 53.e5+ ♔e6 54.♗b3+ ♔e7 55.d5 f6 56.d6+ ♔d7 57.♗a4+ ♔e6 58.d7 ♔e7 59.e6+−
b) 44...h6+ 45.♔h5

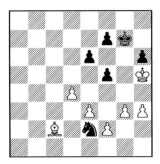

45...♘g1 46.d5! According to Ferenc, this is a stunning idea.

b1) 46...♘xh3 47.d6 ♔f8 48.f3! ♘g5 49.♗d1! ♘h7 50.♔xh6 ♘f6 51.♗a4 ♘d5 52.♔g5!! ♘xe3 53.♔f6 ♘d5+ 54.♔e5 wins as the white king will march to c8.

b2) 46...exd5 47.♗xf5 ♘e2 48.♔g4 ♔f6 49.♗d3 ♘c3 50.♔f4. It is hard to tell whether White's advantage is enough to win. If Black can hold it will require a really turgid defence.

39.♗xd7

Petrosian simplifies to a rook ending. In the case of 4 pawns versus 3 it is useful for the defender to have doubled f-pawns, and maybe here as well.

39...♖xd7 40.♔f3 ♔g7 41.♔f4 ♔f6?

Maybe Black could survive by defending the 8th rank with 41...♖d8.

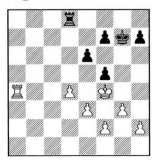

42.♔g5 (42.h3 ♖b8 [42...h5 43.♔g5; 42...♔f6 43.g4] 43.g4 fxg4 44.hxg4 ♖b5 45.c4 h5 46.♖c5 ♖b2 and Black seems to hold) 42...h6+ 43.♔h5 ♖d5 44.♔h4 ♖d8. It is really hard to tell whether White wins here.

According to Timman 41...♖b7! is the correct defence. After 42.h3 (if 42.♖a2 ♔f6 43.h3 h5 the Dutch grandmaster feels that White has practical chances, but the position should be a draw) 42...♖b2 43.f3 h5 44.♔g5 ♖f2 Black seems to hold.

42.h3

According to Timman's tournament book, this was the sealed move.

42...h5?!

It is a bit strange that Tal makes a possible mistake right after the sealed move. Perhaps his health was in such poor shape that he was unable to analyse the adjourned game properly. After 42...♖d8 43.g4 fxg4 44.hxg4 h6 45.f3 ♖d7 Black would surely suffer, but maybe could hold. Timman thinks White wins, but he explains that the white rook moves to d7, which is not possible. Maybe he meant ♖d2, but Black could think of placing his rook on the fifth rank and try to carry out h5. We do not know whether the seconds helped either player when the two Soviets adjourned. We found this question so interesting that we asked about it, but were not able to find an answer. Boris Postovsky asked Averbakh for me, but the old grandmaster was unable to remember.

Berkes kindly offered to look into this position in detail. I have abbreviated his discoveries but, in short, he shares Timman's judgment. The essence of his analysis is that White should probably keep the rook on the fourth rank to defend the d-pawn, then the e-pawn would move to e4. His king moves to g3 in order to stop Black from playing ♔g6 and h5, by playing ♔h4. Here is the main line of Berkes' neat analysis:

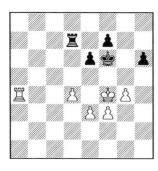

46.e4 ♖d8 47.♔g3! ♖b8 (47...♔g6 48.♔h4 ♖d7 49.f4+−) 48.d5! and according to the Hungarian grandmaster, who analyses this position further, White should win. The position after 48...exd5 49.exd5 can be checked with the Finalgen program. That position is winning for White, and this fact supports the view that Ferenc's evaluation is correct.

43.♖a8 ♖b7?!

This move loses, as it cuts the king off. After 43...♔g6!? 44.♖g8+ ♔h7 45.♖g5 ♔h6 46.h4 ♖d5 Black's

position doesn't fall apart on its own. Maybe he would actually hold it.

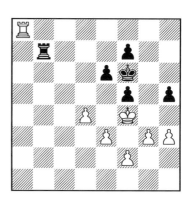

44.♖g8!

Petrosian goes after the h5–pawn by cutting off the king.

44...♖b2 45.♔f3 ♖d2 46.h4 ♔e7
46...♖a2 47.♖g5 ♖a8 48.♖xh5 ♔g6 49.♖g5+ ♔h7 50.g4 f6 51.♖h5+ ♔g6 52.♔g3 with f3 and d5 should win.

47.♖g5 ♔f8

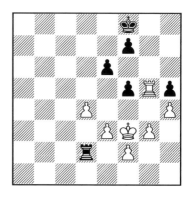

48.♖xh5

White has won a second pawn, but he still has to free his rook.

48...♔g7 49.♖g5+ ♔h7 50.h5
50.g4! f6 51.♖h5+ ♔g6

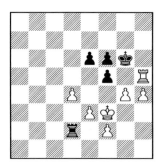

52.gxf5+! ♔xh5 53.fxe6 would win, as Fischer pointed out.

50...♖a2 51.g4

If 51.d5 ♔h6 52.♖g8 ♔xh5 53.♖g7 exd5 54.♖xf7 ♔g6 Black would be very likely to hold.

51...♔h6 52.♖g8 ♔h7

Commentators did not find any improvement for Tal. However, it looks like Black can hold this position with a study-like defence.

52...fxg4+! 53.♖xg4 ♔xh5

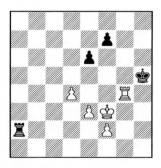

This is an exciting rook ending. The black king is cut off, but the black rook is active. Can it outwit the threatening white king?

a) 54.♖g1 f6! After this move, the black king may move to h6. 55.e4 ♖a3+ (55...♔h6? 56.d5! would win) 56.♔e2 ♖a2+ 57.♔e3 ♖a3+!= This only move holds, whereas 57...♔h6?

58.d5! or 57...♖a5? 58.♔d3! would win for White.

b) 54.♖g7 The rook on the seventh rank is testing, but can't do enough. 54...f6 55.♖e7 ♖a6 56.e4 (56.♔e4 ♔g6=) 56...♔g6 57.♔e3 (57.♔f4 ♖a4!= if it were White to move then f3 or e5 would win) 57...♖a3+! If it were White's move, pushing the f-pawn one or two squares would win. 58.♔e2 (58.♔f4 ♖d3=)

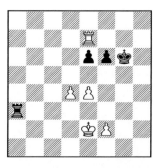

b1.1) 58...♖a2+ 59.♔d3 (59.♔f3 e5=) 59...♖xf2 60.♖xe6 ♔f7=

b1.2) 58...e5 59.dxe5 (59.d5 ♔g5=)

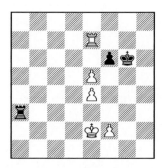

59...f5! 60.♖e6+ ♔g5=

c) 54.♖g2! The rook defends the f2-pawn. This move is more dangerous than it looks.

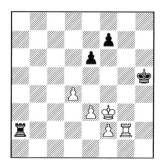

c1) 54...♖d2 55.♖g7 f6 56.♖e7+–

c2) 54...♖a5 Black could try to transfer the rook to f5 and he might survive. 55.♔e4

c2.1) 55...f5+ 56.♔f4 This wins faster than 56.♔d3. Now: 56...♔h6 57.♖g8 ♖a2 (57...♔h7 58.♖e8 ♖a6 59.♔e5 ♖a2 60.♖xe6 ♖xf2 61.d5+–) 58.♔e5 ♖xf2 59.♔xe6 ♖f3 60.d5 ♖xe3+ 61.♔xf5+–

c2.2) 55...♖f5 56.♔d3 The white king reaches the key square (56.f4? ♖a5 [56...f6? 57.♖c2] 57.♖g7 f5+=)

c2.2.1) 56...♔h4

c2.2.1.1) 57.f4 ♔h5 (57...♖a5 58.♖g7 f5 59.♖g5+–) 58.♖c2 ♔g6 59.♖c5 ♖f6 60.♖g5+ ♔h6 61.♔c4+–

c2.2.1.2) 57.e4 ♖f3+ 58.♔e2! (58.♔c4 ♖f4 59.f3 ♖xf3 60.d5 exd5+=) 58...♖a3 59.♖g7 ♖a7 (59...f5 60.e5+–) 60.♔e3 ♔h5 61.d5 e5 62.f4 ♔h6

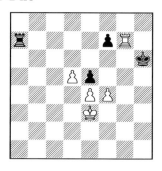

63.♖g3! This prevents Black from checking and taking the f4–pawn. (63.♖g2? ♖a3+ 64.♔f2 exf4=) 63...♖a3+ 64.♔f2 ♖a2+ 65.♔f3 f6 66.fxe5 fxe5 67.♖g8+–

c2.2.2) 56...♔h6 57.♔c4 ♔h7 (57...♖a5 58.e4 f5 59.f3+– or 59.e5+–) 58.e4 ♖f4

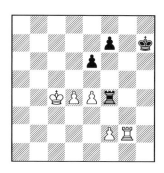

59.f3!! (59.♔d3 ♖f3+) 59...f5 (59...♖xf3 60.d5 exd5+ 61.exd5+–) 60.exf5 ♖xf5 (60...exf5 61.♖h2+!! This traps the rook. 61.♖g3 would win as well) 61.♖e2 ♖f6 (61...♖xf3 62.♖xe6) 62.♔c5 ♔g7 63.♔d6 ♔f7

64.♖e4! (64.♖e1 e5+!!) 64...♖h6 65.♖f4+ ♔e8 66.♖g4 ♖f6 67.f4 ♔f7 (were it again Black to move, then ...♖f5 would hold) 68.♖h4! ♖f5 (68...

♔g7 69.♔e7+−) 69.♖h7+ ♔g6 70.♔xe6 ♖xf4 71.♖d7+−

c3) 54...♔h6 Black is just one tempo short of obtaining the draw. 55.♔e4 f6 (55...♖a3 56.♔e5 ♖a5+ 57.♔f6 ♖f5+ 58.♔e7 ♖f3 59.e4 ♖d3 60.♔xf7 ♖xd4+−)

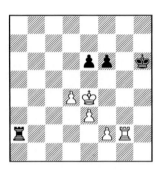

56.♔d3! If Black had managed to stop this move with the rook from d2 or a3, he would have got away with a draw. Now, however, the king reaches the d3-square, although winning from this position still requires quite some skill. 56...f5 57.♔c4 ♖c2+ 58.♔b3 ♖c1 59.♔b2! ♖c8

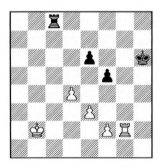

c3.1) 60.f3? Why not start creating a passed pawn? The answer is amazing. 60...♖a8

(60...f4? 61.e4! wins, 60...♖b8+ 61.♔c3

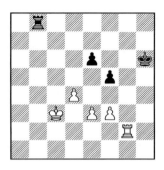

61...♖b1! The rook can start attacking the white pawns. 62.e4 ♖f1 63.♖g3 f4 64.♖h3+ ♔g5 65.d5 exd5 66.exd5=)

61.e4 (61.♔b3 ♖a1!!) 61...fxe4 62.fxe4 ♖a4 63.♖d2 (63.♔c3 e5=) 63...♔g6=

c3.2) 60.♖g1!

c3.2.1) 60...♖c7 61.f3 ♖b7+ 62.♔c3 ♖c7+ 63.♔b4 ♖c2 64.e4 ♖f2 65.e5+−

c3.2.2) 60...♔h5 61.♔b3 ♔h6 62.f3 ♖b8+ 63.♔c4 ♖c8+ 64.♔b4 (64.♔b5? ♖c3!) 64...♖c2 65.e4 ♖f2 66.e5+−

c3.2.3) 60...♖c6 61.f3 ♔h7 62.♔b3 ♖b6+ 63.♔c4 ♖c6+ 64.♔d3 ♖a6 65.e4 ♖a3+ 66.♔e2 fxe4 67.fxe4 ♔h6 68.e5 ♔h7 69.♔d2 ♖f3 (69... ♖b3 70.♖f1+−) 70.♔c2 ♖f8 (70... ♔h6 71.♖g8+−) 71.♔d3 ♖d8 72.♖f1 ♔g7 73.♖f6 ♖e8 74.♔c4 ♖c8+ 75.♔b5 ♖e8 76.♔c5 ♖c8+ 77.♔d6 ♖d8+ 78.♔xe6 ♖xd4 79.♖f7+ ♔g8 (79...♔g6 80.♖f1+−) 80.♖d7! ♖a4 (80...♖f4 81.♔e7) 81.♔e7 ♔g7 (81... ♖a1 82.♖d4! [82.e6? ♔g7!] 82... ♖a7+ 83.♔f6+−) 82.♔e8+ One feels that White wins, but precise play is still required. 82...♔g6 83.♖d6+ (83. e6? ♔f6 84.e7 ♔e6=) 83...♔f5 (83...

♔g7 84.e6+−) 84.e6 ♚e5 85.♖b6 and White would win.

c4) 54...f6 Black still misses a tempo. If the black king stood on h6, it would be a draw.

c4.1) 55.♔e4 ♖d2 or 55...♖a3 would be a draw.

c4.2) 55.e4 ♖a4 56.♔e3 ♖a3+!! 57.♔e2

c4.2.1) 57...♖b3! 58.♖g3 ♖b2+ 59.♔e3 ♖b3+ 60.♔d2 ♖b2+=

c4.2.2) 57...♖c3? 58.♖g3 ♖c2+ (58...♖c4 59.♖d3) 59.♔e3 ♖c3+ 60.♔d2+−

c4.2.3) 57...♔h6! 58.♖g3 ♖a2+! (58...♖a5 59.♔d3 ♖a4 [59...f5 60.exf5+−] 60.♔c3 ♔h7 61.d5+−) 59.♔e3 ♖a3+=

c4.3) 55.d5!! Now it works. Were the black king to stand on h6 then it would not work, and nor would it work if the white king stood on f4! 55...exd5 56.♔f4 ♖a5 (56...♔h6 57.♔f5 ♖a6 58.♖g6+ ♔h7 59.♖xf6+−) 57.♔f5 d4+ 58.♔xf6 d3 59.f3! ♔h4 60.e4!+−

c5) 54...♖a3!! Black's rook takes away the d3-square from the white king. Black wants to push the f-pawn one square. 55.d5 (if any other white

move then pushing the f-pawn one square obtains the draw for Black: 55.♔e4 f6; 55.♔e2 f6; 55.♖g7 f6; 55.♔f4 f6 56.d5 ♖a4+=) 55...exd5 56.♔f4 (56.♖g7 d4) 56...♖a5

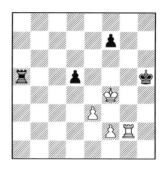

c5.1) 57.♖g7 ♖a2 (57...f6? 58.♖g3+−; 57...♔h6? 58.♖xf7+−) 58.f3 ♖a7 59.♔f5 (59.♖g5+ ♔h6) 59...♔h6 60.♖g2 ♖e7 61.♔f6 ♖e6+ 62.♔xf7 ♖xe3=

c5.2) 57.♖g5+ ♔h6 58.♖g3 ♖b5 59.♔e5 d4+ 60.♔xd4=

c5.3) 57.♔e5 d4+ (57...♔h4=) 58.♔xd4 f6=

Back to the game!

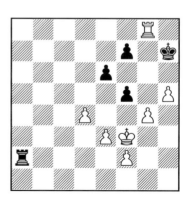

53.♖e8 fxg4+ 54.♔g3 ♔h6

After 54...♔g7 55.♖b8 (55.♖e7 ♖a1) 55...♔h6 56.♖f8 ♔g7 57.♖d8

♖d2 (57...♖b2 58.d5) 58.♖d7 ♖d1 59.d5 exd5 60.♔xg4 White would probably win.

55.♖e7 ♔g7 56.♖c7 ♖b2 57.♖c5 ♔f6

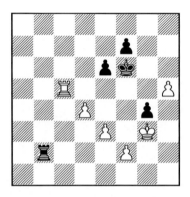

58.d5! ♖b4 59.h6 exd5 60.♖xd5 ♔g6 61.♖d6+ ♔g5 62.h7 ♖b8 63.♖d1 ♖h8 64.♖h1 1–0 Tal lost on time.

Tal played the whole game somewhat optimistically. He probably expected to become champion again, or at least play a match for the title. Had he known what the future would hold, he possibly would have played with more care.

This was Petrosian's first win over Misha. It came at the best moment for Tigran. One can feel that Tal's play was affected by his poor health, but in tournaments only points count. Maybe Tigran was a bit lucky, but one must be good not to let luck slip. Of course, it is sad that Tigran and Misha never played a match against each other (once they played a three player match with Portisch, but they agreed 4 quick draws against each other). It might have been one of the most exciting matches of all time.

In the second round, Petrosian was Black against Korchnoi in a main-line Chigorin Ruy Lopez. Korchnoi was somewhat better for a long time, but was unable to do anything with the position and the game ended in a draw after Victor's 36th move. Petrosian saw 36...e4!, but he did not believe that the size of the advantage was big enough to win. Timman thinks that Petrosian was nervous and before the game he would have been content with a draw.

After the second round, Tal and Fischer both had 0 points. Petrosian must have realised that his chances had improved. Geller and Petrosian made 4 quick draws in the event against each other, starting in round 3, and the evidence suggests they agreed to them in advance, before the tournament (e.g. an interview given by Averbakh with Chess Cafe in 2002). In the fourth round, Petrosian's opponent in a quick draw was Keres. In round 5, Petrosian was Black against Benko. His Modern Defence resulted in a Leningrad Dutch type of position. Petrosian was somewhat better for a long time, but before time control Benko obtained the initiative. Later, he gained a winning position, and Petrosian was very lucky not to suffer his first loss in that Candidates cycle. In the 6th round, Petrosian was White against Fischer and he gained a small edge in the Saemisch King's Indian. Fischer offered a draw after his 25th move. Petrosian could have played on, as he had an edge and Fischer had no chances to win at all, but he accepted the offer. The seventh round, the last of the first cycle, saw Petrosian as Black against Filip. They drew in 14 moves.

After the first cycle, Korchnoi led with 5 points, while Petrosian, Geller and Keres all had 4. In the first game of the second cycle, Tal's illness affected him. In this event, Misha normally played well in the first 4 hours of his games, but dropped his level for the fifth. However, in this game the magician blundered horribly early on. In the 9th round, Petrosian was White against Korchnoi. Petrosian played 3.♕a4+ in the Queen's Gambit Accepted, but Korchnoi fairly easy neutralised Tigran's play. The game was already dead when they agreed to a draw after Korchnoi's 26th move. Then he agreed another quick draw with Geller. Round 11 was another uneventful, quick draw with Keres. In the 12th round, Petrosian was White against Benko. He made a promising exchange sacrifice at the end of the opening. Tigran then won back the exchange a bit too early, Benko equalised, and after Black's 23rd move they agreed to a draw. In round 13, Petrosian played the French against Fischer and got a small edge in the McCutcheon Variation. Bobby was unable to hold. In the 14th round, Petrosian was White against Filip. They played a long line in the ♗f4 Queen's Gambit Declined. Filip

found an imaginative double pawn sacrifice over the board, but soon made a big tactical mistake. Petrosian refuted his move and won it quickly.

At half way in the tournament, Petrosian and Geller held the lead with 9 points. Keres trailed by half a point and Korchnoi by 1. Petrosian had won 4 games and drawn 10. Importantly, he felt he would have enough energy to last the distance.

The organisers tried to treat the players nicely and arranged a 6 day rest on a nearby island. However, spending an extra week in tropical weather may have been demanding. After the tournament, Petrosian told a Polish newspaper that he was not pleased with the conditions. The tournament had lasted a long time. Maybe a Soviet player was simply not allowed to praise organisation by a non-Communist country.

In round 15, Petrosian was White against Tal in a g3 King's Indian. Black equalised, but Tigran came up with a risky idea to grab the a7-pawn. He got away with it and drew. In the 16th round against Victor, Tigran equalised in a main-line Chigorin Ruy Lopez. The level of Korchnoi's moves deteriorated close to time control and Petrosian won a pawn. He simplified to a same-coloured bishops ending and won nicely. Then came the usual two quick draws with Geller and Keres. In the 19th round, Benko played the Reti. The position was balanced for a long time, but Pal went wrong before time control and lost after Tigran's 43rd move. In the 20th round, Petrosian was White against Fischer. The American played the Orthodox Queen's Gambit. They swapped a lot, and agreed to a draw after White's 23rd move.

We look at Petrosian's last game of the third cycle.

Game 109

Filip, Miroslav – Petrosian, Tigran
Candidates Tournament,
Curacao (21), 1962
Pirc Defence

1.d4 g6 2.e4 ♗g7 3.♘f3 d6 4.♘c3 ♘f6 5.♗e2 0-0 6.0-0 ♘bd7
Petrosian is ready to accept a somewhat worse position, as in the ensuing game a fight is almost guaranteed.

7.e5 ♘e8 8.♗f4
White could create complications with 8.e6 fxe6 9.♘g5 ♘df6 and the position would be balanced.

8...♘b6 9.♖e1 c6 10.h3
Filip plays to hold onto the e5–pawn.

10...♘c7 11.♗g3

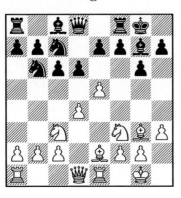

11...f5?!
This move is not the strongest, but it keeps fight in the position. After 11...dxe5 12.♗xe5 ♗xe5 13.♘xe5 White's advantage would be smaller, but with hardly any chances for Black to win.

12.exf6 exf6 13.♗d3
Seven pawns versus seven pawns means that the position is closed, but Filip gained space with his pawns throughout the game and at this stage he just about moves only pieces. In closed positions, one usually should try to gain space, and here this can be done with a nice move: 13.d5! c5 (13...♘cxd5 14.♘xd5 cxd5 15.a4 a5 16.♗b5 and White has an advantage) 14.♕d2 and White's advantage is pleasant.

13...f5 14.♗h4?!
Exchanging the bishop makes Black's position less cramped. The black pieces get more room to manoeuvre. White has nice alternative continuations: 14.♕d2 ♘e6 15.♘e2 ♘d5 16.c4 and White's space advantage would be unpleasant. Or 14.♘e2 ♗e6 15.♘f4 ♗f7 16.h4 and White would be somewhat better.

14...♗f6 15.♗xf6 ♕xf6 16.♕d2 ♗e6 17.♕f4
White's advantage would be small after 17.b3 ♖ae8 18.a4, but if 18.♘e2?! Then 18...♗d5 could be played.

17...♖ad8 18.♕g5?!
Filip plays for a draw.

18...♔g7 19.♕xf6+

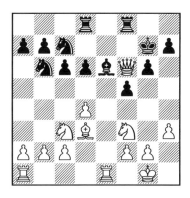

19...♔xf6!

Petrosian is happy to swap queens, and now he improves his king.

20.♘d2

The Czechoslovakian player makes only piece moves.

20...♗f7 21.♗f1

21.♘e2 ♖fe8 22.b3 would be equal.

21...♖fe8 22.♘f3

The knight was here two moves earlier. If 22.f3 White could bring the king to the centre: 22...♖xe1 23.♖xe1 c5 24.dxc5 dxc5 25.♖d1 ♘e6 26.♔f2 and White should not lose.

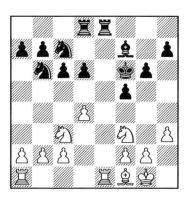

22...g5!

Petrosian gains space with his pawn.

23.♖xe8 ♖xe8 24.♖e1?!

Exchanging rooks helps Black; he is more likely to use his king.

24...♖xe1 25.♘xe1 ♘e6 26.♘e2 f4

26...♘c4 would also be strong. 27.b3 (after 27.♘d3 f4 28.c3 Black would be able to press with 28...♗g6 or 28...♘d2) 27...♘d2 28.c3 f4 29.f3 ♗g6 and Black is much better, maybe even winning.

27.c3 ♗g6 28.♘c1

28.g3 easing the grip on the kingside was worth considering. 28...fxg3 (or 28...♗b1 29.♘c1 ♘a4 30.♗d3 ♗xd3 31.♘cxd3 and White would struggle) 29.fxg3 ♘c4 30.b3 ♘e3 31.♗g2 d5 32.♗f3 ♘d1 and Black would have good winning chances.

28...♘a4 29.♘ed3

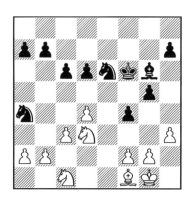

29...c5

Tigran starts biting at Filip's pawn chain. Starting with 29...b5!? was perhaps even more unpleasant.

30.♘b4 (30.f3 c5) 30...♗e8 31.d5 cxd5 32.♘cd3 (32.♘xd5+ ♔e5) 32...d4 and Black would be a pawn up.

30.d5

30.dxc5 ♘exc5 wins.

30...♘f8

Petrosian wants to place his knight on e5, but placing it on f5 was also inviting: 30...♘g7!? 31.c4 ♘f5 32.f3 a6 and Black is almost winning. Black has another strong continuation as well: 30...c4!

31.c4 ♘d7

After 31...♗xd3 32.♘xd3 ♘g6 33.f3 ♘e5 34.b3 ♘xd3 35.♗xd3 ♘c3 Black wins.

32.b3 ♘c3 33.h4 h6 34.hxg5+ hxg5 35.f3

35.a4! resisted more.

35...♘e5 36.♘b2

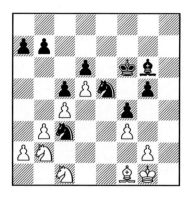

36...a6!

Tigran plans to create a target on c4.

37.♔f2

37.a4 ♗b1!! 38.♗d3 (38.♔f2 ♘a2!) 38...♗xd3 39.♘bxd3 b5 40.axb5 axb5 41.♘b2 bxc4 42.bxc4

♘b1 43.♘b3 ♔f5 and Black is close to winning.

37...b5 38.a4 bxa4 39.bxa4 a5?

It is a pity that Petrosian goes wrong after playing so well. Maybe Filip was short of time and that contributed to this mistake. He has a few good moves: 39...♗c2 40.a5 ♘b1 41.♗e2 ♔f5 42.♔e1 g4 and Black probably wins. Or 39...g4! 40.fxg4 (40.a5 ♔g5) 40...♘xg4+ 41.♔e1 ♘e3 42.♔f2 ♘e4+ 43.♔g1 ♘d2 and White is lost.

40.♔e1 ♗e8 41.♘b3 ♘xa4 42.♘xa4?

Filip seals a losing move. It would be interesting to know whether it just happened like this or whether Petrosian made his last move quickly so that Miroslav would have to seal his move. Keeping the knight would save the game: 42.♘d1! ♘b6 43.♘xa5 ♗a4 44.♘f2. White holds fairly easily as the black king can't go after the a5–knight, but must guard the kingside.

42...♗xa4 43.♘xa5

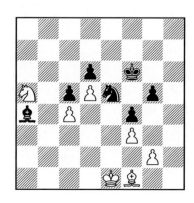

43...♔e7!

The king goes after the knight, which has strayed far from its camp.

44.♔d2 ♚d7 45.♔c3 ♚c7 46.♘b3 ♝xb3!

In the ensuing ending the knight easily outplays the bishop.

47.♔xb3 ♚b6 48.♔c3

48...♘g6

The knight aims to get to e3.

49.♔d3 ♚a5

Now Filip can choose which black piece he allows to invade.

50.♔c3 ♘h4 0–1

After the third full cycle, Keres led on 14.5 points, ahead of Petrosian and Geller on 14. No other player had a chance to win the event, especially as Tal had withdrawn, so the last cycle became shorter. It was by now certain that the challenger would be a Soviet player, so Tal could not have helped anymore. Petrosian had a bye in the first round of the last cycle.

According to Vasiliev, Petrosian felt tired, but thought that the older Keres and Geller were even more exhausted. He had no round 22 due to Tal's withdrawal. In the 23rd round,

Petrosian was White against Korchnoi in an unusual 1.c4 c5. Korchnoi gained the two bishops, but Petrosian had a development advantage. Victor played poorly, not paying much attention to development. Petrosian caught his king and Korchnoi resigned after Tigran's 21st move. The punch that Petrosian delivered can be seen in the It's Your Move chapter.

Fischer made an accusation that the authorities had forced Korchnoi to throw the game. Korchnoi denied it, saying that he just did not know the opening well. Timman does not think Korchnoi lost on purpose. We may never know for sure what happened. Korchnoi indeed played very badly, but he was always known for taking huge risks to capture material, and this time he risked falling behind in development by keeping the bishop pair for too long. In addition, there was no point in the order as it was clear that a Soviet player would win the event. In this round, the tension got too much for Geller, who lost a dramatically seesawing game against Fischer.

In the next two rounds, Petrosian made the usual quick draws with Geller and Keres. The Estonian probably did not care about the moves of the prearranged draw that much. Fischer and Timman both judged the final position as being lost for Keres as White. In the 26th round, Petrosian was White against Benko. He obtained a symbolic advantage in the ♝g5 Grunfeld, as Black had an isolated pawn. Benko exchanged a bit too early, and made a serious mistake in the same-coloured bishops ending. However, Tigran missed a win, and they agreed to a draw after his 42nd move. In the penultimate round, Petrosian was Black against Fischer; he played the Paulsen Sicilian, equalised and offered a draw, which Fischer refused. The game nevertheless ended in a draw after Black's 35th move. Petrosian's last move was pushing his h-pawn to the fifth rank, though he saw that pushing his e-pawn to the fifth rank was also possible. Timman finds it strange that he missed such a chance, which gave him a one-sided endgame with zero risk in playing for a win.

In the penultimate round, Keres lost to Benko, whom he beat in their first three games in Curacao. The standings among the leaders before the last round were Petrosian 17, Keres 16.5, and Geller 16. Petrosian was going to be White against Filip, Keres, the oldest player of the event, had White against Fischer, the youngest, and Geller was White against Benko. Petrosian got a position against Filip in the ♗f4 Queen's Gambit Declined in which he could not play for a win without giving his opponent chances. He thought for 40 minutes on his 15th move and, without making a move, offered a draw. Filip was surprised, but accepted. The game can be seen in commentary to the Petrosian-Lutikov 1966 game in Volume II.

Petrosian knew that the great Estonian had a poor record in the vital games of last rounds of Candidates events. He went for a walk, returning from time to time to take a quick look at Keres's game. That key game also ended in a draw, which meant that he would be Botvinnik's challenger. According to Vasiliev, Keres hurried to be the first to congratulate him. Geller won a lucky game against Benko, but that did not matter anymore.

This was a huge success for Tigran. Tal's health was a bit of luck, and also had Keres been younger, maybe he would have performed better in the last cycle. Still, in recent years Tigran had performed superbly and he played very solidly at the event.

The championship system was heavily criticized by Fischer, who was unhappy that Keres, Petrosian and Geller made 12 quick prearranged draws against each other, which saved a lot of energy. This agreement was not a nice thing to do, but it was not against the rules. So FIDE correctly changed the system and the Candidates Tournament was replaced by knock-out matches. Also, Botvinnik was no longer given the criticised right to a rematch were he to lose his match.

One point was very interesting regarding the last Candidates Tournament of the 20th century: the event generated completely different attitudes from great authors. Kasparov in his section on Petrosian in *My Great Predecessors* spent only one long sentence on the tourney. Timman, on the other hand, many decades after, wrote a whole book on this historical event. It is worth citing how Timman summarised Petrosian's play in his Curacao 1962 book: "With Petrosian one gets the impression that he sometimes held back, that he still had reserves from which he could have drawn if the worst had come to the worst."

Holland – Soviet Union Match

In early June, the Dutch national team hosted the Soviets in Hague. Interestingly, Petrosian was put on board 3 (or he offered to play there) behind Keres and Geller.

In the first game, Petrosian was White against Donner in a 6.♗e2 e5 Najdorf. The Dutch grandmaster played somewhat unusually and Petrosian managed to create holes in Black's pawn chain. Petrosian exploited them and won, the game lasting 31 moves. The second game featured an exchange Queen's Gambit. He equalised as Black and they agreed to a draw after his 18th move. Beating the Dutchman 1.5:0.5 was a reasonable result.

Varna Olympiad

The Chess Olympiad started in the middle of September. Petrosian was selected for second board behind Botvinnik. It was useful to see him in action. Interestingly Spassky, who did not even qualify for the interzonal, played on the third board.

In the first round of the preliminary group, Petrosian did not play against East Germany. In the second round, he was Black against Skold of Sweden. Petrosian got no advantage in a Reverse Dragon, but the Swedish player made a big mistake in the middlegame and Petrosian never let him back into the game. Petrosian was White against Turkey next. He was too strong for his opponent, Suer. After another rest, this time against West Germany, he was Black against Diez del Corral of Spain. Tigran played 5...♘d7 in the Sicilian and made his position a combination of the Najdorf and the Dragon, but his opening was not reliable at the very least. The Spaniard sacrificed a piece for dangerous compensation. However, Diez del Corral soon went wrong. Petrosian took control and won with the extra piece. Against Norway, Petrosian was Black against Johannessen, who played 1.d4 ♘f6 2.♘f3 g6 3.♗g5. Petrosian was unable to avoid exchanges; he played on, but his opponent was good enough to hold. In the next game, Petrosian was Black against Dunkelbaum of Belgium. The Tarrasch transposed into a queenless Queen's Gambit type of middlegame. Petrosian obtained the bishop pair; he pressed until move 43, but had to settle for a draw. In the last round of the preliminary group, he won effortlessly against Anastasopoulos of Greece. Petrosian did not play in the first game of the final group against Bulgaria. We now join Petrosian's game against Gligoric.

Game 110

Petrosian, Tigran – Gligoric, Svetozar
Olympiad Final, Varna (2), 1962

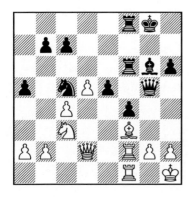

27.♖e1!

Black threatens e4. Petrosian sacrifices an exchange to counter it.

27...♞d3   28.♖fe2   ♞xe1 29.♕xe1

As the black rooks have no open file White is in the game.

29...♖e8

29...b6! Petrosian doesn't mention this tricky move. 30.b3! (30.♖xe5? ♕xe5!! 31.♕xe5 ♖e8 and White would have a difficult endgame) 30...♖e8 31.♞e4 and White would probably hold.

30.c5 ♖ff8

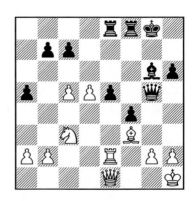

31.♞e4 1/2

In the third round of the final, Petrosian was White against Pietzsch of East Germany. The ♗f4 Orthodox Queen's Gambit resulted in a position with a symmetrical pawn structure. Petrosian nicely obtained domination on the only open file, the c-file. He chopped a pawn, and then his opponent sacrificed a second. Petrosian converted his advantage without any problem. In the next round, he and Botvinnik both took a rest against Argentina. In the fifth round, he was White against Pachman in a reversed King's Indian. The position was balanced for a long time. Closer to the second time control, Pachman made a big mistake and lost.

In the sixth round, he was Black against Dueckstein of Austria.

Game 111

Dueckstein, Andreas – Petrosian, Tigran

Olympiad Final, Varna (6), 1962
Caro-Kann Defence

1.e4 c6 2.d4 d5 3.♘c3 dxe4 4.♘xe4 ♗f5 5.♘g3 ♗g6 6.♘f3 ♘d7 7.♗d3 e6 8.0-0 ♕c7 9.c4

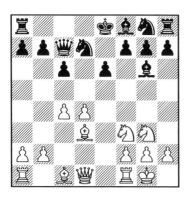

9...0-0-0?!

By not playing the standard h4, White sends the message that he does not mind a peaceful outcome. However, Petrosian also sends a message with his castling that he is looking for a fight. According to the database, Petrosian's move was a novelty, but objectively it doesn't equalise.

10.♗xg6 hxg6 11.♕a4 ♔b8 12.b4

Dueckstein wastes no time in going after the black king.

12...♘h6

Maybe developing the knight with 12...♘e7 was more precise,

as if 13.c5 then 13...♘d5 could be played.

13.♕b3?!

This and Dueckstein's next move are a bit slow. White's attack would be faster after 13.c5! ♘f5 (13...♗e7 14.♖b1) 14.♘xf5 gxf5 15.g3

13...♘f5 14.a4?!

White only concentrates on his attack, but protecting the d4–square with 14.♖d1!? or 14.♘e2!? would still give him an advantage and would be stronger. The latter move should not be met by 14...e5? because of 15.c5.

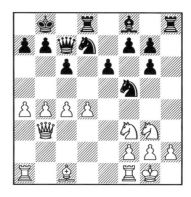

14...e5

Petrosian acts in the centre. 14...♗e7 was also possible.

15.dxe5?!

This capture allows two black pieces to become more effective in the centre. Capturing with 15.♘xf5! would ease Black's pressure on the centre: 15...gxf5 16.c5 f6 (16...exd4 17.g3!) 17.dxe5 ♘xe5 18.♗f4 g5 19.♗xe5 (after 19.♘xe5 fxe5 20.♗xg5 ♗e7 White would be a bit better) 19...fxe5

20.♘xg5 e4 and White would be somewhat better.

15...♘xe5   16.♘xe5   ♕xe5 17.♗b2 ♕c7 18.c5

Dueckstein looks for an attacking chance; bringing a rook to the centre with 18.♖ad1 or 18.♖fe1 would be safer. If the latter move, then 18...f6 or 18...c5 would be fine for Black.

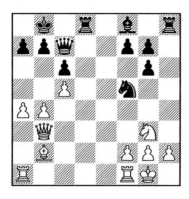

18...a5!

Black weakens the c5–pawn. A surprising idea, as one would expect him to play on the h-file, but he plays actively on the part of the board where White planned to act.

19.♖ad1 ♖xd1 20.♖xd1 ♖h4!

Tigran plays across the whole board; he brings his rook into play in an original way. 20...♘xg3 21.hxg3 axb4 or 20...♔a7 would be fine for Black as well.

21.bxa5 ♗xc5 22.a6

A pawn close to the king can cause problems and can fall as well. Most players who were not world class looked for a draw against Petrosian, but not Dueckstein, who played for a win throughout the game.

a) 22.♕c2 ♕e7 23.♘xf5 gxf5 24.g3 ♖e4 and Black would be sufficiently active.

b) 22.♗c3 ♗xf2+ (Black could play on with 22...♔a7) 23.♔xf2 ♕f4+ 24.♔e1 ♕e3+ 25.♘e2 ♖e4 26.♕b2 ♕g1+ and Black would give perpetual check.

22...b6 23.♖e1

After 23.♘xf5 gxf5 24.g3 ♖e4 25.♗xg7 f4 perhaps White would have a small edge.

23...♔a7

The king is safer on a7.

24.♗e5 ♕d7 25.♘e4 ♗d4 26.g3

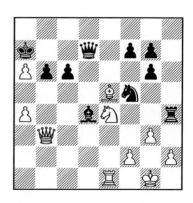

26...♗xe5!?

Petrosian stirs up the position with an imaginative exchange sacrifice. After 26...♖h8 27.♖d1 f6 the position would be equal.

27.gxh4 ♘d4 28.♕d1

28.♕d3 is slightly preferable.

28...♕d5

The queen stands well in the centre. If 28...♕h3?! Then 29.♘g3 would be the answer.

29.♖e3   ♘f5   30.♖e1   ♘d4 31.♕d3

The Austrian player rejects a repetition.

31...f5 32.♘g5

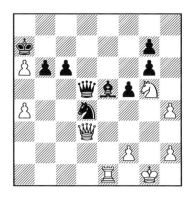

32...c5!

Pushing the c-pawn is an original way of exerting pressure.

33.♖e3 c4 34.♕d1?

White should give back the exchange with 34.♖xe5!. After 34... ♕xe5 35.♕xc4 the position would be equal.

34...♚xa6!?

Tigran plays a good move, not only taking back the pawn, but getting ready to be active. In fact, Black has a forced win with 34... f4, but going for it with possibly little time left would not have been practical. 35.♖e1 c3 36.♕d3 f3 37.♔f1 c2 38.♖c1 ♕c6 39.♘xf3 ♕xf3 and Black would win.

35.♖a3?

If 35.♕f1 then 35...♗f6 stops the exchange sacrifice and threatens to push the f-pawn. 36.♘h3 (after 36.♘h7 f4 37.♘xf6 gxf6 38.♖a3 ♕e6 White would be in trouble) 36...♘c2 (36...♕c6 37.♘f4) 37.♖e2 ♘b4

38.♘f4 ♕d4 and Black would have a small edge.

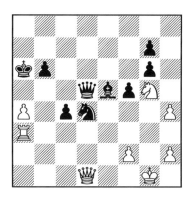

35...♗f6

Out of the blue, White is almost in zugzwang.

36.h3 f4!

Petrosian deprives the rook of squares on the third rank.

37.♕g4

This is White's only active move, but it loses as well. After 37.♔h2 ♗xg5 38.hxg5 f3 39.♖e3 ♕xg5 Black wins.

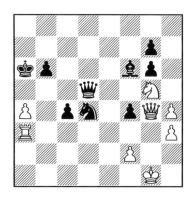

37...♚a5!!

Tigran uses the king as an attacker. Would you believe that in the rest of the game Petrosian will only use his king? It is amazing!

38.♘f3 ♔b4!

This stunning king move wins material.

39.♘xd4 ♔xa3 40.♘c2+ ♔xa4 0–1

They reached time control, but there was no point in playing on. This was vintage Petrosian, but credit to Dueckstein, whose brave attitude helped greatly to bring the genius out of Petrosian.

After this win, Petrosian rested for two rounds, against Romania and Holland. He joined the team against West Germany where he was Black against Unzicker. He played the Modern Defence and he got a tough position in the opening. However, he was able to improve it gradually. He even got an edge after Unzicker blundered a pawn. His opponent kept on fighting until resigning after Petrosian's 72nd move. In the penultimate round, Petrosian was Black against Benko. Tigran wanted to battle it out in the Slav Exchange. Close to time control, Petrosian's play started to get overly risky. Benko, probably in time trouble, missed some clear ways to win. They agreed to a draw after Petrosian's 38th move. In the last round, Petrosian did not play against Hungary.

Petrosian's result was superb; he scored 10 points out of 12 games. He won 8 and drew 4. Botvinnik in total scored 8 out of his 12 games, and it is worth comparing their performance in the final. Botvinnik scored 3.5 out of 6 games against the strongest countries, while Petrosian scored 6.5 out of 8. Maybe Botvinnik's opposition was a bit stronger, but Petrosian clearly performed more impressively.

The Olympiad must have been confidence boosting for Petrosian, and the Soviet team won gold again.

Petrosian remained undefeated the whole year, which was amazing! In early 1962, Fischer said "If Petrosian played more boldly, he would be the strongest player in the world." The results he delivered in 1961 and 1962 proved that in these two years he was the strongest in the world.

Petrosian's results in 1962

Stockholm Interzonal	+ 8 = 14 – 0	15/22 2nd-3rd place
Candidates Tournament, Curacao	+ 8 = 19 – 0	17.5/27 1st place
Holland – USSR Match, The Hague, vs. Donner	+ 1 = 1 – 0	1.5:0.5
Chess Olympiad, Varna, board 2	+ 8 = 4 – 0	10/12
Altogether	**+ 25 = 38 – 0**	**44/63**

Petrosian's Remarkable Exchanges

Exchanging pieces is an important element of any decent player's skill. There were many examples in the selected games where his exceptional talent shone through, but we thought that although some of his games were not worth showing in their entirety, it is worth looking at the parts where these swaps took place. We look at them with light analysis.

A1) Bakhtadze, G – Petrosian, T
Georgian Championship,
Tbilisi, 1944

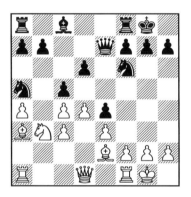

12...♘xb3! 13.♕xb3 ♗g4!

Petrosian obtained a preferable knight to a bishop; he had a small advantage and went on to win.

14.♖a2 ♖ac8 15.h3 ♗xe2 16.♖xe2 ♖c7 17.♖d1 ♕e6 18.♖ed2 g5!? 19.♕b5 ♕f5 20.♔h2 g4 21.♖h1 ♔h8 22.hxg4 ♕xg4 23.dxc5? ♖g8 24.g3 ♕f3 25.cxd6 ♘g4+ 26.♔g1 ♘xe3 27.♕e5+ f6 0–1

A2) Petrosian, T – Zhuk-Tripolitov
Georgian Championship,
Tbilisi, 1945

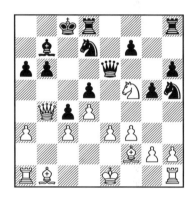

19.♕d6!

White threatens g4 and ♗g3.

19...♖de8 20.♔d2 ♘f4 21.♕xe6 ♘xe6 22.♘d6+ ♔b8 23.♘xe8
Petrosian won an exchange and went on to win the game.

A3) Petrosian, T – Buslaev, A
Tbilisi, 1945

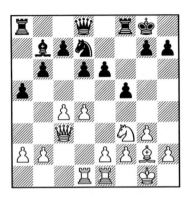

14.♘g5! ♕xg5 15.♗xb7

Petrosian got a small advantage and went on to win the game.

A4) Petrosian, T – Petrovsky, N
Soviet Junior Championship,
Leningrad (3), 1945

14.♗xe4!

With this subtle capture Petrosian uncovers a weakness on e6.

14...dxe4 15.♕e3 f5 16.♖ad1± ♘f6 17.f3! ♘h5?

17...exf3 18.exf3 and White is better; 17...♕c7 18.a4±.

18.fxe4 f4 19.♕f3! ♕g5 20.g4

Petrosian was winning and went on to convert his advantage.

A5) Petrosian, T – Oganesian, S
Yerevan Championship (3), 1948

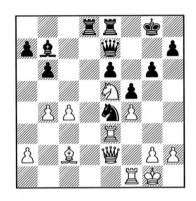

31.♗xe4!

A surprising decision. White wants to base his play on his queenside pawn majority.

31...♗xe4 32.♕b2 ♕d6 33.♖e2

White's plan is h3, ♖f2 and ♖d2, or if needed he can play ♘g4 or ♖c1 and c5.

33...♕d4+ 34.♕xd4 ♖xd4 35.♖c1 ♖ed8 36.♔f2 ♖d2?! 37.g3 ♔f8 38.♔e3 ♖xe2+? 39.♔xe2

White's advantage is considerable and Petrosian went on to win.

A6) Kalantar, A – Petrosian, T
Yerevan Championship (4), 1948

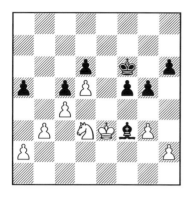

38...♗e4! 39.♔d2 ♗xd3–+

A7) Petrosian, T – Klaman, K
Soviet Championship Semi-final,
Tbilisi (9), 1949
(the game from this book's cover!)

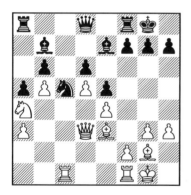

21.♗xc5!

Petrosian could take the knight with the knight as well, it would also give him a considerable advantage. However, he prefers having a knight versus a bishop, and this was a trait especially in the early part of his career.

21...bxc5 22.♘b2! g6 23.♘c4 ♗f6 24.a4 ♗g7 25.♕d2 f5 26.f3 ♖f7 27.♖b1 ♗f8 28.♖f2

Petrosian makes it hard for his opponent to read that he intends to double rooks on the b-file.

28...♗c8 29.♕e1!

The queen still attacks the a5–pawn from e1 and also defends the g3 pawn.

29...♖b7 30.♖fb2 ♗d7 31.♗f1 h5 32.b6 ♖ab8 33.♕xa5 ♕e8 34.♕d2 ♗xa4 35.♘a5 ♖g7 36.♗b5!

This is not the only move, but exchanging the bishop makes the b-pawn event more formidable. Black is hopelessly lost now. Klaman resigned on move 44.

A8) Bondarevsky, I – Petrosian, T
Soviet Championship Final,
Moscow (4), 1951

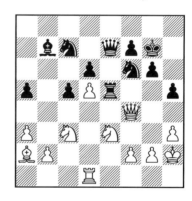

24...♘e4!

With fewer pieces on the board, Petrosian can sense White's vulnerable points.

25.♘xe4

25.♔g1 ♘xc3 26.bxc3 ♘b5
27.♖c1∓.

25...♖xe4 26.♕f3

Here 26...♕e5+ or 26...♖d4 would be close to winning, but Petrosian still won the game.

A9) Simagin, V – Petrosian, T
Soviet Championship Final,
Moscow (14), 1951

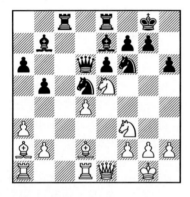

20...♕b8!?

Petrosian starts playing to exert pressure on the long diagonal. Simagin will not play the position well.

21.♗b1?!

21.a4!?; 21.♖ac1!?.

21...♘b6 22.h4? ♘c4 23.♗c1 ♕a8!?

23...♖ed8!?.

24.♕e2?!

24.a4!?.

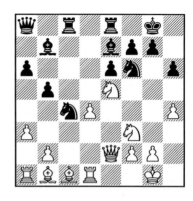

24...♗e4!

Swapping allows Black to pile up the pieces against the isolated pawn and prevents any attack.

25.♖e1 ♗xb1 26.♖xb1 ♕d5 27.g4? ♘xe5 28.♘xe5

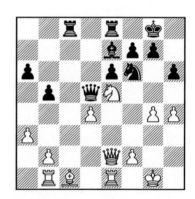

28...♘d7!

28...♕xd4 would be winning as well.

29.♕f3 ♘xe5 30.♕xd5 exd5 31.dxe5 ♗xh4

Petrosian won a pawn and converted his advantage.

A10) Lokvenc, J – Petrosian, T
Austria – Soviet Union Match,
Vienna (1), 1953

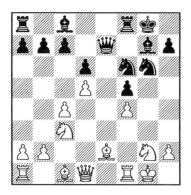

16...♘e4!
Petrosian obtains an edge by exchanging the knight which blocks the diagonal.

A11) Bronstein, D – Petrosian, T
Candidates Tournament,
Amsterdam/Leeuwarden (11), 1956

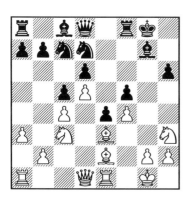

17...♗xc3!

This capture was a revolutionary idea in those days. Petrosian easily obtained a draw with it. Black will get play on the g-file and White can't really activate his dark-squared bishop.

18.bxc3 ♘f6 19.a4 ♔h8 20.♘f2 ♖g8 21.♔h1 ♕e8 22.♖g1 ♕g6 23.♕d2 ♗d7 24.g3 ♖ae8 25.a5 ♖e7 26.♖ab1 ♗c8 27.♖g2 ♖eg7 28.♖bg1 ♘ce8 29.h3 h5 1/2

A12) Petrosian, T – Olafsson, F
Candidates Tournament,
Bled/Zagreb/Belgrade (1), 1959

19.♗c1!
Exchanging the bishop makes it harder for Black to attack.

19...♗xc1
19...♗f6 20.♘e3±.

20.♖xc1 ♖af8 21.♘e3 ♗a8 22.♖c2 ♔h8 23.a4
Petrosian got a somewhat better position and went on to win.

It's Your Move

We show some interesting positions from Petrosian's career. In some cases there are several good possibilities. The solutions are contained at the end of this section. In each position it is Petrosian to move except where stated.

B1) Petrosian, T – Kopelevich, B
Tbilisi, 1944

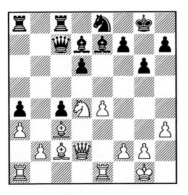

B2) Petrosian, T – Ebralidze, A
Tbilisi Championship (10), 1945

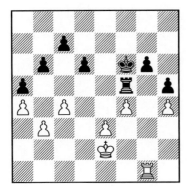

B3) Petrosian, T – Grigoriev, N
Tbilisi, 1945

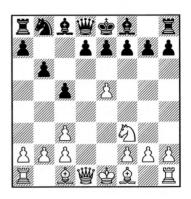

B4) Petrosian, T – Bakhtadze, G
Tbilisi, 1945

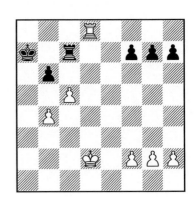

B5) Petrosian, T – Gongadze
Soviet Championship Quarter-Final,
Tbilisi (6), 1947

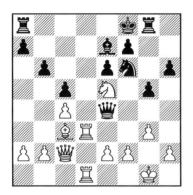

B7) Petrosian, T – Bronstein, D
Soviet Championship Final,
Moscow (11), 1951

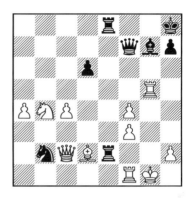

B6) Simagin, V – Petrosian, T
Moscow, 1950

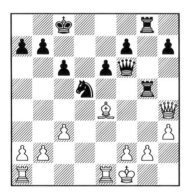

B8) Kotov, A – Petrosian, T
Gagra/Voronovo, 1952

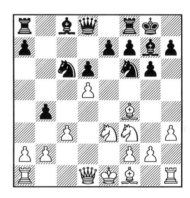

B9) Smyslov, V – Petrosian, T
Candidates Tournament,
Zurich (15), 1953

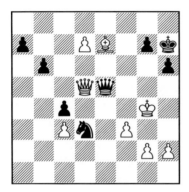

Smyslov to move

B10) Petrosian, T – Corral, H
Uruguay – USSR Match,
Montevideo (1), 1954

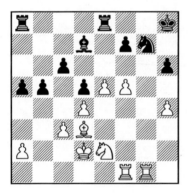

B11) Petrosian, T – Bannik, A
Soviet Championship Final,
Kiev (5), 1954

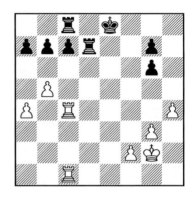

B12) Chistiakov, A – Petrosian, T
Moscow Championship, 1956

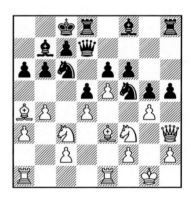

B13) Tolush, A – Petrosian, T
Soviet Championship Final,
Moscow (11), 1957

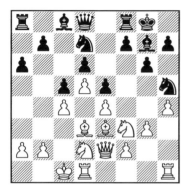

B15) Petrosian, T – Tolush, A
Soviet Championship Final,
Riga (16), 1958

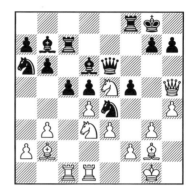

B14) Matanovic, A – Petrosian, T
Soviet Union – Yugoslavia Match,
Leningrad (4), 1957

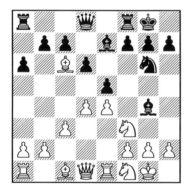

B16) Petrosian, T – Benko, P
Candidates Tournament
Bled/Zagreb/Belgrade (20), 1959

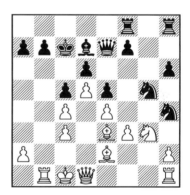

B17) Petrosian, T – Suetin, A
Soviet Championship Final,
Leningrad (2), 1960

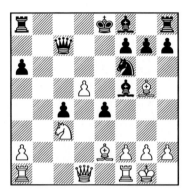

B18) Bronstein, D – Petrosian, T
Soviet Championship Final,
Leningrad (13), 1960

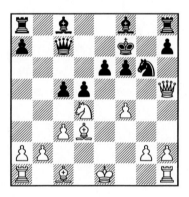

B19) Petrosian, T – Gufeld, E
Soviet Championship Final & Zonal,
Moscow (11), 1961

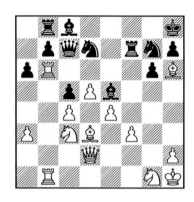

B20) Khasin, A – Petrosian, T
Soviet Championship Final & Zonal,
Moscow (14), 1961

B21) Polugaevsky, L – Petrosian, T
Soviet Championship Final & Zonal,
Moscow (16), 1961

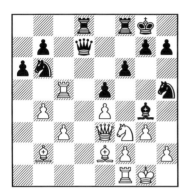

B23) Germek, M – Petrosian, T
Bled (5), 1961

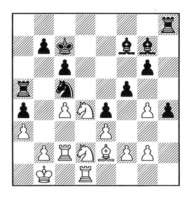

B22) Petrosian, T – Schmid, L
Zurich (8), 1961

B24) Petrosian, T – Pomar, A
Interzonal Stockholm (18), 1962

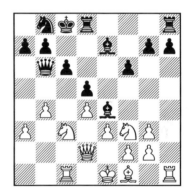

B25) Petrosian, T – Korchnoi, V
Candidates Tournament,
Curacao (23), 1962

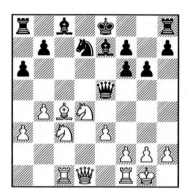

Solutions

B1) Petrosian, T – Kopelevich, B
22.♘f5 gxf5 23.exf5 ♗d8
24.♖xe8+ 1-0

B2) Petrosian, T – Ebralidze, A
42.♔f3! ♖c5? (42...♔f7 and
White is better) **43.e4! c6 44.♔e3
♔f7 45.♔d4 ♔f6 46.♖g2 d5 47.e5+
♔f7 48.♖g5 1–0**

B3) Petrosian, T – Grigoriev, N
**6.e6! dxe6 7.♕xd8+ ♔xd8
8.♘e5 ♔e8 9.♗b5+ ♗d7 10.♘xd7
♘xd7 11.♗f4 e5 12.0-0-0 f6
13.♗xd7+ 1–0**

B4) Petrosian, T – Bakhtadze, G
34.♔e3! bxc5 (34...♔b7
35.♔d4+−) **35.bxc5 ♖xc5 36.♖d7+
♔b6 37.♖xf7 ♖g5 38.g3 ♔c6
39.♔f4 ♖g6 40.h4 ♔d6 41.♔f5
♔d5 42.g4 1–0**

B5) Petrosian, T – Gongadze
**25.♘xf7! ♕xc4 26.♘e5 ♕e4
27.♘d7+ ♘xd7 28.♖f3+ ♕xf3
29.exf3 ♘f6 30.♕e2 1–0**

B6) Simagin, V – Petrosian, T
**22...♖xg2! 23.♕xf6 ♖g1+
24.♔e2 ♖xe1+ 25.♖xe1 ♘xf6**
Petrosian went on to convert his
advantage.

B7) Petrosian, T – Bronstein, D
**41.♗c3! ♖xc2 42.♗xg7+ ♕xg7
43.♖xg7 ♖xc4 44.♖b7** Petrosian

pressed, but Bronstein was able to
hold.

B8) Kotov, A – Petrosian, T
**11...bxc3 12.dxc6 cxb2 13.♖b1
♘e4 14.♗d3 ♕a5+ 15.♔f1 ♗a6**
Petrosian obtained an advantage
and went on to win.

B9) Smyslov, V – Petrosian, T
**47.♕d6!! ♘f2+ 48.♔h4 g5+
49.♔h5** Smyslov was unable to find
this way to win and the game ended
in a draw. Petrosian's previous move
46...♕e5! was a clever try and it
worked.

B10) Petrosian, T – Corral, H
**26.e6! fxe6 27.f6! ♘f5 28.♗xf5
exf5 29.♖g7 1–0**

B11) Petrosian, T – Bannik, A
**40.♔h3! ♔d8 41.♔g4 ♖d6
42.♔g5! c6 43.♖f4!** Petrosian won
the game on move 84.

B12) Chistiakov, A – Petrosian, T
**16...hxg4 17.♕xh8 gxf3 18.♕h5
b5 19.♘xb5 axb5 20.♗xb5 fxe5**
Petrosian was winning and scored a
nice victory.

B13) Tolush, A – Petrosian, T
**14...♘f4! 15.gxf4 exf4 16.♗xf4
♕f6 17.♖dg1 ♕xf4** Petrosian was
winning and went on to win.

B14) Matanovic, A – Petrosian, T
11...♞h4 12.♞1d2 (12.♝d5 ♝xf3
13.gxf3 ♛c8 14.♚h1 ♛h3 15.♞e3
♞xf3 16.♞f1 ♞h4=; 12.♝xb7 ♝xf3
13.gxf3 ♛d7 14.♚h1 [14.♞e3 ♛h3]
14...♛h3 15.♞e3 ♞xf3 16.♞f1
♞h4=) 12...bxc6 13.h3 ♞xf3+
14.♞xf3 ♝xf3 15.♛xf3 ♝f6 16.dxe5
♝xe5 17.♛d3 ♜e8 18.♝e3 1/2

B15) Petrosian, T – Tolush, A
23.dxc5! bxc5 24.♞f4 ♛e7
25.♞xd5 ♝xd5 26.♜xd5 ♞b4
27.♛d1! Petrosian obtained a
clear advantage and defeated his
opponent.

B16) Petrosian, T – Benko, P
26.♝xc5! b6 27.♝e3 ♞g2
28.♝xb6+ axb6 29.♛g1 ♜b8
30.♛xg2 Petrosian won two pawns
and converted his advantage.

B17) Petrosian, T – Suetin, A
16.♝xf6! gxf6 17.♝g4! ♝xg4
18.♛xg4 ♛e5 19.♞xe4 f5 20.♛h5
0-0-0 21.♞d2 c3 22.♞c4 ♛d4
23.♛xf5+ ♜d7 24.♞e5 1–0

B18) Bronstein, D – Petrosian, T
15...cxd4! 16.♝xg6+ hxg6
17.♛xh8 dxc3 18.♛h7+ ♝g7
19.♝e3 cxb2 20.♜d1 ♝a6 21.f5
exf5 22.♛h3 ♛c2 23.♛f3 ♝c4 0–1

B19) Petrosian, T – Gufeld, E
28.♜e6! b5 29.cxb5 c4 30.♜c6
♛d8 31.♝xc4 Petrosian soon won
the game.

B20) Khasin, A – Petrosian, T
13...♞g4 14.♝f2 ♞xf2 15.♜xf2
♛b6 Petrosian won the game on
move 40.

**B21) Polugaevsky, L –
Petrosian, T**
20...♝h3 21.♜a1 ♞f4! 22.♜ca5
♛g4 23.♞c1 ♜d6 24.♜5a2 ♜fd8
25.♞e1 ♞xe2+ 26.♛xe2 ♛xe2
27.♜xe2 ♜d1 Petrosian firmly
converted his advantage.

B22) Petrosian, T – Schmid, L
21.g4! ♞f6 22.gxf5 gxf5
23.♜g1+ ♚h8 24.♜g3 ♜e7 25.♜bg1
♜g7 26.e5 dxe5 27.♛xe5 ♞ce8
28.♜xg7 ♝xg7 29.♜xg7 ♚xg7
30.♛e7+ ♚g6 31.d6 1–0

B23) Germek, M – Petrosian, T
36...f4! 37.♞f1 h3! 38.gxh3 f3
0–1

B24) Petrosian, T – Pomar, A
16.♛a2! ♞d7 17.♞xd5 ♝xd5
18.♛xd5 a5 19.♛xa5 Petrosian won
the game with his 41st move after
using his king nicely in the endgame.

B25) Petrosian, T – Korchnoi, V
14.f4! ♛b8 (14...d6 15.♞e4+–,
14...♛xe3 15.♚h1+–) 15.♝xf7+
♚xf7 16.♛b3+ ♚e8 17.♞d5 ♝d6
18.♞e6 b5 19.♞dc7+ ♚e7 20.♞d4
♚f8 21.♞xa8 1–0

Afterword to Volume I by Tibor Karolyi

As we started researching for this book, my co-author Tigran and I expected to find many undiscovered masterpieces by Petrosian. Yet the quantity of his deep ideas and his power on his good days surprised both of us. Petrosian's career, like Tal's, Karpov's and Kasparov's, featured so many fantastic games that we believe it justified to discuss his career in great detail as we have done in this book.

Originally, we planned to analyse no more than 4 games each year for this book, but our hero delivered so much beauty that we almost always chose more games than that, and once even 8 games (1958). How brilliantly he used his king and how well he manoeuvred his rook was already well-known, but how wizardly he used his knight was new to us. He also played a few great endgames with pawns versus a knight. Also, we see just how important a weapon was his ability to choose between a knight and a bishop. He preferred a knight over a bishop more often than most top players.

Saidy's judgment seems correct: he was a preventer more than a defender. Yet there were events that highlighted where he still had room to improve. The Botvinnik match proved that when he worked under pressure he was able to prepare openings very well. However, often in his tournaments the white pieces meant a smaller advantage for him than for other world class players, long before the computer age. He sometimes unnecessarily got into time trouble or played against his opponents' shortage of time; he rarely had to pay for his mistakes in his opponents' time trouble, though. Further, he rarely made inaccuracies when analysing adjourned games.

But what mostly comes through looking at his games is his unique and exceptional talent; he often uncovered hidden beauty in the game. He was probably more a natural tactician than a strategist, but he became an artist at positional play.

There are several people who helped to raise the level of this book. Tigran's son Vartan Petrosian provided pictures of his family, as well as some background information. It was a privilege to have a foreword written by the three-times Olympic champion Levon Aronian.

The late Peter Szilagyi, chess journalist, and my former trainer, talked about Petrosian at great length. He felt grateful for his indirect career help. Peter was already close to passing away when I was able to bring him some pleasure telling him that I had agreed to write in detail about the great champion. His encouragement to write this book meant a lot to me. Sadly he saw no part in the preparation of this book.

Mikhail Vrona provided a lot of detail on Petrosian's early Soviet tournaments, and he also helped greatly in translating the most complicated parts of certain articles. Regarding the early life of the Maestro, two Georgians helped a lot: Giorgi Khomeriki and the great endgame composer David Gurgenidze, who provided articles about Petrosian as well as some great photos.

I discussed some endgames with Grandmaster Ferenc Berkes, and he spent time on them, deepening our understanding of some positions. Grandmaster Ketevan Arakhamia was kind enough to translate articles written in Georgian. Grandmaster Boris Postovsky helped to get in touch with some people.

Two Dutch players, Rene Olthof and Ton Bodaan, provided details of some tournaments. Sergei Voronkov, Janos Fleisz, Peter Balogh, Oystein Brekke, Svend Steenstrup and Ashot Nadanian also helped. Candidate Master Artur Sarkisian, whose father was a close friend of Petrosian, supplied some great private photos.

We also say thanks to one strong grandmaster who helped, but who asked that we not mention his name. Sorry if anyone was not mentioned.

We hope that the readers enjoyed as much as my co-author Tigran and I did our journey through the first part of the great champion's career, and we very much hope that you will join the second part as well.

Index of Themes

A game is rarely decided by one element; rather, it is usually decided by several ones at once. We have chosen the main elements here. Some games are selected for several motifs. The numbers refer to games.

Endgames

Bishop endings: 15, 26, 75
Fortresses: 39
Knight endings: 48, 80, 98
Knight vs. pawns: 23, 68
Knights vs. bishops: 87, 105
Opposite-coloured bishops: 54, 69, 69
Queen endings: 19, 49, 89
Queen vs. rook endings: 58
Rook endings: 3, 4, 6, 7, 63, 74, 86, 108
Rook vs. bishop endings: 40
Rooks on the 2nd or 7th rank: 26, 57, 79, 82, 83
Zugzwang endings: 4, 7, 48, 80

Printed in Great Britain
by Amazon